FEDERALISM
Mature and Emergent

COLUMBIA UNIVERSITY
BICENTENNIAL CONFERENCE SERIES

"Man's Right to Knowledge and the Free Use Thereof."

The Contributors

Adolf A. Berle, Jr. Henry M. Hart, Jr.
Roy Blough Paul R. Hays
Robert R. Bowie Arthur N. Holcombe
Tom Charlton Clark Charles McKinley
William Diebold, Jr. Arthur W. Macmahon
Noel T. Dowling Franz L. Neumann
John Fischer Ingvar Svennilson
Paul A. Freund David B. Truman
Carl J. Friedrich Herbert Wechsler
John M. Gaus Edward W. Weidner
Milton Handler Kenneth C. Wheare

FEDERALISM
Mature and Emergent

Edited by

ARTHUR W. MACMAHON

NEW YORK
RUSSELL & RUSSELL · INC
1962

Editor's Preface

Federalism, like the companion Columbia Bicentennial symposium on the metropolis in modern life, presents the problem of the free man seeking to achieve the utmost good he can from each of the inevitably mingled elements of centralization and decentralization. The protean nature of federalism draws the analysis upward through all levels of political association.

The content of federalism invites collaboration among disciplines, particularly of students and practitioners of the law and political science. In planning this symposium invaluable help was given by Professor Herbert Wechsler of the Columbia Law School at every stage in conceiving the objectives and methods of inquiry. Acknowledgment is also made of the suggestive preliminary work done by Professor David B. Truman of the Faculty of Political Science.

Illustrations of the realities of a maturing federal system at work could be drawn from almost any field of policy and administration. In view of the fact that another Bicentennial symposium deals with such welfare domains as social security, education, and health, the functional studies that are part of the analysis in this volume are devoted to agriculture, land and water resources, and trade regulation, while the field of labor relations is used to exemplify the degree of central legislative responsibility for the division of jurisdiction among the levels of government.

This symposium traces the federal idea above the level of existing nation states but it touches the problem of international relations only incidentally. The concentration here upon regional efforts in Western Europe is dictated by two considerations; they establish the relevance of the material to a body of essays devoted largely to federalism in action at the national level. The first consideration is the fact that in the regional setting of Western Europe the movement for union is not international in essence but is an attempt to create elements of union which, although novel in scope and texture, are still akin to the developments that have organized political power and achieved common markets through large national states. The second consideration is the fact that in Western Europe things have happened: not only has extensive consultative machinery been set up but also an important functional experiment is at work in the European Coal and Steel Community, and a constitution for a political union has been drafted officially and submitted to the several governments.

The steps in preparing this volume may be briefly described. A score of persons were asked to write chapters on selected aspects. The selection of individuals was guided partly by their interests and special knowledge and in some cases by recent active contact with the subject-matter, as in the case of a Harvard group who had prepared systematic information on federalism for drafting committees in Europe. The chapters in mimeographed form were circulated in advance among sixty-odd persons who attended a three-day Bicentennial Conference on Federalism at Arden House, Columbia University's outpost in the Ramapo Hills for quiet meetings of minds. Subsequently each author revised his draft, aided in many cases by comment at the conference. By permission of the publisher and the university, chapters 7, 10, and 11 were published in advance in the Columbia Law Review of April 1954 and Chapter 12 in the Pennsylvania Law Review of June.

A stenographic record was made of the conference proceedings although with no thought of its publication as such. I have incorporated excerpts from the transcript in the introductory chapters I have written for the second, third, and fourth parts of the book, supplementing my overall introductory chapter in the first part. I have also inserted a few quotations from the transcript among the footnotes in other chapters. In all cases the reference to a "discussion" indicates that the source is the stenographic record of floor discussion at Arden House. Where I thus quote remarks in order to signalize points of disagreement or of consensus, it seems desirable to preserve the original informal phrasing.

This incidental use of the verbatim record of the conference at Arden House is a sign only and no measure of the value of the conference both directly in the development of the chapters in this book and also indirectly. The university's debt to all the participants is accordingly large. In the conduct of the conference itself Professor Aaron Warner of the Department of Economics gave invaluable assistance as did Dr. Fred Burin in editorial matters. Throughout, I gratefully acknowledge on behalf of my colleagues in this undertaking the advice and support of the Director of the Bicentennial, his associates and staff, and Columbia University as a whole.

ARTHUR W. MACMAHON

College of Europe
Bruges

Contents

PART THREE.   Functional Channels of Relationship

PART ONE
Federalism: Its Nature and Role

1

The Problems of Federalism: A Survey

By Arthur W. Macmahon

This symposium treats the federal principle on two levels in several settings. On the national level it is concerned mainly with adjustments in going systems such as the United States but must also take account of nascent federalism in new nations. On the supranational level it is especially concerned with forms of regional union in Western Europe. A paradox runs through these several applications. In the formative stage of federalism, both historically for national states and especially now at the supranational level, the desperate need is a modicum of union where unity is impossible. When federal systems survive and mature, the problem, along with endless practical contrivances for uniformity or concert among the various jurisdictions, appears basically as the double question of the desirability and the practicability of maintaining a decentralized pattern originally dictated by necessity. The disparate compass of our inquiry, by heightening these paradoxical elements, suits the paradox that is at the heart of federalism.

The paradox, indeed, is a phase of man's relation to organization and the profound ambivalence of attitudes today. Politically, man is busy creating new national states while he reaches out for union among and across nations. So far as the spirit of independence breaks up older combinations and systems, nationalism is a decentralizing impulse. Within itself its dominant mood is one of centralization. In such a setting, federalism, if used at all, is an expedient rather than an end. The nation builder who faces surviving diversities within the new national area is inclined to devise a structure that will discourage as well as control them. Nevertheless he must consider how far the recognition of differences is a strategy in the integration of loyalties.

The paradox and the ambivalence must be considered in a context that includes all forms of power. The ultimate desideratum of the free man is the release of personality. Modern man is oppressed by the sense of heavy organization and distant controls; he longs to resolve things into comprehensible and manageable portions. At the same time he values the physical basis of the good life; he must take account of endless elements of interdependence; he must respect the utility of largescale methods. Partly, too, he may be led to favor centralized political power in national states to offset centralized economic power, either by positive intervention or by measures that outlaw barriers or restrictive combinations. In any longrun evaluation of federalism as a desirable arrangement at the national level, therefore, its peculiar method of deconcentrating political power must be appraised in terms of the relation of all forms of power to each other and to an ideal of freedom and tolerance.

I

ESSENTIAL ATTRIBUTES AND THE TEST OF DEGREE

The issue of the adequacy of federalism as a type of structure in meeting free men's needs is blurred by the accommodations that develop in all going federal systems as they mature and in some cases are explicitly provided for in the newer federal constitutions. Such accommodation and adaptation raise the question whether it is possible to speak of a valid pure form that would be desirable to install and practicable to maintain.

From the standpoint of words and meanings it is important to identify the salient characteristics of federalism but self-defeating not to allow for gradations. An exact classification would yield almost as many types as cases. About forty per cent of the world's population live in countries with constitutions that call themselves federal, begging the question whether the purported design exists in reality or is negated by a monolith of party or other dictatorial power. De Tocqueville was speaking of federalism when he made the wise remark that "the human understanding more easily invents new things than new words" and he was deploring the inadequacy of the word to describe what he found in the United States.[1] Yet there is virtue in making such a word do service in varied applications provided it carries an essence or logic that is remembered and respected.

The test on the borders of usage is likely to be one of degree. Thus a federal system distributes power between a common and constituent governments under an arrangement that cannot be changed by the ordinary process of central legislation. This requirement leaves open the question of how additionally difficult must be the method of amendment and how it is to be conducted. A further characteristic of federal systems is that the matters entrusted to the constituent units (whether their powers are residual or delegated) must be substantial and not merely trivial; this, too, is a problem of degree.

Another essential ingredient in federations (as distinguished from looser forms of union) is that their central organs are to some extent directly in contact with individuals, both to draw authority from them through elections and also for the purpose of exacting taxes and compliance with regulations. This principle, however, does not dictate just how much of the central machinery must be so based and so related nor does it preclude indirect methods of federal administration if the surrounding conditions are such that they assure an orderly execution of the central government's will.[2] Still another attribute of federal systems is that the member states have considerable leeway in devising and changing their forms of government and their procedures.[3] This principle, again, does not forbid some standardization from above, both to aid in erecting and maintaining the central organs and also to protect certain minimal institutional forms, rights, and decencies that are deemed more important than autonomy and variation among the constituent governments.[4]

A further essential is the equality of the constituent states, absolute as to legal status but at best relative as to such matters as size, population, and wealth. In these terms the preponderance of Prussia might well justify Heinrich von Treitschke in declaring that Imperial Germany was the very opposite of a federal system. Yet the ideal of equality cannot bar exceptional uses of the federal idea in such arrangements as the union of Eritrea and Ethiopia devised under United Nations auspices—a union that associated an entity of barely more than a million people with a country of fifteen millions. Through all these prime characteristics of federalism runs a discernible logic but the definition is a question of degree.

II

FEDERALISM AS NECESSITY

The case for federalism, we have said, has two aspects: necessity and desirability. Both assume an underlying desire to unite. So far as the case for a composite rather than unitary governmental form rests upon necessity because closer cohesion would be impossible, the question of the desirability of federalism as a method of decentralization is virtually irrelevant. The question may be realistic if a unitary condition is possible at the outset. In such circumstances it is relevant to weigh the advantages and disadvantages of a federal in comparison with a unitary constitution. This option has seldom been open in the past where federal systems have appeared. Thus a choice was hardly possible at the time of the establishment of the United States Constitution although the zest for nation-building was marked enough to invite, on the part of some students of constitutional history, the strained argument that a virtually unitary state was intended and at least lay within reach. Nevertheless there may be new countries, now and in the future, where the forces of nationalism are so composed that it is practical to canvass abstract arguments in the light of federal experience in choosing or rejecting federalism. In older federal systems established through necessity, moreover, the question of the desirability of the decentralized pattern may become relevant when the bonds of union mature to a point that makes a unitary state politically feasible. Even then, in countries like the United States, the discussion is apt to be unrealistic if it assumes a fresh outright choice of basic structure. Rather, the value of constantly renewed analysis of the fundamental considerations of federalism and of comparative federal experience lies in the guidance they bring to bear on the cumulative

choices that are made in the progressive modification or conservation of a
going system. In this spirit, the discussion is hardly less significant for people
who live under unitary constitutions; federalism is not inevitably a halfway
house on a road that leads in one direction only.

Above the level of existing national states, stupendous novelties call for
fresh inventiveness. Nevertheless federalizing efforts may well be attentive to
the conditions that have made unions possible in the past and how the minimal
requirements of durable associations have been met.[5] Much can be learned, too,
from practices under maturing systems in meeting the double problem of interlocking jurisdictions. On the one hand, the solution involves diverse bonds of
functional union that bridge the separate levels; on the other hand, it faces
the need for a degree of integration at each level. The significance of the
methods used in maturity lies partly in the extent to which they rest on
persuasion.

Historically, the explanation of the appearance of federal systems must
take account of two sets of factors: the attitudes that propel and permit a
union as close as a federation but not closer; and the sources of these attitudes.
A. V. Dicey's classic statement, for example, dealt more with resultant attitudes
than their origin when he wrote that federalism "requires for its formation two
conditions." On the one hand, there must be "a body of countries . . . so closely
connected by locality, by history, by race, or the like, as to be capable of
bearing, in the eyes of their inhabitants, an impress of common nationality." On
the other hand, there must exist "a very peculiar state of sentiment among the
inhabitants of the countries, which it is proposed to unite. They must desire
union, and must not desire unity."[6] The primary question, barely hinted at in
Dicey's phrasing, is the reason for the occurrence at particular places and
points in history of so peculiar a state of sentiment.

A striking proportion of federal governments owe their federal character, in
part at least, to the conditions of colonial development. This imprint was
especially likely when the process happened along an extended littoral. The
exploitative tendencies of the home government, perhaps through the haphazard play of mere royal favoritism, encouraged the parcelling out of jurisdictions. Entrance was made at a number of points from which developments
slowly radiated. Land communication was relatively difficult; in any case, the
trade and other relations of new areas producing raw materials tended to be
with the home country or other settled lands. In addition, imperial governments, seeking to divide in order to rule, tended to be lukewarm if not positively
hostile. An illustration of this spirit was Britain's disapproval in 1754 of the
plan of the Albany Congress for intercolonial collaboration. The foregoing generalization about colonial administrative patterns, however, should be qualified
by noting that in Australia, where the divisive imprint of colonial settlement
upon a homogeneous people was so marked that federation was not achieved
until 1900, all parts but Western Australia were originally governed from New
South Wales.[7] Nevertheless the generalization holds generally through the

colonial world; fragmentation could be traced to the center. In some places, as in the Spanish dominion, distrust of inept viceroys led the home power to inject direct representatives below them and thus further to carve up the separate areas of administration.[8] In such ways centers of attention, action, leadership, and loyalty congealed before independence. In Latin America, to be sure, the effect of the colonial administrative pattern struck in two directions. Mainly it helped to draw the lines for the partitioning of the continent into many separate national states. This connection is illustrated in the language of the constitution of Venezuela which says that its territory is "that which belonged to the Captaincy General of Venezuela before the political transformation of 1810." Partly, however, the colonial administrative subdivisions—such as the numerous intendencias in the viceroyalty of La Plata—laid the basis for provincialism and federal sentiment within the separate countries. A somewhat similar influence in a very different setting is the effect of indirect colonial administration working through chieftains and other indigenous political institutions, as in the Malayan union.

In North America the invention of a federal pattern may have been presaged and encouraged by the thinking that attended the attempt to work out a plural theory of the British Empire suited to permit and bulwark colonial autonomy.[9] Present also in many minds was the idea that popular government could be realized best, perhaps solely, in small areas which could meet the needs of defense by associating themselves for the conduct of external affairs. Nevertheless the practical precipitant of federalism when independence came was the parochialism of colonial development in entering upon a continent. The federal solution was consummated by the momentous and pregnant corollary that applied the principle of equality of states to commonwealths formed from the national domain or otherwise, later admitted to the union.[10]

Thus to identify the circumstances of colonial administration as the almost adventitious prime reason why nationhood in so many places took the middle federal course does not belittle the causal role of inherent diversities. In Canada language and religion were more important than topography and administrative organization in evoking the federal solution. In the case of the United States, despite a common language, the depth of the physiographic imprint was signalized by James Madison's remark in the Constitutional Convention of 1787 (according to Yates' minutes) that "the great danger to our general government is that the southern and northern interests of the continent are opposed to each other, not from their differences of size, but from climate, and principally from the effect of their having or not having slaves."[11] He further developed his point that the main differences did not lie between large and small states by adding: "Look to the votes in Congress; most of them stand divided by the geography of the country, not by the size." Only about a year before the Convention met, Madison had written to Jefferson that "of affairs of Georg[i]a I know as little as of those of Kamchatka" and before the Convention was over a delegate from South Carolina, during debate on the power of Congress to stop the importation of slaves, pronounced the interests of the sections of the country "to be as different as the interests of Russia and Turkey."

The outstanding role of colonialism in the origin of modern federations readily invites one to overstate the conclusion that no successful federation has been formed from states that have existed as independent nations for a considerable period of time. Kenneth C. Wheare almost makes this flat declaration in the following chapter. The story of federations on the European continent, I suggest, shows that the generalization should not be made too absolute, although it is true enough to be a warning against false analogy or undue optimism. Its implications are offset, furthermore, by Mr. Wheare's highly suggestive observation that sometimes federations have been established before the sense of nationality was achieved. In any case, when independent countries are brought together, diversities are likely to be more pronounced and lasting than in federations shaped by colonial administration in new lands. To be sure, below the tangles of dynastic history, much that was originally almost sheerly administrative in character has been a precipitant of national divisions within a common culture.

In treating federalism as necessity, because more was impossible, we have stressed thus far the sources of only one side of a "very peculiar state of sentiment"—the aspect that resists unity. The other side is the will to associate. Its source may be traced to two sets of factors. The first is positive compatibility. The second is shared apprehension and mutual defense. Fear has been a dynamic—or at least a catalytic—in most federal undertakings that have been more than imitative. The American states, for example, knew the extent to which their independence had been won in the end as an incident of a European war; not yet secure on the continent and vividly aware of external forces, they feared the risks in division as a fulcrum for intrigue and dissension and an opening for attack. Canadian union in mid-century was influenced by defensive concern. In Australia the tardy movement for federation was quickened in part by the coming of power politics in the Pacific; an immediate factor was the portent of modern Japan as revealed in the closing decade of the century.

Nevertheless man is so made that fear as motive is strangely limited; doubtless it is for the best that it is so.[12] At any rate, fear by itself—short of the fiery crucible—is unlikely to produce combinations that are lasting. The problem of federation today, especially when national units are dealt with, is to find, in addition to well-justified defensive motives, the positive elements that may lie in cultural and economic conditions and needs.

III

INTEGRATIVE ALTERNATIVES

When diversities are faced, as in language or religion, several courses are open. If the sense of identity and difference is strong, it is likely in an age of national self-determination to result in separate countries. This was the course mainly followed after the first world war in the rise of the succession states of the Austro-Hungarian Empire. More recently it was illustrated in the rejection of federalism as a solution of the problems of Pakistan and of Israel. But if schism is resisted and an attempt is made to form a larger state in the face of diversities, the nation-builder confronts several choices. In seeking national strength and cohesion, he may reject the federal idea and create a unitary constitution, provided that the warmth of the nascent nationalism in the new country permits this step. Such was the choice made at the close of the first world war in Czechoslovakia and also in Jugoslavia, after more hesitant weighing of alternatives in the latter instance. Such has been the choice, recently, in Indonesia although here, perhaps, the unitary feature of its constitution (offset, as in Italy, by an emphatic promise of regional autonomy) has been partly a gesture of independence.[13]

Even if the federal pattern is chosen, the emphasis in applying it may be to minimize certain differences by disregarding them. India's policy on linguistic boundaries has afforded a case study in the problem of national integration. In drafting the 1949 constitution it was decided that any reshaping of provincial boundaries along linguistic lines should be viewed coldly and should at least wait until a later time. The preparatory commission that dealt with this issue declared that the "first and last need of India at the present time is that it should be made a nation." It argued that an attempt to reorganize in terms of the various languages—Tamil, Telugu, and others—"would set the ball rolling for the disintegration of the entire country." Despite this decision, India in 1953 was forced to create the new state of Andhra, an entity of twenty millions of people formed from Telugu speaking areas in Madras. This step was reluctantly taken at the cost of risking future defeat for the Congress Party in Andhra and was attended by a further concession in the promise that the government would give early attention to other linguistic claims.

Truly, the choice is a baffling one and the outcome chancy at best when the objective is an integrative loyalty won without the drastic suppression of differences. Even apart from the cultural values that may inhere in diversities, however, their recognition at the outset may be the wisest course. Looking back, one wonders whether in building Czechoslovakia after the first world war it might not have been rewarding to make more formal provision for Slovak autonomy. For the Slovak people's irked sense of subordination to Czech hegemony, as it was viewed, prepared the way for collapse. "The discord between these two branches of the Western Slav family," observed Stephen Bonsal, ". . . made the conquest of their common country by the Germans in 1939 a matter of but a few days."[14] And in Jugoslavia—even disregarding the methods available in this modified Communist regime for maintaining cohesion under federalism—one suspects that the federal features in the Jugoslav constitution of 1946 were a shrewder answer to ethnic particularism than the answer given in 1920 by such nationalists as Pashitch.[15]

An obvious difficulty, however, frequently blocks the use of federalism to recognize differences, to protect minorities, and to maximize government with the consent of the governed by distributing power geographically. The realization of the objective depends upon a neat concentration of national minorities. It is likely, however, that they will be present in many places and in the minority everywhere, subordinate in social prestige, economic power, and influence. When this condition exists, thorough-going federalism may easily result in a kind of feudalism—benevolent, perhaps, but essentially oligarchical in local domination over weaker elements. The situation may indeed be softened by various minor devices: reserved parliamentary seats for certain nongeographical communities, provision for dual or multiple official languages, and like ways. The main relief, however, is sought in central constitutional guarantees, centrally enforced.

The presence of such guarantees in federal constitutions raises a fundamental question in the theory of federalism; the dilemmas involved in their application present the courts with one of the most important, perplexing, and incessant issues in constitutional development. It can be argued that there should be no place in a federal constitution for guarantees that touch matters about which important sectional variations are likely to exist. This argument deserves careful consideration in terms of the nature of the guarantees and of the community they are to cover. Arthur Holcombe, for example, suggests in a later chapter that in the *early* stages of a federal system the guarantees should be mainly against abuse of power by the central government itself. On the main theoretical question, however, there is an affirmative answer apart from the mere fact of the ubiquity of guarantees against member-state action in federal constitutions, not to mention the impulse evident in the European Convention for the Protection of Human Rights and Fundamental Freedoms already accepted by a number of countries. The answer is that the viable theory of modern federalism is based upon respect for personality. If federalism renounces this ideal in strained respect for territorial autonomy, its critics will be confirmed in their belief that protection is best afforded by the leverages of national politics and freedom mainly secured by the nationwide competition of broadly based, responsible parties.

IV

THE QUESTION OF DESIRABILITY

The case for a federal rather than unitary constitution—that is, when it is relevant to canvass the arguments—may be stated summarily under five heads. First, when diversities are pronounced and located with reasonable compactness, the geographical deconcentration of important powers secures greater correspondence between public policies and local majority sentiment on matters entrusted to the constituent governments. Second, by multiplying the independent legislative arenas, the system gives scope for experimentation, followed by imitation. Third, the multiplication of the bodies of elected officials who bear considerable responsibility in their own right broadens the opportunity for political participation. Fourth, the system is suitable for government over large or scattered areas. This argument based on size was stressed in the 1930 report of the Indian Statutory Commission which prepared the way for the Government of India Act, passed five years later, and through this measure helped to shape the present constitution. The commission justified the proposal to change from a unitary to a federal situation in India by saying, in part, "there is a very definite correspondence between dimension of area and population and the kind of constitution that can be operated successfully."[16] In point, too, was the remark of the United Nations Commissioner in Libya, Adrian Pelt, when commenting in his 1949 report on the decision to organize the new state on a federal basis. "The Libyan provinces," he said, "are like islands in an ocean of sand, separated by hundreds of miles of desert wastes."[17] Fifth, federalism lessens the risk of a monopoly of political power by providing a number of independent points where the party that is nationally in the minority at the time can maintain itself while it formulates and partly demonstrates its policies and capabilities and develops new leadership.

Looking back over the foregoing five arguments, it must be conceded as to the first four that the results they contemplate could be approximated in a decentralized unitary state, developed in a tolerant society that believed in diffused initiative. Nevertheless it still can be said that a federal constitution helps by guaranteeing and stabilizing the institutions of regional self-government and by subtly galvanizing them through a heightened awareness of responsibility. Lessons can be read, moreover, in the experience of certain unitary constitutions where seemingly strong mandates for devolution in provinces and communes are largely disregarded. The fifth argument rests upon features peculiar to a federal structure, provided it is not the type that legalizes forceful intervention by the central government; besides, the argument assumes that the surrounding conditions assure competitive politics and orderly elections.

Doubts about the suitability of federal structure for national states under modern conditions—unless federalism is the closest form of organization possible at the time—arise in two directions: in domestic policy and in international affairs. In the background is the question of maintaining cohesion and peace within a composite state.

On the domestic side, the criticism of federalism turns largely on the adequacy of power. For present purposes it will suffice to summarize a formidable and ramified attack in a sentence, assuming the reader will sense the range of applications implied in its phrases. Critics ask whether the central organs in federal systems are competent to provide the desirable degree of uniformity in regulating interdependent matters, whether they can deal effectively with economic entities, whether they can minimize duplication and bring the stimulus of experience and high standards to bear in each field of administration, and whether they can provide the comprehensive equalization that modern societies demand in the relation of governmental services to human needs, on the one hand, and taxable resources, on the other.

From the standpoint of the participation of federally organized nations in international affairs, it is enough here to mention the main clusters of possible difficulties. First is the question of national strength in a world of sovereign states set in the international politics of power. Theoretically at least, a federal state might be so structured as to be at a disadvantage because of lack of power at the center. This lack might affect not only the ability to provide force-in-being but also—and at once more subtly and more seriously—the development of the economic potentials of power so far as these require governmental pre-vision and control. Second is the question of the ability of the central govern-ment in a federal system to participate, with a confidence shared by other peoples, in the full range of international negotiations and agreements that at any point in history is customary in the dealings of nations with each other.[18] It is this angle of American federalism in relation to foreign affairs that the chapter by Noel T. Dowling treats with conservative commonsense inci-dentally to a demonstration of the degree to which the maintenance of internal federal balance rests with the political organs of the central government, in this case the President mainly. Third, the problem of the federal state in interna-tional affairs may be complicated (though not necessarily to the disadvantage of the country in question) by the claim of constituent members for separate representation. Fourth are the possible embarrassments to friendly international relations that may be caused by the action or inaction of the constituent gov-ernments and their subdivisions within the fields left to them by the federal constitution. The central government, for example, assumes few direct respon-sibilities for what happens to or by aliens; full responsibility would hardly be consistent with the federal principle.[19] Fifth is the chance that the decen-tralized structure of a federal state may afford footholds for foreign intrigue and attack through sheer carelessness or as a result of the miscarriage of the attempt to integrate a national loyalty by concessions to the parts. The fore-going five clusters of difficulties are mere possibilities. Doubtless they are mostly chimerical. Nevertheless real problems are faced in the participation of federal states in the world and regional communities. The situation is not without a certain high irony in view of the role that the federal idea is asked to play above the level of existing national states.

The proponents of federalism as the means of maintaining peace while achieving cohesion amid diversity[20] face the disturbing fact that two outstand-ing federal systems were stabilized on the battlefield: Switzerland in the few weeks' war of the Sonderbund in 1847; the United States in a four years' struggle that was one of the greatest wars of the century. It can be said, of course, that at the time neither federal union was mature. Switzerland's consti-tutional structure, indeed, did not become fully federal until 1848 and men found grave ambiguities in the American system. Moreover, if one views fed-eralism as a process of growth, the mere fact that in both cases there was the will and ability to resist secession points to the consolidating influence of federal institutions, however incomplete the form. In addition, looking at the tragic episode of the American Civil War from the standpoint of the future risk of serious armed revolt in federal systems, two things can be said. First one can point to the peculiarly explosive combination of ingredients in secessionist motivation: a vast property interest tied to caste and galvanized by haunting fears; an elaborate legal justification that appealed to the Constitution itself; and a rationalized moral case that sought to turn the tables on northern industrial employers who assumed no responsibility for their workers. It was indeed a singularly potent mixture while on the other side, along with evolving nationalism, were galloping elements of profound moral disapprobation. The second thing to say by way of reassurance about the ability of federations to maintain union without actual resort to arms is to point to the changing technology of weapons and their use. Sir Ivor Jennings puts the matter baldly. "War in a federation," he writes, "is, in modern times, practically impossible." For, he argues, "Modern warfare is a highly complex and technical process requiring not only mechanical armaments, but also highly trained mechanics and a whole apparatus of industrial preparation for war." On these grounds he concludes that "the example of the Civil War in the United States, which causes many prospective 'federalists' to hesitate, is irrelevant." Obviously in the survival of any system of orderly and responsible government, unitary or federal, much depends upon loyalty to the constitutional process on the part of professional soldiers. Ivor Jennings puts his finger exactly though perhaps too casually upon the crucial spot when he remarks: "It is a simple problem of administrative technique, and involves only the maintenance of the morale and the discipline of the armed forces."[21]

But we need not imagine the worst about the embarrassments of federal states in international affairs, nor speculate about the risks of civil war, to admit the gravity of the questions I have summarized, as issues for analysis and not a conclusion, about the inherent desirability of federalism when it is not a sheer matter of necessity.

The chapter of critique by Franz Neumann answers the questions unfavorably. At best he sees federalism as an expedient that particular circumstances may require but which has no values in itself. Indeed, it impedes responsible democratic processes in the nation as a whole and it tends to undermine self-government in local communities—the intimate areas where autonomy is most fruitful. Perhaps Mr. Neumann's focus in the question whether federalism "maximizes freedom" leads him to slight arguments for the inherent desirability of federalism based upon the somewhat different values of harmony through adjustment and compromise among diverse interests. Mr. Neumann believes that his skeptical view about the constitutional partitioning of jurisdiction is confirmed by the "chaos" that he finds reflected in the facts shown in certain of the functional studies in later chapters, as in the handling of land and water resources. On the other hand, it will be observed how

Henry M. Hart, Jr., facing the intricacies of laws and courts, illustrates the viewpoint of those who find positive virtue in the accommodating complexities of the double system of jurisdictions and agencies.

It is worth pausing to raise questions about Mr. Neumann's charge that federalism may weaken self-government in cities and other local units which, he argues, are the prime arenas of political participation. The issue he raises is indeed an important but speculative one. A few things can be said. The premise of the importance of the vitality of local institutions is admitted, although one notes that Mr. Neumann himself qualifies it by his confidence in the potential beneficence of a responsible democratic process carried on over the width of a nation. Nevertheless the creation of some kind of intermediate or regional layer of general government seems inevitable; no country, certainly no large country, has avoided it. Does it make any difference to the vitality of the local institutions below it whether this layer is organized under a federal or a unitary constitution? An offhand answer unfavorable to federalism is prompted by the unsympathetic behavior of many rurally dominated state legislatures in the United States.[22] It is supported, too, by the degree to which municipalities look to the national government for help. But, from the other side, what conclusions may be drawn from the pervasively centralizing effect of the prefecture system in many unitary countries? In the United States, after all, local election of relatively unsupervised local officials has prevailed throughout the country's history. Furthermore, in about half the states the logic of federalism has been projected downward in what is called constitutional home rule for cities. In the play of national-state-local relations, novel units have appeared, evoked by the central government but authorized by enabling legislation in the states: irrigation districts, for example, and more recently soil conservation districts, local housing authorities, and rural electrification cooperatives. Finally it should be noted that the transfer to the state level of many formerly local activities and the assumption by the states, at the request of the localities, of an increasing share of the cost of local functions are phases of the inevitable shift of part of the burden to larger areas. This essential need is a reason why the state governments of the United States, despite mistaken grumbling by some of their partisans, are richer in activities and in this sense more important than at any stage in American history.[23]

From the standpoint of modern economic integration and the way it challenges the adequacy of power in a federal system of government, a different and favorable view of federalism is taken by Adolf A. Berle, Jr. in a chapter that asks fundamental questions about the relationships of property, power, and personality.[24] He views political federalism as an element in a larger complex. Federalism, taken broadly, is conceived in two ways. One embodiment is the constitutional federalism that distributes political powers among levels of government. Historically it has appeared as a centralizing movement, building upward by cessions of power and extending superior but limited controls over larger areas. The other embodiment is the implicit federalism—or quasi-federalism—that in free societies inheres in the relationship between the political structure as a whole and the economic entities and interests that carry on virtually governmental processes within themselves and in their dealings with each other.

Mr. Berle is eloquent about the risks as well as the necessities of power. When he speaks about federalism in the political sense he assumes, as a phase of its essential purpose, that the central organs of the system must be strong enough to enable the government as a whole to play its part as the central mechanism of adjustment within the larger complex. He suggests the variety of organizational forms and relationships and the degree to which power is shared or devolved. He insists upon the need, deeper than contrivance, for a working philosophy.

Where so much is implicit, the grand outlines are felt; only details are visible. Thus (to mention an example not developed by Mr. Berle) there is a federal quality in the relationship of government in the United States to management and labor in the conduct of what Mr. Berle calls administered capitalism. Government at various levels regulates certain aspects of the bargaining process. Nearly everyone assumes, however, that although the government's potential influence is vast, its power is limited as to collective bargaining —the quasi-governmental procedure by which the functional groups adjust their positions in relation to each other. Needless to say, the workability of this profoundly significant type of devolution within an implicitly federal structure depends upon attitudes of mutual respect, shared knowledge, and practical wisdom. In this connection one notes the warning in the chapter by John Fischer about the need for inherent balance. But one should not forget, in asking for an equipoise of diverse forces, that James Madison, in the classic statement in *The Federalist* on the value of conducting government over large areas, spoke not only of the safety produced by a multiplicity of interests and factions but also of government as the regulator of their interfering claims.

V

THE MATURING OF POWERS

Doubts about the desirability of federalism where a unitary constitution is possible would be more convincing if the system had to be conceived always in terms of the traditional model of federal structure—a model, to be sure, that has continuing significance for marginal situations in which union is barely achievable. For national systems generally it is important to note the evolution of federalism as shown in the distribution of powers in existing systems. On the one hand are the types of provisions found in federal constitutions drawn in the last few decades. They represent maturing federalism in the sense that their draftsmen have been able to take account of federal experience and especially of the tasks of government under modern conditions. On the other hand is the outcome reached in the practice in older systems like the United States.

Two questions arise. How far apart are these two developments? What is their cumulative meaning for federalism?

Turning first to recent constitutions, one notes that residual powers belong to the central government in India and in Burma, as indeed was the intention for Canada in the British North America Act. In the Indian constitution the reservation to the central government of all powers not delegated to the states is reinforced by a "Union list" of nearly a hundred items. The matters entrusted to the states run to nearly seventy items, some relatively important. Especially emblematic of a trend in federal thinking is a third list that enumerates about fifty matters over which the central government and the states have concurrent power, subject to the provision that a state law is invalid to the extent that it conflicts with a federal enactment and that a state law may be reserved for the consideration of the President. The significance of the Indian provisions lies in the concept of a hierarchy of policy, not in the itemization which may prove extreme and self-defeating in an organic law.

Elsewhere this significant concept is shown even more clearly in the type of provision that expressly gives the central government a norm-creating or policy-guiding role within broad fields of legislation. Such an arrangement was evident in continental constitutions adopted at the close of the first world war, especially that of Austria. In the Bonn Constitution of 1949—the Basic Law for the Federal Republic of Germany—the description of a field of concurrent legislation (set forth under twenty-three heads) is accompanied by the statement that the central government "shall have legislative rights in this field insofar as a necessity for regulation by federal law exists because: (1) a matter cannot be effectively regulated by the legislation of individual Laender, or (2) the regulation of a matter by a Land law could prejudice the interests of other Laender or of the Laender as a whole, or (3) the preservation of legal or economic unity demands it, in particular the preservation of uniformity of living conditions extending beyond the territory of an individual Land." Moreover, permission and guidance within the field of so-called exclusive federal legislation—defined by a list of eleven items—is implied in the statement that in this field "the Laender shall have powers of legislation only if, and so far as, they are expressly so empowered in a federal law."

It is interesting to ponder on the extent to which a normative technique has evolved in the practice of the older and briefer constitution of the United States. It is no single thing; it is implicit in a host of relationships. The plenary discretion now conceded to Congress in determining the purposes for which interstate commerce may be regulated and the wide meaning of these words open the way for the central government to touch nearly every important economic concern, since by nature a problem that is important is likely to be widespread enough to involve commerce. This fact, to be sure, does not justify complacency about the amount of intrastate activity that is not covered and the consequent risks of invidious competition. Nevertheless the Supreme Court indicates its willingness to respect the intent of Congress by noting committee reports and by giving different degrees of coverage to various shades of statutory language that bears on the relation of intrastate to interstate operations. Congress thus determines the length of its reach. This condition illustrates the tendency of constitutional law to become a question of statutory construction. Congress, thus equipped with incomplete but still expansive regulatory authority (provided it shows clearly how far it deems it necessary to go) and aided by the possibilities of noncoercive action opened by the spending power, can in effect establish fundamental requirements, draw outlines of policy, create germinal points of leadership, and permit various kinds of devolution within such a framework. Some observers, perhaps, will see here a betrayal of the nature of federalism. Others will deplore the clumsiness, indirection, and incompleteness of the guidance or control accomplished in this way. Both viewpoints call for careful analysis. In any case, such is the reality of maturing federalism in systems like the United States. It is proper to ask whether a modern system is workable without these features. I have no hesitation in concluding that it would not be.

If the range of central legislative discretion in this pattern seems almost without limit, one must reflect on the political factors that check its exercise. The resulting controls are dealt with in the chapters by Herbert Wechsler, David B. Truman, and (more broadly) by Arthur N. Holcombe. It will be observed how many elements of political veto are built into such a federal system as the United States. They include, on the one hand, certain features of governmental structure and procedure and, on the other hand, the reflex of federalism in contributing to the decentralization of the great political parties. The operation of the veto can be traced in the way in which Congress has altered in behalf of the states the effect of certain Supreme Court decisions. One believed he saw it reflected in briefs submitted to the Supreme Court for certain states on the issue of segregation in public schools suggesting that, if the Fourteenth Amendment was applicable at all, its application in regard to segregation belonged to Congress.

The discretion conceded to the central legislature in the emergent designs of normative federalism is not inconsistent with—and indeed is in line with—judicial respect for state power. At bottom both attitudes reflect the modesty of enlightened courts. The Supreme Court, to be sure, may not yet always recognize that congressional action is not intended to oust state control. This fact is dealt with by Paul R. Hays in the illustrative chapter on labor relations that points to the increasing responsibility of Congress in clarifying the detailed allocation of jurisdiction between the national and state governments. Nowadays, speaking generally, when the Court deals with the constitutionality of state legislation, respect for the federal principle and for decentralization reinforces the judicial deference toward legislatures on questions of policy. The result is an outlook that, without denying the paramount position of clear assertions of national interest and leadership, seeks to keep open the door for state initiative and action. This attitude is a phase of what may be called the

positive states' rights of state governmental power to act, distinguished from
the misnamed states' rights that are the right of the individual to be left alone
in all matters by all units of government including his own state. It may truly
be said that for a long time after modern industrial problems had to be faced,
the state governments did not have a full chance to show what they could do.
Apart from the disabilities of their own machinery, their power to regulate
economic matters was checked by the substantive twist of the due process
clause in the Fourteenth Amendment, by the scope given to the negative implications of the commerce clause, by the tendency to treat the absence of
congressional action as a prohibition rather than permission, and by the related
tendency in construing national statutes and regulations to resolve doubts
against the consistency and enforceability of state enactments in the same field.

The disposition of the Supreme Court to reverse the situation is a major
chapter in the maturing of American federalism. The attendant problems are
of the greatest. Along with vexing and still unsettled questions about the ability
of the state governments to take advantage of the opportunity to act, singly or
in cooperation with each other, the trend involves dilemmas that make it an
almost tortured field of judicial choice. It presents the question of what personal
rights are so fundamental that they should be protected against state power.
Under the commerce clause it constantly raises the question, in both regulation
and taxation, of the judicial responsibility to maintain the national market
place. No wonder divisions have been frequent and majorities fluctuating in a
Supreme Court that over the last decade and a half has been remarkably of
one mind in accepting the philosophy of a positive role for government in
economic affairs and in feeling deeply about the crisis of liberty in the modern
world.

Apart from constitutional restraints, the obstacles to state action are formidable. Their legislative structure is less easily renovated than their administration; the apportionment of representation between country and city areas
is especially hard to change. Their own constitutions sometimes contain restraints or obsolete complications that it is extremely difficult to dislodge. In
the field of interstate cooperation, devices like the compact seem better suited
to serve mutual needs that arise between adjacent states than to handle strains
between competing states or regions.

Competition among states (even where it does not lead to barriers or aggressive inducements) may make all of them fearful to act even though the realities
behind the alarms would probably be found to be exaggerated if more were
known about the relative weight that businessmen give to various factors—
including elements connected with state regulation and taxation—in deciding
on the location of new businesses, new plants, and the like.[25] Probably the
United States will not develop the rising territorial rivalries that Frederick
Jackson Turner prophesied would come with increasing sectionalism when a
growing and more stationary population pressed upon diminishing resources.
Much of the petty, protective parochialism of the depression period has been

overcome. Nevertheless state governments are active promoters although they may offer less concrete inducements than some cities, presumably acting in programs permitted by state law. The state appeal may be innocent enough and mainly in terms of natural advantages. The Research, Planning and Development Board of South Carolina sponsored a special paid supplement to the *New York Times* of February 8, 1953. Its slogan, "Where Resources and Markets Meet," stressed two basic nonpolitical factors in industrial location. The text (after noting that South Carolina led the states in industrial development between 1948 and 1951) also called attention to "a favorable tax structure that does not penalize industrial expansion." It mentioned the fact that the advance of farm mechanization meant that "for every farm job available, fourteen persons from farm backgrounds must seek other employment." To this estimate it added the argument that "coming as they do from small towns and rural areas, the people of South Carolina who seek places in industry are sound-thinking, conservative, honest, and free from foreign ideologies which have brought turmoil elsewhere."

So far as concerns the provision of the costly services expected of governments, the states are handicapped by the unevenness of their taxable resources apart from all questions of their willingness to act. The longrun view of this matter is admittedly cloudy. Conceivably the surging spread of industry in the United States during the war years and afterward presages a continuing movement that in time will even out the distribution of taxable resources regionally. Many obscure and some novel factors are at work within and outside the major trilogy of influences on industrial location that Calvin B. Hoover called "the three M's—*men, materials,* and *markets.*"[26] The effect of a changing source of material upon the territorial distribution of an industry can be illustrated in the chemical industry's shift from a coal tar to a petrochemistry basis which has been attended by a movement of the industry, once located in the coal-bearing Middle Atlantic states, to the Gulf area and the Middle West. It may be that the future changes in the industrial and urban pattern of the country will be different from those observed in the thirties when decentralization was seen to be "not a scattering of factories up and down the length of the land, but a gradual and limited filling out of the industrial pattern within the major manufacturing regions."[27] If a more thorough-going decentralization gradually industrializes all sections and all states, spottiness will continue within the individual states. In the past, in states like Massachusetts, New York, and Illinois, the spread in average per capita wealth between the wealthiest and the poorest towns or townships has been from five to eight times greater than the spread between the wealthiest and poorest states. This condition within the states is likely to continue. If industry and urbanization should ever become fairly even among all the states, the burden of fiscal equalization would rest at the state level and be carried by state-local fiscal arrangements, projecting the structure of state aid that is already so important. But the nationwide evening out of the fundamental sort we are discussing will be slow if it comes at all. Moreover, the location of industrial wealth in the vital forms reached by income taxation tends to lag behind the spread of industrial equipment. With this patent phenomenon go subtler problems in the relationships of advantage or disadvantage between areas where commerce and finance form around a heavy industrial core and areas that produce raw materials.[28] It is partly a question of the location of ownership but more deeply it is probably a matter of inherent productivity in which industry has an unavoidable advantage in modern economies. In the United States, for a long time at the very least, federalism must make terms with discrepancies in wealth among the states.

These speculative observations invite a passing comment on the related problem of the geography of federal systems. The rational drawing of boundaries (apart from the elements of inertia rooted in history) presents an almost inevitable dilemma. Federalism cherishes the ideals of self-expression and of self-support for the member states. In shaping the areas, should the emphasis be upon as much homogeneity as possible in each of the parts, suiting it for self-expression; or should the emphasis be upon such a spread and balance of resources that it will have within itself the steady basis for enough taxation to ensure self-support? The dilemma is illustrated by asking whether, if state areas in the United States could be recast by some stroke of magic, the ideal plan would provide for a number of great diversified region-states or for a design that would include a number of metropolitan city-states. If the latter course were followed, it would cut them off from the more distant surrounding areas that would be correspondingly handicapped from the standpoint of available revenue. Much could be said for this design in terms of the representative process but it would deepen the fiscal problem of federalism.

VI

ADMINISTRATIVE PATTERNS

The existing fiscal relations among the levels of government are part of the administrative adjustments of federalism. Unfortunately in the study of federal systems the outstanding feature of a distribution of legislative powers policed by a court long invited a neglect of the administrative aspects, including interlevel fusions that involved both laws and administration. In the United States this attitude was encouraged by the nearly complete silence of the Constitution about administrative matters. It was deepened by the historical circumstances and a tradition that made strictly direct federal administration seem an indispensable feature of a true federation. American experience, reacting against the Articles of Confederation although with considerable early dependence upon state facilities, did confirm the essence of truth in Hamilton's observation in the *Federalist* that "a sovereignty over sovereigns, a government over governments, a legislation for communities, as it is a solecism in theory so in practice it is subversive of the order and ends of civil polity, by substituting violence in place of law, or the destructive coercion of the sword in place of the mild and salutary coercion of the magistracy." Ironically, however, in the great case that in 1816 confirmed the power of the United States Supreme Court to review and correct the decisions of state courts on federal questions, the Court found it necessary to repudiate the argument of the Virginia tribunal that under the Constitution, unlike the Articles, the power of the central government was intended to operate only "on individuals in their individual capacity" and that "the constitution of the United States contemplates the independence of both governments." In refuting this view, Justice Story declared: "It is a mistake that the constitution was not designed to operate on states, in their corporate capacities."[29]

Looking at federal systems comparatively, there are many signs of an approach of the direct type of federal administration, so notably though never completely exemplified in the path-breaking practice of the United States, and the indirect type of federal administration more or less characteristic of federalism in European countries in the past. German experience is reflected in the articles of the Bonn Constitution that deal at some length with "the execution of federal laws and federal administration." Direct administration has increased since the seventies but provision is also made for action through the Laender. Meanwhile developments in the United States, as elsewhere, offer much to support the forecast of John W. Burgess who, writing at the close of the nineteenth century, suggested that if federal systems survived after ethnical differences were overcome, "the local governments will become more and more administrative bodies, and less and less law-making bodies."[30] He added a prophecy: "In fact, it looks now as if the whole political world, that part of it in which the centralized form of government obtains as well as that part still subject to the federal form, were tending toward this system of centralized government in legislation and federal government in administration." He wondered whether this was not the ultimate, the ideal, form, at least for great states.

These remarks were indeed prescient if the terms "administrative" and "law-making" are taken figuratively, with an eye to what really enters into the shaping of norms and the outlining of policy. Taking the words in their conventional sense, the activity at the higher level may be administrative while the activity below is legislative. The idea must comprehend an interlocking that is much subtler and more varied than the notion of a simple relationship of principal and agent descending from level to level.

The spontaneous relationships run characteristically in functional channels across the levels of government. This proclivity is richly illustrated in the chapters by John M. Gaus, Charles McKinley, and Milton Handler and in the analysis by Edward W. Weidner of the interplay of professional and other group attitudes in the making of decisions. The fact that elements of natural cohesion exist does not mean that conflict is absent. The extent of the cohesion increases rather than lessens the need for careful attention to the preservation of initiative and experimentation, on the one side, and, on the other, skillful central handling of those aspects of each function which (as John Stuart Mill suggested in some notable generalizations in *Representative Government*) must be dealt with at the center in order to make possible the fruition and spread of ideas engendered at the circumference. Some of the most troublesome problems of adjustment, moreover, lie in the relation at each level of separate functions to the total governmental process at that level. Here federalism complicates a universal problem in government. At the same time it is the vitality of functional union that helps to make federalism workable.

Fiscal relations, quite understandably, involve some of the most serious strains between functional particularism and the ideal of responsible overall policy in separate political units for general governmental purposes. The necessity for interlevel payments is not likely to be overcome by any imaginable reallocation of tax sources in the face of uneven resources. The obvious main lines of reform in the use of interlevel subsidies include, first, the refining of allocation ratios to take fuller account of the need for governmental services in relation to local taxable capacity and, second, broadening the categories in which aid is given. Grants-in-aid, whether from nation to state or state to locality, cannot be viewed as temporary administrative levers for the introduction and spread of novel programs; much of the past use of subsidies in the United States had this coloring. We must at least raise the question of the desirability of a system of unconditional grants allocated among the states by a master formula. Such grants could be supplementary to existing systems of conditional federal aid. In this connection it may be useful to draw upon fiscal experience not only in other federations but also in decentralized unitary governments and in some of the states. In any case it is timely to give more attention to the connection between national-state fiscal relations and overall fiscal policy. The flexible strategies of this policy are especially important in countries which, like the United States, must stress such measures as fiscal policy in seeking to keep governmental influences upon the economy as largely indirect in character as possible. All of the foregoing possibilities challenge the haphazard and unduly piecemeal nature of much federal aid. Nevertheless, whatever steps are taken to meet the problem of reconciling interlevel relations with responsible politics and coordinated policy at each level, it is unlikely (as Roy Blough concludes in his chapter on the fiscal aspects of federalism) that reforms can dispense with linkage along the lines of function.

VII

Supranational Regional Union

On the supranational level in the setting of Western Europe, federal thinking faces novel issues in the fitting of spokes and hub. There is nothing new, of course, in throwing functional strands across international political boundaries. International unions in the past, however, have been mainly advisory or merely administrative. The type of functional union presented in the European Coal and Steel Community has governing powers in its own right. Can such a scheme thrive in isolation? Can a hub be provided into which it can be fitted and other spokes inserted as they are fashioned? Can the old seeming dilemma of the priority of special or general forms of federal union be resolved by creating a broadly based central government which can plan and stimulate while its substantial powers grow by the successive accession of powers agreed to in connection with particular functional controls?

The prospects are brightest on a regional scale where the underlying elements of cultural compatibility are not too attenuated, where common dangers are seen, and where the problems and possibilities of economic interdependence lie close at hand. It can adopt the flexible principle that additional members may join later on the basis of equality. Realistically, perhaps, one may beg as an *a priori* question the problem of the limits of a region and what are likely to be the ultimate viable groupings. In any case the cords of interdependence run beyond the region. Moreover, member states or states asked to be members may seek to retain their links in forms of association that extend into other parts of the world. These ramifying interests at the margins of a supranational regional union seem to call for gradations of relationships with it. It must adjust itself to these peripheral relationships while respecting the principle of federal cohesion it seeks to develop as its core.

FOOTNOTES TO CHAPTER 1

1. *Democracy in America,* Reeve translation as revised by Bowen, edited by Phillips Bradley, New York, Knopf, 1945, Vol. I, p. 158.

2. De Tocqueville did at once service and disservice by the stress that he placed upon a mechanical feature though it was of the utmost importance. He wrote in the first volume of his work, published in 1835 (*op. cit.,* p. 235): "This constitution, which at first sight might be confounded with the federal constitutions which preceded it, rests upon a novel theory, which may be considered as a great invention in modern political science. In all the confederations which had been formed before the American constitution of 1789, the allied states agreed to obey the injunctions of a Federal government; but they reserved to themselves the right of ordaining and enforcing the execution of the laws of the Union. The American states which combined in 1789 agreed that the Federal Government should not only dictate the laws, but that it should execute its own enactments. In both cases the right is the same, but the exercise of the right is different; and the alteration produces the most momentous consequences."

It will be observed that De Tocqueville's essentially pragmatic criterion virtually erases the supposed sharp distinction between "federation" and "confederation" in terms of sovereignty and obligation, as, in the other direction, John C. Calhoun did doctrinally by attempting to pull all federations down to the level of confederations. But De Tocqueville's pragmatic test was not carried far enough and itself solidified into a doctrine.

3. Note the double theoretical implication in the Report of the Conference on the Nigerian Constitution, held in London in July and August, 1953: "The Con-

ference discussed the structure of Government at the Regional level and agreed that there was no need for uniformity." Cmd. 8934.

4. It can be argued, I think soundly, that there is a logic consistent with the spirit of autonomy when pressure from the center on the parts safeguards their inner democratic responsibility which is a source of their continued vitality. In these terms, one may ask why the United States Supreme Court (by a divided vote) held that it could not challenge Georgia's "unit rule" in South v. Peters, 339 U. S. 276 (1950), although it had indeed struck hard at the "white primary" in Smith v. Allwright, 321 U. S. 649 (1944). In posing the question, of course, one is aware of the type of equity power that the Court was asked to bring to bear in the "unit rule" case.

5. Thus when we speak of the weaknesses of the Articles of Confederation, 1781–1789, we may easily overlook not only the lesson that this arrangement was an avenue on the way to the more perfect union of the Constitution but also that the Articles of Confederation were more workable and might have been tinkered into still more workability than history, intent on picturing the triumph of the Constitution, has reflected. Merrill Jensen administers a useful rebuke in a book in which the excess of a virtue, enthusiasm, seems to draw him into an overstatement of his thesis. "The 'critical period' idea," he writes, "was the result of an uncritical acceptance of the arguments of the victorious party in a long political battle." Debate naturally ran hot "because for a moment in history self-government by majorities within particular boundaries was possible. These majorities could do what they wanted and some of them knew what they wanted." Professor Jensen adds: "The movement to strengthen the Articles failed on the verge of success; the movement to call a convention succeeded on the verge of failure." But he observes that: "The weakness of the central government under the Confederation was the weakness of any government that must achieve its ends by persuasion rather than by coercion." *The New Nation, A History of the United States during the Confederation 1781–1789,* New York, Knopf, 1950, pp. 422, 426, 428.

6. *Introduction to the Study of the Law of the Constitution,* Eighth edition, London, Macmillan, 1915, p. 137.

7. Alexander Brady, *Democracy in the Dominions,* Toronto, University of Toronto Press, 1947, p. 124: "The secessions were dictated by the necessity for decentralized administrations at the chief trading ports in which settlers congregated, or through which they passed to the interior." By the middle of the century all except Western Australia, which was organized separately, had achieved self-government with elective legislatures.

8. J. Fred Rippy, *Historical Evolution of Hispanic America,* New York, Crofts, 1932, pp. 124, 174. See also: Lilian E. Fisher, *The Intendant System in Spanish America,* Berkeley, University of California Press, 1929; Karl Loewenstein, *Brazil under Vargas,* New York, Macmillan, 1944. Loewenstein speaks of the "disparity of social development in the different regions" and adds: "For this very reason the country seems predestined to administrative decentralization." (p. 4.) He notes, however, that the "territorial circumscriptions of present-day Brazil are still coincidental with the boundaries of the colonial captaincies; only a few of them have an economic or cultural individuality." Of Vargas he says (writing in 1942): "It is evident that, in condemning federalism and state powers, the regime desires to strike at liberalism and democracy which, under the republic, had made a lasting imprint on the popular mind." (p. 15.)

9. For a restatement of this view, see Robert Livingston Schuyler, "British Imperial Theory and American Territorial Policy—A Suggested Relationship," *Pro-*

ceedings of the American Philosophical Society, vol. 97, no. 4, September 1953, pp. 317–31.

10. On the question of status in the American system, in the discussion Carl Friedrich injected a word of reminder about the fact that "an entirely novel dimension has opened up in American federalism and federal politics with the constitutionalizing of Puerto Rico; and more particularly with the establishment for this particular part of the United States of a commonwealth state." Speaking in terms of the invention of institutional forms, he remarked that it was not only "a new dimension" but also was a reminder "there are conceivably resources yet untapped." (For further comment by Mr. Friedrich, see Chapter 26, notes 34 and 40.) In the discussion, however, Alexander Brady, adverting to the reference to Puerto Rico, remarked that this development was "extremely interesting" but asked whether it had any more bearing on the general situation "than the unique situation of Northern Ireland bears upon the general constitutional nature of the United Kingdom."

11. Elliott, *Debates,* Vol. I, p. 466.

12. Crane Brinton has remarked: "Historically, real federal unions have been relatively few; hard to establish, and limited to groups which already possessed much, and that much positive, not a mere negation like fear, in common." *From Many One: The Process of Political Integration,* Cambridge, Harvard University Press, 1948, p. 105.

13. Lenox A. Mills and Associates, *The New World of South East Asia,* Minneapolis, University of Minnesota Press, 1949: "Some Javanese nationalists disliked the idea of a federal structure for Indonesia. This dislike stemmed from a fear that it meant a Dutch move to divide and rule, but also from a desire to set up a unitary government which would give the concentrated population of Java a practically free hand to rule the whole of Indonesia." (p. 115.)

14. *Suitors and Suppliants,* New York, Prentice Hall, 1946, p. 151.

15. The 1953 revision of the Jugoslavia constitution established a Council of Producers as the second chamber, replacing the Council of Nationalities. It provided, however, that the Federal Council shall be "composed of deputies elected by the citizens in districts and towns on the basis of universal, equal and direct suffrage, and of People's Deputies elected from among their members by the respective Republic Councils of the Assemblies of the several republics and by the provincial council and regional council of the respective assemblies of the Autonomous Province and Autonomous Region." Although the Federal Council "operates as a single House," article 44 states that "its members elected by the representative bodies of the several People's Republics, the Autonomous Province, and the Region shall have special rights fixed by this law." Thus under article 45 they "render decisions separately, as the Council of Nationalities, when on the agenda of the Federal Council are included proposals concerning constitutional changes or the federal economic plan."

On the whole problem discussed in the text, see the doubting comment by Oscar Jászi in his review of the book by Oscar I. Janowsky, *Nationalities and National Minorities,* New York, Macmillan, 1945. Jászi wrote: "Minority problems can be solved only in an atmosphere in which the individual is more highly regarded than the state. That is why we have only one genuine solution of this problem, and this is Switzerland." *Political Science Quarterly,* Vol. 61 (1946), p. 305.

16. *Report of the Indian Statutory Commission,* May 1930, Vol. II, p. 20.

17. *Second Report of the United Nations Commissioner in Libya.* General Assembly Official Records, 6th Session, Supplement 17A, 1929.

18. "A country with a federal system of government is susceptible, because of the demands of its constitutional processes, to a charge of insincerity of purpose in the conduct of its external relations." O. deL. Foenander, *Studies in Australian Labor Law and Relations,* Melbourne, Melbourne University Press, 1952, p. 44.

19. Keller v. U. S., 213 U. S. 138 (1909), in which the Court dealt with a statute that made it illegal to harbor an alien woman for immoral purposes as well as providing for her deportation. The Court said that if the contention of the government was sound, "the power of Congress is broad enough to take cognizance of all dealings of citizens with aliens." In disapproving this view, the Court remarked that although Congress had not attempted to go far into the field, "it may do so, if it has the power. Then we should be brought face to face with such a change of the internal conditions of this country as was never dreamed by the framers of the Constitution."

20. E. A. Freeman, in what remains a classic account of minimal federalism, paid glowing tribute to the Achaean League (281–146 B.C.) as "the first attempt on a large scale to reconcile local independence with national strength." He wrote: "For a hundred and forty years—no short space in any nation's life and a very long space among the few centuries which we call Ancient History—the League had given to a larger portion of Greece than any previous age had seen, a measure of freedom, unity, and general good government, which may well atone for the lack of the dazzling glory of the old Athenian Democracy." And Freeman added: "It was no slight achievement to weld together so many cities into a Union which strengthened them against Kings and Senates, but yet preserved to them that internal independence so dear to the Hellenic mind." Ironically, Freeman's book bore the title: *A History of Federal Government from the Foundation of the Achaian League to the Disruption of the United States.* London, Macmillan, 1863, Vol. I, pp. 709–10. Freeman's projected work was never completed but fragments on later unions of city states were included in a subsequent edition brought out by J. B. Bury in 1893 under the title, *The History of Federal Government in Greece and Italy.*

21. *A Federation for Western Europe,* London, Macmillan, 1940, pp. 10–11.

22. The discussion of the material covered in later chapters took for granted the need for reform in many aspects of state government including legislative apportionment. Charles M. Hardin asked for still closer analysis. "You have to realize," he said, "that political organizations in some of the cities reach out and make deals with the political machines outside." Mr. Hardin added: "The thing that is called for is the kind of analysis that is unfortunately lacking in considerable degree and that is a sort of functional analysis of politics within our states. What groups combine with what; what alliances have there been; what is the trend of these alliances?"

23. William Anderson remarked in the discussion: "The idea that the states have declined in importance and are declining, I think, is unsupported by the weight of evidence that is presented by American history; and I think this is an important fact to keep in mind . . . It seems to me the states never were in history any stronger, any freer, any more active than they are today."

24. An earlier version of Mr. Berle's chapter was delivered as an address at the final open session of the Bicentennial Conference on Federalism.

25. The report of a committee on the New England economy stated: "We strongly recommend that wherever possible the Federal Government should adopt minimum standards of working conditions and social services. In this way the competition among states to improve their competitive position by retarding the growth of their services would be met. Federal standards of minimum wages, hours of

work, factory conditions, benefits under unemployment compensation, and work-men's compensation are among the fields to be covered." *The New England Economy*. A Report to the President transmitting a study initiated by the Council of Economic Advisers and prepared by its Committee on the New England Economy, July 1951, p. xxxii.

26. Calvin B. Hoover and B. U. Ratchford, *Economic Resources and Policies of the South,* New York, Macmillan, 1951, p. 368.

27. Daniel B. Creamer, Jr., *Is Industry Decentralizing?,* Philadelphia, University of Pennsylvania Press, 1935, p. vii.

28. For trenchant comment on this aspect of the problem, see Mabel New-comer's analysis and illustrations: United States Treasury Department, *Federal, State and Local Fiscal Relations,* Washington, D. C., Government Printing Office, 1943, pp. 197–99. Professor Newcomer pointed out that at that time "Only California of the six states with the highest per capita income has unusual mineral, forest, and agricultural resources. The rest have obtained their income from the manufacture, trade, and finance that have been built on the natural resources of other states."

29. Martin v. Hunter's Lessee, 1 Wheaton 304 (U. S., 1816).

30. *Political Science and Comparative Constitutional Law,* Boston, Ginn, 1890, Vol. II, p. 6.

2

Federalism and the Making of Nations

By Kenneth C. Wheare

I

I remember being startled some years ago to read the title of a book by G. H. Calpin about the Union of South Africa. He called it *There are no South Africans*. I had always thought that there were; indeed I believed I had met some of them. Mr. Calpin's opinion was that although people outside the Union thought there were South Africans, in fact when you were inside you realised that there were not. The Afrikaans[1] speaking people, who comprised about sixty per cent of the Union's European population of two and a half million, formed a distinct nation within the Union, cut off by language and national origins and religion[2] from the English speaking people of the Union who looked to Great Britain as their Mother Country. These two nations, if not "warring within the bosom of a single state," were in hostile camps and the result of over thirty years' working of the Union of South Africa inaugurated in 1910— Mr. Calpin's book was published in 1941—was that no sense of common nationality had come to supplement the feelings of distinct nationality which the two European peoples possessed. And if the two European peoples were not South Africans, still less were the eight million Africans, or the one million Colored people (of mixed blood) or the three hundred thousand Asians.

How far Mr. Calpin's argument was exaggerated it is not for me to say. What seems clear, however, is that in the decade or more since he wrote, events in South Africa have tended more to support his argument than to controvert it. There are probably fewer South Africans today than ever before. It is true that Afrikaners and British speak of themselves as South Africans, but for few of them does the term signify a sense of *common* nationhood. For the Afrikaner in particular to be a South African means to be an Afrikaner, and those who do not exhibit those qualities are not really South Africans. Indeed, in his own language he will seldom speak of South Africans; he speaks of Afrikaners and of English.

As I have watched these manifestations of nationalism in South Africa, I have often wondered whether things would have worked out differently if in

28

1909 the people of the four colonies—Cape Colony, Natal, the Orange Free State, and Transvaal—had adopted a federal form of union instead of a unitary form. This is not a completely fanciful speculation, for at the time when the union was being proposed and discussed, it was expected that the federal form would be adopted. The principal official proposal for union—the Selborne Memorandum—was a plan for federation.[3] It is apparent that one of the reasons why federalism was favored in these discussions was that the English speaking people hoped that their national characteristics would be safeguarded in Natal and Cape Colony, while the Afrikaner would have his nationality safeguarded in the Orange Free State and the Transvaal, and that on this basis of security and safeguards a South African nationality might take root and grow.

Looking back upon it, the desire for federalism is not surprising. The two English colonies had only recently been at war with the two Boer Republics. What more natural than that they should prefer a federal to a unitary union. It was indeed surprising that they should be considering a union at all. However, federalism was rejected, and it was the Boer leaders who were largely responsible for its rejection. They saw overwhelming reasons for preferring a unitary form and they felt no serious misgiving about the survival of the Afrikaner nation in a unitary state. History has shown them to be right on this score so far. History has shown the people of Natal to be right also in their misgivings, and today once again the demand is made that the union should become a federation.[4] In May 1953 a Federal Party was inaugurated, depending largely upon Natal for its support, and it aims at securing safeguards both for the English and for the Afrikaans people through federalism, as the only basis upon which the Union can be preserved to make a South African, and not merely an Afrikaner nation.

II

South African politics are complicated and controversial.[5] I am not competent to judge whether their rejection of federalism in 1909 was wrong or whether the acceptance of it today could be right. I have brought South Africa into the discussion because I think a study of its history raises in a very instructive form the question of the value of federalism in the making of nations, and the limitations that are set upon the extent to which it can be used.

What is the role which federalism is expected to play in the making of nations? It is, at first sight at any rate, an appropriate form of government to offer to communities or states of distinct or differing nationality who wish to form a common government and to behave as one people for some purposes, but who wish to remain independent and in particular to retain their own nationality in all other respects. Federal government consists in a division of the functions of government between an independent common authority for the whole country and independent authorities for the constituent parts of the country. In certain circumstances, then, would not this be an appropriate device for bringing nations together, for preserving them, and at the same time developing over and above their feelings of distinct nationality, a sense of common nationality?

There is no doubt that there have been cases in which federalism has performed this role. But it is important to notice why this has been possible. Though differences of nationality and the desire to supplement them by building a common nationality may be an important argument for choosing a federal form of government, it must not be assumed that it will always be regarded as overwhelming. There may be considerations opposed to federalism which prevail. In the making of the Union of South Africa this was what happened. Many of the important leaders in the movement for closer union, such as Smuts, Botha, and de Villiers, thought that federalism brought complications which were not offset by its merits in giving greater security to differing national loyalties. What appears to have clinched the argument against federalism was that the leaders believed that the regulation of the affairs of the native Africans —then, as now, an overwhelming majority of the inhabitants of the Union— could be satisfactorily undertaken only by a unitary state. The function that federalism could perform in solving the problem of national differences was subordinated therefore to what were regarded as more pressing problems. Nationality was not ignored entirely. The equality of the two national languages —Dutch[6] and English—was guaranteed in the constitution, and each of the four colonies was allowed to continue as a distinct province in the new Union with its own provincial council and with equal representation in the Senate or upper house of the parliament of the Union. But the provinces were subordinate units; they were not, like the American states, coordinate with the Union.

Then you find cases not where nationalism is too weak to ensure federalism but too strong to permit it. People of differing nationality cannot form a federal union unless they are prepared to accept a government in which those who differ from them in nationality have some share. In many cases, too, some nationalities must expect that, though they may have their own way in their own state or province of the federation, they will be in a minority in the government of the whole federation. A federal union usually implies, too, that those who join it will expect or be expected to develop some common nationality in addition to their distinct nationalities. When people of different nationalities are unwilling to accept these consequences, federal union cannot be made to fit their case. We have had many examples of this in history. When India approached self-government it was hoped that a federation could be formed in which Hindus, who formed the majority of the population, could be associated with the Moslem minority. Though the Hindus would be in a majority in most of the states of the federation, there would be some states in which the Moslems had a majority—chiefly in the northwest and northeast of India —and in this way it was believed that the distinct cultures of Hindu and

Moslem would be preserved and yet reconciled with a United India and an Indian nationalism. But in 1940 the powerful Moslem organisation, the Moslem League, declared that Moslems were a separate nation and no mere minority community, and that they must be accorded a separate government whose territory would consist of those areas of India in which Moslems had a majority.[7] So in 1947, when self-government came, it was partition and not federation which occurred, and two new States, India and Pakistan, were created.[8] The impossibility of reconciling Moslem nationalism with Hinduism could not be better illustrated than by the fact that Pakistan consists not only of the Moslem provinces in the Northwest of the continent but also of an isolated province of East Bengal, a Moslem island in the midst of the Federation of India, hundreds of miles from the rest of Pakistan. Federalism is almost irrelevant to nationalism as strong as that.

The point may be illustrated in another way by looking at the situation in Nigeria. This British dependency of over twenty million Africans contains within a single government three distinct nations—the Moslems of the North, who occupy over three quarters of the area of the country and comprise over half of the population; the Yoruba speaking people of the western region who comprise about eighteen per cent of the population; and the Ibo people of the eastern region who make up something like twenty-eight per cent of the population. They are now near to self-government, but the Moslems of the North are most reluctant to be associated with a government in which Ibos and Yoruba are to have an important say. At a conference held in London in August, 1953 the first claim of the Moslems was that, if self-government was to come, they must be accorded a separate state. It was only after considerable discussion that they agreed to consider joining in a federation with the peoples of the other two regions. Here is a case where one nation is on the verge of repudiating federation and choosing partition. If the terms of the federation seem to safeguard its national integrity, it will enter into it. Truly, to adapt Mr. Calpin's title, there are, as yet, no Nigerians. The most that can be said is that, as an outcome of the conference in London, followed by a further conference in Lagos, the capital of Nigeria, in January and February 1954, the representatives of the three regions are prepared to try to make Nigerians.

One other case where the strength of nationalism rules federalism out is that of Ireland. Though the Republic of Ireland might be ready to form a federation with Ulster, the majority of Ulstermen are unwilling to submit to a government for United Ireland in which they would be in a minority. Partition in Ireland, as in India and indeed as in Palestine, is the consequence of nationalism so strong that there is no basis upon which even a federal union can be founded.

Not only is it necessary that the minority nation should be willing to join in a union if federalism is to become a possibility; it is necessary also that the nation in the majority should be prepared to tolerate the existence of the minority nation. If the majority regard the existence of national states within the federation, even if they are only minorities in the whole union, as intolerable, then federation is not possible. It may well be that the Afrikaner majority in South Africa today would oppose the notion of transforming the Union from a unitary state into a federation on the ground that Natal, as an English or British enclave, would be a menace to Afrikanerdom. And it would be interesting to know how Englishmen would regard the proposal that the United Kingdom should be transformed into a federation with the autonomous states of Scotland, Wales, Northern Ireland and England![9]

III

One assumption is usually present in any discussion of the use of federalism in making a nation out of differing nationalities. It is taken for granted that the differing nationalities are, in some measure at any rate, territorially segregated. Ideally, of course, it would be best if each area contained its own single nationality exclusively. The federation could then be composed of states none of which contained within its borders any minority group. People do not arrange themselves like that. What is usually regarded as essential, however, is that there should be areas or an area in which each nationality is at least in a majority so that there can be a state or states in the federation to which each nationality can look as to a motherland or national home. If this does not exist, it is difficult to see how federalism, in the ordinary sense of a union of territories, with territorial autonomy, can have much relevance to the problem of reconciling differing nationalities.

In practice this is what has usually happened when federalism has been chosen. In Canada not all French Canadians live in Quebec. They are found in substantial numbers in the Maritime Provinces and in Ontario[10] and their numbers there are growing. It is in Quebec, however, that they are in the overwhelming majority and it is through Quebec's existence as an independent unit in the Canadian federation that French Canadian nationality finds its great safeguard in Canada. So also in the twenty-two cantons of Switzerland, where German, French, and Italian nationalities are associated together in a federation, the people are not arranged exclusively in homogenous national cantons. But there is a German speaking majority in fourteen of the cantons, and a French majority in the three cantons of Vaud, Neûchatel, and Geneva. There is an Italian majority in the canton of Ticino. Each nationality has a part of the federation in which it can enjoy autonomy.

But merely to provide that each nationality shall have its own autonomous area is not usually considered enough. What safeguards are the minority nationalities to receive to ensure that in the conduct of the business of the general government of the whole union their national interests do not suffer? They may be able to preserve their national interests in certain states or provinces where they are in a majority, but this alone provides no guarantee in the general sphere. To meet anxieties of this kind several devices are adopted.

Where nationalities differ in, say, religion or language or laws, provisions are inserted in the constitution of the federation to safeguard these matters in the federal sphere. In the Canadian constitution the equality of the French and English languages is asserted and certain religious rights in education are preserved. In Switzerland, French, German, and Italian are recognised in the constitution as official languages. It is usual in federations for the second chamber or upper house to be composed of an equal number of representatives from each of the states or cantons and in this way minority nationalities may have their position strengthened. In the lower houses, although representation is in proportion to population, there is usually, as in the case of Quebec for example, a minimum proportion or number of seats guaranteed to minority nations. These safeguards in the working of the general government are just as important as the division of powers itself in a federation in encouraging differing nations to unite together to form a new nation. As a rule they are, if not logically, at any rate practically essential adjuncts to a federal structure where differing nationalities are associated together.

IV

In what has been said up to this point, I have tried to analyse in general terms the sort of situation in which federalism might be of value in making a nation out of a group of communities which are themselves of distinct or differing nationality. It is worth while perhaps to look at the way in which, through federation, new nations have been brought into existence. The circumstances differ from case to case and the process is often difficult. There are two or three distinct situations which deserve attention.

First of all there are cases where people of differing nationality are prepared to join in a federation, but they do not yet feel a sense of common nationality. They say, in effect, "We are not Americans yet but we are prepared to try to become Americans." I believe that this is what happened at the time of the founding of the United States.[11] Samuel E. Morison wrote: "Most citizens of the United States in 1790, if asked their country or nation, would not have answered American but Carolinian, Virginian, Pennsylvanian, New Yorker or New Englander." "The United States of 1788 were not a nation by any modern standard."[12] It would not be true, of course, to say that there were no Americans at that time. Many of the Founding Fathers were Americans. James Wilson declared in the Convention: "I am both a citizen of Pennsylvania and of the United States."[13] What is certain, however, is that there were many more people who were prepared to become Americans than were Americans already.

When the French joined with the English in 1867 to make the Canadian federation, they were committing themselves to become Canadians in some sense which they could share with the English. It was far from easy to do. Language was against them. The French-Canadian called (and still calls) himself *Canadien* and his English speaking fellow citizens he called *Anglais.*

In his language there were and are no Canadians, only *Canadiens* and *Anglais*.[14] The making of a Canadian nation has therefore been a delicate and intricate task.[15] A federation, as John Stuart Mill remarked, binds its people "always to fight on the same side."[16] French Canadians and English Canadians have not always agreed upon which side they should fight or indeed whether they would fight at all. Yet the federation has survived the critical stresses of two wars, and in two of its Prime Ministers, Sir Wilfrid Laurier and Mr. St. Laurent, we have not only two great *Canadiens* but also two great Canadians.

There are other examples where the initiation of a federation has meant that differing nations express an intention of trying to achieve in addition a sense of common nationality but are still far from achieving it. The decision of the Nigerian Conferences in London in August, 1953 and in Lagos in January 1954 (already referred to) to attempt a federation meant that the Moslems of the North, the Yoruba of the West, and the Ibo of the East were prepared to try to become Nigerians. So also in April 1953 when representatives of British colonies in the Caribbean decided at a conference in London to support a plan for a federation they were undertaking to try to become West Indians.[17] We may call them West Indians or Caribbeans as we look at them from the outside and they may call themselves that when they talk to outsiders. But most of them are not more than Jamaicans or Trinidadians or Barbadians. Some of them, like the Bermudans, the Bahamans, the British Hondurans, or the British Guianese do not wish to join in any such federation. They do not feel or seek to feel a common nationality with the people of the other islands. The leaders of certain colonies,[18] however, have agreed to support federation and when it comes about the process of making a British Caribbean nation will have begun in earnest. Again when Newfoundland joined Canada as its tenth province in 1949 many of its people must have said: "We shall try to become Canadians, but we shall remain Newfoundlanders still." Indeed a large minority[19] voting against federation in two referenda held in 1948 to determine Newfoundland's future showed that so far as they were concerned, they wished to remain Newfoundlanders and did not wish to try to become Canadians as well.

Consider a different sort of situation. There have been cases where a federation has not been inaugurated until a sense of common nationality had already been fairly strongly developed. The two cases I have in mind are Switzerland and Australia. When the Swiss federation was inaugurated in 1848 the different nationalities in the union had been associated together so long in a looser form of alliance or confederation that they had come to think of themselves not only as German or French or Italian but also as Swiss. Their feeling of being Swiss was no doubt less intense than their feeling of distinct nationality, but it was there. It was possible for them to declare in the preamble to the constitution that they desired not only "to consolidate the alliance of the confederated members" but also to "promote the unity, strength and honor of the Swiss nation." Am I right in concluding that this is something different from

"We, the people of the United States"? Did not the Founding Fathers choose their words carefully? Could they have said "We, the American people" or "We, the American nation"? I believe not.

In Australia the position is hardly free from doubt. The leaders of the federal movement there campaigned for their cause throughout the colonies; the draft constitution was discussed for over ten years and was submitted to the people of the colonies in a referendum. They were persuaded to become Australians and to feel like Australians before they adopted federation. Their sense of Australian nationality was, no doubt, less intense than their feeling of attachment to each separate colony, and there were people who did not feel it at all or felt hostile to it. But it is true to say that there were Australians before there was an Australia.

We can conclude, then, that as a matter of history, federalism has provided a device through which differing nationalities could unite, and, while retaining their own distinct national existence, attempt to create in addition a new sense of common nationality. Nationalism in a federation can be expressed on at least two levels; it is not an exclusive, homogeneous passion.

V

But of course things do not stand still. What happens to the differing nationalities after the federation has been inaugurated and has worked for a period? In some cases it is clear that the feelings of distinct nationality get weaker and the sense of common nationality gets stronger. In Australia and the United States today I suppose it would be thought exaggerated and unreal to speak of the sentiments which people feel towards their states as national feeling. Some states may evoke a stronger loyalty than others, but generally speaking, though state loyalties exist, Americans now, as a result of history, have one nationality and Australians also. Federation has made of each of these people one nation.[20]

It is by no means an inevitable result of federalism, however. French-Canadians are not less a distinct nation in Canada today than they were in 1867. Perhaps more so. As a minority in language and religion upon an English speaking continent, they see policies applied and a type of society developing which they do not entirely approve. There has been a movement in French Canada for the setting up of a separate state of Laurentia, a movement which shows that some French-Canadians at any rate do not want to try to be Canadians. The nationalism of this group is exclusive and intense. They want a single nation, not a multi-national state. And even those French-Canadians who do not go so far as this feel strongly that their distinct nationality must be preserved and entrenched in Canada. It was at the request of the Premier of Quebec, M. Duplessis, that the meeting of Canadian Premiers changed its name in 1950 from Dominion-Provincial Conference to Federal-Provincial Conference. He wished to stress the independent status of Quebec which federation implies against the unitarian notions he saw in the use of the word "Dominion."

Keeping Canada a nation is a principal preoccupation of its statesmen, and it can be achieved only if French-Canadians are certain that Canadian nationality does not exclude or override French-Canadian nationality. Without federalism Canada could not have come into existence, for the people of Quebec would not otherwise have been prepared to try to be Canadians. Without federalism Canada could not continue to exist, for French-Canadians would not feel that their distinct nationality would be preserved—the basis upon which alone they are prepared to think of themselves as Canadians. That Canada has continued for so long and that there are Canadians, French speaking as well as English speaking, is a tremendous achievement, when we remember that it has survived two wars. We forget very often that the making and keeping of a Canadian nation is a continuous, delicate, and intricate process going on unnoticed, not only by people outside Canada but inside it as well.

What Canadian statesmen have always to remember cannot be entirely forgotten by Swiss statesmen. We sometimes forget that the German, French, and Italian peoples of Switzerland live next door to their motherlands. While Quebec, if it seceded from Canada, would be alone on the alien American continent, the nations of Switzerland have somewhere to go. They have links of language and sometimes of religion with peoples just across the border. It is a measure of the success of Swiss statesmanship and of the strength of Swiss national feeling that Hitler's policy of bringing all Germans within one Reich had little appeal to the German Swiss.

Even Australian statesmen, with an homogeneous population to deal with, are not entirely free from worries about possible secessions. In 1933 the people of the state of Western Australia voted in favor of a petition to the British parliament to permit their secession from the Commonwealth. Some Western Australians felt, apparently, that they would prefer not to be Australians any longer.

VI

Difficult as is the task of making and preserving a nation in Canada or Switzerland, it is by no means so difficult as the task of nation building which is now being attempted in British Central Africa where the Federation of Rhodesia and Nyasaland has been inaugurated. Here a nation is to be made not out of two nations but out of two races, the African and the European. It presents what is by far the most difficult form in which the problem of making a nation can arise. I should like to say something about this problem.

Note first a resemblance and a contrast between the position in Rhodesia and Nyasaland on the one hand and the Union of South Africa on the other. They resemble each other in that the non-European population in both cases heavily outnumbers the European. In South Africa there are roughly ten million non-Europeans to two and a half million Europeans. In Rhodesia and Nyasaland there are roughly six million non-Europeans to two hundred thousand Europeans. Most of the non-Europeans in both countries are Africans, but there are also substantial numbers of Indians, Chinese, or Colored people. The non-Europeans outnumber the Europeans not only in the whole of these two countries but in each of their constituent parts—in each of the four provinces of the Union and in each of the three territories (Southern Rhodesia, Northern Rhodesia, and Nyasaland) of the Federation. As against this point of resemblance, there is the difference that whereas in the Union the European population is divided within and indeed against itself into English speaking and Afrikaans speaking nations, in the Federation, though there are some Afrikaners, the European population is substantially united so far as an English speaking people.

At first sight the case for a federation of Rhodesia and Nyasaland, therefore, seems weak or at any rate weaker than in South Africa. There is no division among the European population comparable to that in the Union which led Natal to advocate a federal rather than a unitary union to safeguard the English speaking people. On the other hand, as neither the Europeans nor the Africans (or non-European people) are segregated territorially, there was no ground for arguing that the Europeans or Africans could be given the safeguard which federalism provides of their own autonomous states within the federation. Africans and Europeans are found in all three territories. The argument against federalism which prevailed in the making of the Union of South Africa, namely that the regulation of African affairs must be a central responsibility and that if this were done nothing of importance was left to be regulated by the states of a federation, surely applies with equal force to the union of the Rhodesias and Nyasaland. And indeed this argument was put forward with emphasis by the Europeans of Southern Rhodesia in the course of the negotiations for the federation. In short it may be said that in the Rhodesias and Nyasaland the differences in the European population which in the Union provided the case for federation were absent, while the factors involved in the presence of an overwhelming African population which in the Union provided the case against federation were present. Why then was federation chosen?

The short answer is that those responsible for the African in the three territories differed in their policies and they were prepared to form a union only if each was to be free to continue to carry out its policies in the union. The only way in which this could be done was to leave African affairs so far as possible within the competence of the territories in a federation where each government remained independent within its own sphere. This amounts to an assertion that what in the making of the Union of South Africa was alleged to be unworkable—namely the regulation of African affairs by the separate provincial or territorial governments—can in fact be worked.

A word or two must be said about the position of the three territories in the

Federation of Rhodesia and Nyasaland in explanation of the short answer given above. Before federation, Southern Rhodesia—though not fully self-governing—was in fact almost completely autonomous in its internal affairs. So far as its control over its African population was concerned it was restricted only by the provision that any laws which discriminated between Europeans and Africans must obtain the approval of the government of the United Kingdom. Northern Rhodesia and Nyasaland on the other hand were much more under the control of the United Kingdom, and their policies in regard to Africans were, in effect, the responsibility of the British government. There were differences in the policies of Southern Rhodesia on the one hand, and Northern Rhodesia and Nyasaland on the other, and these differences may be shortly expressed in the following passage from an official study of the subject.

"Policy in Northern Rhodesia and Nyasaland holds that in order to fit the African to take his place in the community as a full partner with citizens of a more ancient civilisation he must be induced to play a full part in the politics and administration of his own area, and must play a direct part in the politics and administration of the whole territory. This is in the belief that without such political education there can be no assurance that the African would be able to play his full part in material and economic development.

"Policy in Southern Rhodesia holds that in order to fit the African to take his place in the community as a full partner with citizens of a more ancient civilisation it is first necessary to make him the equal of his future partner in health, material well-being and education. This is in the belief that without such advancement there can be no assurance that he will be fit to play a full part in the politics and administration even of his own area, let alone the politics and administration of the whole territory."[21]

How far the practical working of Southern Rhodesian policy and of British policy in Northern Rhodesia and Nyasaland differed is a matter of some controversy. The decisive fact for those concerned in negotiating a closer union between the three territories was that an important section of the British people thought there were important differences and, above all, that the Africans thought so. While therefore Southern Rhodesia urged the formation of a unitary state (or "amalgamation" of the three territories) the British, Northern Rhodesian, and Nyasaland governments were unwilling to go further than federation. Their argument was that if Africans and Europeans were to form a partnership as one nation, Africans must believe that their interests would not be prejudiced by the setting up of a union, while Europeans in Southern Rhodesia were entitled to a guarantee that their existing policies could continue if they so wished.

The result is a peculiar form of federation, for the units in it are of different constitutional status. While the territory of Southern Rhodesia continues to enjoy almost complete autonomy, subject only to the approval of the government of the United Kingdom where discriminatory legislation is concerned, the two territories of Northern Rhodesia and Nyasaland remain under the control of the British Colonial Office which retains responsibility for the development of their policies, including their policies towards the African. Within the same federation therefore the units are subject to a different degree of external control by the British government.

VII

Americans will view the working of this experiment with great interest. They may recall that the Federation of Rhodesia and Nyasaland follows, in regard to the African, the same principle which the Founding Fathers embodied in the American Constitution, namely that the regulation of the African or the Negro slave, as was the case in the United States, is confided to the units of the federation and not to the central government. They will notice a difference between the Rhodesian situation and the American, in that while in the Federation the African is in a majority in all three territories, in the United States, though he was very numerous in some states, he was a small minority in others. They will recall also that differences of policy between state and state in regard to the African can lead to the breaking of a federation.

The question which, however, may suggest itself to many Americans, from their own experience of the problem of making Negroes and Europeans feel that they are Americans, is whether federalism alone can do much to achieve this object. Does not the record in the United States show that certain other safeguards are needed in a constitution if the African's position is to be protected and if he is to feel that he is not a second class citizen? Has not the Bill of Rights done as much, if not more, than federalism to make the Negro feel that he is or can become an American? Does not federalism, left to itself, mean that in states where the Negro is in a minority he is treated as something like an equal whereas in states where he is numerous he is debarred from the full exercise of his rights? And must not federalism therefore be supplemented by guarantees such as those embodied in the Fourteenth Amendment, whose effectiveness depends upon the action of an institution of the federation, not of the states, namely the Supreme Court of the United States?

I express these points in the form of questions because I am not competent to make assertions about them so far as the United States is concerned. It may be noticed, however, that in the Federation of Rhodesia and Nyasaland it is clearly recognised that federalism alone is not enough to safeguard the African. I have mentioned already that, though the matters that principally concern the African have been reserved to the territories of the Federation, the legislation of these territories is subject to control by the United Kingdom government, to a small extent in the case of Southern Rhodesia and to a much larger extent in the case of Northern Rhodesia and Nyasaland. But it is well recognised that though matters primarily affecting the African are reserved to the territories, African affairs cannot be segregated entirely and that therefore those matters which the Federation as a whole deals with are likely to affect

Africans in some measure. It is therefore provided that if any federal law discriminates against the African it must be submitted to the British government for its approval.

It is interesting to notice that the device of a bill or declaration of rights, which is found in the American Constitution and in many other constitutions in these days, is not followed in the Constitution of Rhodesia and Nyasaland. Reliance is placed upon the superintendence or intervention of an outside government, the government of the United Kingdom. Where federalism proves inadequate to safeguard African interests, an appeal is made to London.

It is too early yet to judge the prospects of this attempt at making a nation in Africa. At present the European population of the Federation has the major share in the government of the Federation and it may be expected to retain this control for some time. But there are African members in the Federal Assembly —out of nine members representing Africans in a House of thirty-six, six are to be Africans. It is apparent that the task of nation building confronting the Federation is extremely difficult and that there are in effect no exactly comparable precedents to follow. Federalism has some contribution to make in safeguarding the pursuit of different policies in regard to the African and European, as a result of which both races may come to feel a confidence and security upon which partnership and cooperation can be built and can result in a sense of common nationhood. No one can doubt that if federalism can do something to bring about a partnership between the European and African races, it will have achieved its greatest success in history.[22]

VIII

May I add a concluding word about the relevance of all this to the relations between Europeans themselves in Europe? Has not federalism a part to play in bringing the nations of Europe together in a union in which national differences will be protected and national rivalries, if not harmonised, at least rendered less harmful?

My first answer to this question would be to point out that in none of the examples of the making of nations through federalism which I have discussed do we find the federation of states which had existed for any length of time or in any real sense as independent, sovereign national states.[23] Nationality, as we have seen, may express itself in varying degrees. When it finds its expression in a national state and comes to have a history as a national state, the task of making a federal union out of differing nationalities becomes very difficult. So far these difficulties have proved insuperable.[24] It is well to notice that what the advocates of European federation are attempting is something which has never achieved success before. I point this out not to imply that European federation cannot come, but to emphasize the difference between what is being attempted now and what has been achieved in the past.

In the second place I feel tempted to say: "There are no Europeans." I make the remark in the same sense that Mr. Calpin adopted when he said: "There are no South Africans." There is not sufficient common sympathy between the peoples of the national states of Europe, even of Western Europe, for us to say that they have, over and above their national feelings, a sense of common European nationalism. It is quite certain that if Britain is included in one's notion of Western Europe, no such common European nationalism exists. The British are not Europeans though most Americans call them so.

If this is true, it is apparent that a federation of Western Europe, if it is to be inaugurated, must start off with a group of different national states and without a sense of common nationality. That is a drawback, but it is apparent from this paper that federations have been made in similar circumstances. Although the Swiss and Australian federations came after Swiss and Australian nationality, it is fairly clear that the United States and Canada were made before Americans and Canadians. Let us repeat once more, however, that the peoples which made up these federations had not been formerly organised in sovereign, independent national states. There is a difference of degree and perhaps also of kind which is important.

But supposing I am wrong and that there are Europeans. In this case it is well to remember that even when peoples share a common national feeling in addition to distinct national feelings, they do not necessarily desire or need to unite. Australia and New Zealand share a common British nationality, but they do not want to federate. What is more, it is difficult to know why they should. It is well to remember that there are cases in the world of this kind. I do not say that Europe is in this situation. At the same time I think it is right when we consider European federation to ask not only: "Could Europe federate?" but also "Should Europe federate?" But now I begin to trespass upon the province of later chapters in this symposium.

FOOTNOTES TO CHAPTER 2

1. A language descended from Dutch and developed as a vernacular in South Africa.

2. Almost all Afrikaners belong to the Dutch Reformed Church.

3. See A. P. Newton (ed.), *The Unification of South Africa,* London, Longmans, 1924.

4. An eloquent and original plea for federalism is found in A. Keppel-Jones, *Friends or Foes?*, Pietermaritzburg, Shuter & Shooter, 1950.

5. There is a good account in Leo Marquard, *The Peoples and Policies of South Africa,* London, Oxford University Press, 1952, and Sarah Gertrud Millin, *The People of South Africa,* New York, Knopf, 1954.

6. The Constitution was amended in 1926 to make Dutch include Afrikaans.

7. See the Presidential Address of Mr. M. A. Jinnah to the All India Muslim League at Lahore, March 1940. Printed in N. Mansergh, *Documents and Speeches on British Commonwealth Affairs, 1931–1952,* Vol. 2, pp. 609–612.

8. The relevant documents are in Mansergh, *op. cit.*, Vol. 2, section xi.

9. See Cmd. 9059. Report by the Resumed Conference on the Nigerian Constitution.

10. They form 21.5% of the population of the Maritime provinces and 9% of the population of Ontario.

11. In the discussion of Mr. Wheare's views and specifically his suggestion that the United States had illustrated the process of getting "federation first and common nationality afterwards," Henry Steele Commager remarked: "I would be inclined to agree with that, with the qualification of what constitutes Americans . . . But this point, important as it is, must be considered in the light of the further point, which Mr. Wheare has well made, that it came not out of independent states but out of states or colonies which had had only the very briefest experience of quasi-independence, and even that is a matter of considerable controversy."

It may be noted here that in the course of the later discussion Mr. Commager dissented from an attitude reflected, as he saw it, in arguments developed in some of the chapters: the notion that national action is exceptional: "This notion," he said, "runs like a red thread through a good many of the observations here that there is something distinctly abnormal if not improper in national action." (Editor)

12. *History of the United States,* London, Oxford University Press, 1927, Vol. I, p. 10.

13. Max Farrand, *The Records of the Federal Convention,* New Haven, Yale University Press, 1911, Vol. I, p. 413.

14. The resemblance to the Afrikaner in this respect will be noted.

15. See, for example, André Siegfried, *Canada,* New York, Harcourt, 1937, and E. C. Hughes, *French Canada in Transition,* London, K. Paul, Trench, Trubner, 1946.

16. *Representative Government,* Chapter XVII.

17. See *Report by the Conference on West Indian Federation* (Cmd. 8837) and *The Plan for a British Caribbean Federation* (Cmd. 8895).

18. Barbados, Jamaica, Antigua, St. Kitts Nevis and Anguilla, Montserrat, Trinidad and Tobago, Granada, St. Vincent, St. Lucia, and Dominica, make up the 10 units of the proposed federation.

19. In the referendum on June 3, 1948, 63,110 voted for federation with Canada and 91,174 for other forms of government; in the referendum on July 22, 1948, 78,451 voted for federation and 71,217 against.

20. Yet this may be an outsider's illusion. Would the Texan or the Virginian agree? And is not Queensland producing a distinctive people in Australia?

21. *Central African Territories: Comparative Survey of Native Policy.* Cmd. 8235 of 1951.

22. The principal documents are Cmd. 8233 of 1951, *Report of a Conference of Officials on Closer Association in British Central Africa;* Cmd. 8573 of 1952, *Draft Federal Scheme;* Cmd. 8753 of 1953, *Reports by the Conference on Federation;* and Cmd. 8754, *The Federal Scheme.*

23. In the discussion of Mr. Wheare's draft, Carl J. Friedrich remarked: "I noted all the way through Mr. Wheare's paper that he avoids all reference to German experience . . . The development of Germany has perhaps greater reference to the problem now facing us . . . The long tradition in German history in a very strong sense is not of nationality but of community. There certainly was a Germany before there was a German Empire." It may be asked whether Mr. Wheare's dis-

posal of the German example in the following footnote does not put too much stress upon a word that is tied to a question of constitutional form and a form, too, which in the German case had peculiarities that warranted another name and which moved increasingly toward further centralization. (Editor)

24. The case of the union of the German states is sometimes quoted as an example to the contrary. But what the German states formed in 1867 was the North German *Confederation* and the German Empire of 1871 similarly was a confederation, not a federation.

3

Federalism and Freedom: A Critique

By Franz L. Neumann

It will be necessary to define, as briefly as possible, the meaning of the term "federalism" before we can answer the two fundamental questions:
1. Is there a value which inheres in federalism as such?
2. Are there goals that can be attained only through federalism?

I

Have the terms "federalism," "federal government," or "federal state" definable meanings? Even a most superficial study of the various kinds of federal government—those of the United States, Canada, Australia, Switzerland, Imperial Germany, the Austro-Hungarian Dual Monarchy, Weimar and Bonn Germany, the Central African Federation, India, and the USSR, to mention some modern federal states—fails to show any element common to all, except a juristic one. The common element is this: in each, the citizen of the federal state is subject to two jurisdictions: that of the federal government and that of the states.[1] Usually connected to this is a separation of the legislative, administrative, and judicial functions in order to insure the orderly operation of government. The lawyer—and the lawyer alone—is thus capable (and obligated) to make statements concerning federalism that can claim general validity.

Not so the political and social scientist. He will accept a legal definition of federalism, but he must go beyond it. The legal definition of federalism—like all legal definitions—is a negative one. It tells us that we cannot regard a mere treaty system or a confederation of states as a federal system. But it can tell us nothing about the political and social function of the federal system. If we wish to know this, we must ask the two questions: whether federalism as such has a value; and whether certain goals are attainable only through this governmental arrangement.

Posing the questions in such a manner creates extraordinary difficulties. How can one determine whether a certain value inheres in federalism? The federal arrangement operates always within a specific political, social, and cultural setting and the isolation of the federal element from this setting is obviously extremely difficult, perhaps even impossible. Even if we confine the analysis to democratic systems of government, the political and constitutional factors that tend to change the function of federalism are these:

1. presidential or parliamentary democracy
2. separation of powers (checks and balances)
3. the party system;

and the social and economic factors are these:

1. the extent of the pluralistic structure of society
2. the urban-rural ratio
3. the degree of concentration of economic power.

It seems obviously inadmissible to attribute to federalism values which form, in reality, a syndrome consisting of a specific constitutional arrangement within a specific socio-economic structure. What our statements amount to, therefore, is that the value of federalism (as against a unitary state on the one hand, and a looser form of cooperation on the other) can be determined solely through an empirical analysis of a given political system. The need for such an analysis will, moreover, become clearer if we analyze the claims made for the federal, as against the unitary, system.

II

The theoretical argument for federalism revolves around the potential of political power for evil. Federalism is seen as one of the devices to curb the evil use of power by dividing power among a number of competing power-units.

The underlying sentiment—the corruptive influence of power—is often not clearly formulated and the consequences thus not clearly seen.

1. In its most radical form, this sentiment appears in the various anarchist schemes. It has been popular in the anarcho-syndicalist theories and practices of the Latin-speaking countries and with the IWW of the United States. We may find in Proudhon the most precise expression of that trend and a most radical advocacy of "federalism." But one must, of course, not tear the federalist conception of Proudhon from the context of his social and political philosophy. His theory of federalism has nothing in common with that of the federal state; it is rather the very negation of it.

Proudhon indicts capitalism because he finds in it a basic injustice,[2] the exchange of non-equivalents. This injustice comes from two institutions: private property and the state. The property owner is able to draw advantages from the exchange process by selling commodities at prices that are above value, thus imposing a tax upon the social product. It is this exchange relationship which creates the two social classes: the new feudality of owners living on interests, rents, and dividends, and the workers who own no capital except their labor. The state—no matter what its form—is that agency which maintains the exchange of non-equivalents, protects the new feudality, and prevents the uprising of the majority against the minority. This is the sole role of the state which can never, under any circumstances and in any form, change the system, reform it, or create social justice—even when the state is a democracy. Justice can thus be obtained only against the state, against political power, only through a contractual industrial organization[3] of small-scale units.

One may, if one so desires, call this a "federalist" theory, but it is obvious that it cannot help us in our problem of determining whether the federal state, by lessening the corruptive effect of power and thereby increasing political freedom, becomes, on that account, preferable to the unitary state.

2. It is Lord Acton's statement on the corruptive effect of political power which appears to have today the greatest influence. Three statements of his on political power are:

> *a.* ". . . power tends to expand indefinitely, and will transcend all barriers, abroad and at home, until met by superior forces."
> *b.* "History is not a web woven with innocent hands. Among all the causes which degrade and demoralize men, power is the most constant and the most active."
> *c.* To Creighton: "I cannot accept your canon that we are to judge Pope and King unlike other men, with a favorable presumption that they did no wrong. If there is any presumption it is the other way against holders of power, increasing as the power increases. Historic responsibility has to make up for the want of legal responsibility. Power tends to corrupt and absolute power corrupts absolutely. Great men are almost always bad men, even when they exercise influence and not authority: still more when you superadd the tendency or the certainty of corruption by authority. There is no worse heresy than that the office sanctifies the holder of it."[4]

These statements have two aspects. The first one is, indeed, unobjectionable and, of course, not very original. Thucydides said much the same:[5]

> *Melians*—You may be sure that we are as well aware as you of the difficulty of contending against your power and fortune, unless the terms be equal. But we trust that the gods may grant us fortune as good as yours, since we are just men fighting against unjust, and that what we want in power will be made up by the alliance of the Lacedaemonians, who are bound, if only for very shame, to come to the aid of their kindred. Our confidence, therefore, after all is not so utterly irrational.
> *Athenians*—When you speak of the favour of the gods, we may as fairly hope for that as yourselves; neither our pretensions nor our conduct being in any way contrary to what men believe of the gods, or practise among themselves. *Of the gods we believe, and of men we know, that by a necessary law of their nature they rule wherever they can.* And it is not as if we were the first to make this law, or to act upon it when made: we found it existing before us, and shall leave it to exist for ever after us; all we do is to make use of it, knowing that you and everybody else, having the same power as we have, would do the same as we do. (emphasis supplied)

And Montesquieu[6] said this even more clearly. According to him[7] power could be checked only by power—a statement that few would be willing to quarrel with. Not ideologies and beliefs but only a counter-power can check power. In this he applies Cartesian principles and stands in the tradition of Spinoza who saw no way of limiting the state's absoluteness (which was logical consequence of his assumptions and of his geometric method) except by a counter-power.

The Montesquieu generalization is, of course, designed to give his doctrine of the separation of powers an adequate theoretical base. But as little as the theory of separate powers follows from his sociological observation, as little does that of the preferability of the federal state. Bentham[8] rejected the separation of powers not only as incompatible with democracy but also because it could not really maximize freedom if the three organs of government were controlled by the same social group. A quite similar argument can be raised against federalism as a guarantee for liberty. Those who assert that the federal state through the diffusion of *constitutional* powers actually diffuses *political* power often overlook the fact that the real cause for the existence of liberty is the pluralist structure of society and the multi-party (or two-party) system.[9] Federalism is not identical with social pluralism; and neither the two-party nor the multi-party system is the product of the federal state or the condition for its functioning.

3. Whether the federal state does indeed increase freedom[10] cannot be abstractly determined. We have some evidence that the federal state as such (that is, regardless of the form of government) has not fulfilled this role. The German Imperial Constitution certainly created a federal state but there is little doubt that politically it had a dual purpose: to be a dynastic alliance against the forces of liberalism and democracy,[11] and to secure the hegemony of Prussia.[12] One may argue that a unitary state may even have been worse than the federal solution: that is quite possible. Nevertheless one may say, with reason, that the archaic Prussian three-class franchise could not possibly have been introduced as the system for a unitary German state. Thus a unitary German state in all likelihood would have been more progressive than the Bismarckian system. The Austro-Hungarian Dual Monarchy, after the *Ausgleich* of 1867, was an attempt to ensure the rule of the Germans and Magyars over all other nationalities.[13] The Dual Monarchy most certainly did not maximize freedom except for the oligarchies in its two constituent states.

Perhaps more striking are the respective roles of federalism and centralism in the coming to power of National Socialism. Some believe, indeed, that the centralization under the Weimar Republic is wholly or at least partly responsible for the rise of National Socialism. But there is no evidence for this statement— nor indeed for the opposite one. It is certain that Bavaria, with the strongest states' rights tradition, gave shelter to the National Socialist movement and it is equally certain that the federal character of the Weimar Republic did not, after Hitler's appointment, delay the process of synchronization (*Gleichschaltung*) of the various state governments. Nor is there any definable relation between democratic conviction and federalist (or unitary) sympathies. The

National Socialists were both centralists and reactionary, as were the Nationalists. Democrats and Social Democrats were antifederalists and committed to the preservation of political freedom. The Catholic center was not wholeheartedly committed to any position, and the Communists were, in theory, for the unitary state but did not hesitate, during the revolution of 1918, to advocate the secession of Brunswick which they believed they had in their pocket.

4. But perhaps what is meant by saying that federalism maximizes freedom is that only in a democracy does the division of constitutional power among various autonomous territorial units effect a maximum of political liberty; in other words, that democracy and the federal state go together, even that federalism is necessary for democracy. Literally taken, this statement is most certainly untrue. The United Kingdom is a proof against it. Weimar Germany cannot be cited either for or against it. Bavaria—the most states' rights-conscious *land*—was certainly the most reactionary; Prussia, the most democratic. Insofar as the United States is concerned, it seems almost impossible to make any statement because of the extreme difficulty of attributing to the federal system—in isolation from other elements—any specific function. There are, perhaps, some tests like the protection of civil liberties. For a criminal, the federal system has obvious advantages in that it increases his margin of safety from prosecution. The need for extradition may, in isolated cases, permit a criminal to escape punishment. It is doubtful, however, that this can be taken as a compliment to federalism. Of real importance would be a study designed to prove or disprove that the federal nature of American government has strengthened civil liberties. The criminal syndicalism legislation of the post World War I period[14] does not permit us to pass a final judgment. The "red hysteria" of that period "practically assured . . . passage (of this type of legislation) with only slight examination."[15] The bills were passed with "breathtaking swiftness and little debate, or with a great outburst of oratory characterized more by passion, prejudice, and misinformation than by a reasoned effort to get at the facts."[16] There seemed to be a race among the various states for the most drastic legislation, and vested interests, their influence enhanced by the makeup of the state legislatures, pushed through the bills.[17] Simultaneously, efforts to enact a federal bill failed from 1917 to 1920.[18] On the other hand, however, it is possible that without state laws a federal bill may have been enacted, and it is also true that in a few states[19] no legislation was enacted. On the whole, one may perhaps say that the federal system may have speeded up inroads into the civil liberties rather than have protected them.

The same, perhaps, may be said of the present situation.[20] The evidence is certainly too slight to be of great value in determining whether the federal system is preferable to the unitary state as an instrument to preserve or enhance civil liberties. Nor is it likely that convincing evidence can be obtained, since other factors—the plurality of the social structure, the functioning of a truly competitive party system, the strength of a favorable tradition, the intellectual level of the population, the attitude of the courts—do far more easily permit the formation of a counter power against forces hostile to civil liberties than does the federal structure of the government.

5. Lord Acton's statements, however, are also concerned with a second aspect: namely, the corruptive influence of power. This brilliant formula that power tends to corrupt and absolute power corrupts absolutely has attained the position of a classical remark; but, inevitably, it has also become a cliché of which neither the meaning nor the validity is ever questioned. The content of the statement is certainly not very original. While Plato's discussion of the same problem[21] shows a much deeper insight, Lord Acton's has the undoubted merits of brevity and of quotability.

Lord Acton asserts that the character of the man who has power is corrupted by the exercise of power, or as the German adage has it: Politics corrupts the character. This is probably a valid generalization—but what is its significance for politics, in general, and for our problem, in particular? A morally evil ruler does not necessarily make a bad ruler—he may accumulate riches, indulge in all kinds of vices—and yet his rule may be beneficial; while the paragon of virtue may lead his country to destruction. But if we turn from monarchy or tyranny to representative government, the applicability of the formula to politics is quite certainly small.

However, we may well redefine the formula to mean that too much power concentrated in any organ of government has evil consequences for the people and that federalism, by dividing power among independent territorial units, checks these evil potentialities.

Thus redefined, the statement is no longer defensible because the opposite may equally be true. It is, indeed, also true: Too little power tends to corrupt and absolute lack of power corrupts absolutely; or, as Edmund Burke put it: "Nothing turns out to be so oppressive and unjust as a feeble government."[22] One can accept Burke's assertion as absolute truth as little as one can Lord Acton's. Both are partially true generalizations, Burke's being, perhaps, a more realistic description of marginal situations than Lord Acton's. If one shares Burke's hatred of revolution, one may keep in mind that modern revolutions such as the French of 1789, the two Russian ones of 1917, and the German of 1918, had their immediate cause in the lack of power of the central governments and not in the excessive use or abuse of power.

6. It thus seems impossible to attribute to federalism, as such, a value; or to assert that the federal state—as contrasted to the unitary state—enhances political and civil freedom by dividing power among autonomous territorial subdivisions.

III

1. The argument for federalism may, however, have a quite different meaning. It may, in reality, express the theory of "grass-roots" democracy, the view that small-scale units alone permit the practice of democracy and that, conse-

quently, the value of small units must be preserved even in large states so that mass participation in politics will remain a political practice. The most precise formulation of this theory is found in Montesquieu who, through his analysis of the collapse of the Roman Empire,[23] came to the conclusion that democracy, being incompatible with a large empire, can be effectively practiced only by a small territorial entity.[24] Rousseau accepted this view and made it popular.

> In any case, the moment a people allows itself to be represented, it is no longer free: it no longer exists. All things considered, I do not see that it is possible henceforth for the Sovereign to preserve among us the exercise of its rights, unless the city is very small.[25]

But Montesquieu, Rousseau, and *The Federalist*[26] clearly recognized the dilemma of democracy. As Montesquieu put it, "If a Republic is small, it is destroyed by a foreign power; if it be large, it is ruined by internal imperfection."[27] Rousseau virtually copied this question from Montesquieu by continuing the above quotation: "But if it is very small, it will be conquered? No. I will show later on how the external strength of a great people may be combined with a convenient polity and good order of a small state." Both writers, and *The Federalist,* following Montesquieu, suggest federation as a device to attain both external security and internal democracy. It is well to realize that Jefferson, while omitting to copy the chapter on the separation of powers, carefully abstracted this view of Montesquieu.[28]

The Montesquieu-Rousseau theory raises a quite difficult problem: the relation of territorial size to the political structure. This problem has not been adequately discussed since the work of Ratzel.[29] Rousseau's adaptation of Montesquieu's statement raises a second difficulty, namely, the identification of democracy with direct democracy. Rousseau's quotation appears in the chapter entitled "Deputies or Representatives" and is concerned with the demonstration that democracy, being a complete identity of rulers and ruled, cannot be representative government. Yet our theory of democracy (although political scientists quite frequently long for "mass participation in politics") is a theory of representative government, of a form of government which is characterized by the electoral process and by the political responsibility of the representative organs to the electorate. The two doctrines have nothing in common with each other, although the instrumentalities of direct democracy, like initiative, referendum, plebiscite, and recall, may or may not serve as correctives to representative government.[30]

If, therefore, one does not accept the Rousseauist model or agree with Montesquieu's analysis of the cause of the collapse of the Roman Republic, then it is difficult to accept the consequence that a unitary system covering a large territory cannot be a democratic system.

2. Indeed, neither Madison nor John Stuart Mill, to name two, shared this view and yet both were quite deeply attached to the principle of political liberty. Madison wrote:

Was, then, the American Revolution effected, was the American Confederacy formed, was the precious blood of thousands spilt, and the hard-
earned substance of millions lavished, not that the people of America should
enjoy peace, liberty, and safety, but that the government of the individual
States, that particular municipal establishments, might enjoy a certain extent
of power, and be arrayed with certain dignities and attributes of power? . . .
It is too early for politicians to presume on our forgetting that the public
good, the real welfare of the great body of the people, is the supreme object
to be pursued; and that no form of government whatever has any other value
than as it may be fitted for the attainment of this object. Were the plan of the
convention adverse to the public happiness, my voice would be, Reject the
plan. Were the Union itself inconsistent with the public happiness, it would
be, Abolish the Union. In like manner, as far as the sovereignty of the States
cannot be reconciled to the happiness of the people, the voice of every good
citizen must be, Let the former be sacrificed to the latter.[31]

The quotation exhibits a view quite at variance with the Montesquieu-Rousseau theory. It is the power of the central government which appears as the
guarantor of political freedom—against the states. And John Stuart Mill, the
great defender of diversity and individuality, when discussing Italy's future
constitutional structure, reasoned in quite the same terms:

The question may present itself (as in Italy at its present uprising)
whether a country, which is determined to be united, should form a complete
or a merely federal union. The point is sometimes necessarily decided by mere
territorial magnitude of the united whole . . . This obstacle does not exist in
the case of Italy, the size of which does not come to that of several very
efficiently governed single states in past and present times. The question then
is, whether the different parts of the nation require to be governed in a way
so essentially different that it is not probable the same Legislature, and the
same ministry or administrative body, will give satisfaction to them all. Unless
this be the case, which is question of fact, it is better for them to be completely united. . . .
Whenever it is not deemed necessary to maintain permanently in the
different provinces, different systems of jurisprudence, and fundamental institutions grounded on different principles, it is always practicable to reconcile
minor diversities with the maintenance of unity of government. All that is
needful is to give a sufficiently large sphere of action to the local authorities.[32]

3. Yet there is one element of truth in the theory of Montesquieu and Rousseau: the smallest territorial unit—the municipality—is potentially the most
responsive to the will and interests of the people and, consequently, local self-
government must be considered the indispensable cornerstone of a modern
large-scale democracy.

But is it possible to assert that the federal structure maximizes local self-
government and that, in a unitary state, we therefore find a shrinkage of local
powers? At the outset it must be made clear that the federal state, as such, does
not mean strong local government[33] and that, therefore, it is not possible to
answer the question abstractly, but that rather empirical investigations are
necessary. In Weimar Germany the states (*Laender*) were steadily encroach-

ing upon the powers of the municipalities and transformed, on a large scale, municipal into state police power, while the financial resources of the municipalities proved totally inadequate to finance the new and ever-growing tasks of the welfare state.

This may well be a universal phenomenon or it may vary considerably from state to state, or even within each state, according to the size of the municipalities.

4. While we have attempted to demonstrate that there is no necessary connection between democracy and federalism, one may go even beyond it and say that many of the major advocates of federalism are critics, doubters, and even enemies of democracy.[34]

De Tocqueville saw this connection clearly:

> I have already pointed out the distinction between a centralized government and centralized administration. The former exists in America, but the latter is nearly unknown there. If the directing power of the American communities had both these instruments of government at its disposal and united the habit of executing its commands to the right of commanding; if, after having established the general principles of government, it descended to the details of their application; and if, having regulated the great interests of the country, it would descend to the circle of individual interests, freedom would soon be banished from the New World.
>
> But in the United States the majority, which so frequently displays the tastes and the propensities of a despot, is still destitute of the most perfect instruments of tyranny.
>
> . . . when the central government which represents that majority has issued a decree, it must entrust the execution of its will to agents over whom it frequently has no control and whom it cannot perpetually direct. The townships, municipal bodies, and counties form so many concealed backwaters, which check or part the tide of popular determination.[35]

Madison—in the above quotation—implied it. Calhoun in the United States and Konstantin Frantz in Germany are the two best-known theorists of federalism per se, where the connection between federalism and anti-democracy is obvious.[36]

6. We must, therefore, answer our first question as follows: While it is asserted that federalism maximizes political freedom because

   a. it establishes an effective counter-power to the power of the central government;

   b. it curbs the potentialities for evil inherent in power;

   c. it maximizes local government and thus promotes grass-roots democracy;

it has been found that none of the statements can be accepted. It must rather concretely be demonstrated that a federal system is superior to a unitary system in maintaining freedom; that this is attributable to the federal structure and not to the governmental institutions (checks and balances, attitude of the courts, character and orientation of the federal administrative services); or to the nature of the party system (shaped, it is true, by the federal structure); or to the pluralistic and mobile structure of society; or to simply accidental historical circumstances; or to a combination of all or some of these factors.

IV

If federalism, as such, has nothing in it that automatically guarantees the preservation of political freedom, American federalism may have features that have hindered the solution of pressing economic problems.[37] It is not simply that early New Deal legislation was voided by the Supreme Court in the name of the Tenth Amendment. The impact of the American federal system, of the division of powers, on the condition of this country in the thirties was not reassuring.

George C. S. Benson, in his book *The New Centralization*,[38] tried to show how federalism worked in the setting of the Great Depression.

First, he found federalism as an "obstruction of social legislation." The states hesitated to enact this legislation not only for fear of placing their manufacturers at a competitive disadvantage with manufacturers of states that did not regulate wages and hours and provide benefits, but also for fear of driving larger industries into these latter states.[39]

Secondly, there was great disparity among the states' financial resources. Not only were most states incapable of financing serious efforts at reform, but "Complete decentralization—complete local responsibility for governmental services—may then result in a 'spread' between the standards of different districts which would shock even the uncritical believer in a national 'American' standard."[40]

Thirdly, Benson found little evidence that the states were really the "experimental laboratories" they were pictured to be.[41]

Fourthly, the ability of the states to put programs into action in an efficient way was seriously questioned. "With the exception of such cases as those noted on page 13 (auditing systems of Massachusetts, New York, Maryland, Virginia, and New Jersey), state governments are inferior administratively to the federal government. Two thirds of the states lack genuine merit systems for selection of personnel, and only three or four have salary levels sufficiently high to attract competent administrative or professional staffs."[42]

Fifthly, Benson found the functioning of many of the state legislatures faulty because of a lack of time or money for suitable research. "Proponents of states' rights might pause to consider whether the increase of federal activity is not so much a result of superior federal legislative procedure as of superior federal resources."[43]

Lastly, the nature of the economic system is such that its workings were and are obviously not confined to the territory of any given city or state. "As our great business concerns grow more specialized and conduct larger-scale operations in an age of complicated machinery, government cannot be expected to remain simple and pastoral."[44]

In sum, as Professor Key has written, "A characteristic of the federal system seems to be that entrenched interests in the long run can better protect themselves in dealing with state legislatures than with Congress or with federal administrators."[45]

V

The second question, however, still begs an answer: are there goals that can be attained only through federalism? Obviously the answer must be yes, but it requires a careful formulation of the problem.

When the Founding Fathers wrestled with the problem, they did not ask whether they desired a federal state. They rather, and correctly, asked whether there should be a union and how far this union should go. Once the first question had been answered affirmatively, and once it was clear that the existing territorial units could not be extinguished, the necessary result was, indeed, a federal state.[46]

If we apply this to present-day Europe, it seems obvious that one should not ask whether the Western European states should unite into a federal state but rather whether they should cooperate on a permanent basis—politically, as well as economically and militarily. If this is answered affirmatively (and I for one shall not answer a question which is a European responsibility) one must decide what constitutional form this cooperation should take. There exist, obviously, the following alternatives: (1) a tighter treaty system combined with more specialized agencies; (2) a confederation; (3) a federal state; (4) a unitary state with a substantial amount of decentralization; and (5) a unitary state with a centralized administration. The decision what constitutional solution is to be adopted should not be dictated by a doctrinaire preference for a federal state because of its alleged advantages but rather by political considerations such as the need to secure a maximum of popular support, the efficiency of the new constitutional form, etc.

If one simply poses the alternative between a federal state and a continuation of the present system of cooperation, one may wreck the chances for closer integration because those who prefer an expansion of the treaty system and more specialized agencies as well as the advocates of a confederation or a unitary state may be driven into the arms of those who desire no change or are even actively opposed to any form of closer cooperation.

VI

This chapter has tried to show the futility of any discussion of the merits of federalism as an arrangement considered abstractly. There are no values that inhere in federalism as such, and federalism cannot be defended successfully on the grounds that the inevitable tendency of a unitary state is toward political repression. The testimony of history will not support this assertion, nor will it support the assertion that a division of constitutional power is the best guarantee of political freedom. When to these considerations is joined that of the financial inadequacy or political unwillingness of the smaller units to respond satisfactorily to serious economic troubles, then unrestrained adulation of federalism seems all the more unwarranted.[47]

FOOTNOTES TO CHAPTER 3

1. See K. C. Wheare, *Federal Government*, New York, Oxford University Press, 1947, p. 15.

2. Based upon C. Bouglé, *La sociologie de Proudhon*, Paris, A. Colin, 1911; H. Bourgin, *Proudhon*, Paris, G. Bellais, 1901.

3. For details see Alexander Gray, *The Socialist Tradition, Moses to Lenin*, London, Longmans, Green, 1947, pp. 230–256; and G. D. H. Cole, *Socialist Thought, The Forerunners, 1789–1850*, London, Macmillan, 1953, pp. 201–218.

4. Quotations taken from G. Himmelfarb, *Lord Acton, A Study in Conscience and Politics*, Chicago, University of Chicago Press, 1952; a, p. 220; b, p. 139; c, p. 161.

5. Thucydides, *The Peloponnesian War*, Book V.

6. My edition of the *Spirit of the Laws*, New York, Hafner Library of Classics, 1949, XI, 4.

7. See my Introduction, *ibid.*, pp. lvii–lviii.

8. Bowring ed., Vol. IX, pp. 41 *et seq.;* and Elie Halévy, *The Growth of Philisiphic Radicalism*, trans. by Mary Morris, New York, Macmillan, 1928, pp. 458–9.

9. See my Montesquieu Introduction, pp. lviii and lxiv.

10. Cf. Carl J. Friedrich, *Constitutional Government and Democracy*, Boston, Ginn & Co., 1946, pp. 216–7.

11. Rudolf Schlesinger, *Federalism in Central and Eastern Europe*, New York, Oxford University Press, 1945, p. 71.

12. K. C. Wheare, *op. cit.*, p. 29.

13. For details see Oscar Jászi, *The Dissolution of the Hapsburg Monarchy*, Chicago, University of Chicago Press, 1929, pp. 271 *et seq.;* R. Schlesinger, *op. cit.*, pp. 184 *et seq.*

14. See Eldridge Foster Dowell, *A History of Criminal Syndicalism Legislation in the United States*, Baltimore, The Johns Hopkins Press, 1939.

15. *Ibid.*, p. 47.

16. *Ibid.*, p. 55.

17. *Ibid., passim.*

18. *Ibid.*, p. 109.

19. *Ibid.*, pp. 147 *et seq.*

20. For the dismal record of the states in preserving civil liberties, see Walter Gellhorn, ed., *The States and Subversion*, Ithaca, Cornell University Press, 1952.

21. Plato, *Laws*, III, 691:
"Athenian stranger—Nothing can be clearer than the observation which I am about to make.
Megillus—What is it?

Athenian Stranger—That if any one gives too great a power to anything, too large a sail to a vessel, too much food to the body, too much authority to the mind, and does not observe the mean, everything is overthrown, and, in the wantonness of excess runs in the one case to disorders, and in the other to injustice, which is the child of excess. I mean to say, my dear friends, that there is no soul of man, young and irresponsible, who will be able to sustain the temptation of arbitrary power—no one who will not, under such circumstances, become filled with folly, that worst of diseases, and be hated by his nearest and dearest friends . . ."

22. Edmund Burke, *Reflections on the French Revolution* (Everyman's Library), p. 226.

23. *Considerations on the Causes of the Grandeur and Decadence of the Romans,* trans. by Jehu Baker, New York, D. Appleton, 1882.

24. *The Spirit of the Laws,* VIII, 16, and my Introduction, p. xliii.

25. *The Social Contract,* III, xv; transl. by G. D. H. Cole, Everyman Library ed.

26. Hamilton, No. IX.

27. Montesquieu, *The Spirit of the Laws,* IX, i.

28. Gilbert Chinard, ed., *Jefferson's Commonplace Book,* Baltimore, The Johns Hopkins Press, 1926, p. 267.

29. See Friedrich Ratzel, *Politische Geographie,* 3d ed., Munich and Berlin, R. Oldenbourg, 1923.

30. Carl J. Friedrich, *Constitutional Government and Democracy,* Revised edition, Boston, Ginn & Co., 1950, pp. 546–570.

31. *The Federalist,* No. XLV.

32. *Representative Government* (Everyman ed.), pp. 374–5.

33. Roscoe Pound, "Law and Federal Government," in *Federalism as a Democratic Process,* Essays by Roscoe Pound, Charles H. McIlwain, and Roy F. Nichols, New Brunswick, Rutgers University Press, 1942.

Pound equates, or confuses, localism and federalism: "Even if the lines cannot be drawn at any one time absolutely—and in law and politics which deal with life none can be so drawn—the national and the local are distinct at the core, and the experience of English-speaking peoples has shown that local matters are best dealt with in the locality instead of by postulated *ex officio* supermen at a distance." (p. 21).

34. A. V. Dicey, *Introduction to the Study of the Law of the Constitution,* Ninth Edition, ed. by E. C. S. Wade, London, Macmillan, 1950:

"Our survey from a legal point of view of the characteristics common to all federal government forcibly suggests conclusions of more than merely legal interest, as to the comparative merits of federal government, and the system of Parliamentary sovereignty.

"Federal government means weak government.

". . . no more curious instance can be found of the inconsistent currents of popular opinion which may at the same time pervade a nation or a generation than the coincidence in England of a vague admiration for federalism alongside with a far more decided feeling against the doctrines of so-called *laissez faire.* A system meant to maintain the *status quo* in politics is incompatible with schemes for wide social innovation.

"Federalism tends to produce conservatism.

". . . The difficulty of altering the constitution produces conservative sentiment, and national conservatism doubles the difficulty of altering the constitution . . . To this one must add that a federal constitution always lays down general principles which, from being placed in the constitution, gradually come to command a superstitious reverence, and thus are in fact, though not in theory, protected from change or criticism . . .

"Federalism, lastly, means legalism—the predominance of the judiciary in the constitution—the prevalence of a spirit of legality among the people.

". . . Federalism substitutes litigation for legislation, and none but a law-fearing people will be inclined to regard the decision of a suit as equivalent to the enactment of a law." (p. 171–179).

35. Alexis de Tocqueville, *Democracy in America,* New York, Knopf, 1945, Vol. I, pp. 271–2.

36. John C. Calhoun, *A Discourse on the Constitution and Government of the United States,* in *The Works,* Vol. I, New York, D. Appleton, 1854, pp. 168–9, 233–4, 241, 268, 383–6, 392; Konstantin Frantz, *Der Foederalismus als das leitende Princip fuer die sociale, staatliche und internationale Organisation . . . ,* Mainz, Kirchheim, 1879.

37. For a discussion of this situation in Australia, see A. P. Canaway, *The Failure of Federalism in Australia,* London, Oxford University Press, 1930.

38. New York, Farrar and Rinehart, 1941. On this problem see, in addition, Harold Laski, "The Obsolescence of Federalism," *The New Republic,* Vol. 98 (May 3, 1939), pp. 367–69.

39. Benson, *op. cit.,* pp. 23–24.

40. *Ibid.,* p. 30.

41. *Ibid.,* p. 38.

42. *Ibid.,* p. 40.

43. *Ibid.,* p. 42.

44. *Ibid.,* p. 42.

45. V. O. Key, Jr., *Politics, Parties, and Pressure Groups,* Third Edition, New York, Crowell, 1952, p. 102.

46. See Hamilton in *The Federalist,* IX, XV, and the above Madison quotation from *The Federalist.*

47. In preparing this chapter the author had the valued assistance of George A. Kateb.

4

Prerequisites of Balance

By John Fischer

I

The idea of federalism is more alive today than at any time in the last 150 years. Practical men are talking about it in serious terms all the way from Cambodia to Strasbourg; in dozens of countries, especially in Europe, it has moved from the shadowy realm of political theory into the harsh arena of current politics.

The reasons for this suddenly awakened interest are obvious enough. History might be written in terms of the growing size of the political unit—from the family to the tribe; from the tribe to the city state; and so by irregular stages to the nation, the empire, the commonwealth, and to other varied forms of grand-scale social organization. The progression has, of course, been a spasmodic one, and it has been interrupted by many temporary set-backs. Vast units, constructed with much blood and labor, have repeatedly broken down again into more primitive fragments—as in the case of the Roman, the Mongol, the Gupta, the Mohammedan, and the Carolingian empires. Other units—as in ancient Egypt and tribal Africa—have remained relatively stable in size for long periods; and then have suddenly coalesced, or have been forcibly incorporated, into larger political organizations.

Yet when all these spurts, lags, and reversals are scrutinized in long perspective, a trend toward larger political units emerges fairly plain on the graph of history. It is also clear that most men have always viewed this trend with suspicion and hostility. Every step from a smaller unit to a larger one is painful. It disturbs vested interests. Worse still, it confronts everybody with strange and difficult problems of social structure and personal relationship. It forces the people involved to rearrange their loyalties, to get along somehow with aliens, to adjust their lives to a new environment. Usually, too, it means higher taxes.

Quite naturally, therefore, the shift to a wider type of political organization is almost never made voluntarily. It comes—as a general rule—only when it is forced by some overwhelming pressure: the growth of population, military innovations, revolutionary changes in economics or technology, the threat of external enemies. Such pressures commonly are resisted until the last possible moment—and then the new, larger political unit often comes into being (by conquest or, more rarely, by reluctant agreement) with startling rapidity.

One of these periods of sudden transition now seems at hand throughout a considerable part of the world. In Asia, in the Arab lands, in parts of Africa, and in Europe, increasing numbers of people are being driven to recognize that their traditional political patterns are no longer adequate; and they are moving, at widely varying rates of speed, toward more promising forms.

In the so-called backward areas, the typical step is from colonial status to nationhood; and here the vigorous nationalist impulse is often coupled with a groping for larger, sturdier political units: witness Indonesia, Indo-China, and the Pan-Arab movement. Among the Europeans, on the other hand, nationalism appears to have lost most of its vital force. They are realizing—in anguish—that the nation-state which they invented and used with pride for some five hundred years has finally lost its utility. Like the tribe and the walled city, it has become too small to serve as a satisfactory unit for human organization.

For no state in Europe can now perform the functions for which it was originally designed. Standing alone, it can neither feed its people nor defend them. In time of war, national frontiers no longer have any real strategic significance. In peacetime, they have become a faintly comic annoyance—still clogging the natural flow of travel and trade, although an airliner can vault over a dozen of them in a single day. Because they are so obviously anachronistic, the European states no longer command the whole-hearted loyalty of their citizens. Few young Frenchmen—or Italians or Belgians—are eager these days to risk their lives for the glory of the motherland, or even for its survival. Instead of patriotism, the old nationalistic shibboleths are now more likely to evoke cynicism, spiritual lethargy, and despair. Whatever hope the Europeans can muster seems to be focused on new political patterns of one kind or another which appear to be more suitable for the contemporary world.

Two main alternatives present themselves.

One is the Communist prescription. It aims to unite the entire world—eventually—into a single imperium. The characteristics of this universal state are clearly set forth in Marxist doctrine, and are displayed concretely in the present Soviet empire. It is a unitary system—rigid, monolithic, hierarchical, dictatorial, and highly disciplined. Although the Marxist scriptures pay casual lip service to local cultural autonomy, in practice the system cannot tolerate diversity—as the experience of the Russian satellites has well demonstrated. While some of the Communist techniques and economic theories are revolutionary (particularly in a colonial or feudal context), its political pattern certainly is not. On the contrary, it has much in common with one of the most ancient forms of political organization: the absolute monarchy, headed by a priest-king, which was familiar to the Babylonians, the Pharaohs, and the Incas, and until fairly recently to many Europeans. The Communist party serves the traditional roles of a priestly elite, imposing discipline and suppressing heresy in much the fashion of the Holy Inquisition in fifteenth century Spain. (Indeed, the ancient and quasi-theocratic nature of the Soviet state may account, in part, for its appeal to many people of Europe and Asia who feel uneasy with the relatively new-fangled devices of democracy. They find little trouble in fitting a Stalin into the niche previously filled by The Little Father of All the Russias, by a tribal chieftain, a Generalissimo, or a Duce; but because they are long accustomed to rule from above, they find the rigors and obligations of self-government acutely uncomfortable.)

The other alternative is a federal society. Its aim is to harmonize the diverse interests of widely various cultures, traditions, economies, races, and religions into a framework which will serve their common needs. Its characteristics are almost precisely opposite to those of the monolithic Communist system. It attempts to induce strange bedfellows to lie down together in reasonable comfort, or at least toleration, while the Soviet method is strictly Procrustean. A federal system, involving dispersed authority and a large degree of local autonomy, must depend primarily upon the consent of the governed; it can employ coercion only as a last resort, and then very sparingly; else the federation would either split apart or degenerate into a unitary police state.

Obviously it is difficult to make a federal system work satisfactorily. It requires a high degree of political skill and sophistication, not only among the professional politicians but also throughout the whole body of citizenry. Most of all it demands a great deal of forbearance and mutual trust among all its component groups. These are relatively rare qualities; and any federal system will have to operate under apparent handicaps so long as men are selfish, mistrustful, impatient—and so long as it is easier to pull a trigger than to persuade one's opponents and to moderate one's own prejudices.

II

No doubt it is largely historical accident that Russia and America should confront each other as rival examplars of these two competing forms of large-scale political organization.

Their global rivalry of course has other, and perhaps deeper, roots—strategic, economic, and ideological. Nevertheless it is peculiarly appropriate that fate should have chosen the United States as the champion of the federal idea. We invented it—at least in its modern form. We have had more experience than any other people in making it work. It requires extraordinary political talents; and "the genius of the American people is political," as Peter F. Drucker and other shrewd observers have repeatedly noted. Our national saint —Abraham Lincoln—was a politician who spent his life in wrestling with the most profound problems of federalism.

And the concepts and attitudes of a pluralist society are ingrained in all of us from earliest childhood. We practice its disciplines in all of the innumerable voluntary organizations which are such a pervasive (and unique) feature of American life—ranging from high school fraternities to the Federation of Women's Clubs, from the Rotary Club and the Red Cross to the American Federation of Labor and the Farm Bureau Federation. Even our family life is shaped by the habits of democratic federalism—in contrast, for example, with the *Fuehrer* tradition of the German family.

Because democratic federalism has served us reasonably well, and because we are so immersed in it, we tend to think of it as the normal political environment—just as fishes must feel that water is the only healthy environment for any right-thinking creature. Consequently, we are tempted to believe that our institutions should be easily adaptable to other societies, and to wonder —sometimes with impatient irritability—why other peoples, whose own political machinery is so obviously out-worn, do not adopt forthwith a federal pattern modeled on our own.

Although it is natural enough, such a self-righteous and impatient attitude is not likely to prove very helpful, either to ourselves or to our friends abroad. It would, perhaps, be more useful for us to attempt to examine the nature of federalism in a more skeptical and detached light before we leap to any conclusions about its serviceability in other cultures. That, I take it, is one of the purposes of this symposium. In these comments, therefore, I should like to glance at one of the less-frequently discussed problems of a federal system: the problem of balancing power, not simply among the formal political or geographical units which make up the system, but among the great interest groups whose pressures somehow must be harmonized if the federal society is to survive.

III

European political theorists have often pointed to the peculiar advantages which we enjoyed in forming our United States. At the time of the Constitutional Convention, we were a fairly homogeneous people, speaking a common language, worshipping a common God, educated in the generally accepted tradition of John Locke and the British common law, shaped by the common experience of settling a new land. Until recently, we had been united under the British Crown; we had been brought closer together by common grievances, and finally by rebellion against that authority; we had learned to work together under the harsh discipline of war; and we had gained some experience in the arts and difficulties of a common government under the Articles of Confederation.

In addition, we were blessed with two unique political assets which probably can never again be duplicated wherever the question of federalism may be discussed.

1. The United States started with a relatively clean slate. The governmental machinery in each of the thirteen colonies was rudimentary, and the over-

riding authority of the Crown—always tenuous—had been wiped out in the Revolution. As a consequence, there were no entrenched bureaucracies to oppose the new federal regime, no elaborate structures of administration to be knitted painfully together. The enormous advantages of such a pristine beginning can only be appreciated when one contemplates the fearful problem of meshing together the vastly different apparatuses for tax collection, currency management, social security, etc. in such countries as, say, Italy, France, and Germany. Even in the small-scale Benelux experiment with economic cooperation—initiated under relatively favorable circumstances—such obstacles apparently are proving unexpectedly difficult to overcome.

2. In the eighteenth century it was easy to make a distinction between local affairs, which could appropriately be handled by the states, and the matters of general concern which should be delegated to the central authority. The latter were generally held to be defense, foreign affairs, commerce between the states, disputes among the states, and the maintenance of a legal framework within which free enterprise could operate comfortably. As late as 1863, E. A. Freeman could write in his *History of Federal Government* that "a Federal Union, in short, will form one State in relation to other powers, but many states as regards its internal affairs."

Today, however, such a clear-cut division of powers is much more difficult to achieve. As Max Beloff of Nuffield College, Oxford, recently pointed out, "The modern democratic electorate takes no such narrow view of the responsibilities of its rulers. They have to provide not merely law and order and defense, but also social welfare services and above all 'full employment.' The latter objectives can hardly be achieved unless governments have full powers of legislation over the whole economic and fiscal field. It is for this reason that each new federation created has tended to allot more powers to the centre than its predecessors and that within every existing federation the centralizing tendency has been steadily at work and with ever increasing speed."[1]

Moreover, the nature of modern warfare is forcing the federal government to extend its sphere of operations far beyond anything ever contemplated by the Founding Fathers. Because military power has become almost synonymous with industrial strength, the central authority can now discharge its responsibilities for defense only by detailed and large-scale intervention in the economic life of the country. As a consequence, modern constitution-makers face a perplexing task in drawing a sharp line between the role of a federal government and that of its constituent units.

In addition, the balancing of power among the great interests within the union presents a far thornier problem to most would-be federalists of today than it did to Americans in 1787. In our formative period, such interest groups were almost providentially well balanced.

No single religious denomination, for example, was dominant within the thirteen colonies; nor were the differences between the denominations carried to the point of blood-enmity, as they are today between Arabs and Israelis,

Hindus and Muslims, Communists and Catholics. In most of the infant states, the agricultural, manufacturing, and trading interests existed in reasonable equipoise; nowhere did industry overshadow farming as it does today in Britain or Germany—or, for that matter, in Pennsylvania and Massachusetts. The conflict between slave and non-slave interests rested in uneasy deadlock, which was to be maintained—by remarkable feats of political teetering—for more than half a century. The oligarchic and the plebeian elements were so nearly equal in strength that the nation was able to struggle through the Jeffersonian-Jacksonian revolution without any real fear by either side that it might be annihilated by the other.

Perhaps most important of all, the new nation was able to solve—or to by-pass temporarily—many of the most serious conflicts between economic and other groups by the simple expedient of westward expansion. The frontier was an invaluable safety-valve. When a factory worker felt intolerably oppressed, he did not plot revolution; he simply moved beyond the Alleghenies and took to farming free land. Thus, too, did the Mormons escape from a literally murderous religious struggle. And the expedient of admitting new states in pairs, one slave and one free, postponed for a time the irrepressible conflict between South and North.

In spite of these fortuitous (or providential) aids to union, the question which dominated the first seventy-five years of American political life was, quite simply: How can such a federal system be held together against the splintering pressures of divergent interests? From the very beginning, therefore, American politicians were preoccupied with the problem of balancing these pressures against one another. They recognized that no constitutional or legalistic device could save the republic, unless the underlying real forces could be kept in equilibrium. As John Randolph put it: "You may cover whole skins of parchment with limitations, but power alone can limit power."

Nor was it possible to find any single, lasting static solution—for the forces in play were never stable; some were waxing as others waned, and they regrouped themselves in ever shifting combinations. So the indispensable balance had to be achieved afresh, from month to month, by enormous labors of statesmanship.

Out of these labors grew the most distinctive American contribution to political theory: John C. Calhoun's doctrine of the concurrent majority. Because Calhoun was spokesman for a lost cause, and because he evolved his doctrine primarily in defense of the slavery interest, it is sometimes assumed that his ideas were discredited once and for all at Appomattox Courthouse. In fact, however, his theory survived—not so much in the textbooks as in the daily practical operations of American politics. In somewhat modified form, it has become the guiding principle of our public life; and it may yet prove to be our major contribution to the development of federalism in other lands.

First of all, Calhoun argued, no single interest must ever be permitted to become so strong that it could impose its will on the others by force. Moreover, every special interest group—whether racial, religious, regional, or economic—would have to forego the very thought of coercion. The tremendously diverse elements of American society could live together in harmony only so long as each one of them was confident that it would not be destroyed—or even seriously injured—by some temporary combination of the others. No majority, therefore, could afford to use its power ruthlessly. It must always restrain itself to handle tenderly the vital interests of the minority.

Such self-restraint, as Calhoun saw it, was not only statesmanship of the highest order, essential to the preservation of the union; it was also good practical politics. For every American party is simply a temporary coalition of many interest groups.[2] Because the constellation may rearrange itself before the next election, it is never prudent for any politician to alienate irretrievably any group which happens to be, at the moment, in the enemy's rank; tomorrow he may need to bring that particular platoon over to his own side.

In order to assure the necessary degree of restraint—to make certain that each element would always respect the vital interests of every other—Calhoun proposed that every important decision in American life should be adopted only by a "concurrent majority." By this he meant, in effect, the unanimous agreement—or at least the passive consent—of every interested party. Specifically, he asserted that no decision affecting the vital interest of the slaveholders should be forced through over their vigorous objection. By implication he would have given a similar veto to every other special interest, whether it be labor, management, the Catholic Church, or the Western cattlemen.

Because of his deep emotional involvement with the slavery issue, Calhoun was drive to state his doctrine in an extreme and unworkable form. If every sectional interest had been given the explicit, legal veto which he proposed, the government obviously would have been paralyzed—just as the *liberum veto* system once paralyzed effective administration in Poland. But the doctrine became workable in the modified version which has been incorporated into our political practice.

In that version, the idea of the concurrent majority is tacit rather than explicit, a matter of well-observed custom rather than law. For it is the very essence of the concept that it cannot be made legal and official. It can operate effectively only as an informal, highly elastic, and generally accepted understanding. Perhaps the best example is the Quaker church meeting, where decisions are not reached by formal vote at all, but rather by a give-and-take discussion which continues until "the sense of the meeting" emerges and is accepted by everybody present.

Moreover, the doctrine works only if each minority group practices the same self-restraint which it demands of the majority coalition. A special interest cannot afford to use its implicit veto power lightly. This power must be regarded as a strictly defensive weapon, to be unsheathed only when the group's really vital interests are in hazard. When merely casual or fringe interests are at stake, the group does not dare to behave in a doctrinaire or intransigeant fashion; it must make every conceivable effort to compromise, relying on its veto only as a last resort. (The phrase "I don't like it, but I'll go along" is an important key to the understanding of American politics; a key seldom grasped by European politicians who are obsessed with the notion of ideological purity.)

When used with discretion, and in accordance with these accepted rules of the game, the implied veto is an invaluable device for making a federal system work smoothly. But if any player uses it recklessly, the game will break up—or all the other players will turn on him in anger, suspend the rules for the time being, and maul those very interests which he was trying so desperately to protect. The game also will break up if any interest group, or coalition of groups, grows so powerful and arrogant that it frightens the weaker players—thus tempting them to use their veto recklessly.

Something of this sort happened on the only occasion when the American federal system did break down, in the great crisis of 1860. At that time, major economic, moral, and regional interests had been polarized into two hostile coalitions—the industrial, high-tariff, abolitionist North against the agrarian, free trade, slaveholding South. The power of the North grew faster; and as its population and industrial strength became predominant, so its moral fervor became belligerent. The South saw the balance swinging against it, and at the same time lost confidence that the over-weening North would restrain itself to respect the vital Southern interest. ("Power alone can balance power.") So in desperation the South attempted to use its veto in the final, extreme form. The upshot proved that Calhoun's doctrine of the concurrent majority could not guarantee salvation, any more than Randolph's parchment limitations—once real power had slipped irrevocably out of balance.

There is no space here to explore the complex and subtle ways in which the idea of the concurrent majority has been adapted to almost every aspect of the American society. It is enough to note that it has been institutionalized into such diverse forms as the filibuster, the Congressional committee system, and the role of the lobbyists. It governs the make up of cabinets and political tickets. (In New York City, for example, every municipal slate is carefully balanced to include a Catholic, a Protestant, a Jew, and a Negro; and even in the public school system the administrative posts are neatly apportioned on a racial and religious basis.) It determines the selection of presidential candidates—for no man can hope to gain the nomination if he incurs the veto of any substantial group within the party coalition. (Witness the sad case of Senator Robert A. Taft, whose aspirations were repeatedly vetoed by the so-called Eastern or internationalist wing of the GOP.) Comparable traditions govern the internal political life of the American Legion, the Parent-Teachers Association, university student bodies, labor unions, lodges, and churches of all denominations. (A member of the Catholic hierarchy remarked recently in a private conversation that one of its constant problems in America is to maintain an appropriate equilibrium among clerics of Irish, German, Italian, and Polish descent, and to balance the roles and influence of the various religious orders.) The examples could be multiplied endlessly.

From the American experience, then, one is tempted to draw two tentative conclusions:

1. The skillful application of the doctrine of the concurrent majority—with all its implications of toleration and mutual confidence—is probably essential to the successful working of any federal system.

2. The doctrine cannot be applied unless the elements of real power are kept in reasonable balance; for whenever the balance is upset, toleration and confidence will almost certainly give way to arrogance and mistrust.

IV

If these assumptions are at all valid, then the obstacles to federation in Western Europe appear all the more formidable. The potentially predominant strength of Germany, for example, is understandably frightening to the lesser Continental states, particularly France; and the central problem, therefore, becomes the finding of some method to balance the economic, military, and political power of Germany.

One conceivable solution would be to throw onto the scales enough British and American power to serve as make-weight; but that course would lead to something far wider and more complicated than a mere European union. It would seem to imply some kind of tripartite confederation, involving the United States, the British Commonwealth, and a federated Western Europe— that is to say, three separate federations of very different character, linked together in a loose but mutually supporting confederacy. This notion has been much discussed in England and on the Continent, but the details never emerge very clearly—just enough to indicate that this would be one of the most appallingly complex and unmanageable structures ever devised by the human mind.

Moreover, such a solution would raise new problems of balance because American power almost certainly would dominate any grouping in which we might participate; and however benevolent that power may seem to us, it inevitably makes the weaker partners uneasy. (That, indeed, seems to be the chief sore point in the North Atlantic Treaty Organization, and the prime cause of anti-Americanism abroad.)

Even if some answer could be found to these prime questions of structural equilibrium, many other factors would still be fantastically difficult to balance in any conceivable European system. The obvious differences in population, wealth, distribution of resources are discouraging enough. Even worse, perhaps, are the intangible differences—the highly-developed political skills of Britain, Switzerland, and the Scandinavian countries, for instance, as contrasted with France and Italy, not to mention Spain.

And how long would it take to cultivate the habits of mutual trust and toleration which a federal system seems to demand? The national rivalries, the barriers of language, the cultural antipathies, the inescapable burdens of history, all present handicaps unknown to American federalism. Furthermore, the existence of large Communist parties in several European countries raises a special kind of obstacle; for they would not be dedicated to making the system work, but rather to its destruction.

V

These gloomy speculations are not intended to indicate that the prospects for the growth of federal institutions abroad are entirely hopeless. They are merely meant to suggest that the problem is more difficult than the casual American observer might suspect; that the American pattern is not likely to produce a wearable political garb for other peoples without a lot of tucks and patching; and that the tailoring process may require a long time.

The seemly course for us, therefore, might be to present our experience for what it is worth—granting that to others it may not be worth much; to offer more encouragement and less exhortation; and to cultivate the golden virtues of modesty and patience. For the development of workable federal systems in Europe, Asia, and elsewhere must be solved—if it is solved at all—by the peoples who must live within these systems. And however difficult and distasteful the federal solution may be, it will not be quickly dismissed as hopeless—simply because the chief other alternative is likely to appear even more distasteful, as knowledge of the nature of the Communist imperium becomes more widespread throughout the world.

FOOTNOTES TO CHAPTER 4

1. "The 'Federal Solution' In Its Application to Europe, Asia, and Africa," a paper delivered before the University of Leeds, March 12, 1953, and printed in *Political Studies,* Vol. 1, No. 2, June 1953.

2. It is the Continental European habit to form coalitions *after* an election; while in America this process is carried out *before* the election, within the capacious framework of the two omnibus—rather than ideological—parties. This difference in custom often makes it difficult for Europeans to understand American politics, and vice versa.

5

Evolving Capitalism and Political Federalism

By Adolf A. Berle, Jr.

I

INTRODUCTION

Two centuries is a short span in the time-count of history. Measured by the expansion of men's minds and lives, the span may be long indeed.

Federalism did not exist as an effective conception until thirty years after King's College was founded. Now it is accepted as the principle which determined the national course of the United States; which is appealed to as a possible unifying principle in the economics of Western Europe; which is taken as a guide line offering the only tangible hope of resolving the millennial divisions of the Greco-Roman world; which is used even by our intellectual opponents in the Soviet constellation; and within whose framework are constructed visions and dreams of a world order struggling to be born.

There is promise here, and danger too. The institution has proved its power and offers vast prospect of future usefulness.

There is danger lest, as the institution gains in force, the personalities of men and their individual and diverse hopes, thoughts, achievements, and possibilities may be submerged. The present world appears to demand more delegation of power, more powerful federalisms at the very time when protection of man and his individual personality appears most needed.

The turbulences of the twentieth century, however inconclusive, have settled three questions for the time being. One is that no nation taken by itself can militarily defend its existence alone in the modern world. So we work with an inter-American general staff, with the prospect of a European army, with the distant hope of a United Nations security force. The second is that no country taken by itself alone can hope to maintain the standards of production, distribution, and economic progress demanded by a modern population. So we struggle, not without success, towards realizing in the Schuman Plan the creation of the sovereign authority of the European Coal and Steel Community.

The third is that technical progress expresses itself economically in great measure through huge business or quasi-economic entities—the large corporation or the large cartel. So, in the United States as elsewhere in the western world, the most significant area of business is occupied by enterprises country-wide and often international in scope. So also, though without benefit of con-stitutional sanction, sometimes with and often without legal recognition, cartels or aggregates of economic interests—as, for example, the oil industry—carry on coordinated international and frequently worldwide operations.

These are three powerful forces driving historic entities into arrangements for common action. They seem to apply to the new, nongeographical entities like corporations as well as to the older historical entities known as nation-states.

Concurrently, the twentieth century exhibits a no less powerful demand for individual, local, national, and regional self-determination as pressures mount, forcing pooling of interests and common action. Demands become louder that colonies should be made independent, that national cultures shall not be sub-merged, that individuals shall express themselves freely. If the twentieth cen-tury demands a higher factor of common action in the field of defense, peace-keeping, and economics, it is equally asserting individualist claims of the smallest groups from Icelanders to IndoChinese, from Slovaks to Maoris. But these increase rather than decrease the intellectual claims of federalism. For federalism provides a conception in which the individual, the locality, the historic entity retains existence for the precise purpose of defending and ex-pressing the individual and local values considered important by it. Abdications of power to a central unit are designed precisely to defend all that can be maintained of the autonomy and individuality of the surrendering group. Much of the success of the American federal experiment rests on the aptness of the federal instrument in just this respect. The federal system can recognize, pre-serve, and defend diverse individual and parochial values at the same time that it unites forces necessary for the common welfare and the common defense.

The United States stands committed to federalism and its achievements have made federalism an avenue of hope in a troubled world. Yet in its hour of success, the greatest problems are foreshadowed. To some of these we must turn.

II

FEDERAL ELEMENTS IN THE TREND OF TWENTIETH CENTURY CAPITALISM

In our span of two centuries, it seems, the world has achieved more technical progress and more domination over physical forces than in all previously recorded history. Concurrently (perhaps as a result) the number of people in the world has vastly increased. In 1755 Dr. Samuel Johnson glumly estimated the population of the world at "about one billion, chiefly fools." In 1954 the population of the world consists of approximately two billions and a half, though no one has estimated its wisdom. In the United States alone, population has increased by thirty millions in the last twenty years, with more rapid increase promised for the future. Communication has pushed these millions into intimate contact. Congress, originally designed to be convened four months after election so that representatives from outlying parts of the country might perhaps reach Washington in time for the sessions, can now call a representative from the farthest part of the United States in twelve hours. Communication no longer is limited to "post offices and post roads," confided to the central government so that mails might be carried without political obstruction. Radio waves, knowing nothing and caring less about either state or international boundaries, reach their targets within a split second. "Freedom of the press," designed as a negative protection to local communities, must now involve positive policies of direction and control of radio networks whose instantaneously transmitted news and editorial coverage rivals, if it does not surpass, that of all the newspapers combined.

In companion development, steady evolution of economic organization appears to be forcing a new federalism of its own. The chief elements are here given in shorthand.

Propelled by growth of massive enterprise, four main categories of federalist economics are discernible. *First,* a group of industries, national in scope, but assimilated to the common law conception of "public utilities" and "affected with a public interest"—transportation, communications, electric light and power, natural gas, and the like. These have steadily gravitated towards governmental and even central governmental control. *Second,* a group of industries providing products or services deemed necessary by the community, and dominated by so small a group of enterprises that a measure of national planning and control, set up by or in cooperation with government, has been found necessary by the community or by the industry, or both. *Third,* a group of industries supplying products or services deemed necessary or much desired by the community whose operations are concentrated in a small number (usually three, and rarely more than six) of large enterprises. In these there has not yet been violent impact with the community, but the industrial concentrate has achieved, informally, its own planning and coordinating mechanism. This is the phenomenon of unregulated "oligopoly." And, *fourth,* a group of enterprises recently brought into existence by and largely conditioned upon the needs and desires of government. This, a new, powerful, almost unstudied group, is rapidly rising to cardinal importance.

Without attempting to review the mass of detail indicated by this catalogue, a few illustrations will suffice to prove the point.

In the *first* category, the transportation industry, originally local, private, and individual, has now become a congeries of great enterprises brought under central regulation as the community became convinced that centralized control was the only avenue of safety. The political upheaval known as the "Granger Movement" broke the path; its first fruit was the Interstate Commerce Commission, weakly formed in 1887, which secured its substantial powers from the government of President Theodore Roosevelt in 1903. Intended for railroads, this central regulative authority now controls and guides truck, autobus, and internal water transportation. A parallel body, the Civil Aeronautics Board, rises to assume control over air transport, as the Federal Maritime Board guides, and in a measure creates, overseas shipping. Impact of a great but immature industry on the community compelled, in 1935, authorization of the Federal Power Commission to act as control agency for great parts of the electric light and power industry. More recently, this body has begun to control still newer industries—for instance, the natural gas industry.

In these and many like cases the community demanded, and in a measure imposed, centralized control over the industry.

In the *second* category, federal planning for essential industries, the most striking example is petroleum. There, a federal system of national planning was set up more by the desire of the industry than by requirement of public opinion. Its first form was a code under the National Recovery Act of 1933. Later, a modified form of the system was made permanent through a triad of governmental acts: administrative action through the United States Bureau of Mines which regularly estimates demand for petroleum products; treaty action by the oil-producing states through the Interstate Oil Compact of 1935, with congressional approval, which arranged for state action adjusting local production to the demand estimates; the whole enforced by the national "Connally Hot Oil Act" forbidding shipment of petroleum in interstate commerce unless a certificate shows that it has been produced in accordance with production controls. Analogous though less detailed planning and control were demanded and secured by the sugar industry through the Sugar Act of 1947.

In the *third* category falls a powerful and growing group of industries which have not come under continuous governmental control, perhaps because through wisdom or good fortune neither the community nor the industry feels need of relief, but which nevertheless have achieved (in effect) an extra-legal federal system. The copper and steel industries, for example, when not under defense control regulation, operate essentially through a "price leadership" system; this, taken in connection with the fact that capital expense is huge and free entry into the field difficult, supplies a pattern typical of many basic industries. Indeed, throughout most of the American industrial field the pattern has come to be concentration of half or more of the industry in the hands of three or four very large corporations, alongside of which twenty or more small competitors live without great expansion.

In one form or another these concentrations have steadily sought, or been forced into seeking, some nationwide central planning nucleus. Sometimes this is done illegally, and an antitrust prosecution results. More often it is done by seeking legislation or by securing administrative cooperation of some branch of the federal government. (Accurately understood, the large corporations are the greatest federalists of them all.)

The *fourth* category, possibly destined to become the greatest heir of the technology of coming years, is pure economic futurism.

Here enterprises of national scope, though nominally private, are in fact inextricably intermingled with the national state. The aircraft production industry, for example, one of the largest in the country, is in private hands; but 95 per cent of its product is sold to the United States government, its operations are powerfully influenced by government needs, while an indeterminate amount of its plant was constructed and much of it is still owned by the central government. Its patents, processes, designs, and technical information form a crazy-quilt mixture of the results of public, private, and combined research and development. In this category also falls much of the new electronic industry emerging from modern invention; into it are steadily being drawn even the great electrical manufacturing companies built up prior to World War II. Atomic energy in various phases now is emerging as a probable industrial base; but atomic energy, the product and monopoly of the national government, was wholly brought into existence by the government with taxpayers' money. Industry based on it, at least for a time, is bound to be indissolubly linked to the central political state.

The four categories, thus illustrated, cover at least half of all of American industry. Unquestionably they include its most essential fields. They must be taken in the framework of a banking and currency system controlled in most of its major functions by the Federal Reserve Board and the United States Treasury—a huge extension of the centralizing principle in federalism through its entry into many fields of American production and distribution. Within this outline, the outlines of a federally-managed economy emerge.

Capitalism of the mid-twentieth century consequently is coming to turn, not on the "verdict of the market place," so dear to our grandfathers, but on administrative decisions, governmental or private, whose impact is nationwide. We may risk coining a name. Professor Kenneth Galbraith of Harvard called it a system of "countervailing power." Yet it outpasses that. The force of autonomous collective units, seeking and increasingly finding a central planning nucleus in American economics, is already so strong that we have a system which may fairly be called "administered capitalism" in place of an economy resting wholly on market balance.

This has come about gradually, and even without clear intent. Expansion of technical information, new ability to organize, community desire for the products and services, engendered large-scale enterprise. But large-scale enterprises do not "compete" in the same sense as do thousands of small scale enterprises. Rather they struggle with each other, but the result of their contest is sometimes monopoly and commonly concentration of the industry in not more than five huge corporations. The community clearly wants the products and services in quantities and at prices which only vast corporations can offer. Beyond avoiding monopoly, public opinion really wished not to break them up but to exact standards of performance. The corporations on their side almost always seek economic arrangements looking towards stability of price and supply, permitting predictability in the results of operations. The result has been a series of national plans, industry by industry, in varying degree of development, which already cover much of American economic life. The added impact of governmentally developed technology and of the central government as principal buyer, emerging chiefly since the beginning of World War II, obviously expands still further the area of federal influence.

The conclusion is clear enough. Dynamic forces in American economics have engendered, and are compelling, intense evolution of the federal system in a vast area of life formerly considered outside the range of the central government, if not outside the scope of government at all. "Administered capitalism" appears to be the result.

In terms of political organization, this presents a novel problem. Classic American federalism did not contemplate a government which carried on any great part of the activities of production and distribution. Hamiltonian "Federalism" unquestionably did contemplate a central government which superseded much of the state power in establishing rules within which "commerce" in its present meaning would be carried on. Few, if any, classic federalists foresaw a time in which great, nonterritorial organizations would be the chief productive and distributive agencies: they did not foresee the growth of the modern corporation. Still less could it have been imagined that concentrates of great corporations would find need for national organization within their own industries, increasingly requiring some central nucleus for planning, stabilization, and policy-making; in a word, that (outside the political form of the American government) nonterritorial economic organizations would arise; and that these, while insisting on a high degree of liberty of action, would also seek an equivalent of federal organization. Lacking material for prophecy, the end result scarcely has been foreshadowed, namely, the growing tendency to bring these aggregates, industry by industry, into more or less recognized political relationship with the American government. Yet this is precisely what has been happening. Nongovernmental organizations—corporations—seek central organization among themselves. This apparently proves insufficient, and some fragment of the power of national political government is needed to complete the organization. This perhaps may fairly be called economic federalism, though the component units begin by being nonpolitical in origin and nature.

No historical analogue for this situation is known to the writer. Nor is it necessary at this time to attempt a forecast of its evolution, except to note an unbroken trend during the past half century. Nonpolitical economic centralization, which guards a high degree of autonomy in great corporations yet increasingly delegates certain powers to a central group, which in turn seeks authority and legitimacy from the central government, can fairly be described as federalist. But it is federalism developed from a new type of component unit, towards new types of central organization, eventually drawing the composite governmental system of the United States into new fields and new responsibilities.

III

THE RISE OF ECONOMIC RESPONSIBILITY IN POLITICS

At this point, it is submitted, the political philosophers and political scientists are urgently paged by history. Rarely, perhaps, has an academic discipline been so squarely challenged. It must consider objectives, derive principles, sketch out and evaluate the techniques of the emerging system.

Physical scientists, engineers, business organizers, economists, financiers, production managers, have already had their assignations and have met them. Together they have forged instruments, physical and organizational, capable of production beyond past dreams. These are capable, apparently, of accomplishing a distribution which (however imperfect) has lifted material standards of living of the American people far beyond any other group in the world. In doing so, they have brought about a state of affairs permitting, indeed requiring, conscious political determinations in areas heretofore decided automatically without benefit of government, formal or informal. Prior to the emergence of administered capitalism, the economic balance arrived at in the market place determined events. As the market decision was understood to be the resultant of all the community choices, the verdict was considered "right" in the sense that it most reflected the positive choice of the community. The businessman was released from considering whether his price was just or extortionate, whether wages he paid were fair or were oppressive, whether his suppliers were adequately or inadequately compensated. The market settled that; it alone could judge and correct misjudgment. Attempt to judge otherwise was considered impracticable, dangerous, and therefore "wrong."

Even today, conservative economists like Hayek and von Mises insist that market determination is the only system of judgment consistent with freedom. Advent of administered economics, they believe, foreshadows coming serfdom. Perhaps so; only the future can tell. But the gods of mid-twentieth century economics have not offered us a system in which the economy is not administered, or any practical avenue of retreat to the world of Adam Smith. They have only offered us choice of the degree of administration and of administrators: officials of the state, reserve bankers, appointive federal commissioners; legalized action by managers of great corporations under some governmental plans; informal concurrence of action by the managers of great corporations in concentrated industries; agencies or officers controlling the new mixed state-private industries which flourish on the base of governmentally developed technology.

With this has passed the old and happy dispensation from responsibility for moral, philosophical, political, and social decisions in economic affairs. Absolution from responsibility is no longer accorded by verdict of the market place.

Complete in its time, this absolution was a luxury for which we may well be nostalgic. But it has gone. Great corporations and concentrates do not automatically sell in the highest market—frequently, as was recently the case with the motor, the steel, and the electrical industries, they do their best to require that a price lower than that readily attainable shall be collected. They do not always buy in the cheapest market: the Interstate Oil Compact which raised the price of crude oil was positively insisted on by an industry which knew very well that it could not go on drawing raw material from the ground at less than cost of production. Decisions made in running a great business now become determinations with more or less predictable effect on building, maintaining, or guiding the life of the community in a manner and direction chosen by the administrators. Of interest is the fact that this is not power they particularly sought. Most of them, probably, would have preferred the old dispensation. Neither is it power they can decline to use. Still less is it power that the community can afford to ignore.

IV

THEORY OF POWER AND PROPERTY

But power, its organization, the results which may be attained by it, the administration of it, the possible checks and balances upon it, the forces released, canalized, and repressed by it, and the values which it should foster, lie squarely within the province of political science.

Regrettably, in our span of two centuries, no progress in political theory and science comparable to that made by its companion disciplines seems to have occurred, and almost none as democratic political theory. Currency of the phrase, "political science," and the creation of a faculty at Columbia University to study and teach it, took place only in the late nineteenth century. The last great political hypothesis was Marx's *Capital,* the first volume of which was published in 1867, to be completed (by Friedrich Engels from Marx's notes) in 1894. Heinrich von Treitschke about the same time (1895) was formulating his philosophy of the State as concrete embodiment of highest morality. But both these discarded the principle of individual freedom of choice, and with it the first premise of democracy.

Democracy, as we understand it today, still is working chiefly on the seventeenth and eighteenth century hypotheses of John Locke based on faith in individual men under a system of tolerance (1688), of David Hume and his Utilitarian school (1750), and of Jeremy Bentham and his "laissez-faire" philosophy (1781). These last were roughly contemporaneous with Jean Jacques Rousseau and the French Physiocrats whose philosophical work began to appear about 1750. Later political philosophers, notably John Stuart Mill and Herbert Spencer in the nineteenth century, explained old rather than pioneered substantial new theories of political action. Our twentieth century has not as yet produced even any great reinterpretation of older theories. In result, we enter a period in which men have unexampled power and responsibility to shape at least the economic destinies of themselves and of their communities—with unexampled absence of criteria to guide and judge action.

Now the federal system of the United States was constructed by statesmen who intended to give governmental reality to the philosophy of Locke and Rousseau. The bills of rights of the various state constitutions, emerged or emerging, and the first ten Amendments of the American Constitution, were statesmanlike translation of Locke's free individual mind, Rousseau's Social Contract, into workable government institutions. The Federalist fathers had in their minds a conception of man and of each man; the government they constructed was designed to protect and foster these conceptions in the framework of the military and economic data of the time. Since then, the data have changed and analysis of them has lagged. Thanks largely to the speculative work of Taussig and Seligman and the sheer genius of Wesley Clair Mitchell in devising scientific measurement, a beginning has been made on the economic side. We have not yet caught up in the pure science of politics. Such work as has been done suggests the scope and type of problems which will be presented.

The relationship of property and power as a matter of pure theory may be approached (as is attempted in intensive seminar groups in the Columbia Law School) by taking the large corporation as the subject of classical study. The modern corporation plainly lies in that no-man's land where economics, law, and political science converge; and it is an important and durable institution in the twentieth century. By observation and analysis of its impact on the twentieth century community and consideration of the social phenomena comprehended within its scope, some elementary principles might be derived.

One conclusion which appears justified by evidence is here presented.

Property and power are not different from each other but are different phases of the same phenomenon, namely, man's relation to other men with respect to goods and services.

Possessory property—individual holding of physical matter capable of being possessed or segregated—is the extreme negative end of the spectrum; the "property right" being primarily the power to exclude everyone but the holder from contact, possession, or enjoyment. The opposite end of the spectrum is naked political power—such as that disposed of by, let us say, a despot or perhaps a Communist commissar.

To become viable, the negative right of exclusion constituting possessory property must be diluted through relations with other men. The property right of exclusion is necessarily weakened as other individuals are admitted to relationship. As these relationships grow and become more complex, property becomes significant increasingly in its relation to organization. As organization increases in size and scope, capacity to direct the actions and attitudes of other men simultaneously increases while possession and exclusion progressively lose importance. In the large corporation, possessory property has become attenuated, sometimes to the point of invisibility. Its processes of production, exchange, distribution, development of the art, and so on, depend on its organization and the capacity to direct men which flows from it, far more than on its base in physical things; it has become primarily an instrument of power. The classic "owner" is merely a holder of paper with expectations; his search for "profit" has become the hope that men directing the organization will find it expedient to deal with him in accordance with the results of the enterprise and his hope of reward.

At the opposite or power end of the spectrum, like attenuation takes place. Absolute power has to be delegated, and consequently diluted, to attain results. Apparently this can only be done by creating, and continuing, more or less predictable relationships between the holder of power and the men with whom he must share it to carry out any project or to achieve any given result. As the scope of any task increases, the extent of this dilution increases with it and the demands of the men in the resulting organization for predictable position, relationship, and reward, become more intense. In the decadence of any power system, individuals to whom power has been delegated stake out claims to their particular sector, demanding the right to transmit the power by inheritance or perhaps by sale, and if tangible base (such as land) can be found, to reduce it eventually to a possessory base. The feudal system was essentially a power system. In its decadence, its economic base, land, was reduced to possession. As possession was subdivided, the end-result was the system of possessory property, especially based on land, which existed in England when the United States attained its independence, and which was the chief economic organization of the United States during the early nineteenth century.

The reverse process—gradual change from a system of individual possessory property towards a system of organized power—became apparent in the late nineteenth century. The modern corporation was the chief instrumentality. It collectivized property and organized power. As of today, 135 industrial corporations "own" and carry on roughly 45 per cent of the property and operations of all American industry (the estimate is that of Professor Adelman of Massachusetts Institute of Technology). In the process of acquiring this position, they have been compelled to organize the activities literally of millions of men. The "possessory" element still inherent in their titles to their factories is perhaps exercised by their night watchmen, their janitors, or their gate-keepers. The real base of their operations lies in their capacity to put together the minds and activities and actions of many thousands or perhaps hundreds of thousands of men and women, thereby obtaining the widespread results which have characterized American economic life. The phenomenon observed above—the growth of "administered capitalism"—measures almost precisely the transition from a system of small-scale possessory property towards a power system.

As far as we can observe, the power system thus emerging is in essence federalist. It contemplates autonomous economic organizations—corporations. It engenders loose relationships between these organizations, usually for the purpose of stabilizing or apportioning markets. The long history of prosecutions under the antitrust laws reflects the opposition of the American political state to this process when it is carried out outside the framework of political government and federal law. But increasingly these loose aggregations seek and obtain legal sanction for a centralized vehicle of limited power over them through congressional action or through the operation of an administrative branch of the political government. Since it is nationwide in scope, the ensuing organization is both federal in the theoretical sense of the term and Federalist in the Hamiltonian sense. It is occupying an increasing area of American life and activity—a great accretion of economic function in which the political state is coming to have a notable part.

Implicit in this thesis is a corollary. The difference between a system of statist power and a system of non-statist power (the large private corporation, concentrate, cartel, or democratically regulated industry) is not a difference in kind, but a difference in philosophical objective and content. If our thesis is correct, a socialist commissariat is in essence merely an extreme form of economic organization—a corporation carried, let us say, to exponent $(n-1)$. If the corporation does not produce the same result as the socialist commissariat (as happily it ordinarily does not), the reason does not inhere primarily in the law of its being. Rather it lies in the fact that the corporation itself, as well as its surrounding community, chooses that it shall do and refrain from doing certain things which the socialist commissariat does not do or insists upon doing. To that end the community erects, with the positive assent or at least the acquiescence of the individuals composing the corporate organization, guiding standards, safeguards, and limitations.

This difference in objective with attendant creation of limits, safeguards, incentives, and so forth, is essentially a political choice—politics (here used in the academic sense) being, as always, dominated by acceptance of certain determining philosophical values.

If we maintain (as most of us do) the soundness of the premise of John Locke and his conception of a free intellectual self-determining man, the twentieth century political scientist has a pretty problem set out for him. The French Physiocrats, Jean Jacques Rousseau, and early nineteenth century American statesmen, including Jefferson, proposed to foster the Lockean man by assuring reasonable distribution of property. Private property as we understand it today was insisted on by the French Physiocrats as the only possible guarantee of individual freedom. Jefferson consequently hoped for a country in which no one was very rich and no one was very poor; well distributed property plus universal education gave the Lockean man his best defense and offered him his best opportunity. Now, it seems, this private property changes, twists, and dissolves into component particles of power under the impact of twentieth century organization and technology. In great areas of life the old possessory property is merely for consumption purposes; production increasingly falls into the hands of great organizations which are essentially power mechanisms. In these there are no "proprietors"—merely employees of different degree of power status. But corporations do not have bills of rights written into their charters. What are the means and what are the instruments and institutions by which the Lockean man can be given base, guarantee, defense, and take-off in this emerging organization of affairs? Inquiry research (as in the Columbia Law School) has not yet produced the answer. It has perhaps approached a statement of the problem.

V

STATESMAN'S CHOICE

If the foregoing is soundly based, it becomes clear that the philosophical content of institutions, even more than their structure, is the determining factor. The same power institution may enslave men or compel them into a conformist bee-hive pattern—or may liberate them in realizing within viable limits their own potentialities through free and self-determining life, as the dual quality of federalism did for the nascent United States. But how to guide the vast twentieth century revolution in the latter course?

Recourse to history steadies one's nerves. It is easy to forget that the great rights we consider foundation stones of democracy and guarantees of freedom within it were not worked out within the background of democratic nineteenth century America, but were forged in the teeth of Norman, Angevin, and Tudor dictatorships. They were enlarged under feudal and semifeudal oligarchies. The ancient right to appeal to the "conscience of the king" through his Chancellor antedated Magna Carta; that document, indeed, required that his conscience be located at a determined, accessible place—which is why equity courts still sit at Westminster. The right to trial by one's peers was exacted against the opposition of Angevin King John. Freedom of the judiciary was maintained in the teeth of the Stuart kings. The rights of free press and of habeas corpus were made good long before modern democracy had been brought into being by eighteenth century philosophers. Political democracy, as we now have it, is expression, not source, of the conception of man as a self-determining personality, claiming the freedoms and accepting the responsibilities of a constantly widening community. The success of American federalism is due in no small measure to the fact that, even as it has organized the growing community posed by modern economic and technical development, its statesmen have usually sought to carry forward and protect this philosophical conception of the free man and set up political checks and balances adapted to that end.

Now we seem to be faced with still greater extension of the federal principle, under impulse of unlimited military and economic imperatives. Its national achievements have led to its use as an instrument of regional consolidation. Distant dreams arise that some day it may become worldwide. Also, it is generally posited that, to be free and intellectually self-determining, men must have at least a minimal measure of economic welfare with as wide measure of opportunity for individual economic improvement as circumstances permit. Technical advance has made it clear that both minimal measure of welfare and wide range of economic opportunity are attainable. The second half of the twentieth century appears likely vastly to expand the possibilities, and achieve a measure of their attainment. When Columbia University was founded, a man's problem was usually whether he could live at all. Increasingly in years to come, he will know that he can live with a measure of safety and comfort; his question will be, how does he wish to live? How to attain, not merely subsistence, but "the good life"? These possibilities of choice, with the profound responsibilities implied in them, lay beyond dreams of the most daring in 1754. In 1954, they become sober preoccupation of statesmen, businessmen, and scholars.

In the military field we have learnt that no nation now in existence is capable of defending itself alone. But the processes of military defense are no longer separable from other aspects of national life. They involve canalizing effort in all fields of occupation: scientific, economic, political, perhaps even cultural. A composite army like that of the United Nations in Korea, or that contemplated in the European Defense Community, is more than the collection of detachments under common theatre command which sufficed in World War I and even in World War II. Finance, industry, technology, transport, indeed organization of all the component elements, have to be coordinated not only at the point of command but through all of these processes in each of the countries involved. If Arnold Toynbee is right, and cultural penetration at any point draws with it a pervasive cultural interaction, exigencies of common defense are laying the foundation of a nascent international federalism, whether we like to recognize it or not. This imposes itself; it is the price of such precarious safety as we have yet attained. Statesmen consequently must consult and consider and choose what ideas, what systems, what techniques of communication, what pervasive forces can and should be selected to construct and hold together the defense structure.

Thus we return to the point of departure of this chapter. The deep forces exacting enlargement of the community—national and international—are sufficiently plain. They will impose themselves. But the values declared, expressed, forwarded, and maintained within this growing federalism are not imposed: they are distinctly matter of choice. At once the philosophers, the political scientists, the teachers, the writers, assume the determinative role. Alexander Hamilton decisively won the debate on the mechanical side. The community insists on growing, and to achieve this an ever greater measure of function must be transferred or subordinated to the power of the central state and ultimately to the community of states. Thomas Jefferson unquestionably triumphed in the philosophical discussion. The objective and concern, the guiding principle and essential safeguard of federalism is its capacity and its will to foster the self-determining free individual, using its component parts to that end. Its political mechanisms must conform to that purpose—else it becomes another form of mere centralized power, and travels the old path of past king-states. Therefore, it must give the greatest measure of responsibility to local entities. Therefore, it must maintain legal institutions apt to protect individuals against invasion of personality. Therefore, it must pursue economic policies affording possibility for individuals to reach and hold an economic station upon which personality can be developed. The successors of Jefferson and Hamilton, and the political philosophers and scientists who must equip them, are presented a task as difficult and as splendid as any yet offered by history.

VI

PHILOSOPHER'S RENDEZVOUS

Surveying the forces at work and their possible results in the generation to come is a sobering, even a frightening, experience. The stakes, in the United States alone, are stupendous.

There will not be wanting philosophies urging the causes of groups and of men who seek to use the implacably growing economic and miiltary organization to gain for themselves power, mastership, and empire. Increase in numbers may enhance richness of culture—but pressure of population can be used to degrade masses to helot status. Transport may enrich contact—but it can be used to intensify the bitterness of struggle. Communication may transmit education to millions—or be used as a new instrument to whip up mobs unexampled in number, force, and ferocity. Economic welfare can lead to finer individual development; it can also conduce to personal decadence. Instrumentalities of economic progress may be used to invade, stifle, and strangle personality, binding thought and spiritual development into dead conformity, even as they offer bait of safety and material well-being. Always there have been dictators who bought power with them and theorists who justified the result. In our time we have seen nationally organized mobs, inspired by demagogues, delighting in sadistic hatred, and economic systems built on the security of serf-labor. The greater the gift of power, the greater the possibility of its perversion.

There are today, there will be in the future, national and international political struggles perhaps of titanic proportions. In the universities we have faith no force will arise so powerful, no struggle so deadly, that it can put out the eternal lights, nourished in the philosophical and spiritual heritage of our civilization and perpetually kindled anew in dreams of the human mind and heart. In George Herbert Palmer's luminous phrase, dreams are dangerous things, apt to be fulfilled. Now, as always, as men think, so are they.

So long as free universities stand throughout the world, we must resolve that there shall always be dreamers who assault the gods of the possible; philosophers who apprehend eternal values and humanists who trust free men to seek and realize them. There must be scholars of politics and law who study to see that these vast instruments, in being and in birth, are made to serve man and not to enslave him. There must be teachers assuring that the materials of freedom are transmitted to coming generations.

In a world now torn and wounded, we can understand the bewilderment of great masses and sympathize even with the faint and the fearful. Our modern struggles in their essence are as old as the history of man. In humility let it be recalled that one thousand years before Christ, a statesman-poet also survey-ing a world in travail prayed for his people:

> "They know not; neither will they understand; they walk on in darkness; all the foundations of the earth are out of course."

The answer came:

> "I have said, ye are gods; and all of ye are children of the Most High."

PART TWO
Basic Controls in a Maturing System

6

Introduction

By Arthur W. Macmahon

The group of chapters that follow deals with basic controls in maturing federal systems as illustrated by the United States. The first section stresses the extent to which the balancing mechanisms are located in a political process that is fundamentally conditioned by the structural characteristics of federalism itself. The political process operates on and mainly through the central legislative body which increasingly becomes an arbiter of the allocation of powers between nation and states. In the second section the analysis passes to the courts and the law, reexamining the mood and method of judicial review, on the one hand, and, on the other, the continuing responsibility and creative opportunities of courts, especially in view of the interstitial, incomplete, and often interlocked nature of national statutes in relation to the main bodies of law and administration in a federal system. The third section exemplifies the allocating duties of the prime political organs: Congress and the President. The field of labor relations is examined to illustrate the responsibility that now rests on Congress to arrange the distribution of power between nation and states. The President's discretion in negotiating treaties and executive agreements is considered in terms of his obligation to respect the spirit of the federal system while serving as initial umpire of the scope of the central government's jurisdiction made necessary by the country's position in the world.

I

The analysis by Herbert Wechsler of the political process as the primary control and safeguard of decentralization is the more impressive because it comes from a lawyer. He writes as a believer in the values of diversity and deconcentration. His emphasis upon the decentralized nature of American politics and legislative methods is written in the spirit of reassurance. For the overtones answer those who are worried about the degree of potential power conceded by courts nowadays to the central political organs. Written from such a standpoint, with an eye to the role of the political process as shaped by federalism in guaranteeing the survival of a federal division of powers, Herbert

Wechsler's treatment may strike some as too passive in its acceptance of the loose texture of national politics in the United States.

The political party is a crucial link in the analysis. It is the link between the social pluralism of an equipoise of interests (extolled by John Fischer) and federalism as a juristic device and a form of political structure. How important is the reflex of federalism upon the nature of the party system? Many factors are at work: not merely other structural elements (such as separation of powers as practiced in the United States contrasted with cabinet government in Canada and Australia) but also, and perhaps even more crucially, the relative importance of the older vertical divisions of geographical sectionalism based upon what I have ventured to call commodity-consciousness, compared with horizontal cleavages along lines of income level or occupation attendant on emergent group demands for new types of governmental intervention or service and resulting shifts in the level of political attention. David B. Truman undertakes to disentangle this complex of influences upon the nature of parties and political processes in federal systems.

Certainly federalism is a main factor in this complex. In the United States it seems destined to remain the most durable of the influences at work. So far as students of politics emphasize the need for internal party discipline they may deplore not only the effect of federalism but even federalism itself. Nevertheless they must concede that the existence of autonomous areas of political attention and action (galvanized by their legal status under federalism) makes it likely, in Arthur Holcombe's terms, that the American political party will be more suited to moderate among geographical sections and even classes than to coordinate its own factions. This moderating role, as Mr. Holcombe points out, is performed simultaneously by both parties. Whatever one may think about the desirability of the reflex of federalism in politics, it is clear that federalism as a structure automatically reinforces itself, quite apart from the constitutional allocation of power and the doors of potential action that are opened or kept locked by high courts.

The whole process undoubtedly must be viewed in the perspective urged by William Anderson in the discussion. "The American system," he remarked, "provides a series of appeals from one center of power to another, to another, to another, over a wide range." He added: "We have here a complex of forces, sources of decisions, powers, whatever you want to call them, which in a sense have to be taken into account as a totality; and to talk about a balance with only one of these facts in mind, I think, is to talk without using the knowledge that we actually have about the various sources to which an appeal can be made in reaching decisions in this country."

II

Against the background of arbitrament by a decentralized political process that revolves around the central legislative body, Paul A. Freund examines the role of the high court as umpire of a federal system. In the United States, truly, constitutionalism is curiously paradoxical. One suspects, without boasting, that its quality is part of the mood if not the exact method of humane and orderly life and progress. It is related to the art of being at once general and specific; absolute and yet relative; fixed and still tentative. The constitutionalism of the United States may be described in a crude metaphor by saying that the prescriptions of a written constitution, without losing their essences, are dissolved in the situational ways of thinking characteristic of the common law. The ideals they embody are held in solution while retaining their absolute quality as potentials. They are precipitated from time to time in specific factual settings.

As to the role of the United States Supreme Court in passing upon the constitutionality of legislation, some will ask whether nowadays the Court is not doing too little rather than too much. Many things combine to hold its hand. Much of its caution does not bear upon federalism as such but upon the difficulty of reconciling limited government with the principle of responsible government through elections and majority rule. The polity of positive government is assumed by the Court. The ideal of experimental federalism enters to plead a double case for resolving doubts in favor of the constitutionality of state laws: that they reflect the choices of responsible legislative bodies; and that these legislatures are local. A judiciary sophisticated by the cumulative critique of generations of searching constitutional scholarship may thus find a double ground for hesitation even when the legislation is challenged as an invasion of guarantees as fundamental as freedom of speech. On such matters (as also in censoring certain political practices in the states) the rationale of Court review—I venture to suggest again at the risk of seeming to play with words—may well be to conceive the apparatus of government by discussion as a gigantic procedure and thus to bring judicial protection in this field within the logic of procedural due process. But I am aware that the application of such a rationale is not simple in a revolutionary age when agitation appears in novel forms and pursues a self-contradictory end.

So far as concerns judicial reluctance to upset national economic legislation, we have already pointed to the prior inhibitions that are inherent in the political process under federalism. Many tasks remain for the courts. Willard Hurst, in off-hand comment during the discussion stimulated by the views of Paul Freund, remarked that in the past "The melodrama of judicial review has warped American legal scholarship very considerably." He went on to say that "the really important area of judicial contribution to policy-making is in the field of the interpretation of statutes." Thus oriented, he argued, the judicial process has advantages in meeting the problems of creative adjustment. "On the whole," he suggested, "it takes less money, less organized unity, to fight most lawsuits than it does to organize a lobby for federal, state, or local legislatures." A second advantage, he said, lies in the fact that "we live in a society that necessarily places a higher and higher premium on matter-of-fact decisions and the matter-of-fact decision is a hard thing to get in legislative tribunals; but when we deal with a court, for all its frailties, we deal with an institution which has a tradition quite favorable to matter-of-fact analysis." Courts, he added, have the final advantage of being "in relatively continuous operation."

The possibility of administrative means of adjustment, it will be observed, is hinted at by Paul Freund in speculating about a body that would resolve conflicts over the taxation of interstate business. His tone is skeptical as it was when in the discussion he raised the question of an administrative tribunal to pass on trade barriers "on the notion that a commission would have the advantages of continuing preoccupation with the problem, of ability to employ experts, and, perhaps above all, powers to formulate rules in advance of a detailed sort rather than simply to approve or disapprove what it finds to have already been adopted by the states." Mr. Freund's tentative question (raised, he said, because a conference should "talk about Utopia as well as America in 1954") did not draw any favorable comment. Nevertheless it should be noted that within certain special fields, national administrative bodies now set limits to state action. Thus in railroading the Interstate Commerce Commission guides state regulation incidentally to its own control and its orders stand if the Court deems that its findings are sufficient to sustain them. The significance of this development is not entirely undermined by William Anderson's reminder in the discussion that the national regulatory bodies deal in large part with matters that arise in private disputes, quite unlike what would be involved in administrative action which directly limited the scope of state taxation.

The chapter by Henry M. Hart, Jr. takes account of the daily tasks of administering a double system of law through a double system of courts. Basically he finds the combination not only workable but also suited to the needs of a large and diverse society in which activity from the center enters interstitially in the total body of governmental action which in turn is only an interstitial element in ordinary living. During the discussion several allusions were made to the exceptional nature of the dual court structure in the United States among the federal systems of the world. By implication and in his general tone, Mr. Hart answers both the question and the criticism behind it by portraying the system as more than merely practicable. In the discussion he brushed aside as immaterial (whether literally true or not) the complaint of one versed in the ways of federal courts that one-third to one-half of their time may be taken with questions of jurisdiction, sometimes ending in the frustration of both parties. The critic thought he saw in this phase of the complexities of federalism an aspect of a more general tendency in the political institutions of the United States: a tendency "to conceal responsibility in government." Mr. Hart does not waver in his faith in federalism as a method of accommodation when, in his chapter, he points to missed opportunities for judicial creativeness.

Mr. Hart's concern with laws and courts does not invite him to expand the hints he gives about the role of administration, broadly considered, in supplying impulses and channels for uniformity in the law itself. This need is not sweeping nor often literal, as Mr. Hart points out. At crucial points, however, uniformity is indispensable in a mobile society and in an economy that is at once interdependent and competitive. It would be fatuous to minimize the obstacles that federalism puts in the way of uniformity in statute law. The condition is especially marked in a system like that of the United States. Its constitution leaves the main bodies of civil and criminal law to the states while regulative action by the central government rests upon a few ramifying shelves of power —regulation of interstate commerce, mostly—not (as in some other federal systems) upon the assignment to the central government of legislative responsibility for whole phases of economic life. The handicaps to statutory uniformity, moreover, are increased by certain incidental features of American federalism. The sheer number of states (though not disproportionate to the total population in comparison with other federal systems) multiplies the opportunities for variation. Rivers are frequently used as state boundaries, disregarding the truth of Lord Curzon's remark in a classic lecture on *Frontiers* that "the teaching of history is that rivers connect rather than separate." Indeed, practically the only considered respect for this principle was shown in the drawing of the state boundary lines east of the Hudson River and north of the Merrimack. The prevalence of river boundaries resulted in the fact that important cities, rising on the water courses that marked natural trade routes regardless of the medium, are frequently on the borders of states, not at the center. Much essentially local traffic is thus turned into interstate business. In 1927, before modern communciation had worked its full effect, a survey of 683 principal retail shopping areas in the country showed that 58 of them crossed state lines. In wholesaling activities the overlapping was even more striking. An atlas of wholesale grocery territories published in the same year by the United States Department of Commerce remarked that "the inland water routes which played such a large part in the opening up of the west at an early date dictated the location of the present railway centers with the result that many of the major distribution points of today are actually situated on the state boundaries . . ."

Unifying factors were at work in the United States, of course, notably the basis of the common law in all but one state. Historically its harmonizing role in American federalism can hardly be overstated. As time went on, however, its influence was weakened by two developments. The judiciaries of the various states, as they grew older, became more attentive to their own lines of precedent and less disposed to follow the leadership of certain of the older state benches. Further dispersal came when statute law—a necessary instrument of progress—increasingly supplemented or supplanted common law rules. Meanwhile no substantial contribution to overall uniformity resulted from the effort of the United States courts after 1842 to take advantage of their jurisdiction in suits between citizens of different states in developing a body of federal common law applicable to questions "not at all depending upon local statutes or local usages of a fixed or permanent operation" and "especially to questions of general commercial law." This attempt proved to be a complication rather than a cure. The state judiciaries were not disposed to follow the doctrinal lead of the national courts. The result was to create double rules of law within states where the law impinged upon ordinary living, Mr. Hart's cogent criterion of the places where simplicity and uniformity are desirable. In 1938 the attempted shortcut to uniformity in commercial law begun in 1842 was abandoned by the Supreme Court. These developments are among the many intertwined legislative strands and interacting judicial responsibilities traced by Mr. Hart.

As for interstate action in securing uniformity in statute law, much copying goes on from state to state in a federal system. A crude, never completed, but in the aggregate substantial progress toward similarity results from the imitativeness of states. There is in fact little original legislation. When once a suggestion catches root somewhere and flourishes the seeds drift down the wind. Such a tendency would come if only because it is the line of least effort for many draftsmen. Indeed, the imitation of distant sister states is sometimes too exact, perhaps when a stenographer mistakes the cut-off mark in the passage that is being copied. The compiled laws of North Dakota at one time not only defined the term "port" but also stipulated that vessels must be taken in and out of ports by pilots. Whatever the source of this requirement (it may have been the excellent laws of New York), enough salt and tar found its harmless way into the code to allay in the reading, even on a sun-bathed prairie, nostalgia for masted water-fronts and the open sea. But to observe and generally to commend the prevalence of considerable spontaneous copying from state to state does not deny the need for methods of comparison, evaluation, and communication without which the experimental initiative of individual states fails to bear its proper fruit. It does not lessen the importance of concerted approaches to uniformity. Spontaneity by itself remains sporadic.

Only limited results, however, have been achieved by the organized effort carried on since 1890 through the Conference of Commissioners on Uniform Laws. After sixty years only five of its model statutes had won substantially universal adoption by the states. Its success in terms of general acceptance was understandably confined to matters like negotiable instruments, bills of lading, warehouse receipts, and sales—matters of pressing convenience, mutually interesting to bars and business groups, and not likely to present issues of social conflict. Even when models have been enacted by legislatures, dispersal has followed through variant judicial interpretations or amendments. In appraising future possibilities, however, allowance should be made for the fact that only in recent years has the movement focused in the Council of State Governments, linked to political and legislative leadership in the several states, been available to help the small groups of virtually volunteer draftsmen who have constituted the commissions on uniform state laws. These elements now have the collaboration of the American Law Institute, a semi-public body dedicated mainly to harmonizing and progressive restatements of the common law.

In the field of statutory uniformity a new test has been presented to the states in the Uniform Commercial Code, completed in 1949. It combines and replaces the model acts on negotiable instruments, warehouse receipts, sales, bills of lading, stock transfers, and trust receipts. The code declares that "it has been recognized for some years that these acts needed substantial revision to keep them in step with modern commercial practices and to integrate each of them with the others." The self-declared basis of the code is the concept "that 'commercial transactions' is a single subject of the law, notwithstanding its many facets," and that "The act purports to deal with all the phases which may ordinarily arise in the handling of a commercial transaction, from start to finish." As an aid to uniformity in the interpretation of the code, it declares that "The official comments of the National Conference on Uniform Laws and the American Law Institute may be consulted by the courts to determine the underlying reasons, purposes and policies of this Act and may be used as a guide in its construction and application." The commercial code, in short, is a fresh opportunity as well as challenge. Assuming the best, however, its coverage is limited; it is confined mainly to the special fields in which the movement in the past has been fairly fruitful. Even within this domain it remains to be seen how far the movement can be carried and stabilized without federal legislation or an interstate compact, the difficult expedient mentioned by Mr. Hart.

Speaking generally, it must be admitted that the prospects of statutory uniformity by state action are modest. Fortunately the need is limited. Identical legislation even in matters of common concern is less important than is often assumed. The crucial requirement is agreement at key points. These deal with what may be called standards in a broad sense of that word. The impulse comes from many sources. It may come from the central government's statutes or regulations, perhaps incidentally or perhaps as a deliberate feature of the normative role of which I spoke in an earlier chapter. The source may be an association of officials; their name is legion and their types many. In any case, the characteristic channel of the impulse is administrative. The results may appear in either law or administration or in a combination of elements. Often the most fruitful arrangement is the statutory adoption by reference of an extrinsic standard which itself is capable of growth, thus ensuring a dynamic type of uniformity. When such an arrangement adopts changes prospectively, it needs the approval of an imaginative judiciary attentive to the actualities of government and the true intent of legislatures. A court ill serves the ideal of the rule of law and the vitality of legislative bodies if it holds, as once did an Ohio court and indeed others, that the statutory recognition of the *United States Pharmacopoeia* (a vast body of definitions and the like revised every ten years) applied to the edition extant when the law was passed, not to the current edition. The learned court attributed to the legislature a learning even vaster, at least more technical, in assuming it had read these thousands of pages of fine print and chemical symbols when it originally adopted the publication as a standard in the regulation of foods and drugs.

III

The field of labor relations is used by Paul R. Hays as an example of the way in which the maturing federalism of the United States confronts Congress with the task of working out a rational allocation of responsibilities among the levels of government. His chapter is a case study in the ability of the central legislature to manage federalism. The Supreme Court has conceded the authority to Congress. How adequately has Congress faced the challenge and performed the task? Not at all well thus far, Mr. Hays concludes, but he is not less insistent that it is Congress that must perform the task. It must proceed selectively. The outworn formulas do not suffice. The assignment of phases of the subject must be made with an eye to consequences in the economy, especially the way in which variant labor practices and their regulation affect interstate economic competition.

In approaching this example of the role of Congress in the interlevel allocation of precise responsiblities, the reader will note differences of opinion about the relative competence of legislature and court in handling the problem. The range of the difficulties was illustrated in the discussion by Thomas Reed Powell's allusion in another connection to the riddles faced in trying to draft a congressional formula for the taxation of commercial air-fleets at their home ports. In the consideration of Paul Hays' views on labor relations, Henry Hart remarked: "Mr. Hays seems to me to leave the solution of the problem to Congress, and I suggest that is too easy a solution." He asked Mr. Hays to "name an instance in the 164-odd years of the Constitution's history in which the Congress has confronted a problem of this sort—not a focused problem but a general problem of making a systematic and rational (in his terms) allocation of power between nation and states—in which that has ever been done." For one thing, he added: "Groups do not form behind proposals for a rational and general reallocation of governmental powers." Yet Mr. Hart admitted that the Supreme Court had failed to disentangle the problem. The solution, he thought, illustrated the future constructive role of systematic collaborative analysis by social scientists and lawyers as an aid to the judicial process. This meant "general analysis, not of specific interest needs." Paul Hays countered by saying that, as to the division of interlevel responsibilities in labor relations: "I just do not agree that the Court can possibly solve the problem in terms of the present legislation." At the same time he conceded that "it seems to me a question of degree." Much must be left to the Court to allocate but, he said, "I would be clear as to what part was being left to the Court and I would leave that part to the Court rationally, say, on the basis that the Court was better equipped for making the allocation." Nor did Mr. Hays believe that the field of labor relations was a unique example of an unavoidable but still undischarged central legislative responsibility in managing the federal system.

Since Willard Hurst's remarks, already quoted, were echoed by Henry Hart in his disagreement with Paul Hays about the practicability of legislative adjustment, it is appropriate to note Mr. Hurst's comment at another point in the discussion. To be sure, his suggestion has a somewhat different bearing and implication. Speaking generally about the limitations on separate state action, he said: "There is not only the question of allocation of power but there is also in operation something of a law of the limitation of the energies, imagination, and will; and that is a phenomenon of twentieth century government in contrast to the early development of insurance regulation, say, which was relatively simple and straightforward. The twentieth century presents us with problems of government whose cause and effect are quite complex and they require a great deal of tracing through with several sets of analysis to see wherein the public interest lies. There is some evidence in the last fifty years that there just does not exist the amounts of imagination and will within the confines of most states to mobilize the aggressive minority pressure to get something done about it; and that perhaps nothing but a nationwide forum would mobilize the energies and imagination to handle such problems."

The emphasis upon a primary congressional responsibility for a rational and selective interlevel rearrangement of jurisdiction in terms of economic consequences does not preclude, as Mr. Hays points out in passing, the usefulness of administrative agreements between national and state agencies. He deplores the rigid statutory qualification which since 1946 blocked the fruition of the budding cooperation that was developing between national and state boards. Ideally the complementary sharing of jurisdictions within the field of labor relations must be worked out with the aid of flexible administrative devolution upon bases provided in the law which will be subtler than the over-simple distinction between interstate and intrastate activities.

In the field of foreign relations, the chief executive holds the initiative in umpiring the division of powers in the federal system. Noel T. Dowling succinctly puts the case for a statecraft of commonsense that will respect the spirit of federalism while it takes account of the imperative necessities of international negotiation and binding agreement. Mr. Dowling soundly observes that presidents loyal to the constitutional system will not invoke the treaty power for purposes of internal reform. On the other hand, where the objective rises inherently from foreign affairs, the ability of any modern nation to enter into commitments must accommodate itself to the content of international dealings. This is a reasonable view of the original intent as well as the evolution of the Constitution of the United States; more than that, it is a corollary of true national self-interest. But to say this does not simplify the judgments required of leaders under federal constitutions. Along with restraint, they must respect the need to deal with countries of many constitutional types; they must be aware of the indispensability of confidence on the part of other nations and of the importance of morale in the affairs of the vaguely emergent world community.

SECTION ONE

THE POLITICAL PROCESS

7

The Political Safeguards of Federalism: The Role of the States in the Composition and Selection of the National Government

By Herbert Wechsler

Federalism was the means and price of the formation of the Union. It was inevitable, therefore, that its basic concepts should determine much of our history. The more important fact is that they shape government, law, and politics today. Nor is this merely illustration of the insight that the lives of nations, like the lives of individuals, are permanently influenced by the experience of infancy. In a far flung, free society, the federalist values are enduring. They call upon a people to achieve a unity sufficient to resist their common perils and advance their common welfare, without undue sacrifice of their diversities and the creative energies to which diversity gives rise. They call for government responsive to the will of the full national constituency, without loss of responsiveness to lesser voices, reflecting smaller bodies of opinion, in areas that constitute their own legitimate concern.

No form of government can serve these values with complete efficiency, no set of mechanisms can perfectly discriminate between the polar claims so patently involved. No single form or mechanism will give equal service under different circumstances or function with the same results at different times. But in a time when federalism must appear to many peoples as the sole alternative to tyranny, there is a special value in examining American experience, the more so since we face important issues of direction ourselves.

I

Our constitution makers established a central government authorized to act directly upon individuals through its own agencies—and thus they formed a nation capable of function and of growth. To serve the ends of federalism they employed three main devices:

> They preserved the states as separate sources of authority and organs of administration—a point on which they hardly had a choice.

97

They gave the states a role of great importance in the composition and selection of the central government.

They undertook to formulate a distribution of authority between the nation and the states, in terms which gave some scope at least to legal processes for its enforcement.

Scholarship—not only legal scholarship—has given most attention to the last of these enumerated mechanisms, perhaps because it has been fascinated by the Supreme Court and its interpretations of the power distribution clauses of the Constitution. The continuous existence of the states as governmental entities and their strategic role in the selection of the Congress and the President are so immutable a feature of the system that their importance tends to be ignored. Of the Framers' mechanisms, however, they have had and have today the larger influence upon the working balance of our federalism. The actual extent of central intervention in the governance of our affairs is determined far less by the formal power distribution than by the sheer existence of the states and their political power to influence the action of the national authority.

The fact of the continuous existence of the states, with general governmental competence unless excluded by the Constitution or valid act of Congress, set the mood of our federalism from the start. The first Congress did not face the problem of building a legal system from the ground up; it started with the premise that the standing *corpus juris* of the country was provided by the states. As with the law, so with the courts. One federal Supreme Court was essential and the Constitution gave a mandate that it be established. But even the establishment of lower courts was left an open question by the Framers, as was the jurisdiction to be vested in any such courts as Congress might establish—within the limits that the Constitution set. Congress was free to commit the administration of national law to national tribunals or to leave the task to the state courts, sworn to support the national supremacy within its proper sphere.[1] Even the appellate jurisdiction of the Supreme Court was subject to congressional control.

National action has thus always been regarded as exceptional in our polity, an intrusion to be justified by some necessity, the special rather than the ordinary case. The point of view cuts even deeper than the concept of the central government as one of granted, limited authority, articulated in the Tenth Amendment. National power may be quite unquestioned in a given situation; those who would advocate its exercise must none the less answer the preliminary question why the matter should not be left to the states. Even when Congress acts, its tendency has been to frame enactments on an *ad hoc* basis to accomplish limited objectives, supplanting state-created norms only so far as may be necessary for the purpose. Indeed, with all the centralizing growth throughout the years, federal law is still a largely interstitial product, rarely occupying any field completely, building normally upon legal relationships established by the states. As Henry Hart and I have put it elsewhere: "Congress acts . . . against the background of the total *corpus juris* of the states in much the way that a state legislature acts against the background of the common law, assumed to govern unless changed by legislation."[2] As a state legislature views the common law as something to be left alone unless a need for change has been established, so Congress has traditionally viewed the governance of matters by the states.

The tradition plainly serves the values of our federalism in so far as it maintains a burden of persuasion on those favoring national intervention. New York, for example, faced the need for rent control after the need was deemed to have passed in most parts of the country. Should a national program have been continued when New York and every other state was competent to launch a program of its own, adapted to its special needs? Under such circumstances national action has consequences that are plainly undesirable. On the one hand, it is likely to impose control in areas where the politically dominant local judgment finds control unnecessary. On the other hand, it is likely to attenuate the rigor of control in areas where it is really needed. For if the need is not severe the country over, the terms of national legislation will be shaped by a Congress in which the hostile sentiment has a large influence, rather than by a legislature more generally sensitive to the need. This was, of course, the actual experience with federal control of rent throughout the later post-war years.[3]

The political logic of federalism thus supports placing the burden of persuasion on those urging national action. Though the explanation is the same, it is more difficult to find support for the commonly fragmentary quality of many national enactments, with their resultant ambiguity as to how far they supersede state law entirely and how far they call for integration with it. This is a point that has a special visibility to lawyers, for the federal-state adjustments called for by such ambiguities present problems of enormous difficulty to the courts.[4] The issue is perhaps most striking in the common case where federal law defines powers, rights, or duties without attention to resulting liabilities or remedies, raising the question whether these are matters to be governed by state legal systems or determined by the independent judgment of federal courts.[5] To explore these matters is beyond my present purpose. I adduce them only to support my thesis that the existence of the states as governmental entities and as the sources of the standing law is in itself the prime determinant of our working federalism, coloring the nature and the scope of our national legislative processes from their inception.

II

If I have drawn too much significance from the mere fact of the existence of the states, the error surely will be rectified by pointing also to their crucial role in the selection and the composition of the national authority. More is involved here than that aspect of the compromise between the larger and the smaller states that yielded their equality of status in the Senate. Representatives no less than Senators are allotted by the Constitution to the states, although their number varies with state population as determined by the census. Though the House was meant to be the "grand depository of the democratic principle of the government,"[6] as distinguished from the Senate's function as the forum of the states, the people to be represented with due deference to their respective numbers were *the people of the states.* And with the President, as with Congress, the crucial instrument of the selection—whether through electors or, in the event of failure of majority, by the House voting as state units—is again the states. The consequence, of course, is that the states are the strategic yardsticks for the measurement of interest and opinion, the special centers of political activity, the separate geographical determinants of national as well as local politics.

Despite the rise of national parties, the shift to popular election of the Senate, and the difficulty of appraising the precise impact of such provisions on the legislative process, Madison's analysis has never lost its thrust:

> The State governments may be regarded as constituent and essential parts of the federal government; whilst the latter is nowise essential to the operation or organization of the former.[7]
>
> A local spirit will infallibly prevail much more in the members of Congress, than a national spirit will prevail in the legislatures of the particular States.[8]
>
> Even the House of Representatives, though drawn immediately from the people, will be chosen very much under the influence of that class of men, whose influence over the people obtains for themselves an election into the State legislatures.[9]

To the extent that federalist values have real significance, they must give rise to local sensitivity to central intervention; to the extent that such a local sensitivity exists, it cannot fail to find reflection in the Congress.[10] Indeed, the problem of the Congress is and always has been to attune itself to national opinion and produce majorities for action called for by the voice of the entire nation. It is remarkable that it should function thus as well as it does, given its intrinsic sensitivity to any insular opinion that is dominant in a substantial number of the states.

III

The point is so clear in the Senate that, as Madison observed of the equality accorded to the states, it "does not call for much discussion."[11] The forty-nine votes that will determine Senate action, even with full voting, could theoretically be drawn from twenty-five states, of which the combined population does not reach twenty-nine millions, a bare 19 per cent of all state residents.[12] The one-third plus one that will defeat a treaty or a resolution of amendment could, equally theoretically, be drawn from seventeen states with a total population little over twelve millions, less than that of New York. I say theoretically since, short of a combination to resist an effort to impair state equality within the Senate (which the Constitution purports to place beyond amendment) or to diminish the political power of the smaller states in other ways, a coalition in these terms is quite unthinkable. The fact remains that in more subtle ways the Senate cannot fail to function as the guardian of state interests as such, when they are real enough to have political support or even to be instrumental in attaining other ends. And if account is taken of the operation of seniority within the Senate, of the opportunity of Senators to marshal individual authority, not to speak of the possibility of filibuster, this power of negation, vested in the states without regard to population, multiplies in many ways. Given a controversy that has any sectional dimension, it is not long before the impact of this power is perceived.[13]

Nor is it only power of negation. To be sure, on any direct show of strength in passing legislation, a Senate majority based on the states must be supported by a House majority based on population and must also avoid a veto by the President. But power to enact is rarely based on such a test—and when it seems to be, there sometimes is involved a merely token process. Legislation rests in practice on a balancing of interests, a give and take that calls for coalition and for compromise, a strategy that may involve a present sacrifice to hold or win future support.[14] In this dynamic interchange, a latent power of negation has much positive significance in garnering the votes for an enactment that might otherwise have failed. This is the point at which state equality may well present the largest difficulties, but the issue is beyond the range I have undertaken to explore. It is enough for present purposes to show how far the composition of the Senate is intrinsically calculated to prevent intrusion from the center on subjects that dominant state interests wish preserved for state control.

IV

Even the House is slanted somewhat in the same direction, though the incidence is less severe. This is not due appreciably to the one seat reserved for every state regardless of its population, nor to the mechanics or the mathematics of congressional apportionment, though they present their problems.[15] It is due rather to the states' control of voters' qualifications, on the one hand, and of districting, on the other.

The position with respect to voters' qualifications derives from the constitutional provision that fixes the electorate of Representatives (and of Senators as well since the Seventeenth Amendment) as those persons who "have the qualifications requisite for electors of the most numerous branch of the State Legislature."[16] Subject, then, to the prohibition of the denial of franchise because of color, race, or sex, embodied in the Fifteenth and Nineteenth Amendments and the radiations of the equal protection clause of the Fourteenth, the states determine—indirectly it is true—the electorate that chooses Representatives.[17] The consequences of contracting the electorate by such devices as a poll-tax are, of course, incalculable, but they tend to buttress what traditionally dominant state interests conceive to be their special state position; that is the point of the contraction. This sentiment, reflected in the Representatives that these constituencies send to Congress, is not ordinarily conducive to support for an adventurous expansion of the national authority, though there have been exceptions, to be sure.

The Fourteenth Amendment purports to put in the hands of Congress a remedy for such diminution of the electorate. It directs that the census figure determinative of the number of a state's representatives be reduced on the apportionment to the extent that the right to vote "is denied to any of the male inhabitants of such state, being twenty-one years of age and citizens of the United States, or in any way abridged, except for participation in rebellion, or other crime." The remedy has proved unworkable in practice by reason of the difficulty of the quantitative investigation needed,[18] not to speak of the political problems that an effort to employ it would present. Federal abolition of the poll-tax is periodically urged in Congress, with extensive hearings on the measure, but there are grave doubts with respect to its constitutionality and no real prospect of its passage.[19]

State control of congressional districting derives from the constitutional provision that the "times, places and manner of holding elections for Senators and Representatives, shall be prescribed in each State by the Legislature thereof."[20] The same clause provides, however, that "Congress may at any time by law make or alter such regulations. . . ." Though the matter has been disputed, it seems plain that state control thus rests entirely on the tolerance of Congress.[21] Until congressional action was taken in 1842, there was variation in state practice. Alabama, Georgia, Mississippi, Missouri, New Hampshire, New Jersey, and Pennsylvania elected Representatives on a state-wide basis by general ticket, while Maryland, Massachusetts, New York, Virginia, and South Carolina were committed early to the district basis. The act of 1842 made districts "composed of contiguous territory" mandatory, though leaving districting to the respective states.[22] Even this mandate was initially defied in four of the general-ticket states, with the House seating their elected Representatives despite the state's recalcitrance as to the method of selection. Omitted in 1850, the mandate was repeated in later acts and was extended in 1872 to require that the districts contain "as nearly as practicable an equal number of inhabitants."[23] The requirement of contiguity was further supplemented in 1901 to call for districts of "compact territory."[24] These provisions were repeated in 1911[25] but the Congress failed to reapportion after the census of 1920. The legislation of 1929, as amended,[26] establishing the present framework, provides for an automatic reapportionment upon the President's report (unless Congress directs otherwise). It directs the course that must be followed in the election of Representatives when a change from prior methods is required by an alteration of their number as a consequence of the apportionment and the state has failed to prescribe what the change shall be.[27] Beyond this, however, it lays down no requirements at all. The district system thus rests wholly upon state initiative at the present time. More important, the delineation of the districts rests entirely with the states.

It is well known that there are great discrepancies in district size in many multi-district states, paralleling for Congress the discrepancies, to forego harsher terms, that prevail in districting for the state legislatures.[28] A recent study estimates that in the spring of 1952, 115 of the 435 congressional districts showed variation as to size larger than 15 per cent above or below the state average, the maximum above the average being 129.8 per cent in Texas and, below the average, 51.3 per cent in South Dakota (where there are only two districts).[29] Writing before recent redistricting in some fifteen states, Professor Holcombe's committee of the American Political Science Association said:

> The Committee has noted with concern the great disparities in the 1950 populations of existing Congressional districts. Take 350,000 as roughly the average in a district. In one state, there is a district under 175,000; six others under 250,000; three between 500,000 and 700,000, and one exceeding 900,000. In many states, the spread between 1950 population in the smallest and the largest existing district in the State is two or three hundred thousand.[30]

The committee proposed a remedy which was in turn proposed to Congress by President Truman in his message of January 9, 1951, reporting the reapportionment.[31] The main features were these: (1) that Congress restore the earlier requirement of single-member districts composed of contiguous and compact territory and containing as nearly as practicable the same number of inhabitants; (2) that it forbid deviations in excess of 50,000 above or below the norm of 350,000 persons to a district; (3) that Congress itself take measures to eliminate a larger variation, even to prescribing the redistricting in cases where the state persists in deviating from the standard thus laid down. Needless to say, no action has been taken on the message.

It may be said, and perhaps rightly, that the situation with respect to districting, while detracting from the equality of popular representation in the House, has little bearing on the role of Congress in preserving federalist values. I am not so sure. It is significant, for one thing, that it is the states that draw the districts; one can hardly think the district lines would be the same had they been drawn from the beginning by Congress. Beyond this, however, the general motive and tendency of district deviations has quite clearly been to reduce urban power, not in the meaning of the census classification[32] but in the sense of the substantial cities. The tendency is so appreciable that a recent article assures the readers of a small town magazine that while cities or towns of under 10,000 coupled with the farms account for only 51 per cent of the entire population, residents of such areas are numerically dominant in 265 of the 435 congressional districts, accounting for the choice of 61 per cent of the House (including 18 of the 21 committee chairmen) in addition to their numerical dominance in the choice of 75 per cent of the Senate.[33] Traditionally, at least, a more active localism and resistance to new federal intrusion centers in this 51 per cent of Americans than in the other 49 per cent. I should suppose that this is likely to continue; and that the figures, therefore, have some relevancy to an understanding of why presidential programs calling for the extension of national activity, and seemingly supported by the country in a presidential election, may come a cropper notwithstanding in the House. Such hostility to Washington may rest far less on pure devotion to the principle of local government than on opposition to specific measures which Washington proposes to put forth. This explanation does not make the sentiment the less centrifugal in its effects. Federalism would have few adherents were it not, like other elements of government, a means and not an end.[34]

V

If Congress, from its composition and the mode of its selection, tends to reflect the "local spirit" predicted by Madison, the prime organ of a compensating "national spirit" is, of course, the President—both as the Chief Executive and as the leader of his party. Without the unifying power of the highest office, derived from the fixed tenure gained by his election and the sense that the President speaks for and represents the full national constituency, it would be difficult to develop the centripetal momentum so essential to the total federal scheme. No modern President can doubt that one of his essential functions is to balance the localism and the separatism of the Congress by presenting programs that reflect the needs of the entire nation, building the best coalitions that he can for their enactment,[35] using the prerogatives and prestige of his office to that end.[36] That this has been accomplished, on the whole, despite the role allotted to the states in the selection of the President yields more support than Bagehot realized for his great dictum that "the men of Massachusetts could . . . work *any* Constitution."[37]

Familiar though they are, the constitutional provisions governing our presidential choices should be noted. The electors, in whom the initial choice is vested, are appointed by the states in the manner provided by each state's legislature.[38] Their number reflects the compromise concerning representation in Congress, being determined by the number of Representatives allotted to the state on the apportionment plus the two Senators that each state is assured. A majority of all the votes is necessary for election by electors. If it is not obtained by any candidate, the choice among the three who lead in electoral votes devolves upon the House of Representatives voting not as individuals but by states, with each state granted equal voice and a majority of all required for election.

Had these provisions worked out as the Framers contemplated, with the electors as an independent agency of choice, it is hard to think that there would often have been an electoral majority; the electors would have functioned merely as a nominating body, with selection falling mainly to the House voting under the rule of state equality. It is not comfortable to conjecture how far this result might have reduced the President to a mere agent of the states, exacerbating the intrinsic localism of the Congress, losing the unifying thrust for which the Presidency stands. It is uncomfortable also to reflect that only the rise and success of the two-party system, buttressed by the general ticket method of selecting the electors (under which a state's votes are cast as a unit), prevents that result today.

The drift to the general ticket was inevitable, given the demand for popular participation in the choice and the fact that the choice of electors by districts, which Madison averred the Framers mainly contemplated,[39] would normally divide the state's electoral votes. The states that used the district method early found themselves forsaking it, unwilling to accept such diminution in their influence on the election, unless the method that effected the division were decreed for all.[40] The most important consequence for present purposes is that the casting of the electoral votes in state units yields electoral majorities despite third party candidates, as in 1860 and 1912, while any system that reflects internal differences of opinion in the states might send the election to the House. Minority opinion is washed out within the states; it works no fragmentation of their electoral votes.

Fortunate though the result has been in keeping presidential choices from devolving on the House, the system still presents important difficulties.[41] The fact that electoral votes are allocated to the states means that the votes of individuals vary in influence depending on the size of the electorate within the states where they are cast.[42] Whatever merit there may be in the egalitarian objection, the state allocation must be taken as a datum of our federalism that is probably beyond the reach of an amendment. The other problems are, in any case, more serious. The system cannot meet third party threats with any confidence if the third party has sufficient sectional strength to win state pluralities and thus to make a substantial showing in the electoral vote. If this contingency befalls, there is great danger of the choice devolving on the House.[43] Moreover, disregard of the minorities within each state and of the size of the plurality by which a state is carried contracts the basis of our presidential politics by focusing prime attention on the large and doubtful states. In addition, since small margins of difference may determine large and possibly decisive groups of electoral votes, voting blocs that may appear to hold the balance of decision in pivotal states are granted disproportionate political importance. Finally, there is the risk that a candidate may be defeated on electoral votes, even though he has a solid popular plurality.[44]

It is much easier to state these difficulties than to find solutions to them, though more proposals of amendment have been offered on this subject than on any other aspect of the Constitution. Whatever may be said in principle for simple popular election, it would so diminish the political importance of the states of small electorates that it has no hope of adoption. Any method for dividing a state's electoral votes is clearly unacceptable so long as the House chooses on a vote by states on failure of electoral majority; more elections would devolve upon the House. The real question is whether a division plan is workable upon a basis that either permits election by plurality, whatever its dimensions, or vests the election in the Congress as a whole, voting *per capita*, unless one candidate obtains a specified percentage of the electoral votes (40 per cent in the proposal last brought to a vote). Such plans have been advanced throughout our history, calling either for determination of the electoral votes by districts or for a proportional division of each state's votes in accordance with the choices expressed by its voters.[45] A proportional division resolution has had the steady support of both Judiciary committees in recent years;[46] it passed the Senate by the requisite two-thirds in early 1950 but failed by a substanial margin in the House.[47]

There is something to be said for the proportional division plan, even beyond the point that it would be a gain for the Republic to eliminate the present possibility of House selection on a plane of state equality. Division would deny to voting blocs within a state any disproportionate strategic importance. Moreover, absent intense sectional concentration of voting allegiance, proportional division should provide a better mirror of popular opinion than the present system. But intense sectional concentration of allegiance does exist and it exists, moreover, in the states where the voting population represents the smallest fraction of the total population that determines the number of electoral votes. The division plan would greatly increase the relative influence of these states and reduce that of the states with large electorates, accustomed to a close division in their voting. In the election of 1900, for example, where McKinley had a popular plurality of 861,459, the division system would have elected Bryan because of the relative unity of his southern vote.[48]

To make the point in more detail, I cite the 1944 election, but the evidence that it affords is typical of most. The twelve southern states polling a total vote of 5,609,320 gave Roosevelt a plurality of 2,263,270, which brought him 138 electoral votes and yielded none to his opponent. Division would have cut his lead to 65+, giving him 99+ and Dewey 33+, with 4+ for minor candidates. California, Illinois, Michigan, New York, and Pennsylvania—the five states with the largest voting population—all have active party competition. They cast a total vote of 20,621,569, returning a Roosevelt plurality of 1,026,-256, giving him 135 electoral votes to 25 for Dewey, an advantage of 110. But proportional division would have brought this lead to less than 10, producing 83+ for Roosevelt to 73+ for Dewey. Thus a plurality within the single party states would have had an average worth of three times that given to a similar plurality in the states with the largest voting populations and the keenest party competition.[49]

The impact of the change is illustrated by considering its probable effect on party practice. Where the conventions now place emphasis upon the large and doubtful states, proportional division would inevitably turn it to the South —the Democrats to seek to hold their large advantage, the Republicans to reduce what would otherwise be a destructive lead. If the present emphasis on the pivotal states presents the evils that I have already noted, it has at least the virtue of its limitations: on the whole, it centers party thought upon the needs and claims of the most numerous among us, compensating for the diminution of the influence that the electoral system gives their individual votes and balancing somewhat their under-representation in Congress. To shift this emphasis to the states which now combine the smallest of electorates with an exceptional influence in the Congress would present comparable evils, in directing political appeals to a limited area, without the mitigation of comparable gain.

The answer given is that the proportional division would provide its own corrective of this danger by creating party competition where it now is lacking; that this in turn would create pressures for enlarging the electorate and thus would bring two-party politics to the affected states. If this prediction is correct it is a potent answer—but the trouble is that it may turn out to be wrong. The change might work *per contra* to solidify adherence to one party and intensify desire for restriction of the franchise in order to retain the larger influence that solidarity would yield. The other states would then have no defense but imitation, as the states that first chose electors on a district basis felt impelled by those that would not risk division to adopt the method that made unity the rule. But such an increase in the single party states would hardly leave us with the sense that we had made any advance. The people of the states of large electorates, confronted with this further diminution in the influence accorded to their numbers, may well prefer not to reflect their own internal difference of opinion, lest they imperil values larger than those involved in their differences, including their capacity to disagree.

What I have said about proportional division applies on the whole to the proposal to require choice within the states by one-vote districts rather than by the states at large.[50] Though it would be more difficult to show the consequences in detail, this method also would enhance the influence of single party states at the expense of those that show a close division, with the consequences that I have described.[51]

In net result, the present practice with respect to electoral votes seems likely to endure; and since the House vote by states on failure of an electoral majority is probably unchangeable alone, that feature of the system will probably remain as well, despite the weight and historicity of the objections to it.

Federalist considerations thus play an important part even in the selection of the President, although a lesser part than many of the Framers must have contemplated. A presidential candidacy must be pointed towards the states of largest population in so far as they are doubtful. It must balance this direction by attention to the other elements of the full coalition that is looked to for an electoral majority. Both major parties have a strong incentive to absorb protest movements of such sectional significance that their development in strength would throw elections to the House. Both must give some attention to the organized minorities that may approach balance of power status in important states, without, however, making promises that will outrun the tolerance of other necessary elements of their required strength. Both parties recognize that they must appeal to some total combination of allegiance, choice, or interest that will yield sufficient nationwide support to win elections and make possible effective government.

The most important element of party competition in this framework is the similarity of the appeal that each must make. This is a constant affront to those who seek purity of ideology in politics; it is the clue, however, to the success of our politics in the elimination of extremists—and to the tolerance and basic unity that is essential if our system is to work.[52]

The President must be, as I have said above, the main repository of "national spirit" in the central government. But both the mode of his selection and the future of his party require that he also be responsive to local values that have large support within the states. And since his programs must, in any case, achieve support in Congress—in so far as they involve new action—he must surmount the greater local sensitivity of Congress before anything is done.

VI

If this analysis is correct, the national political process in the United States —and especially the role of the states in the composition and selection of the central government—is intrinsically well adapted to retarding or restraining new intrusions by the center on the domain of the states. Far from a national authority that is expansionist by nature, the inherent tendency in our system is precisely the reverse, necessitating the widest support before intrusive measures of importance can receive significant consideration, reacting readily to opposition grounded in resistance within the states. Nor is this tendency effectively denied by pointing to the size or scope of the existing national establishment. However useful it may be to explore possible contractions in specific areas, such evidence points mainly to the magnitude of unavoidable responsibility under the circumstances of our time.

It is in light of this inherent tendency, reflected most importantly in Congress, that the governmental power distribution clauses of the Constitution gain their largest meaning as an instrument for the protection of the states. Those clauses, as is well known, have served far more to qualify or stop intrusive legislative measures in the Congress than to invalidate enacted legislation in the Supreme Court.

This does not differ from the expectation of the Framers quite as markedly as might be thought. For the containment of the national authority Madison did not emphasize the function of the Court; he pointed to the composition of the Congress and to the political processes. So in his letter to Everett, written in 1830, he summarized the views that he had often stated:

> as a security of the rights and powers of the states in their individual capacities ag[ainst] an undue preponderance of the powers granted to the Government over them in their united capacity, the Constitution has relied on 1. The responsibility of the Senators and Representatives in the Legislature of the U.S. to the Legislatures & peoples of the States. 2. The responsibility of

the President to the people of the U. States; & 3. The liability of the Ex. and Judiciary functionaries of the U.S. to impeachment by the Representatives of the people of the States, in one branch of the legislature of the U.S. and trial by the Representatives of the States, in the other branch; the State functionaries, Legislative, Executive & judiciary, being at the same time in their appointment & responsibility, altogether independent of the agency or authority of the U. States.[53]

The prime function envisaged for judicial review—in relation to federalism —was the maintenance of national supremacy against nullification or usurpation by the individual states, the national government having no part in their composition or their councils.[54] This is made clear by the fact that reliance on the courts was substituted, apparently on Jefferson's suggestion,[55] for the earlier proposal to give Congress a veto of state enactments deemed to trespass on the national domain. And except for the brief interlude that ended with the crisis of the thirties, it is mainly in the realm of such policing of the states that the Supreme Court has in fact participated in determining the balances of federalism.[56] This is not to say that the Court can decline to measure national enactments by the Constitution when it is called upon to face the question in the course of ordinary litigation; the supremacy clause governs there as well. It is rather to say that the Court is on weakest ground when it opposes its interpretation of the Constitution to that of Congress in the interest of the states, whose representatives control the legislative process and, by hypothesis, have broadly acquiesced in sanctioning the challenged act of Congress.[57]

Federal intervention as against the states is thus primarily a matter for congressional determination in our system as it stands. So too, moreover, is the question whether state enactments shall be stricken down as an infringement on the national authority. For while the Court has an important function in this area, as I have noted, the crucial point is that its judgments here are subject to reversal by Congress, which can consent to action by the states that otherwise would be invalidated. The familiar illustrations in commerce and in state taxation of federal instrumentalities do not by any means exhaust the field.[58] The Court makes the decisive judgment only when—and to the extent that—Congress has not laid down the resolving rule.[59]

To perceive that it is Congress rather than the Court that on the whole is vested with the ultimate authority for managing our federalism is not, of course, to depreciate the role played by the Court, subordinate though it may be. It is no accident that Congress has been slow to exercise its managerial authority, remitting to the Court so much of what it could determine by a legislative rule. The difficulties of reaching agreement on such matters, not to speak of drafting problems of immense complexity, lend obvious attractiveness to the *ad hoc* judicial method of adjustment. Whether Congress could contribute more effectively to the solution of these problems is a challenging and open question. The legislative possibilities within this area of our polity have hardly been explored.

FOOTNOTES TO CHAPTER 7

1. For Justice Story's view that Congress was obliged to vest full jurisdiction over federal matters in a federal court either originally or on appeal, see Martin v. Hunter's Lessee, 1 Wheat. 304, 328 (U.S. 1816); Joseph Story, *Commentaries on the Constitution,* Boston, Little, Brown & Co., 1833, Vol. III, p. 449. The position was recently supported by Professor Crosskey. See William W. Crosskey, *Politics and the Constitution in the History of the United States,* Chicago, University of Chicago Press, 1953, Vol. I, pp. 612 *et seq.* It seems, however, to be plainly contrary to the purport of one of the major compromises of the Constitutional Convention. See Henry M. Hart, Jr., and Herbert Wechsler, *The Federal Courts and the Federal System,* Brooklyn, Foundation Press, 1953, pp. 17–18. It was, of course, rejected by the Congress in the framing of the Judiciary Act of 1789 and the rejection has prevailed. See Charles Warren, "New Light on the History of the Federal Judiciary Act of 1789," *Harvard Law Review,* Vol. 37, p. 65, 1923; Henry M. Hart, Jr., "The Relations between State and Federal Law," below, p. 186.

2. Hart and Wechsler, *op. cit.,* 435.

3. On the dissatisfaction in New York with the progressive relaxation of federal rent control, culminating in the substitution of state control pursuant to the "local option" provision of the federal act of 1949, 63 Stat. 18, 26 (1949), 50 U.S.C. App. § 1894(j) (Supp. 1952), see Teeval Co. v Stern, 301 N.Y. 346, 93 N.E. 2d 884 (1950); Temporary City Housing Rent Commission, *Control of Evictions and of Residential Rents by New York City,* 1950; *Report of New York State Temporary Commission to Study Rents and Rental Conditions,* New York Legislative Documents No. 49, 1950; Herbert Wechsler, "Next Steps in Rent Control," *The Record,* Vol. 5, p. 126, 1950.

4. Taft-Hartley is a good example. See, *e.g.,* Garner v. Teamsters Union, 346 U.S. 485 (1953); Hart, "The Relations between State and Federal Law," below, p. 207. The problems of federalism in labor relations are considered by Paul R. Hays in Chapter 12, below.

5. See Hart, "The Relations between State and Federal Law," below, pp. 183–192; Herbert Wechsler, "Federal Jurisdiction and the Revision of the Judicial Code," *Law and Contemporary Problems,* Vol. 13, p. 241, 1948.

6. George Mason in the Convention; see Jonathan Elliott, *Debates on Federal Constitution,* Philadelphia, J. B. Lippincott Co., 1876, Vol. V, p. 136.

7. *The Federalist,* Lodge edition, New York, G. P. Putnam's Sons, 1888, No. 45, p. 288.

8. *Ibid.,* No. 46, p. 294.

9. *Ibid.,* No. 45. pp. 288–89.

10. Many members of Congress have, of course, served previously in state government. For an analysis of the prior state service of the Senate in the Eightieth Congress, including twenty-eight former governors, see Arthur N. Holcombe, *Our More Perfect Union,* Cambridge, Harvard University Press, 1950, pp. 205–06.

11. *The Federalist,* Lodge edition, New York, G. P. Putnam's Sons, 1888, No. 62, p. 385.

12. The states referred to and their populations (according to the 1950 census) are:

Arizona	749,587	New Mexico	681,187
Arkansas	1,909,511	North Dakota	619,636
Colorado	1,325,089	Oklahoma	2,233,351
Connecticut	2,007,280	Oregon	1,521,341
Delaware	318,085	Rhode Island	791,896
Idaho	588,637	South Carolina	2,117,027
Kansas	1,905,299	South Dakota	652,740
Maine	913,774	Utah	688,862
Mississippi	2,178,914	Vermont	377,747
Montana	591,024	Washington	2,378,963
Nebraska	1,325,510	West Virginia	2,005,552
Nevada	160,083	Wyoming	290,529
New Hampshire	533,242		

The last apportionment allots these states 86 Representatives in a House of 435.

13. Any judicious estimate upon this point must take account of Lindsay Rogers' thesis that, sectional controversies apart, the Senate has traditionally taken a much broader and disinterested view of public questions than the House. See Lindsay Rogers, *The American Senate,* New York, Knopf, 1926, especially chap. 4.

14. See, *e.g.,* John Fischer, "Unwritten Rules of American Politics," *Harper's,* Vol. 197, p. 27, November 1948; Arthur N. Holcombe, *op cit.,* pp. 208–10; Bertram M. Gross, *The Legislative Struggle,* New York, McGraw-Hill Book Co., 1953, especially pp. 148–50.

15. See Laurence F. Schmeckebier, *Congressional Apportionment,* Washington, Brookings Institution, 1941; Lawrence F. Schmeckebier, "The Method of Equal Proportions," *Law and Contemporary Problems,* Vol. 17, p. 302, 1952; Walter F. Willcox, "Last Words on the Apportionment Problem," *Law and Contemporary Problems,* Vol. 17, p. 290, 1952.

16. U.S. CONST. Art. I, § 2.

17. See United States v. Classic, 313 U.S. 299, 314–15 (1941).

18. See Schmeckebier, *op. cit.,* pp. 94–96. See also *ibid.,* pp. 97 *et seq.* for the suggestion that the purpose of the unenforceable provision of the Fourteenth Amendment should be achieved by a further amendment basing the apportionment of representatives on the number of votes cast in a state rather than on population.

19. See the testimony of Charles Warren, expressing hostility to the poll-tax but also opposing the constitutionality of federal abolition even in federal elections. *Hearings before Committee on House Administration on H.R. 29,* 80th Cong., 2d Sess. 145–162 (1948). Both Judiciary Committees have consistently reported in support of abolition. See, *e.g.,* SEN. REP. No. 1225, 80th Cong., 2d Sess. (1948); H.R. REP. No. 947, 80th Cong., 1st Sess. (1947). Though the measure has passed the House by overwhelming votes, see, *e.g.,* 89 CONG. REC. 4889 (1943), it has not been brought to a decision in the Senate. Compare the curiously different voting in the House on the war-time proposal to facilitate the vote of service personnel by distribution of a federal ballot, which, despite reliance on the war powers of Congress, was opposed on constitutional grounds. See 90 CONG. REC. 1229–30 (1944). Is it too cynical to suggest that voting on the poll-tax abolition bills is partly influenced by knowledge that they are foredoomed to failure in the Senate?

20. Art. I, § 4.

21. For an excellent account see J. Francis Paschal, "The House of Representatives: 'Grand Depository of the Democratic Principle'?", *Law and Contemporary Problems,* Vol. 17, p. 276, 1952.

22. 5 STAT. 491 (1842).

23. 17 STAT. 28 (1872).

24. 31 STAT. 733–34 (1901).

25. 37 STAT. 13 (1911).

26. 46 STAT. 26 (1929), as amended, 55 STAT. 761 (1941), 2 U.S.C. § 2a (1946).

27. *Id.* § 2a (c).

28. See Willard Hurst, *The Growth of American Law,* Boston, Little, Brown & Co., 1950, pp. 41–43; Lashley G. Harvey, "Reapportionment of State Legislatures—Legal Requirements," *Law and Contemporary Problems,* Vol. 17, p. 364, 1952; Charles W. Shull, "Political and Partisan Implications of State Legislative Apportionment," *Law and Contemporary Problems,* Vol. 17, p. 417, 1952.

29. See James E. Todd, "The Apportionment Problem Faced by the States," *Law and Contemporary Problems,* Vol. 17, p. 337, 1952.

30. "The Reapportionment of Congress," *American Political Science Review,* Vol. 45, p. 154, 1951.

31. 97 CONG. REC. 114 (1951).

32. The 1950 census classifies the "urban" as opposed to "rural" population on a basis that includes as "urban" all persons living in places of 2,500 or more inhabitants, whether incorporated as cities, towns, boroughs or villages or unincorporated places outside any urban fringe. See Bureau of Census, *Census of Population: 1950,* Washington, U.S. Government Printing Office, 1952, pp. xv–xvii.

33. Pathfinder, The Town Journal, June, 1953, pp. 26–27.

34. For an interesting comment on this aspect of the matter in relation to Australian federalism see Percy H. Partridge, "The Politics of Federalism," in *Federalism: An Australian Jubilee Study,* Sawer edition, Melbourne, F. W. Cheshire Proprietary Ltd., 1952, p. 174.

35. On the weak hold of party ties on voting in the Congress, and especially the Senate, see *e.g.,* HOLCOMBE, *op. cit.,* pp. 152, 215.

36. *Cf.* Sydney Hyman, *The American President,* New York, Harper & Brothers, 1954, pp. 52–53: "His problem would be simplified if the coalition he built for an election-day victory remained stable. But it does nothing of the sort. . . . To get any kind of measure enacted, the President has to build a special coalition for the immediate object in view." See also, *e.g.,* Woodrow Wilson, *Constitutional Government in the United States,* New York, Columbia University Press, 1908, chap. 3; E. P. Herring, *Presidential Leadership,* New York, Farrar & Rhinehart, 1940; James Rowe, Jr., "Cooperation or Conflict?—The President's Relationships with an Opposition Congress," *Georgetown Law Journal,* Vol. 36, p. 1, 1947.

37. Walter Bagehot, *The English Constitution,* St. Louis, Central Law Journal, 1914, p. 296.

38. Only the time when the electors shall be chosen and the day when they shall vote are explicitly subjected to control by Congress. But since the electoral votes are counted in joint session of both Houses, it became accepted that theirs is the agency to settle issues that arise upon the counting. The aftermath of the Hayes-Tilden controversy was the act of February 3, 1887, 24 STAT. 373, 3 U.S.C. § 6 (1946), designed to refer disputes as to the validity of state electoral votes to the state's courts, so far as possible.

39. Letter to George Hay, August 23, 1823, quoted in Max Farrand, *The*

Records of the Federal Convention, New York, Henry Holt & Company, 1937, Vol. III, pp. 458–59.

40. *Cf.* Jefferson to Monroe, January 12, 1800: "All agree that an election by districts would be best if it could be general; but while 10 states choose either by their legislature or by a general ticket, it is folly & worse than folly for the other 6 not to do it." *Works of Jefferson,* Ford edition, Boston, A. W. Elson & Co., 1905, Vol. IX, p. 90.

41. For a more extended analysis of these problems than is presented here, see Herbert Wechsler, "Presidential Elections and the Constitution: A Comment on Proposed Amendment," *American Bar Association Journal,* Vol. 35, p. 181, 1949; Wechsler, "The Lodge-Gossett Plan," Fortune, June, 1949, p. 138. Much of the following material is reproduced from these papers, with permission of the publishers.

42. Thus in the 1948 election the ratio of electoral to popular votes ranged between 1 to 161,000 in California and 1 to 18,000 in South Carolina.

43. With 39 electoral votes for Thurmond in 1948, small shifts of votes in Ohio and California, which Truman carried by 7,107 and 17,865 respectively, would have sent the election to the House—where incidentally, only twenty-one state delegations were controlled by non-dissenting Democrats, twenty were Republican controlled, and three were evenly divided. The four Thurmond states could thus have blocked any selection in the House or forced it on their terms. See Wechsler, "Presidential Elections and the Constitution," *loc. cit.,* p. 181.

44. Hayes prevailed in the disputed election despite Tilden's plurality of over 250,000—even on Republican claims. Cleveland's lead of almost 100,000 did not prevent the choice of Harrison in 1888. Wilson needed his advantage of 3,806 in California in the 1916 election though a reversal there would have left his national plurality at almost 600,000. The shift of only 29,000 votes in California, Illinois, and Ohio would have elected Dewey in 1948, though Truman prevailed by 2,000,000 in the country.

45. For a summary of the history of these proposals, see Wechsler, "Presidential Elections and the Constitution," *loc. cit.,* p. 271.

46. See, *e.g.,* SEN. REP. NO. 1230, 80th Cong., 2d Sess. (1948); SEN. REP. NO. 602, 81st Cong., 1st Sess. (1949); SEN. REP. NO. 594, 82d Cong., 1st Sess. (1951); H. R. REP. NO. 1615, 80th Cong., 2d Sess. (1948); H. R. REP. NO. 1011, 81st Cong., 1st Sess. (1949); H. R. REP. NO. 1858, 81st Cong. 2d Sess. (1950); H. R. REP. NO. 1199, 82d Cong., 1st Sess. (1951). Senator Ferguson and Representative Case both filed dissenting reports in 1949. See SEN. REP. NO. 602, Part 2; H. R. REP. NO. 1011 at 27. For the modification proposed by Mr. Case, see 96 CONG. REC. A890, 891 (1950).

47. The Senate vote was 64 to 27 in favor of the resolution, the House vote 210 to 134 against. 96 CONG. REC. 1278, 10427 (1950).

48. See the testimony of Basil Brewer, publisher of the New Bedford Standard-Times, *Hearings before Subcommittee of Senate Committee on the Judiciary on S.J. Res. 2,* 81st Cong., 1st Sess. 141–42 (1949).

49. The point is made with greater emphasis by pointing to the situation in 1944 within individual states. California with 3,520,549 votes yielded Roosevelt a plurality of 475,599. Proportional division would have meant that this advantage was worth less than 4 electoral votes. New York gave Roosevelt a lead of 316,591 on a total vote of 6,316,790. Under division the electoral advantage would have been but slightly more than 2. Yet South Carolina with 103,375 votes and a

plurality for Roosevelt of 86,054 would have produced an electoral lead of almost 7 votes. So Mississippi would have counted over 7 in return for a plurality of 155,773 among 180,080; and Texas, showing an advantage of 630,180 out of 1,150,330, would have contributed a lead of almost 13 votes.

50. For a contrary view, see *e.g.*, Lucius Wilmerding, Jr., "Reform of the Electoral System," *Political Science Quarterly,* Vol. 64, p. 1, 1949.

51. See the study by Professor Ruth C. Silva (App. A-J) in *Hearings before a Subcommittee of the Senate Committee on the Judiciary on S.J. Res. 8, 17, 19, 55, 84, 85, 95, 100,* 83d Cong., 1st Sess. 230, 237–46 (1953).

52. See Fischer, note 14 above.

53. *Writings of James Madison,* Hunt edition, New York, G. P. Putnam's Sons, 1910, Vol. IX, pp. 383, 395–396.

54. See, *e.g., The Federalist,* Lodge edition, New York, G. P. Putnam's Sons, 1888, No. 44, p. 283; *ibid.,* No. 45, p. 288; Madison: Letter to Everett, note 53 above; Letter to Thomas Ritchie, Dec. 18, 1825, *op. cit.* Vol. IX, p. 231; Letter to Jefferson, June 27, 1823, *ibid.,* pp. 137, 140–44; Letter to Spencer Roane, June 29, 1821, *ibid.,* p. 65; Paul A. Freund, "Umpiring the Federal System," Chap. 10, below.

55. See his letter to Madison, June 20, 1787, quoted in Charles Warren, *The Making of the Constitution,* Boston, Little, Brown & Co., 1928, pp. 168–69.

56. Of the great controversies with respect to national power before the Civil War, only the Bank and slavery within the territories were carried to the Court and its participation with respect to slavery was probably its greatest failure. The question of internal improvements, for example, which raised the most acute problem of constitutional construction, was fought out politically and in Congress. After the War only the *Civil Rights Cases* and income tax decisions were important in setting limits on national power—until the *Child Labor Case* and the New Deal decisions. The recasting of constitutional positions since the crisis acknowledges much broader power in the Congress—as against the states—than it is likely soon or ever to employ.

57. Surprisingly, Chief Justice Arthur Vanderbilt ignores this point in his recent lectures urging judicial control of congressional expenditures. See Arthur T. Vanderbilt, *The Doctrine of the Separation of Powers and its Present-Day Significance,* Lincoln, University of Nebraska Press, 1953, pp. 135–40.

58. See Paul A. Freund, "Umpiring the Federal System," p. 160, below; Herbert Wechsler, "Stone and the Constitution," *Columbia Law Review,* Vol. 46, pp. 785–93, 1946.

59. The judicial function in relation to federalism thus differs markedly from that performed in the application of those constitutional restraints on Congress or the states that are designed to safeguard individuals. In this latter area of the constitutional protection of the individual against the government, both federal and state, subordination of the Court to Congress would defeat the purpose of judicial mediation. For this is where the political processes cannot be relied upon to introduce their own correctives—except to the limited extent that individuals or small minorities may find a champion in some important faction. See Stone, J., in United States v. Carolene Products Co., 304 U.S. 144, 152–53n. 4 (1938).

8

Federalism and the Party System

By David B. Truman

In the representative governments characteristic of the Western World the interdependence of constitutional forms and types of political party is a fact, obvious enough in its simple statement, but complex and baffling when the observer undertakes to explain these interrelations as they bear upon past changes in the political life of a people or to anticipate the form and direction of developments in the future. The need to organize and to lead a mass electorate has given rise, even in political systems paying the merest lip-service to the values of democracy, to party forms basically different from the cliques and cabals which bore the name in an age when the political drama was played before a smaller and more select audience. Constitutional practices, whether formal and written or informal and customary, have presented the engineers of power with both advantages and handicaps in terrain and material to which their structures have been adapted, especially in systems where an attachment to constitutionalism has imposed limitations upon the techniques and tactics of the politician.

Yet even the most superficial glance at these interdependent elements will indicate that the cast has altered the mold, whether subtly and implicitly, as in the case of the American Electoral College, or directly and openly through formal amendments and legislative enactments. A search for origins and for trends is thus bedeviled by the tendency to treat in linear, cause-and-effect terms a relationship which is circular and elusive. At whatever point the circle is entered appear the dangers of assumptions too hastily made and generalizations too easily arrived at. These dangers are augmented when the constitutional structure to be examined is federal, where diversity of practice and complexity of organization are endemic.

The questions that make this interdependence significant lie close to the core of the underlying paradox of federalism.[1] In the formative phase of a federal system the question of survival—of maintaining a minimal degree of union and of giving some measure of reality to formal powers of central direction—challenges the adaptive and adjusting potentialities of party, even in the context of a restricted electorate. Maturity, on the other hand, focuses upon the party system, as the representative device most responsive to the underlying values of personality, such questions as whether the perpetuation of decentralizing forms must eventuate in restricting a centralized power to govern which a developing popular consensus would otherwise support; whether federalism, as structural fact rather than as doctrine, must spawn an extra-constitutional system of party power which places limits upon the adaptability of the scheme as a whole and forces a choice between an inhibiting political veto and a drastic alteration of the whole pattern, perhaps through violent means.

I

To speak loosely of "the party system," especially when dealing with federalism in the United States, is to run the risk of begging the central question in this inquiry, for the nature of the party enterprise rests on the extent to which the elements collectively designated by the term actually constitute a system. Differentiating factors of structure and function bisect the "system" from various directions and in bewildering fashion, creating patterns of autonomy and subordination, some stable and some fluid, which seriously embarrass generalization.

The structural elements of party can be classified in the conventional fashion —following the formal, frequently statutory provisions for the diversity of committees, conventions, and individual functionaries—by national, state, and local levels. Such classification, while formally appropriate, is likely to take insufficient account of the extent to which the persistent and effective relationships among men and groups of men active in party affairs are clustered around one or a number of individual offices located on one or two or all three levels of the formal hierarchy.

It is a commonplace to point out that the party on the national level in the United States is, and throughout the country's history has been, focused on the presidency. Such national or interstate machinery as exists is primarily, though not exclusively, concerned with the nomination and election, perhaps especially the renomination and reelection, of a President. So much is this the case that, despite the practice by both parties since 1928 of maintaining at least a nuclear national headquarters in continuous operation and despite the normal efforts of the defeated presidential candidate to give substance to his titular leadership, the party which has failed to win the White House presents a somewhat truncated, if not fractionated, appearance, which it is likely to retain until after the next nominating convention. Moreover, when the presidency is not at stake both parties show strong symptoms of "mid-term atomization."[2]

The essential supportive structures for members of the Congress typically are not national or interstate. The chairmen and staffs of the national committees provide some services and assistance for duly nominated candidates for the Congress. The organizationally separate and often jealously independent campaign committees maintained by the "parliamentary" parties in the Senate and the House of Representatives seem to perform much the same sort of function, although their activities have never been closely studied.

The party in the Senate and the House of Representatives is not without significance as a means of allocating positions of power and influence in the legislative branch or even as a vehicle for the formulation of public policy,[3] and the "record" of the congressional parties is not irrelevant to the fortunes of aspirants for election or reelection to the Congress. But the risks and sanctions to which most members of Congress are particularly sensitive have their focus within the states and localities. The relationships which the legislator has established and maintained within the constituency are primary and crucial; others are secondary and incidental. This seems to be the case despite the evidence that, especially in the case of the House of Representatives, the bulk of the voters in general elections cast their ballots on the basis of party preference rather than attachment to the personal qualities of individual candidates for the national legislature; that is, party percentages in most districts tend to shift in the same direction. This is the case in presidential years, when the party is in a sense symbolized in the person of the chief candidate, but is equally apparent in the midterm elections.[4] This paradox seems to point to the underlying significance of the nominating as against the electoral function of party structure, of which more will be said below.

At the state and local levels the structural patterns are varied and complicated, but not essentially different in kind. The significant organizations in the states may be centered upon the governorship, with control reaching down effectively into the counties and municipalities, or upon the United States Senators or upon both in some form of combination. Specialization in the localities may be built individually or in combination around the positions of mayors, sheriffs, or other prime sources of patronage and power such as the office of surrogate in the counties of New York State. Such specialized structures may include a variety of other elective offices, such as seats in the state legislature, in the United States House of Representatives, and even in the Senate. As often as not, however, congressional candidates will operate through more or less independent organizations of their own creation, even in the general election campaign. In the case of Representatives, this is often a reflection of the relative indifference of the more inclusive state and local organizations toward the congressional ticket, as compared with more lucrative sources of patronage. Senators may function independently for quite different reasons. Not only are they more conspicuous in the political affairs of their constituencies and secure in their positions for a longer period of time, but also they are likely to command other means of political power in greater abundance, including federal patronage.

The structural scheme of parties in the American federalism thus displays a confusing complexity, both in its formal aspects and in its informal operation. The system, to the extent that it can be given the name, is composed of a tremendous variety of elements imperfectly and rather unpredictably articulated, capable of showing a remarkable degree of separatism and autonomy. Moreover, the degree of articulation which exists to make the system is of a peculiar sort. The relationships between the more obscure and the more prominent elements in the system show a defensive, unilateral quality. In areas where general elections mean anything, it is a rare local or state party unit which, personal and factional feuds aside, is indifferent to the vote-pulling power of those occupying the principal positions on the ticket. But the concern is in a sense parasitic, to derive support from the leading figure on the ticket rather than to supply it. Given the tendency of voters, even when the form of the ballot does not help, to simplify their tasks by voting a "straight ticket," state and local elements are understandably interested in a nominee at the top of the list who may carry the whole slate into office with him. But these segments of the system are able, in marked degree, to cut themselves off from the head of the ticket when the latter is regarded as a handicap and succeed with remarkable frequency in checking the effects upon them of a swing of voting sentiment adverse to the occupant of the top place.[5] Similarly, there are significant relationships between the presidential party and the "constituency parties," illustrated by the common appeal by a member of the Congress for executive adoption of a particular policy or for a favorable presidential announcement in order to improve the prospects of hard-pressed candidates in special areas, but these carry no guarantee of reciprocal support either on the floor of the Congress or in subsequent election campaigns.

II

Although the system—made up of the presidential parties, the "parliamentary" parties, the constituency parties, and the various other state and local aggregations—is structurally unstable and disjointed, the distribution of power within it is not even or merely haphazard. Here again, however, the danger of hasty generalization is great. It is customary to refer to the distribution of power within the American party system as decentralized. This is the generally accepted view, yet its implications in the context of federalism and for possible future trends are not clear unless some account is taken of the relative significance of the various functions of the party and of the degree of decentralization of power in connection with the most important of them. Parties, in any representative system, perform a composite of functions, including nominating candidates for public office, mobilizing an electorate for their support, distributing patronage and other perquisites of public position, developing and protecting those formulas for social adjustment and accommodation which we collectively refer to as public policies, and a host of less obvious and self-conscious services. In different places and at different times one or another of these may be more conspicuous than the rest, which vastly complicates the tasks of historians and comparative analysts of the political process. Except perhaps in those political situations where a basic consensus is lacking or is being challenged, however, the nominating function seems to be the most fundamental or at least the most persistently focal. This has been strikingly the case in the United States since at least as far back as the caucuses and juntos of the later colonial years and, especially on the national level, conspicuously so since the great changes in the period associated with the name of Andrew Jackson, when the presidential party assumed most of the characteristics it displays today. It is around the nominating function that the states in recent decades have constructed the most elaborate and complicated systems of statutory regulation, and the intensity of feeling associated with the spread of the direct primary in the first decade of the present century reflected in part a recognition of the fundamental importance of the nomination process. James Bryce made no more acute observation concerning the American scene than he did when he noted that the nomination of candidates for public office was not only the most important but the most distinctively American function of party organization.[6]

It is in connection with the nominating of candidates that the decentralization of power in the American party system is most apparent. Looking at the presidency it is clear that the changes in practice which developed in the eighteen-twenties—changes largely of degree, perhaps, but of such measure that their significance can scarcely be exaggerated—involved an increase in the importance of localism in the selecting process. The congressional caucus had been the instrument of a limited and comparatively homogeneous national elite, disposing of an office which had little of the quality of popular symbolism that it possesses today. Its members were not, of course, lacking in attachment to states and sections, but theirs was a national and central power reflecting the effects of close association in the institutional frame of the national legislature. The shift of initiative to the state legislatures and later to the national delegate conventions was a response to demands from more heterogeneous elements in the population and eventuated in a shifting of the power of decision, if not of initiative, from the national to the state or local level.

In Jackson's day, and for decades thereafter, the utility of the national convention lay not only in the announcement of a defensible nomination, but also in the sharpening of an effective electoral mechanism. In fact, the first national convention of the Democratic party was apparently more a rally to spur Jackson's state and local cohorts into vigorous activity than a device for selecting the candidate, as, in fact, conventions in which incumbent Presidents have sought renomination have usually been ever since. In later years the leaders of state and factional delegations had not only convention votes to market among the managers of aspiring candidates but also a canvassing and electoral organization as well. Both were needed, even though the former were of more immediate importance.

Perhaps the most significant, if largely undocumented, change in recent years, a change which may account for some of the recent criticism of the national convention, is that the electioneering functions of the presidential party have become increasingly centralized while the power over nominations remains decentralized. Although those voters who alter their choices late in the campaign may be strongly influenced, as the survey studies indicate, by personal solicitation,[7] the presence of the presidential candidates in every living room, by way of radio and television, reduces the need for an army of canvassers in presidential campaigns as the development of the metropolitan press alone never did. In recent presidential elections both the behavior and the informal testimony of many urban functionaries support this interpretation; the circulars and posters are still distributed to the local clubs and headquarters, but the effort necessary to put them in the hands of individual voters is recognized as being of little or no value. State and local leaders are not powerless or completely unnecessary in the electioneering efforts of the presidential party, but both central direction and central execution of a presidential campaign have become in recent years not only a possibility but in large measure an actuality.

Yet the nomination function, excepting the renomination of an incumbent President, remains essentially decentralized. Despite such devices as the presidential primary and the centrally directed pre-convention efforts of the leading aspirants, local and frequently extraneous considerations not only enter into but even dominate the selection of delegates and the horse-trading decisions behind the scenes at the convention. In fact, the evidence clearly suggests that in areas where one-party dominance, as in the South, operates to avoid disturbance to distinctive local practices, the only significant function of a state party may be to select reliable delegates to interstate party councils. The leaders of the presidential party may no longer need to rely heavily upon a decentralized machinery for conducting an election campaign, but they are still dependent on forging a cohesive coalition of state and local leaders for the opportunity to conduct one.

Decentralization of the nominating function is more striking and more significant as it affects Senators and Representatives. Regardless of the method of selection, by one or another form of the predominant direct primary or by convention, the influences which are chiefly responsible for the selection of candidates are local rather than national. The importance of this fact is merely underscored by the evidence that, under normal conditions, in about half the congressional constituencies, success in the primary is tantamount to election.[8] This is typically due to the "one-party" complexion of many such areas, but it may result as well from the individual candidate's effectiveness in creating or associating himself with an organization within the constituency which can assure his selection or redesignation. The implications for the party system are much the same in either case.

Even a casual glance at the career lines of Senators and Representatives, as well as of state and local officials from whose ranks they are normally recruited, will indicate that most of them have had long and intimate association with the areas which they represent, more than is required by the symptomatically significant custom demanding residence in the district from which the legislator is chosen. No precise data on this point exist in the literature, but the impression is that a member of Congress is more likely than the average of the population to have been born, raised, educated, and trained in the area from which he is chosen. A constituency, perhaps especially an urban one, may take up a comparative newcomer who has achieved sudden prominence, but his survival is likely to depend ultimately upon his knowing his constituency, not in abstract, intellectual terms, but through supportive associations with individuals and groups. He must have satisfactory "connections," either with the leadership of a dominant party organization or with influential individuals primarily concerned with assuring his continuance in office or a combination of the two.

These connections may not be able to assure his election; the fortunes of the national party may be ebbing so rapidly that nothing can assure his individual survival or the nominee of the opposing party may more successfully exploit local dissatisfactions. But the aspirant will have no chance even to face these risks, except as he chooses to attempt a normally unsuccessful "independent" candidacy, unless he has the support necessary for nomination.

The structure responsible for nominating the legislative candidate need not be parochial or anti-national in its attitudes. This is not its principal significance but rather the fact that it is the locus of discretion in the nominating process. In its operations it need display no dependence upon, no functional association or identification with, the leadership of the presidential or the "parliamentary" party. Bryce made the point effectively in a brief comparison of local party organizations in Britain and the United States:[9]

> An organization which exists, like the political associations of England, solely or mainly for the sake of canvassing, conducting registration, diffusing literature, getting up courses of lectures, holding meetings and passing resolutions, has little or no power. . . . But when an organization which the party is in the habit of obeying, chooses a party candidate, it exerts power, power often of the highest import. . . .

Decentralization of the functions of nominating and promoting the election of members of the Congress is reflected in a lack of cohesion on important policy matters within the "parliamentary" parties—within the party in either House and between the party in one chamber and "the same" party in the other —and in fairly frequent rejection of the legislative leadership of "the party's" President when it "controls" the White House. It is too easy to underestimate the influence of party affiliation upon legislative voting and to ignore the evidence that it is more reliably predictive of such behavior than any other factor so far identified.[10] But on controverted issues of prime significance the leaders of the "parliamentary" parties not infrequently find themselves in the minority among their nominal following or split into two opposing wings, and the Administration may have to count on appreciable support from a segment of the "opposition" in Congress for the enactment of a basic portion of its legislative program, often despite extraordinary efforts by a popular President through public appeals and pronouncements, efforts which depend for effectiveness upon their infrequent use.

This state of affairs leads to criticism of the party system and demands for party "responsibility" by those who desire a central place among the functions of party for the formation of a more coherent and enforceable program. Of such criticisms the recent report of the American Political Science Association's Committee on Political Parties may be taken as representative.[11] A common shortcoming of such appeals, illustrated in the committeee's proposals, is that in their enthusiasm for programmatic elegance they tend to underestimate the significance of the decentralized nominating function. It seems unlikely that any amount of policy talk in local meetings or of platform writing by interstate bodies will increase discipline within the congressional parties or cohesion within the Administration as a whole, unless they are preceded by a centralization of the risks and sanctions associated with the selection of candidates for seats in the legislature. It may be doubted, in fact, whether in any party system dominated by two major aggregations, even in a country less extensive and socially less complex than the United States, cohesion is provided primarily by the programmatic element rather than by a central leadership whose policy tendencies are but vaguely known and whose displeasure with a parliamentary follower is enforceable at the nominating stage. If the legislator's risks are localized, he will look in that direction when making difficult choices on matters of public policy.

III

The American party system thus tends to be characterized by decentralization of power with respect to its most crucial function, by structural confederation, and by a lack of coherence in matters of major policy. What have the facts of federalism to do with this? To what extent is this an inescapable consequence of the federal system itself? Federalism, by the constitutional protection of constituent governments, creates at least the possibility, as Herbert Wechsler has argued,[12] that the states will control the composition and influence materially the legislative processes of the national entity. If, as Arthur Holcombe suggests, the national political party is the principal agent for restricting these tendencies,[13] its effectiveness in the United States has been something less than complete. Is the molding force of the federal system itself such that a party system operating within it must inevitably show the characteristics of political organizations in the United States?

This is a question of considerable importance for an understanding of the American experience and for an estimate of its potentialities in the future. It is a question which the Committee on Political Parties tends to avoid by treating party organization as a matter dissociated from that of governmental structure. Thus it asserts that: "In the case of the American party system, the real issue is not over the federal form of organization but over the right balance of forces within this type of organization."[14]

The basic political fact of federalism is that it creates separate, self-sustaining centers of power, privilege, and profit which may be sought and defended as desirable in themselves, as means of leverage upon elements in the political structure above and below, and as bases from which individuals may move to places of greater influence and prestige in and out of government. This does not mean simply that a socio-economic interest group, dominant within a state or, more typically perhaps, a group of contiguous states, will utilize state powers to protect itself from assault both from within the area and from the national center. This is true enough; it merely restates the facts underlying the original choice of a federal rather than a unitary structure for the second American constitution, and it points to the familiar fact of sectional politics present through most of our history and recurrent with each wave of state creation.

The separate political existence of the states in the days of the nation's industrial and political maturity, on the other hand, provides effective access to the whole governmental structure for interest groups whose tactics may be local or sectional but whose scope is national. Separatism, whether within the federal system or in the form of a specious demand for making a governmental activity "independent of politics" at whatever level of the structure, has frequently been a refuge for interests bent on defensive or evasive action, and the "states' rights" argument has often had about it an air more of expediency than of principle. This is not new. But it is the fact of federalism which permits an interest group or other enterprise of national scope, in alliance with lesser interests which may be primarily local or sectional, to prevent or negate action on the national level and to insure inaction or indulgence in the states. It was not merely Yankee stubbornness and dedication to local self-government which in the thirties prevented federal action to foster integrated development of the Connecticut River Valley. Such sentiments may have been more than mere expedient romanticism, and they might alone have affected the outcome of the proposal and the fortunes of elected state officials and members of Congress, but they received significant support and direction from private utility interests whose reach was nationwide.[15] Nor were the interests exclusively local or sectional, though such were allied at least peripherally, which induced the Congress to alter in favor of state action a Supreme Court decision asserting or permitting national control of insurance. These illustrations are not cited by way of indictment but merely of illustration. In the maturity of the federal system the existence of the states as self-contained centers of power permits the use of them and associated party units by interests which are state or local only in a tactical sense. This is not equivalent to the separatism of a geographically defined interest, though it appears in the same garb and owes its significance as a technique to the continued existence of the states as power centers. Its effects on the party system are conducive to neither centralization nor cohesion at the national level.

In viewing the states as channels of access for interest groups, however, it is easy to forget that elective positions within the states, especially the governorships, are prizes in themselves and that the political "game" may be merely a means from the viewpoint of the interest group leader but is likely to be an end in itself for many of the more active partisans. It is perhaps a commentary on the instrumental, almost a-political attitudes of many academic observers of politics that they lay such stress upon the American parties as alliances of socio-economic interest groups. They are, of course, alliances of groups, but parties are not distinguishable exclusively or even primarily in terms of their socio-economic policy content. In varying but important measure they are purely political, focused upon securing and holding power for their leading elements as an end in itself. The grand patterns of sectional and perhaps class alliances which have successively dominated our presidential politics for periods lasting up to several decades can in the large view perhaps be explained most meaningfully in terms of socio-economic interest. But at shorter range the detailed patterns take on a more exclusively political appearance.[16] There is here no intended implication of petty place-seeking but rather a suggestion that to aspire to be among those who govern and to associate for that objective as an end in itself is both normal and honorable. The evidence which indicates that enduring attachment to a party is for many voters a loyalty independent of, though not dissociated from, socio-economic interest[17] supports the assumption that similar attachments to party, clique, and faction exist among the more active elements in political organizations.

The significance of this point in the present context is that, given the multitude of elective positions in the system (only partially a consequence of federalism) and given the absence of a clearly defined and recognized path from one position to another in the loose hierarchy of political careers (a consequence more of a decentralized party system than directly of federalism itself), conflicting but interdependent clusters of loyalty and aspiration build up around various positions in the governmental structure. Thus, within a given "party," the career aspirations and prospects of a state governor, a United States Senator, and a member of the House of Representatives are likely to be ambiguous to one another or to others in the political structure with whom they must deal. Each may want one of the other offices; the governor and Senator may both have presidential ambitions which are mutually exclusive; the Senator or the Representative, though occupying a "national" office, may hope to move to the governorship and is likely to be far more closely dependent upon the state governor, from considerations either of preference or of expediency, than upon the leaders of the "parliamentary" party or upon a President bearing the same party designation. This is a simplified and hypothetical example,[18] but it illustrates the role played by the offices established in the federal structure, and especially the state governor, in fractionating and decentralizing the party system, in encouraging the development of largely independent, hostile, and internally cohesive factional groupings.

The connection between these tendencies and the existence of federalism should not, of course, be overstated. The basic phenomenon of clique and personal rivalry is familiar enough in all organizations, including political parties. The point of significance here is the extent to which the federal structure tends to give these free rein. It is symptomatic of the function in the party system of state political positions, especially the governorship, that of the forty-three major candidates in the twenty presidential elections from 1876 through 1952 (counting three candidates in the elections of 1912, 1924, and 1948), only seven, excluding the thirteen incumbent Presidents, came to the nomination directly from a national political position, such as a seat in the Congress or a cabinet post; five were nominated from non-political positions of national or regional importance, and the remaining eighteen were drawn from state political roles, mostly governorships. Such nominations are, of course, available under normal conditions only to governors of the large doubtful states, but the disruptive potentialities of the governorships are not confined to presidential races. The governor who merely seeks to retain his office through an effective organization covering major sections of the state is in a position to influence the fortunes and the choices of members of Congress, and a Senator or Representative who is aiming at the governorship is likely to be peculiarly solicitous of interests located in his home state.[19]

These three factors derived from the existence of the states as separate and largely self-sustaining power centers—channeling the claims of local socioeconomic interest groups, inviting their use as leverage against federal action by interests which are only tactically local, and providing for competing and frequently incompatible nuclei of decentralized intra-party conflict—are, of course, interrelated. In various combinations they go a long way toward indicating that there is something inherent in federalism which induces decentralization and lack of coherence in a party system.

But it is not sufficient merely to show that federalism has had some effect upon the nature of the party system. The important question of how much effect it has remains unanswered and to a precise degree unanswerable. It can easily be pointed out that decentralization and lack of cohesion frequently are apparent within the state parties, where factors other than federalism are influential. Could the like of these account in considerable measure for the peculiarities of the system as a whole? Would the American party system have developed essentially its present characteristics if the Founding Fathers had established a unitary constitution? The question is hypothetical but not irrelevant.

IV

Before turning to an examination of some of the influences other than federalism that have molded the American parties, it may be instructive, or at least suggestive, to examine briefly two other federal systems, Canada and

Australia, for evidence of similar effects of federal organization. The comparison cannot be conclusive, since, as in all such efforts, it is impossible to differentiate the effect of other influences and state in precise terms the consequences of basic constitutional structure. But contrasts may be revealing even when comparisons cannot be made with exactness.

In both Canada and Australia the major parties are obliged, especially in the former, to take account of the geographically defined differences which underlie the federal structure. Viable national political structures, as would be expected, must reckon with sectional issues, attitudes, and interests. Yet despite this obvious fact both have seen the development of national parties more centralized and considerably more cohesive than those in the United States.[20]

In Canada there is considerable variation in the formal structures of the major parties, and within the parties the patterns differ from one province to another and between rural and urban constituencies, as in the United States. In Quebec, whose politics are not unlike those of the American South, parties are more loosely organized, and purely personal and factional influences have considerable significance. At the national level the only party organization of importance is the parliamentary party. Below that is the somewhat more complex provincial party organization and the constituency (riding) organization.

The fact of federalism introduces potential cleavages into the party system, yet normally the leader of the parliamentary party, especially if he is also Prime Minister, can count on the disciplined support of those elected with him, and a majority Government usually can survive throughout its permissible statutory life of five years. In Dominion elections, to be sure, it is not unusual for the outcome nationally to be affected by the existence of local or provincial hostilities clustered around other points in the federal structure and largely irrelevant to national questions.

Such centrifugal influences as exist within the Canadian parties seem to be associated, as in the United States, with decentralization of the nominating function and with the use of provincial governmental positions as points of resistance. Nominations for the Dominion parliament are made by the constituency organizations through various procedures generally lacking the complexity of their American equivalents, a point perhaps not without significance. These constituency organizations, perhaps especially in Quebec, are a good deal more independent in their decisions than are those in Britain, and the provincial and national parties have no formal or acknowledged power to withhold designations or to control the local decisions. A member of parliament who is not in the best of standing with the Government may be renominated if he nevertheless retains the confidence of the constituency committee, but this is less likely to occur if he is known to be in disfavor, and the national party leader may, especially if he is Prime Minister, be able to punish, by indirect means, the recalcitrant by seeing that he is deprived of his nomination.

The national party's organized contact with the individual voter is through the mechanism of the provincial party association, which directs the electioneering efforts in the constituency. The provincial organization has dual loyalties, to the national party and to the provincial leader. These may become divided, as happened in the not entirely unprecedented break in 1940 between Prime Minister Mackenzie King and Mr. Mitchell Hepburn, the leader of the Liberal Party in Ontario and the provincial prime minister. In a fashion not unrecognizable to Americans, the latter made use of his position in the provincial government to embarrass the national leadership. Clokie's comment on the incident was that it illustiated "one of the penalties paid for federalized politics when there is no appropriate political organization to coordinate the entire national party."[21] This was an extreme case; the more common threat is merely that the provincial party will be more interested in winning power in the province than in promoting the interests of the national party leadership.

The Canadian party system thus shows the influences of the federal structure, but it is in rather sharp contrast to the United States in degree. This is not the place to attempt an exhaustive analysis of the reasons for the contrast, but one or two prominent factors should be cautiously mentioned. These seem to be associated with the parliament-cabinet system, operating under conditions at least analogous to those in Britain. In this connection it is tempting to seize upon the absence of a separation of powers as the crucial element, but as a simple constitutional fact it is not convincing. However, the consequence that it involves no separate popular election of the head of the government is significant, in that it implies narrowing and rather sharply defining the alternative lines of succession to the positions of principal influence. The subtle differences in the role of prime ministers, at the national level and in the provinces, flowing from retention of representatives of the Crown in the chiei ceremonial positions, are not unimportant. But the chief fact seems to be that the positions of provincial prime ministers, to say nothing of a variety of other governmental and nongovernmental positions, are not points from which direct succession to the most important political post can take place. As a point of leverage the provincial prime ministership, or leadership of the minority party in a province, may be useful, but it is not readily convertible into peak national leadership. In fact, it appears that sectional hostilities are more likely to focus upon a provincial leader than upon a Dominion statesman. The advantages of political ambiguity, which adhere to the governor of an important state or to a presidential aspirant whose prominence rests on a nonpolitical career in the United States, lie with the experienced politician at the national level. This seems to produce a somewhat cooptative pattern of succession which, buttressed by a skillful and thoroughly un-British use of patronage when the party is in power, increases dependence upon the party leader. In the hands of a gifted politician such as a Laurier or a Mackenzie King—historically not unimportant political facts in themselves—the system can produce long and durable national leadership and reduce the disruptive influences of federalism to a minimum.

Associated with and in some instances flowing from these basic factors are a number of supportive influences of apparently less fundamental importance, such as the power of dissolution, simpler and less frequent elections, resulting in a more informal and less sustained party activity at the local level, and the striking dominance of the national party leader. The last of these involves an assumption within the constituency that a member of parliament will support his party in the legislature or resign, which considerably reduces the significance of decentralized nominations.

The main features of the Australian situation are succinctly expressed by Louise Overacker in the closing sentences of her informative study:[22]

> In spite of its federal structure and a strong sense of particularism among the member states, unified, disciplined parties with Commonwealth-wide organizations developed. Even the Senate, created to safeguard state interests, has become a body in which divisions are along strict party lines.

This state of affairs is traceable to the existence of the remarkable Australian Labor Party, not only in the sense that it applies most completely to that party but also because the A.L.P., far more than the Liberal Party in Canada, has developed a structural pattern to be imitated by other political groupings as well as a substantive position for them to react to.

Superficially the structure of the A.L.P. resembles the general pattern in Canada. However, the primary emphasis given to the movement has not only attached extraordinary importance at both the state and Commonwealth levels to the parliamentary caucus, which the elected member is pledged to support, but has also produced a federal structure of state and interstate conventions whose relations with the parliamentary parties in the matter of policy-making are not always clear or harmonious.

While discipline within parliamentary parties is high, it is not always so striking in the structure as a whole, and decentralization is even more conspicuous. State party leaders have successfully repudiated the positions taken by federal leaders in referendum campaigns, and the leader of the party in New South Wales was able for five years, from 1932 to 1937, to dominate the party within the state even though his group had been formally expelled by the federal party. These occurrences are not necessarily typical or increasing in frequency, but they point to the fact of federal structure as a source of decentralizing leverage. Ambiguity in lines of succession is not as marked as in the United States, but its equivalent seems to be supplied by control by the state leadership over nominations, both state and federal, and over the financing of campaigns. The influence which they can thus exercise over the composition and conduct of the parliamentary parties appears to warrant Overacker's characterization of them as "masters in their respective bailiwicks" and "lords of their own domain."[23]

Parliamentary discipline is less marked and decentralization is considerably more evident in the new Liberal Party, as in its predecessors, but its tendencies seem to be in the direction of a development similar to that of the A.L.P. The Country Party, clearly more a product of underlying social differences than of the structure of federalism itself, has never achieved a strong central organization.

At least in the case of the A.L.P. the contrasts with the American situation seem, as in Canada, to be more marked than the similarities. For this the parliament-cabinet system, with its partial reflection of British practices, is undoubtedly in part responsible. The importance of the individual national party leader is not as great as it has been in Canada, but, in the hands of a John Curtin, it is apparently possible so to use the machinery of party conference, caucus discipline, and the solidarity pledge as to offset state control of nominations.

But the chief significance of the Australian system for Americans is that matters of constitutional form are far less important than in Canada. The degree of discipline and of centralization which marks the A.L.P., and its rivals by partial adaptation, is fundamentally a reflection of underlying social conditions. Early land policies and patterns of settlement, imposed upon the peculiarities of Australian geography, and a course of economic development which restricted the emergence of a significant middle class and the dominance of middle-class values, resulted in the early appearance of a highly class-conscious labor movement unlike anything in the United States or Canada. Australian politics have been proportionally bitter and marked by lines of conflict drawn in class terms. Their significance is that these lines cut across geographic jurisdictions and minimize, even if they do not eliminate, the centrifugal effects of constitutional structure. These lines, moreover, are old, older than Australian federalism itself. As Overacker puts it, "Not only does the Australian Labor Party antedate federalism but in a sense it became a national party even before Australia was a nation."[24]

The Canadian and Australian experiences thus seem to indicate that, although the structural fact of federalism produces tendencies toward decentralization and lack of cohesion in the party system, a variety of other political or social influences may minimize the effect of such tendencies sufficiently to permit the development of a centralized power to govern consistent with the degree of underlying popular consensus. In the American case, apparently, these additional political and social facts have accentuated or at least perpetuated the centrifugal tendencies.

V

It seems clear that the structural fact of federalism is not alone sufficient to account for the peculiar characteristics of the American party system, though it may be fundamental. Additional influences must be identified and accounted for. Yet any effort to identify the additional forces in the American experience and to assess their relative importance is, in a sense, likely to be artificial. It sets the analyst to the unenviable task of cutting apart what is a seamless web of multivariant and interdependent factors with the prospect that he will end up with a set of separate elements whose chief significance lies in their inter-action.

The foregoing discussion of Canada and Australia suggests the relevance of the separation of powers, the constitutional arrangement which seems to attract the attention of critics most easily. If the present analysis is sound, however, it is not the partial constitutional isolation of executive from legislative func-tions or the accompanying system of checks and balances that is of chief in-terest. Attempts to encourage or to develop means for improving communica-tion and collaboration between the White House and the Congress are, in this context, essentially palliatives, though commendably constructive ones of con-siderable potential significance. It is the separate election of chief executives at both levels, and perhaps all three, which seems relevant here. Governors have often succeeded in imposing their leadership upon state legislators and presidents have with varying degrees of success bridged the long mile from Capitol Hill to 1600 Pennsylvania Avenue. Nevertheless the separate election of chief executives has multiplied and thereby rendered ambiguous the lines of succession within the governmental structure, and ambiguity of this sort seems almost certain to encourage independence and parallelism in party structures rather than coherence and centralization. As long as Presidents may be re-cruited from Congress, from the governorships, or from the cabinet (as well as from outside of political life), and as long as men in any of these positions may reasonably aspire to any of the others, decentralization and lack of coherence are likely to appear in many subtle but significant ways. The hypothesis is rhetorical, but if gubernatorial aspirants could be recruited only from within the state legislature or only from among the principal executive positions and if presidents were drawn exclusively from the Senate, or, in Jeffersonian fashion, from the hierarchy of the cabinet, the reasons for independent and poorly articulated party structures would be reduced.

But if the separation of powers is relevant, it is not sufficient. Such elements of structure would not alone be controlling, particularly in face of the kinds of factors which originally produced a federal scheme and which give it vitality today. Looking broadly at such factors over the sweep of the years, one gets the impression that, with one great exception, our politics has been carried on at relatively low temperatures. Except for the conflicts leading up to the Civil War, the issues generally have been of moderate intensity or, when heated or persistent, have been considerably tempered by a timely improvement in prices or in the level of industrial and commercial activity. Operating in the context of a large domestic market and a rapidly expanding economy, unrestricted by the kinds of factors which stoked the fires of conflict in Australia, our politics has been occupied with parceling slices of a pie that has had a way of expand-ing when awkward choices were imminent, not only over the relative sizes of the portions, but over who might partake and who must go without. Un-til very recently, moreover, our controversies have been for the most part domestic.

Our domestic, low-temperature quarrels have taken full cognizance of the geographically defined diversities which are still a reality within the country. In fact, the system has frequently exaggerated them; in a viable polity, and the survival value of the American scheme need not be argued, cleavages along local or sectional lines are not likely to dominate the scene in the presence of intersecting issues of great significance, especially if the latter have their origin on the international plane. In the absence of such issues, and occasionally in default of a recognition of their import, Americans have been able to engage in locally or regionally based disputes which have not infrequently had the appearance of political luxury. The argument is not that all these geographically defined issues have been without substance, although some of them clearly have, but rather that their prominence is in part owing to the absence of more intense, intersecting issues and that collectively their impact on the party system has been decentralizing and disintegrative. These conditions, if this estimate is valid, may help account for tendencies toward a decentralized politics within many of the states as well as in the nation as a whole.

In no respect is the quality of American politics, in contrast with Australian, more clearly indicated than in the labor movement. No substantial proportion of American wage earners has ever developed strong class attitudes. Given our characteristically uninhibited methods of settling and exploiting a rich and virgin continent, the steadily expanding economy, and the resulting high social mobility, the dominant values of the society have been "middle-class" and individualistic. So thoroughly have these values been accepted by the wage-earning population that the labor movement throughout its history has been haunted by the problem of cohesion. For decades this problem was dealt with in the organized sector of labor more by a reliance on differences within the working-class population than on cleavages between class groupings. From the "plain people" movements of the eighteen-sixties to the industrial unionism of the nineteen-thirties and nineteen-forties, American workers have been more likely to divide along sectional, commodity, even ethnic and religious lines— all essentially decentralized—than to consolidate along the shadowy boundary of social class. For good or ill, the American political system has not been faced with the intersecting issues churned up by a class-conscious labor movement.

A further consequence of the low-temperature, domestic quality of American politics is the high visibility of the organized interest groups which have developed around the lines of cleavage and specialization in a complex, industrialized society. Many of these are local or sectional only in a tactical sense, as noted earlier, but all of them are on occasion highly significant, in the absence of other sorts of controversies, as elements in the calculations surrounding the nomination function, even though they may not be overtly active in this respect. Moreover, even when, in partial consequence of their own characteristically federal structures, they have been rent by divisive controversy, their local or state components are no less likely to be influential in the facilitation or disruption of political careers and in the determination of legislative action at state and national levels.[25]

In this connection it is worth while to point out that a considerable element of localism has inevitably been injected into American politics, regardless of constitutional structure, by such factors as the patterns of immigration from Europe. Immigration itself has rarely provided a controversy of national scope, and nativist movements have been conspicuous on occasion but of no lasting significance. Ethnic issues as such, perhaps excluding the Negro question, have not had the impact on national politics that they have had, for example, in Canada. But with the tendency for individual nationality groupings to concentrate in particular areas, especially in the cities, and to find in their common rootlessness and frequently in the experience of discrimination and exploitation a basis in addition to national origin for cohesion and interdependence, they have constituted a means to power and influence for locally oriented political organizations outside and inside their own ranks.

It is these geographically defined factors, accentuated by a low-temperature, domestic politics, which give major force and relevance to the possibility of state control over the composition of the national governing bodies, through the electoral college and related means, which Herbert Wechsler points out in his chapter. Structural elements in the system—some, it is argued here, inherent in federalism—alone encourage an irreducible minimum of decentralization and disruption in the party system. But it is as these reflect the underlying pace of the political process and as they are harnessed to regionally differentiated issues and clusters of organization that they find their most impelling dynamic.

As in other national systems, moreover, there are additional governmental arrangements which support and in some instances reflect the decentralizing tendencies apparent in the process as a whole. Not the least important of these is the practice of frequent elections specified by the calendar and the related constitutional provision for unequal terms of office. Decentralizing in intent, they have operated to accentuate localized concerns, especially in the midterm primaries and elections at the national level. But in a system in which any election may be relevant to all others in an area, whether they are held simultaneously or not, the very frequency of elections and campaigns can accentuate and exploit local and transitory animosities and consolidate localized patterns of control. This point has never been more dramatically illustrated than it was in the tragic years leading up to the Civil War. During the decade of the eighteen-fifties "the baneful influence of elections almost continuously in progress, of campaigns never over,"[26] accentuated local and sectional hostilities. Aided by the fact that at that time elections to the Congress were not held at a uniform date throughout the nation, the upthrust of localism further crippled already imperfect efforts to forestall a fatal break. In Nichols' words, "The incessant procession of artificially ordered election conflicts frequently meant nothing more than the routine return of pleasurable electioneering excitement; but in the 1850's it had become dangerous." "It was," he points out, "harder for the statesman at the capital city to calm the emotions stirred in these countless local contests when their representatives brought them to Washington."[27]

The difference between this fateful decade and the more normal course of our politics is one of degree, the more so as a multiplicity of local elections may support a professionalized corps of politicians whose organized relationships within the area can be utilized to resist an effort at centralization.

A representative and significant response to such an effort is provided by the Hatch Act of 1939. Stimulated by Franklin Roosevelt's awkward and ill-fated attempt at a "purge" of rebellious Representatives and Senators in the Democratic primaries of 1938, a bipartisan combination in the Congress took steps to forestall the possibility that a centralized party leadership could be built upon presidential patronage, through the device of a statutory prohibition against political campaign activity by federal employees below the policy-forming level, whether they are in the classified civil service or not. This was an effort at insurance against an extremely remote contingency, since the requirement of senatorial confirmation and the practice of senatorial courtesy have made patronage a comparatively feeble instrument of centralized leadership except in the opening months of an Administration or for purposes of securing renomination for an incumbent President. It is impossible to estimate precisely the effects of this restriction or of the comparable provision in the 1940 legislation restricting the annual expenditures of national committees, but at minimum their enactment testifies to the strength of the decentralizing tendencies.

VI

In a federal system decentralization and lack of cohesion in the party system are based on the structural fact of federalism, but, it has been argued here, the degree to which these become the dominant characteristics of the distribution of power within the political parties is a function of a variety of other governmental and social factors which are independent of the federal structure or are merely supportive of its tendencies. Within the American structure there clearly are limits beyond which centralization and coherence in the parties may not go. Nevertheless, accepting the argument that the national political party is the most responsive instrument of restraint upon federalism's centrifugal tendencies, it may be appropriate briefly to inquire into the circumstances which might produce a gradual shift in the locus of power within the American parties.

It seems clear that the prospects for such a shift must rest fundamentally upon the emergence or intensification of a dominant and persistent set of interests and issues which will tend to cut through rather than to unify constituencies, especially the states, and which demand standardized national solutions. These would imply a more intense and urgent, perhaps a more explosive, politics; that would seem to be the price of change. Here is not the place to attempt a detailed examination of any such issues, but it seems entirely possible that their most likely source would lie in the problems of an increasingly urbanized and industrialized society, as Arthur Holcombe suggested more than twenty years ago in his anticipation of the replacement of sectional by class politics.[28] Another complex of such issues may emerge or may be in process of emerging out of the problems besetting the new American leadership on the international scene.

Neither of these complexes of issues appears to hold much promise of startling immediate developments within the party realm. In the unlikely event of an increasingly even industrialization of all the states, it is by no means certain that an expanding economy will not so check the importance of intersecting issues of full employment, social security, and the like, that the demands of commodity and of section will still be dominant. Nor in such circumstances is it at all sure that leadership forces will not prefer the occasional inconveniences of a decentralized politics to the less manageable potentialities of an opposite trend. And in the realm of foreign policy it is by no means clear that an emerging consensus on direction and general posture will not leave the center of the stage free for geographically defined issues of pace and of precise application.

These obstacles aside, the dominance of issues capable of dividing major constituencies internally presupposes their emergence or evocation in sections now monopolized by a single party and the development of a vigorous and genuine bipartisan pattern. This result is not likely to be the work of a single day and not only because of the stubborn disinclination of voters to alter partisan attachments once they have been formed, though this is a factor of no inconsiderable importance. Rather, as V. O. Key has amply demonstrated in his study of the South, a single-party monopoly based on the assertion or defense of a dominant sectional interest tends to inhibit the identification and expression of intersecting national issues. It induces a fluid factionalism along personal and clique lines incapable of the organization necessary to sustained expression of such issues from within and to effective response to their assertion from without.[29] Moreover, the purely political advantages of a one-party monopoly are considerable and not to be surrendered without resistance. Only the most intense conflict over persistent issues is likely to prevail over efforts by an invigorated majority party to capture the leadership of an emerging opposition and to hamstring its efforts with all the statutory and polemic resources at the command of an entrenched group.

The federal structure itself imposes no insuperable obstacles to a shift in the locus of power within the party system, but it seems improbable that the country will soon dispense with the talents of the politician skilled in the manipulation and reconciliation of decentralized and recalcitrant power blocs.

FOOTNOTES TO CHAPTER 8

1. See the opening chapter in this symposium by Arthur W. Macmahon.

2. The phrase is V. O. Key's. See *Politics, Parties, and Pressure Groups*, 3d edition, New York, Thomas Y. Crowell Company, 1952, p. 515.

3. Julius Turner, *Party and Constituency: Pressures on Congress*, Baltimore, The Johns Hopkins Press, 1951.

4. See the data presented in Key, *op. cit.*, chap. 17, and his paper, "The Veterans and the House of Representatives: A Study of a Pressure Group and Electoral Mortality," *Journal of Politics*, Vol. 5 (1943), pp. 27–40. This pattern is not to the same degree discernible in the case of Senators, since they are likely to enjoy a greater degree of personal prominence.

5. This point is tentatively demonstrated in V. O. Key, Jr., "Partisanship and County Office: The Case of Ohio," *American Political Science Review*, Vol. 47 (1953), pp. 525–32. Cf. Harold F. Gosnell, *Machine Politics: Chicago Model*, Chicago, University of Chicago Press, 1937.

6. James Bryce, *The American Commonwealth*, 2d edition, New York, Macmillan and Company, 1891, Vol. II, p. 73.

7. Paul F. Lazarsfeld, Bernard Berelson, Hazel Gaudet, *The People's Choice*, 2d edition, New York, Columbia University Press, 1948, pp. 150–158.

8. Cortez A. M. Ewing, "Primaries as Elections," *Southwestern Social Science Quarterly*, Vol. 29 (1948–49), pp. 293–98; Malcolm Moos, *Politics, Presidents, and Coattails*, Baltimore, The Johns Hopkins Press, 1952.

9. Bryce, *op. cit.*, Vol. II, p. 76.

10. Consult the evidence in Turner, *Party and Constituency*. Turner's data are confined to the House of Representatives.

11. *Toward a More Responsible Two-Party System*, A Report of the Committee on Political Parties, American Political Science Association, Supplement, *American Political Science Review*, Vol. 44, No. 3, Part 2 (September, 1950). Also published as a separate volume (New York, Rinehart and Company, 1950).

12. Herbert Wechsler's chapter in this symposium.

13. See the chapter by Arthur N. Holcombe.

14. *Toward a More Responsible Two-Party System*, p. 26.

15. William E. Leuchtenberg, *Flood Control Politics: The Connecticut River Valley Problem, 1927–1950*, Cambridge, Harvard University Press, 1953.

16. I am here dissenting in part from the view expressed by John Fischer in his contribution to the symposium. Cf. my comments in *The Governmental Process*, New York, Knopf, 1951, pp. 279–81, 509–10, and *passim*.

17. There are interesting data on this point in the recent study of the 1952 presidential election by Angus Campbell, Gerald Gurin, and Warren E. Miller: *The Voter Decides*, Evanston, Illinois, Row, Peterson and Company, 1954.

18. In some states, of course, party organizations have been disciplined enough to establish a relatively clear and enforceable *cursus honorum*, as recently in Virginia. See V. O. Key, Jr., *Southern Politics in State and Nation*, New York, Knopf, 1949, chap. 2.

19. The basic incompatibility of elements in the party structure is underestimated

in the report of the Committee on Political Parties when it looks to local party meetings to give local party organizations "a stronger sense of loyalty to the entire party" and when it proposes a Party Council "representative" of various elements, including the party's state governors. See *Toward a More Responsible Two-Party System*, pp. 39 ff., 47.

20. In this section I have relied heavily upon Alexander Brady, *Democracy in the Dominions*, 2d edition, Toronto, University of Toronto Press, 1952; Robert M. Dawson, *The Government of Canada*, Toronto, University of Toronto Press, 1947; H. McD. Clokie, *Canadian Government and Politics*, 2d edition, London, Longmans, Green and Company, 1945; and Louise Overacker, *The Australian Party System*, New Haven, Yale University Press, 1952.

21. Clokie, *op. cit.*, p. 95.

22. Overacker, *op. cit.*, pp. 327–8.

23. *Ibid.*, pp. 100, 319.

24. *Ibid.*, p. 30. For a comment on similar phenomena in interest-group organization, cf. Truman, *op. cit.*, p. 121.

25. See Truman, *op. cit.*, chaps. 2, 6, 10, and *passim*.

26. Roy F. Nichols, *The Disruption of American Democracy*, New York, Macmillan, 1948, p. 515.

27. *Ibid.*, pp. 5, 7.

28. Arthur N. Holcombe, *The New Party Politics*, New York, W. W. Norton, 1933.

29. Key, *Southern Politics*, chap. 14 and *passim*.

9

The Coercion of States in a Federal System

By Arthur N. Holcombe

The coercion of states, which are members of a federal system, by the government of the system, in order that they may perform the obligations of membership in a satisfactory manner, presents one of the most difficult problems of federal politics. For a principal purpose of federation is to secure peace and freedom from forcible constraint for the federated states, and the coercion of a state by its own federal government seems to be incompatible with the nature of a well-ordered federal union. But deliberate and persistent refusal by a state to perform properly its obligations to a union of which it is a member is also incompatible with a well-ordered federal union. The supremacy of a federal government within its proper sphere seems to require the submission of the states to authentic federal power, even if that submission must be procured by military force. On the other hand, a decent respect for the opinion of the people of a state calls for the employment of political rather than military methods to induce a state to accept an appropriate adjustment of a conflict between state and federal interests.

I

How difficult this problem may be of solution is strikingly illustrated in the pending project of a constitution for a European federal union.[1] The constitution study committee of the European Movement, which took the initial lead in working out the details of a federal constitution for a European union, had given this problem careful thought. In their draft submitted to the official Constitutional Assembly there was a provision that, if the government of the union should find that the constitutional order, democratic institutions, or fundamental freedoms had been gravely violated in any member-state, without the established authorities in that state being able or willing to protect or restore them, the union government might intervene until the situation should again become normal. It was further provided that in such a case the measures taken by the union government should be submitted without undue delay for the approval of the union parliament. The intention of these advocates of

European federal union was clear. The union government should have authority to coerce a member state without waiting for the previous advice and consent of the union parliament.

The official Constitutional Assembly was unwilling to accept this proposal. Their draft constitution provided merely that the Federal Executive Council, if it should find coercion to be necessary and proper, could prepare a plan for federal intervention in a member-state, with the advice and consent of the Council of National Ministers, and should submit it to the union parliament for approval. The framers of the draft constitution recognized the importance of the problem of coercion, but were reluctant to approve effective measures for its solution. They were ready to agree that the union government should guarantee the maintenance of constitutional democratic governments in the states. But they were not prepared to authorize the prompt use of force by the government to make that guarantee good except when federal aid should be requested by a state government.

The problem of coercing states in a federal system is more important and urgent in connection with plans for strengthening the United Nations and giving the organization the authority which may be necessary and proper for achieving the high purposes set forth in the preamble of its Charter. The United Nations have already taken an important step toward the achievement of its purposes by adopting the Universal Declaration of Human Rights, thereby establishing what Lincoln happily termed standard maxims for free society. The rights of individuals mark the limits of the power of governments in their dealings with their subjects and a universal declaration of rights gives the sanction of all mankind to the efforts of portions of mankind in particular states to go forward in the development of their civil liberties. But many of the member states of the United Nations are politically backward and their institutions fall far short of what would be required to assure to their peoples the enjoyment of the blessings of the kind of liberty envisaged by the framers of the Universal Declaration of Human Rights. Have the United Nations a responsibility to help the peoples of backward countries in their struggles to compel their governments to show greater respect for their rights, and, if so, what practical measures can they employ to bring about a closer approximation to the established standards of civil liberty?[2] For five years the United Nations Commission on Human Rights has been wrestling with this problem, but up to now all efforts to draft a Covenant of Human Rights, providing for the effective enforcement of the rights asserted in the Universal Declaration, have failed. Agreement upon a plan for coercing backward member states has been impossible.

The United Nations must presently consider other steps toward the achievement of its high purposes, which can hardly be taken without raising similar questions concerning the relations between member states and the general international organization. How can there be any effective limitation of national armaments without some intervention in the arming, training, and disciplining of troops by the governments of member states? How can there be any effective measures against aggression without control over international airways, international waterways, and strategic land routes? Above all, how can there be effective action to keep the peace without adequate means of raising necessary revenues for supporting the proper activities of the United Nations? None of these things can be done without finding a satisfactory method of compelling member states either to take indicated action through their own governments or at least to keep their governments from obstructing necessary action by the United Nations.

II

The coercion of states in a federal system of government, which may be defined provisionally as the use of military force by the general government of the system for the purpose of compelling member states to perform their duties under the constitution of the system, may seem at first thought an essential means of maintaining the system in good working order. If the general government can not compel obedience by the state governments to the laws of the land, above all to the constitution itself, which is presumably the supreme law of the land, how, a reflective observer may ask, can the integrity of the system be preserved? The member states in a federal system possess important powers. Are they not to be held responsible for the exercise of these powers with a due regard for the rights and interests of the other states and also for those of the people of the system as a whole? And how can they be held to an effective responsibility unless the general government can intervene with the force that may be necessary for the faithful execution of its own constitution and laws despite the failure of state governments to do what may be properly required of them?

The framers of federal constitutions have always recognized the existence of this problem. General governments in federal systems possess important powers and must be able to function efficiently if the purposes of such systems are to be realized. The privileges and immunities of citizens of the federal system must be protected and preserved; the rights of member states in their relations with one another must be defended; and the governments of member states must be kept in their proper places. If military force can not be employed by the general government against member states, when apparently necessary for the discharge of its obligations, how shall the federal system be maintained? Is the government of such a system to have responsibilities without adequate powers for their performance?

The discussions of this problem at the meetings of the European Movement's constitution study committee and of the official Constitutional Assembly seem to have covered the theoretical aspects of the problem thoroughly. There is no really satisfactory theoretical solution of the problem. If a federal government possesses a constitutional authority to intervene by force in the government of a state for the purpose of insuring the state's performance of its duties as a member of the federation, there is no adequate constitutional barrier against the conversion of the federation into a centralized state by a vigorous and resolute central government. If it does not possess such authority, there is no adequate assurance that the federal government can maintain the character of the system when vigorous and resolute state governments take full advantage of their constitutional freedom to go their own ways. For a better understanding of the nature of modern federalism it is necessary to turn from theory to experience.

The framers of the Constitution of the United States were well aware of this problem.[3] In the original draft of the Virginia Plan the sixth resolution provided that the national legislature, as its authors described the new body which was to succeed the Continental Congress, should have power "to call forth the force of the Union against any member of the Union failing to fulfill its duty under the articles thereof." This provision of the Plan, which would have authorized the government of the United States to coerce member states by the use of military force, presumably commanded the support of the Virginia delegation at the time of its introduction into the Convention. James Madison, the Plan's principal author, was a persistent advocate of a strong national government and may well have believed at this early stage of the proceedings that military coercion would be an indispensable means of compelling uncooperative states to live up to their obligations under the proposed articles of union. But a few days later, when this resolution came up in the Convention for consideration, Madison moved that it be postponed, observing, according to his own report, that "the more he reflected on the use of force, the more he doubted the practicability, the justice and the efficacy of it, when applied to people collectively and not individually."[4]

Madison had evidently been troubled in his own mind about this feature of the Virginia Plan and was quickly persuaded that the military coercion of states had no proper place in a well-conceived plan for a federal system of government. His "Notes on the Debates" disclose his sober second thoughts on the subject. "A union of states containing such an ingredient," he declared, "seemed to provide for its own destruction." The use of force against a state would look more like a declaration of war than an infliction of punishment; and would probably be considered by the party attacked as a dissolution of all previous compacts by which it might be bound. He hoped, he concluded, "that such a system would be framed as might render this recourse unnecessary." The postponement was agreed to without objection.

What Madison had in mind for the purpose of rendering recourse to the military coercion of states unnecessary became clear a few days later when the provision in the Virginia Plan for a congressional veto upon state legislation came up for consideration in the Convention. Madison declared at once that a congressional negative, as he termed it, on state laws was the proper alternative to military coercion of the states, and was necessary because the latter

was (in his words) "visionary and fallacious." The Convention, however, was
not ready to accept this conclusion. The New Jersey Plan for a more perfect
union, which was prepared shortly thereafter, revived the provision for military coercion. Its sixth resolution proposed that "if any state . . . shall oppose or prevent the carrying into execution of such acts or treaties (that is,
acts or treaties under the authority of the United States), the Federal Executive
shall be authorized to call forth the power of the Confederated States . . .
to enforce and compel obedience. . . ."[5]

This proposal touched off the debate which had been postponed when the
corresponding provision of the Virginia Plan was before the Convention.
Edmund Randolph objected that the kind of coercion proposed by the authors
of the New Jersey Plan was "Impracticable, expensive, cruel to individuals."[6]
George Mason exclaimed that "fire and water themselves are not more incompatible than such a mixture of civil liberty and military execution."[7] Mason was
thoroughly aroused by William Paterson's acknowledgment that the New Jersey
Plan could not be enforced without military coercion. "Rebellion is the only
case," Mason declared, "in which the military force of a state can be properly
exerted against its citizens." Luther Martin presently ended the debate with the
suggestion that "the federal plan of Mr. Paterson did not require coercion any
more than the national one (of the Virginia Planners)."[8] Nothing more was
heard on the floor of the Convention about the military coercion of member
states until weeks later, when Madison tersely observed in another connection
that "the practicability of making laws with coercive sanctions, for the States
as political bodies, had been exploded on all hands."[9] Like the Virginia delegation, the Convention as a whole, on giving the problem careful consideration
concluded that the military coercion of states was out of place in a well-ordered
federal union. But the Convention could not finally accept Madison's alternative of a congressional veto of state legislation. The majority of the delegates
eventually preferred, and Madison and his associates ultimately accepted, the
method of judicial review as that best suited to maintaining the supremacy of
the constitution and laws in a well-framed federal system.

III

How the military coercion of states in a federal system would actually work
in practice was left by all the speakers in the Convention to the imaginations of
the delegates. But there are federal systems where this method of federal execution is deliberately provided for in the written constitutions, and experience dis-
closes the implications of the method. In the Latin American republics of
Argentina, Brazil, and Mexico the framers of the federal constitutions recognized the existence of the problem, which had disturbed the authors of the
Virginia and New Jersey plans at Philadelphia in 1787, and, unlike their
North American precursors, adopted the practice of military coercion as a
regular method of keeping states in their proper places in the federal system.[10]

The North American Constitution indeed does authorize the Congress to provide for calling forth the militia to execute the laws of the Union, suppress insurrections, and repel invasions, and the explicit guarantee of a republican form of government to each state doubtless implies a duty on the part of the federal government to use these or other forces under circumstances which remain conveniently indefinite. But the constitutions of the Latin American federal systems make explicit all, and presumably more than all, that is implicit in the North American system.

The Argentine constitution, for instance, which was drafted by statesmen professing great respect for the principles of the Constitution of the United States, and obviously trying to introduce those principles into their own country, offers an instructive comparison with the North American model. The central government of the Argentine Republic is expressly authorized by this constitution to intervene in the provinces in order to guarantee the republican form of government, and also when requested by the provincial authorities, in order to maintain them in power, or to restore them to office, if they shall have been deposed by sedition or by invasion from another province.[11] The use of the expression "to intervene" suggests a wider latitude of discretion on the part of the Argentine central authorities than was deemed necessary or proper by the framers of the Constitution of the United States. The record shows that in fact the power of federal intervention in the provinces has undergone what must seem to North Americans an astonishing development. Combined with the power to declare a state of siege in cases of domestic disturbance, it has enabled the central authorities, particularly the President, to intervene in provincial politics to an extent that has profoundly affected the nature of the federal system.

The procedure of intervention is for the President, having determined that the republican form of government in a province has been subverted or is threatened with subversion, to appoint a federal commissioner and supply him with sufficient force to establish his authority in the province. This is done with the approval of the Congress if it is in session; otherwise on the President's own responsibility. The commissioner may, and usually does, supplant the governor and legislature of the province and sometimes also the judges, restores or maintains order, holds fresh elections, inaugurates a new and more satisfactory government, and then makes his final report to the President. In the eighty years following the final establishment of the Argentine federal system in 1860 there were one hundred twenty-nine cases of federal intervention in the provinces.[12] None escaped, and most were subjected to federal intervention many times. In forty-six cases federal intervention was authorized by the Congress, but in a large majority of the cases the President acted on his sole responsibility.

The frequency of federal intervention has increased in the present century. President Irigoyen, who was responsible for twenty-two interventions during his first term of six years, frankly employed the power for the purpose of strengthening the position of the Liberal Party, which he headed, in the provinces. General Uriburu, who intervened in twelve provinces (all of which then possessed Liberal Party governments) within a week after his seizure of power on behalf of the Conservatives, was equally frank in his employment of this political weapon for partisan purposes. It was not always necessary for the provincial government to be actually threatened with subversion. It was enough that the President desired to have the government of a province subverted in order to replace political opponents with his own followers.

The practice of federal intervention in Argentina can be understood only as an incident in the operation of the Argentine system of party government. The practical capacity of a President to carry on the government of the country is of course, as in the United States, partly a function of his own personality. But in a country as far advanced as Argentina on the road to effective constitutional government, the management of the Congress by the President can not be satisfactorily accomplished by open violence or thinly veiled intimidation. It has been found more acceptable, under what may perhaps be described as normal circumstances, to gain a dominating influence over the Congress by collusion with the provincial governors and manipulation of the provincial elections. If the provincial governors are not sufficiently cooperative, a federal intervention can be arranged. The resulting party system is doubtless more personal than that in the United States, but clearly more political and less militaristic than that in many Latin American countries.

In Brazil also federal intervention is closely connected with the operation of the party system.[13] The Brazilian party system resembles the Argentine in many respects, though no single Brazilian state stands out above the others like the province of Buenos Aires in Argentina. In Brazil there are two leading states which contend with one another for primacy in national politics, and as long as each is willing to share the control of the national government with the other, successful presidential leadership under the forms of party government faces a similar problem of aligning a majority of the lesser states, and consequently of the Congress also, with the presidential party. While the gauchos and the landed oligarchy in general maintained their class ascendancy in the politics of these two federal republics, the system of party government served tolerably well to reconcile the practice of personal dictatorship with the fiction of constitutional government without too much open resort to military force. But in recent years the growth of urban industry, modern capitalism, and a class-conscious proletariat has complicated the traditional pattern of party government and opened the way for the demagogic dictatorships of Vargas and Peron.

In both Argentina and Brazil the practice of federal intervention is associated with the use of the state of siege as instruments of executive leadership in the systems of government. The authors of the Brazilian Constitution of 1891 were greatly influenced by the Argentine Constitution of 1853 as well as by that of the United States, and in both countries the intention was clear to make the presidency a more powerful office than had been deemed prudent by the North American founding fathers. By a declaration of a state of siege the President can suspend the personal rights guaranteed by both the federal and state constitutions with the consent of the Congress, if it happens to be in session, or otherwise without it. Thus alleged threats to the republican form of government in a province or a state or to the peaceful execution of federal laws anywhere enable the chief executive to intervene at discretion (subject to the approval of the Congress, when in session) and to assert his personal authority in a state or locality by such display of force as may be necessary until fresh elections, conducted under the supervision of his own agents, confirm the ascendency of his partisans. A Vargas or a Peron can connive at the creation of circumstances, particularly when their Congresses are not in session, which can be made to appear to justify excessively arbitrary and tyrannical proceedings on their part, and yet in countries so far advanced on the road toward stable governments of law and not of men, as Americans like to say, public opinion imposes no inconsiderable limits on the discretionary authority even of such masterful or, perhaps it should be said, domineering leaders.

IV

Supreme Court judges, both in Argentina and in Brazil, have studied the North American precedents and shown much interest in such significant cases as *Luther vs. Borden* and *Texas vs. White*.[14] The distinction between justiciable and political questions, which afforded much comfort to United States Supreme Court judges reluctant to clash with the political arms of the government in dealing with Dorr's anaemic rebellion in Rhode Island, was manifestly insufficient to afford guidance to their hard-pressed successors, when trying to deal with the much more difficult problems growing out of the far greater rebellion which broke out in South Carolina in 1861. Constitutional lawyers in the United States tend to ignore the problems which were left unsettled by the Supreme Court during the period of Civil War and Reconstruction, as if the uniqueness of the occasion excused their refusal to face the lessons of the experience. Constitutional lawyers in the two greatest Latin American republics lack the same pretext for ignoring the implications of these decisions. The historic importance of the relations between the military and civil authorities in these federal republics, on the contrary, caused them to make the most of the North American precedents.

The case of *Luther vs. Borden*[15] was comparatively simple. Political reformers in Rhode Island grew impatient with the resistance of backward-looking politicians in power in that state to the democratic trend of the times and appealed from the verdict of elections under the ancient state constitution to the arbitrament of arms. Neither of the parties had any heart for hard fighting, both preferring the rule of law under the federal Constitution. The question was, what did the federal constitutional guarantee of a republican form of government to the states require of the federal government under the circumstances? Was the federal government bound to secure for the embattled Rhode Islanders the blessings of a democratic republic in accordance with the spirit of the age, or must it prevent changes in an established form of state government except by political methods, even though the authorized method under the old state constitution was so undemocratic as to defeat the will of a majority of the people of the state?

Most of the Supreme Court judges at the time were, or had been, Jacksonian Democrats, but they showed little of Jackson's readiness to shoulder responsibility or of his fondness for combat. Their refusal to say what was a republican form of government necessarily left to the political branches of the federal government the responsibility for determining what the constitutional guarantee required of the federal government, and the convenient distinction between a political and a justiciable question served to cover their negative attitude with a garment of respectability. An Andrew Jackson in the White House might have found a way to decide such a political question. The man in the White House happened to be John Tyler, who was no Jacksonian Democrat and even less inclined than the Supreme Court judges to mingle in a quarrel not of his own choosing. Congress was permitted to decide the question by the simple expedient of not challenging the title to seats of the Senators and Representatives from Rhode Island who had been elected under the authority of the established state government.

Abraham Lincoln was neither an Andrew Jackson nor a John Tyler, and the Supreme Court judges who owed their appointments to him were also men of different temper from most of those who happened to be sitting on the high court at the time of Dorr's rebellion. History has chosen to call the rebellion with which Lincoln had to deal by an equivocal name, and in recent years the public taste has even seemed to favor the acceptance of the Southern term for the Civil War, doubtless out of consideration for the feelings of the vanquished, since there is no better reason for calling it the War between the States. Lincoln himself never conceded that he was waging a war against any of the states, preferring at first to regard his warlike activities as no more than necessary and proper measures for discharging his duty to take care that the laws of the United States be faithfully executed. Later he was forced to consider what measures he should adopt to reestablish state governments in areas where resistance to federal laws had resulted in the disappearance of state governments able and willing to perform the duties of such governments under the federal Constitution.

Lincoln showed great indifference to what he considered to be nonessentials in developing a policy for the reconstruction of state governments in the South. He saw no need to decide whether the Southern ordinances of secession had taken the southern states out of the union or not. He was satisfied to find men in those states ready and willing to operate state governments under the federal Constitution, when he was able to give them the necessary protection against violent interference by the misguided individuals who were resisting the authority of federal laws. He did not deny that there might be other ways of insuring domestic tranquillity in the sorely troubled union than that contemplated by his reconstruction policy, but he did insist that he was entitled to try his method until some other was provided by law. And he did not hesitate to use the pocket veto in order to frustrate the effort of Congress to make a law which would provide a different and in his opinion less promising method.

Under Lincoln's less politic and less effective successor Congress forced the adoption of its own method of reconstruction. *Luther vs. Borden* seemed to justify action of some kind by the Congress for the purpose of making good the guarantee of a republican form of government in the southern states, but there was difference of opinion concerning the constitutionality of the particular means employed by the Congress for this purpose. Congress did what it could by the use of its power to regulate the appellate jurisdiction of the Supreme Court to prevent the judges from treating this constitutional question as justiciable and thus settling, if able, the validity of the congressional method of reconstruction. But Congress could not prevent the Supreme Court from deciding, if it wished, the great, though not completely conclusive, case of *Texas vs. White*.[16] A majority of the Supreme Court, including a majority but no more than a majority of the judges appointed by Lincoln, held that the question was justiciable and that the federal union was an indestructible union of indestructible states.

This decision clearly justified what Lincoln had done toward reconstructing the union but it left persistent doubt concerning the constitutionality of some of the later actions of the Congress. More than two-thirds of the Senators and Representatives in the Congress presumably believed that what they did for the purpose of reconstructing the union was within their constitutional power, since they passed the Reconstruction Act over the presidential veto. If the question was a political one, as the judges in *Luther vs. Borden* seemed to have conceded, Congress had acted within its rights. A noncooperative President, such as Johnson, had only himself to blame if he could not make the Congress accept his views concerning the proper distribution of power between the President and the Congress under the section of the Constitution which guarantees a republican form of government to the states. Practical people are content to leave unsettled what can not be conveniently settled if the achievement of their major objectives is not obstructed thereby. The constitutional question could be regarded as closed by subsequent generations in the reconstructed union. But Latin Americans, living under different political conditions in their federal unions, could not be so easily satisfied with the official interpretation of the great North American model constitution.

The judicial theory of the process of reconstruction, set forth by the majority of the Supreme Court in *Texas vs. White,* was formally challenged by the dissenting judges. One of them, Justice Grier, had been a Jacksonian Democrat and later a member of the majority of the Court in the great case of *Dred*

Scott vs. Sandford.[17] He was an active participant in the intrigue that led President Buchanan to connive at the judicial effort to take the problem of slavery in the territories out of politics by denying the power of Congress to make the Missouri Compromise. Grier regarded himself as a judicial and political realist and, viewing the actual condition of the South under the congressional policy of reconstruction realistically, he concluded that the major-generals in command of the military forces, occupying the administrative regions into which the South had been divided in pursuance of the Reconstruction Act of March 2, 1867, were the dominating facts in the situation and that the assumed existence of the southern states was a meaningless fiction. This was a view of the process of reconstruction after the Civil War which could be readily understood by Argentinian and Brazilian judges and politicians, although presidents in the Argentinian and Brazilian federal unions were likely to be more successful in the management of congresses than hapless Andrew Johnson, and consequently the distribution of power between the presidents and the congresses in cases of federal intervention in the provinces and states was likely to take a different form than in the United States.

The two other dissenting judges in *Texas vs. White,* Justices Swayne and Miller, were Union Republicans. They concurred in the judgment of the Supreme Court in *Texas vs. White,* but were dissatisfied with Chief Justice Chase's opinion. Though they did not take the trouble to set forth a systematic and comprehensive statement of their own theory of reconstruction, it is evident that they thought Chase had said either too much or too little. He could have disposed of the case before the Court without propounding the theory that the union was an indestructible union of indestructible states. He could not have disposed of the widespread doubts concerning the validity of the process of congressional reconstruction without analyzing further the nature of the constitutional guarantee of a republican form of government to the states which were or had been members of the union. If Swayne and Miller could have persuaded a majority of the Court to adopt their view of the nature of this guarantee, they would presumably have written an opinion designed to dispel the existing doubts concerning the constitutionality of the congressional policy of reconstruction. Be that as it may, the result of the decision was to leave the full significance of the guarantee of a republican form of government judicially undetermined. This has happily been no serious inconvenience to the people of the United States. The precedent, however, has been duly noted in the Latin American federal unions and has doubtless encouraged to some extent the tendency there for politicians to make the most of the distinction between justiciable and political questions.

V

In the Latin American federal unions federal intervention in the government of the provinces and states has provided a method of virtually coercing the provincial and state governments. One result has been to bring about a greater degree of centralization in the government of the federal unions themselves than was presumably intended by the framers of the union constitutions. Another has been to supply a great deal of evidence tending to confirm the opinion of the framers of the United States Constitution that the coercion of states by military force is a practice to be avoided in the interest of domestic tranquillity. In the United States Lincoln's theory—that the central government, in its use of force to insure domestic tranquillity, deals only with individuals who resist the authority of the nation's laws and does not recognize the existence of the governments such persons may claim to represent in the course of their unlawful resistance to its authority—has been tacitly accepted as authentic. How far the political branches of the central government may go in protecting the union against the subversive acts of such individuals is a political question which future Presidents and Congresses will have to decide, if and when circumstances require such decisions.

This traditional reluctance to coerce states by forcible federal intervention in the affairs of their governments, rather than the theoretical distinction between justiciable and political questions, has limited the role of the judiciary in the adjustment of interstate controversies.[18] In general the Supreme Court of the United States has made an excellent record in the adjudication of interstate controversies when the controversies have been of such a nature that the judgments of the Court could be executed by proceedings against individuals. This has been true even in those cases where the individuals were state officials, provided that the execution of the judgment has not required a positive act by an official but merely that he refrain from action objectionable to the Court. The record has not been so good, however, in cases where the execution of a judgment would have required positive action by state officials, particularly in cases where the officials were elective officers, above all governors and legislators. In such cases, uncertainty concerning the possibility of compelling state officers to take the action desired by the Supreme Court has seemed to constrain the Court to act rather as an instrument of mediation and conciliation than as a true judicial body.

The most impressive illustration of this self-imposed limitation upon judicial power is the long series of suits brought by Virginia against West Virginia in order to force the latter to assume its proper portion of the Virginia state debt as it stood at the time of the separation between the two states.[19] Nine times Virginia appeared before the Supreme Court before the controversy was settled. In the course of the proceedings the Court successively decided that West Virginia ought to assume a fair portion of the debt, determined what the portion was, asserted that it had authority to enforce the satisfaction of Virginia's just claim against West Virginia, and announced that it would listen to arguments concerning the method of enforcing its judgment, whether by seizing and selling property belonging to the State of West Virginia, levying a tax upon its people, or issuing bonds in its name and paying over the proceeds to the State of Virginia. Repeatedly in successive stages of the litigation the Court postponed action on the ground that it could not assume a self-respecting state would persistently refuse to discharge its just obligation to another state, but each postponement was followed after an interval by a fresh appearance on the part of Virginia before the Court with a fresh plea that West Virginia had done nothing to justify further delay.

Eventually, more than half a century after the original separation between the states, the Court was able to postpone hearing arguments concerning the method of enforcing its judgment on the ground that such a proceeding was not proper in a suit between states at a time when the United States was engaged in a foreign war of such magnitude as World War I. At last the Court's patience and forbearance was rewarded by an agreement between the states which rendered further judicial proceedings unnecessary. The outcome may be acclaimed as a triumph for the Court in its self-assumed role as a mediator and conciliator of interstate controversies, but the question still remains judicially undetermined how a judgment against a state involving a large pecuniary payment to another state is to be executed if the government of the debtor state fails to make a timely settlement with its creditor in accordance with the decision of the Court.

In the recent case of *Dyer vs. Sims,* in which West Virginia was again involved in a controversy over the payment of money to meet an. interstate obligation, the Supreme Court showed more confidence in its practical capacity to get its judgment faithfully executed.[20] In this case a West Virginia state auditor had blocked the payment of a share of the expenses of the Ohio River Valley Water Sanitation Commission, assessed against that state, on the pretext that the compact itself, under which the agency was operating, was one which the state government had no right to make under the state constitution, and the West Virginia Supreme Court had declared that the auditor had construed the state constitution correctly. All the other Ohio River Valley states, which were parties to the compact, were interested in the outcome of the case, although the proceedings took the form of a suit by an officer of the Commission against the West Virginia auditor and was brought originally in the West Virginia courts. Ordinarily the United States Supreme Court would accept the construction put upon a state constitution by the highest state court, and in this case it might have been supposed that the federal Supreme Court judges would have hesitated to involve themselves in a controversy with such high officers of a state government as the members of the state Supreme Court over the interpretation of its own constitution. The United States Supreme Court decided unanimously, however, that West Virginia should pay its share of the expenses of the water purification district though the judges were unable to agree upon the reasons for the decision.

In this case circumstances strongly favored the federal judiciary in any clash of authority with the state government over the enforcement of its judgment. The case had originally been brought in the name of individuals so as to camouflage the conflict of interests between different states, and the government of West Virginia did not present a united front in the proceedings, since the state legislature had originally approved the compact and presumably believed that it was not beyond its power to do so. Nevertheless the dignity of the state was involved by the action of its Supreme Court, and the legislature might have made an issue out of the reversal by the federal Supreme Court of the state court's interpretation of its own constitution. Perhaps the magnitude of the political issue was obscured by the triviality of the financial obligation actually involved in the litigation. Perhaps the myth of state sovereignty had lost so much of its earlier potency that state politicians were no longer interested in challenging undramatic federal encroachments on the traditional reserved powers of the states. Be that as it may, the United States Supreme Court made its decision without hesitation and the state of West Virginia accepted the result without resistance.

In general the distinction between justiciable and political questions seems to lose importance as a weapon in the struggle between federal and state power with the decline of the myth of state sovereignty in this neotechnical age. Popular acceptance of the judgments of the federal courts becomes easier in cases where state interests or state pride may be involved. Federal judges may still plead nonjusticiability in cases involving the processes of constitutional amendment and of congressional reapportionment and redistricting, but apparently they now face most of the issues that are presented to them without giving much, if any, thought to the problem of coercing states which might be reluctant to accept their decisions. Certainly the combination of politicians to bring about a reversal of the federal courts' decisions in the submerged oil lands cases shows that there is plenty of vitality in the fiction of state sovereignty in cases where important interests are involved. But important interests, as these cases plainly disclose, will appeal from the judicial power to the political when the audacity of the proceeding appears to be justified by the size of the stakes. Politicians, like judges, seem inclined under the changing conditions of modern times to pay less heed than formerly to the distinction between justiciable and political issues, and the national politicians with a growing sense of competence venture to assume responsibility for the settlement of controversies which in earlier years would have been left to the politicians of the particular states most directly concerned.

VI

Under the changed conditions the principal agent of coercion, if a state must be compelled to yield to the opinion of the nation, is the national political party. Political issues, as distinguished from justiciable ones, are issues over which people will fight, but in a constitutional state the fighting will be kept on the plane where political parties wage their contests for control of a government without recourse to physical force or violence. In ordinary matters which judges find to be within their competence their decisions will be accepted without protest even if important state interests are involved, and the protection of the legitimate interests of the states, like that of the United States, becomes a normal function of the federal courts. In extraordinary cases, where the courts might feel competent to act, the party politicians may choose to operate under the impulse of the normal political motives, and federal intervention in what might be regarded by state interests as an affair of the state takes the form of a campaign for federal legislation. But the national political parties are themselves federations of state factions, and the nature of such parties imposes natural limits upon the practical capacity of national politicians to take effective action. The relations between the parties and the judiciary are absorbed into the general system of checks and balances. A serviceable equilibrium seems to be maintained.

These tendencies in the development of the American federal system are well illustrated by the treatment of the freedmen after the Civil War. Old-fashioned federalism would have left the protection of the civil rights of the freedmen to the state governments. A much more nationalistic type of federalism might have insisted upon a new and more elaborate definition of the republican form of government which would have prevented the reconstructed southern states from resuming their place in the union until the equality of the freedmen before the laws of the states, and in the practical administration of the laws as well, had been secured to the satisfaction of the dominant party in the national government. The Fourteenth Amendment supplied an answer to the problem of reconstruction which held fast to a middle way. The authority of the Congress and the President to treat the interpretation of the constitutional guarantee of a republican form of government to each state as a purely political question was radically restricted.

Instead of a partisan political definition of the meaning of the words "republican form of government" there was an attempt to define in the Constitution itself the rights of freedmen on the same basis as the rights of other persons who were or might become citizens of the United States. Thus the actual determination of the rights of the freedmen might be transformed from a political into a justiciable question. In fact the federal courts were reluctant to assume this responsibility until the passage of time and the improvement in the economic and social condition of the Negroes gradually brought about a better adjustment between the ways of life of the two races. The Supreme Court refused to construe the privileges and immunities of citizens of the United States in such a way as to disturb the slow natural process of adjustment.[21] It put enough meaning into the new guarantees of personal rights to keep the racial question out of national politics, but not enough to freeze any temporary nonpolitical adjustment into a permanent relationship.

Eventually the climate of opinion moderated to the point where national party leaders began again to talk about a settlement of the racial problem by national legislation, but meanwhile the judges were at last handing down

decisions in the course of ordinary litigation between individuals which promised to make the guarantee of due process of law an acceptable substitute for an
interpretation of the guarantee of the privileges and immunities of citizenship
which would secure for the descendants of the slaves a position equal to that
of free white men in the American republic. What neither the force of arms nor
the more subtle coercion of political leaders at the head of national parties
had been able to accomplish, the federal courts are gradually bringing to pass
by the creation of an ever-broadening series of precedents.[22] The episode
records the working of an important principle of political science. When in the
fullness of time a political question becomes justiciable, the problem of coercing states in a federal union loses its importance so far as that particular
question is concerned. Until that time is reached, American experience suggests that what politicians can not readily achieve by the political techniques
of compromise and pacific adjustment had better be left undone unless the tension of unadjusted controversy threatens to provoke conflicts fatal to the
existence of the federal union itself.

If the Latin American federal unions seem indifferent to this lesson of
North American political experience, the answer is not obscure. There is a
larger problem than that of coercing the members of a federal union with
which their statesmen have to deal. That is the problem of maintaining the
supremacy of the civil authorities over the military. The experience of modern
times offers no better solution for this problem than the organization of political
parties strong enough to command the respect of generals as well as the support
of voters. Whether there be two major parties or a larger number seems to be
less important than that there be free competition between parties for the favor
of the public. A monopolistic position for a single party offers little promise of
a solution of the problem unless the party so conducts its affairs as to assure
that the powers which it ostensibly exercises in the name of the people are
actually exercised with their unconstrained and ungrudging consent. The monolithic party states of our times have not yet demonstrated that this can be done.

The experience of modern federal systems everywhere seems to show that
the two problems, that of guaranteeing a republican form of government to the
member-states and fundamental freedoms to their peoples and that of preserving the supremacy of the civil authorities over the military, are closely related.
There are two ways of dealing with the latter problem. One is to keep the military power weak, which was the American way for many years. The other is to
make the civil power strong. This means more than the elaboration of schemes
on paper for the distribution of powers among the various agencies within the
system. It means the political education of the people and also the strengthening of the social classes which have the most to gain from the preservation of a
reign of law instead of a government of men. In modern democracies, these
classes are the middle classes.

American experience makes one political principle clear. The best instrument of a politically intelligent people is a well-developed party system, capable

of stimulating the enterprise of politicians content to rule under the law and of maintaining free competition between them. The free enterprise system in politics is the best answer to the schemes of political regimentation so energetically but unwisely pressed upon the nations in recent years by false friends of mankind. If there must be coercion, the answer offered by Abraham Lincoln is still the world's best answer to the basic problem. Let coercion be confined to the coercion of individuals in the name of the law, and let the process, so far as is humanly possible, be judicial rather than militaristic.

VII

The practical operation of the federal systems of the United States and leading Latin American republics seems to show that the political theorists in the European Movement's constitution study committee, who prepared the first draft of a federal constitution for "Little Europe," possessed a less realistic understanding of the proper role of force in a federal union than the more experienced politicians who dominated the proceedings in the official Constitutional Assembly which revised the first draft. The essential character of a federal union seems to be better protected when sharp conflicts of interest between the central and state governments are reserved for adjustment by strictly political methods than when they are exposed to attempts at settlement by military force. Force may be properly exerted against lawless individuals, but in a true federation has no proper place in determining the relations between the union government and member-states unless there is violent aggression by one or more of them against others. Even if the lawless individuals happen to be the chief officers of a state, American experience shows that they should be dealt with as individuals rather than as spokesmen for a state, if the federal union is to retain its essential character. Violation of this principle of federal politics threatens the destruction of the federation, either by converting it into a centralized state or by bringing about its dissolution.

It may be argued that this principle of federal politics is not applicable to the proposed constitution for "Little Europe," since in any case that instrument of government does not provide for a true federal union. To those who make this argument it may be conceded that the draft constitution approved by the official Constitutional Assembly left the character of the proposed federal union in doubt, because of the powers of obstruction reserved to the Council of National Ministers representing the governments of the member-states. Doubtless the position of the union government needs to be strengthened if the advantages of a federal system are to be fully realized. But the effort should not be made to strengthen the proposed union government by authorizing military intervention with the governments of member-states at the discretion of the union government. It is the legislative authority of the union parliament, not the military power of the executive, that needs strengthening if the proposed European union is to be a genuine federal union.

More important perhaps is the applicability of this principle of federal politics to plans for strengthening the Charter of the United Nations. It is difficult to believe that this immature agency of international politics can become a satisfactory instrument of the common purposes of mankind without being transformed into a genuine federal union of peace-loving states. Acceptable arrangements for the limitation of national armaments and the preservation of international peace depend upon the grant of suitable law-making powers to a general international organization. But authority to coerce member-states by military force is neither a necessary nor a proper means of maintaining the supremacy of a universal federal union within its legitimate sphere. The principle that guilt is personal must be embodied in the scheme of federal union, even when the persons concerned happen to be officers of member-states. The object of international police actions must be restricted to the coercion of lawless individuals; the actions themselves are rightly distinguished from anachronistic wars against states. In this respect the proceedings in Korea have been in line with the sound development of a universal federal union.

The problem of coercing member-states in a federal system will arise in a new form in connection with the general review of the United Nations Charter, which will be in order in 1955. Advocates of the greater use of political instead of military methods for the settlement of international controversies will doubtless urge at that time the strengthening of the United Nations. The simplest and surest way to bring about a greater use of political methods in the settlement of international controversies is to grant to the organization suitable legislative powers. The vesting of legislative powers in the United Nations General Assembly and Security Council, or in new agencies created for the purpose of exercising such powers, will form a more perfect union of the nations constituting a genuine federal system with limited but important law-making authority. The question will have to be faced, to what extent shall the member-nations be employed as agents of the union, and how shall they be compelled to perform the duties which may be imposed upon them?

This is not a new problem for the statesmen of the United Nations. Already the adoption of a Universal Declaration of Human Rights by the United Nations General Assembly has raised the question, what shall be done to secure the enjoyment of these rights by the peoples of different member-nations? Shall each member-nation be free to pay as much or as little respect to the articles of this international bill of rights as it pleases? If so, it is easy to imagine that among the sixty member-nations, with their widely various traditions and practices in such matters as the legal relations between the individual and the state, there will be not a few which will give slight attention to the enforcement of these hard-won, and in many parts of the world up to now little honored, rights. The Universal Declaration might eventually acquire under such circumstances an uncertain moral force, but it would remain without legal effect in the member-nations whose law-makers might choose to ignore it.

The United Nations Commission on Human Rights has sought to avoid such an unsatisfactory result by drafting a Covenant of Human Rights which would provide legal sanctions for the proclaimed rights of mankind. The ratification of the proposed Covenant by a member-nation would create an obligation towards other member-nations which might likewise ratify the Covenant to transform an ideal standard of human relations into an enforceable body of laws. But what if a member-nation should neglect to enforce these laws and its people should be thereby denied the enjoyment of the proclaimed rights of mankind? Will the United Nations have guaranteed the substance, if not the form, of a democratic republican government to the peoples of the member-nations who become bound by the Covenant? What, if anything, shall it do to enforce the provisions of the Covenant?

The Commission on Human Rights, though possessing in its membership legal and political talent of a high order, has been unable to find an acceptable solution of its problem. It is evident that the problem can not be solved without vesting important law-making powers in the United Nations. The United Nations, following the example of the United States with its first federal bill of rights, might make a modest beginning in the enforcement of such rights by restricting their application to the relations between individuals and the United Nations itself, leaving for a time the application of its provisions to the relations between individuals and their respective national governments to the discretion of these national governments. This was the status of the fundamental freedoms proclaimed in the American Declaration of Independence down to the adoption of the Fourteenth Amendment to the federal Constitution after the Civil War. Though this forbearance on the part of the federal government to interfere in the domestic affairs of the states did not prevent the war, it certainly eased the way for the gradual development of a sense of loyalty to the union which made its survival and ultimate strengthening possible.

In general the statesmen of the United Nations may be expected to go ahead deliberately with proposals for granting legislative powers to the infant organization. To assume obligations such as the Latin American federal unions have assumed for maintaining the republican form of government in their member-states means an amount of interference with the governments of the member-nations which would make for less rather than greater tranquillity in the contemporary world. The more modest responsibilities assumed by the government of the United States respecting preservation of basic human rights in the states furnish a more suitable model for the builders of the new federal system with limited powers which, it may be hoped, will emerge from the deliberations of the United Nations statesmen in the years immediately ahead. The right principle of coercion is the Lincolnian. The true function of the government of a successful general international organization is to keep the peace by keeping individuals in their proper places rather than by trying to coerce member-states.

FOOTNOTES TO CHAPTER 9

1. See Constitutional Committee of the *Ad Hoc* Assembly. Draft Treaty embodying the Statute of the European Community. Published by the Secretariat of the Constitutional Committee, Paris, 1953. See also *Mouvement Européen Comité d'Etudes pour la Constitution Européenne. Parallele entre le Project de Traité adopté par l'Assemblée "Ad Hoc" et le Projet de Statut établi par le Comité d'Etudes pour la Constitution Européenne. Bruxelles, 1953.*

2. See Hersh Lauterpacht, *International Law and Human Rights,* New York, F. B. Praeger, 1950.

3. See 69th Congress, 1st Session, House Document No. 398. *Documents Illustrative of the Formation of the Union of the American States.* Washington, U. S. Govt. Printing Office, 1927, p. 117.

4. *Ibid.,* p. 131; see also pp. 174–5.

5. *Ibid.,* p. 207.

6. *Ibid.,* p. 214.

7. *Ibid.,* p. 244.

8. *Ibid.,* p. 246.

9. *Ibid.,* p. 380.

10. Argentine Constitution of 1853, Articles 4, 23, 67, 86; Brazilian Constitution of 1891, Articles 6, 24, 48, 80; Mexican Constitution of 1857, Article 29.

11. L. S. Rowe, *The Federal System of the Argentine Republic,* Washington, Carnegie Institution, 1921. See especially Chapter VII, "Principles and Practice of Federal Intervention."

12. Austin F. MacDonald, *The Government of the Argentine Republic,* New York, Crowell, 1942. See especially Chapter IX, "Federal Intervention."

13. Herman G. James, *The Constitutional System of Brazil,* Washington, Carnegie Institution, 1923.

14. Santos P. Amadeo, *Argentine Constitutional Law. The Judicial Function in the Maintenance of the Federal System and the Preservation of Individual Rights.* New York, Columbia University Press, 1943. See especially Part II, "Division of Powers in the Federal System," Chapter IV.

15. 7 Howard 1 (U.S. 1849).

16. 7 Wallace 700 (U.S. 1868).

17. 19 Howard 393 (U.S. 1857).

18. A. N. Holcombe, *Our More Perfect Union,* Cambridge, Harvard University Press, 1950, Chapter XI, "The Supreme Court and the States," pp. 389–394.

19. Virginia v. West Virginia, 246 U.S. 565 (1918).

20. 341 U.S. 22 (1951).

21. The Slaughterhouse Cases, 16 Wallace 36 (U.S. 1873).

22. Sweatt v. Painter, 339 U. S. 629 (1950); McLaurin v. Oklahoma State Regents, 339 U. S. 637 (1950); Brown v. Board of Education of Topeka and companion cases, 347 U. S. 483 (1954).

SECTION TWO

THE COURTS AND THE LAW

10

Umpiring the Federal System

By Paul A. Freund

It is a commonplace that the great divisive contests in American history
have been played out across the boards, as it were, of the Supreme Court.
There, as in the sublimation of a morality play, have passed in review before
a tribunal of authoritative critics the dramatic conflicts over slavery, the contest between land and water transportation, the struggle of industrial competition against the forces of concentration, the clashing interests of workers,
consumers, and investors, and the claims of dissenting groups and individuals. A federal system presupposes diversity and must cope with corresponding tensions. Does it assume also a judiciary vested with the role of arbiter?

I

THE ROLE OF THE COURT

The Anglo-American tradition has accustomed us to identifying with judges
the task of constitutional arbitration. Elsewhere, however, the practice has
not been standardized. The example of Switzerland reminds us that a federation, while entrusting review of state authority to a national judiciary, may
reserve for the people the function of deciding whether a national law is consistent with the constitution. The French Constitution of 1946 suggests another
device which might be adapted to a federation; it establishes a Constitutional
Committee, elected in part by the National Assembly at the beginning of each
annual session, to which is confided the task of determining whether the laws
passed by the National Assembly require amendment of the Constitution. The
contemporary Constitution of Yugoslavia, inverting the practice whereby a
government may seek from the judiciary a constitutional decision, authorizes
the Federal Supreme Court to apply to the Federal People's Assembly for a
decision on the conformity of federal laws with the Federal Constitution.[1] Thus
is the rule of law accommodated to the environment of this or that brand of
democracy. In the United States the Senate might have been employed as an
arbiter of constitutional disputes between states and nation, as Madison tentatively suggested,[2] but such a role would very probably have intensified the

159

identification of the Senate with local interests. From this point of view an important function of the judiciary is to relieve the legislators of the task of resolving conflicts between local power and national concern—a task which might have been felt to call for a duty of insularity.

Even in the United States, however, the conflicts between localism and centralism are by no means resolved wholly by the apparatus of judicial review. It is part of our political theory that each department of the government has responsibility in the first instance for interpreting and applying the Constitution as a limitation on its own action. The President's use of the veto on constitutional grounds, if not overridden by Congress, will foreclose the courts from receiving the question of constitutional law. Congress, moreover, enjoys considerable authority over the jurisdiction of the federal courts, which it can exercise to cut off the appellate jurisdiction of the Supreme Court, as it did in the Reconstruction era,[3] or to place limits on the jurisdiction of the lower federal courts.[4]

Furthermore, on interstate commercial relations Congress can overturn a judgment of the Court under the interstate commerce clause by announcing a judgment of its own on the question whether the subject requires uniformity of regulation, if any is undertaken, or permits diversity of treatment.[5] Similarly, Congress can waive the immunity of its agencies from state taxation or may, within limits, confer an immunity that the courts would not by themselves have recognized.[6] The recent legislation following the decision on offshore oil deposits testifies to the assumed authority of Congress to yield to the states what in the judgment of the Court belonged to the nation.[7] Many an interstate bone of contention is amicably divided under compacts between the states with the assent of Congress—in lieu of submission to the process of litigation. And in the crucial area of fiscal relations the leverage exerted by a federal grant-in-aid or a federal tax mitigated by a conditional credit may determine the balance of state and national functions and promote a degree of uniformity quite outside the framework of the judicial process. While the Court may be called upon to pass on the scheme's legitimacy, the particular provisions of the plan will be determined by political forces responding to economic pressures, whether in matters of inheritance taxation or unemployment insurance or loans and grants for municipal hydro-electric plants.[8] The overwhelming effect of the federal taxing power and its supremacy is pointed up by the recent experience of Australia and to some extent of Canada, where federal-state fiscal relations have resolved themselves into round-table bargaining for federal funds.[9] Although this experience has been less extreme with us, it does point to at least a potential truth in the observation of Karl Loewenstein that "A state with a federal income tax is no longer a genuinely federal state."[10]

The role of the judiciary is limited not only by the resourcefulness of other branches of government but also by the complexes of private power that lie outside the framework of constitutional limitations. Whether we are to enjoy a free national market, as the commerce clause envisaged, depends as much upon the practices of business enterprise as upon the governmental acts of member states. While a state may not by legislative fiat permit its commercial resources to be developed for local enjoyment and forbid their export to other states,[11] the Constitution is silent and neutral on the power of private groups thus to restrict the market. The Constitution reflects an eighteenth century faith in economic liberalism. In this sense Professor Loewenstein is right in stating: "Federalism is a product of liberal thinking. It applied the (relative) freedom of the individual to the (relative) freedom of organization of territorial entities. It thrives as long as a free economy thrives. Speaking again sententiously: Economic planning is the DDT of federalism."[12]

But this is only to say that economic relations are in large part outside the province of those self-executing constitutional mandates which can be enforced solely through judicial control. These relations are remitted to the legislative power, so that the Sherman Act has become as important to the maintenance of the free national market as the commerce clause. Moreover, the implication that economic control is synonymous with centralization is not quite true. In more than one segment of the economy we have employed the resources of cooperative federalism to integrate local planning with national policy. The federal "hot oil" statute which forbids the interstate shipment of oil produced in excess of state quotas is an example;[13] another is the federal assistance given to the state-controlled marketing of the raisin crop in California.[14] Our concern with these devices is that, once the general pattern is validated by the Court, the structure and balance of forces, both private and public, which shape the federal system are left to the working of politics. Thus the courts may be conceived as umpires determining what kinds of contests are permissible, leaving the choice of contests and the detailed rules to be worked out by the immediate participants.

With these qualifications in mind we turn to the experience of the Supreme Court in keeping the public power of nation and states within constitutional bounds.

II

THE RECORD OF THE COURT

It is a first principle of effective federal government, as of all government, that the cloth must fit the figure, and no less so when the figure expands in size and changes its dimensions. From time to time this working principle has been threatened by decisions of the Court. The *Dred Scott* case[15] was perhaps the most dramatic, though it is doubtful whether the gathering tensions in the nation could have been allayed by a decision recognizing power in the national government to deal with slavery in the territories. Following the Civil War the Reconstruction Acts were diluted in the *Civil Rights Cases*,[16] which reflected the sentiment that reunion called for a mitigation of the upheaval produced by the Reconstruction legislation. But even within the confines of the Fourteenth Amendment as there interpreted—as applicable to state action and not to that of public utilities—considerable scope was left for Congress to promote universal standards of civil rights under the Amendment's enabling clause.[17] Regardless of the problems which may have troubled the Supreme Court in deciding the cases on segregation in the public schools, it is scarcely to be doubted that if Congress itself had pronounced the doom of segregated primary education in the public schools the mandate would have been cheerfully accepted by the Court. And in the white primary cases, the company town cases, and the restrictive covenant cases, the Court has shown that the concept of private action must yield to a conception of state action where public functions are being performed or a state agency is the dominant source of discrimination.[18] If Congress were to address itself to a revision of the archaic and patchwork civil rights legislation it would find, within the limits set by the Court, substantial latitude for extending the standards of uniformity governing the area of civil rights.

In the field of economic regulation there have been impediments, serious but not insuperable. It is noteworthy that only in the case of the income tax was it found necessary to overcome by constitutional amendment a Supreme Court decision in the economic field.[19] Of the several constitutional amendments which have been submitted by Congress to the states and not ratified, only the child labor proposal reflected an effort to surmount a Supreme Court decision.[20] The early decisions under the Sherman Act, holding woodenly that manufacture is not commerce, were short-lived.[21] And although the conception of national economic power had not crystallized by the time of the New Deal, there were decisions, particularly those involving the regulation of transportation and restraints of trade, which would have sufficed in the hands of a Marshall to validate the major measures taken in the depression. The Court indicated its different temper clearly enough when antitrust precedents which had been applied to labor activities were held inapplicable to sustain federal regulation of trade practices and labor conditions in the same industries under the NRA and the Bituminous Coal Act, and when the transportation precedents were denied application to the Railroad Retirement Act.[22] Government by the judges, in the sense intended by critics of judicial review here and abroad, was upon us. The intimate story of the Court's subsequent shift remains to be told, but it would appear that, like Margaret Fuller, the judges decided to accept the Universe. Our system of judicial review produces frustrations but has a saving quality of resiliency.

In a successful federalism opportunities must be seized for a wide variety of experiments in cooperation. The conventional picture of a modern federal system with apoplexy at the center and anemia at the extremities is not an inevitable one if various kinds of circulatory pumps are utilized. The Court has been particularly successful in finding vindication for these experiments and indeed in stimulating them. "Undoubtedly," Chief Justice Fuller observed in *Leisy v. Hardin,* "there is difficulty in drawing the line between the municipal powers of the one government and the commercial powers of the other, but when that line is determined, in the particular instance, accommodation to it, without serious inconvenience, may readily be found, to use the language of Mr. Justice Johnson, in *Gibbons v. Ogden* . . . in 'a frank and candid cooperation for the general good.' "[23] The cooperation thus invited has taken many forms and has been hospitably received. The device of the Webb-Kenyon Act,[24] "divesting" articles of their interstate character upon reaching a state, is the most familiar. The constitutional doubts about it were serious enough to induce President Taft to veto that act, and it was preserved as a model only by virtue of the overriding of the veto.[25] It was argued that Congress could not "delegate" its power over interstate commerce; that Congress could not regulate commerce in a non-uniform way; and that since the Constitution gives the states explicit authority to act with the consent of Congress in the case of state taxation of imports and exports, the maxim *expressio unius* precludes this kind of arrangement under the commerce clause.[26] Formidable as these objections may seem, they have been unavailing to prevent a flexible and resourceful cooperative federalism.

Cooperation has taken other forms. The device of a conditional grant by Congress to the states has furnished the basis for a federal-state unemployment insurance program, providing a measure of uniformity of standards but with local administration and enough diversity to embrace both the Wisconsin plant-reserve system and the more common state-wide pooled insurance fund. In judicial administration, too, working methods of cooperation have been devised and successfully executed. The diversity of citizenship jurisdiction of the federal courts is a familiar instance, under which a cause of action resting on state law is adjudicated in a federal tribunal according to federal procedure. Conversely, Congress may require the state courts to entertain causes of action under federal law, as for example under the Federal Employers Liability Act and the Price Control Act, at least where there are state tribunals competent to adjudicate comparable cases under their own law.[27] Again, compacts between the states with the consent of Congress have received a full measure of encouragement from the Court, even where some adroit skirting of state constitutional obstacles has been required.[28]

When all of this has been said, it remains true that the role of the Court in these matters has been simply to place its imprimatur upon measures and devices worked out by the legislatures. If judicial review in a federal system were to be appraised solely on the basis of control over national legislation or cooperative measures, the cost in terms of doubt and occasional delay would outweigh the value. But judicial review is intended preeminently as a restraint on state action, and it is to that field that we must turn for a proper evaluation of the role of the Court—perhaps most vividly performed in its judgments on state measures affecting interstate commerce.

Here the Court has been more successful in its specific practical judgments than in the formulation of governing standards. The Court has worked with standards too frequently mechanical and formalistic. Where does national power end and state power begin in the control over goods shipped from one state to another? When Marshall invented the original-package formula he was perhaps drawing, in typical lawyer's fashion, on a concept from another branch of juristic learning, the criminal law, where the doctrine of "breaking bulk" had been devised to extend the notion of larceny to the case of a servant who, having been entrusted with goods, converted them to his own use.[29] At all events, the original-package doctrine in constitutional law soon reflected the inadequacies of reliance on a mechanical formula to resolve claims of power. A state, it is now clear, may exclude diseased or falsely labeled products in whatever package, and on the other hand it may not prohibit the resale of goods, even after the original package is broken, if its permission to sell is conditioned on a minimum price paid by the seller to an out-of-state producer.[30] No more workable have been the formalistic tests essaying a distinction between laws regulating commerce and those regulating health or safety. A state law limiting the speed at which an interstate train may travel is, to the pragmatic eye, a regulation neither exclusively of commerce nor exclusively of safety but is rather something of both, and we do not escape a hard question of judgment by converting the problem of accommodation into one of semantics.

Another standard which the Court has employed to test the regulatory power of the states is the rule that a state law may not discriminate against interstate commerce. But discrimination does not wear its badge upon its sleeve, and certain forms of legislation may, depending on the point of view, be regarded as discrimination or simply as equalization. Consider, for example, the recent case involving the ordinance of Madison, Wisconsin, which prohibited the sale of milk as pasteurized unless it was processed and bottled at an approved plant within five miles of the center of the city.[31] To Justices Black, Douglas, and Minton the measure was a legitimate one for the control of sanitary standards, applicable alike to local and out-of-state dealers. To a majority of the Court, however, the ordinance was an illegitimate promotion of a local monopoly of the business of pasteurization. The majority pointed out that the city might maintain its sanitary standards for milk by excluding milk not pasteurized in accordance with the standards enforced by the city, without requiring that the process be carried out at a local plant. This suggestion is a happy illustration of the technique of adjusting the claims of local welfare to those of the national market by insisting that restrictive measures in the state of destination interfere no more with interstate commerce than is consistent with the satisfaction of a genuine local need. But the suggestion raises the more general question whether equalization enforced by a state—in requiring that interstate operations measure up to local standards—is consistent with the constitutional demands of a national market.

It would be easy to answer the problem of state-imposed equalization by setting up one or another polar formula, as, for example, that equality is not discrimination or that enforced equality is a form of flexible tariff which it was the purpose of the commerce clause to forestall. In fact, the Court has slipped between the horns of the dilemma. States may not exclude goods from other states manufactured under conditions of child labor or other substandard working conditions; indeed it was this inability, coupled with the Court's decision striking down the Federal Child Labor Act, that created a no man's land in the federal system until the Child Labor case was overruled.[32] Nor may a state, to protect its local system of minimum prices for producers, prohibit goods from being brought in and sold if they were purchased outside at less than the prices set by law within.[33] But a rather different approach has been taken to the problem of taxation. The sales tax, which it was assumed could not be imposed by the state of destination in respect of goods ordered from without, placed purely local sales at a competitive disadvantage if the state of origin had no sales tax or was likewise powerless to impose one on interstate transactions. The competitive gap was closed through the introduction of a compensating use tax in the state of destination; by this device purchasers are taxed (the sellers being made liable for collection) but a credit is allowed for any sales tax paid on the same transaction. Thus the purchaser from a local seller pays only the sales tax; the purchaser from an out-of-state seller pays the corresponding use tax; and the tax burden on the competing transactions is equalized. This device has passed muster in the Court.[34] But it would be extremely unsafe to regard this judgment as a germinal decision forecasting approval for other forms of state equalization of interstate and local tax burdens.

The Court has power to allow or disallow state taxes but not to alter or set terms, and the mesh of its net is consequently coarse. The question is whether it is coarser than it needs to be. Is there any justification for the rule of thumb that the obligation of a business engaged in both intrastate and interstate commerce to pay a license tax depends on whether the taxing statute imposes the exaction on account of the intrastate commerce or indifferently on account of both?[35] Is the rule formalistic only, without rational basis in the protection of interstate commerce? Two possible grounds of support have been advanced. It is said, first, that the enterprise must be free to give up its intrastate business and escape the tax on the rest, and if it is thus free the tax is validly imposed. But where the enterprise, though legally free to withdraw from intrastate business, could not do so in practice because that intrastate business is necessary to the profitability of the whole, the test appears a barren one.[36] Secondly, it is argued that a license tax "on" interstate as well as intrastate activities would subject the enterprise to the threat of expulsion from interstate business for failure to pay the tax. But this ground would be more persuasive if and when the state resorted to exclusionary sanctions rather than the normal modes of tax collection.[37] The real danger lurking in the formal subject of a tax is something different: the selectivity of the tax may conceal a discrimination against those economic functions that are interstate, and its burden may more readily be shifted to those outside the state. In this view the Court has understandably looked askance at selective license fees of fixed amount, varying widely among classes of enterprise—as, for example, the license fees on "drummers."[38] But the Court has not always focused squarely on this element of possible discrimination and perhaps cannot be expected to, given an admittedly wide area of permissible classification in a state's taxing system.

If we turn from the formal subjects of taxation to the measure of the tax, federalism presents still greater complexities. Seizing both horns of the dilemma, one horn playing the melody that interstate commerce must be free of taxation and the other that even interstate commerce must pay its way, the Court has scarcely resolved the dissonance. But a purer tone would give a poorer tune. If the states may tax interstate commerce but not too much, the Court's role is to decide how much is too much. Here enters the concept of allocation. Like the ideas of discrimination and equalization, it is a most suggestive criterion which calls for some care in application.

At least three levels of problems are encountered in judging allocation formulas. First, the formula should be germane to the subject or base of the tax; the measure should be relevant to what is being measured. A property tax on mobile railroad cars calls for an allocation formula designed to yield the average daily presence of cars within the state, as if the tax were imposed on tax day once a year.[39] But even the concept of presence can prove to be a stumbling block, as in the case of aircraft. Shall these be taxed on the basis of an allocation of the total fleet which takes account of miles flown over the state or only on the number of planes arriving and departing, and if the more complex formula is used how shall the ratios be weighted in the allocation formula?[40] How shall net income from interstate business be apportioned? How much weight should be attributed to the presence of manufacturing facilities and how much to the presence of customers who have bought the product? The Court has been quite tolerant of allocation formulas save where they confer a strikingly inappropriate share of the total on a given state.[41] Perhaps tolerance has proceeded too far at times, particularly where the erratic operation of the formula has been excused by invoking as the subject matter of the tax the convenient vagueness of a franchise to do business.[42] These problems of allocation, it will be observed, would exist even if each state were to adopt the same formula. In constitutional terms, they present problems of territorial reach under the due process clause.

But in most instances, absent a uniform act or an interstate compact, it is artificial to assume that each state will adopt the same formula, and so a second layer of problems is reached—the pyramiding of local taxes by reason of different allocation formulas in various states. To the extent that the several formulas adopted in different states are intrinsically reasonable, more than one hundred per cent of the income or property of an interstate enterprise may be taken in the aggregate as a tax base. The commerce clause thus reinforces the due process clause and may be thought to call for enforced selection of a single formula for a given class of taxes. This step the Court has been unwilling to take, as it has been unwilling for most purposes to utilize the full faith and credit clause in order to impose a single choice-of-law rule on the states in questions of conflict of laws.[43] If it is implicit in the commerce clause that an interstate business shall not be subjected to multistate fiscal charges greater in the aggregate than would have been imposed had the same volume of business been carried on within one state, the Court may be thought to be remiss in its duty toward the protection of interstate commerce.

Manifestly, however, such an ideal is incapable of achievement by the judicial process. This realization brings us to the third level of complexity. Not only is it impracticable to compare the burdens under different forms of taxation in the varying tax patterns of the several states, ranging from extraction taxes through property taxes to payroll and other excises, but even a common allocation formula for a particular tax gives no assurance of a nicely limited aggregate burden. For the allocation controls only one factor in the tax; the rates and valuations may differ from state to state and thus produce a total tax quite different from that which would have been imposed on the total enterprise had it been conducted wholly within any one state. No court can be expected to set the rates and assessment levels for a state, so long as there is no improper discrimination within the state.

The impulse at this point is to suggest the establishment by Congress of an administrative commission which would take over the function of resolving these contests over the taxation of interstate business. Such a commission would function under both the commerce clause and the enabling clause of the Fourteenth Amendment. It must be acknowledged that a commission would enjoy the strategic advantage of having power to prescribe rules and formulas instead of merely issuing assents or vetoes. The commission would presumably acquire expertise in measuring the economic consequences of various forms of taxation. By taking continuous thought it could elaborate more comprehensively than the Court has done a philosophy of protection for interstate commerce. It could tell us what it means for interstate commerce to pay its way and whether interstate commerce is paying more or less than its way under a variety of fiscal burdens.

Attractive as is the case for an administrative commission, we face the basic query whether we are prepared to pay the price for this greater certainty and clarity. If a commission were to move substantially beyond the point of the Court's control of taxation, it would have to cut deep into the taxing systems of the state, determining tax rates and valuations for interstate business much as the Interstate Commerce Commission does in the more limited area of railroad charges. In any event, when we enter so sensitive and vital an area as taxation, we may be unprepared to accept the edict of a body which is neither so detached from the pressures of the interested parties as the Supreme Court nor so frankly responsive as the Congress. Perhaps here, as in our party system and elsewhere, a little fuzziness and untidiness at the edges, a little ground for maneuver within the confines of federalism, is an indispensable price for loyalty to the system. The problem of judicial review merges here into the larger problems of popular government and custom.

III

CONDITIONS FOR THE SUCCESS OF JUDICIAL REVIEW

The first requisite for one who sits in judgment on legislative acts is that he be a philosopher. He must be able to see social and economic measures under the aspect, if not of eternity, at least of a wide perspective. When critics of judicial review speak of government by judges they refer in the main to review under such vague rubrics as due process of law and equal protection of the law; but review of the federal balance is not essentially of a different order. The limitations of minds conditioned to a familiar pattern of government intervention are exposed no less in judging issues of federal-state power than in weighing claims of individuals against government. Indeed, it would be the grossest fiction to ignore the fact that the issues of federalism are contests between persons in private character and others in official character, whatever the legal framework of the controversy. In this respect our judicial process, which frequently leaves the claims of state or federal power to be asserted by private persons in opposition to duties imposed by the other sovereign, and which may thus seem to favor an artificial mode of presentation, is actually showing a high degree of realism.

When our judges refused to apply the precedents of the antitrust laws to other federal controls imposed on the same industries but reflecting a different economic philosophy—when, that is, the NRA and the Bituminous Coal Act were held to be beyond federal power—the judges were imprisoned by the same formulas that had become notorious in review under the due process clauses. The phenomenon is not peculiarly American. In Canada and Australia, where "government by judges" does not include judicial vetoes under a due process clause, the same confusion of the familiar with the permissible has confounded the umpiring of the federal system.[44]

The years 1935 to 1937 were years of decision in Canada and Australia as well as in the United States. The Canadian New Deal program of the Bennett administration came before the Privy Council in a group of cases in 1937. In order to appreciate the results, it should be remembered that under the British North America Act (1867) the Dominion has power "to make Laws for the Peace, Order, and good Government of *Canada,* in relation to all Matters not coming within the Classes of Subjects by this Act assigned exclusively to the Legislatures of the Provinces." For "greater Certainty, but not so as to restrict the Generality of the foregoing,"[45] exclusive legislative authority was conferred on the Dominion Parliament over some twenty-nine classes of subjects, including trade and commerce, bankruptcy, the criminal law, and banking; each province, at the same time, was authorized to legislate in relation to such matters as incorporation of companies with provincial objects, direct taxation within the province, and property and civil rights in the province. Over the subject of agriculture (as well as immigration) Dominion and provinces were given concurrent jurisdiction, the Dominion to prevail in case of conflict. Despite these sweeping grants of power to the Dominion, motivated in 1867 by the example of the weakness of the American union, the Privy Council struck down Dominion statutes providing for unemployment insurance, minimum wages and maximum hours of labor, and marketing quotas for agricultural products.[46] But the entire New Deal program was not destroyed: statutes authorizing creditors' compositions for farmers were sustained, as were prohibitions on secret rebates and price discriminations engaged in to eliminate competition.[47] The pattern of decisions is less explicable in terms of a constitutional division of powers than in terms of a conception that the function of government is to maintain a free field with no favor and not to rationalize or supersede managerial planning.

The Australian experience has been similar. Rejecting the double listing of the Canadian constitution, the Australian constitution of 1900 resembles ours in its plan of enumeration of national powers, including legislative authority over trade and commerce. Section 92 declares: "On the imposition of uniform duties of customs, trade, commerce, and intercourse among the States, whether by means of internal carriage or ocean navigation, shall be absolutely free." This mandate, with its somewhat rhetorical flourish at the end, was designed to end customs barriers between the states—what had come to be termed the barbarism of borderism. In the hands of the judges, however, it has become a banner of free enterprise. Not only state legislation imposing marketing quotas on agricultural products, but also national legislation of the same kind, has been overturned.[48] Indeed, the Bank Nationalization Act, under which private banking would have been taken over entirely by the Commonwealth, was wrecked on the reef of Section 92, in spite of the constitutional powers of the federal government to legislate with respect to banking and to acquire property for public use.[49]

All of this suggests that in the selection of judges for a supreme tribunal in a federation, much more is to be looked for than conventional professional attainments. It is hardly the supreme qualification for a constitutional judge that he be expert in the drawing and interpretation of wills, or even that he be experienced in the ordinary judicial business of courts having little or no responsibility in the decision of constitutional questions. As Professor Chafee remarked concerning the opposition to the appointment of Mr. Hughes as Chief Justice, it is less revealing to examine the list of clients in the nominee's office than to investigate the books in his library.[50]

If the first requisite of a constitutional judge is that he be a philosopher, the second requisite is that he be not too philosophical. Success in the undertaking requires absorption in the facts rather than deduction from large and rigidly held abstractions. The constitutional judge is an architect, one who tempers the vision of the artist with a reliable knowledge of the strengths and

weaknesses and availability of materials. Some of the least satisfactory constitutional decisions, as the experience in Canada particularly illustrates, have
taken the form of advisory opinions rendered without benefit of a detailed
factual record.[51] In the familiar phrase, judgment from speculation should
yield to judgment from experience.

These reflections have a bearing on the organization and procedures of a
judiciary in a federal system. Review by the supreme tribunal ought not be
precipitate. Ordinarily it should await the development of a body of evidence
illuminating the actual working of the laws in question. There should, at the
same time, be sufficient flexibility in procedure to expedite cases where excep-
tionally prompt decisions would be more desirable than a fuller development
of the facts. A certain amount of discretion with regard to expedition or
temporizing ought to be left to the court, at the risk of criticism that the
court is avoiding unpleasant duties. Is not this the lesson to be drawn from the
recent experience in Germany, when the Court at Karlsruhe avoided a decision on the validity of the European defense treaties in advance of the vote on
ratification and the national elections? The Court was thus able to avoid en-
tanglement in the political process, to remind the executive and legislative
branches in effect that their responsibility could not properly be shifted to
the Court, and withal to preserve the prestige of an institution which must
secure its position for inescapable tasks in the future.

In suggesting that the judges must be philosophers and yet not too philosophical, I am side-stepping the question, fascinating in academic circles,
whether pragmatism is a philosophy or an excuse for not having a philosophy.
However that may be, one can find in the thought of John Dewey a highly
relevant warning against the needlessly divisive influence of abstract philosophic premises, and an appeal to the process of accommodation and adjustment for the business of living which is exemplified in the adjudicating function
of a constitutional judge.

> What we want light upon is this or that group of individuals, this or that
> concrete human being, this or that special institution or social arrangement.
> For such a logic of inquiry, the traditionally accepted logic substitutes dis-
> cussion of the meaning of concepts and their dialectical relationship to one
> another. The discussion goes on in terms of *the* state, *the* individual; the
> nature of institutions as such, society in general.
>
> We need guidance in dealing with particular perplexities in domestic life,
> and are met by dissertations on the Family or by assertions of the sacredness
> of individual Personality. We want to know about the worth of the institution
> of private property as it operates under given conditions of definite time and
> place. We meet with the reply of Proudhon that property generally is theft,
> or with that of Hegel that the realization of will is the end of all institutions,
> and that private ownership as the expression of mastery of personality over
> physical nature is a necessary element in such realization. Both answers may
> have a certain suggestiveness in connection with specific situations. But the
> conceptions are not proffered for what they may be worth in connection with
> special historic phenomena. They are general answers supposed to have a uni-

versal meaning that covers and dominates all particulars. Hence they do not assist inquiry. They close it. They are not instrumentalities to be employed and tested in clarifying concrete social difficulties. They are ready-made principles to be imposed upon particulars in order to determine their nature. . . .

The waste of mental energy due to conducting discussion of social affairs in terms of conceptual generalities is astonishing. How far would the biologist and the physician progress if when the subject of respiration is under consideration, discussion confined itself to bandying back and forth the concepts of organ and organism: . . . Not only does the solemn reiteration of categories of individual and organic or social whole not further these definite and detailed inquiries, but it checks them. It detains thought within pompous and sonorous generalities wherein controversy is as inevitable is it is incapable of solution. It is true enough that if cells were not in vital interaction with one another, they could neither conflict nor cooperate. But the fact of the existence of an "organic" social group, instead of answering any questions merely marks the fact that questions exist: Just what conflicts and what cooperations occur, and what are their specific causes and consequences?[52]

This philosophy (or lack of philosophy) has come to be regarded as peculiarly American. In speaking of university studies in the social sciences in pre-war Germany, Franz Neumann has pictured the transition from that environment to America:

The whole theoretical-historical approach is (or rather was) accompanied by contempt for Anglo-American philosophy. I still hear the sneers of my philosophy professor about Locke, Condillac, and Dewey, while Whitehead was treated with silence then as now.

Thus, on the whole, the German exile, bred in the veneration of theory and history, and contempt for empiricism and pragmatism, entered a diametrically opposed intellectual climate: optimistic, empirically oriented, a-historical, but also self-righteous.[53]

The question is thus raised whether the pragmatic institution of judicial review is possible in a federal system only where deep philosophic cleavages do not exist—whether judicial review is in fact a luxury reserved for those communities which can afford to focus attention on methods and arrangements rather than on basic conceptions of freedom or property or the state. It has indeed been suggested that judicial review in America is a corollary of our philosophic poverty. Louis Hartz has recently written:

Looked at from a slightly different angle, however, it is this unanimity around the Lockean idea which makes the institution of judicial review, apart again from the matter of federalism, a meaningful thing. When half of a nation believes in Locke and half in Filmer or Marx, the result is not law but philosophy. *Inter arma leges silent.* But when the whole of a nation agrees on Locke, the idea of settling ultimate issues of public policy through adjudication logically arises, since the problem is then not one of principle, but of application. America's famous legalism is thus the reverse side of its philosophical poverty in politics, both of which, like its pragmatism, trace back in large part to a deep and implicit liberal general will.[54]

Although Professor Hartz excludes from his analysis judicial review in matters of federalism, the exclusion may be an unnecessary concession, inasmuch as the process can involve issues as deep-cutting as those subsumed under other constitutional provisions. Thus the question of segregation in the public schools is an issue of federalism, stemming from the post-Civil-War mandate that in matters of civil rights we are to be one people governed by national and not state standards. And so, with federalism presently an object of world fascination, the question raised by Professor Hartz must be faced if we are to consider whether our experience has relevance for other peoples— whether the institution of judicial review in a federal system is an exportable product.

The philosophic unity which can be pointed to in America serves to conceal conflicts over programs of action which may be at least as intense as those to be found in countries where controversy over philosophic premises is more rampant. We may all be said to accept the institution of property in America, and yet this attachment to a common concept did not forestall the tension of the sit-down strikes in the depression of the nineteen-thirties, nor was the tension dissipated because the workers appealed to the notion of a property right in their job and the employers to a property right in the premises. While we may all profess allegiance to the constitutional principle of the free exercise of religion, the practical issue of state aid to religious schools is not thereby averted; under the common standard are ranged those who insist that religion presupposes a religious element in education, as well as those who maintain that religion is best served through divorcement from secular education. The pragmatist is obstinate enough to insist that the most meaningful unities and disunities are to be found in the realm of programs of action rather than in philosophic slogans. If this is so, the judicial process as it has evolved in this country is not without meaning for other communities.

That meaning may be found, not in the arrogant assumption that principles may be dispensed with, but in the introduction of mediating principles between the large constitutional or philosophical concepts to which some or all of a community pay tribute and the common problems of reconciliation which beset the modern state. In the same symposium at which Professor Neumann spoke of the social sciences, the theologian Paul Tillich described the way in which Europe and America made their distinctive contributions in the realm of theology:

> The difficulties, stressed by Continental theology, in applying the absolute principles of the Christian message to concrete political situations, were met by American theological ethics in a rather ingenious way. One found that between the absolute principle of love and the ever-changing concrete situation, middle axioms exist which mediate the two. Such principles are democracy, the dignity of every man, equality before the law, etc. They are not unchangeable in the sense in which the ultimate principle is, but they mediate between it and the actual situation. This idea prevents the identification of the Christian message with a special political program. It makes it, on the other hand, possible for Christianity not to remain aloof from the actual problems of man's historical existence.[55]

The role of the courts in maintaining a working federalism is precisely this task of mediation between large principles and particular problems, the task of interposing intermediate principles more tentative, experimental, and pragmatic. The courts are the sub-stations which transform the high-tension charge of the philosophers into the reduced voltage of a serviceable current. At the risk of making oneself an exhibit of Professor Neumann's self-righteous scholar and a caricature of Professor Hartz's American constitutional lawyer, one may suggest that judicial review in a federal system is an exercise in the kind of thinking most needed in the modern state. For judicial review is not merely a derivative from a society in agreement on fundamentals; in itself it is an educative and formative influence which, like the legal idea of a fair trial, may have consequences beyond its immediate application for the mind of a people.[56] It would be a happy augury if a people were to become better empiricists in the process of becoming more effective federalists.

FOOTNOTES TO CHAPTER 10

1. Constitution of the French Republic, Art. 91; Constitution of Switzerland, Art. 113; Fundamental Law of Yugoslavia, Arts. 16, 34(6).

2. Madison's proposal was in fact broader. He addressed it to the motion of Charles Pinckney, made in the Convention on June 8, 1787, that the national legislature be given the power "of negating all laws to be passed by the State legislatures which they may judge improper." *Documents Illustrative of the Formation of the Union of the American States,* 1927, p. 758. Supporting the motion, Madison "confesses it is not without its difficulties on many accounts—some may be removed, others modified, and some are unavoidable. May not this power be vested in the senatorial branch? they will probably be always sitting." *Ibid.,* p. 759. An earlier version of Pinckney's motion, providing for a negative by two thirds of the legislature on all state laws "interfering . . . with the general interests and harmony of the Union," was opposed by Madison as being imperfectly drawn. *Ibid.,* p. 604.

3. *Ex parte* McCardle, 7 Wall. 506 (U.S. 1868).

4. See Henry M. Hart, Jr., "The Power of Congress to Limit the Jurisdiction of Federal Courts: An Exercise in Dialectic," *Harvard Law Review,* Vol. 66, p. 1362, 1953, reprinted in Henry M. Hart, Jr. and Herbert Wechsler, *The Federal Courts and the Federal System,* Brooklyn, Foundation Press, 1953, pp. 312–39.

5. *In re* Rahrer, 140 U.S. 545 (1891); Pennsylvania v. Wheeling and Belmont Bridge Co., 18 How. 421 (U.S. 1855); see Note, "Change in Constitutional Doctrine Through Legislation," *Harvard Law Review,* Vol. 63, p. 861, 1950.

6. See Helvering v. Gerhardt, 304 U.S. 405, 411 n.1 (1938).

7. 67 STAT. 29 (1953), 43 U.S.C.A. § 1301 *et seq.* (Supp. 1953); United States v. Texas, 339 U.S. 707 (1950); United States v. California, 332 U.S. 19 (1947); Rhode Island v. Louisiana, *motion to file bill of complaint denied,* 22 U.S.L. Week 4171 (U.S. Mar. 15, 1954).

8. Steward Mach. Co. v. Davis, 301 U.S. 548 (1937); Florida v. Mellon, 273 U.S. 12 (1927); Duke Power Co. v. Greenwood County, 91 F.2d 665 (4th Cir. 1937), *aff'd,* 302 U.S. 485 (1938).

9. See Kenneth C. Wheare, *Federal Government,* 2nd edition, New York, Ox-

ford University Press, 1951, pp. 114–25; K. H. Bailey, "Fifty Years of the Australian Constitution," Australian Law Journal, Vol. 25, pp. 323–25, 1951; F. R. Scott, "Centralization and Decentralization in Canadian Federalism," Canadian Bar Review, Vol. 29, p. 1120, 1951. See also, for Australia, H. P. Brown, "Some Aspects of Federal-State Financial Relations," in Federalism: An Australian Jubilee Study, Sawer edition, Melbourne, F. W. Cheshire Proprietary Ltd., 1952, p. 49; for Canada, William A. Mackintosh, "Federal Finance," in Federalism: An Australian Jubilee Study, p. 80.

10. Karl Loewenstein, "Reflections on the Value of Constitutions in Our Revolutionary Age," in Constitutions and Constitutional Trends Since World War II, Zurcher edition, New York University Press, 1951, pp. 191, 211.

11. Hood & Sons v. Du Mond, 336 U.S. 525 (1949); Pennsylvania v. West Virginia, 262 U.S. 553 (1923); cf. Hudson County Water Co. v. McCarter, 209 U.S. 349 (1908); Geer v. Connecticut, 161 U.S. 519 (1896); Lincoln Smith, The Power Policy of Maine, Berkeley, University of California Press, 1951.

12. Loewenstein, "Reflections on the Value of Constitutions in Our Revolutionary Age," loc. cit., pp. 211–12.

13. 49 STAT. 31 (1935), 15 U.S.C. § 715(b) (1946).

14. Parker v. Brown, 317 U.S. 341 (1943); Griswold v. President of the United States, 82 F.2d 922 (5th Cir. 1936).

15. Dred Scott v. Sandford, 19 How. 393 (U.S. 1857).

16. 109 U.S. 3 (1883).

17. U.S. CONST. AMEND. XIV, § 5.

18. Smith v. Allwright, 321 U.S. 649 (1944); Marsh v. Alabama, 326 U.S. 501 (1946); Shelley v. Kraemer, 334 U.S. 1 (1948); Barrows v. Jackson, 346 U.S. 249 (1953).

19. Pollock v. Farmers' Loan & Trust Co., 157 U.S. 429, 554 (1895).

20. Hammer v. Dagenhart, 247 U.S. 251 (1918). For a list of constitutional amendments submitted by Congress to the states but not adopted, see H.R. Doc. No. 211, 83d Cong., 1st Sess. (1953).

21. Compare United States v. E. C. Knight Co., 156 U.S. 1 (1894), with Swift & Co. v. United States, 196 U.S. 375 (1905), Northern Securities Co. v. United States, 193 U.S. 197 (1904), and Addyston Pipe & Steel Co. v. United States, 175 U.S. 211 (1899).

22. Compare Local 167 v. United States, 291 U.S. 293 (1934), with A. L. A. Schechter Poultry Corp. v. United States, 295 U.S. 495 (1935); Coronado Coal Co. v. UMW, 268 U.S. 295 (1925), with Carter v. Carter Coal Co., 298 U.S. 238 (1936); New York Cent. Securities Corp. v. United States, 287 U.S. 12 (1932), with Railroad Retirement Bd. v. Alton Ry., 295 U.S. 330 (1935).

23. 135 U.S. 100, 125 (1890).

24. 37 STAT. 699 (1913), 27 U.S.C. § 122 (1946).

25. See Clark Distilling Co. v. Western Md. Ry., 242 U.S. 311, 325 (1917).

26. Ibid. at 325–31.

27. Testa v. Katt, 330 U.S. 386 (1947).

28. West Virginia ex rel. Dyer v. Sims, 341 U.S. 22 (1951).

29. Brown v. Maryland, 12 Wheat. 419 (U.S. 1827).

30. Baldwin v. G. A. F. Seelig, Inc., 294 U.S. 511 (1935); Crossman v. Lurman, 192 U.S. 189 (1904).

31. Dean Milk Co. v. City of Madison, 340 U.S. 349 (1951).

32. Hammer v. Dagenhart, 247 U.S. 251 (1918), *overruled,* United States v. Darby, 312 U.S. 100 (1941); *cf.* Leisy v. Hardin, 135 U.S. 100 (1890).

33. Baldwin v. G. A. F. Seelig, Inc., 294 U.S. 511 (1935).

34. Henneford v. Silas Mason Co., 300 U.S. 577 (1937). Not all use tax statutes grant a credit for out-of-state sales taxes. See James A. Maxwell, *The Fiscal Impact of Federalism in the United States,* Cambridge, Harvard University Press, 1946, p. 301. It has been suggested that this failure is not fatal, since the state of delivery could employ a general use tax without any sales tax, thus avoiding even the semblance of discrimination inasmuch as there would be no deduction for sales taxes anywhere. See Thomas R. Powell, "New Light on Gross Receipts Taxes," *Harvard Law Review,* Vol. 53, pp. 930–31, 1940. The problem is minimized if the state of origin cannot in any event levy a sales tax on an interstate sale. Adams Mfg. Co. v. Storen, 304 U.S. 307 (1938).

35. Sprout v. City of South Bend, 277 U.S. 163 (1928).

36. Cf. Pacific Tel. & Tel. Co. v. Tax Comm'n, 297 U.S. 403 (1936).

37. See St. Louis S.W. Ry. v. Arkansas, 235 U.S. 350, 368–69 (1914); cf. Hill v. Florida, 325 U.S. 538, 546–47 (1945) (Stone, J., dissenting).

38. See, *e.g.,* Memphis Steam Laundry Cleaner, Inc. v. Stone, 342 U.S. 389 (1952) (alternative holding); Nippert v. Richmond, 327 U.S. 416 (1946); Robbins v. Shelby County Taxing Dist., 120 U.S. 489 (1887).

39. Johnson Oil Refining Co. v. Oklahoma, 290 U.S. 158 (1933).

40. See Minn. Laws 1945, c. 418, § 5, for a three-factor allocation formula, adopted after taxation of an entire fleet based in Minnesota was upheld in Northwest Airlines v. Minnesota, 322 U.S. 292 (1944); *cf.* Mid-Continent Airlines v. Nebraska State Board of Equalization and Assessment, 157 Neb. 425, 59 N.W.2d 746 (1953).

41. Compare Underwood Typewriter Co. v. Chamberlain, 254 U.S. 113 (1920), with Hans Rees' Sons, Inc. v. North Carolina, 283 U.S. 123 (1931); Pullman's Palace Car Co. v. Pennsylvania, 141 U.S. 18 (1891), *with* Union Tank Line Co. v. Wright, 249 U.S. 275 (1919).

42. *E.g.,* Ford Motor Co. v. Beauchamp, 308 U.S. 331 (1939) (capital stock, surplus and undivided profits the base; gross receipts the allocation fraction); Illinois Central R.R. v. Minnesota, 309 U.S. 157 (1940) (tax measured by railroads' gross earnings, imposed in lieu of all other taxes and sustained as a property tax, calculated by ratio of freight car miles within the state to total system car miles). In the latter case the taxable earnings were the net credit balance remaining after subtracting the carrier's obligations for rental of cars of other carriers on its lines from its credits for rental of its cars to other carriers on their lines. Both amounts were allocated by the car mileage ratio, and only carriers having lines within the state were taxed. The smaller the amount of trackage in the state the smaller is the amount subtracted as car rental debits and the larger the tax. If this paradoxical result is to be avoided by viewing the tax as one in lieu of a tax on cars or on credit balances for car rentals, the exemption of carriers having no lines in the state would seem to violate the equal protection clause.

43. Elsewhere I have discussed more fully the Court's reluctance to prescribe rules for choice of law. Freund, "Review and Federalism," in *Supreme Court and Supreme Law,* Cahn edition, Bloomington, Indiana University Press, 1954, pp. 105–07.

44. At this point I have drawn on an earlier study which pursues the comparison in greater detail. Freund, "A Supreme Court in a Federation: Some Lessons from Legal History," *Columbia Law Review*, Vol. 53, p. 597, 1953.

45. 30 Vict., c.3, § 91.

46. Attorney Gen. Can. v. Attorney Gen. Ont., [1937] A.C. 355 (P.C.); Attorney Gen. Can. v. Attorney Gen. Ont., [1937] A.C. 326 (P.C.); Attorney Gen. Brit. Colum. v. Attorney Gen. Can., [1937] A.C. 377 (P.C.).

47. Attorney Gen. Brit. Colum. v. Attorney Gen. Can., [1937] A.C. 391 (P.C.); Attorney Gen. Ont. v. Attorney Gen. Can., [1937] A.C. 405 (P.C.).

48. James v. South Australia, 40 C.L.R. 1 (Aust. 1927); James v. Cowan, [1932] A.C. 542 (P.C.); James v. Commonwealth, [1936] A.C. 578 (P.C.). Since this paper was written, Lord Wright, who participated in the decision of *James v. Commonwealth* in the Privy Council, has published a remarkable *mea culpa*, acknowledging that Section 92 should be regarded as simply a prohibition on interstate fiscal barriers, in his suggestive phrase a *laissez-passer* and not a *laissez-faire* clause. Lord Wright, "Section 92—A Problem Piece," *Sydney Law Review*, Vol. 1, p. 159, 1954.

49. Commonwealth v. Bank of New South Wales, [1950] A.C. 235 (P.C. 1949), *affirming* 76 C.L.R. 1 (Aust. 1948).

50. Zechariah Chafee, Jr., "Charles Evans Hughes," *Proceedings of the American Philosophical Society*, Vol. 93, p. 272, 1949.

51. See Freund, "A Supreme Court in a Federation: Some Lessons from Legal History," *loc. cit.*, p. 613.

52. John Dewey, *Reconstruction in Philosophy*, enlarged edition, Boston, Beacon Press, 1948, pp. 188–89, 198–99.

53. Franz L. Neumann, "The Social Sciences," in *The Cultural Migration: The European Scholar in America*, Crawford edition, Philadelphia, University of Pennsylvania Press, 1953, p. 19.

54. Louis Hartz, "The Whig Tradition in America and Europe," *American Political Science Review*, Vol. 46, p. 997, 1952.

55. Paul J. Tillich, "The Conquest of Theological Provincialism," in *The Cultural Migration: The European Scholar in America*, pp. 138, 145–46.

56. Compare the observation of Professor Goodhart: "in time legal thinking tends to influence lay thinking, and I believe that the average Englishman's dislike and distrust of rumour and scandal in political and social life is due in part to the fact that he has been taught that hearsay evidence is not to be believed." Arthur L. Goodhart, *English Law and the Moral Law*, London, Stevens & Sons, Ltd., 1953. p. 136.

11

The Relations between State and Federal Law

By Henry M. Hart, Jr.

I

INTRODUCTION: THE RELATION BETWEEN PRIVATE ORDERING AND OFFICIAL LAW

The law which governs daily living in the United States is a single system of law: it speaks in relation to any particular question with only one ultimately authoritative voice, however difficult it may be on occasion to discern in advance which of two or more conflicting voices really carries authority. In the long run and in the large, this must be so. People repeatedly subjected, like Pavlov's dogs, to two or more inconsistent sets of directions, without means of resolving the inconsistencies, could not fail in the end to react as the dogs did. The society, collectively, would suffer a nervous breakdown.

Yet the sources of the laws which say what Americans can, may, or must do or not do and what happens if they act differently, or which seek to influence by official action what they are able or choose to do on their own account in the infinity of situations in which they have to decide whether to do or not do something, are exceedingly diverse. The problems of developing the necessary mechanisms for evoking or enforcing harmony are correspondingly complex.

Historically, the law begins and has to begin at the grass roots. Currently and continuously in the continuous current of time the same thing is true. For the function of law is the function of settling the problems of people who are living together in a condition of interdependence. These problems first make their appearance at the level of everyday life, and the shape of the problems as they present themselves for official settlement is the shape which has been given them by the successes or failures of the manifold processes of private adjustment. Governmental action may and constantly does alter the conditions of collaboration among the people in a society. So doing, it may change the nature of the problems pressing for solution, solving some, modifying

177

others, and creating still others. But what the government never can do, whatever techniques of legislation it employs, is to change the way in which the problems keep coming to it, emerging at the level of private activity with the gloss of private adjustments and maladjustments already put upon them. This is a fact of social dynamics which not even the masters of Soviet Russia may escape.

The fact is important for our purposes for several reasons. It poses the broad challenge which confronts any system of law, federal or otherwise. Official law must do more than "eliminate the negative" of undue disparity between the criteria of official and of private action. It must "accentuate the positive" of so guiding and channeling the processes of private autonomy and adjustment as to release to the utmost the enormous potential of the human abilities in the society—its ultimate and most significant resource.

In any system of government, responsibility for doing these things is divided among the government's various branches. In a federal system, it is further divided between the federal government and the governments of the states and their political subdivisions. This brings into focus our central question. Are we to regret this as a confusing and debilitating fractionalization of authority? Or are we to rejoice in it and capitalize upon it as a multiplication of opportunities and resources for fruitful action?

The question obviously cuts deep into basic issues of how governments ought to function and how they can best function. If one conceives of the job of governing as a job of affirmative direction of social affairs, with responsibility, in Professor Fuller's expressive phrase, of "planning for determinate ends,"[1] then a federal organization will necessarily appear inefficient. To make a large-scale organization manageable there must be decentralization in any case, but the guiding geniuses of a central command would naturally prefer to have the lines of authority run straight from them to the remotest of their delegates. If, on the other hand, one thinks of private activity as the prime motive power of social life, the test of efficiency is different. The job of government appears then as a job of providing a favorable framework for collaborative living—as a job, in other words, of planning for such *"indeterminate* ends" as establishing justice, insuring domestic tranquillity, providing for the common defense, promoting the general welfare, and securing the blessings of liberty to the members of the society and their posterity.

In this view of government as more significantly a facility than a control, the existence of varied facilities, providing alternative means of working out by common action, through various groupings of interest, solutions of problems which cannot be settled unilaterally, appears as an enrichment of equipment for successful social life. Constitutional impediments to centralized direction, in those matters in which there is no compelling need for national action, appear as safeguards against impairments of the viability of the social mechanism as a whole. The resulting disparities in the formal law of different states are notable chiefly as reflections of a necessary independence and even competition in the wise guidance of social affairs, entailing in most cases no sacrifice of any comparably important social value.

In this view, moreover, the mere complexity of the legal system for purposes of comprehensive summary is seen to be irrelevant. For legal and governmental systems are not designed for simple ease of nutshell description any more than for ease of central command. The systems are to be judged from the point of view neither of officials nor of expositors but from that of the people whose activities they are supposed to facilitate. Workable clarity for them is what is important. While, as already suggested, multiple avenues of relief from difficulties are an advantage to people, uncertainties about jurisdiction to resolve the difficulties are not; and these need to be minimized. But disputes about social relations being the exception rather than the rule, intricacies in the remedial law, large though they may bulk in the professional concern of lawyers, are of relatively minor concern in the system generally. In a well-operating society the overwhelming mass of actions and transactions never come into question—in court or elsewhere. The main desideratum is the clarity and rightness of the primary law which governs these transactions and constitutes accordingly the basic framework of everyday life.

II

The Structure and Dynamics of Growth of the Federal System

A. The State Systems

Nowhere is the theory and practice of American federalism more significantly revealed than in the constitutions of the states. These constitutions assume responsibility for dealing, and claim authority to deal, with the whole gamut of problems cast up out of the flux of everyday life in the state, save only in the particular respects in which the federal Constitution or statutes deprive the states of any competence whatever or provide for an overriding or displacing federal law. They announce clearly, in Madison's words, that whereas the powers of the federal government "consist of special grants taken from the general mass of power [we, the state governments] possess the general mass with special exceptions only."[2]

The state constitutions establish institutional structures adequate to this conception. It is important to observe in broad outline how these institutions characteristically operate, disregarding for the moment the federal elements in the system.

At the base of the structure are the institutions of local government. These institutions serve as the first level of official adjustment of hosts of problems, and often as the final level. For present purposes it is enough to note the existence and importance of these local authorities, without attempting to examine their internal structure and operation.[3]

In the structure of statewide institutions, the state courts have served historically as the initial agency of official settlement for most of the problems of private behavior which have failed of satisfactory adjustment at either the private or local level. These include courts of general jurisdiction over all persons and matters within the state's power. As such, they have had at their command a theoretically complete set of answers for every claim of breach of private duty that might be brought before them. Here, in the principles of decision guiding the courts of the forty-eight states, are the great and immensely valuable reservoirs of underlying law in the United States, available for the resolution of controversies for which otherwise there would be no law.

In every state except Louisiana, this underlying law was at first largely decisional law, drawn as best the courts could from what they understood to be the English common law, or from so much of that law as they believed to be adaptable to American conditions,[4] and reshaped thereafter, with varying degrees of skill and insight, to conform to changing customs and shifting trends of legal thought. Upon the foundation of this underlying law the state legislatures over the years have built a superstructure of supplementary or superseding statutory law, designed to deal with the felt inadequacies of the preexisting judge-declared law. The legislatures, in other words, have functioned characteristically as a second level of official adjustment of problems which failed of satisfactory adjustment at the private, local, and initial judicial levels. Some states have enacted almost comprehensive codes, but without attempting to displace the common law.[5] In others, statutory law has been of *ad hoc* or limited application, designed often only for the needs of the moment. Codes and statutes alike, however, have drawn upon the underlying principles developed by the decisional process, and alike assume their continuing vitality and growth.

As agencies of creative legal development, courts have the great virtue of being accessible, regularly and as of right. Litigants with an appropriate interest are free always to come before them as one-man lobbies, as Professor Hurst has put it,[6] seeking clarification or correction of the law. Legislatures, in contrast, meet only in intermittent and short sessions, with much of their attention devoted to tasks of governmental housekeeping having no direct bearing on the body of permanent law. With respect to this body of law, they have and must have a crucially important discretion to legislate or not to legislate. In the exercise of this discretion legislatures perform an indispensable function as agencies of second resort for general review of the judgments of social policy implicit or explicit in the decisions of the courts. Actually, however, only a small part of the annual output of the state legislatures is concerned simply with the revision of such judgments. The significant fact about legislatures as law-making agencies is that they have at their disposal a great variety of techniques for dealing with social problems which are not open to the courts. State statutory law reflects predominantly this capacity of a legislature to introduce novel techniques of social control. The federal system has the immense advantage of providing forty-eight separate centers for such experimentation.

Virtually the whole of judge-made law exemplifies the technique of *regulation*—that is, the control of conduct by means of the statement of judicially enforceable duties. These include various duties of public officials in relation to private citizens. But primarily they are duties of private persons in relation to each other or to the public—sometimes duties to do or refrain from doing described kinds of things, such as murder, theft, or careless driving; and sometimes more general, open-ended duties to carry out the terms of duly formulated private arrangements of various kinds, such as contracts or wills.[7]

Most of judge-made law, moreover, is in the pattern of *self-operating* regulation. The duties are made known in general terms, or assumed to have been adequately known, in advance of the time for compliance, so that they can operate without official intervention in the particular situation. Official intervention occurs only in a very minor fraction of instances, when a claim of noncompliance is made after the event in support of an effort to invoke a judicial sanction. This characteristic method of the common law, employing only the after-check of a public or private remedy for breach of duty, is the most flexible and least constraining of all the techniques of coercive governmental action. Together with the basic public services provided largely at the local level, it constitutes the main framework of social control in each of the states.

A considerable proportion of statutory law is likewise regulatory in character. Sometimes the legislature merely codifies a self-operating scheme of control along lines developed originally by the courts. Sometimes it intervenes only to revise the content of such a scheme in specified respects, without affecting its method of operation, although this usually occurs in situations where the changes introduced would have been beyond the power of judicial innovation.[8] Alterations in regulatory law, however, more often involve the introduction of administrative devices for the formulation and enforcement of private duties, including not only rule-making but also a great variety of case-by-case techniques, such as licensing and other prior checks and various forms of administrative adjudication.

A still larger body of statutory law reflects a decision to resort to non-regulatory modes of control. These include the method of *direct government action* affecting the physical equipment of the society or the economic or other abilities of its members, as by building highways and bridges, giving pensions or other forms of economic assistance, maintaining schools and colleges, or conducting a host of other forms of governmental enterprise. They include, moreover, attempts to influence private conduct by the method of *persuasion and publicity,* or by the method of *financial inducement* through such means as subsidies and other grants, homesteads, and bilateral contracts. They may include, on occasion, resort to the method of *direct coercion* of persons and property without the necessity of intervention by the courts, as in the summary destruction of food thought to be dangerous to public health. In the case of all these primarily non-regulatory methods of control, there is commonly present, of course, the possibility of limited regulation of official action through judicial enforcement of constitutional or other restraints.

The technique of control which the legislature chooses, assuming it to be valid, is determinative of the later dynamics of growth of the state's law with respect to the matters in question. If the new statute remains subject only to judicial interpretation and enforcement in the same fashion as the pre-existing judge-made law, the courts retain responsibility as the first-line agency of official settlement of the ensuing uncertainties and problems. If, on the other hand, the legislature resorts to an administered scheme of control, then first-line responsibility passes to the administrative agency, subject or not subject to a second-line judicial review. In either event the problems, as before, are the problems which emerge from the successes and failures of private adjustment and local self-government within the framework of the new conditions. And the legislature continues to function in its characteristic reviewing capacity, with discretion to intervene again or not to intervene, subject always to the further and continuing review of the electorate.

B. The Superstructure of Federal Law and Institutions

At the cost of perhaps dangerous oversimplification it can be said broadly that federal substantive law operates in relation to state law in two principal ways. As to certain matters, federal law assumes and accepts the basic responsibility of the states, and seeks simply to regulate the exercise of state authority.[9] As to other matters, federal law displaces state law, in whole or in part, and itself takes over, *pro tanto,* the basic task of governance of private activity.[10]

The most important of the federal restraints upon the exercise of state authority are embodied in the federal Constitution and are enforceable in appropriate judicial proceedings without further action by Congress.[11] This body of law thus grows mainly by the familiar process of judicial elaboration of grounds of decision. To be sure, Congress has a considerable power to supplement and revise judicially-developed law in this area, especially remedial law. Notably is this true under the express grants of implementing power such as those in the full faith and credit clause and the Fourteenth Amendment.[12] But no aspect of the federal statute book is more striking than its reflection of the gingerly fashion in which this authority has been exercised.[13]

In a few of the spheres of affirmative federal governance the federal courts, like their state counterparts, have assumed a responsibility for the initial development of law, prompted only by a grant of jurisdiction. Maritime law is the most conspicuous example, although there are others which will be noticed hereafter.[14] In such cases Congress has been left in the position characteristic of the state legislatures, reviewing and supplementing, by the techniques of enactment, the underlying body of federal decisional law. But the body of federal law directly governing private activity springs mainly from a statutory base.

The predominantly statutory character of this body of law is not a reflection simply of preference, within the federal regime, for legislative rather than judicial initiative. It reflects, instead, an essential aspect of the relation between the federal and state governments. In some important but relatively few respects the constitutional grants of power to the United States have been treated as a federal occupation of the field, neutralizing further attempts to exercise state power.[15] For the most part, however, the Constitution has been read as proceeding upon precisely the opposite principle. Broadly speaking, the legal systems of the states have been competent, historically, to handle most of the immediate exigencies of government, even in spheres which were subject to a power of control by the United States. In most of these spheres, accordingly, the plan of the Constitution has permitted the state systems to continue to operate until such time as the United States chose to intervene. Federal intervention has been thought of as requiring special justification,[16] and the decision that such justification has been shown, being essentially discretionary, has belonged in most cases to Congress. Over the years, in other words, Congress has functioned as a tribunal of further review of a special type, available for the solution of problems which have failed of solution, or are thought to have failed of solution, at any of the levels of state action.

In the exercise of this discretion to substitute a federal plan of action for the diversities of state action, Congress has been free to make a choice from among the same varieties of legislative techniques earlier described in the case of the states. In practice, indeed, its choice has been freer, since the more ample fiscal resources of the federal government have permitted more frequent resort to techniques of control depending upon large expenditures.[17]

As in the case of the states, the choice of technique which Congress makes is determinative of the later dynamics of development of the new body of federal law. Either the courts alone, or an administrative agency alone, or agency and then courts, take over the immediate responsibility for further development, subject in the same way to the further and continuing review of Congress and the electorate. It is worthy of special note that when a federal administrative agency is created there often comes into existence not only a new place of resort for private persons for the solution of troubling problems but also a new and flexible method of cooperation between the states and the United States.[18]

The federal law which governs the exercise of state authority is obviously interstitial law, assuming the existence of, and depending for its impact upon, the underlying bodies of state law. What is less obvious is that the same thing is true of what has been called the law of affirmative federal governance. As will be emphasized later, Congress rarely enacts a complete and self-sufficient body of federal law.[19] The federal statutes are full of references, both explicit and implicit, to the law of some state. As a result, legal problems repeatedly fail to come wrapped up in neat packages marked "all-federal" or "all-state." It is necessary to dissect the elements of the problems and identify those which depend upon state law and those which depend upon federal. When mixed problems of this kind arise in state court litigation the state court must necessarily decide the federal questions, and *vice versa*.[20]

The complexities thus created are greatly enhanced by the circumstance, of enormous significance in American federalism, that state courts are regularly employed for the enforcement of federally-created rights having no necessary connection with state substantive law, while federal courts are employed for the enforcement of state-created rights having no necessary connection with federal substantive law. The states have no more conspicuous role as agents of the nation[21] than in the judicial enforcement of federal statutes.[22] And the federal courts, by virtue especially of the much-debated grant of jurisdiction in controversies between citizens of different states, have a major responsibility to enforce state law.[23] In so enforcing substantive rights and duties created by the other system, each of the two systems of courts employs its own rules of procedure[24] and to some extent its own remedial concepts. To the problems of disentangling federal substantive law from state substantive law are thus added problems of disentangling substantive law, state or federal as the case may be, from federal or state procedural and remedial law.

III

The Problems of Concurrent Judicial Power

Some of the important problems arising from this partly concurrent jurisdiction of the state and federal courts in the enforcement of federal and state law call for exploration at this point. For the basic pattern of federal-state relationships has been clarified in considerable part as a by-product of the efforts of the courts to solve these problems.

A. The Clarification of the Function of the State Courts as Expositors of State Law

Crucial in the process of clarification was the recognition of the state courts as occupying a position of authority in the state systems comparable to those of the state legislatures and chief executives.

The Constitution need not have accorded the state courts such a position. The Australian constitution, for example, gives the High Court of the Commonwealth plenary authority to review state court decisions on questions of state as well as federal law. The administration of justice thus becomes essentially a federal function, though exercised largely through the subordinate tribunals of the states. By virtue of its general appellate jurisdiction and the obligation of the state courts to accept its decisions as binding precedents, the High Court is enabled not only to coordinate federal law but to establish uniformity throughout the Commonwealth in many matters of state law.[25]

It is a central fact of American federalism that the Supreme Court of the United States has never had such responsibility or power.[26] The fact, of course, affects not only the position of the courts and the immediate outcome of litigation but also the whole structure and dynamics of the state and federal systems.

1. *The Common Law as State Law.* The fact would be less important if a more spacious view had been taken of the scope of federal law. The first clause of Article III, Section 2, of the Constitution provides that the judicial power shall extend to "all Cases, in Law and Equity, arising under this Constitution, [and] the Laws of the United States," as well as under federal treaties. Exploiting various ambiguities of eighteenth century thought and speech, Professor William Crosskey has recently argued that the English common law—that is, that part of the system of the English law as a whole which was found by the courts to be adaptable to American conditions—was thought of as part of the "Laws of the United States" within the meaning of this language.[27] In 1789 the ambit of state statutory and constitutional law was narrow. The "general mass" of matters, in Madison's phrase, were governed by the unwritten law inherited from England. Treatment of this law as a "law of the United States" for the purpose of Article III would thus have transferred to the federal courts the "general mass" of judicial law-declaring power. The Supreme Court could have been authorized to review any decision of a state court not controlled by state statute or special provision of a state constitution. And the inferior federal courts could have been vested with jurisdiction, regardless of the citizenship of the parties, of any case arising under the unwritten law.

Such a grant of jurisdiction would obviously have neutralized the function of the state courts as initial agencies for official adjustment of the general mass of problems of social living in each state. It would have transferred this function to the federal courts, to be exercised on the basis of an assumed body of national rather than local customs and expectations. But since the supremacy clause is limited to those "Laws" of the United States which are passed by Congress pursuant to the Constitution, it would have left the state legislatures in the position of second-line agencies of adjustment reviewing the adequacy, from the local point of view, of the first-line adjustments arrived at by the national courts. The local adjustments of the state legislatures would in turn have been subject to national legislative review under the substantially plenary powers to override state law which Professor Crosskey elsewhere attributes to Congress.[28]

2. *The State Courts' Freedom to Disregard Supreme Court Precedents on Questions of State Law.* Professor Crosskey advances another suggestion, both in addition and in the alternative, which would have had even more far-reaching effects in destroying the position of state courts as authoritative and independent branches of functioning systems of state government. He points out that the Supreme Court was certain to have frequent occasion to pass upon questions which were indubitably questions of state law, as indeed it has had, particularly in diversity cases coming from the lower federal courts. The suggestion is that such decisions, once made, were thereafter to be binding upon

the courts of the state whose law was in question, and that the failure of a state court to respect such a decision would in itself constitute a denial of a federal right reviewable and reversible by the Supreme Court.[29] The responsibility for the development of each state's law would thus have been divided between the Supreme Court and the courts of the state, the occasions for the Supreme Court's intervention being determined by the accidents of what state questions happened to come before it in cases otherwise within its jurisdiction.

Professor Crosskey's suggestions have contemporary interest only as invitations to speculation about the possible effects of plans of federation so fundamentally at variance with the actual one. The historical arguments in their support are couched mainly in terms of inferences of what the Framers took for granted as obviously desirable or appropriate.[30] But the Judiciary Act of 1789, which is a good index of the consensus of 1787, gives these arguments small comfort. Far from giving the lower federal courts a broad common law jurisdiction, Congress withheld from them any general jurisdiction whatever even in cases arising under the federal Constitution, statutes, or treaties.[31] And, although Professor Crosskey argues that the act gave the Supreme Court jurisdiction to revise the judgments of state courts on direct review on the ground either of a misinterpretation of the common law or of a failure to follow a prior Supreme Court decision on a matter of state law, no lawyer, so far as can be discovered, ever ventured to take this position before the Court.[32]

3. *The Limits of the Supreme Court's Ancillary Jurisdiction to Decide Questions of State Law.* Actually, the twenty-fifth section of the First Judiciary Act was carefully drawn to limit the Supreme Court to the consideration of federal questions. It expressly denied jurisdiction to reverse state court decisions on any ground save that which "immediately respects" a claim of federal right.[33] Congress gave the Court no authority to review decisions of state courts in cases of diverse citizenship, nor in any other of the Article III classes of cases in which jurisdiction depends simply upon the character of the parties without regard to the law to be applied. Nor has it ever done so since. So completely did Congress conceive of the Court as an agency only for vindicating federal authority, rather than for the coordination even of federal law, that it limited the Court's jurisdiction strictly to cases in which the state courts had *denied* claims of federal right. Not until 1914 was the Court given the function of policing the mistaken acceptance of such claims and so enabled to enforce nationwide uniformity in the interpretation of federal law.[34]

The conception of the Supreme Court's appellate jurisdiction over the state courts as limited to the review of federal *questions* in cases, rather than extending to the decision of *cases* as a whole, received its crucial test in 1875, after Congress had struck out the sentence limiting review to error which "immediately respects" the federal question.[35] In *Murdock v. City of Memphis*[36] the Court decided that this repeal was to be explained on other grounds, and that it should not be understood as evincing an intention drastically to revise the established structure of state and federal relationships. So doing, it avoided decision of the constitutional question, which it nevertheless noticed, whether Congress would have power to authorize the Court to reverse the judgments of state courts in matters of state law unrelated to the vindication of any claim of federal right.[37]

The issues of power thus undecided were far-reaching. On the assumption that the Court's decision of the state questions in such cases would have been binding thereafter on the state's courts, the rejected claim was only another version of Professor Crosskey's second suggestion, earlier mentioned. On the assumption that the Court's decision of the state questions would have been good only in the case at bar, or in future cases in federal courts, the proposal was one for a spurious federal law, dependent for its application upon which case found its way into which court.

Upon the twin pillars of *Martin v. Hunter's Lessee*,[38] upholding the Supreme Court's power to revise the judgments of state courts on issues of federal law, and the reaffirmation in *Murdock v. City of Memphis* of the lack of any general power to reexamine issues of state law, the Supreme Court through the years has built up a body of jurisdictional determinations which serve also to draw the main lines of demarcation between the authority of the state legal systems and that of the federal system.[39]

4. *The Authority of State Court Decisions in the Lower Federal Courts.* One of the most baffling phenomena of American legal history is the Court's long delay in requiring that state court decisions be consistently accepted as guides also to decision in the lower federal courts. Jurisdiction in the first instance, unlike appellate jurisdiction, is unavoidably jurisdiction to decide whole cases and not merely questions in cases. Given the interstitial nature of federal law, the lower federal courts from the beginning were constantly confronted with the necessity of deciding questions of state as well as of federal law, not only in diversity but often in non-diversity cases.

The draftsmen of the great statutory charter of federalism, the thirty-fourth section of the First Judiciary Act, undertook to tell the lower federal courts how to deal with such questions. But they did so in a way which, with one exception, seems almost perversely uninformative. The section provided:

> That the laws of the several states, except where the constitution, treaties or statutes of the United States shall otherwise require or provide, shall be regarded as rules of decision in trials at common law in the courts of the United States in cases where they apply.[40]

The crucial ambiguity was the meaning of "laws." By common consent the "laws" of a state included valid state statutes and constitutional provisions in matters of substantive right.[41] They came quickly to include also interpretations of these enactments by the state's own courts and, in addition, decisional rules of the state courts on matters, such as title to land, which were felt to be of peculiarly local concern.[42] In 1842, however, the Court decided in *Swift v.*

Tyson[43] that the Rules of Decision Act did not apply to a question of unwritten law, described as one of "general jurisprudence," which was felt to involve interests transcending those of any single state.

The issue in *Swift v. Tyson* was a plainly substantive question of the liability of a drawer of a bill of exchange to a later holder in good faith. The ruling that the federal court was free to decide such a question without regard to the decisional rules of any state court was thereafter applied not only in the field of unwritten commercial law generally but in various other fields of basic common law, notably tort law.[44] The questions involved, however, were all of a type which the Supreme Court plainly would not review on writ of error from a state court. Thus the Court was saying that a question of substantive right which was one of state law for the purposes of the twenty-fifth section of the First Judiciary Act was a question of some other kind of law for the purposes of the thirty-fourth section. In the nineteenth century view this other kind of law was no doubt still state law, but state law of a kind which federal courts were as competent to ascertain as state courts, if not more competent. But since the decisions of the Supreme Court with respect to this kind of law were treated as binding in all federal courts sitting in any of the states,[45] the law involved was obviously also a kind of federal law. Obviously, too, it was a spurious federal law, depending for its application upon the unpredictable contingency of litigation and the accident of federal jurisdiction of the controversy, of precisely the kind which the Court declined to sponsor in *Murdock v. City of Memphis.*

When *Swift v. Tyson* was decided, the conception of questions of general commercial law as depending essentially upon the discerning ascertainment and wise application of principles common to the English-speaking world, rather than upon any "law" peculiar to a particular jurisdiction, was "congenial to the jurisprudential climate of the time."[46] But in 1842, and increasingly with the passing years, it was or should have been apparent that the wisest of judges would differ upon such questions. Such differences, between two coordinate systems of courts each respecting its own rather than the other's precedents,[47] were bound to yield, and did yield, a steadily growing disparity of subordinate and related rulings. The result was to subject citizens at the crucial level of everyday activity to dual and often inconsistent systems of substantive law, without means of foretelling which system, in the unforeseeable contingency of litigation, was going to apply. The decision in *Erie R.R. v. Tompkins*[48] in 1938 put an end to this offense to the most basic concepts of justice according to law.

The significance of *Erie* in terms of state-federal relationships, however, lies deeper. The federal courts in the era of *Swift v. Tyson* had put themselves in the position of denying the authority of state courts as coordinate organs of the state governments in wide areas over which the Constitution assigned legislative power and responsibility to the states. The *Erie* case left in its train many unresolved questions, presently to be examined.[49] But the questions were left to be resolved as questions only of choice between state law or federal law. The case put a period, with an exclamation point, to the notion that the decisional rules of the state courts had a status inferior to state statutes in the spheres, whatever they were, in which state law governed.

B. The Obligation of State Courts to Enforce Federal Law

In the early days of the republic, as is well known, challenge was directed not to the denial of the Supreme Court's jurisdiction to reverse state court decisions on matters of state law but to the Court's assertion of *any* jurisdiction to reverse state courts, even on grounds which were plainly federal. The challenge, decisively rejected in *Martin v. Hunter's Lessee*[50] and *Cohens v. Virginia*,[51] seems singularly implausible today. Its acceptance would have been in the teeth of the universal understanding of the Framers, as disclosed in the convention records.[52] Functionally considered, it would have struck a body blow at the apparent plan of the Constitution for the enforcement of federal law.

If federal law were not to be flouted outright, or reduced to confusion by the conflicting interpretations of state courts, Congress would have been forced to establish a structure of federal trial courts vastly more elaborate than it actually did. In the large class of cases in the state courts in which federal questions emerge only at an advanced stage in the proceedings, it would have been necessary to provide for removal in the midst of consideration from the state to the federal court.[53] Perhaps more significant still, in the substantial class of cases in which process must run to a state officer, the United States would have lost its capacity to make use of the state courts as intermediaries for the communication and enforcement of federal commands.

Congress, of course, is not required to employ the state courts as federal instruments. It can give the lower federal courts exclusive jurisdiction in any of the classes of cases enumerated in Article III, or provide for removal from the state court to a federal court at the option of a litigant, usually the defendant.[54] In a few cases of doubtful soundness, involving actions against federal officers, the Supreme Court has discovered in the silence of Congress, or in the Constitution itself, an implied exclusion of the state courts.[54a] But the normal assumption and the normal practice is what Hamilton predicted it would be in the *82d Federalist*. Absent a special prohibition, express or implied, the state courts enforce federal law as they do their own.[55]

Whether they can always be compelled to do this is a different matter. The supremacy clause, of course, makes plain that if a state court undertakes to adjudicate a controversy it must do so in accordance with whatever federal law is applicable.[56] The doubt concerns a state court's power to decline to adjudicate—a question which is likely to arise only in cases in which the plaintiff bases his action upon a claim of federal right. If an action so founded belongs to a type of which the state court has been given jurisdiction under state law, it seems clear that the court may not decline to entertain it on any ground which involves a discrimination against a federal interest.[57] Probably it must assume jurisdiction in such a case, even in the absence of discrimination, if Congress has so directed.[58] But whether the states are under a constitutional obligation to provide courts of competent jurisdiction for the enforcement ot federal rights of action, if no such courts otherwise exist, and, if so, how the obligation can be made effective, remains uncertain.[59] The uncertainty illustrates again the great fact of political science that ultimate questions often do not have to be faced in successful collaborative living.

Of greater everyday importance are questions of the ways in which state courts enforce federal rights. The general rule, bottomed deeply in belief in the importance of state control of state judicial procedure, is that federal law takes the state courts as it finds them. For example, state rules about the ways in which claims for relief, or defenses, or counter-defenses, must be asserted may ordinarily be applied also to federal claims and defenses and counter-defenses, providing only that the rules are not so rigorous as, in effect, to nullify the asserted rights.[60]

The Supreme Court in recent years has been disturbed by the recognition that differences between state and federal procedure may sometimes lead to different results in actions to enforce federally-created rights of which state and federal courts have concurrent jurisdiction.[61] The disturbance is a phase of the phantasy, which for fifteen years has bemused the Justices, that in determining the difference between substance and procedure it is possible to reason backwards from the results of a litigation to the basic premises of decision.[62] In a clearer view it will be seen eventually that what is essential is that different courts should accept the same basic premises of decision in those respects which are important to the generality of people in everyday, prelitigation life.

Some differences in remedy and procedure are inescapable if the different governments are to retain a measure of independence in deciding how justice should be administered. If the differences become so conspicuous as to affect advance calculations of outcome, and so to induce an undesirable shopping between forums, the remedy does not lie in the sacrifice of the independence of either government. It lies rather in provision by the federal government, confident of the justice of its own procedure, of a federal forum equally accessible to both litigants.[63]

C. The Obligation of Federal Courts to Enforce State Law

The most acute of the problems involved in the effort to use the federal courts to enforce state law grow out of the diversity jurisdiction, although questions of state law come constantly into issue also in cases in which the federal courts are engaged primarily in the enforcement of federally-created rights.

The problems are illuminated by a relatively narrow group of exceptions which the Supreme Court has carved out, by implication, from the general grants of federal jurisdiction. Thus the federal courts will not probate wills or administer decedents' estates, nor grant divorces or interfere in other matters of intimate domestic relations, such as the custody of children.[64] Here, in effect, the Court is saying that a unitary administration of the law is indispensable. And so it recognizes a sphere of jurisdiction impliedly reserved exclusively to the states. In a closely related type of situation, where the state creates a new kind of statutory right dependent for its implementation on administrative action, the federal courts perforce have had to treat the right as non-negotiable, and to recognize that the jurisdiction of the state tribunals is exclusive.[65] Even where the right has been susceptible of enforcement by federal courts, they have often leaned toward abstention in favor of the states.[66]

In general, however, the obligation to administer state law in any case within a valid grant of federal jurisdiction has been accepted. The basic issue of constitutional division of function involved in such a case was settled in *Erie* so as to oblige the federal court to follow, on a plainly substantive question, the decisional rules of the courts of the state whose law was properly applicable. The decision, however, focused attention on a series of problems which had been recurrent long before *Erie* in the numerous situations in which the federal courts had from the beginning declined to take an independent view of questions of state law. Partly by heightening awareness of the significance of issues of federal-state relationships, and partly by increasing the frequency with which questions of choice of state or federal law arose, *Erie* induced a reexamination of these problems. In the course of this reexamination the Supreme Court since 1938 has persistently depreciated the foundations of principle of Justice Brandeis' opinion and moved steadily in the direction of degradation of federal justice.

1. *Modes of Ascertaining State Law.* The first of the problems concerns the weight to be given by federal courts to the decisions of inferior state courts. The suggestion seems never to have been seriously made that the courts of the states are formally bound by the decisions of federal district courts or even of federal courts of appeals on questions of federal law. Yet after *Erie* the Supreme Court, abandoning earlier holdings,[67] solemnly held that on a question of state law even the highest federal court was bound by an obviously unsound decision of a state trial court of statewide jurisdiction.[68] A labored opinion was required to release the federal courts from the bondage even of an unreported decision of a state trial court of limited territorial jurisdiction which no other state court would have felt called upon to follow.[69]

The healthy development of law is paralyzed without the creative participation of courts. If federal courts, in the exposition of state law, are not to have the freedom at least of the state courts immediately inferior to the state's highest court, federal justice in such matters is doomed to be second-rate justice, and the state systems will lose the benefit of valuable contributions to their growth.[70]

2. *Substance and Procedure.* A second group of problems concerns the extent to which distinctively federal remedies and rules of procedure may be

applied in actions to enforce state-created rights, when the result of the application may be to affect the outcome of the litigation.

Almost simultaneously with *Erie* the Supreme Court promulgated the Federal Rules of Civil Procedure, establishing in actions at law a new policy of
procedural uniformity in federal district courts sitting throughout the nation.[71]
The question was insistent and still is: To what extent must the new rules
yield, in diversity actions, to the procedural rules of some state court?[72] More
difficult even than questions of procedure were questions of remedy. For a century and a half the lower federal courts, sitting in equity, had administered a
uniform system of federal equitable remedies drawn from the remedies developed by the English chancellors.[73] The new federal rules abolished the distinction between law and equity but, despite confusion on the point, left remedies
seemingly unaffected.[74] Thus the essential questions posed by *Erie* remained:
Could a federal district court in a diversity case now grant a remedy, equitable
or otherwise, which the courts of the state creating the underlying rights in suit
would deny? Could it deny a remedy which those courts would grant?[75]

Thus far the Supreme Court's decisions on these matters seem to be founded
on no higher principle than that of eliminating every possible reason for a
litigant to prefer a federal to a state court.[76] The principle having no readily
apparent stopping place, the reach of the decisions is unclear. What is more
important is the triviality of the principle. The more faithfully it is carried out
the more completely the constitutional and statutory grants of diversity jurisdiction are emptied of intelligible meaning.[77] The principle passes over the
essential rationale of the *Erie* opinion—the need of recognizing the state courts
as organs of coordinate authority with other branches of the state government
in the discharge of the constitutional functions of the states—and most of the
battery of considerations marshalled by Brandeis as reasons for respecting the
constitutional plan.[78] Indeed, the Court seems never clearly to have recognized
the distinction between this constitutional problem of *Erie* itself and the col-
lateral problem, with which it has since been concerned, of the dividing line
between state substantive law, both statutory and decisional, and federal
remedial and procedural law. In effect the Court has singled out as the master
key to this second problem a relatively minor consideration which Brandeis
mentioned only in passing—the undesirability of affording any incentive for
forum-shopping as between state and federal courts sitting in the same state.[79]

The triviality of this fear of forum-shopping which has so obsessed the Court
is shown by the fact that it would disappear as a relevant factor if Congress
were to equalize, as perhaps it should, the power of in-state and out-of-state
citizens to invoke federal jurisdiction in a diversity action.[80] The Court would
then be forced to confront the deeper questions at issue. Why is it an offense
to the ideals of federalism for federal courts to administer, between citizens of
different states, a juster justice than state courts, so long as they accept the
same premises of underlying, primary obligation and so avoid creating uncertainty in the basic rules which govern the great mass of affairs in the ordinary

processes of daily living?[81] Was Hamilton wrong in saying that the assurance of the due administration of justice to out-of-state citizens is one of the great bonds of federal union?[82]

3. *The Question of Which State's Law.* In its handling of a third problem the Court has paralyzed the capacities of the federal courts to further one of the central desiderata of a federal system. Uniformity of formal doctrine throughout the forty-eight states is occasionally desirable, and where that is so a uniform federal substantive law provides the best means of securing it. But uniformity of obligation as between particular individuals, regardless of the locus of litigation, is almost invariably desirable; and the essence of this can be achieved without enacting uniform substantive laws. The promotion of this kind of uniformity, so far as this can be accomplished without sacrifice of greater values, is one of the functions of the principles of the conflict of laws.

The courts of the states, however, differ in their views of these principles. To the extent that the Supreme Court is willing to invoke the full faith and credit and due process clauses in the resolution of these differences, means of federal coordination are available.[83] But the Constitution, as the Court interprets it, often fails to give an answer. Where this is so, the Court has held that a federal district court, in an action between citizens of different states involving a problem of choice of state law, must follow the conflicts rules of the courts of the state in which it is sitting.[84]

The theory of the Constitution remits citizens of the same state to the courts of their own state (or of any other state having jurisdiction) for the settlement of many matters that may arise between them. There is sound reason for including among these matters many questions of the choice of the appropriately applicable state law. It does not follow that these questions should be similarly disposed of when they arise between citizens of different states. The questions are essentially federal, in the sense that they involve, by hypothesis, more than one state. To the solution of no other type of controversy is the diversity jurisdiction better adapted.[85] This is true alike of conflicts problems which involve a choice of law for purposes of final adjudication and of those problems which involve a choice for the purpose of determining whether to adjudicate.[86]

The Rules of Decision Act says that "the laws of the several states" are to be followed only "in cases where they apply." The federal courts are in a peculiarly disinterested position to make a just determination as to which state's laws ought to apply where this is disputed. By disabling them from doing this, the Supreme Court has not only impeded the development of a sound body of private interstate law but has placed it within the power of a plaintiff who can find the defendant in a state where he wants him to make the choice of law for himself.[87] Justice is not ordinarily served by putting it in the hands of one of the litigants.

IV

FEDERAL REGULATION OF THE EXERCISE OF STATE AUTHORITY

A. Federal Requirements of the Affirmative Exercise of State Authority

Federal law often says to the states, "Don't do any of these things," leaving outside the scope of its prohibition a wide range of alternative courses of action. But it is illuminating to observe how rarely it says, "Do *this* thing," leaving no choice but to go ahead and do it. The *Federalist* papers bear ample witness to the Framers' awareness of the delicacy, and the difficulties of enforcement, of affirmative mandates from a federal government to the governments of the member states.[88]

The Constitution counts upon the necessary participation of the states in the electoral process not by direct command but by the incentive of not losing the opportunity of participation. In similar fashion Congress now elicits desired affirmative performances from the states by attaching them as conditions to the receipt of federal grants-in-aid. If we search the Constitution for provisions which have the appearance of affirmative requirements, two of the most striking are those which call for the surrender of fugitive slaves and fugitives from justice. But the first was disembowelled by the *tour de force* of *Prigg v. Pennsylvania*,[89] and the second was flatly held, in *Kentucky v. Denison*,[90] to be judicially unenforceable. "And we think it clear," said Chief Justice Taney in the latter case, "that the Federal Government, under the Constitution, has no power to impose on a State officer, as such, any duty whatever, and compel him to perform it."[91] Taney's statement can stand today, if we except from it certain primary duties of state judges and occasional remedial duties of other state officers. Both exceptions, it will be observed, involve enforcement through the orderly and ameliorating forms of the judicial process. In any event, experience with the exceptions does little to bring into question the principle of the rule.

The judges of the state courts are not only sworn to support the Constitution, like other state officers, but are bound also to observance of federal law by the special direction of the supremacy clause. This may on occasion require them, specifically and affirmatively, to enter a particular judgment, as in complying, for example, with the injunction of the full faith and credit clause. State courts ordinarily fulfil such obligations without question. But Congress nevertheless has recognized the possibility of conflict and authorized the Supreme Court, in its discretion, to avoid it by entering judgment itself. The imbroglio of *Martin v. Hunter's Lessee* suggests the wisdom of making this alternative available.[92]

Judicial mandates to non-judicial state officers to enforce either primary or remedial duties requiring the performance of affirmative acts are relatively infrequent. Lower federal courts may *prohibit* state officers, in their individual capacity, from taking action under color of office in violation of law.[93] But an action to compel the performance of an affirmative act would encounter, ordinarily, the bar of the Eleventh Amendment. Whether a writ of mandamus to compel performance of a ministerial duty would be regarded as an action against the state is not altogether clear.[94] But it is significant that a practice of issuing such writs to state officers has never become established.

In cases coming to the Supreme Court from the state courts the Eleventh Amendment is inapplicable.[95] Here, not infrequently, federal law is able to take advantage of state practice authorizing writs of mandamus or their equivalent to state officers and to utilize the processes of state courts for their enforcement. But the Supreme Court, as already noted,[96] shies away from directing remedial measures calling for action by the state legislature. The Eleventh Amendment is inapplicable also in suits between states brought in the original jurisdiction of the Supreme Court.[97] Here, in a very few instances, the problem of compelling a state legislature or state executive officers to perform affirmative acts in redress of a prior wrong has been starkly presented. Nothing in the outcome suggests the utility of such a method as a frequent instrument of federal control.[98]

B. *Federal Prohibitions of State Action*

Most of the commands which federal law directs to the states and to those acting under color of state authority are initially negative, although on occasion an affirmative order, such as a judgment for money damages, may follow from the breach of a prohibition. One important group of these prohibitions—the type mainly considered under this heading—seeks to protect private individuals against abusive state action. Here federal law functions, so to speak, as a policeman of the decencies of civilized government, recognizing the responsibility of the states for the day-to-day task of governing but telling them to carry it out without infringement of federal standards. The prohibition against trying a defendant on a capital charge without providing him with the assistance of counsel is one of innumerable examples. A second and closely related type of prohibition is concerned with the protection not only of private interests but of the governmental interests of sister states, as where a state is forbidden to apply its own law in derogation of the authority or effectiveness of the more appropriately applicable law of another state. Here federal law functions as umpire among the states, subordinating, in the interest of a more harmonious union, governmental claims which might be valid if advanced by independent nations. Closely related to this second type of prohibition is a third, in which federal law restrains the operation of state law because it interferes with the effective discharge of responsibilities for the governance of private activity which have been assumed by the United States. The determination of what constitutes such an interference raises problems dealt with in the fifth part of this chapter. Most of what is here said, however, concerning technical problems of jurisdiction and other problems of choice of law is applicable to all three types of proscriptions.

1. *Federal Law as a Shield*. The negative commands of the federal Constitution and statutes are enforced almost exclusively through the courts, federal or state. In some instances their violation gives rise to affirmative rights of action against the offender. But their more conventional operation is by way of defense, counter-defense, or other objection to judicial proceedings founded primarily on state law. It will be useful to examine these simpler situations at the outset.

Predominantly, although not exclusively, what the United States polices by means of these proscriptions is abusive action by state legislatures and administrative officers, even though the policing occurs at the point of judicial enforcement.[99]

In some instances the phrasing of the Constitution invites the confinement of the prohibition to action based upon statute, as, for example, when it forbids any state "to pass any Bill of Attainder, ex post facto Law, or Law Impairing the Obligation of Contracts."[100] In the case of the contract clause, the Supreme Court has adhered to this view in the face of earnest contentions that state court changes in decisional law, even though not founded on statute, may also defeat contractual expectations in a fashion inconsistent with the constitutional policy.[101]

The situation with respect to the Fourteenth Amendment's pervasive guarantees of due process of law and equal protection of the laws is more complex. These injunctions are in part addressed, specifically, to the mode of exercise of state judicial authority. But their effect in this regard has been largely confined to the control of judicial procedure.[102] A handful of Supreme Court decisions have condemned aberrational judgments of the state courts in the field of conflict of state laws.[103] And, of course, constitutional policies help to guide the courts in the interpretation of state statutes and administrative regulations. But federal law has operated only in rare instances to restrain the state judges in the elaboration of the states' unwritten substantive law.[104] Perhaps judges are less likely than other officials to develop unreasonable principles of action. The fact remains that the practical impact of federal proscriptions of abusive state action, outside the field of judicial procedure, has been the result largely of findings of abuse by legislative or administrative officers.

The prohibitions of the Fourteenth Amendment are, of course, addressed only to state action. When a state court, or a federal court in the name of state law, is asked to enforce a state statute or an administrative determination which is properly challenged under the Fourteenth Amendment, there is seldom any doubt that state action is involved, and that the substance of it must be squared with the Amendment's provisions.[105] But what if enforcement is sought not of an officially-formulated command but of an agreement or other command of private persons?

The use of the Fourteenth Amendment as a sword against private orderers who want only to be free of official interference raises difficult problems, considered below. Where, however, the private orderers themselves appeal to the courts for enforcement of their arrangements, or the state appeals in their behalf, and the Amendment is invoked as a shield, most of these difficulties would seem, in principle, to disappear. It may be assumed, for example, that private persons are free to discriminate against one another on grounds of race, color, or previous condition of servitude. But if they embody such a discrimination in a restrictive covenant and a court, upon their application, orders its enforcement, the state is no less involved than if a city council had embodied the discrimination in a municipal ordinance and sought to enforce that. So at least the Supreme Court held in *Shelley v. Kraemer*.[106] There remain, to be sure, elusive possibilities of differences in the content of due process and equal protection when the state is merely giving official backing to private arrangements in the context of private relationships, rather than framing the rules itself in the context of coercive governmental control.[107]

The defensive use of federal proscriptions of abusive state action of course raises other problems than the reach of the proscriptions. If the proceeding is a civil action, for example, there may be problems of original federal jurisdiction. In the absence of diversity of citizenship a federal district court cannot ordinarily entertain a civil action which has its immediate foundation in state law, no matter what the federal questions which loom ahead in the path to final decision.[108] Hence, most civil cases of this type are decided in the state courts, as, of course, are virtually all criminal cases.[109] In the state courts, as already noticed, the actions are subject to the normal rules of practice and procedure in those courts, including rules for the assertion of constitutional or other rights.[110] Beyond this, a whole series of complexities may arise with respect to the relationship of state and federal substantive law.

The party who is opposing the claim of federal right has, of course, to establish his own claim under state law, including its premises of fact. If he fails in that, the federal issue will be irrelevant. Intermingled state questions of this kind may be of great variety. They sometimes include questions about the unwritten law of the state but more often questions of interpretation of the state statutes or administrative orders or regulations of which enforcement is sought. State constitutions, moreover, have their own proscriptions of the abusive exercise of state authority, and a claim of state constitutional right commonly appears as an alternative to the claim of federal right.

To questions of the kind just described are added still others when the party advancing the claim of federal right has himself to predicate that claim upon an assertion about state law. Such a situation is the reflection of one of the most interesting facets of federal law, in which it undertakes to give federal protection against infringement by the states of rights which the states themselves have created. Property is not to be taken without due process of law, but the existence of a property interest which is susceptible of being taken is a question of state law.[111] Statutes are not to be enacted and applied so as to impair the obligation of contract, but whether a valid contract was ever made the obligation of which could be impaired, and, if so, what the obligation was, are again matters of state law.[112]

All these complexities are a challenge to accurate analysis. In a federal trial court, once jurisdiction is established, the trial judge must sort out the state from the federal issues in order to determine the relevant materials for decision. In framing his decision he must give due weight to the long-established canon of federal law which enjoins the court to avoid the adjudication of a federal constitutional issue if the case can fairly be disposed of on a nonconstitutional ground.[113] In cases arising in the state courts, problems of identifying the applicable law become entangled also with problems of appellate jurisdiction.

If a state court disposes of a case on a federal ground, constitutional or otherwise, the Supreme Court will examine the record closely to make sure that the decision did not rest also upon independent and adequate state grounds, rendering the federal question moot.[114] If, on the other hand, the state court disposes of the case on state grounds, to the prejudice of a claim of federal right, a much more delicate question is likely to be presented. Federal law must not be evaded or defeated by misapplication of state law. Yet the suggestion of evasion or defeat is a serious one. In this type of situation, and this alone, the Supreme Court has asserted an ancillary jurisdiction to reexamine rulings of state courts on questions of state law which "immediately respect" a rejected federal claim to make sure that they provide an adequate and independent ground of judgment.[115] But it usually softens the assertion with expressions of deference, and exercises the jurisdiction only with hesitancy.

2. *Federal Law as a Sword.* Attempts to use the Constitution and the federal statutes as a sword instead of a shield in litigation attacking an exercise of state authority raise additional questions which are among the most far-reaching in the whole field of civil and other liberty.

An initial and basic question concerns the reach of the constitutional provisions, and particularly the Fourteenth Amendment, when employed as a basis for an affirmative right of action. The jurisdiction of the lower federal courts to entertain any action to enjoin a state officer from violating the Fourteenth Amendment was for years challenged on the ground that if the complaint did not run afoul of the Eleventh Amendment it must necessarily fail to state a case under the Fourteenth. The challenge was buttressed by the argument that the federal government ought not prematurely to condemn a state for action which perchance the state itself did not authorize, and which, through its own constitution, it might even have prohibited. Only after the highest available state court had sanctioned the abuse complained of as consistent with state law, it was urged, should the proscriptions of the Fourteenth Amendment be regarded as coming into operation.

The Supreme Court's answer was that the constitutional proscriptions of action by a "state" are directed to abuses under color of state authority as well as to those which are actually authorized.[116] The answer has obvious relevance

not only to the important issue of district court jurisdiction immediately involved but also to the power of Congress, generally, to create civil and criminal remedies for violations of the rights guaranteed by the Amendment. The
power must at least reach all actions by persons purporting to hold state office
and to act under its authority, if the actions are of a kind that a state statute
could not expressly sanction.[117]

How much further it reaches remains uncertain. Attempts, on a wholly different theory, to reach admittedly private action on the ground that it interferes with the enjoyment of privileges under federal law are outside the present
discussion.[118] Conceivably, under the theory here in question, all kinds of un-
authorizable private action tolerated by state law and taken under its general
governance might be regarded as action under authority of the state. But it
seems unlikely that the Supreme Court will or should go so far. The outer
limits appear to be marked by a few marginal instances of private action under
special privilege of state law, or under special circumstances giving the action
the practical effect of official action.[119]

Assuming that prohibited state action is involved, complex questions remain
as to the nature and sources of the offensive remedies available. The normal
remedy for abuse of state authority, as of federal, is the last-ditch remedy of
defense. A claim of an offensive remedy commonly introduces complicating
factors of competing public interests. Thus actions for money damages, if not
brought simply for restitution, may involve grave issues of possible discouragement of official action in good faith.[120] Suits for preventive relief by way of
injunction or declaratory judgment entail dangers of undue or premature interference with state governmental processes.[121]

The states, it is plain, are free to give such remedies as they choose for violations of federal rights by state officials, provided only that the remedies do
not conflict with any provision, express or implied, of federal law.[122] The
proviso suggests the range and difficulty of the potential problems. Federal law
may also provide its own remedies, with or without benefit of an act of Congress—the Supreme Court never having clearly explained when and why such
an act is necessary or unnecessary.

The intricacy of analysis to which such problems are susceptible is illustrated by the history of federal injunctions against state officers. These injunctions were originally sanctioned, and the bar of the Eleventh Amendment
avoided, on the theory that an individual could be enjoined from taking action
which in the absence of official justification would amount to a trespass, and
that the federal question of the existence of a valid justification could thus be
determined as an incident of the suit to prevent the trespass.[123] The analysis, it
may be inferred, ran something like this: (1) the general grant of federal
equity jurisdiction authorizes a federal equitable remedy for breach of a duty
created by state as well as by federal law, where the legal remedy is inadequate; (2) a trespass is a breach of duty under state law; (3) under state law,
a showing that the defendant acted in an official capacity pursuant to a state

statute is a defense to an action of trespass; and (4) as a matter of federal law, such a defense is not available if the statute under which the defendant justifies his conduct violates federal law. The Court, however, came to neglect the second and crucial link in this chain of reasoning and ceased to inquire whether the acts complained of did, indeed, constitute a breach of duty under state law. By almost imperceptible steps it appears to have come to treat the remedy of injunction as conferred directly by federal law for any abuse of state authority which in the view of federal law ought to be remediable.[124] A host of restrictions developed partly by act of Congress and partly by federal judicial decision have emphasized the federal character of this remedy.[125]

The other major preventive remedy, the declaratory judgment, was introduced into federal law by act of Congress.[126] Prior to the enactment of the Federal Declaratory Judgment Act the Supreme Court had declined to recognize state acts of this kind as authorizing a federal district court sitting in the state to give such a judgment[127] while at the same time accepting state court judgments under such acts, in cases of actual controversy, as a basis for appellate review.[128] The precise consequences of a federally authorized remedy of this kind, in relation both to federally-created rights and state-created rights, remain uncertain.[129]

With respect to substituted relief, the Court has recognized, as in the case of equitable remedies, a non-statutory federal right of action against a state tax collector, as an individual, to recover taxes collected in violation of federal law.[130] But rights of action for damages from violation of the federal Constitution, other than by way of restitution, it has been unwilling to recognize on its own motion.[131] *A fortiori,* criminal prosecutions for such violations have had to be authorized by statute.[132] Within limits, Congress has created such remedies, both civil and criminal, in the Civil Rights Acts, and today the most frequently litigated questions of the validity of state action turn on the construction of these acts.[133]

V

The Roles of State and Federal Law in Programs of Affirmative Federal Governance

When federal law, instead of simply regulating the exercise of state authority, turns to take up itself the task of affirmative governance of private activity,[134] it might be supposed that state law would cease to play a significant part—save only at the periphery marking the outer bounds of federal power. Precisely the contrary is true. It is in this sphere that the essentially incomplete and interstitial nature of federal law is most conspicuously revealed.

A. Non-User of Congressional Power

At the root of the situation is a fact of federal dynamics already mentioned.[135] The Constitution does not attempt itself to block out fixed spheres of state and federal responsibility. In a few particular matters it deprives the states of competence, forcing action by the United States if any action is to be taken at all.[136] For the most part, however, it does no more than sketch a delegation of federal powers, leaving to Congress, and in a measure to the federal courts, a broad discretion in deciding whether power should be exercised, and indeed a considerable freedom even in determining whether such power exists. In wide areas, accordingly, a state law continues to operate not by virtue of the Tenth Amendment but by virtue only of the non-exercise of latent federal powers, furnishing impressive evidence of the practical worth of the state governments.[137]

Having this discretion not to act at all, Congress *a fortiori* has discretion to act only for a limited purpose. And when it thus confines its assertion of authority, the precise location of the outer bounds of power may remain ambiguous. The Constitution, for example, empowers Congress "to dispose of and make all needful Rules and Regulations respecting . . . Property belonging to the United States." Grants pursuant to the exercise of this power are the foundation of a large proportion of the land titles in the country. Conceivably, Congress might have attempted to impose conditions on these grants governing the rights and powers of grantees and subsequent holders. But as the Supreme Court has read the legislation it provided instead that the interests of the grantees should be assimilated into the general mass of property interests in the state, and subject thereafter to the governance of the general land law of the states.[138] Again, Congress has exercised its constitutional authority to provide for the issuance of patents for inventions. But the patent laws, as construed, confer only a narrow right to exclude other persons, on certain conditions, from the use of the invention. State law governs transfers of this federal interest and contracts concerning it.[139] And in another early instance the Court upheld the power of Congress to create the Bank of the United States and to authorize it to sue and be sued in a federal circuit court. But it assumed that state law would determine the rights and duties of the bank incident to ordinary banking transactions.[140] To add a similar recent example from among a host of others, the Court has decided that the statutes providing for federal licensing of radio broadcasting stations and federal approval of transfers of licenses are not to be construed as removing contracts concerning the operation of the stations and transfers of their property from the basic control of state law.[141]

Holdings such as these result in subtle and often highly complex interrelationships between state and federal law. The relationships must be unravelled in determining the applicable legal materials, and not infrequently they are decisive of the jurisdiction of a state or federal court.[142] But beneath the technicalities lie far-reaching considerations of policy in the distribution of governmental "say." In the processes of congressional enactment such considerations may sometimes come to the surface and receive explicit treatment. Far more often the issues are either unnoticed or remitted *sub silentio* to later judicial determination. Here is a characteristic and portentous aspect of the Supreme Court's role in shaping the working structure of the federal system. It is a noteworthy but little noticed fact of our political history how often issues which might have been resolved in favor of nationwide uniformity have been resolved instead in favor of decentralization.

Closely related questions may be raised in the interpretation of the silence of the Constitution as well as of Congress. Thus a federal injunctive remedy against unlawful acts of federal officials seems to be recognized as implied in the Constitution, or in the general grant of equity jurisdiction, where the requisites of equity and other jurisdiction are satisfied.[143] But, as in the case of corresponding remedies against state officials, the courts seem to have treated a remedy in damages as dependent upon an act of Congress. The anomaly may thus result of an exclusive state remedy for violation of a federal constitutional right.[144]

B. Release of Federal Control

Much simpler for courts and lawyers, but significant also for our general theme, are the situations in which Congress expressly releases a federal control previously in effect. This has not uncommonly happened after the Supreme Court has found in the Constitution an implied exclusion of state authority, in the absence of congressional action. Shares of stock in national banks, for example, were originally held to be immune from state taxation, but Congress later gave consent to such taxes, upon conditions.[145] An analytically similar situation results when Congress lifts a prior statutory prohibition. Thus after the Sherman Act had been held to invalidate certain kinds of interstate contracts for resale price maintenance, Congress amended and then reamended the act to permit the operation of state fair trade laws in those states which chose to enact them.[146] For jurisdictional purposes it is reasonably clear that claims which are made enforceable in this fashion arise under state and not federal law, even though the validity of the claim may depend upon a disputed point of construction of the federal permission.[147] For the larger purpose of understanding federalism, what is illuminating is that Congress should so often elect to give the permission, preferring state determinations to the imposed uniformity of a federal rule even after the Supreme Court has resolved the issue the other way.

C. Adoption (or Absorption) of State Law

Even more significant because much more pervasive are the situations in which Congress adopts state law as its own, incorporating it by reference so to speak, for the solution of problems arising in an area of inescapable or assumed federal responsibility. Not infrequently the adoption is express. Thus procedure in actions at law in the lower federal courts was for years regulated in large part by a direction to "conform, as nearly as may be" to the practice prevailing in the courts of the state in which the federal court was sitting.[148] The new rules of federal civil procedure are still replete with references to state law in relation to particular matters.[149] And when in 1946 Congress moved at long last to subject the United States to suit upon certain tort claims, it chose to allow recovery only "under circumstances where the United States, if a private person, would be liable to the claimant in accordance with the law of the place where the act or omission occurred."[150]

In an accurate analysis, it seems, state law cannot be said to operate of its own force in such situations. The case is rather one in which "the state law has been absorbed, as it were, as the governing federal rule"—a rule which "does not owe its authority to the law-making agencies of" any state, but is "ultimately attributable to the Constitution, treaties or statutes of the United States."[151] But there is illumination, again, in the fact that Congress should choose to make the reference, by absorption or otherwise.

For every instance in which Congress has made the choice expressly there are dozens in which it has left it uncertain. In such cases the Court has come to recognize, with increasing candor in recent years, its duty to make the choice in Congress' behalf. "In absence of an applicable Act of Congress," in the blunt language of Justice Douglas, "it is for the federal courts to fashion the governing rule of law according to their own standards."[152] Again and again the Court has found "reasons which . . . make state law . . . the appropriate federal rule"[153] in matters which beyond doubt are basically federal. Thus state law has been applied in determining whether a judgment for the United States in an action to recover taxes illegally exacted from an Indian should include interest.[154] And when Congress creates a new statutory right of action for the recovery of damages but fails to specify any period of limitations, the inference has seemed irresistible that some limitation must have been intended and, in default of any federal measure, the Court has turned to state law.[155]

D. Federal Decisional Law

To put the problem as one of choice, to be exercised in the light of "appropriate considerations of 'public convenience,' " is, of course, to imply the possibility of rejecting the state reference. This obviously assumes that it is a proper function of the federal courts in proper cases to fill in the interstices of congressional enactments by developing a uniform body of federal decisional rules. The same assumption is involved in the class of cases earlier considered[156] in which the question is whether a statute is to be read as permitting a pre-existing body of state law to continue to operate of its own force, or as displacing it by some uniform federal law. In both classes of cases the Court has shown itself willing on occasion to assume this responsibility. Indeed, the history of the federal common law, in this sense of separate bodies of federal decisional rules to govern particular matters, as distinguished from a general system of decisional law, goes back almost to the beginning of the republic.

Justice Jackson has given a succinct explanation: "Were we bereft of the common law, our federal system would be impotent. This follows from the recognized futility of attempting all-complete statutory codes, and is apparent from the terms of the Constitution itself."[157] If the moral of the cases earlier considered is that uniformity, even within the scope of federal power, is not an invariable desideratum in a federal system, here is the other side of the coin. In different contexts the need for uniformity may be so pressing that sole responsibility for establishing it, or for working out the content of the needed regulation, cannot feasibly be entrusted to a legislature.

Most of the early instances of judicially-developed federal law were outgrowths of grants of jurisdiction to the federal courts, posing the problem of finding appropriate grounds of decision. Perhaps the simplest illustration is the grant of original jurisdiction to the Supreme Court to determine controversies between states. On occasion, the law of one or the other of the contending states may be relevant, and the Supreme Court may draw upon it, although usually asserting the power to judge the state law for itself. But when the controversies concern such questions as interstate boundaries or the apportionment of the waters of an interstate stream, it is often manifestly inappropriate to apply either state's law. The consequence has been the development of a body of federal decisional rules, derived by the Court from "principles of established credit in jurisprudence," and applied in the light of the apparent needs of the situation.[158]

In admiralty, the quasi-exclusive grant of jurisdiction to the federal courts, the absence in the states of any complete system of maritime law and remedies, and the tradition of the maritime law as a separate corpus of law claiming the respect of all maritime nations, have combined to induce a uniform development of the traditional principles of admiralty in the federal courts, although with occasional absorption of supplementing state law.[150]

The admiralty experience is noteworthy as having provided an especially severe test of the genuinely federal character of these bodies of federal decisional rules. The jurisdiction, while formally exclusive, was qualified by the famous saving clause, "saving to suitors, in all cases, the right of a common law remedy, where the common law is competent to give it."[160] For more than a century and a quarter it seems to have been generally supposed that this clause authorized the states to administer, through traditional non-maritime remedies, a distinctive and independent system of state substantive law side by side with the separate federal admiralty law.[161] The system of state remedies, however, was necessarily incomplete. In no view did any single state have legislative jurisdiction to deal authoritatively with problems of maritime law generally. Thus Congress had obviously to be recognized as possessing general legislative jurisdiction in admiralty matters,[162] whatever might be the peripheral powers of the states in relation to transactions and events within their borders.[163] In result, the administration of the saving clause threatened to bring about a dual system of federal-state substantive law involving in reverse precisely the evils of *Swift v. Tyson*. The same logic of federalism which underlay *Erie* eventually prompted the Supreme Court to hold that the state courts in saving clause cases must respect the same principles of substantive obligation which the federal courts enforced in admiralty.[164] By a curious quirk of intellectual history the critics of Justice Brandeis' conclusion in *Erie* have tended often to applaud the reasoning of Justice McReynolds in *Southern Pacific Co. v. Jensen* and *Chelentis v. Luckenbach S.S. Co.,* and *vice versa.*

The history of federal crimes illuminates the general problem of a federal decisional law with an illustration of a contrary conclusion. The First Judiciary Act gave the federal courts jurisdiction of "all crimes and offenses cognizable under the authority of the United States."[165] But the Court refused to read this grant of jurisdiction as authorizing punishment of crimes which had not been defined by statute.[166]

The question of common law crimes has often been confused with the question of the status of the common law, generally, as a law of the United States.[167] But in truth the issues were very different. With respect to offenses within the territorial jurisdiction of the states, state law was available to carry the main burden of maintaining public order, and indeed was undisplaceable. What was at stake, therefore, was the propriety of trying to work out by the judicial process the shadowy line between offenses against the states and those which affected distinctively the peace and dignity of the United States.[168] With respect to offenses committed in federal enclaves and on the high seas, on the other hand, what was involved was the existence of a vacuum of law until such time as Congress got around to filling it. The experience in this latter aspect illustrates vividly the perils of depending upon a legislative body as a first-line agency for the basic development of law.[169]

In again illuminating contrast is the history of the law governing the proprietary legal relationships of the United States. The First Judiciary Act gave the lower federal courts jurisdiction, concurrent with the courts of the states, of most civil actions in which "the United States are plaintiffs, or petitioners."[170] When the United States began to bring conventional civil actions to enforce proprietary interests, this grant of jurisdiction appeared as a clear direction to adjudicate, and the answer of no-law was never seriously entertained.[171] Save for one modern aberration,[172] it never has been. But years passed before the Court clarified the question whether the law being applied was uniform federal law or state law, either borrowed or operating of its own force.

The Court's opinions, although vacillating and conflicting in their suggestions, were long open to the interpretation that the United States, while protected by the Constitution from discriminatory state action, and perhaps certain other special forms of state control, was nevertheless governed generally in its ordinary proprietary relations by state law.[173] Recent decisions, profiting from the sharpened sense of state-federal relations induced by *Erie,* have made clear that this is not so. The Court has plainly recognized the basic authority of federal law and has followed the approach already outlined to determine whether in a particular situation federal law should be read as absorbing state law or as providing its own uniform rule.[174] The decisions permit the conclusion that the same approach is applicable when the United States, having consented to suit, is made a defendant in a proprietary action—save, of course, where Congress has foreclosed the issue as it did in the Federal Tort Claims Act.[175]

Against this background it is not surprising that a growing body of decisions are finding in the interstices of federal legislation an authorization to develop uniform decisional rules governing many kinds of legal relations between private persons. Should a federal statutory right of action be regarded as cut off by a state statute of limitations when the right is equitable in nature and the traditional limitations principles of federal equity are available as guides to decision?[176] Should the provisions of the Hepburn Act restricting the classes of persons to whom railroads may give free passes be read as precluding the application of state law to determine the validity of a railroad's effort to limit its liability to a free rider in a permitted class?[177] Congress having enacted an elaborate scheme of regulation of other aspects of the interstate transmission of messages, should state law continue to answer questions of a carrier's liability for a libel published by delivery of an interstate message, or for negligent delivery?[178] In recent cases posing these questions the courts have examined the possibility of treating state law as absorbed into federal law or, as the case might be, as permitted by federal law to continue to operate of its own force. But in each case the question was answered in favor of a uniform federal rule.

What is ironical is that this trend toward federal uniformity, involving as it does the sterilization *pro tanto* of both state courts and state legislatures as agencies of growth in the law, has been accompanied by a trend toward diffidence in the creative exercise of federal judicial power after federal concern has been asserted.[179] The result is to thrust upon Congress a burden of exclusive responsibility for the interstitial development of legal doctrine— a burden which it is wholly unequipped to bear.[180] But this latter trend has never been adequately thought through, and can be expected to pass.

Other cases cast the choice in favor of state law.[181] But the decisions yield no simple rule of thumb for choosing. They cannot. Particularly is this so in the subtler situations in which federal legislation is building upon legal relationships established by the states and its power is one of characterization only and not of alteration of the substance of the relation. Federal tax law, for example, can say what state-created interests are to be taxed, and can characterize them in any way it chooses; but it cannot create the interests.[182] Similarly, federal bankruptcy law can dissolve state-created interests in any way it thinks equitable; but it is hard to see how it can create, or recognize in liquidation, interests which never had any existence under state law.[183]

E. Problems Resulting from Choice of Uniformity or Diversity

An answer even to a real choice between federal uniformity and state diversity does not put an end to the problems. This is so whether the answer is given in express terms by Congress or worked out by implication by the courts.

If the answer is in favor of federal uniformity, questions may still exist whether parallel or partly parallel remedies continue to be available under state law. The Supreme Court's recent decision that federal provisions for the administrative redress of unfair picketing preclude any state action by way of an additional or different remedy suggests the occasional magnitude of such issues.[184] When parallel remedies are permitted, and both remedies are judicial, intricate questions of jurisdiction and procedure may be presented if an effort is made to secure enforcement of the state remedy in a federal court.[185]

If, on the other hand, the answer is in favor of state diversity, two major types of problems may ensue.

The ambiguities of Section 301(a) of the Taft-Hartley Act suggest one of these. The sub-section attempts to give the federal district courts jurisdiction of actions for violation of certain collective bargaining agreements affecting commerce, "without regard to the citizenship of the parties."[186] Is this grant vulnerable, as not grounded in Article III, if it is interpreted as leaving questions of the validity and interpretation of such agreements to the continued governance of state law? Or does Congress have power to protect acknowledged federal interests by providing nothing more than a federal forum for the application of state substantive law? The problem may arise not only in situations such as Taft-Hartley in which Congress has undoubted power, if it chooses to exercise it, either itself to enact a body of substantive law or to direct its creation by the courts, but also in situations in which the only federal power is one of protecting a federal interest from the discriminatory application of state law.[187]

The second type of problem is more pervasive and far-reaching. When Congress does remit matters to state law in any of the ways that have been described does it have the power to say which state's law? If, as almost invariably happens, it has not said expressly which state law is to govern, should the federal courts work out a federal answer? Or should they leave it to the plaintiff, within the limits of the applicable venue and process requirements, to determine the answer for himself? This distinct and vital aspect of the problem of a federal law of conflict of state laws the Supreme Court has scarcely yet noticed.[188] But it seems plain that decisions reached in the context of the diversity jurisdiction cannot foreclose judgment in a context in which federal interests are directly, and often vitally, concerned.

F. State Accommodation to Federal and Other States' Law

Congress, within the limits of its delegated powers, and the federal courts, within the interstices of the Constitution and federal statutes, are of course the principal instruments for the development of uniform federal law, where that is necessary or desirable. There remains to be noticed the part which the states may play to the same end.

To the extent that both states and nation are engaged in the same kind of governmental activity, the federal Constitution leaves each state free to secure uniformity of written law within its own borders by making the provisions of federal law applicable in its own sphere of concern. Thus federal regulations of interstate commerce may be extended to local commerce; proceedings in state courts may be made subject to the provisions of the federal Rules of Civil Procedure; many if not all the provisions of federal income tax statutes and regulations may be utilized for purposes of state income taxation. What is remarkable is that the states have so seldom found federal statutes and administrative regulations thus adaptable to their own needs.[189]

State law, of course, is not transformed into federal merely by phrasing it in federal language. The identical language may receive differing interpretations at the hands of state and federal courts. So far as the federal Constitution is concerned, there is nothing to prevent a state legislature from dealing with this difficulty by directing the state courts to conform as nearly as may be with federal interpretations.[190] But can the legislature, or the state court by construction of the state statute, go further and, in effect, make the interpretation of the federal language, even when employed for state purposes, a federal question subject directly to authoritative resolution by the Supreme Court?

Despite contrary intimations in a few recent Supreme Court decisions,[191] time and mature reflection seem likely to yield the answer that they cannot. The situation must be sharply distinguished from that in which state law refers to federal, interrelating its own law with it but without seeking to enlarge the sphere of primary federal governance. Thus a state may give a stockholder in a state-created corporation a right of action to prevent the directors from investing in illegally issued securities, and a question may arise whether federal securities were or were not legally issued. Again, a state may confer a private right of action for breach of a federally imposed duty, and a question may arise whether the federal duty has indeed been violated. In such cases as these the Supreme Court will treat the point of federal law as presenting a genuinely federal question, reviewable on certiorari or appeal from a state court's decision.[192] But it is a different matter to permit the legislature of a single state to alter the distribution of federal and state powers by making federal law directly controlling in a sphere of exclusive state responsibility. Plainly the state could not unilaterally appropriate the services of federal administrative agencies in this fashion. There seems to be no better reason why they should be able thus to appropriate the services of the federal courts.[193]

The states may seek to deal with the problem of disparity of written law as between one state and another by the device of enacting uniform statutes. The last half century has witnessed a great body of uniform legislation of this character.[194] Moreover, a state which wishes to make the effectiveness of its own statute contingent upon the enactment and consistent administration of another state's law may do so by the device of reciprocal legislation.[195] Here again, however, one of the main sticking points is the problem of securing uniform judicial interpretation.[196] No state has thus far experimented with the possibility of designating some other state as lead-dog and requiring conformity to the interpretations of that state's courts. And the Supreme Court thus far has been unable to find a federal question in a mere difference of opinion about the meaning or application of uniform or reciprocal statutes of different states.[197]

Conceivably these difficulties might be met by the device of compacts among states, which of course require the consent of Congress.[198] Such compacts have often been used as vehicles for carrying out enterprises of common concern to two or more states, particularly in relation to the conservation of natural resources.[199] And the Supreme Court has said that questions about the execution, validity, and meaning of congressionally-approved compacts are federal questions, determinable on review of state court decisions.[200] The suggestion has been made that uniformity of interpretation of the proposed Uniform Commercial Code might be achieved by embodying the Code in a compact and securing its approval by Congress.[201] The question is whether mere uniformity in the regulatory law to be applied in the courts of different states is an appropriate subject of agreement among them. Or, perhaps more accurately, granting that federal question jurisdiction is an appropriate incident of compacts involving programs of joint governmental action by two or more states, does it follow that such jurisdiction can be made an end in itself when joint action is not proposed?[202] If these questions are answered in the affirmative, one can envision some future movement for a Bricker-like Amendment to dispel fears of the possibility of extension of federal authority implicit in this use of the treaty powers of the states, with the safeguard only of a majority vote in Congress.

VI

CONCLUSION: THE NATURE AND DIMENSIONS OF THE PROBLEM OF COORDINATION

We could have, in principle, a perfect uniformity of law in the United States—at a price. We could have it by establishing a single legislature, a single system of courts, a single chief executive, and a single phalanx of executive departments and administrative agencies, each possessing within its sphere a nationwide and general jurisdiction.

So Procrustean a solution of the problems of federalism is unlikely to find wide favor. Wholly apart from the natural inertia of institutions, one can discern two major reasons why this is so. The first is the workaday reason of administrative feasibility. In this nation of one hundred and sixty millions, the sheer volume of governmental business would prevent the promise of uniformity in principle from being realized in practice. No informed observer can suppose that any of the three branches of the federal government, as now organized, could long avoid breakdown under the load of total governmental responsibility. And no experience on the face of the globe, past or present, shows how to blueprint a plan of reorganization to enable the load to be carried. The second reason is more basic. Common sense and the instinct for freedom alike can be counted upon to tell the American people never to put all their eggs of hope from governmental problem-solving in one governmental basket.

Among drastic structural changes perhaps the most nearly thinkable is the substitution, at least in part, of a single system of courts for the existing dual system. The main outlines of the scheme to which the architects of such a reform would be driven can be foreseen: state trial courts for both state and federal business, with the possible exception of a few highly specialized federal courts; federal courts of appeals for the review of state court decisions turning upon federal questions; and a coordinating and largely discretionary review of decisions of the federal courts of appeals by the Supreme Court. The net gain from this reorganization would be the elimination of some hard technical problems of jurisdiction and of post-*Erie* distinctions between substance and procedure.[203] The great if indeterminable loss would be the substantial sterilization of Congress as an agency of reform of trial procedure, the abandonment of an independent federal judiciary and of the federal jury as instruments of protection of federal rights at the trial level, and the sacrifice of the possibility of further contributions to legal thought of the kind which a separate corps of federal trial judges have been able to make in the past.

If the possibility of major structural change be discarded, the principal problems created by the established division of governmental authority, it is suggested, are six-fold:

First. The adequacy of existing federal powers to establish nationwide uniformity (a) of legal doctrine and (b) of administrative policy; and, if they are inadequate, the best means of enlarging them. The extent of the non-use of existing federal powers is persuasive of the conclusion that this problem, if it is a problem at all, is of concern only in a few highly specialized areas.

Second. The criteria which should guide Congress in deciding whether to exercise the powers to promote uniformity which it now has, and the courts in determining whether Congress *has* exercised the powers. In the future as in the past, Congress is likely to make decisions of this kind only under the pressure of immediate and strongly-felt political interests, and then only with respect to the principal points of controversy. The opportunity for long-range and systematic thinking lies with the courts and the legal profession, with such help as political science can muster. In no other area of federalism is there greater need for such thinking and for judicial opinions which reflect it and hence carry with Congress the weight which only disinterestedness and sound reasoning can command.

Third. A reconsideration and clarification of the bases of jurisdiction of the federal district courts. The time has long been overdue for a full-dress reexamination by Congress of the uses to which these courts are being put—a need only faintly reflected in this chapter.[204] Short of such a reexamination, there is both opportunity and need for the courts to narrow the areas of uncertainty in the application of the lines of jurisdiction which Congress has drawn, and of the criteria for deciding in a particular case whether a federal court should exercise a jurisdiction which Congress has conferred.[205]

Fourth. Assuming the continuance of a concurrent jurisdiction of state and federal courts, the best ways of securing uniformity of legal obligation regardless of which system of courts exercises the jurisdiction, without sacrifice of the necessary or useful independence of either the federal or state governments. What is here needed is little more than restoration of the nerve to grapple intelligently with the familiar and entirely manageable problems of the distinction between substance and procedure. The job is not beyond the reach of effective legislation, but it ought mainly to be done by the courts.

Fifth. The best ways of securing uniformity of legal obligation regardless of whether litigation is brought within the borders of one state or another, without sacrifice of the necessary or useful independence of any of the governments involved. This chapter has suggested that these problems cannot be satisfactorily solved solely by means of a further constitutionalizing of conflict of laws doctrines. The decision in *Klaxon Co. v. Stentor Electric Mfg. Co.*[206] needs to be reexamined, and the unexamined questions of the conflict of state laws adopted or referred to by federal law need to be met.

Sixth. The adequacy of the existing powers of the states to establish on their own motion near-equivalents of federal uniformity by compact with other states, by uniform or reciprocal legislation, by adoption of federal law, or otherwise.

These are large problems, as the legal and governmental problems in a large country can be expected to be. But in a just perspective of social institutions which appraises them with satisfaction at the extent to which they succeed in making encroachments upon chaos, rather than with pain at the extent to which they fall short of naively assumed possibilities of perfection, the problems will appear relatively minor, and impressive mainly as evidence of the sound architecture and good working order of the system as a whole. Imagination and intelligence need to be applied to their solution. But these qualities imply the wit not to be deluded by little-minded assumptions about the value of doctrinal uniformity and symmetrical organization charts. They imply the discernment to see that a political system which maximizes the opportunities for coping effectively with the problems of social living is better than one which minimizes them. This means a federal system.

FOOTNOTES TO CHAPTER 11

1. Suggested to him by the discussion in Barbara A. Wootton, *Freedom Under Planning,* London, G. Allen & Unwin, Ltd., 1945, chap. 2.

2. *Writings of James Madison,* Hunt edition, New York, G. P. Putnam's Sons, 1910, Vol. 9, pp. 199–200.

3. In Chapters 15, 16, and 17, below, John M. Gaus and Charles McKinley discuss the special role both of regular county governments and of local special-purpose districts in the administration of agricultural and other natural resource programs. These chapters and the excerpts from the discussion of problems of federal fiscal policy illustrate the ways in which direct relations may be established between the central government and local governmental units—with the federal government, indeed, sometimes serving as place of appeal or alternative resort to the states in the attempted solution of local problems.

4. This statement oversimplifies a complex story. The states all inherited a body of colonial statutes. The decisions of their courts were influenced by local customs and decisional rules developed during the colonial period and varying from the common law, although deriving from it. The colonists were influenced, too, by customary practices of the many local courts in England as well as by the law of the king's courts. Finally, English statutes enacted before settlement were commonly regarded as included in the reception. In this and other regards, reception statutes in varying terms induced varying attitudes in different states. See, generally, Mark De Wolfe Howe, *Readings in American Legal History,* Cambridge, Harvard University Press, 1949, pp. 1–71; Roscoe Pound and Theodore F. T. Plucknett, *Readings on the History and System of the Common Law,* 3d edition, Rochester, Lawyers Cooperative Publishing Co., 1927, pp. 306–49; Zechariah Chafee, Jr., "Colonial Courts and the Common Law," *Proceedings of the Massachusetts Historical Society,* Vol. 68, p. 132, 1952; Julius Goebel, Jr., "King's Law and Local Custom in Seventeenth Century New England," *Columbia Law Review,* Vol. 31, p. 416, 1931; Ford W. Hall, "The Common Law: An Account of its Reception in the United States," *Vanderbilt Law Review,* Vol. 4, p. 791, 1951; Ford W. Hall, "An Account of the Adoption of the Common Law by Texas," *Texas Law Review,* Vol. 28, p. 801, 1950. The influence of the Spanish and French law made itself felt in many of the states of the South and Southwest; see last citation above.

5. See, *e.g.,* CAL. CIV. CODE § 22.2 (Supp. 1953): "The common law of England, so far as it is not repugnant to or inconsistent with the constitution of the United States, or the constitution or laws of this state, is the rule of decision in all the courts of this state." For a concise summary of the fate of the nineteenth century code movement in New York, see 1 MCKINNEY'S CONS. LAWS OF N.Y. ANN. IX-XXXVII (1942). And see generally, Clarence J. Morrow, "Louisiana Blueprint: Civilian Codification and Legal Method for State and Nation," *Tulane Law Review,* Vol. 17, pp. 387–415, 1943. As to Louisiana, see further, Harriet S. Daggett, Joseph Dainow, Paul M. Hebert, and Henry G. McMahon, "A Reappraisal Appraised: A Brief for the Civil Law of Louisiana," *Tulane Law Review,* Vol. 12, p. 12, 1937.

6. In discussion at the Bicentennial Conference on Federalism quoted above in Chapter 6.

7. The latter duties are the product of unilateral, bilateral, or group exercise of a great variety of private powers constituting in the most literal sense private law-making—a phenomenon which needs to be distinguished from other forms of

private ordering that do not receive or depend upon the affirmative backing of government. Private lawmaking powers are one of society's great instruments in the decentralization of capacity to command the exercise of public authority. The parallels between private and public lawmakers and their respective counsel, in terms both of necessary skills and of social responsibility, have been insufficiently explored. See generally, David F. Cavers, "Legal Education and Lawyer-Made Law," *West Virginia Law Review,* Vol. 54, p. 177, 1952.

8. On the difference between judicially-developed law and statutory law, see the illuminating analysis in Ernst Freund, *Legislative Regulation,* New York, Commonwealth Fund, 1932, particularly chap. 1. The scope and limits of the creative powers of courts is one of the most neglected problems in American legal thought. Cf. Fred V. Cahill, *Judicial Legislation,* New York, Ronald Press Company, 1952.

9. Relationships of this kind are examined more particularly in Part IV.

10. Some typical relationships of this kind are discussed in Part V.

11. *E.g.,* Art. I, § 10: "No State shall enter into any Treaty, Alliance, or Confederation; grant Letters of Marque and Reprisal; coin Money; emit Bills of Credit; make any Thing but gold and silver Coin a Tender in Payment of Debts; pass any Bill of Attainder, ex post facto Law, or Law impairing the Obligation of Contracts, or grant any Title of Nobility.

"No State shall, without the Consent of the Congress, lay any Imposts or Duties on Imports or Exports, except what may be absolutely necessary for executing its inspection Laws: . . .

"No State shall, without the Consent of Congress, lay any Duty of Tonnage, keep Troops, or Ships of War in time of Peace, enter into an Agreement or Compact with another State, or with a foreign Power, or engage in War, unless actually invaded, or in such imminent Danger as will not admit of delay."

Art IV, § 1: "Full Faith and Credit shall be given in each State to the public Acts, Records, and Judicial Proceedings of every other State. And the Congress may by general Laws prescribe the Manner in which such Acts, Records and Proceedings shall be proved, and the Effect thereof."

Art. IV, § 2: "The Citizens of each State shall be entitled to all Privileges and Immunities of Citizens in the several States.

"A Person charged in any State with Treason, Felony, or other Crime, who shall flee from Justice, and be found in another State, shall on Demand of the executive Authority of the State from which he fled, be delivered up, to be removed to the State having Jurisdiction of the Crime.

"No Person held to Service or Labour in one State, under the Laws thereof, escaping into another, shall, in Consequence of any Law or Regulation therein, be discharged from such Service or Labour, but shall be delivered up on Claim of the Party to whom such Service or Labour may be due."

Art. VI: ". . .

"This Constitution, and the Laws of the United States which shall be made in Pursuance thereof; and all Treaties made, or which shall be made, under the Authority of the United States, shall be the supreme Law of the Land; and the Judges in every State shall be bound thereby, any Thing in the Constitution or Laws of any State to the Contrary notwithstanding.

"The Senators and Representatives before mentioned, and the Members of the several State Legislatures, and all executive and judicial Officers, both of the United States and of the several States, shall be bound by Oath or Affirmation, to support this Constitution; . . ."

AMEND. XIII: "§ 1. Neither slavery nor involuntary servitude, except as a punishment for crime whereof the party shall have been duly convicted, shall exist within the United States, or any place subject to their jurisdiction.

"§ 2. Congress shall have power to enforce this article by appropriate legislation."

AMEND. XIV: "§ 1. All persons born or naturalized in the United States, and subject to the jurisdiction thereof, are citizens of the United States and of the State wherein they reside. No State shall make or enforce any law which shall abridge the privileges or immunities of citizens of the United States; nor shall any State deprive any person of life, liberty, or property, without due process of law; nor deny to any person within its jurisdiction the equal protection of the laws.

"§ 5. The Congress shall have power to enforce, by appropriate legislation, the provisions of this article."

AMEND. XV: "§ 1. The right of citizens of the United States to vote shall not be denied or abridged by the United States or by any State on account of race, color, or previous condition of servitude.

"§ 2. The Congress shall have power to enforce this article by appropriate legislation."

AMEND. XIX: "The right of citizens of the United States to vote shall not be denied or abridged by the United States or by any State on account of sex.

"Congress shall have power to enforce this article by appropriate legislation."

12. See these and other enforcement clauses in note 11, above.

13. See Robert H. Jackson, "Full Faith and Credit—The Lawyer's Clause of the Constitution," *Columbia Law Review,* Vol. 45, p. 1, 1945; Robert K. Carr, *Federal Protection of Civil Rights: Quest for a Sword,* Ithaca, Cornell University Press, 1947; *To Secure These Rights,* The Report of the President's Committee on Civil Rights, New York, Simon & Schuster, 1947.

14. See Part V-D, below.

15. See note 136 below.

16. For an illuminating discussion of the political and other reasons for this attitude, see Wechsler, *The Political Safeguards of Federalism: The Role of the States in the Composition and Selection of the National Government,* Chapter 7, above.

17. The *Fiscal Aspects of Federalism* are considered by Roy Blough, Chapter 20, below.

18. These administrative relationships are a principal concern of the chapters cited in note 3 above, and also of Chapter 19 on *Decision-Making in a Federal System* by Edward W. Weidner.

19. See Part V.

20. The *"vice versa"* needs to be qualified by the developing doctrine which permits and sometimes even requires a federal court to abstain from the exercise of jurisdiction in favor of a state forum. See notes 66 and 121 below. But no such doctrine is available to relieve a state court having jurisdiction of the duty to exercise it and come to a decision.

21. See the excellent essay by Arthur N. Holcombe, "The States as Agents of the Nation," *Southwestern Political Science Quarterly,* (now *Southwestern Social Science Quarterly*), Vol. 1, p. 307, 1921. Reprinted in *Selected Essays on Constitutional Law,* Chicago, Foundation Press, 1938, Vol. III, p. 1187.

22. See Part III-B below.

23. See Part III-C below.

24. See text below accompanying note 60, and Part III-C-2.

25. Section 73 of the Commonwealth Constitution provides:

"The High Court shall have jurisdiction, with such exceptions and subject to such regulations as the Parliament prescribes, to hear and determine appeals from all judgments, decrees, orders, and sentences:

"I. Of any Justice or Justices exercising the original jurisdiction of the High Court:

"II. Of any other federal court, or court exercising federal jurisdiction; or of the Supreme Court of any State, or of any other court of any State from which at the establishment of the Commonwealth an appeal lies to the Queen in Council:

"III. Of the Inter-State Commission, but as to questions of law only:

and the judgment of the High Court in all such cases shall be final and conclusive.

"But no exception or regulation prescribed by the Parliament shall prevent the High Court from hearing and determining any appeal from the Supreme Court of a State in any matter in which at the establishment of the Commonwealth an appeal lies from such Supreme Court to the Queen in Council. . . ."

All the Australian states having received the common law of England, it will be observed that these provisions enable the High Court to coordinate decisions upon all questions of unwritten state law. To the extent that the states enact uniform statutes, the interpretation of state statutory law may also be coordinated. The policy of the High Court is to accord great deference to English decisions, thus promoting uniformity in the English common law generally. See Zelman Cowen, "The Conflict of Laws: The Experience of the Australian Federation," *Vanderbilt Law Review*, Vol. 6, p. 644, 1953.

The Commonwealth has created a few specialized inferior federal courts, but federal jurisdiction in the first instance is exercised primarily by the High Court Justices and by the state courts. See K. H. Bailey, "The Federal Jurisdiction of State Courts," *Res Judicatae*, Vol. 2, p. 184, 1940–41.

26. It is to be observed that the Court as now constituted could not possibly discharge such a responsibility.

27. William W. Crosskey, *Politics and the Constitution in the History of the United States*, Chicago, University of Chicago Press, 1953, especially Vol. I, chaps. 18–20.

28. Professor Crosskey develops at great length the thesis that Congress was intended to have general power to legislate in furtherance of all the objects of government stated in the Preamble to the Constitution, and that neither the express enumeration of congressional powers in the original Constitution nor the limitation of the Tenth Amendment impugns this conclusion. CROSSKEY, *op. cit., passim*, especially Vol. I, and more particularly Part III, entitled "A Unitary View of the National Governing Powers." At the same time he recognizes that the so-called unwritten or customary " 'Laws of the United States,' were not to be regarded as part of 'the *supreme* Law'; and unlike that 'Law,' . . . they were, and still are, *alterable by state legislation,*" *ibid.*, Vol. I, p. 622 (italics in original). The latter conclusion, however, is qualified by the argument, elsewhere advanced, that the states were to be without power to legislate in any way inconsistent with the various branches of the law of nations as then understood, including the law merchant. *Ibid.*, Vol. I, pp. 321–22, 638–40, 652.

29. See *ibid.*, chap. 21, "The National Judicial Powers under an Eighteenth-Century Interpretation: Herein of These Powers with the Second Category of 'Cases' Minimally Taken."

30. Compare the elaborate introduction to the thesis respecting the national status of the common law in chapters 18 and 19 with the paucity of data in support of the thesis itself in chapter 20.

The thesis that all Supreme Court decisions were to be binding as precedents upon the state courts seems chiefly to rest, question-beggingly, upon the constitutional statement in the Preamble of the purpose to "establish Justice," and the constitutional description of "the supreme Court" as "supreme."

31. And instead of extending the diversity jurisdiction to all controversies "between citizens of different States," Congress carefully limited it to those cases where prejudice was to be feared, in which "the suit is between a citizen of the State where the suit is brought, and a citizen of another State." There was also a jurisdictional amount requirement of $500.

Professor Crosskey speaks of the First Judiciary Act as "almost diabolically contrived to render both the national trial courts, and the Supreme Court of the United States, unpopular; to delay and difficilitate the systematic exposition of the new judiciary powers; and thus to postpone and, haply, to prevent the long-desired judicial reform which the Constitution had been expected to inaugurate." *Ibid.,* Vol. II, p. 756. Elsewhere he asserts that in withholding "from the courts it set up, certain of the powers that the Constitution, upon a straight-forward reading, plainly makes mandatory for them . . . the First Congress, it appears, acted unconstitutionally." *Ibid.,* Vol. I, p. 610. He promises that "The reasons for this action, or inaction, on the part of Congress, will be considered in a future volume." *Ibid.* Pending the appearance of this volume, it is possible to think that the misreading of the Constitution is Professor Crosskey's and not that of the First Congress.

32. Professor Crosskey cites no such case, and none has been found.

Early arguments for treating the common law as in some sense a law of the United States were addressed to two problems very distinct from that of appellate jurisdiction over state courts. The first was the question whether the federal courts had jurisdiction to punish offenses against the United States which had not been defined as crimes by act of Congress. As to this see text following note 165. The second was the question of the law governing controversies between citizens of different states in federal circuit courts in the absence of an applicable state statute. See Part III-A-4.

In such cases as Jackson *ex dem.* St. John v. Chew, 12 Wheat. 153 (U.S. 1827), counsel showed their understanding that a writ of error would not lie to review an adverse decision of a state court on a common law question by omitting to apply for such a writ and instead pressing the same claim in a new action, founded on diversity of citizenship, in a federal circuit court. See also Daly's Lessee v. James, 8 Wheat. 494 (U.S. 1823). When common law questions, or other state questions, were presented in cases involving also a genuinely federal question, Court and counsel alike seem to have treated the question of jurisdiction over the common law or other state question as turning upon whether that question was one which "immediately respects" the federal question. See note 33. See, *e.g.,* Smith v. Maryland, 6 Cranch 286, 304–05 (U.S. 1810); Martin v. Hunter's Lessee, 1 Wheat. 304, 355–60 (U.S. 1816); Matthews v. Zane, 7 Wheat. 164, 201, 206 (U.S. 1822); and Crowell v. Randall, 10 Pet. 368, 392–97 (U.S. 1836), reviewing earlier cases.

Professor Crosskey's elaborate argument, *op. cit.,* Vol. II, pp. 719–53, that the response of the bar and the Pennsylvania state courts to the Supreme Court's decision in Huidekoper's Lessee v. Douglass, 3 Cranch 1 (U.S. 1805), shows a contemporary understanding that such decisions were precedents binding the state courts falls to the ground, other weaknesses aside, in the face of the fact that writs of error to state courts were never taken to urge such a position. The issue was finally settled in a diversity action in which a federal circuit court had adhered to an earlier Supreme Court decision on a point of interpretation of a Tennessee statute in disregard of later Tennessee decisions to the contrary. The Supreme Court held that this was wrong, with Justice Baldwin alone dissenting. Green v.

Neal's Lessee, 6 Pet. 291 (U.S. 1832). See also Shelby v. Guy, 11 Wheat. 361, 366–69 (U.S. 1826).

33. 1 STAT. 73, 86–87: ". . . But no other error shall be assigned or regarded as a ground of reversal in any such case as aforesaid, than such as appears on the face of the record, and immediately respects the before mentioneu questions of validity or construction of the said constitution, treaties, statutes, commissions, or authorities in dispute."

34. See the summary of the statutory development in Henry M. Hart, Jr., and Herbert Wechsler, *The Federal Courts and the Federal System,* Brooklyn, Foundation Press, 1953, pp. 400–03.

35. Judiciary Act of 1867, 14 STAT. 385.

36. 20 Wall. 590 (U.S. 1875).

37. On the limited power which the Court has always asserted to reexamine determinations of questions of state law which do not constitute an "adequate and independent" ground of disposition of a case involving a claim of federal right, see text following note 114.

38. 1 Wheat. 304 (U.S. 1816), discussed in Part III-B.

39. See, *e.g.,* the cases collected in Hart and Wechsler, *op. cit.,* pp. 435–545.

40. 1 STAT. 92 (1789).

41. But see the dictum in Watson v. Tarpley, 18 How. 517, 521 (U.S. 1855), and the discrediting comment in Burns Mortgage Co. v. Fried, 292 U.S. 487, 495 (1934). As to state statutes in federal equity, see the references in note 73 below.

42. As to statutory interpretation, see McKeen v. Delancy's Lessee, 5 Cranch 22, 32 (U.S. 1809); Elmendorf v. Taylor, 10 Wheat. 152, 159–60 (U.S. 1825); Green v. Neal's Lessee, 6 Pet. 291, 297 (U.S. 1832); Bucher v. Cheshire R.R., 125 U.S. 555, 584 (1888). For later and, as it now appears, aberrational qualifications, see Hart and Wechsler, *op. cit.,* pp. 617–20.

As to decisional rules in "local" matters, see Sim's Lessee v. Irvine, 3 Dall. 425, 447 (U.S. 1799); Jackson *ex dem.* St. John v. Chew, 12 Wheat. 153, 167 (U.S. 1827); Wheaton v. Peters, 8 Pet. 591, 658–59, 687–91 (U.S. 1834).

43. 16 Pet. 1 (U.S. 1842).

44. The opinion of Justice Brandeis in Erie R.R. v. Tompkins, 304 U.S. 64 (1938), reviews the development.

45. In Baltimore & Ohio R.R. v. Baugh, 149 U.S. 368, 370, 388 (1893), extending the doctrine of *Swift v. Tyson* to the field of torts, the Court spoke of the case as involving "not a question of local law, to be settled by an examination merely of the decisions of the Supreme Court of Ohio, . . . but rather one of general law, to be determined by a reference to all the authorities, and a consideration of the principles underlying the relations of master and servant." But when it came to examine the authorities it said that "it is enough . . . to refer to those in this court." Lower federal courts, of course, treated these as controlling.

46. See Justice Frankfurter in Guaranty Trust Co. v. York, 326 U.S. 99, 103 (1945).

47. Justice Story no doubt counted upon the prestige of the Supreme Court to induce the state courts to accept its views. Sometimes this happened, but more often it did not. See Erie R.R. v. Tompkins, 304 U.S. 64, 74 (1938).

48. 304 U.S. 64 (1938).

49. See Part III-C below.

50. 1 Wheat. 304 (U.S. 1816).

51. 6 Wheat. 264 (U.S. 1821).

52. In the debate on whether to authorize or direct the establishment of inferior federal courts, all hands agreed that review of state court decisions would be available as one means of vindicating federal rights, the argument of the states' righters being that this was enough. See Hart and Wechsler, *op. cit.*, pp. 17–18.

53. Congress, of course, has power to provide for such removal, but for the most part it has sought to make cases removable, if at all, only at the outset of the proceedings. See *ibid.*, pp. 375–80, 763.

54. See *ibid.*, pp. 373–80, 1019–21.

54a. See Tarble's Case, 13 Wall. 397 (U.S. 1871) (habeas corpus in behalf of federal prisoner), with which compare McClung v. Silliman, 6 Wheat. 598 (U.S. 1821) (mandamus to federal officer). The problem of a state court's power to issue a writ of injunction to a federal officer is still unresolved. See Brooks v. Dewar, 313 U.S. 354 (1941). Since virtually all actions against federal officers in state courts are now subject to removal to a federal district court at the option of the defendant, 62 Stat. 938 (1948), 28 U.S.C. § 1442 (Supp. 1952), whatever basis may once have existed for an implied exclusion of state court jurisdiction seems to have disappeared. See generally Hart and Wechsler, *op. cit.*, pp. 388–90.

55. See, *e.g.*, Claflin v. Houseman, 93 U.S. 130 (1876). Statistics on the volume of this litigation are, unfortunately, unprocurable, but the volume is undoubtedly large.

56. A point which escaped the New York Court of Appeals in Wasservogel v. Meyerowitz, 300 N.Y. 125, 89 N.E.2d 712 (1949). See also Lynbrook Gardens, Inc. v. Ullmann, 291 N.Y. 472, 53 N.E.2d 353 (1943). The point is assumed in numerous decisions reversing state court judgments for further proceedings in accordance with federal law. See, *e.g.*, Ward v. Love County, 253 U.S. 17 (1920); Iowa-Des Moines National Bank v. Bennett, 284 U.S. 239 (1931).

57. McKnett v. St. Louis & S.F. Ry., 292 U.S. 230 (1934).

58. *Cf.* Testa v. Katt, 330 U.S. 386 (1947).

59. In General Oil Co. v. Crain, 209 U.S. 211 (1908), the Court said plainly that the Tennessee courts could not refuse, on the ground that the courts of the state were without jurisdiction, to entertain an action to enjoin a state taxing official from enforcing a tax alleged to violate the federal Constitution. But since it went on to uphold the tax on the merits, the incipient conflict never came to a head. In post-conviction efforts of state prisoners to secure release on the ground that they were convicted in violation of the federal Constitution, the Court has spoken repeatedly of the obligation of the states to provide an adequate corrective process for certain kinds of claims. But the Court has not so far sought to enforce such an obligation by direct command to hear a claim, apparently assuming rather that the ultimate sanction is federal habeas corpus. See, *e.g.*, Young v. Ragen, 337 U.S. 235 (1949); Marino v. Ragen, 332 U.S. 561 (1947). See, Hart and Wechsler, *op. cit.*, pp. 474–77, 512–17.

60. See, *e.g.*, Davis v. Wechsler, 263 U.S. 22 (1923), and Patterson v. Alabama, 294 U.S. 600 (1935), with which compare Herndon v. Georgia, 295 U.S. 441 (1935), and Parker v. Illinois, 333 U.S. 571 (1948).

61. Brown v. Western Ry., 338 U.S. 294 (1949); Dice v. Akron, C. & Y.R.R., 342 U.S. 359 (1952), both Federal Employers' Liability Act cases.

62. Compare the parallel problem of federal court enforcement of state-created rights in diversity litigation, discussed in Part III-C.

63. Most actions under federal statutes are removable by the defendant without

regard to the amount in controversy, although the amount is required if jurisdiction has to be established under 28 U.S.C. § 1331 (Supp. 1952) in combination with § 1441 (b). The irony of the cases cited in note 61 above is that the plaintiffs, to whose benefit the rulings redounded, had deliberately chosen a state court, and the statute under which they sued was one of the few in which Congress has expressly prohibited removal.

64. See generally Hart and Wechsler, *op. cit.,* pp. 1001–18.

65. Administrative questions, calling for an exercise of administrative discretion, do not present a "case" or "controversy" within the grant of federal judicial power in Article III of the Constitution. See, *e.g.,* Federal Radio Comm'n v. General Elec. Co., 281 U.S. 464 (1930), with which compare Federal Radio Comm'n v. Nelson Bros. Co., 289 U.S. 266 (1933). But review of a state administrative determination, or further proceedings predicated upon it, may present a justiciable case cognizable in a federal district court. Such review is ordinarily postponed until state administrative remedies have been exhausted. See, *e.g.* Porter v. Investors' Syndicate, 286 U.S. 461 (1932); Prentis v. Atlantic Coast Line Co., 211 U.S. 210 (1908). For illustrations of the difficulties in determining the nature of the state proceedings, and in ascertaining when and whether federal jurisdiction may later attach, see Chicago R.I. & P. R.R. v. Stude, 346 U.S. 574 (1954); Commissioners of Road Improvement District No. 2 v. St. Louis S.W. Ry., 257 U.S. 547 (1922); Upshur County v. Rich, 135 U.S. 467 (1890); Snook v. Industrial Comm'n of Illinois, 9 F. Supp. 26 (E.D. Ill. 1934).

66. In Burford v. Sun Oil Co., 319 U.S. 315, 326 (1943), a divided Court held that a federal district court ought to decline to review a complex state administrative order, even on a complaint presenting federal questions, in order not to interfere with the relationship of the state courts as "working partners with the Railroad Commission in the business of creating a regulatory system for the oil industry." See generally Hart and Wechsler, *op. cit.,* pp. 869–85.

67. For examples of the Court's pre-*Erie* attitude, see Beals v. Hale, 4 How. 37, 54 (U.S. 1846); Erie R.R. v. Hilt, 247 U.S. 97, 100–01 (1918); Graham v. White-Phillips Co., 296 U.S. 27, 30–31 (1935).

68. Fidelity Union Trust Co. v. Field, 311 U.S. 169 (1940), a decision buttressed by several similar holdings at the same term.

69. King v. Order of United Commercial Travelers, 333 U.S. 153 (1948).

70. See Arthur L. Corbin, "The Laws of the Several States," *Yale Law Journal,* Vol. 50, pp. 775–76, 1941.

71. In equity, admiralty, and bankruptcy the tradition of uniform federal procedure had been long established. But until the issuance of the Federal Rules of Civil Procedure in 1938, pursuant to authority given by Congress in 1934, 48 STAT. 1064, 47 U.S.C. § 151 (1946), procedure in actions at law in the federal courts was governed by a series of requirements, of varying content and often highly uncertain scope, to conform to the procedure of the courts of the state in which the federal court was sitting. 17 STAT. 196 (1872). See generally Hart and Wechsler, *op. cit.,* pp. 577–90.

72. In two notable instances the Court has avoided the issue by construing the rules so as to avoid any conflict. Palmer v. Hoffman, 318 U.S. 109 (1943); Cohen v. Beneficial Industrial Loan Corp., 337 U.S. 541 (1949). In a third case presenting the sharpest apparent conflict Justice Douglas avoided shedding light on the problem by ignoring it, enforcing in the face of Federal Rule 3 ("A civil action is commenced by filing a complaint with the court") a state rule that an action is not commenced for the purpose of the statute of limitations until personal service is made.

Ragan v. Merchants Transfer & Warehouse Co., 337 U.S. 530 (1949). That Congress lacked power to protect plaintiffs who comply with federal rules from the impact of such a state doctrine as that involved in the *Ragan* case seems inconceivable. That a competent draftsman would write a rule like Rule 3, deliberately intending not to give such protection, is equally hard to credit. The only remaining possibility is that Justice Douglas may have thought that the application of the rule in *Ragan* would have abridged substantive rights in violation of the Enabling Act. 48 STAT. 1064 (1934), 47 U.S.C. § 151 (1946). It seems unlikely that such a position could survive a full and candid examination. For general discussions, see the materials cited in Hart and Wechsler, *op. cit.*, p. 677.

73. On the tradition of federal equity, see Guaranty Trust Co. v. York, 326 U.S. 99 (1945); Alfred Hill, "The Erie Doctrine in Bankruptcy," *Harvard Law Review,* Vol. 66, pp. 1024–35, 1953; Note, "The Equitable Remedial Rights Doctrine: Past and Present, *Harvard Law Review,* Vol. 67, p. 836, 1954; Hart and Wechsler, *op. cit.*, pp. 640–59.

74. The confusion has been compounded by the opacity of the 1948 revisers of the Judicial Code in dropping as obsolete the historic requirement, traceable back to the First Judiciary Act, that "suits in equity shall not be sustained in either of the courts of the United States, in any case where plain, adequate and complete remedy may be had at law."

The assertion in the text is difficult to document, except by the absence of Supreme Court decisions to the contrary. It may draw support from the provision of the Enabling Act, 48 STAT. 1064 (1934), 47 U.S.C. § 151 (1946), that the rules "shall neither abridge, enlarge, nor modify the substantive rights of any litigant."

75. As pointed out in the next sub-section, the more recent Supreme Court decisions do not pose the issues this way: they ask only what the courts of the state in which the federal court is sitting would do.

The decisions to date permit the conclusion that a federal court in such a case may *not* grant a remedy which the state court would deny, even though the state court's denial would be without prejudice to the underlying substantive right. See, *e.g.*, Guaranty Trust Co. v. York, 326 U.S. 99 (1945) (opinion silent whether right was forum-created or out-of-state-created); Angel v. Bullington, 330 U.S. 183 (1947) (out-of-state-created right); Woods v. Interstate Realty Co., 337 U.S. 535 (1949) (forum-created right); Ragan v. Merchants Transfer & Warehouse Co., 337 U.S. 530 (1949), see note 72 above (opinion silent whether right was forum-created or out-of-state-created); First National Bank of Chicago v. United Air Lines, 342 U.S. 396 (1952) (out-of-state-created right); Wells v. Simonds Abrasive Co., 345 U.S. 514 (1953) (out-of-state-created right).

But the Court has not yet overruled such cases as Guffey v. Smith, 237 U.S. 101 (1915), where an oil and gas leasee out of possession was given specific relief in federal court although the state court would have given only damages; and the *York* opinion, above, purports to save at least some of them. That a federal court may not give a declaratory judgment in a diversity action merely because the courts of the forum state are not authorized to give declaratory relief still seems incredible.

The answer to the second of the two questions in the text would seem in principle to be yes, of course—providing the federal courts merely decline to adjudicate and do not purport to settle substantive rights inconsistently with applicable state law. Thus the Norris-La Guardia Act, 47 STAT. 70, (1932), 29 U.S.C. § 101 (1946) would still seem to be constitutional, even in states which are generous with labor injunctions. But the disposition in Venner v. Great Northern Ry., 209 U.S. 24 (1908), would now have to be a remand to the state court, or dismissal without prejudice, rather than dismissal on the merits.

76. Or, as Justice Jackson has put it, "Most of these decisions are actuated by a laudable but undiscriminating yen for uniformity within the forum state." Wells v. Simonds Abrasive Co., 345 U.S. 514, 519, 521 (dissenting opinion). Two of the most influential, but interestingly different, statements of the governing criterion are Justice Reed's in Klaxon Co. v. Stentor Elec. Mfg. Co., 313 U.S. 487, 496 (1941) ("the principle of uniformity within a state upon which the *Tompkins* decision is based"), and Justice Frankfurter's in Guaranty Trust Co. v. York, 326 U.S. 99, 109 ("The nub of the policy that underlies *Erie* . . . is that for the same transaction the accident of a suit by a non-resident litigant in a federal court instead of in a State court a block away, should not lead to a substantially different result").

77. It must be inferred that the present members of the Supreme Court believe that the framers of the diversity clause, and the successive Congresses which have acted under it, were moved only by a desire to afford out-of-state litigants the protection of the superior, or potentially superior, personnel, fact-finding processes, and housekeeping rules of the federal courts. Even these, it should be observed, are capable of disturbing the "equal administration of justice in coordinate state and federal courts sitting side by side." If they do not succeed in doing it, there seems to be no point to them.

78. See the parts of the opinion marked *"First"* and *"Third"* which purport to state the controlling rationale. 304 U.S. at 71–74, 78–80.

79. In the part of the opinion marked *"Second,"* Justice Brandeis discussed "experience in applying the doctrine of *Swift v. Tyson"* and noted the "injustice and confusion incident to" it, but observed that "the doctrine has not been without defenders" and stated expressly that the "injustice and confusion" were not in themselves a sufficient reason to abandon *Swift v. Tyson.* "But the unconstitutionality of the course pursued has now been made clear and compels us to do so." 304 U.S. at 74–78. In discussing the "injustice and confusion" he refers repeatedly to "discrimination" in favor of non-citizens and says that "the doctrine had prevented uniformity in the administration of the law of the State." But he was speaking in reference to lack of uniformity in substantive law, and appears to have had this in mind rather than mere lack of identical outcome of litigated cases.

80. If the parties are of diverse citizenship, and other requisites of jurisdiction are satisfied, the plaintiff can choose a federal court and make that choice final, whether he is an in-state or out-of-state citizen. If the plaintiff in such a case chooses a state court, the defendant can reverse his choice and remove to the federal court— if but only if he is an out-of-state citizen. 28 U.S.C. § 1441 (b) (Supp. 1952), in conjunction with § 1332 and § 1391 (a). Save for a short period from 1875 to 1887, Congress has acted on the apparent assumption that an in-state citizen ought not to be heard to complain of an outsider's satisfaction with his own state's courts.

81. Cf. notes 61–63 above, and accompanying text.

82. "It may be esteemed the basis of the Union, that 'the citizens of each State shall be entitled to all the privileges and immunities of citizens of the several States.' And if it be a just principle, that every government *ought to possess the means of executing its own provisions by its own authority,* it will follow, that in order to the inviolable maintenance of that equality of privileges and immunities to which the citizens of the union will be entitled, the national judiciary ought to preside in all cases in which one State or its citizens are opposed to another State or its citizens. To secure the full effect of so fundamental a provision against all evasion and subterfuge, it is necessary that its construction should be committed to that tribunal which, having no local attachments, will be likely to be impartial between the different states and their citizens, and which, owing its official existence to the Union, will

never be likely to feel any bias inauspicious to the principles on which it is founded."
The Federalist, Lodge edition, New York, G. P. Putnam's Sons, 1888, No. 80, p.
497; (italics in original).

83. See Elliott E. Cheatham, "Federal Control of the Conflict of Laws," *Vanderbilt Law Review,* Vol. 6, p. 581, 1953; note 103 below.

84. Klaxon Co. v. Stentor Elec. Mfg. Co., 313 U.S. 487 (1941), accepting the
analysis in Sampson v. Channell, 110 F.2d 754 (1st Cir.), *cert. denied,* 310 U.S.
650 (1940). See also Griffin v. McCoach, 313 U.S. 498 (1941). In *Erie* itself,
Justice Brandeis seemed to assume that a federal court should think for itself on
conflicts problems. See 304 U.S. 64, 80 (1938). The whole Court assumed the same
thing in Sibbach v. Wilson & Co., 312 U.S. 1 (1941).

85. Compare Hamilton in note 82 above.

86. *Klaxon,* above note 84, involved a problem of the first type and *Griffin,*
seemingly, a problem of the second type. But Justice Reed's opinions in the two
cases discussed both types indiscriminately, without recognition of the highly significant differences between them.

It is difficult to understand why federal policy required, in *Klaxon,* the denial
to a New York plaintiff forced to bring suit in Delaware of interest on a verdict
which the New York and perhaps other state courts would have allowed, merely
because Delaware state courts would not have allowed it. But it is far more difficult
to understand why the merest local rule denying a state forum to an out-of-state
claim, without any attempt to question the underlying substantive claim, should
require also the denial of a federal forum in the same state, as held in the cases cited
in note 75, above. The latter difficulty Justice Jackson has recently twice recognized,
carrying with him Justice Minton and in the second instance Justice Black also.
See his dissenting opinions in First National Bank of Chicago v. United Air Lines,
342 U.S. 396, 398 (1952), and Wells v. Simonds Abrasive Co., 345 U.S. 514,
519 (1953). Other Justices seem surely destined to see the same light.

87. See Justice Jackson, dissenting, in Wells v. Simonds Abrasive Co., 345
U.S. 514, 519 (1953). Prevailing doctrines both of state court jurisdiction and of
federal venue often give plaintiffs a wide choice among territorial units in which
to sue.

88. See, particularly, Hamilton's argument in No. 15, and the development of it
in Nos. 16–22. The problem of *The Coercion of States in a Federal System* is discussed in Chapter 9 by Arthur N. Holcombe.

89. 16 Pet. 536 (U.S. 1842). The Court held that the obligation to secure the
return of fugitive slaves rested on the United States in view of the act of Congress
undertaking to deal with the subject. It left open the question whether the United
States could compel state officers to act, in effect, as federal agents in carrying out
the obligation.

90. 24 How. 66 (U.S. 1861).

91. *Ibid.,* at 107.

92. See the references to this and other instances of state court recalcitrance in
Hart and Wechsler, *op. cit.,* pp. 420–21.

93. *Ex parte* Young, 209 U.S. 123 (1908). See also Part IV-B below.

94. Probably it would not be, on the theory that the writ was directed "not against
the sovereign, which has already sanctioned the act, but against the recalcitrant
agent who refuses to obey the express instruction of his principal." Recent cases,
Harvard Law Review, Vol. 67, p. 1081, 1954. Board of Liquidation v. McComb,
92 U.S. 531, 541 (1875); Rolston v. Missouri Fund Comm'rs, 120 U.S. 390, 411

(1887); cf. Houston v. Ormes, 252 U.S. 469, 472–74 (1920); Minnesota v. Hitchcock, 185 U.S. 373, 386 (1902). In view of the historic restriction of jurisdiction to issue writs of mandamus to the courts of the District of Columbia, the issue is likely to arise, if at all, only on an application for a mandatory injunction. See Hart and Wechsler, *op. cit.*, pp. 1180–87.

95. Cohens v. Virginia, 6 Wheat. 264, 407 (U.S. 1821).

96. See note 59 above.

97. Principality of Monaco v. Mississippi, 292 U.S. 313, 328–29 (1934).

98. See Hart and Wechsler, *op. cit.*, pp. 246–47.

99. On the much-misunderstood theory of judicial review, see Marbury v. Madison, 1 Cranch 137 (U.S. 1803); Frothingham v. Mellon, 262 U.S. 447 (1923); Hart and Wechsler, *op. cit.*, pp. 75–217.

100. See note 11 above.

101. See Tidal Oil Co. v. Flanagan, 263 U.S. 444 (1924), explaining, among other cases, Gelpcke v. City of Dubuque, 1 Wall. 175 (U.S. 1864), with which compare Railroad Co. v. McClure, 10 Wall. 511 (U.S. 1871).

102. See, *e.g.,* Twining v. New Jersey, 211 U.S. 78, 90–91 (1908), considering and upholding the validity of an application of a judicially-developed rule permitting a jury in a criminal case to be instructed that they might draw an unfavorable inference against the defendant from his failure to testify: "The judicial act of the highest court of the State, in authoritatively construing and enforcing its laws, is the act of the State. . . . The general question, therefore, is, whether such a law violates the Fourteenth Amendment." See also Brinkerhoff-Faris Trust & Savings Co. v. Hill, 281 U.S. 673, 680 (1930).

For a collection of cases on the constitutionality of state judicial procedures, many involving the application of state statutes and many not, see Paul A. Freund, Arthur E. Sutherland, Jr., Mark De Wolfe Howe, Ernest J. Brown, *Constitutional Law: Cases and Other Problems,* temporary edition, Boston, Little, Brown & Co., 1953, Vol. II, pp. 902–1089.

103. See, generally, Cheatham, note 83 above.

In Kryger v. Wilson, 242 U.S. 171, 176 (1916), Justice Brandeis said: "The most the plaintiff in error can say is that the state court made a mistaken application of doctrines of the conflict of laws in deciding that the cancellation of a land contract is governed by the law of the *situs* instead of the place of making and performance. But that, being purely a question of local common law, is a matter with which this court is not concerned."

Nevertheless, in a few instances the Court has found due process limitations upon a state court's choice of law. *E.g.,* New York Life Ins. Co. v. Dodge, 246 U.S. 357 (1918). In a few other cases, not always clearly distinguished, the Court has held that the full faith and credit clause required respect for the "public Acts," as distinguished from judgments, of another state. These "Acts" include statutes. *E.g.,* Order of United Commercial Travelers v. Wolfe, 331 U.S. 586 (1947); John Hancock Mutual Life Ins. Co. v. Yates, 299 U.S 178 (1936). And in at least one instance the Court has spoken of "the faith and credit . . . to which local common and statutory law is entitled under the Constitution and laws of the United States." Magnolia Petroleum Co. v. Hunt, 320 U.S. 430, 436 (1943). A much more fully developed body of law expresses federal requirements of faith and credit to judgments of the courts of sister states. See Willis L. M. Reese and Vincent A. Johnson, "The Scope of Full Faith and Credit to Judgments," *Columbia Law Review,* Vol. 49, p. 153, 1949. See generally Freund *et al., op. cit.,* Vol. II, pp. 459–60.

It should be noted that the local substantive law rule assertedly misapplied by a state court may be either decisional or statutory. But the choice of law rule being reviewed is usually decisional, statutes rarely settling conflict of laws questions.

104. The few cases are reviewed in Shelley v. Kraemer, 334 U.S. 1, 14–18 (1948), which invalidated the application of a judicially-developed doctrine permitting judicial enforcement of racially restrictive covenants.

105. Questions of standing to challenge constitutionality may be involved if the objection is addressed to the effect of the statute upon persons other than the objector. See Hart and Wechsler, *op. cit.*, pp. 176–92.

106. Note 104 above.

107. See, *e.g.*, Marsh v. Alabama, 326 U.S. 501 (1946).

108. See note 53 above. In its interpretation of the statutory grants of federal jurisdiction, the Court has steadily sought to develop criteria which will enable jurisdiction to be determined at the outset of the proceeding rather than making it dependent upon the unpredictable contingencies of the defenses or replications which may be made. See Hart and Wechsler, *op. cit.*, pp. 748–97.

109. All criminal cases save those which Congress has made removable to a federal district court. See 28 U.S.C. § 1442 (Supp. 1952), Tennessee v. Davis, 100 U.S. 257 (1880).

110. See note 60 above.

111. See, *e.g.*, Demorest v. City Bank Co., 321 U.S. 36 (1944).

112. See, *e.g.*, Indiana *ex rel.* Anderson v. Brand, 303 U.S. 95 (1938). On federal protection of state-created rights generally, see Hart and Wechsler, *op. cit.*, pp. 465–70.

113. See Ashwander v. Tennessee Valley Authority, 297 U.S. 288, 346–48 (1936) (Brandeis, J., concurring); Liverpool, N.Y. & P.S.S. Co. v. Emigration Comm'rs, 113 U.S. 33, 39 (1885). For an important application of the canon where federal law was invoked offensively, see Siler v. Louisville & N. R.R., 213 U.S. 175, 193 (1909).

114. See, *e.g.*, Fox Film Corp. v. Muller, 296 U.S. 207, 210 (1935); Murdock v. Memphis, 20 Wall. 590, 635–36 (U.S. 1875); and other cases in Hart and Wechsler, *op. cit.*, pp. 435–545.

115. See *e.g.*, Ward v. Love County, 253 U.S. 17, 22 (1920), and cases cited. In the *Ward* case itself federal law was used offensively. The Court recognized that a state rule forbidding the recovery of illegally collected taxes in the absence of a showing that they had been paid under protest could properly be applied in an action to recover taxes collected in violation of federal law, but held that the ruling that the payment in question had been voluntary was "without any fair or substantial support." On the other hand, the Court overrode as in violation of federal law a state rule requiring a showing that the proceeds of the tax were still in the hands of the collecting officers.

116. Home Tel. & Tel. Co. v. Los Angeles, 227 U.S. 278 (1913); see Hart and Wechsler, *op. cit.*, pp. 820–33.

117. See Chief Justice Stone in Snowden v. Hughes, 321 U.S. 1, 11 (1944): "And state action, even though illegal under state law, can be no more and no less constitutional under the Fourteenth Amendment than if it were sanctioned by the state legislature."

118. Cf. note 134 below; see *e.g.*, REV. STAT. § 1980 (1875), 42 U.S.C.A. § 1985 (3) (Supp. 1953), giving a right of action to any person injured by a conspiracy of two or more persons, under color of office or otherwise, to deprive him

of certain federal rights, and 28 U.S.C. § 1343 (1) and (2) (Supp. 1952), giving the district courts jurisdiction of such actions. For the problems involved in this provision, see Collins v. Hardyman, 341 U.S. 651 (1951).

119. As for example the cases upholding federal claims against election officers in assertedly private and unofficial primary or pre-primary elections. Terry v. Adams, 345 U.S. 461 (1953); Smith v. Allwright, 321 U.S. 649 (1944). See also the recent cases considering the outer limits of permissible federal criminal prosecution for violation of civil rights. Williams v. United States, 341 U.S. 97 (1951); United States v. Williams, 341 U.S. 70 (1951); Screws v. United States, 325 U.S. 91 (1945); United States v. Classic, 313 U.S. 299 (1941).

120. See "Note on Accountability in Damages for Official Misconduct," in Hart and Wechsler, op. cit., pp. 1215–24.

121. The elaborate safeguards, both statutory and judge-made, which have been thrown about such actions are summarized in Hart and Wechsler, op. cit., pp. 843–90. Among the limitations, too complex to be examined in this chapter, are those which seek to deal with the dilemma of a federal court when jurisdiction is invoked on the basis of a claim of right the validity of which depends upon certain issues of state law. The Supreme Court has indicated that in some circumstances a federal court, while retaining jurisdiction, should withhold the exercise of it until appropriate proceedings have been brought in the state courts to resolve the doubtful issues of state law. Railroad Comm'n v. Pullman Co., 312 U.S. 496 (1941). In other hard-to-distinguish circumstances, the Court has said that the federal court should relinquish jurisdiction to the state court over state and federal questions alike. See Alabama Pub. Serv. Comm'n v. Southern Ry., 341 U.S. 341 (1951); Burford v. Sun Oil Co., 319 U.S. 315 (1943). For this and other aspects of these problems, see Hart and Wechsler, op cit., pp. 862–85, 1052–85.

122. There may, for example, be federal limitations based on federal concepts of justiciability. See, e.g., Doremus v. Board of Education, 342 U.S. 429 (1952); Coleman v. Miller, 307 U.S. 433 (1939); Hart and Wechsler, op. cit., pp. 165–66.

123. See the careful statement by Justice Matthews in In re Ayers, 123 U.S. 443, 499–506 (1887). The opinion speaks only of actions for "trespass or detinue" against individuals "guilty of personal trespasses and wrongs." In the era of the "general jurisprudence" of Swift v. Tyson there was no occasion for more particular reference to state law.

124. The crucial advance, seemingly, was in Ex parte Young, 209 U.S. 123 (1908), where the personal wrong complained of consisted of threats of a multiplicity of prosecutions, a very dubious tort under state law. The present attitude can be seen in Chief Justice Vinson's opinions in Georgia R.R. & Banking Co. v. Redwine, 342 U.S. 299, 304–06 (1952), and Larson v. Domestic & Foreign Commerce Corp., 337 U.S. 682, 704 (1949), dealing with a parallel problem of suits against the United States, both of which speak of the Constitution as if it not only conferred the remedy but also carved out an implied exception to the bars of the Eleventh Amendment and the doctrine of sovereign immunity. For jurisdictional purposes, certainly, it has long been recognized that injunction proceedings against both state and federal officers are "Cases arising under this Constitution."

125. See note 121 above. These restrictions have been applied only in actions in the federal district courts and presumably are not relevant in state court actions. See notes 61–63 above and accompanying text.

126. 48 Stat. 955 (1934), 28 U.S.C. §§ 2201–02 (Supp. 1952). See generally Hart and Wechsler, op. cit., pp. 135–56.

127. Liberty Warehouse Co. v. Grannis, 273 U.S. 70, 73 (1927).

128. Nashville, C. & St. L. Ry. v. Wallace, 288 U.S. 249 (1933). The *Wallace* case followed a series of cases which had suggested that no such judgments were reviewable. *E.g.,* Liberty Warehouse Co. v. Burley Tobacco Growers Co-op. Marketing Ass'n, 276 U.S. 71 (1928).

129. As to state-created rights, see note 75 above. The Court has indicated unwillingness to permit the new remedy to enlarge the federal question jurisdiction of the district courts, apparently applying the test of whether such jurisdiction would have existed in a coercive action by either party against the other. Skelly Oil Co. v. Phillips Petroleum Co., 339 U.S. 667 (1950); see Hart and Wechsler, *op. cit.,* pp. 774–77. See note 108 above.

130. *E.g.,* Ward v. Love County, note 115 above.

131. See Note, "Federal Jurisdiction in Suits for Damages Under Statutes Not Affording Such Remedy," *Columbia Law Review,* Vol. 48, pp. 1093–95, 1948.

132. See text below following note 165.

133. See Note, "The Proper Scope of the Civil Rights Acts," *Harvard Law Review,* Vol. 66, p. 1285, 1953; Comment, "The Civil Rights Act: Emergence of an Adequate Federal Civil Remedy?," *Indiana Law Journal,* Vol. 26, p. 361, 1951.

134. If the concept of "affirmative governance" appears confusingly vague, the following more precise definition may be substituted: Any exercise of federal governmental power involving the imposition of a legal duty upon private persons, or affecting private persons in any other way than by giving them a liberty or immunity from the exercise of state authority or a right of action for the wrongful exercise of state authority. The distinction, like many another, may seem to be a merely technical one in its borderline applications, but it points to a grouping which has significance for many purposes both of analysis and of understanding.

135. See text following note 15.

136. As, for example, in many of the prohibitions of Art. I, § 10, some of which, it will be observed, are absolute in terms, and others of which leave open the possibility of action with consent of Congress.

Other limitations have been drawn by the courts by implication from the Constitution, such as those which restrain the states from interfering with the appropriate functioning of the federal government and its instrumentalities. See Freund *et al., op. cit.,* Vol. II, pp. 679–712. The implied limitation upon certain kinds of state regulation of interstate commerce in matters viewed as "imperatively demanding a single uniform rule" were originally regarded as drawn from the Constitution. Cooley v. Board of Wardens, 12 How. 299, 319 (U.S. 1851). More recently they have often been treated as resting rather upon the more pliable will of Congress, as evidenced by its failure to legislate affirmatively. The problems, including those of congressional power to admit state regulation, are discussed in Thomas R. Powell, "Business Taxation and Interstate Commerce," *Proceedings of the National Tax Association* 1937, pp. 338–39, 1938. See also Henry W. Biklé, "The Silence of Congress," *Harvard Law Review,* Vol. 41, p. 200, 1927. The cases are collected in Freund *et al., op. cit.,* Vol. I, pp. 118–56, 310–678.

It is noteworthy that the commerce limitations operate almost exclusively as barriers to state taxation and special forms of statutory regulation without prejudice to the continued application of the basic decisional and other standing law of the states. For the application of this standing law to the United States and its instrumentalities, see text following note 170.

137. The evidence is the more impressive, currently, in view of expanded concepts of the reach of latent federal powers, particularly over commerce.

138. See, *e.g.,* Joy v. St. Louis, 201 U.S. 332, 342 (1906), holding that the question whether one claiming title to land under a United States patent is entitled to land formed by accretion after the patent was issued "is a question of local or state law, and is not one of a Federal nature."

139. See, *e.g.,* Luckett v. Delpark, Inc., 270 U.S. 496, 510 (1926): ". . . where a patentee complainant makes his suit one for recovery of royalties under a contract of license or assignment, or for damages for a breach of its covenants, or for a specific performance thereof, or asks the aid of the Court in declaring a forfeiture of the license or in restoring an unclouded title to the patent, he does not give the federal district court jurisdiction of the cause as one arising under the patent laws." See also American Well Works Co. v. Layne & Bowler Co., 241 U.S. 257 (1916), holding that an action for damages to business caused by a threat to sue under the patent law arises under and depends on state law. In these cases, it will be observed, a federal question concerning the validity or scope of the patent may become relevant or even be decisive of the litigation. But a federal district court lacks jurisdiction, in the absence of diversity of citizenship, because the cause of action is created by state law. For the nicety of some of the problems of this type, see Hart and Wechsler, *op. cit.,* pp. 754–58.

140. See Osborn v. Bank of the United States, 9 Wheat. 738 (U.S. 1824), and the companion case of Bank of the United States v. Planter's Bank of Georgia, *ibid.,* p. 904.

141. Regents of the University System of Georgia v. Carroll, 338 U.S. 586 (1950); Radio Station WOW, Inc. v. Johnson, 326 U.S. 120 (1945).

142. They control the jurisdiction of the Supreme Court on review of state court decisions for reasons already discussed, see Part III-A-3. They are of particular importance in relation to the federal question jurisdiction of the federal district courts because of the Court's insistence, in the interpretation of the statutory grant, that the existence of jurisdiction be determinable at the outset of the case. Sometimes this is accomplished through the formula used in the patent cases, note 139 above, that "a case arises under the law that creates the cause of action," and sometimes through a somewhat broader test of whether it necessarily appears from a well-pleaded statement of the plaintiff's case that a claim under federal law is an essential ingredient of it. See generally Paul J. Mishkin, "The Federal 'Question' in the District Courts," *Columbia Law Review,* Vol. 53, p. 157, 1953; Hart and Wechsler, *op. cit.,* pp. 758–777.

143. See notes 124 and 131 above.

144. Justice Black's opinion in Bell v. Hood, 327 U.S. 678 (1946), may be thought to require qualification of these statements. But it does not if the unappealed decision of the district court on the remand is sound, as it seems to be. Bell v. Hood, 71 F. Supp. 813 (S.D. Cal. 1947).

145. The original immunity was derived from McCulloch v. Maryland, 4 Wheat. 316 (U.S. 1819), invalidating a tax on the early Bank of the United States itself. The National Banking Act of 1863 was amended in 1864, 13 STAT. 99, to authorize non-discriminatory state taxes on the shares of national banks. See REV. STAT. § 5219 (1875), as amended, 12 U.S.C. § 548 (1946). The power of Congress to give the permission was upheld by a divided Court in Van Allen v. Assessors, 3 Wall. 573 (U.S. 1865).

146. The story is summarized in Note, "Fair Trade and Horizontal Price Fixing: Their Status Since the Second Schwegmann Case," *Yale Law Journal,* Vol. 63, p. 538, 1954.

147. The leading case is Gully v. First Nat. Bank in Meridian, 299 U.S. 109

(1936), holding that an action to collect state taxes on national bank shares, note 145 above, arises under the state taxing statute.

148. See note 71 above.

149. See the list of references in Hart and Wechsler, *op. cit.*, p. 589.

150. 28 U.S.C. § 1346(b) (Supp. 1952).

151. See Justice Frankfurter in Board of County Comm'rs v. United States, 308 U.S. 343, 349–50, 351–52 (1939).

152. Clearfield Trust Co. v. United States, 318 U.S. 363, 367 (1943).

153. *Ibid.*

154. Board of County Comm'rs v. United States, note 151 above.

155. See Note, "Federal Statutes Without Limitations Provisions," *Columbia Law Review,* Vol. 53, p. 68, 1953; Cope v. Anderson, 331 U.S. 461 (1947). For situations in which the Court draws the contrary conclusion that the matter is one to be governed by a uniform federal rule, judicially developed, see Part V-D. See generally Note, "Clearfield: Clouded Field of Federal Common Law," *Columbia Law Review,* Vol. 53, p. 991, 1953.

156. See Part V-A.

157. D'Oench Duhme & Co. v. Federal Deposit Ins. Corp., 315 U.S. 447, 465, 470 (1942) (concurring opinion).

158. The phrase is Justice Jackson's in the *D'Oench Duhme* opinion, above note 157, at 472. On the law applied in suits between states, see, particularly, Connecticut v. Massachusetts, 282 U.S. 660 (1931), and Kentucky v. Indiana, 281 U.S. 163 (1930). See also West Virginia *ex rel.* Dyer v. Sims, 341 U.S. 22 (1951); Hart and Wechsler, *op. cit.,* pp. 243–45.

159. See generally Hart and Wechsler, *op. cit.,* pp. 481–83, 785–90. State wrongful death acts are the leading example of absorption. See Levinson v. Deupree, 345 U.S. 648 (1953); The Hamilton, 207 U.S. 398 (1907). See also Just v. Chambers, 312 U.S. 383 (1941), absorbing a state statute for survival of claims against a deceased tortfeasor.

160. 1 STAT. 77 (1789). Among the many annoying because probably meaningless but possibly meaningful changes made by the 1948 revisers of the Judicial Code was the revision of this language to read, "saving to suitors in all cases all other remedies to which they are otherwise entitled." 28 U.S.C. § 1333(1) (Supp. 1952).

161. The question, however, was seldom faced squarely, and it is difficult to be certain what the prevailing opinion was. See E. Merrick Dodd, "The New Doctrine of Supremacy of Admiralty over the Common Law," *Columbia Law Review,* Vol. 21, p. 647, 1921; Note, "State Common Law in Maritime Jurisdiction," *Columbia Law Review,* Vol. 47, p. 1364, 1947; Note, "The Expansion of Federal Question Jurisdiction to Maritime Claims: A New Jurisdictional Theory," *Harvard Law Review,* Vol. 66, p. 315, 1952.

162. See, *e.g.,* Panama R.R. v. Johnson, 264 U.S. 375, 385–87 (1924), and Note, "From Judicial Grant to Legislative Power: The Admiralty Clause in the Nineteenth Century," *Harvard Law Review,* Vol. 67, p. 1214, 1954.

163. The leading case in the historical development, Southern Pacific Co. v. Jensen, 244 U.S. 205 (1917), concerned a peripheral problem of this type. The Court set aside an award under a state workmen's compensation statute to a stevedore injured while unloading a vessel. The currently doubtful questions center upon the law applicable in this marginal area potentially within the legislative jurisdiction of both states and nation. See, *e.g.,* Davis v. Department of Labor, 317 U.S. 249 (1952).

164. See, following Southern Pacific Co. v. Jensen, 244 U.S. 205 (1917); Chelentis v. Luckenbach S.S. Co., 247 U.S. 372 (1918); Garrett v. Moore-McCormack Co., 317 U.S. 239 (1942); *cf.* Pope & Talbot, Inc. v. Hawn, 346 U.S. 406, 409–11 (1953); Caldarola v. Eckert, 332 U.S. 155 (1947).

165. 1 STAT. 79 (1789).

166. United States v. Hudson & Goodwin, 7 Cranch 32 (U.S. 1812) (indictment for libel on the President and Congress); United States v. Coolidge, 1 Wheat. 415 (U.S. 1816) (indictment for forcibly rescuing a prize captured by American privateers).

167. As it is in Crosskey, *op. cit.*, Vol. II, pp. 766–85.

168. See the Hudson & Goodwin case, note 166 above, and consider the range and character of the problems that would have been involved in deciding, case by case, exactly which common law crimes under what circumstances constituted crimes against the United States.

169. See Hart and Wechsler, *op. cit.*, pp. 1090–95. The perils are epitomized by the fact that as late as 1950 it was possible for a federal district court to hold that a murderous assault on an airplane flying over the high seas from Puerto Rico to New York must go unpunished for want of a federal statute anticipating with sufficient precision the possibility of such an offense. United States v. Cordova, 89 F. Supp. 298 (E.D.N.Y. 1950). In the District of Columbia these difficulties were avoided by the holding that the antecedent common law of crimes of Maryland and Virginia survived when the District was formed by cession from these states. United States v. Watkins, 3 D.C. 441, 452 (1829); cf. 2 STAT. 103 (1801), DeForest v. United States, 11 App. D.C. 458 (1897); Tyner v. United States, 23 App. D.C. 324, 358 (1904); see D.C. CODE § 22–107 (1951).

170. 1 STAT. 78 (1789). See 28 U.S.C. § 1345 (Supp. 1952).

171. See, *e.g.*, Dugan v. United States, 3 Wheat. 172 (U.S. 1818); United States v. Buford, 3 Pet. 12, 28 (U.S. 1830); United States v. Tingey, 5 Pet. 115, 127–28 (U.S. 1831); Cotton v. United States, 11 How. 229 (U.S. 1850).

172. United States v. Standard Oil Co., 332 U.S. 301 (1947).

173. See, *e.g.*, Cotton v. United States, note 171 above, at 231: "As an owner of property in almost every state of the Union, they [the United States] have the same right to have it protected by the local laws that other persons have." See also Mason v. United States, 260 U.S. 545 (1923).

174. Clearfield Trust Co. v. United States, 318 U.S. 363 (1943); United States v. Standard Oil Co., note 172 above; see Hart and Wechsler, *op. cit.*, pp. 483–84, 685–91.

175. See note 150 above; Munroe F. Pofcher, "Choice of Law, State or Federal, in Cases Involving Government Contracts," *Louisiana Law Review*, Vol. 12, p. 37, 1951.

176. See Holmberg v. Armbrecht, 327 U.S. 392 (1946).

177. See Francis v. Southern Pacific Co., 333 U.S. 445 (1948).

178. See O'Brien v. Western Union Tel. Co., 113 F.2d 539 (1st Cir. 1940); cf. Western Union Tel. Co. v. Boegli, 251 U.S. 315 (1920). See generally Hart and Wechsler, *op. cit.*, pp. 685–706.

179. See the refusal, after holding state law inoperative, to deal on the merits with a claim by the United States of a somewhat novel right of action in United States v. Standard Oil Co., 332 U.S. 301 (1947), the refusal, after a similar holding, to reexamine a completely outmoded federal judicial decision in Francis v. Southern Pacific Co., above note 177; and the similar disclaimers of competence

even to grapple with the merits of the issues presented in Halcyon Lines v. Haenn Ship Ceiling & Refitting Corp., 342 U.S. 282 (1952), and United States v. Atlantic Mutual Ins. Co., 343 U.S. 236 (1952). It is illuminating to compare Justice Black's eloquent protest against the trend in his dissent in the *Francis* case (sympathetic facts involving damages for the family of a deceased railroad employee) with his later opinions, violating the same principles even more egregiously, in *Halcyon* and *Atlantic Mutual* (facts involving business interests).

180. See Hart and Wechsler, *op. cit.,* pp. 706–08.

181. See notes 151–155 above. See also United States v. Gerlach Live Stock Co., 339 U.S. 725 (1950); First Iowa Hydro-Electric Cooperative v. FPC, 328 U.S. 152 (1946); RFC v. Beaver County, 328 U.S. 204 (1946).

In the *Beaver County* case Congress had expressly subjected "any real property" of various government agencies to state taxation "to the same extent according to its value as other real property is taxed," and the question was whether the term "real property" was to be defined in accordance with some uniform federal rule or in accordance with state law. The Court pointed out that a uniform federal definition would serve little purpose since the tax rates would vary in any event. The convenience of not having to develop a body of federal decisional law to deal with the problem should also be noticed.

For a much more debatable reference, see the now long-established holdings that the effect of a judgment of a federal trial court is to be determined in accordance with the law of the state in which the court sits. Dupasseur v. Rochereau, 21 Wall. 130, 134 (U.S. 1875); Metcalf c. Watertown, 153 U.S. 671 (1894); cf. Provident Savings Life Assurance Soc'y v. Ford, 114 U.S. 635, 641–42 (1885).

182. See, *e.g.,* Crooks v. Harrelson, 282 U.S. 55 (1930) (what property of decedent is "subject to the payment of charges against his estate and the expenses of its administration" governed by state law); Edmond N. Cahn, "Local Law in Federal Taxation," *Yale Law Journal,* Vol. 52, p. 799, 1943; Covey T. Oliver, "The Nature of the Compulsive Effect of State Law in Federal Tax Proceedings," *California Law Review,* Vol. 41, p. 638, 1953.

183. So, at least, it was hard for Justice Frankfurter to see, concurring in Vanston Bondholders Protective Comm. v. Green, 329 U.S. 156 (1946). See also Alfred Hill, "The Erie Doctrine in Bankruptcy," *Harvard Law Review,* Vol. 66, p. 1013, 1953.

184. See Garner v. Teamsters Local Union No. 776, 346 U.S. 485 (1953). Problems of this kind are discussed by Paul R. Hays, in Chapter 12. See also a recent article by Archibald Cox, "Federalism in the Law of Labor Relations," *Harvard Law Review,* Vol. 67, pp. 1297–1348, 1954. Similar problems in other fields are legion.

185. See, *e.g.,* the problem in Fay v. American Cystoscope Makers, Inc., 98 F. Supp. 278 (S.D.N.Y. 1951), *Harvard Law Review,* Vol. 65, p. 1443, 1952.

186. 61 STAT. 156 (1947), 29 U.S.C. § 185 (Supp. 1952).

187. For the view that such a protective jurisdiction should be recognized, see Hart and Wechsler, *op. cit.,* pp. 744–47.

188. See Hart and Wechsler, *op. cit.,* pp. 696–97. The problem would be acutely presented in Austrian v. Williams, 198 F. 2d 697, (2d Cir.) *cert. denied,* 344 U.S. 909 (1952), *Harvard Law Review,* Vol. 66, p. 527, 1953, if the Virginia statute of limitations differs from that of New York.

189. See Samuel Mermin, " 'Cooperative Federalism' Again: State and Municipal Legislation Penalizing Violation of Existing and Future Federal Requirements," *Yale Law Journal,* Vol. 57, p. 201, 1947, including the bibliography at 1

n. Professor Mermin discusses the problem of the constitutional limits upon the delegation of state legislative powers, under the states' own constitutions, which has often impeded adoption of federal statutes and regulations as they may be changed from time to time in the future.

190. On the procedure of federal courts, compare the Federal Rules of Decision Act and the Federal Conformity Act. See note 71 above.

191. See Standard Oil Co. v. Johnson, 316 U.S. 481 (1942); cf. Flournoy v. Wiener, 321 U.S. 253 (1944).

192. See, e.g., Moore v. Chesapeake & Ohio Ry., 291 U.S. 205 (1934); Smith v. Kansas City Title & Trust Co., 255 U.S. 180 (1921), with which compare Miller's Ex'rs v. Swann, 150 U.S. 132 (1893). The Smith case held that a stockholder's action of the kind mentioned in the text arose under the laws of the United States for purposes of the original jurisdiction of the federal district courts. Cf. note 142 above. In the Moore case, in which the question of breach of federal duty entered the litigation only by way of replication to a defense, the Court held that original district court jurisdiction was lacking, while recognizing that the question of the validity of the replication would be open on review of a state court decision. See generally Hart and Wechsler, op. cit., pp. 450–53, 758–69.

193. The problems are discussed in an admirable note, "Supreme Court Review of State Interpretations of Federal Law Incorporated by Reference," Harvard Law Review, Vol. 66, p. 1498, 1953.

194. See Robert Braucher, "Federal Enactment of the Uniform Commercial Code," Law and Contemporary Problems, Vol. 16, pp. 101–04, 1951.

195. See Legislation Note, "Reciprocal and Retaliatory Tax Statutes," Harvard Law Review, Vol. 43, p. 641, 1930.

196. There are, of course, other difficulties. See Robert Braucher, "Commercial Code in Massachusetts," Harvard Law School Record, Vol. 18, p. 1, 1954, listing as the "four principal goals which have not been met by uniform legislation, but which might be achieved by interstate compact: (1) a uniform effective date, (2) uniformity of original provisions, (3) uniformity of interpretation, (4) uniformity of amendment."

197. See, e.g., Massachusetts v. Missouri, 308 U.S. 1 (1939); cf. Worcester County Trust Co. v. Riley, 302 U.S. 292, 298–300 (1937).

198. See Art. I, § 10, note 11 above.

199. See Frederick L. Zimmermann and Mitchell Wendell, The Interstate Compact Since 1925, Chicago, Council of State Governments, 1951; Felix Frankfurter and James M. Landis, "The Compact Clause of the Constitution—A Study in Interstate Adjustments," Yale Law Journal, Vol. 34, p. 685, 1925. On the problem of international unification of private law, and the policy of the Department of State to avoid use of the treaty power to override state law, see Kurt H. Nadelmann, "Ignored State Interests: The Federal Government and International Efforts to Unify Rules of Private Law," University of Pennsylvania Law Review, Vol. 102, p. 323, 1954.

200. See West Virginia ex rel. Dyer v. Sims, 341 U.S. 22 (1951); Delaware River Joint Toll Bridge Comm'n v. Colburn, 310 U.S. 419, 427 (1940); Hinderlider v. La Plata River & Cherry Creek Ditch Co., 304 U.S. 92 (1938). In the Hinderlider case, the Court reversed a state court decision holding that an interstate compact on water rights was invalid because it affected appropriation rights guaranteed by the state's constitution. Presumably, also, a question arising under a compact might be made the foundation of an action in a federal district court.

201. See Braucher, note 196 above, discussing a suggestion of three Massachusetts legislators. If the cases in note 200 above are applicable, it would follow that any state court case under the Code would be subject to Supreme Court review, irrespective of any conflict in interpretation. It would seem to follow also that a case asserting a right under the Code could be brought in a federal district court under 28 U.S.C. § 1331 (Supp. 1952) without regard to diversity of citizenship, if more than $3,000 were in controversy. But Congress would have power to withhold district court jurisdiction and to limit the Supreme Court's appellate jurisdiction to cases of conflict, if that were thought desirable, and probably to shut off appellate jurisdiction altogether. See Hart and Wechsler, op. cit., pp. 312–40.

202. Compare the provisions of the Waterfront Commission Compact between New York and New Jersey, upheld against constitutional attack on other grounds in Linehan v. Waterfront Comm'n, 116 F. Supp. 683 (S.D.N.Y. 1953), and Staten Island Loaders v. Waterfront Comm'n, 117 F. Supp. 308 (S.D.N.Y. 1953).

203. It will be observed that to the extent that problems of jurisdiction are coterminous with problems of choice of state or federal law they would not be eliminated. To the extent that the uniform protection of federal rights in the state courts requires the overriding of state procedural or remedial law, problems of distinguishing between substance and procedure would likewise survive.

204. See Herbert Wechsler, "Federal Jurisdiction and the Revision of the Judicial Code," *Law and Contemporary Problems,* Vol. 13, p. 216, 1948.

205. See, *inter alia,* Hart and Wechsler, *op. cit.,* pp. 177–85, 862–85.

206. See note 84 above.

LEGISLATIVE AND EXECUTIVE RESPONSIBILITIES IN MANAGING A FEDERAL SYSTEM

12

Federalism and Labor Relations: A Case Study of Congressional Responsibility

By Paul R. Hays

I

INTRODUCTION

A federal constitution may carefully define the spheres in which the federal government or the constituent states shall operate to the exclusion of the other, or it may leave the allocation of functions to future determination. In the United States the allocation of control over labor relations under the constitutional power of Congress "to regulate commerce with foreign nations, and among the several states" may be looked upon as a continuing process of adjustment of the federal relation. The power to regulate may be left to the states, prohibited to the states, taken over by the federal government, or given or returned to the states from time to time as occasion for change arises.

Until recently the federal Supreme Court assumed the power to allocate control as between states and nation. By means of a generally restrictive, though somewhat flexible, definition of "commerce," the Court gave extensive powers to the states to the exclusion of the federal government. Influenced, however, by the trend toward national integration, particularly notable in the increase in size of operating economic units and greatly accelerated by economic depression, and recognizing the inadequacy of judicial machinery and doctrinaire solutions to meet the growing complexity of the economic problems with which it was faced, the Court, finally, by broadening its definition of commerce, relinquished to Congress the power to allocate control over labor relations.

The Supreme Court's action was generally considered to be a part of a growing tendency toward "centralization" and it is probable that the Court looked upon its transfer of power to Congress as in fact a recognition of the need for national, rather than state, regulation of labor relations. There is, however, nothing in the American constitutional system which designates the Court as the sole guardian of the federal system. After all, the framers of the

Constitution provided that the legislature, not the court, would reflect in its structure the continuing existence of the states. There are many instances of congressional action, such as those involving state regulation of intoxicating liquor, insurance, and offshore oil, which indicate that on occasion Congress can be an even more zealous guardian of federalism than the Court. The federalist idea is deep rooted in the American people. It is shared alike by Presidents, judges, administrators, and members of Congress and it is always a major factor in the actual process of allocation of power, wherever the power to make that allocation may lie. Moreover, the nonideological pressures which favor "centralization" and "uniformity" are frequently balanced by others which favor state control and local variation. Study and experience have shown that the exercise of power by one government has been ineffective or less effective than when exercised by the other. These considerations lead in practice to the accommodation of the constitutional system to new and changing needs, with no major impairment of basic aspects of its federal structure. The method of entrusting to the federal government the function of continuous constitutional revision, whether the power of allocation of control is in the hands of the Court or of the legislature, does not by any means necessarily lead to the concentration of power in that government to the exclusion of the states.

There are, moreover, extremely important reasons for preferring that Congress rather than the Court administer the federal system in a field as complex as the field of labor relations. The allocation of power in such a field must be worked out for each situation with careful consideration of a large number of economic, sociological, political, and administrative factors. The legislative method is better adapted to the requirements of this type of thoughtful planning than is the judicial method.

At the present moment there is a constitutional crisis in this field. In exercising its new function Congress has made what has proved in experience to be an unsatisfactory allocation of power as between state and nation. The problem of reallocation is now before it as possibly the most important problem in labor relations facing the country today. It is equally important as a problem in federalism since it involves the question of whether a flexible federal system can be successfully administered by the national legislature in a field of intricate complexity.

II

THE COURT TRANSFERS POWER TO CONGRESS

In 1937 the Supreme Court of the United States relinquished its control over the administration of the federal system in the field of labor relations.[1] The Court, in ceding to Congress practically unlimited power to control all aspects of the production and distribution of goods, left no significant elements of regulation in this field to the exclusive power of the states. Not only may Congress regulate labor relations in interstate commerce but it may regulate those relations which "affect" interstate commerce.[2] Its power, moreover, does not depend on "any particular volume of commerce affected more than that to which the courts would apply the maxim *de minimis*."[3] "Congress' power to keep the interstate market free of goods produced under conditions inimical to the general welfare . . . may be exercised in individual cases without showing any specific effect upon interstate commerce . . . ; it is enough that the individual activity when multiplied into a general practice is subject to federal control . . . , or that it contains a threat to the interstate economy that requires preventive regulation."[4]

At about the same time that the Court relinquished to Congress the function of allocation of power over labor relations under the commerce clause, the long history of Court regulation of this field under the "economic" interpretation of the due process clauses also came to an end. Beginning in 1940, however, the Court, now basing its action on the constitutional protection of personal freedoms, resumed its power to regulate an important segment of the field. In a series of cases involving picketing the Court undertook to formulate a new system of limitations on legislative controls.[5] The allocation of this power to the Court promptly proved to be unworkable and unrealistic and it was generally disregarded by the states, which continued to regulate picketing with little change from former practice. After a few years the Court in effect abandoned its "picketing doctrine" and returned the regulation of picketing substantially to the status in which it stood prior to 1940.[6]

Other efforts to induce the Court to return "to the due process philosophy that has been deliberately discarded"[7] have been largely unsuccessful. The power of the Court over regulation of the right to organize and the right to strike have been confined to very narrow limits.[8] The Court, however, has decided certain cases involving racial discrimination in such a way as to suggest the possibility of its playing a role of great importance in the regulation of the whole field of collective bargaining.[9] Faced with this possibility in a recent case which did not present the element of racial discrimination, the Court, while denying recovery and somewhat limiting the implications of its prior decisions, did not indicate clearly a disposition to take itself out of this new field of regulation.[10] Some of the lower federal courts, however, have shown decided reluctance to accept further regulatory power.[11]

Whatever may develop to be the Court's future course in accepting or rejecting the temptations afforded by the due process clauses, there can be no doubt that the general field of regulation of labor relations is now within the power of Congress.

III

CONGRESS AS GUARDIAN OF THE FEDERAL SYSTEM

The advantages of a flexible federalism which permits the allocation and reallocation by varying methods and in varying degrees of the power to regulate labor relations have not in practice been fully realized. Congress has not yet understood fully the implications of the Court's transfer to it of the duty of allocating power. It has been slow to grasp the fact that the long history of the guardianship of federalism in this area by the Court has ended. In adopting the Taft-Hartley Act Congress failed to give necessary consideration to the problem of allocation of power in the federal system. Confusion has resulted in the absence of clear allocation in the statute itself and practical difficulties have arisen where allocations have proved to be unworkable. The Court in its effort to complete the task of allocation which Congress left half-done has added to the number of practical difficulties. Congress now has before it the problems raised by its original failure to give sufficient attention to the federalist impact of its action.

The picture thus presented does not reveal any weakness in the federal structure itself or, indeed, provide any basis for doubt as to the advantages of the flexibility in that structure which is applicable to the regulation of labor relations. If all decisions as to allocation of power were invariably made with the most carefully reasoned consideration for the best possible operation of the federal system, there would still arise situations in which the careful calculations proved to be wrong, as well as situations in which changes in the facts on which calculations were based demanded revision of the scheme of allocation. Moreover, the method of leaving to the courts or to administrative tribunals the working out of some of the details of distribution of power may provide in many instances an opportunity to complete the allocation of power in accordance with demonstrated needs in particular situations. But, although flexibility provides the possibility of keeping a federal constitutional system workable in its application to the complex and changing demands of the regulation of labor relations, the implications of this for federalism must be understood and carefully considered by Congress if unnecessary confusion and difficulty are to be avoided.

As practical problems have multiplied the need for careful consideration of the many interrelated factors which must enter into a decision as to the manner in which power should be allocated, the processes of case by case decision have come to be less and less adequate to the demands of the situation. The Court has done well to leave larger and larger areas to Congress, and, by the enormous enlargement of the concept of interstate commerce and, to some extent, the withdrawal from the field of "economic due process," to turn over to Congress a large part of its duties as keeper of the federal system.

The failure of Congress fully to assume its new obligations, as well as the inadequacy for practical purposes of the methods available to the Court to supplement the action of Congress, are illustrated in ten cases arising out of the National Labor Relations Act.[12] The Court on several occasions has remarked on the failure of Congress to indicate clearly in the act the boundaries of state and federal power. "Congress has not seen fit," said Mr. Justice Jackson, "to lay down even the most general of guides to construction of the

Act, as it sometimes does, by saying that its regulation either shall or shall not exclude state action."[13]

An examination of the legislative history of the original National Labor Relations Act shows that little attention was paid to the federalist aspects of the legislation. And, though the Labor Management Relations Act of 1947, because of its greater reach, added enormously to the problems of federalism, they received even less attention than at the earlier period. There are a few quotable generalizations about federal preemption and there is some reference to state action, but the very case in which these are most confidently relied on[14] almost certainly reached the wrong conclusion as to the congressional intent.

The difficulties which have resulted from the failure of Congress clearly to allocate power and from the unworkable allocations made by the Court in some of the cases it has decided, have alerted Congress and the interested parties to the problem, and in the recent hearings before the Senate Committee on Labor and Public Welfare on proposed revision of the act much consideration was given to it. The record of these hearings, however, indicates that there still is little comprehension on the part of either Senators or others of the complexities inherent in the application of a flexible federalism to the field of labor relations.

Once the Court had surrendered to Congress the duty to allocate between state and nation the power of regulation in this field, theoretically the only duty the Court had was to determine in each case presented to it what Congress had decided to do in this regard. The Court had already developed certain guides supposedly applicable to this situation. Had Congress "laid hold" of the very matter which the state sought to regulate? Did the attempted state regulation "conflict with" the federal regulation which Congress had adopted? But the concept of identity of subject matter is itself an abstraction since in the cases which came before the Court, the state was not seeking to regulate situations in which the federal government had already acted but often situations in which state regulation seemed desirable because the federal government had *not* acted. The Court has had to decide whether Congress intended "to preempt the whole field" or whether congressional silence with respect to particular situations was to be interpreted to mean that those situations were to be left to the state to regulate or were to be left "unregulated."

Mr. Justice Frankfurter, particularly in dissent, has argued that the Court should in these matters accord a presumption of validity to regulation by the state.[15] Whatever virtue this position may have when supported by argument based upon implications from the federal system itself, it seems to be a sound reflection of the congressional intent. Study of the legislative history of the two acts and of the structure of the acts themselves leads to the conclusion that Congress went about discharging its new function as guardian of federalism in this field largely by taking for granted a complete system of state regulation and seeking to superimpose on the state regulation, federal regulation of some aspects of the field. Although, as has been said, there is little discussion of the problems of federalism, what little there is is almost invariably in defense of particular provisions of the act as *not* depriving the states of power to regulate.

If the "intent" of Congress may be derived from the attitude of Congressmen in general as to state regulation of this field, and not only from express comments on particular aspects, the legislative history of the two acts taken as a whole, and the comments of Senators at the recent hearing on proposed amendments, would support the contention that Congress intended rather to supplement state regulation in the field than to displace it. For example, Mr. Hartley said, in answer to a question as to the effect of the federal law on Wisconsin law: "This will not interfere with the State of Wisconsin in the administration of its own laws."[16] Senator Taft said: "I may say that we never intended any preemption of the field. The Supreme Court has gone beyond what we intend."[17] "In general, I am quite willing to leave it to the states, the control of anything that we can do."[18] "Of course, I do not offhand see why the states cannot handle a local public utilities strike, a street car strike, or anything else, as well as the Federal Government. . . . Do you think there should be some legislation at least to stop this preemption doctrine?"[19] Senator Smith said: "Of course, if you say to any section of this country, not necessarily to the South, but also to some of the Western States, 'we are going to tell you what kind of law you are going to have for the relationship between management and labor in your State,' you are not going to create a healthy atmosphere by such legislation being forced down their throats. . . . Let me remind you that, as we all know, we had a problem in the South that led to our Civil War, and we are still trying to heal the wounds of that conflict. We have here in our Congress, in our own Senate, representatives of the Southern States. We are trying to heal those differences and bring about mutual understanding. But the mere passage of legislation to be superimposed on any one area of the country is not going to solve the problem."[20] Senator Goldwater demanded to know on what a witness based the statement that "the laws of the United States shall be supreme law of the land." When told that the statement was based on the Constitution, Senator Goldwater asked, "The Congress has to be given that right by the States by agreement; is that right?"[21] The Senator was so deeply shocked by the statement that he later repeated it to another witness and asked, "Do you feel, as attorney general of Nebraska, that that is a true statement, that in this particular field the Federal law is the supreme law of the land?"[22] The hearings before the House Judiciary Committee on the recent New Jersey-New York Waterfront Commission Compact contain repeated indications of impatience with any questioning as to the provisions of the Compact, on the ground that what the states want to do is no concern of Congress, although the Compact regulates labor relations in an industry of vital importance to interstate and foreign commerce.

Yet a majority of the Court in passing on state legislation which was claimed to be beyond state power under the Labor Management Relations Act has tended consistently to find that the Congress intended to allocate power to the federal government to the exclusion of the states.

Although the National Labor Relations Act declares in the most general terms the rights of "employees" to engage in collective bargaining and other types of "concerted activities," the system of regulation set up by the act protects them in the exercise of these rights only from interference by employers. It seems possible that Congress "intended" to regulate rights between employers and employees which were not at the time of the adoption of the act the subject of affirmative regulation by the states. Whether it "intended" to deny to a state the power to regulate, as, for example, by requiring a majority vote of employees before strike action can be taken, is highly doubtful. Yet it is the Court's view that Congress has excluded the states from the regulation of all those activities which the act declares to be the rights of employees.[23]

Congress has set up an administrative tribunal, the National Labor Relations Board, to determine in situations involving alleged interference by employers whether the activities interfered with are or are not of the type which the act protects from such interference and, if the employer claims that he interfered with employees because they engaged in activities which are not so protected, whether or not they did in fact engage in such activities. But where it is the state, rather than the employer, which attempts to regulate, the National Labor Relations Board will frequently have no power to act at all because no employer interference is alleged. Under the Court's interpretation of the act a question arises as to who is to decide in such a case whether the activities are of the type protected by the act and whether the employees engaged in such activities.[24]

The National Labor Relations Act gives employees the right "to bargain collectively through representatives of their own choosing" and provides a procedure to protect them in such choice from interference by their employer. Did Congress "intend" to exclude a state from regulating such choice by, for example, providing that an ex-convict could not serve as a representative? It seems unlikely; yet the Court appears to believe that the act is so to be interpreted.[25]

A holding of the Court that Wisconsin could regulate mass picketing and violence was largely based on the view that the National Labor Relations Act did not purport to regulate these activities.[26] This is only partly true since in deciding a question of employer interference the National Board must frequently determine whether employees engaged in such activities. But more important, the amended act, which added certain direct prohibitions on the activities of labor organizations, *does* regulate mass picketing and violence. Does this mean, by the Court's criterion, that Congress intended to withdraw from the states the power to control violence on a picket line—that, for example, the state's police could not keep pickets from destroying the plant? Obviously Congress had no such intention.

The Court has held that where the Congress chose to regulate strikes which create a national emergency, its rejection of proposed legislation which would have regulated local emergencies as well indicates an intention that local emergencies should be "unregulated."[27] It seems much more likely that Congress "intended" to leave such regulation to the states.

The Court, like Congress, has not fully realized the implications of its surrender of power over the administration of federalism in the field of regulation of labor relations. It has failed to recognize that Congress, too, can be a keeper of federalism. The Court has appeared to assume that once Congress was given the duty of allocation of power between state and nation, it would promptly allocate power to the federal government. By tending to construe the intent of Congress in the direction of taking power rather than of leaving it to the states, the Court underestimates the power of federalism as an affirmative concept of government and as a basic element in American political thought.

IV

THE ADMINISTRATION OF THE FEDERAL SYSTEM BY CONGRESS

The very complexities which have made it impossible for the Court to administer the federal system on a case by case basis in this field have also made impossible the simple solution which Congress apparently intended for the federalist aspects of the problem it faced. The elements of central regulation can be carefully fitted into a system of state regulation. They cannot be superimposed on it.

The difficulties which the Labor Management Relations Act poses for the federal system are not to be solved, then, by the Court's seeking to ascertain the intent of Congress, but only by Congress itself. Congress now has the duty of "accommodating" federal and state power in this field and, as the long history of federalism indicates, it is not a duty which can properly be discharged in any off-hand way.

General formulas will not suffice. In the course of the recent hearings on proposed amendments to the Labor Management Relations Act, representatives of management advocated again and again "a stronger federal law" and at the same time "leaving more room for the states to act." The Senators, like Taft, who were beginning to realize the complexities of federalism tried without success to induce these witnesses to suggest specific applications of their general formulas. Frequently the non-lawyers seemed to be parroting the opinions of their counsel. The lawyers were little more helpful. Their formulas were derived from the decisions which the Court had had to abandon as inadequate when they relinquished to Congress the administration of federalism in this field.

The fact is that, as the Court recognized, the old distinctions such as "local and national" are no longer sufficient and Congress cannot allocate power on the basis of such distinctions any more successfully than could the Court

Certain aspects of activities which under the old formulas are "national" in character should be subject to state control; some "local" activities must be controlled by the federal government. After all, the formula "local or national" was invented, and was useful, only in determination of the now-settled issue of limitation on congressional power. The present issue is an entirely different one—the issue of where power can most desirably be allocated in a federal system such as ours.

The National Labor Relations Board has formulated certain rules of thumb based on size to govern its determinations as to when it will and when it will not take jurisdiction. But distinctions of mere size of operation have already been found insufficient. Not only did the Board even in its original formulation treat some categories, such as war industries, on bases other than mere size, but from time to time it has had to depart from the rules as originally formulated.

In order to be successful in its administration of federalism in the field of labor relations Congress will have to give up reliance on preexisting formulas and on simple solutions and turn to such basic considerations as the effect of specific allocations of power on the national economy. The simple solution, for example, of the problem of economic competition among the states is uniform federal regulation. Forty years ago manufacturers operating in Massachusetts felt that they could not compete with those operating in North Carolina if they were not as free as were those in North Carolina to employ young children at low wages. Today the same problem of competition is raised with relation to state limitations on the closed shop. In fact every difference in wages, hours, and working conditions is to some extent relevant to competitive status. Since the simple solution of total federal regulation is not acceptable and since the federal system is going to be preserved in the field of labor relations, Congress has the problem of determining which aspects require national regulation in order to eliminate or reduce competition and which may be allocated to state regulation, either because the preservation of federalism is more important than the elimination of competition or because their effect on competitive status is so slight as not to justify national regulation.

There are also basic problems which may be called sociological. However narrowly the policy of the act is defined in terms of preventing interruptions to the free flow of commerce, actually it must be looked upon in a much larger way as free enterprise's answer to socialism. It assures the freedom of the worker to organize, to increase his bargaining power, and to participate in the determination of his own economic destiny. And by giving him this status it gives him the *opportunity* to better his economic condition instead of granting him benefits directly through the machinery of government. But control and regulation of this power are as necessary with respect to the organizations of labor as they are with respect to the organizations of capital. The problem of federalism is, then, what part the federal government and what part the states should play in protecting and in limiting these rights.

In the decision of these basic questions there is the need to consider the problem of effective administration of standards. Which government is better able to achieve results which both are seeking? In some particulars the answer is obvious. For example, effective control of violence in connection with labor disputes is going to continue to be the duty of the state merely because Congress is not going to create a national police force for this purpose. Such a conclusion can be thought of as arising from basic assumptions of the federal system itself. But there are other problems to be solved in empirical terms. State labor relations boards where they exist have, in general, acted more promptly and, therefore, more effectively than has the National Board. Are there not some aspects of the labor relations picture where prompt and effective action is more important than that the action should be exactly the same action which the National Board would have taken in the same circumstances? There is an obvious need for more careful supervision of the large and ever-increasing union "welfare" funds. Has state supervision of insurance in general, which Congress has in a sense endorsed,[28] proved sufficiently effective so that power over these funds should be allocated to the states? Is there in fact such a need for uniformity in the administration of collective agreements that the federal courts must be given a mandate to develop a body of law applicable to this matter? What role can state mediation and conciliation agencies play in the peaceful settlement of disputes?

This is not the place to suggest solutions for these problems. The important point is that there is no single simple solution. The field of labor relations is a field of enormous varied complexities. The Court, as it began to realize the complex nature of the problem of allocation of power, also realized that the facilities available to it in the judicial process of case by case decision were inadequate to provide solution. Congress has the facilities and is now called upon to use them thoughtfully and wisely in the discharge of its duty to administer the federal system.

V

METHODS OF ALLOCATION OF POWER

Congress has available to it and has used a number of different methods of allocating between the state and the federal government the power to control labor relations. It has sometimes given that power to the federal government and expressly excluded the states, as in Section 14(a) of the National Labor Relations Act which provides that "no employer subject to this Act shall be compelled to deem individuals defined herein as supervisors as employees for the purpose of any law, either national or local, relating to collective bargaining." It has sometimes expressly allocated power to the states, as in Section 14(b) of the National Labor Relations Act which provides that "nothing in this Act shall be construed as authorizing the execution or application of agreements requiring membership in a labor organization as a condition of employment in any State or Territory in which such execution or application is prohibited by State or Territorial law." Congress has sometimes itself established certain minimum standards, leaving it to the states to regulate in the area above these minima, as in the Fair Labor Standards Act, Section 18 of which provides that "No provision of this Act or any order thereunder shall excuse noncompliance with any . . . State law . . . establishing a minimum wage higher than the minimum wage established [by the Act] or a maximum workweek lower than the maximum workweek established under this Act, and no provision of this Act relating to the employment of child labor shall justify noncompliance with any . . . State law . . . establishing a higher standard than the standard established [by the Act]." Congress has also used the method, as in the case of unemployment compensation, of allocating control to the states while at the same time securing, through the "spending" power, the adoption by the states of certain minimum standards.

There are cases in which Congress may properly employ the method of leaving some details of power allocation to be completed by the Court. For example the Fair Labor Standards Act regulates wages and hours only in the case of employees who are "engaged in commerce or in the production of goods for commerce." The Court must complete the allocation of power by determining on a case by case basis to which employees the statute applies and which employees are left subject to regulation by the states.[29] Whether or not this is the best method of allocation, it is one in which the Court should have special skill, after its many years of defining commerce for purposes of power allocation. The Court also properly participates in the allocation of power in cases in which, for example, it interprets the express exemptions of congressional legislation, such as the exemption of agricultural labor under the Fair Labor Standards Act or of independent contractors under the National Labor Relations Act. This type of determination is, of course, thought of as "statutory interpretation" and in fact it shades off at one end of the scale into a mechanical application of a determination actually made by Congress. But frequently it is much more, and the Court, applying the same types of criteria as Congress itself applies to the problem, is actually participating jointly with Congress in the distribution of power. The real difference between the Court's function when it is determining allocation on the fundamental bases of constitutional power, e.g. deciding that the states shall have the power of regulation to the exclusion of the national government, and when it is determining allocation on some other basis, is, of course, that its determination is conclusive in the former instance and cannot be reversed by Congress, whereas in the latter instance Congress may decide upon a different distribution.[30] It is interesting to note in this connection that while the Court clearly has the final word on the allocation of power exclusively to the states, Congress appears to have the final word in the converse situation. If, for example, a state, succumbing to Petrillo's arguments, should by statute require that every theater have an orchestra of live musicians, theoretically the Court could determine that the state had the power so to regulate with respect to small local theaters but that such a regulation of large theaters or chain theaters was an unwarranted burden on commerce.[31] The determination of the Court giving to the state the power over local theaters, to the extent that its determination was based on constitutional power to regulate, would be final and Congress would not be able to change it. But Congress could reject that part of the determination which *excluded* the state from regulating the larger theaters and reallocate that power to the state.[32]

There is no fundamental objection to Congress' using the technique of delegating to the Court the duty of completing an incomplete allocation of power. It is in fact frequently a useful technique, since it can provide a certain flexibility for the treatment of special situations. The difficulty arises when Congress fails to provide proper guidance to the Court in making such determinations. The National Labor Relations Act, for example, regulates certain aspects of labor relations but does not clearly provide whether the power is given to the states to regulate other related aspects. It regulates some matters in certain ways and does not make it clear whether the states are to have power to regulate those same matters in other ways. It gives employees the right to choose bargaining representatives but does not indicate what power the states may have to limit the choice by, for example, forbidding convicted criminals from acting as such representatives.[33] It gives power to a national agency, the National Labor Relations Board, to determine the employees' choice of representatives when application is made to that Board for such a determination, though there is no requirement whatever that any such application be made and no prohibition on the functioning of a bargaining representative in the absence of such a determination. Since the act is silent on the subject, the question arises as to whether a labor organization which wishes to function as a bargaining representative and which may do so without any recourse to the Board, can properly apply to a state agency for a determination of the question of whether it is the choice of the employees.[34] The act provides (Section 7) that "employees shall have the right to self-organization, to form, join or assist labor organizations, to bargain collectively through representatives of their own choosing, and to engage in other concerted activities for the purpose of collective bargaining or for other mutual aid or protection, and shall also have the right to refrain from any or all such activities." Other sections of the act set up an elaborate system to protect employees from interference by employers and labor organizations in the exercise of these rights. Except in the one instance of Section 14, already referred to, nothing is said about state power to regulate these same rights. May a state forbid certain types of concerted activities such as recurrent work stoppages?[35] May a state require a majority vote before employees can strike[36] or forbid strikes in essential industries, by substitution of compulsory arbitration?[37] The act empowers the National Labor Relations Board to determine whether there has been violence in connection with a strike and in certain cases to prohibit such violence. Are the state police and the state courts therefore deprived of the power to deal with violent conduct where it is a part of a labor dispute?[38]

Congress left it to the Supreme Court to complete these imperfect allocations of power and in the cases cited in the foregoing footnotes the Court undertook to do so. In these instances the result of the joint work of Congress and the Court has proved to be unsatisfactory and unworkable. The states have, in the main, disregarded the allocation and, in the absence of a more practical definition of their powers, continued to regulate most matters in accordance with former practice.[39] The problem of reallocation has become, and is recognized to be, one of the major problems of revision of the Taft-Hartley Act.

Congress has also allocated to the federal government a large segment of the regulation of labor relations by Section 301 of the Labor Management Relations Act, which gives the federal courts jurisdiction in cases involving breach of collective agreements. Although the full implications of this section are not yet clear, it appears that the effect of the statute is to create a new uniform federal common law applicable to all collective agreements and to displace existing state regulation of this subject.[40] It seems probable that, although the state courts will have the power to continue to pass upon such cases, they will be required to apply the new federal law.

The allocation of power to the federal government through the method of giving jurisdiction to the federal courts without at the same time providing by statute for the substantive rights to be enforced in those courts is novel. There is considerable doubt that Congress actually intended to give the federal courts the exclusive power to provide substantive regulation for this important area of the field of labor relations, since the principal evil which the Congress sought to correct was the impossibility of suing incorporated unions as legal entities under the procedure of some states.[41] It may be that Congress intended to employ a different method of distributing power between state and nation by merely making the federal courts available for the enforcement of state substantive regulation. However not only are there serious analytical objections to this view, since it is hard for lawyers to believe in the existence of substantive regulations for which there is no method of enforcement, but also there is some doubt as to whether, under Article III, Section 1 of the Constitution, Congress has the power to provide that questions arising under the common law of a state become questions arising under the laws of the United States by the mere action of giving jurisdiction over such questions to the federal courts.

Another method of allocation of control over labor relations which Congress has used is that of delegating to an administrative tribunal discretion to determine within a limited area what powers should be exercised by the federal government and what by the states. Before the adoption of the Taft-Hartley Act, though no express statutory basis for the practice existed, the National Labor Relations Board by agreement with state boards, and particularly with the New York State Labor Relations Board, shared with these boards a number of fairly important aspects of the regulatory power.[42] Section 10(a) of the Taft-Hartley Act provides that "the Board is empowered by agreement with any agency of any State or Territory to cede to such agency jurisdiction over any cases in any industry (other than mining, manufacturing, communications and transportation except where predominantly local in character) even though such cases may involve labor disputes affecting commerce, unless the provision of the State or Territorial statute applicable to the determination of such cases by such agency is inconsistent with the corresponding provision of this Act or has received a construction inconsistent therewith."

In the Board's view none of the state statutes is consistent with the national act. The agreements which existed prior to the inclusion of this provision in the act have therefore been abrogated and no cession has been made.

The Board, which has had at all times since its inception more cases than it could handle effectively and expeditiously, has adopted the practice of declining to accept jurisdiction in instances where in the Board's view the effect of the activities involved is primarily local rather than national. This practice apparently has the approval of the courts. The Supreme Court has said of it, "Even when the effect of activities on interstate commerce is sufficient to enable the Board to take jurisdiction of a complaint, the Board sometimes properly declines to do so, stating that the policies of the Act would not be effectuated by its assertion of jurisdiction in that case."[43] Since the Board does not "cede" jurisdiction to any state agency in these cases and since presumably a state agency cannot act in the absence of such cession—if it could (so runs the argument) there would be no need to provide expressly for cession—these cases are left to a limbo of nonregulation by either power, although there is clearly no policy justifying this result, since actually the only reason they are not handled by the Board is that the Board is too busy to handle them. In order to illustrate the defective operation of this allocation of power we may assume that on a small local building project there is activity which amounts to a secondary boycott of the type which is prohibited by Section 8(b) (4) of the National Labor Relations Act. The Board declines jurisdiction, not on the ground that the activity does not affect commerce but on the ground that the project is essentially local in character. The state, it is held, cannot act because Congress has allocated the power to the federal government. An activity which both the nation and the state have made unlawful is permitted to continue because the details of the allocation of power have not been adequately worked out in the joint action of Congress and the Board. Naturally the states have rejected this result and have continued to act in absence of effective federal regulation.[44]

Delegation to the Board of power to allocate to state agencies certain aspects of labor relations is a highly useful device in the administration of a flexible system of federalism in this field. Unfortunately Congress failed to make wise use of it in the present act. There have been before Congress several bills which would give the Board this power. These bills, however, fail to take full advantage of the opportunity to develop a plan for division of power based upon thoughtful study of relevant political, economic, and social factors. They reflect rather the simplistic interstate-intrastate analysis which the Supreme Court discarded as inadequate. To the extent, however, that the bills suggest a division based on considerations of administrative convenience and therefore permit reinstitution of the former "agreement" system, they would free the Board from the restrictions imposed by the act in its present form.

A novel method of allocation of the power to regulate labor relations is the recent New Jersey-New York Waterfront Commission Compact. In this instance Congress gave its consent to a statute enacted by the legislatures of the two states which regulates certain important aspects of labor relations in one industry. Although, contrary to testimony presented at the hearing before the House Committee on the Judiciary, the provisions of the Compact conflict with provisions of the National Labor Relations Act in a number of important particulars, the Compact is presumably a law of the United States within the meaning of Article VI of the Constitution.

Congress, then, has available to it a number of techniques for solution of its federalist problems, including establishment of minimum standards, encouragement of state legislation, and delegation of discretionary powers of allocation in limited fields to courts and administrative tribunals. Doubtless others can be devised. It may be that a procedure resembling Madison's rejected notion of a veto on state legislation would permit a large measure of state regulation and at the same time protect against extreme action by a single state.

VI

FLEXIBLE FEDERALISM AND MULTIPLE SOLUTIONS

Congress also has facilities for breaking its problem down into its many parts and treating them separately and differently where the realities of the situation require separate and different treatment. The variety of problems is endless and each type may require a different federalist solution. Congress has given to the federal government control over the basic right to organize and to bargain collectively. What limitations should states be permitted to impose on the activities incident to those rights? The states have been given power with respect to compulsory union membership. Are there other powers which the states can best handle, such as the power to regulate strikes, picketing, and secondary boycotts? How should power be divided with respect to the proper subjects of collective bargaining? What of the myriad problems which arise in connection with intra-union affairs, the right to membership, the right against discrimination, the right to have a voice in the union government? What of welfare funds and the check-off and bribery of union officials? What of inter-union relations and rivalries, such as jurisdictional strikes? Each of these problems is in fact a host of problems and it may be desirable to treat each of that host separately and differently in respect to distribution of power.

It may develop that different types of industries require different treatment. The problem of compulsory union membership on the railroads is governed by federal law. In respect to other industries Congress has allocated power over this matter to the states. Congress has chosen to regulate strikes in certain types of industries which create a "national emergency." Would it be well to leave to the states the control of strikes in these same industries which create a "local emergency"?

The changes which develop with the passage of time may indicate that particular distributions of power should be revised from time to time. In time of war, for example, it may be thought necessary to allocate to the federal government certain powers which in time of peace are given to the state, as when the orders of the National War Labor Board superseded the Wisconsin law on compulsory unionism, while the state law automatically regained validity with the conclusion of hostilities.[45]

This flexible federalism also allows for trial and error. The allocation by the Court of power to the federal government, through "interpretation" of the Labor Management Relations Act, has proved unworkable in several respects. Congress is now called upon to reallocate these powers to the states. There is no reason why this should not be a continuous process as particular allocations are shown to be desirable or undesirable in the way in which they actually work out.

FOOTNOTES TO CHAPTER 12

1. National Labor Relations Board v. Jones & Laughlin Steel Corporation, 301 U.S. 1 (1937).

2. National Labor Relations Board v. Jones & Laughlin Steel Corp., note 1, above.

3. N.L.R.B. v. Fainblatt, 306 U.S. 601, 607 (1939).

4. Mandeville Island Farms v. American Crystal Sugar Co., 334 U.S. 219, 236 (1948).

5. Thornhill v. Alabama, 310 U.S. 88 (1940); Milk Wagon Drivers Union v. Meadowmoor Dairies, Inc., 312 U.S. 287 (1941); American Federation of Labor v. Swing, 312 U.S. 321 (1941); Bakery and Pastry Drivers v. Wohl, 315 U.S. 769 (1942); Carpenters and Joiners Union v. Ritter's Cafe, 315 U.S. 722 (1942); Cafeteria Employees Union v. Angelos, 320 U.S. 293 (1943).

6. International Brotherhood of Teamsters v. Hanke, 339 U.S. 470 (1950). See also Giboney v. Empire Storage and Ice Co., 336 U.S. 490 (1949); Hughes v. Superior Court, 339 U.S. 460 (1950); Building Service Employees International Union v. Gazzam, 339 U.S. 532 (1950).

7. Lincoln Federal Labor Union v. Northwestern Iron & Metal Co., 335 U.S. 525 (1949).

8. See Lincoln Federal Labor Union v. Northwestern Iron & Metal Co., above,

note 7; International Union v. Wisconsin Employment Relations Board, 336 U.S. 245 (1949); Thomas v. Collins, 323 U.S. 516 (1945).

9. Steele v. Louisville & N. R. Co., 323 U.S. 192 (1944); Brotherhood of Railroad Trainmen v. Howard, 343 U.S. 768 (1952).

10. Ford Motor Co. v. Huffman, 345 U.S. 330 (1953).

11. See, for example, Williams v. Yellow Cab. Co., 200 F. 2d 302 (C.A. 3d, 1952); Courant v. International Photographers, 176 F. 2d 1000 (1949).

12. Allen-Bradley Local v. Wisconsin Employment Relations Board, 315 U.S. 740 (1942); Bethlehem Steel Co. v. New York Labor Relations Board, 330 U.S. 767 (1947); Hill v. Florida, 325 U.S. 538 (1945); La Crosse Telephone Corp. v. Wisconsin Employment Relations Board, 336 U.S. 18 (1949); Algoma Plywood & Veneer Co. v. Wisconsin Employment Relations Board, 336 U.S. 301 (1949); International Union v. Wisconsin Employment Relations Board, 336 U.S. 245 (1949); Plankinton Packing Co. v. Wisconsin Employment Relations Board, 338 U.S. 953 (1950); International Union v. O'Brien, 339 U.S. 454 (1950); Amalgamated Ass'n v. Wisconsin Employment Relations Board, 340 U.S. 383 (1951); Garner v. Teamsters Union, 346 U.S. 485 (1953).

13. Bethlehem Steel Co. v. New York State Labor Relations Board, 330 U.S. 767, 771 (1947). See also International Union v. Wisconsin Employment Relations Board, 336 U.S. 245, 252 (1949); Garner v. Teamsters Union, 346 U. S. 485, 488 (1953).

14. Amalgamated Assn. v. Wisconsin Employment Relations Board, note 12.

15. See especially his dissenting opinion in Hill v. Florida, note 12, above, and his concurring opinion in Bethlehem Steel Co. v. New York State Labor Relations Board, ibid.

16. *Congressional Record,* June 4, 1947, pp. 6383–4.

17. Sen. Comm. on Labor and Public Welfare, 83rd Cong., 1st Sess., *Hearings on Proposed Revisions of the Labor-Management Relations Act of 1947,* p. 284.

18. *Ibid.,* p. 286.

19. *Ibid.,* p. 721.

20. *Ibid.,* p. 1538.

21. *Ibid.,* p. 606.

22. *Ibid.,* p. 879.

23. See especially Amalgamated Association v. Wisconsin Employment Relations Board, note 12, above.

24. See International Union v. Wisconsin Employment Relations Board, *ibid.*

25. See Hill v. Florida, *ibid.*

26. Allen-Bradley Local v. Wisconsin Employment Relations Board, *ibid.*

27. Amalgamated Assn. v. Wisconsin Employment Relations Board, *ibid.*

28. 59 Stat. 33, 34; 15 U.S.C. §§ 1011–1015.

29. See, for example, Kirschbaum Co. v. Walling, 316 U.S. 517, (1942); Borden v. Borella, 325 U.S. 679 (1945); 10 East 40th Street Bldg. v. Callus, 325 U.S. 578 (1945).

30. For example, the Congress, dissatisfied with the allocation of power made by the Court in National Labor Relations Board v. Hearst Publications Inc., 322 U.S. 111 (1944), provided for a different distribution by an amendment to Section 2(3) of the National Labor Relations Act. See *Report of House Committee on Education and Labor on the Labor-Management Relations Act,* 1947. H. Rep. 245,

80th Cong., 1st Sess., p. 18. (In deciding on the content of classifications of employees who are included in the act or exempted from its provisions, the Court does not necessarily determine the question of whether Congress "intended" that employees not covered by the act should be subject to state regulation or should be "unregulated." See, however, Utah Valley Hospital v. Industrial Commission, 199 F. 2d 6 (C.A. 10th, 1952), holding that nonprofit hospitals which are exempted from the act are subject to state jurisdiction.)

31. See Southern Pacific Co. v. Arizona, 325 U.S. 761 (1945), where the Court so held with respect to a state law limiting the length of trains, one of many such laws passed by legislatures under the guise of safety legislation, but actually largely at the instance of the railroad unions whose purpose was, like Petrillo's, to make more work for their members.

32. See Prudential Insurance Co. v. Benjamin, 328 U.S. 408 (1946).

33. See Hill v. Florida, 325 U.S. 538 (1945).

34. See La Crosse Telephone Corporation v. Wisconsin Employment Relations Board, 336 U.S. 18 (1949).

35. See International Union v. Wisconsin Employment Relations Board, 336 U.S. 245 (1949).

36. See International Union v. O'Brien, 339 U.S. 454 (1950).

37. See Amalgamated Association v. Wisconsin Employment Relations Board, 340 U.S. 383 (1951).

38. See Matter of Thayer Company, 99 N.L.R.B. 165 (1952). In this case the Massachusetts courts prohibited a strike on the ground that it was (1) in violation of a contract and (2) accompanied by violence. The Board subsequently held the contrary as to both counts. In effect the Board holding was that the Massachusetts courts had prohibited the exercise of a right guaranteed by federal law.

39. See Montgomery Bldg. and Construction Trades Council v. Ledbetter, 256 Ala. 678, 57 So. 2d 112 (1952) (appeal dismissed on ground that certiorari was improvidently granted, 344 U.S. 178 (1952)); Kincaid Webber Motor Co. v. Quinn, 362 Mo. 375, 241 S. W. 2d 886 (1951); Erwin Mills v. Textile Workers Union, 234 N.C. 321, 67 S.E. 2d 372 (1951); Wortex Mills v. Textile Workers Union, 369 Pa. 359, 85 A. 2d 851 (1952); Williams v. Cedartown Textiles, Inc. 208 Ga. 659, 68 S.E. 2d 705 (1952); Lion Oil Co. v. Marsh, 220 Ark. 678, 249 S.W. 2d 569 (1952); Sommer v. Metal Trades Council, 40 Cal. 2d 392, 254 P. 2d 559 (1953); Russell v. Int. Union, 258 Ala. 615, 64 So. 2d 384 (1953); Kinard Construction Co. v. Bldg. Trades Council, 258 Ala. 500, 64 So. 2d 400 (1953); Goodwins Inc. v. Hagedorn, 303 N.Y. 300, 101 N.E. 2d 697 (1951); State v. Dobson, 195 Or. 533, 245 P. 2d 903 (1952). But see Norris Grain Co. v. Nordaas, 232 Minn. 91, 46 N.W. 2d 94 (1950); Garner v. International Brotherhood of Teamsters, 373 Pa. 19, 94 A. 2d 893 (1953); Faribault Daily News v. ITU, 236 Minn. 303, 53 N.W. 2d 36 (1952); State v. Montgomery Ward, 233 P. 2d 685 (1951), certiorari denied 342 U.S. 869; Ryan v. Simons, 302 N.Y. 742, 98 N.E. 2d 707 (1951), certiorari denied 342 U.S. 897; Costaro v. Simons, 302 N.Y. 318, 98 N.E. 2d 454 (1951); McNish v. American Brass Co., 139 Conn. 44, 89 A. 2d 566 (1952).

40. See Shirley-Herman Co., Inc. v. International Hod Carriers, 182 F. 2d 806 (1950); Textile Workers Union v. Aleo Mfg. Co., 94 F. Supp. 626 (D.C.N.C., 1950); International Union v. Dahlem Construction Co., 193 F. 2d 470 (C.A. 6th, 1951); Fay v. American Cystoscope Makers, 98 F. Supp. 278 (D.C.N.Y., 1951); Hamilton Foundry & M. Co. v. International M. & F. Wkrs., 193 F. 2d 209 (C.A. 6th, 1951), certiorari denied 343 U.S. 966,

41. See *Report of the Senate Committee on Labor and Public Welfare on the Proposed Federal Labor Relations Act of 1947,* S. Rep. 105, 80th Cong., 1st Sess., pp. 15 ff.

42. See Bethlehem Steel Co. v. New York State Labor Relations Board, 330 U.S. 767, 783–797 (1947).

43. N.L.R.B. v. Denver Bldg. and Const. Trades Council, 341 U.S. 675 (1951). See also Haleston Drug Stores v. N.L.R.B., 187 F. 2d 418 (C.A. 9th, 1951), cert. den. 342 U.S. 815. In Joliet Contractors' Assn. v. N.L.R.B., 193 F. 2d 833 (C.A. 7th, 1952), the court held that the Board had abused its discretion in refusing to exercise its jurisdiction in a case involving certain building operations which the Board had found to be "essentially local in character."

44. See cases above, note 39.

45. See Algoma Plywood and Veneer Co. v. Wisconsin Employment Relations Board, 336 U.S. 301 (1949)

13

The Problem of the Federal State in Foreign Affairs

By Noel T. Dowling

This chapter is limited to the problem arising from the scheme of federalism under the Constitution of the United States as it stands today, and it will be concerned with two points. The first point: that, as a matter of *power,* the national government is fully equipped for the conduct of international affairs and is not handicapped by the fact that ours is a federal system. Even on this point, our principal concern will be, not with the whole power, but with so much of it as underlies treaties affecting the internal law of the United States. The second point: that, as a matter of *policy,* the fact that ours is a federal system has, or ought to have, a large influence in the formulation of any program leading to a treaty which, either by itself or with the aid of an act of Congress, will become effective as domestic law.

At the outset it is well to recall a distinction in the structure of our federal system and to take note of certain current discussions, all having to do in one way or another with the power of the United States for the conduct of international affairs. The distinction is between questions relating to the *distribution* of power within the federal system, on the one hand, and those relating to the *limitations* upon power, on the other. The former have to do with the maintenance of the federal system—the respective roles of nation and states; the latter have to do with the preservation of individual rights—the extent of governmental interference with the liberties of the people. For present purposes we are concerned only with the former.

The current discussion we need to note is on a recent proposal, popularly known as the Bricker Amendment, to amend the Constitution on the subject of treaties and executive agreements. The text is in the footnote;[1] if adopted, the amendment would effect large changes in the scheme of federalism. Thus, as far as the internal law in the United States is concerned, the amendment would do away with the self-executing effect of treaties and would abolish the doctrine that Congress may implement treaties with laws it has no power otherwise to pass; it would make executive agreements subject to the limitations imposed on treaties by the amendment and establish power in Congress to regulate all such agreements. The fact that the amendment failed of passage in the Senate does not render an analysis less important.

The major aim of the proposed amendment was to provide safeguards against apprehended abuses of power in the conduct of international affairs.[2] Apprehension rests on the view that, as respects the internal law of the United States, the power now vested in the national government for the conduct of international affairs is excessive and involves danger to the federal system[3] as well as to the liberties of the people.[4] Supporters of the amendment look with special apprehension on the many international arrangements, such as the Covenant on Human Rights, in process or contemplated under the United Nations.

I

FEDERAL SYSTEM AND NATIONAL POWER

The first thing to be said on the point that the government of the United States is fully equipped for the conduct of international affairs is that the power to make treaties has been expressly placed in that government. More particularly it is given to the President, subject to the check of advice and consent by the Senate.[5] Whatever the treaty power may be, whatever it may include, the totality belongs to the national government. And, as if to make assurance doubly sure, power is denied to the states.[6] Here is a clear example in the Constitution itself of something entrusted to the nation and foreclosed to the states. As a consequence not much room is left for talk about the reserved powers of the states.

A second thing to be said is that the treaty power can reach and control matters normally within the power of the states. Almost from the beginning, as shown by *Ware* v. *Hylton*[7] in 1796, it was held that state laws relating to local matters went down in the face of the provisions of a treaty. The most conspicuous example of the reach of the treaty power is in the land cases, such as *Hauenstein* v. *Lynham*[8] in 1880, where a treaty enabling aliens to inherit land within a state was sustained as overturning a law of the state prohibiting such inheritance. It would be difficult to find a subject matter over which a state had a more clearly recognized historic power and as to which no power was delegated to Congress.

A third thing to be said is that a treaty itself may fix the rule of law binding on individuals and enforceable in courts. It is settled law that a treaty can have (in popular terms) a "self-executing" effect. The cases mentioned in the preceding paragraph illustrate this capacity of treaties. There the treaties were aptly phrased to become effective as domestic law without the aid of legislation. Whether a treaty shall so operate of its own force or require implementation by Congress is a question to be determined in the process of making the treaty. Whether a given treaty is self-executing may become a question for the courts if the treaty is invoked in a case.

Finally, it has to be said that the lawmaking power of Congress may be employed in furtherance of treaties, and—an important point—that Congress can thereby make laws which, absent the treaty, it would have no power to enact. Though this result seems implicit in the cases already mentioned, it took a decision by the Supreme Court in 1920 to make it explicit and well known. That was *Missouri* v. *Holland,* familiarly known as the *Migratory Bird Case*.[9] A suit was brought by the State of Missouri to stay the operation of an act of Congress for the protection of certain migratory birds, the principal objection being that the statute was an invasion of the powers of the state. The statute in question was passed by Congress in order to give effect to a treaty between the United States and Great Britain. A similar law enacted prior to the making of the treaty had been declared unconstitutional by the lower federal courts as an interference with matters reserved to the states. The issue in those cases never reached the Supreme Court for decision, and when it was sought to be raised in *Missouri* v. *Holland* the Court put it to one side as of no consequence. Even if the decisions by the lower courts were right, said the Court, they could not be accepted as the test of treaty power: it was enough for the new statute that it was in pursuance of the treaty.

This feature of *Missouri* v. *Holland* has been magnified by the critics of the doctrine that a treaty can enable Congress to pass statutes on subjects not otherwise within its delegated powers. The case seems to be regarded as the source of that doctrine. But the rule of *Missouri* v. *Holland* did not steal its way into our law. It came as a normal development from the earlier decisions on supremacy of treaties over state laws. There is, as it seems to me, less of a constitutional shock in saying that Congress can carry a treaty into effect on matters normally belonging to the states than in admitting a treaty can do it alone.

So much for the power to make treaties. But, though it is not a matter for detailed discussion here, something needs to be added about the power of the President to enter into agreements (other than treaties) with foreign governments. As in the case of treaties, it took a decision by the Supreme Court to publicize the scope and effect of executive agreements. *United States* v. *Belmont*[10] was a suit by the United States to recover from a New York banker certain sums owned by a Russian corporation and deposited by it with the banker. Russia had dissolved the corporation and taken over the assets. The United States claimed them under an assignment embodied in diplomatic correspondence with Russia. The lower courts gave judgment against the United States holding that it would be contrary to the public policy of New York for the government to recover.

The Supreme Court reversed the judgment. "We do not pause to inquire [said the Court] whether in fact there was any policy of the State of New York to be infringed, since we are of the opinion that no state policy can prevail against the international compact here involved." But the Court went further and said that while the rule of supremacy in respect of treaties is established by the express terms of Article VI, "the same rule would result in the case of all international compacts and agreements from the very fact that complete power of international affairs is in the National Government and is not and cannot be subject to any curtailment or interference on the part of the several States." In respect of all international compacts and in respect of our foreign relations generally the Court concluded that state lines disappear. "As to such purposes, the State of New York does not exist."

The strong national doctrine of *Belmont,* like that of *Missouri* v. *Holland,* is a normal development from earlier cases. Since the President has power to conduct the affairs of this country with foreign governments, he has the primary responsibility of determining whether to do it by means of a treaty or of an executive agreement. If the agreement is valid, it must prevail over state law standing in the way of its enforcement; otherwise, the power of the national government would be subject to restriction by the action of an individual state. The power of the President in making executive agreements was elaborated and strengthened in *United States* v. *Pink.*[11]

In the above described area of the law under the federal system such a proposal as the Bricker Amendment would make several changes. Thus, as already suggested, it would eliminate the self-executing effect of treaties and substitute the rule that a treaty can become effective as internal law only when made so by an act of Congress. By providing that Congress can implement a treaty as internal law only with laws it could pass in the absence of the treaty, the amendment would eliminate the doctrine exemplified by *Missouri* v. *Holland.* Also, by the further provision that executive agreements shall be subject to the limitations imposed by the amendment on treaties, executive agreements would have no self-executing effect as internal law and Congress could pass only such laws to make them so effective as it would have power to enact in the absence of the agreement. The merits of the proposal are not before us, but it may be remarked in passing that if the amendment, taken as a whole, were adopted it would seriously interfere with the conduct of international affairs.

Under the Constitution, then, as it stands today the situation is clear. The government of the United States is invested with ample power for the conduct of international affairs, and the power is undiminished by the fact that ours is a federal system.

II

Federal System and National Policy

The national government being possessed of ample power, the problem of the federal state in the actual conduct of international affairs becomes essentially one of policy. And the most I can do on that aspect of the matter is to point up the nature and weight of the responsibility resting on the President in the making of treaties (or executive agreements) which affect the internal law of the United States, and to suggest that for the discharge of that responsibility

something of guidance and warning can be drawn from an attentive consideration of the federal system.

The recent experience of the United States in connection with the Covenant
on Human Rights will provide a background for, and some illustration of, what
is to be said in the ensuing discussion. Enough of the story for this purpose
can be quickly told.

The Covenant, as is generally known, was but one of the features in the
large movement which had many separate beginnings but which has been
made into a major program under the auspices of the United Nations. From
the beginning the United States played a leading part. We helped see to it that
the Charter of the United Nations spoke broadly on the subject, and when
machinery was set up and put in motion for securing more specific action, we
continued as an active participant. We joined in the formulation and adoption
of the Universal Declaration of Human Rights. That document, however, was
not designed to have legal effect but rather to be a statement of aims and
aspirations. At that stage there was no particular problem; the Declaration as
adopted covered a wide variety of subjects.

But in the next stage, when the task was begun of incorporating some of
those rights into a Covenant, trouble arose. The Covenant, unlike the Declaration, was intended to have legal effect. It was to constitute a treaty with the
force of such a document under our Constitution. Without going into detail
on the content of the Covenant, it is enough to say that the rights included
were much more extensive than those in our own Bill of Rights, and that,
unlike our own scheme of protection against *official* action, the Covenant extended to *private* action as well. The Covenant became so broad that, if
adopted by the United States as a treaty without more, it would have brought
into congressional power (under the doctrine of *Missouri v. Holland*) a wide
array of subjects at present within the powers of the states. It would have constituted a broad centralization of power in Washington.

As an offset to the centralizing consequence there was proposed what has
come to be known as the Federal State Article.[12] For our purposes the significant provision was that the Covenant "shall not operate so as to bring within
the jurisdiction of the federal authority of a federal State . . . any of the matters referred to in this Covenant which independently of the Covenant, would
not be within the jurisdiction of the federal authority." Manifestly, the aim of
the Article was to prevent the operation of the doctrine of *Missouri* v. *Holland.* Disavowal of that doctrine put the United States in the position of refusing to exercise a power admittedly available for the protection of human
rights. Such refusal, to say the least, did not enhance the standing of the United
States as a defender of those rights.

Whatever may be said of the United States' approach to and participation
in the effort on the Covenant, the Federal State Article was a matter of high
importance. Without the Article or some other device for a like result (perhaps appropriate reservations by the Senate in giving consent), the wide content

of the Covenant and its centralizing effect were such as to foreclose its acceptance as a treaty. Even with the Article, assuming a satisfactory one could be
written, the prospect of acceptance was clouded. Many people came to believe
that the project of the Covenant[13] as a treaty ought to be given up and that
other means be devised for the protection of human rights.

That is what the Administration decided to do. On April 7, 1953, in a message to the members of the United Nations Commission on Human Rights,
President Eisenhower called the Universal Declaration of Human Rights "a
significant beacon in the steady march towards achieving human rights and
fundamental freedoms for all" and said "there is need for a new approach to
the development of a human rights conscience in all areas of the world."[14]
The Secretary of State made the position more explicit in a letter to the Representative of the United States on the Human Rights Commission. The United
States Government, he wrote, "has reached the conclusion that we should not
at this time become a party to any multilateral treaty such as those contemplated in the draft Covenants on Human Rights, and that we should now work
toward the objectives of the Declaration by other means." And on April 8,
1953, in a statement before the Human Rights Commission the representative
of the United States outlined three principal proposals as "other means" toward the desired end, namely,

> that the Commission institute a study of various aspects of human rights
> throughout the world, . . .
> that annual reports on developments in the field of human rights be pre-
> pared by each member Government with the assistance of a national advisory
> committee, . . .
> that the United Nations establish advisory services on specific aspects of
> human rights along the lines of the advisory services now being provided in
> the economic, social, and public administration fields. . . .

So, on this single expedition in the conduct of international affairs, the
problem of the federal state has contributed to, if it has not been the prime
cause of, a decisive and surprising change in the position of the United States.
Even without the benefit of hindsight we can put down a number of questions
on whether the United States should have joined in the movement for such a
treaty as the Covenant on Human Rights. With such hindsight, the questions
become sharper and more substantial; and most of them have a certain relevancy for the future in respect of any treaty affecting the internal law of the
United States.

To catalog some of the questions. In the circumstances of the time and
especially in view of the fact that the Universal Declaration of Human Rights
was already an accomplished fact, just what was expected to be gained on the
international scene by virtue of a treaty in furtherance of the protection of
human rights? In what respect and to what extent would the cause of human
rights be advanced on the domestic scene, and was such advancement among
the primary aims? Was the treaty a necessary next step—or could the same,

or similar, results on the international scene be obtained by other means? Would it have been better to proceed piecemeal rather than by an all-inclusive plan? Was it contemplated that the treaty would bring about a shift in the existing division of powers between the states and nation? How extensive would the shift be—more precisely, what power did Congress have to legislate on the subject matter of the treaty and how much would be added as a result of the treaty? Were the international advantages so desirable that they justified the shift of power from the states to Congress? Was full consideration given to the prospect that, the ultimate content of the treaty being determined by an assemblage in which the United States had only a single vote, the treaty might include matters making acceptance by the Senate impossible? Was it assumed that difficulties concerning a shift of power in the federal system could be overcome by inclusion in the treaty itself of such a provision as the Federal State Article? Were the advantages and disadvantages of the Federal State Article carefully weighed in terms of the effect on our negotiating position and on world opinion from our insistence on such an article?

Of such are the questions the President must consider when he enters upon the making of a treaty which, alone or with congressional implementation, will become effective as internal law in the United States. In what respect can it be said that from an attentive consideration of the federal system the President may find guidance and warning for dealing with those questions?

To begin with—to put a practical aspect of the matter first but not to dwell upon it—the President carries a heavy political responsibility. He must take into account the limits of approval by the Senate—how far can he go and still gain that approval? In the Senate, because of its structure and tradition and sense of responsibility, any proposal which involves a possible redistribution of powers between the nation and the states will be subjected to the most searching examination. Witness the opposition to single pieces of proposed legislation on subjects normally considered within the powers of the states— such, for example, as the poll tax.

It does not belittle the importance of the political aspect of the President's responsibility to say that it involves considerations of political prestige and "face." These considerations supply a powerful stimulus to the President so to fashion a treaty program as to keep it within the range of probable acceptance by the Senate; for failure in the Senate may easily appear as a rebuff to his leadership at home and abroad. It may cause him subsequent embarrassment in his conduct of international affairs: it may adversely affect the standing of the United States in world opinion.

But there is a still heavier responsibility. By way of contrast to the political aspect, this is of a constitutional character. For, while it is not the conventional way of putting the matter, I think it permissible and appropriate to say that the President is under a constitutional duty to preserve the federal system. Not, I add at once, the federal system precisely as it stands today, with its present distribution of powers between nation and states; but the federal system none the less. Powers can be shifted from the states to the nation (*Missouri v. Holland* takes care of that), but the scheme of federalism frowns upon a shift unless it is for, and then only to the extent of, a clear need on the international scene.

"Constitutional duty" is the best term I can think of to make emphatic the responsibility of the President when he undertakes the making of a treaty which disturbs the balance of power between nation and states. On domestic matters, when an act of Congress is called in question as intruding upon the states, it falls to the Supreme Court to hold "with a steady and even hand, the balance between state and federal power," and the Court makes its decision on the basis of an ascertainable, even if not sharply fixed, scope of powers delegated to Congress. But here, in respect of treaties, the President himself, within the limits of senatorial consent, determines what the treaty power shall extend to. That is itself a decision under the Constitution—a decision, indeed, which as matters stand today is not subject to review in the courts. If, then, it is incumbent on the Supreme Court never to forget that it is a Constitution being expounded, the President should be animated by a like remembrance. In any event, where treaties are concerned, the balance between nation and state depends in the first instance on the President's own steady and even hand.

For further emphasis upon his responsibility, there is the reminder that the treaty power was not designed as a means of reform within the states or as a short cut for more power in Washington. The federal system presupposes a substantial amount of government in and by the states and it affords considerable room for trial and error. It may come to pass, by reason of domestic shortcomings or the rise of problems beyond the competency of the states (alone or with the leadership and support of the national government), that new or larger national powers may be needed in order to deal effectively with such problems. But that is not the prime business of treaties. The very presence of the amending process in the Constitution shows another way to that end. It is of course true that some gains in internal reform can be achieved by means of the treaty power, but I think such gains must be kept in perspective as by-products rather than the main output.

The results of what I have been trying to say can be reduced to brief and simple terms. So far as the government of the United States is concerned, the solution of the problem depends essentially and singularly upon the qualities of statesmanship in one man, the President. The Founding Fathers saw to it that he was invested with ample power to face the other nations of the world, and they gave him a federal system in which to work. They placed upon him a vast responsibility for the conduct of international affairs. And upon him they pinned both hope and faith that in the fullness of his vision of things abroad he would not lose sight of essentials at home.

FOOTNOTES TO CHAPTER 13

1. In June 1953 the Senate Committee on the Judiciary, by a divided vote, recommended the adoption of an amendment to the Constitution reading as follows:

"Section 1. A provision of a treaty which conflicts with this Constitution shall not be of any force or effect.

"Section 2. A treaty shall become effective as internal law in the United States only through legislation which would be valid in the absence of treaty.

"Section 3. Congress shall have power to regulate all executive and other agreements with any foreign power or international organization. All such agreements shall be subject to the limitations imposed on treaties by this article.

"Section 4. The Congress shall have power to enforce this article by appropriate legislation.

"Section 5. This article shall be inoperative unless it shall have been ratified as an amendment to the Constitution by the legislatures of three-fourths of the several States within seven years from the date of its submission."

The foregoing text evolved from the Committee's consideration of a Resolution introduced by Senator Bricker and 63 other Senators. (Senate Report No. 412, 83d Congress, 1st Session.)

2. Supporters of the amendment do not limit the case merely to apprehended abuses. Thus, it is suggested that under the treaty provisions in the United Nations Charter (particularly Articles 55 and 56 relating to human rights and fundamental freedoms) Congress may already have been vested with power to legislate on broad subjects not within its present powers but reserved to the states. Again, the Judiciary Committee says that "the committee could almost take legislative notice of abuses by the executive branch in the conclusion of executive agreements. . . ." (p. 34)

3. Contrariwise, an occasional voice is heard from abroad that there is too little power. The thought there seems to be that under the present Constitution, framed for a bygone age and ill-suited to the diplomatic needs of today, we are geared for isolation and not for dealing with worldwide problems.

4. Apprehension about individual rights arises from the question whether the treaty power is limited, for example, by the provisions in the Bill of Rights. The Bricker Amendment is intended to allay such apprehension by the inclusion of Section 1 which declares that a "provision of a treaty which conflicts with this Constitution shall not be of any force or effect."

5. "He [the President] shall have power, by and with the advice and consent of the Senate, to make treaties, providing two-thirds of the Senators present concur; . . ." Article II, Section 2.

6. "No State shall enter into any treaty, alliance or confederation; . . ." Article I, Section 10.

7. 3 Dallas 199 (U. S., 1796).

8. 100 U. S. 483 (1880).

9. 252 U. S. 416 (1920).

10. 301 U.S. 24 (1937).

11. 315 U. S. 203 (1942).

12. Drafting a satisfactory article has proved a difficult task, and the text has

been revised from time to time. The following is the text submitted by the United States, Australia, and India in 1952:

"1. A federal State may at the time of signature of ratification of, or accession to, this Covenant make a Declaration stating that it is a federal State to which this Article is applicable. In the event that such a Declaration is made, paragraphs 2 and 3 of this Article shall apply to it. The Secretary General of the United Nations shall inform the other States Parties to this Covenant of such Declaration.

"2. This Covenant shall not operate so as to bring within the jurisdiction of the federal authority of a federal State making such Declaration, any of the matters referred to in this Covenant which independently of the Covenant, would not be within the jurisdiction of the federal authority.

"3. Subject to paragraph 2 of this Article, the obligations of such federal State shall be:

"(a) In respect of any provisions of the Covenant, the implementation of which is, under the constitution of the federation, wholly or in part within federal jurisdiction, the obligations of the federal government shall, to that extent, be the same as those of Parties which have not made a declaration under this Article.

"(b) In respect of any provisions of the Covenant, the implementation of which is, under the constitution of the federation, wholly or in part within the jurisdiction of the constituent units (whether described as states, provinces, cantons, autonomous regions, or by any other name), and which are not, to this extent, under the constitutional system bound to take legislative action, the federal government shall bring such provisions with favorable recommendations to the notice of the appropriate authorities of the constituent units, and shall also request such authorities to inform the federal government as to the law of the constituent units in relation to those provisions of the Covenant. The federal government shall transmit such information received from constituent units to the Secretary General of the United Nations."

13. As a matter of fact, there were late in 1953 two draft Covenants: one on Civil and Political Rights (consisting of 52 Articles), and one on Economic, Social, and Cultural Rights (30 Articles).

14. This and other quotations in this paragraph are from Press Release No. 1688, April 9, 1953, by the United States Mission to the United Nations.

PART THREE
Functional Channels of Relationship

14

Introduction

By Arthur W. Macmahon

A pervasive theme in these chapters is the sense of function in interlevel relationships. It presents in many guises certain problems that attend the formation of vertical networks within separate subject-matter fields of governmental activity. These complex developments, so characteristic of modern federalism, must be considered in juxtaposition to political power and administrative integration at each level. The four chapters of the first section illustrate the variegated patterns that exist. Their designs can be seen best in the context of particular domains of public policy and administration. Their meaning for the understanding of federalism as a phenomenon of growth can be appreciated only when they are traced in some detail, with attention to substance, to law, to informal as well as formal organization, and to the politics of groups. These illustrative treatments are followed in the second section by two chapters that deal with the same realities more generally. The first is concerned with the location of decision-making in the patterns of functional relationship. It refutes the notion of a simple opposition of levels of government; it refines the idea of centralization by showing the degree to which policy rises from below in functional channels and leadership depends upon persuasion. The second chapter is addressed to crucial fiscal issues in federalism: tax sources and interlevel subsidies.

I

The threads of agricultural policy and administration traced by John M. Gaus involve the story of the origins and development of cooperative federalism in the United States. Its methods suited a welfare polity. The great commodity controls of recent farm policy, however, though partly decentralized administratively, did not develop through grants-in-aid to state agencies. The opportunity provided at one time by the law was generally disregarded by the states. I am not sure that Mr. Gaus attaches enough significance to this fact in its bearing upon the difficulties of state-by-state intervention in factors of production and price; indeed, he does not quite close the door on the possibility and, in truth, it must be admitted how numerous are the indirect forms of national support that might be devised. In the administration of agricultural programs generally, Mr. Gaus's analysis reveals not only the use of existing or freshly evoked local units of government in the play of cooperative federalism but also, as he puts it, a large amount of downward stimulation and underwriting of state and local activities by the central government. He points out that many of the complications that beset such federal relations are not due to federalism as such. They are aspects of unsolved organizational difficulties in the government as a whole, including both its executive and legislative branches.

The same point is made in Charles McKinley's chapters on federal relations in the handling of land and water resources. He writes anxiously and even exigently, with a sense of tightening needs and with emphasis upon national responsibility. He reveals clashes of policy in which state officialdom makes common cause with private interests. He shows how little zest states have shown to finance costly undertakings. In land management he records some weakening of standards, at least some temporary postponement of goals. Yet he does not overlook the pioneering role of certain states nor minimize the importance of their powers and controls especially in view of the preponderantly private ownership of the resources that must be protected.

On the possibility of handling water resources in part by interstate compact, Mr. McKinley's views may seem to some unduly skeptical. He does remark that critics of the compact device carried too far in recent years the deflation of certain earlier expectations. He mentions progress in the use of the compact, especially in establishing not only agreement but also continuing administrative machinery. Basically, however, he questions the desirability and the practicability of creating intermediate regional entities by interstate action, even if they involve the national participation that some plans contemplate. Such schemes, he fears, might open the way for state particularism.

Looking beyond Mr. McKinley's skeptical appraisal of interstate compacts in the particular context of water resources, the student of federalism must indeed have doubts in the light of the history of compacts generally. They have brilliantly demonstrated their utility in two sets of circumstances. Mainly they have thrived on contiguity, where adjacent states have been drawn by close common concerns into contractual relationships with each other. Such concerns are mutual; they are not necessarily friendly. The other occasion for successful compacts has been for administrative action on matters of some urgency and general convenience where overt opposition was inconceivable, as in the handling of parolees and certain other phases of nationwide crime control. The compact is hardly suited to resolve the collisions that so often lie between regions rather than within them. Even between adjacent states the steadying effect of the Supreme Court continues to be useful occasionally in developing and applying what it once called a common law of interstate relations, if only to provide base points for supplementary agreements and administrative action.

In drawing illustrations from trade regulation as a broad functional field, Milton Handler has two main objectives. First, he demonstrates the diversity of existing relationships. Second, he seeks to answer the question whether federalism in the United States is a bar to effective trade regulation. He concludes that it is not an obstacle if the will exists to use the tools at hand. This favorable answer is made possible partly by the new dispensation in constitutional law. The means at hand include state action, either separately or in cooperation. It is interesting to note, however, that while Mr. Handler views antitrust policy as the most signal governmental influence upon economic organization, he treats as immaterial the fact that such state antitrust laws as exist have gone so largely unenforced. Is he unduly complacent? Is his outlook on this matter consistent with his general attitude toward federalism? So far as antitrust action goes, Mr. Handler's preference is not to enlist state participation but rather to secure more adequate support for the enforcement of the national act. The uncertainties that attend and handicap the development of the law and its administration, he remarks, are society's own perplexity about size, competition, and other riddles of economic power and progress. In the case of unfair competition, Mr. Handler suggests that the more limited reach of the Federal Trade Commission leaves room for state assistance. Ironically, under Congress' devolutionary deference to state trade laws, state activity has tended to weaken rather than stiffen the national antitrust policy.

These four functional studies indicate most of the tendencies and many of the devices of cooperation in federal systems although some of the latter would be even more apparent if the chapters dealt with fields like social security. Collaboration proceeds on two axes: horizontally, from state to state; vertically, from nation to state or state to nation. The two axes are properly complementary, not alternative. The emphasis, however, may lie on one or the other. The question how far interstate cooperation can be a substitute for national action is an issue of some importance in the United States. So too is the further question whether, when the nation acts, it should participate cooperatively, as in unemployment insurance, or proceed directly, as in old age and survivors insurance.

Along the horizontal axis run relationships that are partly legislative, partly administrative, and in the latter case partly formal, partly informal. On the legislative side they range from sporadic copying of each other's laws, at one extreme, through the concerted drafting of models, reciprocal legislation, and finally interstate agreements made by executive officers on relatively minor matters or compacts approved by the legislatures and Congress, at the other extreme. Administratively the states share information informally; more formally, they may arrange to perform services for each other; they may virtually confer power on each other, as by accepting the other's inspections; they may even participate jointly in such work. Through the associations of officials that exist in every branch of administration, they collaborate in drawing up standards for voluntary adoption—standards that, as we have said, are often recognized by reference in state legislation. The associations, furthermore, help to lay the personal bases for informal dealings too varied to classify.

On the vertical axis, national-state cooperation may go no further than similarity in laws and regulations with little or no administrative contact. National statutes, or regulations issued under them, may be used by the states as models for provisions applicable to intrastate activities. The model may be deliberately drawn as such and offered to the states. The national standard may be adopted by reference, perhaps with automatic acceptance of future changes. The last arrangement, however, may involve the issue of alleged improper delegation of legislative power although myriad instances exist in practice without the question being even raised.

On the vertical axis, too, mutual administrative dealings may develop. The standards under laws at both levels may be drafted by a joint committee or like device. Joint boards or at least joint hearings may be used in handling situations subject from different angles to both national and state control. In various phases of law enforcement, more or less formal arrangements may be made for the lodging of complaints and the initiation of prosecution. Personnel may be loaned; training may be given to employees from the other level. All of these relationships may be laid down in written agreements or memoranda of understanding that often describe themselves as contracts. By such means the respective facilities can be combined or the respective fields of jurisdiction defined and provision made for the cross-transfer or devolution of items of business.

The levels of government, moreover, may be bridged by investitures of power from one level to the other. The possible forms are extremely varied; in many cases the underlying nature of the relationship as a conferral of power is not readily apparent. State officers may be given authority under the laws of the United States. The state courts enforce certain classes of rights so created. On the administrative side, the investiture may be personal as in the designation of individuals as collaborators, deputies, or the like. The investiture may be implicit in a scheme of virtually substitute administration under which the states control certain matters and the national law becomes operative only if such control is lacking. Nor does the bridging of levels by conferrals of power run only from nation to states. National officers may be given authority under state law. Usually the advantage is mutual although the purpose may be to equip them for their national duties or to borrow them incidentally as state agents. Where state law requires intrastate compliance with national standards and inspection, as in aeronautics, the states in a sense use the nation as their agent. The foregoing list is a bare indication of the variety of interlocking forms developed in the practice of federal administration in the United States.

The prevalence of such relationships in federal systems like the United States, broadly characterized historically by their emphasis upon direct federal administration through the central government's own exclusive agents, confirm the impression of an approximation in the world of federal types. From the other side, an increased amount of direct federal administration appeared in the constitutions of countries like Germany which had leaned heavily upon the facilities of member states. Important differences remain, of course. In the United States the practical mutuality that attends most of the relationships just listed should not conceal the fact that constitutional systems like the United States do leave problems of control as a matter of legal obligation. The imposition of indirect federal administration in terms of centrally enforceable command is subject to the doctrine, among other limitations, that neither the nation nor the states can put burdens upon the other level of government.

The important exception has been in judicial law enforcement, as Mr. Hart has shown. Here the central government's right to impose an obligation and to control its performance is aided by a double circumstance: the prerogative of the national judiciary to review and to correct the action of state courts on federal questions; and (along with the "supremacy clause") the basic idea that any court has the duty to apply all relevant law from any source to any case that falls within its jurisdiction. This double circumstance is reinforced by the professional compatibilities of training, outlook, and method that mark judiciaries at all levels within a common legal system even when, as in the United States, judges are drawn from the practice of law and not specially prepared for judicial office.

In the course of American history the use of state facilities has gone through a cycle that has closed under profoundly altered circumstances. At the outset under the Constitution considerable use was made of state instrumentalities despite the wish to by-pass the states in avoiding the weaknesses of the Articles of Confederation. Little administration existed except through courts. Cogent reasons suggested the national use of state tribunals, at least alternatively. The needs of the time and the receptive attitude of the state judiciaries were illustrated in the remark of a Pennsylvania judge in 1824: ". . . although inconvenience is no justification for usurpation of power, yet as the court does not see how this conflicts with the constitution of the United States, the inconvenience may be considered; and it would be an intolerable inconvenience and grievance, in an action for a petty penalty, to drag a man from the most remote corner of the state, to the seat of the federal judiciary." (*Buckwalter v. U. S.*, 11 S. and R. 193, 197) In the same spirit, as late as 1835 and in the State of South Carolina, a decision reversed a lower court and insisted that jurisdiction be taken because "the constitutional legislation of the United States is the command of South Carolina as well as of the United States." (*State v. Wells*, 2 Hill 687, 695) Four years later, however, a judge in the same state held: "The consideration of the convenience of the citizen does not weigh a feather with me . . . I sit here to administer the laws of South Carolina; and in the discharge of my appropriate duties, find ample occupation for all my time and ample employment for all my powers. I do not come here to enforce the criminal laws of the United States, whose government in that regard is a foreign government." (*State v. McBride,* 1 Rice 400, 404) His refusal indeed was in line with a trend illustrated by the stand of a New York court as early as 1819. As Charles Warren once remarked, the states generally were drawing away in self-defeating caution and exclusiveness. Meanwhile transportation was improving and the central government's network was being extended, as in the creation in the forties of United States commissioners to handle certain preliminaries of judicial action. Meanwhile, too, the strains of the slavery issue were putting their distorting imprint upon many phases of constitutional interpretation and practice.

One need recall only the latest stage of the cycle. It was signalized in 1947 by the vigorous language of the Supreme Court in holding that a reluctant state court must assume jurisdiction under the congressional price control law. This development (though in essence only a reaffirmation) is a significant phase of cooperative federalism. In spirit at least the doctrine may have broader long-run implications. As things stand in constitutional systems like the United States, however, no general right exists to compel the acceptance of administrative, as distinguished from judicial, obligations. The basis is mainly voluntary. This fact emphasizes the roles of professional morale, of persuasion as an administrative art, and of the motivation and support of interlevel relationships by services-in-aid and grants-in-aid. These relationships merge in the formidable fiscal problems of federalism in modern societies. Here the issues are not only technically economic and administrative; they also involve profound collisions and consequences in the adjustment of forms of wealth and its distribution.

II

The analysis of decision-making by Edward W. Weidner is supported by the unique series of intensive field studies of interlevel relationships within the state of Minnesota—national, state, and local—which Mr. Weidner helped to direct as the associate of William Anderson. The findings as reflected in the present chapter illuminate the overall view of criss-crossing sympathies and strains. The groups involved are: first, the more or less professionally trained civil servants within a particular function at all levels; second, the politically responsible officials at each level, especially officials with legislative or general administrative responsibility; third, the political officials of other states having different conditions, views, and ambitions; and fourth, the professional and clientele organizations that parallel the function in question, often subdivided in terms of special interests. In these circumstances it is idle to conceive a simple juxtaposition of levels, national and state. The sense of level as level seems to be felt strongly only by the political officials. Moreover, there is seldom agreement among them from state to state. The variations of viewpoint on the same level reflect the differences that help to explain and justify the existence of federalism itself. The militant awareness of state level as such is most likely to be felt by an organization like the Council of State Governments, mainly professional in staff but dedicated to serve the officials generally at the level in question.

Most associations are instinct with function. Until the rise of the Council of State Governments after 1925 one might well have concluded that in the United States the vital associations would remain of that character. There was much in the faltering story of the Governors' Conference to support such a prophecy. Nor was this dim view necessarily refuted by the important role played in Australia by the meetings of prime ministers; after all many different factors were present there, including cabinet government at the state level and a small number of states. The Council of State Governments, however, has shown that in the United States a vital, overall, multifunctional center can be created for service, negotiation, and pressure. What is its ideological destiny in the maturing federalism of the country?

In the discussion of the draft of his chapter, Mr. Weidner summarized an impression that rises in the study of intergovernmental relationships as illustrated in Minnesota. "The striking conclusion," he remarked, "is that if you analyze the devices used in national-state and state-local relations as to their authoritativeness, their severity, if you will, to the techniques used, you will discover no discernible difference in the techniques used in national-state and state-local relations." It will be observed that his chapter does indicate that the legal position of the states in a federal system has some effect upon the attitudes of political officers at the state level. Moreover, the similarity of methods that Mr. Weidner stressed in the discussion must be viewed in the light of the extent to which the tradition of self-government by locally elected officers has given a partially federal quality to state-local relations in the United States, quite apart from specific state constitutional provisions.

The perplexities of federal finance analyzed in the chapter by Roy Blough are aggravated versions of a problem faced wherever government is conducted over a considerable area by separate political subdivisions with independent taxing powers and uneven resources, because of a spotty distribution of taxable wealth, while a central government exists with taxing powers over the whole area. Under the equalitarian ideas and electoral pressures of modern government a demand will develop to overcome in some way the discrepancies between the need for governmental services (corresponding roughly to the distribution of population but affected by conditions such as relative sparsity or density and relative per capita wealth) and the ability of the various local governments to supply the needed services from local tax resources.

In such situations there is bound to be recurrent agitation in the hope that somehow the basic problem can be removed at a stroke by a reallocation of tax sources. Ordinarily the emphasis in such agitation is upon the separation of sources so that any one source (or, more realistically, any one type of tax) is used only by one level of government. As a practical matter, however, the reallocation of sources is more likely to take the form of the entrance of various governmental units into lucrative tax fields hitherto novel for them but already tapped by another level, as when municipalities in the United States began in recent years to tax incomes under the name of payroll taxes. Needless to say, the interlevel sharing of certain taxes on the basis of the place where the tax is collected may sometimes be an administrative convenience but, by definition, cannot equalize conditions among areas.

Mr. Blough belittles the alleged evils of overlapping taxation as such. He does not look for magic in any reallocation of sources. On this matter he doubts the usefulness of grandiose inquiry. Such adjustments as are feasible (possibly in gasoline taxation, for example) should be piecemeal. In the discussion on this point, James A. Maxwell said of Mr. Blough's preference for the piecemeal rather than the overall approach: "I suspect this is very much the way it may well be but it is not the way it ought to be . . . I would prefer an overall examination once in a while by a body as close as may be to a Royal Commission." Nevertheless none who discussed Mr. Blough's views dissented from his conclusion that in the face of modern necessities no rearrangement of tax sources could avoid the need to meet the problem in part by a transfer of costly services to larger governmental units or, alternatively, interlevel payments of some kind.

On the question of the type of interlevel subsidy, it will be observed that Mr. Blough resolves doubts against the use of socalled block or unconditional grants except, perhaps, in time of depression. A basic reason is that he does not believe national support should be given except for purposes related to national interest, which in his view is always tied to particular functions despite the pervasive elements of interdependence in contemporary society. He proposes a reasonable middle course between block grants and the highly segregated grants-in-aid that have prevailed in the United States. In the discussion John E. Burton endorsed this line of reform although expressing interest in the possibilities of some form of block grants. On the general question of federal aid he said: "We have accomplished great good with these grants-in-aid . . . but there have been evils" apart from "a form of coercion in three billions of dollars that is parcelled out by the federal government to the states." Waste, he argued, results from "the manner in which these grants are appropriated piecemeal—some forty or fifty of them." The main defect is a kind of distortion at the state level where a specific federal grant may "force the state to divert moneys that it might want to spend in certain areas to the federally supported area, and it does not have sufficient capacity to do much more than to meet the federal money that it has to match." Mr. Burton added: "I would like to see a great number of appropriations to the fullest extent consolidated into a smaller number of appropriations and on an equalized basis.' This step in itself would bring changes in the nature of supervision.

Mr. Burton had something of this in mind in urging that an effort be made to "find a broader basis of compliance than the detailed rules and regulations that now go with the multifarious programs that we have." He spoke of the possibility of creating "a new agency, a federal-state agency, that could be the umpire of state compliance for federal aid." Mr. Blough in the discussion questioned the desirability of such an overall agency; the control, he believed, should be exercised by national officials close to the substance of the work in each of the broad functional fields. William Anderson, too, disapproved any central joint body except on an advisory basis. He believed that "the state governments and the local governments should have every means of access to the federal authorities." He added: "I would like to see this relationship formalized to some extent by the establishment of some advisory body representing the local, the state, and the federal governments which could be a continuing body for research and development." The basic allocations, however, should rest with Congress. Mr. Anderson did not approve anything like the Australian Loan Council. He did not mention the fact but it may be noted that on this body the Commonwealth has two votes and a casting vote; it can be and indeed has been outvoted. On the question of possible new machinery in the United States, Frederick L. Bird suggested that steps should be taken "to see some means devised which would bring constantly to the attention of the Executive Office of the President and of Congress the probable effect of proposed national policies on the finances of state and local governments." He declared that "too often policies are considered as though the national government were a unitary system and without careful consideration of the fiscal effect on the other components of the federal system."

Throughout the discussion there was general acceptance of equalization as an objective in grants-in-aid and of the corollary necessity to revise the traditional schemes for the apportionment and matching of funds. It was assumed that no grounds exist for believing that the fiscal position of the states will become equal in the predictable future. To be sure, mention was made of the fact that in the decade ending in 1951 the spread between the states with the highest and the lowest per capita income dropped from the ratio of 1:4.8 to 1:2.7. On the question of further stress upon equalization as an objective in subsidy policy, James A. Maxwell sounded a note of caution against the misdirection of national resources by the permanent subsidizing of uneconomic areas. It will be noted that Roy Blough, consistently with his concept of national interest, would keep equalization objectives subordinate to the support of particular functions, however broadly defined. As time goes on and with the development of such functions, he suggests that the stress upon equalization (as distinguished from stimulation) might well increase so that the wealthier states would receive little or no aid. On this last point, I venture to argue that, however small the share of the stronger states, they should never be eliminated from a cooperative undertaking. The very strength that makes aid to them unnecessary for equalization purposes also makes their self-reliance and administrative endowments useful counterweights in maintaining resilient management in the program as a whole.

The bearing of anticyclical fiscal policy upon the financial problems of federalism is only impliedly dealt with in the chapter by Mr. Blough although in the discussion he showed his sympathy for developments in the handling of grants that will take this factor into account. Ideally the mobile strategies of a planned relationship among the levels of government must pay attention to rates of expenditure and to the abilities to tax and borrow as well as to rates of taxation in relation to the movements of the economy. In the discussion the growing awareness of the problem and its bearing upon a reorientation of techniques of grants-in-aid was reflected in remarks by Frederick L. Bird, among others. He said: "We would like to see the means of more harmony in fiscal policy among national, state, and local governments. You will recall the disharmony in the depression in the thirties when federal spending for public works was largely offset by the discontinuation of state and local spending for that purpose." Nevertheless, in view of the unavoidably continuous normal duties of local units with increasing costs and their limited borrowing power in times of depression, the burden of accommodating government to the economy must rest heavily upon the central government. Mr. Bird suggested that the future policy might well include "a clear recognition by the national government on some predetermined basis that it has the responsibility to help maintain the fiscal stability of state and local governments in a severe business depression."

The hopeful emphasis, of course, is upon the preventive aspects of anticyclical policy. A hint of fresh thinking about the articulated handling of federal aid may be noted in the 1949 congressional act for slum clearance and community redevelopment. It provided that in any year the stated limits for bond issues and capital grants might be raised by the President on the advice of the Council of Economic Advisers as to the general effect upon conditions in the building industry and the economy; it also stipulated that the number of authorized units of low rental housing might be increased or decreased in the light of such advice. Doubtless the attempt in the United States to take thought and to devise procedures about this phase of federal finance has only begun. Attention may well be given to certain elements of flexibility illustrated in Australia. Where the ability of the central government directly to influence the rates of deceleration or acceleration of state expenditure and taxation is as limited as in the United States, the main indirect remedy, partial at best, is the spread of economic sophistication among the people and among officials at all levels of government.

Mr. Blough in his limited space chooses not to discuss the federal angle of state-local financial relationships, beyond observing that they have many similarities to national-state patterns and problems. In the discussion, John E. Bebout voiced a municipal point of view. "Too many of our states too much of the time," he said, "treat their cities more or less like conquered provinces —with a combination of oppression, meddling, and neglect." In view of the nature of many state governments, both politically and administratively, he defended the tendency to bypass the states on many matters. "One of the great safeguards in the federal system for a local government," he concluded, "lies in the fact that, while it is created and legally subject to state law, it can because of fiscal and other arrangements appeal over the head of the state. And get federal aid, federal technical assistance, and federal encouragement."

The question is an open one in the evolution of federal systems. At the present stage in the renovation of state governments in the United States, it is difficult to speculate about an ultimate pattern of national-state-local relations. Many longrun considerations point to the desirability of a downward interlevel continuity in functional developments which will draw the initiative, support, and coordinating influence of the intermediate level into each program. But there is also much in the genius of federalism that argues permanently not only for decentralization but also for flexiblity, variation, and multiple avenues of contact and appeal. As things stand in the United States, alert and active state governments can earn the right to participate in the development of the great functions.

ILLUSTRATIVE STUDIES OF FUNCTIONAL FIELDS

15

Agricultural Policy and Administration in the American Federal System

By John M. Gaus

In the United States we have meant by a federal system a joining of partially or wholly separate political units with one another by a compact under which each preserved its corporate personality with certain duties and powers while becoming a part of a comprehensive new political system to which duties and powers were also allocated. The terms of the compact were not to be changed formally by any one party or corporate unit alone, but only by a special process of amendment whereby a wide basis of consent would be guaranteed. In fact an equality of representation of the units within one legislative chamber of the whole was made absolute.

The possibility of a balance and federating of major economic interests was suggested, a half-century after the winning of independence, by John C. Calhoun. He argued that in some degree the states as geographic units tended to be the seats of particular economic interests. The Senate might therefore be viewed as roughly representing the major commodity, processing, financial, shipping, and other interests. Some forty years ago, the late Charles A. Beard returned to this theme in a discussion of politics and economics. In the decade in which he wrote there was a rising interest among students of government in theories of pluralism and a federalism of interests, of guilds, or corporations was envisaged. Ideas of this kind in fact found favor in the constitutions and political movements at the close of the First World War. The Soviet system was at one time thought to reflect them, as also the Italian Fascist corporation and the constitution of the Weimar German Republic in Article 165. It is ironic that in the evolution of substantive policy and its administration, a kind of federalism of functions has been developing with us, while the countries in which a functional or interest federalism was being claimed went the way of single-party machine and personal dictatorships. Our own system, as it was emerging from the Second World War, was such that an observer could state, in writing of "The Future Organizational Pattern of the Executive Branch," that "in federal relations with states and localities, it is evident that cooperation along the pattern of functional union will remain the tendency of the social service state as well as in policing activities."[1]

American public policy and administration of functions primarily relating to agriculture offer examples of this mingling of both geographic and functional federal systems. This is to understate and oversimplify a complex of activities and organizations. We are confronted with the raw and semiprocessed materials of a variety to challenge every branch of our study and every fashion in emphasis, from the intricacies of audit of expenditures to the sociology of power. One might have thought that the very origins of the term agriculture —the cultivating of the field—would firmly root the structure of its public relations to the ground, to a field or fields whose proprietors and cultivators would determine its plan of management for themselves as far as possible, and join them with those for other fields and their cultivators in public housekeeping where collective effort might be needed on a widening geographic base alone. And that thread is present still. But it would require the imagination and pen of Edmund Burke, as in his inspired account of the social compact, to hint at the range and depth of considerations that are revealed in public agricultural policy. It reflects myriad compacts across multiple areal units, levels of government, substantive activities and commodities, and considerations of the time-periods which must be kept in mind for the application of decisions.

I

A dispassionate record of legislation reveals that from the beginning of the republic, in its days as a Confederation, agriculture was enmeshed in not only the larger economy but also the exercise of national powers. The conspectus of *Farm Policies of the United States, 1790–1950,* presented by Murray R. Benedict,[2] begins with land policy, and discusses money, tariffs, transportation, and farmer organizations as introductory to the appraisal of agricultural policies during the present century. For however fundamental is the actual physical cultivation of the field for production, that production, as a Chief Justice has stated of a comparable situation, is not undertaken "in an intellectual vacuum."[3] The factors of physical environment mingle with those of man-made institutions of communication, price, and market to evolve a rough and ready federal system of farm and market, of producer, processor, distributor, and consumer. Successive application of science to human activities, additions to, and shifts in the distribution of population change what a farm family may do in relative isolation within their fences and what they must do with others beyond the fences to facilitate, or even make possible, the satisfaction of their needs. While the early public policies directly related to agricultural production were those of the states, chiefly for encouragement through bounties for the supply of particular foods and fibres and the financing of prizes at fairs and exhibitions, the land policies of both state and national governments affected the location, tempo, and nature of settlement. Despite the misgivings of many legislators as to constitutionality, and indeed after the departure of the members from the southern states, Congress passed three important acts in 1862 that set a policy of national-state participation that not only persists but also has been expanded to include local governmental units.

The Homestead Act used national power and property to give freer access to the public domain to owner-occupier-operator farmers and thus also to scatter settlement more rapidly and widely across the continent. The Morrill Act fostered education in agriculture and engineering through grants by the national government to the states. A third act established a new unit in the national government, "A Department of Agriculture, the general designs and duties of which shall be to acquire and diffuse among the people of the United States useful information on subjects connected with agriculture in the most general and comprehensive sense of that word." In later years, the policy of land dispersal was, after the disposal of most of the good land, to be reversed by policies reflected in the setting aside from sale of forest reserves and then of managed range lands in the public domain. The encouragement of higher education in agriculture was to be extended by grants for experiment stations, money grants in larger amounts and for varied subjects, and a "cooperative" extension system that enlisted participation of national, state, and county governments—and what was more, local associations of primarily but not exclusively farmer membership that were shortly to join both within states and among states as a federation of Farm Bureau federations.

These well known facts are recalled here because they illumine attitudes toward and actions taken in the use of our federal system in agricultural policy at many points. For example, among the effects of the Homestead Act was the use of a settlement policy for the more arid regions (against which Major John Powell was to protest strongly in his famous report) that delayed long a reconsideration of land policies affecting grazing, arable, and forest land uses most suitable to the variations of soil and climate, and the units and services of local government. The grant-in-aid principle applied to the fostering of state agricultural education was to be copied for other functions, and to fix in the minds of many, especially in the land grant institutions, a constitutional theory of aid from, plus autonomy toward, the national government—and also toward the state government. This theory pivoted on the notion of an exclusive and single channel of national participations in agricultural policy, so far as the state and the farmer were to be affected, via the autonomous land grant institutions. It is true that these views were modified with the rise of regulations affecting the physical flow of commodities in interstate and foreign commerce, beginning with the adoption of standards and inspection whereby a loss of foreign markets in meats might be averted and the importation of diseased livestock prevented. Intrastate commercial regulation came to be vested chiefly in state departments of marketing, or agriculture and marketing, although the land grant institutions have been employed at times and for certain commodities. Another exception to the relationship established in agri-

cultural education is in the allied field of forestry, where the connection between the two levels has been chiefly between state forestry or conservation
departments and the Forest Service.

The widening of functions or programs has sometimes created a problem
of obtaining a better focus of policies administered in two different agencies
on more than one level. The recognition of the importance of the farm wood
lot and the need for extension work in forestry with farmers, and of vocational
education in agriculture in high schools, illustrate this administrative heritage
of policies of grants-in-aid or other forms of collaboration that affect different
aspects of the same function yet have historically been assigned to different
units both at Washington and in the states. Thus the conduct of federal relations—that is, relations to national, state, and local agencies—is entangled
with the planning and administration at each level of policies which require
comprehensive balance and detailed integration yet are split up among various agencies on that level. While this problem may not be exclusively inherent
in a federal system, it is fair to admit that a federal system exacerbates it. And
it invites the rise of organizations of those directly affected which enter the
political-administrative arena to obtain their desires in unified policy and administration by "pressures" all along the line in promoting collaboration of all
the parts at every level.

The attitude toward the distribution of functions between national and state
governments, and indeed toward the relative extent of the use of government
generally, reflected in the legislation of 1862 (as well as for a long time afterward) may be viewed as a tide ebbing away from a Marshall interpretation of
the federal system. Any governmental relation to production was a matter for
the states—and then chiefly in bounties and aid through research and education. Commercial regulations to facilitate the producer might be state for
intrastate transactions, national for interstate and foreign commerce. The purpose was primarily to facilitate the marketing process. The role of the national
government was that of giving away lands, both to individuals and to the
states, and fostering education and the gathering and distribution of information. In all this we witness not so much the peculiarities of agricultural policy
as the condition of the arts, the size and distribution of population, and their
interaction with one another and with the physical environment.

II

In 1910, in a Commencement Address at the University of Indiana, Frederick Jackson Turner[4] noted that "As land values rise, as meat and bread
grow dearer, as the process of industrial consolidation goes on, and as Eastern
industrial conditions spread across the West, the problems of traditional
American democracy will become increasingly grave. . . . The time has come
when University men may well consider pioneer ideals, for American society
has reached the end of the first great period of its formation. . . . The times call

for educated leaders. General experience and rule-of-thumb information are inadequate for the solution of problems of a democracy which no longer owns the safety fund of an unlimited quantity of untouched resources. Scientific farming must increase the yield of the field, scientific forestry must economise the woodlands, scientific experiment and construction by chemist, physicist, biologist and engineer must be applied to all of nature's forces in our complex modern society. The test tube and the microscope are needed rather than the axe and rifle in this new ideal of conquest. . . . But quite as much in the field of legislation and of public life in general as in the industrial world is the expert needed. The industrial conditions which shape society are too complex, problems of labor, finance, social reform too difficult to be dealt with intelligently and wisely without the leadership of highly educated men familiar with the legislation and literature on social questions in other states and nations."

The accuracy of prophecy and diagnosis in this statement concerns us here less than its portrayal of atmosphere and attitude. It throws light on agricultural policy and administration within the federal system from the time of the Interstate Commerce Act in 1887 to the catastrophe of the first World War. The national legislation affecting agriculture in this period was not directly concerned with the control of production. The debates over tariff, credit, and monetary policy which affected agriculture along with other economic activities were to have more sharply focused direction later in the establishment of a farm credit system under the national government but with an encouragement of semi-autonomous cooperative associations. However, the most important of the shifts and reversals of larger national policies that directly affected agriculture were in natural resources policies. These inevitably affected the population, activities, and tax base of state and local governments as well as the decisions of farm and ranch owners and operators. They included the establishment of national forest reserves in the public domain, later assigned to a Forest Service of the Department of Agriculture for custody and administration; of a Department of the Interior Reclamation Service for administering a policy of development of irrigation in arid lands; and of the fostering through grants-in-aid of cooperative U.S.-state forest protection on the watersheds of navigable streams. These and related subsequent policies, such as the establishing of the Grazing Service in 1934 and the ending of the traditional land disposal program, warrant examination in any review of our experience in the agricultural functions of a federal system.

The fact should be noted that the surviving public domain was almost entirely in the more arid and mountainous parts of the West where population was sparse and water a decisive factor in determining land use. This gave those states in which the public domain was the dominant type of ownership the greatest stake, whether in the effect upon settlement or upon income from the land, in policies of disposal or of management of national forests and range lands. A rancher supplementing his own acres by the lease of grazing rights on public lands might have to deal with the Forest Service (Department of Agriculture) and the Grazing Service (Department of the Interior). The presence in several western states of so predominant a land-owner as the United States —and that land-owner one who operated administratively at least through two or more agencies, each zealous to advance a cause born in a period of militant reform and growing to maturity amidst conflict—is again illustrative of the complication and intermingling of interlevel relations with those between functional agencies. There would come a time when the policies of the Reclamation Service would be attacked as adding to an existing surplus of farm production and at a cost, moreover, not justified in comparison with the same expenditure in the improvement of lands in some other region. The retort to this would stress the importance of further population and general economic development precisely in the area of the project.

With the expansion in national forest programs to include the purchase of lands in eastern and southern states for national forests, and of cooperation with those states (as well as all the others) in blocking up public lands to create areas adequate for future permanent location of wood-using industries, and with new methods of lumbering, transport, and processing, the importance of the farm wood lot or the forests held in smaller parcels has come to be recognized. Here again is the need for a nice adjustment in advisory and extension work between agencies within a single department and joining the national, state, and local levels so that specialized extension work, soil conservation payments, soil conservation district programs, and those of the national and state forest agencies will supplement each other. And here again the local and state governments and the citizen consumers of and payers for their services have a major interest.

The coming to the Secretaryship of the Department of Agriculture in 1913 of David F. Houston, after the long regime of James Wilson, may be viewed in retrospect as marking other shifts of emphasis that have affected the extent and distribution of activities. His interest in general economic policy and awareness of the changing setting of agriculture led him to establish in his office a nucleus of personnel to study problems of marketing and distribution which laid the ground for more extended legislation to facilitate orderly marketing. It also became the forerunner of the Bureau of Agricultural Economics, established by the elder Wallace when Secretary, which was to supply a staff of economists and other social scientists much as Turner had called for. After 1900 there had been a development of agricultural economics from the pioneering work of H. C. Taylor, G. F. Warren, and others chiefly in the land grant colleges or, like W. J. Spillman, within the older natural science bureaus of the department whose studies in farm management could no longer be confined within the fences of the farm.

The recognition in the research and instruction in agricultural education of economic, and shortly thereafter, rural social problems has more than a substantive importance. The study of these matters was not only brought within the national department, but in addition their introduction coincided with the beginning of an equipment of the Office of the Secretary for the consideration of general policies. Could there be some balance achieved between and across the attitudes and programs of the individual bureaus, so that their operations in the field might take account of one another and of state and local conditions? This problem had become the more urgent with the proliferation of agencies and programs and the widening of discretionary power. At one time it was considered possible to channel much of the program of the department, and in particular that relating to "education," through the land grant institutions, and the establishment of the cooperative agricultural extension program seemed to offer the device through which, along with joint planning of research by the department and the state agricultural experiment stations, this might be accomplished.

The establishment of the Agricultural Extension Service under the Smith-Lever Act in 1914 marked a further application of the policy of 1862 whereby the national government fostered education and research in agriculture through grants to the states. It was built on various types of extension work already under way and fostered and supported often by a local county "bureau" that maintained an "agent" from private funds or a mixture of private and public contributions. The Smith-Lever Act provided that county agents were to be joint agents of the national department and of the state colleges of agriculture. "Since the colleges needed local financial support and wanted to make use of local leadership," states Dr. Gladys Baker,[5] "they in turn redivided their authority with county boards, governing advisory committees, and farm bureau organizations. Thus the county agent became the joint representative of the United States Department of Agriculture, the state agricultural college, and his individual county." With a more permanent base supplied by the grants to the states under the act and stimulated by the use of the system during World War I for increasing the production of foods and fibres, the local bureaus increased greatly in number, federated by states, and finally in 1920 brought the state federations in the American Farm Bureau Federation.[6] A measure that on the surface would seem to be of interest primarily as an example of national-state relations in a federal system thus produced a third-level partner. And it provided the groundwork of "a related organization of farmers that has had much to do with the course of agricultural policy in the decades since 1920."[7]

The cooperative extension system has played so important a part not only in the actual administration of agricultural policy but also as an illustration of a method possibly applicable to other programs, and therefore has been so much debated, that we should attempt to clarify here certain underlying assumptions. We should note, however, that from the beginning there was some ambiguity about these and throughout its history the extension system has illustrated the wide range of interpretation which federal institutions by their nature seems to permit.

First, the extension system seems to be a further application of the principle earlier applied in U.S.-state cooperation in agricultural research through the support by national grants of state agricultural experiment stations: namely, that the conditions peculiar to states and to smaller areas within states—such as differences in soil or climate—should be recognized and reflected in programs. Extension work carried this principle down to the ultimate farm or at least to the groups of farms and the problems and potentialities of farm conditions typical of, or substantially present in, a county. The research and information of the national department, through the facilitation of the Extension Office in that department, and the findings of the state college and experiment station were to be channeled through, and interpreted to, the local farms by the county agent.

A second basic assumption was local participation in the educational process through groups which would indicate what were the appropriate problems to be dealt with and what use to make of the characteristic technique of "demonstrations." These programs were subject also to the state extension organization with its director and staff of specialists in various subject-matter fields located at and tied in various ways to the college with its program of residence instruction and to the agricultural experiment station.

At the time of its origin, a further assumption would seem to be that the farmer who received the knowledge thus made available (presumably with his participation in testing its applicability to local conditions) would employ it as a free enterpriser in charge of his own operating unit, which we may view as a self-contained farm. Such use as he made of the educational opportunities thus made available would presumably be mingled with his knowledge generally and applied in his own farm management plans and in his activities in the market as buyer and seller. Not collective action (except such as might follow by accident, so to speak, from the general influence of new knowledge widely made available) but individual action as qualified by new knowledge and its communication was the essence.[8]

It followed that the county agent was not an administrator enforcing collective rules, in the ordinary sense, but a teacher in adult education beyond the campus of the college. And the American tradition in public administration emphasized the autonomous nature of the system and the necessity for "keeping it out of politics." It may be added in this connection that the tendency has been for a decline of the proportion of the costs contributed from nongovernmental sources, and the almost complete financing of the work from national, state, and county appropriations.

Certain of these principles have become so influential among those most concerned with agriculture that either they have been in part incorporated in other programs or remain as a standard whereby those programs have been appraised. Thus, the idea of participation by the farmers at the local level in agricultural policy formulation was applied to the new Agricultural Adjustment Administration. Its central program, however, went beyond the use of the fruits of public research and called for induced collective action to affect the market, even providing in certain circumstances after the use of a referendum for coercive action supported by the sanctions of public law. The market and price system was increasingly national and international; even the local markets (as in milk, for example) were affected by, and affected, national (or "interstate") markets and prices since milk-sheds crossed state lines. What is more, the commodities raised and consumed on the farm might affect market and price.[9] The public regulation of the market required the use of the only legal power of sufficient reach, that of the national government. Yet so strong was the tradition of local participation that the devices of administration of county and local community elective committees, first on a commodity, then a general program basis, were built into the administrative structure of regulation. This shift and widening of function in national action therefore should be examined here because it has contributed so greatly to the present complexities of our federal system.

The conception of national powers prevailing in the early quarter of this century and into the thirties denied the right of the national government to reach at least directly the production phase of industry and agriculture, since the tendency of interpretation of Article I, Section 8, in the light of the Tenth Amendment, confined the area of its jurisdiction to foreign and interstate commerce with an emphasis on transportation across state lines or activities directly affecting such commerce. Agricultural policy proposals for improving the farmer's economic position were therefore directed on the national level to general issues of banking, currency, the tariff, transportation, and the breakup or regulation of monopoly, so far as these could be based upon the "enumerated" powers, and those "necessary and proper to them," whether through taxation and spending or in more direct terms.

III

The catastrophe of World War I profoundly affected our entire economy. The readjustments at its close struck most deeply an expanded agriculture. It was at this precise moment that the national department was being equipped with a Bureau of Agricultural Economics whereby the earlier programs of research in plant and animal industry were being supplemented by research in economic questions. Inevitably these tied the study of agriculture into that of every factor in the economy and, in view of the profound changes in our position in world economy, to an examination of international and national markets and prices. The apparent imbalance between farm-produced commodities and farm-purchased goods, revealed sharply by the newer focus of attention and research, could hardly be reached by tariffs for a country that was exporting. Nevertheless, the influences previously noted, as well as the constitutional position, concentrated the attention of farmers, of business men and manufacturers affected by them as purchasers, and analysts of the situation generally upon the search for a remedy in measures roughly equivalent to the tariff as well as through market controls. Some "conservationists," including foresters, land economists, and farm management experts were moving toward a conception of land use policy that would have later relevance to the larger issues. But for the most part thinking about the "farm relief" problem centered upon finding some "parity" for the farmer (viewed as less able to adjust his production to markets) through the use of national powers which alone could stretch across the market at home and reach into the wider international market—as tariffs did. The building of a legislative program proceeded across party lines, commodity by commodity, by types of farming region by region, distorting but utilizing the lines of congressional representation by states and districts. The presidency resisted capture, yet, with the election of Herbert Hoover, was required to produce an alternative in the form of an encouragement of and public financial aid to an attempt at market controls through cooperative marketing and the financing of "surpluses."

But as the problem persisted, the idea was developed of reaching down to the farm to induce a limitation by the farm owner or operator of production to meet estimated market needs. With the Democratic Party victory in 1932, attributed in part to support from farmers and others who desired a program that would go beyond that of the Farm Board (some of whose members had publicly stated that a public regulation of production would be necessary to secure a rise in farm prices), an attempt to meet both the substantive economic and the constitutional points was reflected in the use of payments to farmers joining, through the device of referenda, in the adoption of quotas of acreage adjusted to market estimates and reimbursed from funds raised by processing taxes on the commodity. Although the law was a national statute, administered by a national department, aimed at a national-international objective, so strong was the tradition and conception, as we have seen, of national, state, and local cooperation represented by the land-grant agricultural institutions and procedures that the administration of the act at the local and state levels was placed in part in committees elected by participating farmers. The state and county extension personnel were in many states employed not only in giving farmers information about the act but also as administrators in the system, such as committee secretaries.[10] Nevertheless the general philosophy behind the program with its employment of large-scale national intervention reaching down to the decisions as to land use of the participating farmer seemed to be a sharp break with the assumptions concerning extension work as "educational" we have already noted. In actual operation the opportunities for differences in outlook, personality, and agency corporate feeling could arise frequently and in many places as the new agency got under way.

The original program was invalidated when in 1936 the Supreme Court[11] declared the basic provision unconstitutional. The "power to confer or withhold unlimited benefits is the power to coerce or destroy," stated Justice Roberts, and this regulation of "production" brought the measure within the reservation set forth in the Tenth Amendment. The effect on the place of agricultural policy in a federal system was to shift the objectives of the adjustment program in a hurriedly passed new act (the Soil Conservation and Domestic Allotment Act of 1936) to an emphasis on soil conservation and on income rather than on price. Adjustment plans for a farm would be drafted in terms of soil conservation objectives ("soil-conserving" as against "soil-depleting"), with payments for execution of the plans to be made from general appropriations and not an earmarked processing tax. Since most "soil-depleting" crops were cash crops in which major surpluses had produced low prices, it was hoped that the original goal of affecting price and income could be reached through this spending for the public welfare in terms of soil protection and improvement. Two years later the Agricultural Adjustment Act of 1938 incorporated these and other provisions including marketing quotas and loans for withholding supplies from the market. The Supreme Court, in 1939, in the case of *Mulford v. Smith*[12] speaking again through Justice Roberts, modified the earlier Butler case decision of 1936. "It established the power of the Federal Government to regulate the quantity of a commodity which could be sold, a type of regulation which in practical effect would control the amount produced in an interstate industry."[13] A later decision of the Court voiced by Justice Jackson in the case of *Wickard v. Filburn*[14] extended further the power of the national government to regulate the farm management policies of the farmer. The issue centered in the right to control the acreage of a commodity in the program used for consumption on the farm and thus not entering the market at all physically, but, it was argued, exercising some influence upon the market. "Even if appellee's activity may be local," stated Justice Jackson, "and though it may not be regarded as commerce, it may still, whatever its nature, be reached by Congress if it exerts a substantial economic effect on interstate commerce, and this irrespective of whether such effect is what might at some earlier time have been defined as 'direct' or 'indirect'."[15]

One part of the Soil Conservation and Domestic Allotment·Act that has special relevance to our theme, contained in sections 7 to 17 inclusive, made possible the administration of the program by the states. A transfer of this task with an allocation of the necessary funds from the national government to the states could be made with the approval of the Secretary of Agriculture, contingent upon the passage of state laws and the submission of state programs in sufficient number and adequate to achieve the purposes of the act. By 1938 twenty-five states had passed laws framed to meet these provisions. One other state has since then, in 1949, legislated on this point. No state, however, submitted a program until 1951 when Mississippi did so, but its plan did not receive the approval of the Secretary. It is conceivable that with a shift in emphasis from the objective of affecting national and international markets and general price and income factors in the economy to assisting individual farm planning this possibility of transfer of administration to the states might be utilized. Such a shift would affect the land use policies and administration of both the national and state governments. The evolution of those policies in the past two decades throws further light on the operation of our federal system.

The mounting interest in studies of land use had been stimulated in the twenties by growing tax delinquency in various regions and resultant problems of employment in areas cleared of commercial forests yet largely unsuitable for agriculture, and of financing relief and other local services. An emphasis upon timber as a crop requiring wise land management for both the large forest and the wood lot was being advocated by many foresters. Wisconsin pioneered in a new program that combined land zoning and a forest crop law; New York[16] with a program of purchasing areas of "submarginal" land for reforestation, supplementary to its existing extensive state parks largely not available for forest management. Land grant colleges were active in the development of studies and proposals, as were certain officials in relevant agencies of the U.S. Department of Agriculture, and a first National Land Utilization Conference was held in Chicago in 1930.

When the Roosevelt Administration came into office in 1933, an early and major effort to stimulate employment through public works that would avoid competing with private business found in both the older conservation tradition and these more recent applications of land study lines of fruitful activity, and as "reform" mingled with "recovery," a wiser management of the national estate was envisaged in the light of changes in population and the quantity and quality of remaining resources. The evolution of thought and action was speeded up by a series of natural catastrophes, including major floods and drought in several regions. The fact that the new Tennessee Valley Authority was commissioned to develop its program in the light of the multiple interrelated uses of a watershed, and was a major center of public debate and attention, gave a new and more widely dispersed awareness of our dependence on a nice and complex adjustment to our physical environment.

Among the older agencies concerned with some important part of these issues were the Forest Service in the Department of Agriculture and the Land Office in the Department of the Interior. The new Secretary of the latter department, Harold Ickes, had interested himself in conservation matters and was an heir of the old Theodore Roosevelt Progressive Party. He was designated Public Works Administrator by the President and was thus concerned to "prime the pump" by loans and grants that would stimulate employment by all levels of government. In addition to the stepping up of public forest programs, a new Civilian Conservation Corps recruited from unemployed youth served the dual purpose of supplying them with work and pay, and various conservation projects with assistance—among them soil conservation activities. A program for the purchase of submarginal lands, the resettlement of the occupiers (some in new settlements designed for a balance of agriculture and industrial employment), and the reallocation of use of land was initiated in a Resettlement Administration which came increasingly, however, to concern itself with the rehabilitation of farm families on relief through grants, loans, and a more intensive type of guidance than was characteristic of extension work. This agency was incorporated into the Department of Agriculture and later renamed the Farm Security Administration and still later the Farmers Home Administration; in its direct line of operation down to the farm family it had importance for the local townships and counties, struggling with the heavy burdens of relief. A Soil Erosion Service begun in the Department of the Interior with funds allotted from P.W.A. was in 1935 transferred to the Department of Agriculture and reestablished by statute as the Soil Conservation Service. The Director was Hugh H. Bennett of the Bureau of Chemistry and Soils, a pioneer in soil conservation in much the way of Gifford Pinchot in forestry (arousing also powerful loyalties and enmities). The idea of soil conservation, reinforced by some of the activities of the C.C.C. and dramatized by dust storms that even left a residue in the metropolitan cities of the eastern seaboard, attracted wide public interest.

As the program evolved from the stage of physical demonstrations made possible by the C.C.C., it took the form of encouraging the states to pass legislation whereby soil conservation districts might be established locally, governed by boards of supervisors (a title borrowed from county government) elected by the participating members, and with power to enforce certain regulations upon members aimed at soil conservation and to contract with the Service to supply technical advice and assistance. State legislation has also provided for state soil conservation commissions chiefly for insuring the fulfillment of conditions required for the establishing of a district.[17] Some of the more enthusiastic advocates of the soil conservation district as an administrative device thought of it as a possible point of application for all programs of the national department affecting land use. Thus by 1936 an acute stage had been reached in the problem of bringing the various programs initiated in the stress of the depression and early New Deal, as well as older ones, into a more sensible fitting-together as they reached the ultimate operating unit of the farm. Their integration was needed so that the farmer could make a more useful selection and adaptation of them to his own farm management plans and practice, and the expenditures on the programs be more carefully and efficiently made.

Some advocates hoped that the areas of the districts would be determined by natural watersheds requiring common conservation treatment, rather than by historic county lines. But the districts are only another type of the independent units marked in local government generally, as was noted by some thoughtful students of local government concerned at the proliferation of separate "special districts." Such observers were at the outset doubtful of the wisdom of the department's policy of pressing upon the states the enactment of legislation authorizing a new unit of government whose activities would affect land use and hence the tax bases and services of local governments, already complicated by semi-autonomous units, sometimes partly financed by state grants-in-aid. School districts, drainage districts, and water districts already existed. Those who had struggled to find some more focused and responsible structure of local government were skeptical of adding another unit, despite its tempting claims to fit both physical environmental conditions and a doctrine of "democratic control at the grass roots." Actually the notion of adapting boundaries to watersheds has largely, if not entirely, been abandoned under the counterpressure of the claims of county boundaries, voiced in part by county-conditioned land-grant institution personnel on state soil conservation committees. It should be added that these committees, however, have had increasing injections of representation from the personnel of the district supervisors, thereby strengthening the tradition of autonomy of functional representation as against all-purpose, total-program legislative and executive units of government. This development has been furthered by the organization of the National Association of Soil Conservation Districts, an organization increasingly active in defending the Service and the districts against the opposition of the land-grant institutions (whose national organization with continuing representation at Washington is the Association of Land Grant Colleges and Universities) and the American Farm Bureau Federation. The program of C.C.C. demonstration projects gave way to a servicing of the districts by the increasing career personnel of the Soil Conservation Service through a national, regional, and state organization that included research as well as operating functions. As the emphasis, already noted, of the A.A.A. (later Production and Marketing Administration) shifted to "soil conservation payments" as a device for limiting production and increasing incomes from commodities, and as the threat to a reduction in such payments led to still other "pressure groups" (such as the National Association for the Promotion of Soil Conservation),[18] the stage was not only set but even crowded for trouble.

The views of land-grant institution personnel may perhaps too succinctly be summarized not as due to original sin but as centered in the claim that the Soil Conservation Service program was essentially one of education and but little different from that of the Extension Service; that its research also duplicated (though superficially and with distorting emphasis upon physical works of an engineering type) farm management planning that should rather aim at a balanced economic program for each farm into which physical soil erosion prevention elements should be fitted. And it was held that the Service's program created a new direct line by-passing the one through the state land-grant institutions (a development, as we have noted, already under way in forestry, powerfully present in the A.A.A.,—and also evident in credit programs).

IV

Even before World War II revealed the stresses, gaps, and overlaps in the wide range of national, state, and local programs and policies not only within but also between departments, there had been moves, after the rush of activity in the early years of the New Deal, to reappraise both content and organization. As we have noted, the Butler decision, for one thing, forced this, although such appraisals were already under way in the Office of the Secretary, the Program Planning Division of the A.A.A., and at many points all along the line.[19] A general atmosphere conducive to such effort was set by the Report of the President's Committee on Administrative Management in 1937 and various reports of the National Resources Committee (later recreated as the National Resources Planning Board). To single out the federal system aspect from the welter of economic, party, personal, and other forces at work is to court almost certain distortion, but the risk must be run. An early move was the establishment in 1937 in the Office of the Secretary of the Office of Land-Use Coordination under the then Director of Information, a career public servant, Milton Eisenhower, who was to be active in reorganization studies and proposals for many years. Its purpose was as a staff agency without line authority to review all programs of the department with the object of preventing contradiction and conflict among them at their point of ultimate application in land use and to serve as a means of liaison and representation on interdepartmental committees and with other departments, such as Interior, that touched land use functions.[20]

The problem of policy coordination on one level, complicated enough, is intertwined with the distribution of each activity among the areal levels and jurisdictions.[21] To attempt coordination of A.A.A., S.C.S., and the Extension Service, not to mention the Reclamation Service and the Grazing Service, would require at the very least agreements across bureaus and between the national department and state land-grant institutions. The new Office therefore at once tackled this problem. In 1938 the first fruits were visible in a scheme that sought at once to move toward a process and structure which, given good will, would help to solve both. It was embodied in the agreement between representatives of the department and of the land-grant institutions arranged at Mt. Weather, Virginia, which has given its name to the document. Its essence was neither agency consolidation nor a shifting of functions from one level to another, but rather a continuing process of land-use planning from county to national department as a basis for all relevant programs. "The document provided for the establishment of a nation-wide system of county land-use planning committees, to be set up by each state Extension Service. Each county committee was to consist wholly of farm people, with the county agent as nonvoting secretary, but a subcommittee was to include local officials of the Agricultural Adjustment Administration, the Soil Conservation Service, and the Farm Security Administration. The state organization was to consist primarily of governmental officials under the chairmanship of the state Extension director, with a representation of farmers. These committees had a twofold purpose: coordination of existing agricultural programs and planning of land use."[22]

In the same year, structural changes in the department ordered by the

Secretary linked the Mt. Weather Agreement to the Bureau of Agricultural Economics, which was "to serve as a general agricultural program planning and economic research service for the Secretary and the Department as a whole. . . . In this manner unified departmental planning which encompasses erosion control, rehabilitation, price stability, marketing, production adjustment, security of farm tenure, forest, wild-life, and soil conservation, can be provided for the nation, for watersheds, for type-of-farming regions, and for appropriate areas."[23] The plan also provided an Agricultural Program Board consisting of a number of bureau chiefs under the chairmanship of the head of the Office of Land-Use Coordination, and it contemplated the establishment by him during the year of regional coordinators in the southern and northern Great Plains. Milton Eisenhower was continued as chief of the Office of Land-Use Coordination and Howard Tolley named chief of the Bureau of Agricultural Economics. All operating phases of physical land-use programs were to be centered in the Soil Conservation Service.

This effort to move toward both vertical and horizontal integration of programs and policies had less than a year to get under way before the second World War broke out in Europe and two years later engulfed us fully. From its beginning thinking in the various agencies and in farm organizations went back to the tremendous effect of World War I on American agriculture. The administrators sought to appraise policies and programs that might be needed in the greater catastrophe that first loomed ahead, then struck in the tragedy of Pearl Harbor. It is impossible to improvise "reorganizations" and the adaptation of programs as complex as the land-use planning project which reach into hundreds of counties. From the point of view of effective land-use planning (in itself a term needing careful definition), it would have been wiser to devise a procedure whereby a few pilot demonstration counties might have been set up and the system expanded on the basis of an appraisal of their experience and their use in training personnel. But this single point of view did not exist; for, as we have seen, there was need to repair the strained relations between agencies both vertically and horizontally. It is not clear how much the ultimate rejection of the land-use plan through congressional action was due to the opposition of the American Farm Bureau Federation (Grant McConnell calls the program and organization "the first victims of the Farm Bureau War"), how far to the skepticism of land-grant institutions, and how far to jealousy among national agencies about the assignment of responsibilities for "planning"—an ambiguous term, then growing ever more suspect.[24] The conflict has been described in terms of a power struggle. The problem of agricultural policy in a federal system is much more complex, of course, but clearly it was the concern of every association to claim at least to be the spokesman of its constituency. The significant fact in this situation has been the apparent fear of permitting regular official use of committees of farmers in the A.A.A.-P.M.A. programs for administrative action or (as in the land-use, soil conservation, extension, and land-use planning programs) for advice and knowledge relevant to the formulation of policy. This uneasiness has been reflected not only by the voluntary farmer associations whose officials owe their positions and importance to their presumed ability to voice farmer sentiment accurately. When linked to the delegation of discretionary power to administrative officers, it has merged in a general line of attack by party and legislative leaders. Throughout administration a constant necessity exists both to spell out the details of an act, and also to appraise its effects as a basis for legitimate advice to the law-making body as to desirable amendments and changes. Where the department fell into a pit that in part at least was of its own digging lay in stressing that administrative participation by the farmer-elected committees was to insure a product that would be "the farmers' own program." It was natural that a "farmers' own program" welling up "from the grass roots" would invite attack, both on grounds of substance and also on grounds of the method it embodied, by associations whose position and prosperity seemed to be endangered. This attack was pursued in legislative halls and among members wanting value for their dues.

We must hasten over the subsequent efforts to "reorganize" agriculture in government. No essentially or radically new issue, argument, or device has emerged from the experience with the "War Boards" during the war, the earlier post-war proposals, the proposals of the Task Force or the Commission on the Reorganization of the Executive Branch of the Government, the reorganization measures of Secretary Brannan, nor from the current proposals of Secretary of Agriculture Benson. All have been incidental to the contemporary larger policies of government—the waging of war, demobilization from the war effort, and the ebb and flow of representation in Congress, the presidency, and the parties of varying shades of general doctrine and dogma on social, economic, and political policy. Any specific program must remain tethered to the problem of policy-making within and across departments on each level, and between the three constituent levels of the federal system, local, state, and national. The question of what belongs functionally and structurally in the Department of Agriculture (for example, rural electrification, forests, all land policy, as against the claims of the Department of the Interior) continued to be, inevitably, a question pertinent not merely to national government but also, as we have seen, to the relations between the national, state, and local governments. National policies continued to be stimulants and underwriters of state and local action, in spite of popular conceptions of an unswerving march of centralization and a one-way shift of state activity to the national level. The catastrophic effects of war and rumors of war in a world of garrison states, and the application of science and of devices of economic interdependence, continued to lift the production for market in our economy to the level of interstate commerce. These developments were not confined to the United States; they were at least equally reflected in the federal systems of Canada and Australia, or the "tight little" unitary system of the United Kingdom, where a national ministry, county agricultural committees, and interest associations were also intermingled in the larger setting of a parliamentary system of government with its presumably more sharply focused processes of policy making.[25]

V

The reader who has plodded through this description of complexity may properly ask, at the end, for some more generalized view of what it all portends for a federal system of government employed to formulate and execute agricultural policies.[26] A "level of government"—national or local—should so far as humanly possible be an effective operating unit, with the area, population, resources, and legal power adequate to the policies whose decision is its assignment and responsibility. In an economy based on private ownership, the basic unit in agriculture is the farm itself, and its government for decision-making is the farm family. Whatever comes to it from any unit of government has to be fitted into the family decisions; and therefore it is wisdom both to encourage the tapping of the knowledge and will of the family in the formulation of those policies and also to try to prevent whatever comes to it from being confused, contradictory, and irrelevant to or even destructive of its peculiar combination of producing and consuming elements and its needs and resources.

Some of its needs require immediate cooperating and facilitating joint services with neighbor farms and villages. Primary schools and roads are illustrative. Here is involved not the farm as such—although it is unique in our economy as both a place of work and a home at the same time—but rather the farm family as persons, with children needing schooling. And the appropriate area will change with the wider use, for example, of the automobile. Nevertheless there seems to be a permanent case for some fairly intimate operating unit for local consumer public services which range from police to schools.

Another operating unit is the national state which in the future perhaps may share more widely with international operating units its responsibility for the public stake in basic determinations of policies relating to the interdependent economy of money, prices, markets, transport, and the plexus of economic institutions within which every enterprise is conditioned.

In most countries another level exists between locality and the national state, either because of some historical experience as a separate political entity or as a supplier of specialized collective services that are uneconomic for the smaller units to maintain, or as the supervisor of local government.

Then there are regions determined by important single or grouped multiple factors related to the physical environment whose possible needs for consideration in the formulation of government policy may not be served by existing units. Examples are watersheds, areas based on types-of-farming or commodities, or metropolitan regions.[27]

Our federal system has shown itself reasonably adequate to the use of these types of operating units, so far as agricultural policy is concerned, and has reflected the changes in technology, the economy, and in political ideas through legislation, administration, and adjudication with no great lag in the response, although with the necessity of adapting programs to the prevailing interpretations such as noted in this chapter. The policies have not been toward "centralization" or "decentralization" in absolute terms, but in general have been adapted to equip the different operating units, at the regional and local as well as national and state levels, with a role in a two-directional flow of policy making. The result is a complex system which in its operation produces, as we have seen, a kind of federalism of functional and interest groups that form in part to secure their objectives through pressing for common tendency and interpretation throughout the levels.

The major difficulties in this use of the federal system therefore appear to be those of insuring some unity and integration of policy in the relation of agricultural to other public policy, and among agricultural policies, at each level against the resistances of agency corporate outlook and the special economic, commodity, or regional bias of the contending interest groups. It is this problem (universal in government in the United States) which exacerbates the general solution of interlevel relations envisaged in the more traditional and conventional type of concept of federalism, and which is central to the current struggles to achieve "reorganization."[28]

We may wisely and humbly emphasize that whatever the quality of organization and procedure, the possibility of successful control or modification of forces affecting agriculture through public intervention is circumscribed. We are dealing with a complexity of sensitive and interdependent factors difficult to analyse and predict. They include the vagaries of nature, catastrophic events, and the intricacies of markets and technological change. These play upon the making of decisions by millions of individuals. Too much must not be expected or promised in the effort to guide or counter-coerce these forces through collective action.[29]

The line of attack which seems most fruitful would emphasize first the bending of every effort to assist the farm family in making its farm plans a "balanced" type that would best incorporate the facilities available to it from public sources at every level, in line with the family's own resources and preferences. "Farm planning" begins, and ends, literally at home; but the farm home reaches out through lines of activity and association. Here again we must be humble in our expectations. Even to reach a substantial portion of the commercial farms would place a strain on our resources of knowledge, personnel, and income. Too great a confidence in the efficacy of public action may be paralleled by similar uncritical enthusiasm for individual farm planning programs. The gap between promise and performance with both may have, and has had, bad consequences.

There are, however, local public interests other than agricultural in land-use programs, and a serious problem (present at every level) is that of bringing

the special agricultural programs—buttressed by their autonomous soil conservation districts, P.M.A. committees, and advisory committees, and by the
too glib slogans of keeping them "out of politics" and as the "farmers' own
program"—into harmony with the community concern in wise land use as a
base of all public services. The old land-use planning process, broadened by
representation from the general organs of local government, would seem to be
the way that must eventually be trod—not the making of a final "plan," but
a continuing process of policy review, problem analysis, and learning to work
together and to use the resources of national and state governments to supplement and not supplant the local.

At the national level, the problem is interwoven with that of improvement
in responsible policy making in Congress, the parties, and the executive departments generally. One need here only point up its application to the Department of Agriculture in terms of strengthening the processes and structure there
for a wider view across agency lines, governed by the remembrance that the
ultimate application of most policy is at the farm operating unit, or the
stomach of the consumer. Probably the designation of one office as "the planning staff" for the department would be fatal again; and we are learning that
the task and challenge is to tap the operating forces, facilitate the flow of
experience and knowledge, and evoke and encourage the wider view even
within the specialized units.[30] The task to which the department committed
itself—in land-use planning and staffing itself for better preparation of program proposals to Congress and discretionary powers within its own agencies—
remains essential in realizing the value of a federal system, however inadequate
may have been the immediate measures that were adopted in the Mt. Weather
agreement.

These questions of policy and of party, legislative, and executive relations
become more urgent in agricultural matters with the decline in the proportion
of farm population to the total, the rise of metropolitan regions, and the
inexorably increasing pressure of an industrial society on natural resources.
They are made even more urgent by the international situation. Does this
mean that the states are outdated? Certainly not in their legal powers and the
potentiality of their contribution to improvement in agricultural administration.
But the insistence of many that they be made more important among the operating units overlooks their present lack of any single unified land or natural
resources or agricultural agency with operating functions and powers adequate
to what they might usefully do. Should the provisions of the Soil Conservation
and Domestic Allotment Act of 1936, subsequently renewed, that would permit a transfer of administration and funds to the states for carrying out the
purposes of the act be utilized, the administration of state land policy would
be further complicated. The present state laws on this, with two exceptions,
vest any such responsibility in the governing bodies of their respective land-
grant institutions. But the land-grant institutions have a very difficult educational task before them in both instruction and research in determining their

best role in the higher education of the state, in adapting the social sciences and the humanities more effectively to their older curricula, and clarifying with each student the public and local and regional setting of his special studies and field. For them to undertake to be also the general state agricultural administrative agency would seem to be unwise at a time when they are properly beginning to see the study of public policy as a part of their responsibility. It is clear, too, that they should divorce themselves from any organized interest group in the financing and policy making of their services.

There remain the problems of regions not coterminous with states through interstate cooperation or national-regional action calling for state participation to adapt and utilize national and regional programs advantageously to the state; and policy and surveillance over the entire range of local government. "The states are in the middle," but their use of this position remains dependent on the improvement of general governmental structure and process, and the adequacy of their resources, so widely varied among the states, to financing, staffing, and operating agricultural—and any other—programs.

As agricultural policy is more clearly diagnosed as an essential part of politics, interwoven with these other aspects of the life of nation, state, and locality, the opportunity is at hand for a greater use of parties as a medium for mingling urban and rural outlooks and for mitigating the exclusiveness in the outlooks of the organized interest groups. "Democracy at the grass-roots" is not democracy if it is separated off, partial, and exclusive. Here again, we are led back to, and close upon, the note that the successful use of a federal system in one type of function involves all of the basic problems of politics.

FOOTNOTES TO CHAPTER 15

1. Arthur W. Macmahon, in *The American Political Science Review*, Vol. 38 (Dec. 1944), p. 1191.

2. New York, The Twentieth Century Fund, 1953.

3. Chief Justice Hughes, in NLRB v. Jones and Laughlin Steel Corporation, 301 U.S. 1, 41–42 (1937).

4. Frederick Jackson Turner, *The Frontier in American History*, New York, Holt, 1920, ch. 10, "Pioneer Ideals and the State University," pp. 281, 284, 285.

5. Gladys Baker, *The County Agent*, Chicago, University of Chicago Press, 1939, p. 45. This is the classic account. See also Grant McConnell, *The Decline of Agrarian Democracy*, Berkeley, University of California Press, 1953, ch. 5.

6. Cf. *ibid.*, pp. 50–52.

7. Benedict, *op. cit.*, p. 154.

8. Note how the distinction in speech and writing between "action programs" and the presumed research and education activities was stressed in disputes over the programs of the New Deal. It was overlooked that the department had long-established "action" programs as in forestry and market regulation and facilitation that included cooperation with state agencies other than the land-grant institutions, and that to pour research findings into the consciousness of the producer was in

fact to influence his action, granted that it was in a form different from direct cash payments. Furthermore, in the differing uses of these opportunities by different farmers—or their non-use—the less efficient, so the assumption runs, would help-fully bankrupt themselves out of farming—and the market. Here is an origin of opposition to programs for rehabilitation of farmers on relief such as those of the Resettlement-Farm Security Administrations.

9. See Wickard v. Filburn, 317 U.S. 111 (1942).

10. Thereby also helping to finance the system, hard hit by slashed local and state budgets.

11. U.S. v. Butler, 297 U. S. 1 (1936).

12. 307 U.S. 38 (1939).

13. Robert L. Stern, "The Commerce Clause and the National Economy, 1933–46," *Harvard Law Review,* Vol. 59 (1946), p. 692.

14. 317 U. S. 111 (1942).

15. On this case see the interesting discussion by Stern, *loc. cit.,* pp. 901–909, with his conclusion that "the opinion makes it plain that Congress can control all the necessarily interrelated operations of an interstate industry, no matter how 'local' particular transactions may appear to be when viewed in isolation."

16. Significantly under Governor F. D. Roosevelt, whose policies as President were shortly to reflect these developments in his own state—and estate.

17. There is an excellent account of the districts in W. Robert Parks, *Soil Conservation Districts in Action,* Ames, Iowa State College Press, 1952. The growth of the movement is illustrated by these facts he presents (p. 8): 48 states have passed authorization legislation and over 2400 districts have been created covering 4,871,000 farms and ranches and 883,353,000 acres as of 1952.

18. A much later organization. There had, in various quarters, been great fear of organizing of the A.A.A. committee members after the earlier precedent of the farm bureaus; it had been staved off, but the charge has been made that they were utilized in the political party sector of policy formulation. This was particularly deplored by many in the American Federation of Farm Bureaus, the land grant institutions, and the Republican Party.

19. See John Gaus and Leon Wolcott, *Public Administration and the United States Department of Agriculture,* Chicago, Univ. of Chicago Press, 1940, esp. chaps. 14, 15, 16, 17.

20. An almost Freudian situation existed between the two departments, since forestry and now soil conservation activities had been shifted from Interior to Agriculture.

21. The best general discussion of this problem is James Fesler's *Area and Administration,* University, University of Alabama Press, 1949; the most revealing case study is Charles McKinley's *Uncle Sam in the Pacific Northwest,* Berkeley, University of California Press, 1952.

22. McConnell, *op. cit.,* pp. 116, 117. The agreement is given in Gaus and Wolcott, *op. cit.,* Appendix B, with other documents relevant to the reorganization of the department in 1938. McConnell describes subsequent developments with particular emphasis on the part played by farm organizations. See also Charles Hardin, *The Politics of Agriculture,* Glencoe, The Free Press, 1952.

23. Memorandum of the Secretary, H. A. Wallace, Oct. 6, 1938.

24. The land-use planning program was described in an excellent study by Ellen Sorge (Mrs. Robert) Parks entitled "Experiment in the Democratic Planning of

Public Agricultural Activity," a doctoral thesis in political science at the University of Wisconsin in 1947. This is a valuable study that includes a history of the episode, an appraisal of the causes of its discontinuance, and a diagnosis of the situation which has continued to the present time, although there have been further efforts, as under Secretary Brannan, to develop closer working relations, for example, between the P.M.A. and the S.C.S. in the field. I am informed also of various efforts in some counties in different states to salvage benefits from the movement by local cooperation among agencies and with farmer committees, notably in Michigan. Mrs. Parks' concluding statement is: "Today (1947), therefore, the basic problems in public agricultural administration, which the democratic agricultural planning process was designed to solve, are still unanswered. The need for developing over-all integrated agricultural policy, for bringing representative farmer experience and attitudes into the development of public agricultural programs, for securing an optimum of local adjustment in national programs, and for developing fruitful working relationships with the Land Grant Colleges has not yet been adequately filled."

25. Note, e.g., *Federal Agricultural Assistance Programs, Canada, 1900–51*, by Marjorie R. Camerson and Frank Shefrin (mimeo.), published by the Department of Agriculture of Canada, Ottawa, 1952. I record gratefully the use of seminar reports (typed) on "Coordination of Federal-State Agricultural Policies and Programs in Australia," by Jack N. Lewis, and on "The Ecology and Coordination of Government Service in the Agricultural Program of Nova Scotia," by W. A. Jenkins, both prepared in the spring of 1953.

26. I am grateful for the opportunity of reading, during the preparation of these pages, some as yet unpublished papers on the problems dealt with here that were sent me by their authors, Professors W. Robert Parks of Iowa State College and Ernest Engelbert of the University of California at Los Angeles. Four of these papers were presented at the "National Work Conference on Public Policy" at Green Lake, Wisconsin, September 8–11, 1953, namely, "Federal-State Relationships in Agriculture" and "Goals of Democracy," by Professor Parks, and "Political Party and Pressure Group Considerations in Agricultural Politics" and "Agriculture and the Political Process," by Professor Engelbert. I have also had the privilege of reading Professor Parks' "The Political Process and Land Tenure Goals," presented at the National Land Tenure Workshop at Black Duck, Minnesota on August 24, 1953. Any merit in my own observations will probably have seeped in from these and the writings of other younger scholars, such as Charles Hardin and Vincent Ostrum, who are pioneering in these fields; but the weaknesses of thought and presentation remain, alas doggedly, my own!

27. The governmental problem is discussed in *Regional Factors in National Planning and Development,* National Resources Committee, Washington, U.S. Government Printing Office, 1935. See also James Fesler's *Area and Administration.*

28. These are well set forth in Charles McKinley's *Uncle Sam in the Pacific Northwest* and John D. Black's *Federal-State-Local Relations in Agriculture,* Planning Pamphlet no. 70, National Planning Association, February, 1950.

29. Charles M. Hardin, commenting on the problem of the vagaries of nature and otherwise, pointed in the discussion to the following facts: "If one studies farm prices on September 15 from 1945 through 1953, he sees that cotton has varied 33 per cent; corn, 53 per cent; oats, 80 per cent; etc. Corn was $1.78 in 1947, $1.16 in 1948; prices for fluid milk varied 45 per cent between 1949 and 1952. These figures omit the wide swings in beef cattle prices. In cotton, after three years of production with averages between 15 and 16 million bales, we carried over 8,700,000 bales into the 1950 season. This was almost precisely what our domestic mill consumption

was in 1949. Since we were exporting only 4 to 6 million bales, marketing quotas were necessary under existing farm legislation. We cut from 27 to 22 million acres; but actually less than 19 million acres were harvested; the boll weevil infestation was severe; production was less than 10.5 million bales; but Korea had increased the demand, and in October, 1950, export quotas were announced for cotton. The following year nearly 27 million acres were produced, and we were again plagued by surpluses." (Editor)

30. Note the discussion of this in Paul Appleby, *Big Democracy,* New York, Knopf, 1945.

16

The Impact of American Federalism upon the Management of Land Resources

By Charles McKinley

A sense of urgency is abroad lest the natural resource base for our American civilization fail us. This anxiety, aroused by events, discussion, and public policies during the days of the New and Fair Deals, has been heightened by the war-revealed critical shortages in the domestic supplies of strategic materials and the approaching depletion of high quality domestic deposits of base minerals like iron, copper, lead, and bauxite ores. The dramatic reversal of the prewar birth rate revives the prospect for a burgeoning population. These new Americans will greatly expand the demand for all the materials essential to a high-level economy. Finally, we take seriously our front rank position in the resistance of the noncommunist world to the revolutionary expansionism of Russian-led world communism. Whether or not we teeter on the brink of a third world war, the present world rearmament race and the competition between the United States and Russia in material aid to other peoples seem to make unprecedented demands upon our physical as well as cultural resources.

This new resource situation has recently been outlined in the reports of the President's Water Resources Policy Commission released early in 1951, and in the so-called Paley Commission's report on material resources published in 1952. While they reveal that our problems are not primarily those of resource exhaustion, they do indicate shortages of particular minerals and of water in a number of areas. The mineral resource problems that lie ahead are principally those of higher cost, unless technology improves more rapidly than seems assured. Water policy issues center around comprehensive river basin multiple purpose planning, proper watershed management, deficiencies of water data, questions of who shall administer, who shall pay, and the adequacy of state laws governing the use of water. Neither study was directed primarily toward the problems of agricultural land but neither could avoid them. Here again the basic issue is not imminent shortage but wise management of what we have and improved agricultural technology.

The mere statement of these problems suggests the need for public authority on a national or international scale. Here the American federal system of divided powers confronts a crucial test. For if, in general, the bulk of our best land and most important minerals has passed to private ownership, then the role of the American states which in legal theory monopolize the police power over the use of private property must be made to harmonize with national policy. Similarly the division of legal authority which recognizes the states' title to the appropriation of water for beneficial use while the nation controls its use for navigation and interstate commerce, poses another set of key problems for governance under our federal system. Even the apparently simple question of the proper management of publicly owned land, which in the western states is predominantly retained in federal ownership, includes many complex relations with states, counties, and private owners.

I

FEDERALISM AND THE MANAGEMENT OF PUBLIC LAND RESOURCES

I turn first to the impact of our federal system upon the management of our public "wild land" resources, though it will be quickly apparent that this is in many respects interlocked with important private land policies and operating relationships.[1] In this matter I shall confine my attention to situations found in the public land states of the West; even there I shall omit consideration of the limited though important acreages within the National Parks, the national game refuges, and the Indian reservations, and include only the vaster areas comprising the National Forests and the picked-over but extensive residue of the public domain. In these areas I am concerned with the issues of national-state-local-private relationships which their management has entailed.

The fact that conservation management by the national government of its landed estate really started with the National Forests under Gifford Pinchot needs no belaboring here. But it is well to recall that until recent years national forest management was centered around the functions of fires, insect and disease protection, and grazing management.

The prevention of fire or its prompt suppression has been an elemental requirement vital to all owners of timber land as well as to the dependent public. Nevertheless, it was not until the disastrous fires on the west slope of the Cascades in the summer of 1902 swept over at least seven hundred thousand acres of green timber and snuffed out the lives of thirty-five people that private timber owners and the states of the Pacific Northwest awoke to the need of organized, cooperative fire protection, compulsory patrol laws, and a code of forest fire practices. From 1905 to 1912 private protective associations sprang up throughout the timbered areas of Washington, Oregon, California, and the panhandle of Idaho, and took the lead in forest fire protection.[2] This coincided with the transformation of the old Bureau of Forestry into the U.S. Forest Service and the dispatch by Gifford Pinchot of his young forester disciples of conservation to the National Forests to begin a vigorous management program, with special stress on fire control. An even greater disaster which struck in the summer of 1910 in the Bitter Roots and Coeur D'Alenes of northern Idaho, and which took a toll of three million acres of timber and eighty-five lives, finally awakened national, state, local, and larger private timber owners to the realization that they must either hang together in furnishing fire protection or burn together.[3] As a consequence in part Congress in 1911 passed the Weeks Act which offered national grants-in-aid to protect state and private timber. Since many state governments not only had large public forest acreages of their own (today estimated in the neighborhood of twenty-seven million)[4] but also monopolized the legal power to compel private owners to join in a fire protective program, they had perforce to be part of any effective protection programs. On the foundation laid by the Weeks Act and the McNary Act of 1924 (with its 1944 amendment) has been built an increasingly efficient three-way partnership between the Forest Service, state forestry departments, and associations of private timber owners.[5] Thus has been bridged the legal gap inherent in a federal system of divided powers.

This program has also been of great and increasing value to all the timbered states, though those of the southeast were slow to take full advantage of it. By 1950, forty-three states and Hawaii had joined this partnership, leaving only the five timberless prairie-plateau states of Kansas, Nebraska, North Dakota, Wyoming, and Arizona outside the program. Out of approximately 426 million acres of state and private forest and watershed lands needing fire protection, more than 360 million were by 1952 under organized protection.

It is to the leadership and supervision of the U.S. Forest Service that this fire protection system owes its stimulus, its improvements in fire planning, personnel training and management, and the application of improved suppression techniques. As a matter of fact it was the Weeks and Clark-McNary legislation that first led to the establishment of many state forestry departments staffed by competent foresters, a movement of great importance not only to this program but to the expansion of state forestry management in other directions also.

While no formal merit system has been required for the selection of state forest fire control staffs, the Forest Service did insist on the employment of competent wardens and supervisors as a condition of grant approval. Thus, without benefit of state legislation, spoils politics in the staffing of state forestry departments underwent accelerated erosion.

Building on this successful pioneer cooperative scheme came other facets of national-state, public-private forest collaborative land management. A program of federal subsidizing of the state production and distribution of trees at nominal cost for reforestation on state land and on farm wood lots soon followed and was expanded in 1951 to include any timberland owners. At present forty-three states and two territories are in this program.[6]

Forty-five states aided by federal funds and Forest Service guidance now employ trained extension foresters to bring the gospel of good wood lot management to farmers and small timber tract owners. Nearly three fourths of the private forest land is owned by about 3,500,000 farmers and 750,000 small-town business and professional men. Potentially these lands are highly productive but they universally suffer from neglect or bad management.

The Norris-Dixey Act of 1937 was intended to bring direct case work assistance to the management of farm wood lots. This was included in the farm planning program of the Soil Conservation Service. Since 1945 the Forest Service has supervised this program. It works through the state foresters who, with the approval of the Forest Service, now hire and supervise about two hundred and fifty farm foresters who work directly with farmers in selected counties in thirty-eight states. This program was expanded to include direct assistance to all small timber land owners and small mill owners by the Co-operative Forest Management Act of 1950.[7] The task of securing conservation practices by these millions of small owners will be a slow, expensive, and up-hill job. Without national stimulus and financial aid it would not even be under way.

The research programs of the Forest Service were for many years the principal sources of information for improved forest management for all types of owners. This was also true at first for wood utilization research. However, private industry soon expanded this activity, and in recent years the states have added their efforts to improve both utilization and forest management knowledge. Nearly one-half of the estimated three and a half million dollars spent in 1951 for forest research by states and private agencies goes into projects planned and organized jointly with the Forest Service, "with mutual agreement on what the program will be, how the work will be done and how the financial load will be shared. In cooperative research some problems are attacked jointly, the cooperators merging their facilities and personnel; others are divided into segments under correlated arrangements."[8]

The toll of timber taken by insects and plant pests often exceeds even that of fires. Because these biological menaces are likewise blind to ownership boundary lines, mastery of pest control must also be a cooperative undertaking. Hence come frequent appeals from the states and private owners for federal funds and administrative leadership to deal with special pest problems. In 1947 Congress put forest pest control on a basis similar to that of fire control, with the federal Bureau of Entomology and Plant Quarantine in the role of technical leader, with the four federal agencies having timber management responsibilities participating, and with financial aid to encourage private-owner cooperation. The precise arrangements for participation vary from one pest infestation problem to another, but in the three years after the enactment of the national pest control law, eight states centered responsibility for their part in these programs upon their state foresters.[9]

The interlevel operation of this program as illustrated by experiences in the Pacific Northwest has been very close knit and highly successful.[10]

While the current retreat from national leadership in resource development may change the intergovernmental relationships in some of the forest land programs, none of those reviewed above is likely to be greatly modified. They have become too fully embedded in a web of interlocking practices, buttressed by the consensus of the forestry profession and the timber industry.

When we inquire into other aspects of the forest resource problem the federalism answer is not so clear. First let us note the quality of management of state owned timber lands. Here the situation seems very uneven, though careful studies of state management operations are few and precise information is hard to obtain.[11] Of the three Pacific Northwest states, most rapid headway has probably been made in Oregon which, however, had the smallest forested estate left to manage. By the time forest conservation had found an appreciative public, Oregon had squandered most of its valuable timber holdings. Nevertheless, it still had a sufficient number of isolated school land sections within National Forest boundaries to permit an exchange during the thirties for a solid block of about seventy thousand acres on the edge of one of the National Forests. This was transferred from the State Land Board—the general custodial agency for Oregon's residual federal land grants—to the Board of Forestry and the state forester for management. To the last agency have gravitated the cutover tax-reverted lands which the counties have been transferring to the state during the past twenty years. This includes most of the great Tillamook burn of 1932 which, under a rehabilitation program started in 1949, is undergoing reforestation and receiving very expensive special fire protection. Today, under the state forester's competent and well staffed control are nearly three-fourths of a million acres of forest land which in time will play an important part in tree production and in supplying raw material for the economy of the state.[12] On the other hand, there still remain numerous small timbered tracts under the control of the State Land Board, so scattered as to defy economic state management.

Statehood came to Idaho and Washington nearly a half century later than to Oregon. The improvident disposal policies pursued by the older states made some impression upon the early law makers of these two states, who specified either in the state constitution or in statutes a minimum acre sale price of ten dollars for their land endowments. This requirement so throttled sales that each state still has large, though dispersed, acreages of virgin, burned-over, and cutover timber lands for permanent management. The areal dispersion is not so great as in the older public land states because, in addition to the two-section gift out of every township for public school support, other sizeable acreage allotments for the support of institutions of higher education, the penitentiary, charitable institutions, public buildings, and so forth, were given to the states for their later selection. As a result since 1950 about half of Idaho's state owned timber lands, totaling more than four hundred thousand acres, has been grouped under its state forester into five state forest blocks for full scale management. Approximately the same amount of timber land is so scattered as to defy continuous economic management.

Yet aside from fire control, Idaho state forest management until very recently was minimal. The first professionally trained state forester was appointed only five years ago. Under his leadership, backed by better state financial support, with the forward looking cooperation of the state land commissioner (under whose jurisdiction come all state timber sales), forestry on the state's property in Idaho has been making rapid strides. Yet because there is no formal merit system in Idaho state service, except for the Social Security-aided agencies and the State Game Department, the quality of personnel depends upon the changing agency heads.

The state of Washington, which owns approximately eighteen per cent of all standing timber in the state, still denies to its state forester management functions other than fire control, reforestation, and the supervision of the tax-reverted county lands held in trust by the state.[13] The constitutionally elected state land commissioner, flanked with an ex-officio state land board with which he is often politically in conflict, "manages" the state's school and most other grant lands.[14] The atmosphere of county court house politics, not untainted by scandal and operational laxness in handling timber sales, still surrounds these agencies. As in Idaho, no statutory merit system protects the personnel of the land commissioner's department, nor has custom yet furnished alternative safeguards. Other management duties on state forest lands are split between the land commissioner and several boards, so that responsibility is thoroughly confused. No classification of the state's lands has been made to guide sale and harvest policies. While fire control on state and private lands and the enforcement of the recently adopted act regulating a few of the cutting practices on private timber lands are handled by the state forester's trained staff, elsewhere the job of managing state owned lands in Washington has not attained a high standard.[15]

The hottest spot in the relationships between state and national forest agencies and policies has to do with the control of private forest cutting practices. For some years the U.S. Forest Service, backed by the Secretary of Agriculture, has been pushing for public regulation of private timber harvesting as essential to a sufficient national timber supply and to watershed protection. In private hands lie seventy-five percent of the nation's forest lands and ninety percent of its timber production.[16] The most recent proposals of the Forest Service call for national laws setting the harvesting standards, with administration by those states choosing to enforce them, but with federal control in states unwilling or unable to provide adequate administration.[17] Beginning with the Oregon Forest Conservation Act of 1941, as subsequently amended, a start toward the state regulation of private harvesting practices has been made.[18] This law established an annual permit system for loggers and timber owners as condition for harvesting timber; it required the leaving of seed trees sufficient to restock the land and the disposal of slash without injury to the trees left standing or to young growth. The act as defined by regulations laid down by the state forester and approved by his forestry board would allow that officer to reforest the land and assess the costs against any violator. Undoubtedly this law, like its counterpart statutes later adopted by Washington, Maryland, and California, was enacted to forestall federal regulation.[19] It was not enforced until the end of the war. Since then, and partly as a consequence of penalty amendments which facilitate enforcement, the Oregon state forester's organization has begun to give reality to these cutting regulations.[20]

It would be agreed, I think, that these laws will not of themselves produce either sustained yield forestry or watershed protection. Nevertheless, they do constitute important beginnings in those directions.

The adjustment of National Forest wildlife programs to our scheme of divided powers may be noted here. Gifford Pinchot clearly included wildlife conservation programs in his plans for management. He took the position that if the states did not develop proper fish and game policies the Forest Service, as the agent for the national sovereign, might do so within the National Forests. But in practice this right has not been asserted. Instead the states have been encouraged to improve their wildlife activities and the Forest Service field men have become highly valuable collaborators in the analysis of problems of management, in the enforcement of state game laws, and in the application of the many management improvement programs.

There have been long-standing difficulties in obtaining state action to keep some species of wildlife—particularly deer—which have multiplied rapidly in recent years, in balance with the supply of forage. This has been especially hard to solve where the game habitat cycle crosses state boundary lines. One example is the interstate deer herd that winters in the forests of northern California and summers in the Fremont forest in Oregon. For years this constituted a problem of bistate and interlevel disharmony. The United States Forest Service, whose browse was being injured, has been the chief catalytic agent in finally precipitating an agreement that promises a solution.

The adoption of improved wildlife management practices by the states in recent years is probably the most striking achievement in state conservation efforts.[21] This is in part the result of federal grant-in-aid assistance under the Pittman-Robertson Act which is administered by the U.S. Fish and Wildlife Service. This program, financed jointly by national and state funds, has stepped up the use of research in state management; it has improved the quality and increased the number of state wildlife staff; and it has greatly expanded the facilities, land and structures, for effective wildlife programs.

National-state-private relationships in range management reveal a less successful operation of our complex federal system. At the time the National Forests were first placed under management, the grass, browse, and soil on many of the high mountain meadows had been terribly depleted, especially in the more arid parts of the West. Earlier unregulated use of the livestock men left a heritage of problem areas with depleted forage and eroding soil. While improved management since 1905 has alleviated this situation there are still many "sore spots." Some of these will not heal until grazing is prohibited or greatly reduced. Time after time rehabilitation efforts have been checked or rendered less than adequate by the intervention of special circumstances: two world wars which emphasized all-out production of meat; financial hardship resulting from over-commitment of the industry during the first World War and sudden price deflation thereafter; and prolonged drought accompanied by economic collapse.

Despite these impediments the greatest headway toward sustained yield range management made by the public land agencies is to be found on the National Forests and on the pastures created from the dry-farm repurchase areas by the Soil Conservation Service. This constructive improvement has required as a tool the extensive development of range research. Thus the Forest Service has become the principal center of information for improved range management available to all range land owners, national, state, and private. Even though some of the state college experiment stations have also undertaken range research and the Soil Conservation Service has done some outstanding development of range grasses, the chief restorative techniques, such as range reseeding, sage brush removal, soil stabilization on mountain meadow slopes, deferred and rotation grazing, etc., have developed out of the studies and experiments of the oldest national range management agency.

As in the case of forests, there is an interlocking management relationship between the national, state, and private range lands. Domestic livestock, and to a lesser degree the browse-eating big game, move back and forth in accordance with the seasons, from the valley and low-bench privately owned lands to the intermingled state and national grazing district lands, on to the summer mountain meadows of the National Forests. Depletion on one kind of grazing land, resulting from mismanagement or natural causes, has a definite and sometimes immediate impact upon the other range ownerships and their freedom to pursue their own programs. Division of the national range lands between the Forest Service and the Bureau of Land Management makes this situation even more difficult of successful administration.

Operation under differing congressional and administrative policies concerning permittee user rights, fees for forage, the administrative influence of livestock advisory boards, standards of grazing management, participation by the states in range improvements, etc., has furnished excellent opportunity for private livestock interests, through their well organized national associations, to play the laxer or more favorable policies of one national agency against the other, and to use as a weapon the demand to transfer federal grazing lands to the states. The cry of states' rights in the controversy over public range land management is a thinly veiled disguise for the abandonment of range conservation, though it is not only in the public interest but also in the *long run* interest of the livestock industry. This is pretty evident in view of the kind of management practiced thus far by most of the western states in the handling of their own grazing lands.[22]

Until the enactment of the Taylor Grazing Act the states had paid virtually no attention to sustained yield management of their remaining grazing lands. Though some of it was leased to private operators, most of it, like the federal domain public ranges, was left to the tender mercies of those private livestock operators who were the most successful at aggressive and illegal range preemption.

The Taylor Grazing Act as amended by the Pierce Act permitted the states to incorporate their range lands into the district management program and to receive rental payments in return. While considerable state land was thus early incorporated into the district program, most of it (at least in the Pacific Northwest) has been withdrawn in late years because (as a result of the rising values of forage after 1940) the states have been able to make more money by direct leases to stockmen. Their concern has been immediate income, not range land restoration, long run productivity, or watershed protection.

This short run crowding of the forage by the states is partly the result of long established habit; but it is also partly excusable by the terms of federal grants to the states. The school lands were given to provide endowment income. Hence state sales and leases have in most instances been made with an eye to immediate cash return. The state agencies supervising these range properties have too often thought of themselves as investment organizations and have had little or no interest in or experience for a land management job. Thus the state land board in Oregon has spent no money for conservation practices or for range improvements, although in the early forties it had nearly seven hundred thousand acres of range land under its jurisdiction.[23]

The brightest spot among the Pacific Northwest states (and possibly in all the western states save Montana) is Idaho. Except for some improved policies adopted during the late twenties under the leadership of Land Commissioner I. H. Nash, this is a late development.[24] Because the state constitution has been construed to require that all revenues received from the sale or leasing of school lands be impounded for school endowment purposes, it has been necessary to obtain special legislative appropriations for management purposes.[25]

The management policies adopted for grazing lands a few years ago under the recent Land Commissioner Edward Woozley have been officially described as follows:

> The land pattern of most open ranges makes it mandatory that cooperative management programs be effected. Federal lands, state lands, and privately owned lands many times are side by side on open ranges. Stock drives, water holes and other factors make each of these ownerships an integral part of the total range. For these sales of grazing lands have been scrutinized very carefully and where a complete disruption of an existing range is evident we have declined the sale.
>
> The invasion of noxious and poisonous weeds, particularly halogeton, has necessitated joint control programs. We are also attempting to rebuild our ranges through brush eradication, development of additional water holes, range reseeding and the construction of drift fences. Some progress is being made along these lines. One field man has been given the job of classification

of all our state owned range land to determine the present carrying capacity and to suggest practical means of improving range for feeding additional numbers of livestock. When the classification is completed these lands will be catalogued for rental purposes in their proper order and we will attempt to follow market trends in setting rentals.[26]

This statement not only reveals the joint concern of nation, state, and private owners in the handling of particular range areas because of the complex ownership pattern and the physical dependence of one unit upon the other for feasible livestock operations, but also indicates the urgency of state conservation leasing policies adjusted to this physical situation.

The trouble with the Idaho program (as with those of other western states) is the gross inadequacy of its field force and its lease supervision. In addition, the absence of a merit system has meant that each time a political change brings in a new land commissioner a new set of field officers usually appears. It is utterly impossible to assure either efficiency or continuity under such circumstances regardless of how enlightened the state management policy may be. This was one of the many reasons advanced by Idaho Land Commissioner I. H. Nash, as a member of President Hoover's 1929 Committee on the Conservation and Administration of the Public Domain, against the President's suggestion that the states should take over the administration of all surface resources on federal domain lands.[27]

One other illuminating experience for federalism in range management is the spread of grazing associations in the northern Great Plains states, beginning with organization in 1928 by the stockmen of Custer County, Montana, of the historic Mizpah-Pumpkin Creek Association. It took a special act of Congress to transfer to the association for joint management purposes twenty-five thousand acres of public domain land needed to round out this first venture in pooling private, state, county, and national grazing land for sustained yield management.[28] This advance in range management has been the fruit of state laws (first enacted in 1933 by Montana) in the Great Plains region and of cooperative national administrative policies followed by the Resettlement Administration (or its successors), the Soil Conservation Service, the Grazing Service and its successor, the Bureau of Land Management. By 1940 Montana had forty such associations to which had been entrusted the management of nearly thirteen million acres of pooled private, state, county, and federal grass lands. In Montana but not in all the other states a state agency (the Grass Conservation Commission) has supervised the creation of grazing districts and the organization of the cooperative associations.

The Montana law in effect gave "legislative endorsement of the range management policies of the Grazing Service and the Soil Conservation Service, and the individual operator using district-controlled lands is usually subject to the same type of regulations set up by those agencies."[29] The federal range management agencies turned over in trust to these associations the management in accordance with their carrying capacities of national range lands (including the large acreages repurchased as submarginal for cash cropping) on generous rental terms. The Soil Conservation Service, as the administrative heir of the repurchased farm lands and the special agent of the nation for spreading the gospel of conservation farm land management, also lent the associations its technical assistance in range problems and in spreading interest among livestock men and the local public in the use of this cooperative, collective tenure method of range management. In a few cases the Farm Security Administration made loans to the associations for constructing range improvements or land purchases. Where the associations operated largely on national public domain lands, as many in Montana have done, their management relations with the Bureau of Land Management and the Soil Conservation Service have been particularly intimate.

II

FEDERALISM AND THE MANAGEMENT OF PRIVATELY OWNED NON-URBAN LAND RESOURCES

While publicly owned lands greatly contribute to the protection of our watersheds and to the production of timber, wildlife, livestock, and minerals, it is the privately owned farming lands upon which our American civilization chiefly depends for its principal supplies of food and much of its fibre. But the use of these lands is only indirectly the subject of central governmental action. Under our federal system any public interference with a private owner's use of his land is the function of the states.

Even though many still regard as absolute the right to do as one pleases with his own property, the states have for many years recognized the legitimacy of drastic controls to meet such urgent threats or emergencies as the spread of insect pests, noxious weeds, and plant diseases, or the ravages of forest fires. Public intervention to regulate private land management in these cases has been fully accepted as a proper function of the states. Even such exceedingly drastic actions by public agents as the destruction of diseased orchard trees without compensation, or the performance of weed eradication or fire suppression with the costs charged against the private owner, are universally approved as justifiable state or local regulations and have been sustained by the courts.[30] In many of the timbered states, the private owner of timber land or wood lots has long been compelled by taxation or by the threat of state intervention for which he must pay, or both, to protect his trees against fire.

But such acquiescence in public interference with private ownership rests upon the idea of a temporary emergency or of imminent irreparable damage to adjacent private owners. Intervention by the state or its local agents in private land use meets stronger resistance when the benefits of such interference are much more diffused in time or incidence. It is to the "cheek by jowl" life in urban communities that we must turn for the origins of the recent, broader proposals to regulate private agricultural and forest land. Rural land-zoning laws and land-use regulations are the legal offspring, perhaps one should say the step-children, of urban zoning statutes.

Rural zoning is of many varieties and serves diverse purposes but our concern is primarily with what Erling Solberg in his recent analysis of state enabling acts and local zoning ordinances has called "open-country-use" rural zoning,[31] that is, the effort to encourage the best long run treatment of those vast areas that produce our major supplies of agricultural and timber raw materials.

The pioneer regulation was made by Wisconsin. The cut-over timber lands of the sandy soiled areas between the Great Lakes were submarginal for farming, even under good price conditions. The decline of agricultural prices during the twenties, accentuated after the financial crash of 1929, created such human distress and such havoc in local government finance and services that private decisions about land use could not longer be left uncontrolled. So the state adopted a rural zoning statute permitting county or town boards to create forestry or recreational zones and general agricultural zones—along with other zoning restrictions—as one means to bring the use of land into line with its basic potentialities. Forest and recreation zones were drawn which prohibited farming and year-long residence in those regions where such uses were incompatible with the capabilities of the land and would result in individual and public bankruptcy.

The Wisconsin example has been followed, with some changes, in Michigan, Minnesota, and to a much more limited extent in Washington. At least one ordinance in Colorado also provides for forest conservation districts.[32] There are also several states in which "rural communities concerned about the destruction or impairment of agricultural soils by strip mining have adopted ordinances prohibiting or regulating such operations."[33]

Despite the fact that by 1949 one hundred and seventy-three counties in twenty-three states had rural zoning ordinances, the evidence indicates that except for areas along the Great Lakes in northern Minnesota, Wisconsin, and Michigan, in the unorganized towns of Maine, and a few scattered locations in other parts of the nation, rural land zoning has done little toward bringing privately owned agricultural and forest land into adjustment with its best sustained use.[34] The large volume of discussion and study during the thirties which pointed toward land classification and rural zoning as one of the principal devices to be relied upon seems to have produced very modest results.

So it is to the initiative and support of the national government that we must look for most of the headway that has been made in stimulating private owners of agricultural and forest land toward a more provident use of these resources.[35] To be sure the states have been drawn into the programs as essential collaborators, and, however reluctant some of them were in the beginning, a wholehearted mood of cooperative effort seems now to be firmly established. I turn to a brief review of these national-state-local programs.

Professor Gaus has traced the origin and early development of the Soil Conservation Service and its administrative vehicle, the state-created soil conservation district. While the latest available count shows 2,570 of these new units of local government, which include nearly six-sevenths of the entire agricultural area of the United States, it should at once be added that "basic" farm plans are in effect for only about one-fifth of the district farms, including about a fifth of the total farm and ranch acreage.[36] Additional conservation treatment is being given land on farms without "basic" plans.

Even though a close scrutiny might modify these statistics (since practices once established may be abandoned without penalty), this rapid spread across the nation's private farmland of so much in the way of improved management practices geared to perpetual productivity is a great achievement. That it has not been as fast, complete, or assuredly permanent as desired does not alter this conclusion. Nor is it the result solely of this one program of intergovernmental collaboration between the Soil Conservation Service, the states, and the local soil conservation districts. Once the evangel of soil conservation had begun to win popular acceptance, many private institutions embraced the faith, particularly when the faith was buttressed by sound business considerations. The banks handling agricultural paper or mortgages, the insurance companies owning large numbers of farms, the creditors of farm borrowers, the farm machinery companies finding new demand for conservation equipment, the mail order houses which prosper when farmer incomes are high and stable, and other private citizens have added support to the official programs.

Included in the impact of our national system on this resource management change were several other bureaus in the U.S. Department of Agriculture, namely: the Farm Security Administration (which survives vestigially as the Farmers Home Administration), the Farm Credit Administration, and the Production and Marketing Administration. The first two agencies brought many of their borrowers into the district programs, but the PMA—the most ubiquitous, affluent, and charitable agency of the departmental family—has probably exercised the strongest supplementing influence.[37]

It was the intention of the national department as reflected in its "standard" act that the local soil conservation district should perform two major tasks: (1) induce farmers to adopt plans to modify practices and land use so that every acre would be used in accordance with its capability, thus stopping accelerated erosion and conserving fertility; and (2) adopt compulsory land use regulations that would prevent or control erosion. To achieve these purposes the districts were to contract with farmers to furnish them technical, financial, and material assistance. In addition they might conduct research in erosion control, develop land use plans and programs for their districts, conduct demonstration projects, build and maintain structures, and the like. But they were not to have taxing or bonding power. These financial limitations compelled the districts to seek gifts in the form of technical assistance, equipment, labor, or money. The first three the Soil Conservation Service was prepared to give, but it was hoped that other national, state, or local agencies might augment its assistance. In fact the SCS became the principal and in most cases the sole source of effective aid so that the districts were soon regarded, even by district supervisors, as "Soil Conservation Service" districts.[38] The whole administrative organization of the SCS was realigned to suit the district aspect of its work.

Why did the Department of Agriculture assume the role of local government procreator instead of using the county government as the vehicle for its attack upon the problem of private land management? No doubt the Wallace regime was unwilling to draft the county agent-extension service organization for another action program as it had done for the crop restriction program in 1933. To use the county for the SCS work might have seemed to make that inevitable. Other reasons were the general backwardness of the county as an efficient or responsible unit of local government; the preoccupation of its officials with matters not related to soil conservation; the desire to lodge local control with that vocational group primarily affected by the program; and (most frequently voiced) the conviction that conservation farm planning and operation could succeed only if geared into unified watershed treatment. Obviously county boundaries had only accidental relationships to this physical area concept.[39]

Though the district was undoubtedly conceived as the federal government's chosen instrument the "standard act" did not bypass the state government. It provided for a state committee to assist in the organization of the districts, select two of the five board members, and, after a district was established, act as an advisory and informational agency.

While the early state laws followed this general design, later statutes and amendments have tended to increase the operational influence of the state body over the districts. The Missouri, Wisconsin, and Pennsylvania state committees have a tight administrative rein over their districts, acting as buffers between the districts and the national agencies.[40]

In modifying the "standard act" conceptions the most tight-reining states like Missouri doubtless responded to the political influence of the land-grant colleges with their suspicion of the Soil Conservation Service and of "federal domination." Until recently the representatives of the state colleges plus their Farm Bureau or Extension farmer friends have dominated the state committees.

As Professor Gaus has suggested, a counterpoise to this tendency and to the influence of the SCS bureaucrats is the organization of Soil Conservation District Supervisors and their farmer friends. These associations are not only carrying the ball for state appropriations for the districts and for federal appropriations for the SCS (as well as supporting the latter against hostile administrative rearrangements at the hands of Congress or the Department of Agriculture) but also they are taking the farmer member places on the state committees which originally went to the Farm Bureau or the Grange (or in some Great Plains states, to the Farmers' Union), sometimes by explicit direction of the legislatures. Professor Parks summarizes the current contrasting tendency as follows:

> ... after 1944, almost all state laws providing for farmer members specified that these farmers also were to be district supervisors or representatives of the supervisors' associations. The California, Michigan and Vermont laws set up the specification of being a district supervisor. Georgia, in 1945, specified that the farmer members are to be members of the Board of Directors of the Georgia Association of Soil Conservation District Supervisors. North Carolina, in 1947, added to the membership of the state committee the President, first Vice-President and the immediate past President of the state Association of Soil Conservation District Supervisors. By 1952 thirty-two state committees had farmer members who were not legally designated as representatives of any farm organization. Four states—Georgia, New York, Oklahoma and Texas—have all-farmer committees. In twelve other states, farmers constitute a majority of the committee membership.
>
> The state committee has thus far been largely regarded as a body without an organizational personality, without institutional drives and ambitions of its own—an organ, in short, designed for state college or SCS control. Yet, the factors are all present for its becoming an independent institutional personality which will accept control from no other agency. As its power in the district grows, as it has increased funds to dispense, as it develops its own organization and staff, as it gains its own organized popular supports, it is likely to develop its own organizational interest and views in conservation activity.[41]

The field organization of the Soil Conservation Service has of course been designed to facilitate its relations with the state committee and the state colleges. The latter have inevitably been drawn into the program, whether they liked it or not, since their experimental work and technical skills as well as the Extension Service educational facilities had to be utilized even if with ill grace —and the response was often cordial.[42]

Yet the regional structure of the agency was intended to resolve both policy and technical questions at the regional level where pressure from state agencies was least. This pattern of regional control of the lower units in the field structure and of decentralization from Washington to the region, while disliked by the land-grant colleges and their farm pressure group friends, illustrates the kind of administrative adaptation to our federal constitutional system that after 1933 became characteristic of national land and water programs.[43] While it was in part a structural response to the inadequacy of state boundaries for field supervision (due to work load-cost, span of control, and other operating characteristics) it was also one means of easing and adjusting the pressures of state officialdom.

In the case of the Soil Conservation Service, however, regionalization has also functioned, probably without intention, as a device for modifying the application of national agency policy to meet not only the great variability in physio-agronomic conditions in so vast a country but also the variable political conditions. The early uniform national stipulations laid down as conditions for aiding districts included:

1. The incorporation in their state laws of standards necessary for carrying out a well rounded soil erosion control and conservation program. States that withheld powers necessary to this purpose, or failed to give the districts the power to make and enforce land use regulations were not to be given the use of mechanical equipment or plants, until they did conform.

2. Districts must develop basic programs stating their conservation goals.

3. In the subsequent memorandum of understanding the district must agree to formulate work plans for these goals, make written agreements acceptable to SCS with individual farmers binding them to carry out the agreed practices as conditions of federal assistance.

4. The work-plan content must include detailed conservation practices and administrative arrangements. If approved by SCS a supplemental agreement pledged SCS assistance to the district, while the district agreed to limit its aid to lands either covered by cooperative agreements or owned, leased or operated by the district. It also assumed responsibility for records of SCS materials used, and for maintenance of SCS equipment loaned to it. The SCS regional offices were authorized to approve the work plans.

The key to the ultimate effectiveness of the entire soil conservation program was the application in good faith by the cooperating farmer of the practices specified by his farm plan. Consequently the SCS conditioned its assistance upon the use of an agreement between the district and the farmer which would not only mark out these practices and the timing to be followed, but also would stipulate that if the farmer did not perform them, the district might terminate the agreement and the farmer should reimburse it for labor, materials, and equipment used.

This series of "contractual instruments" may make it appear that the national government, through its assistance to these local units, had achieved controls over the use of private land comparable to those established by such unitary governments as Great Britain with its legal authority over private ownership of agricultural land. But such appearance is deceiving. For not only is a minority of land and ownership as yet included in the district programs but also the national policy minima and the farmer cooperative obligations have undergone a process of accelerated erosion since the brave New Deal days.

No effort has ever been made to enforce the penalty clauses against farmers who have disregarded their conservation commitments and their inclusion in the agreements has in large part been discontinued. The minimal statutory conditions for federal assistance have also been greatly softened. In effect there are today no minimum national standards for state legislation in the establishment of soil conservation districts.

A similar tendency prevails with regard to district programs, many of which are now accepted with only the sketchiest indication of objectives. And as for work plans, the attitudes of regional offices toward district discretion have varied widely. Recently they have pursued an increasingly relaxed policy in which good general intentions are allowed to do duty for concrete and specific practices, task assignments, area priorities, etc., until the district shall be ready with its annual plan of activity. No district has ever been refused service because of inability to agree with SCS upon a program, plans, or working relationships.

Nor has the Service ever used sanctions such as cancellation of the agreement or withdrawal of services when a district board has failed to live up to its explicit obligations.

The early national policy emphasis on "complete" farm planning was stated by Service Chief Bennett in 1937 as follows:

> . . . a partial program for a given farm does not meet the essential requirements of a good soil conservation program and is, therefore, not acceptable. The program for each farm . . . must call for the *full* treatment of *every* acre affected and for the employment of *all* measures and practices needed to provide that treatment. Otherwise the Soil Conservation Service fails to discharge its full responsibility.[44]

But district supervisors, responsive to local farmer sentiment, were prone to push the type of program that was immediately profitable and popular and were, moreover, convinced that acceptance of the whole program would come later if not all practice changes were required simultaneously. There was also the constant example of the AAA which after 1937 was handing out cash payments for single or limited conservation practices. No farm plan to guide that program was required.

The influence of supervisor pressure, field complaint and connivance with adulterated interpretations, the Gresham's law of interagency competition, and the war, still further eroded the original standards.

The culmination of this relaxing process came in 1951 and 1952 when Secretary Brannan ended the competition between the SCS and the PMA by reorganizing their relationships so as to harmonize the two conservation programs at the county level and by making the SCS responsible for the technical phases of both of them. SCS field technicians now assist PMA farmers in their limited practices even though they do not become district cooperators and are thus not committed to complete farm planning and conservation management. Yet the Secretary of Agriculture as late as April 1952 reemphasized the national goal of embracing "every acre of farm land . . . in soil conservation districts." He also asserted as the ultimate objective a scientifically developed, technically sound conservation plan for each farm.[45]

The second half of the original soil conservation district task was the adoption and enforcement of land use regulations to prevent erosion. Even if farmers rejected the program of affirmative assistance or failed to live up to the district-farmer agreement, they would still have to so treat their lands as to preserve the top soil. By the end of 1951, however, only eight districts in the entire United States were enforcing land-use ordinances. Six of these were in the "dust bowl" section of southeast Colorado, one was a sandy-soiled district in southwest North Dakota, and the eighth was in the shifting sand-dune

Pacific littoral west of Astoria, Oregon.[46] Seven other Colorado districts had at some time adopted such ordinances but these are no longer in effect because of a 1945 amendment to the state law requiring reenactment by a greatly increased majority or because of changes in local sentiment. Those regulations, however, which require the owners to perform certain practices to abate soil blowing have been so successful that the Colorado legislature in 1951 applied them to the entire state, to be enforced by the boards of county commissioners.

Despite the emphasis that the "standard act" placed on the right of the district to issue and enforce land-use regulations, the early state legislative acquiescence in this policy has been sharply reversed. Today sixteen states deny all regulatory authority to the districts.[47] It is clear from the Colorado experience that absentee land owners and their local representatives and the real estate speculators, when beaten by local sentiment, have been able to exert such powerful influence upon the state legislature as to render the exercise of regulatory authority over land use by the districts very difficult or precarious. The climate of farmer and public opinion has so changed since the distressed thirties that there is no appreciable public support for the police power mode of obtaining better land management even for the most badly adjusted lands.

It would be too simple to explain the weakening of these national standards and policies solely by the division of our constitutional system of powers between nation and states. The war brought a reversal of earlier national agricultural policies. Emphasis shifted from restrictive policies, favorable to many conservation practices, to all-out production and to a price policy designed to bring in much formerly submarginal land. The gospel of soil and fertility conservation so strenuously preached during the thirties was drowned out after Pearl Harbor by the evangel of patriotism to which clung seductively the certain prospect of returns beyond anything farmers had experienced since the days of World War I. No wonder that farm plans went by the board as farmer after farmer broke his conservation rotations to reap the golden harvest offered by returning moisture and high guaranteed prices. From this jettisoning of farm planning standards the original SCS policies never recovered.

While a number of influences have contributed to this result, special note should be taken of the pressure from the unofficial district supervisors' organizations. The district system has bred a new genus of local farmer-administrators who, as they appeared over the length and breadth of the land, were bound to concert their efforts. The Department of Agriculture had created them. It has encouraged their associations and used them to help fight its battles for funds and administrative protection in state legislatures and in Congress. Although the district was the ideological creation of the national department, the states were its legal parents and the national agency had become in important respects the captive of its creatures, which had in sixteen years gained experience, confidence, and independent political strength. One gains the impression from Charles Hardin's acidulous account of the "Soil Conservation Service in Politics" that all the benefits of this alliance have been for the federal bureaucrats in whose hands the districts have been complaisant puppets.[48] But the later and more complete study of the soil conservation districts by Professor Parks is replete with indications of political influence flowing in the opposite direction. If, as he maintains, the district "supervisors have always leaned to the belief that any combination of practices acceptable to the farmer was a suitable basis for extending district assistance," (p. 100) then the supervisor-customer point of view has prevailed in the evolution of federal agency policy.

Our federal political system, as it has related to the task of bringing conservation practices to the management of private agricultural lands, has thus not only stimulated the elaboration of a strong bureaucracy but likewise has generated parallel semipublic or private federations of political influence. What persists and gets itself applied in the way of national land resource policies depends in considerable part therefore on the efficiency of these associations, their breadth of membership, their economic and social status, their ability to attach to themselves influential "friends" from other segments of the farm and urban population, and the skill of their leaders. They have had the basic political advantages inherent in the divorce of legal authority from national will as well as those which flow from the contradictions within the national willing process, so much accentuated by checks and balances.

Nor does the different type of organization under the aegis of the Tennessee Valley Authority for similar national purposes within the counties of the seven-state valley tell a tale of greater national policy penetration. Quite the contrary, if the evidence of Selznik is to be credited. There the existing state and county organizations were employed to administer the farm land-use program. TVA controls over state and county performance were so gossamer thin that no accurate quantitative summary of conservation achieved by federal expenditure for these national objectives has been possible. Both experiences suggest the insubstantiality of the fear of "federal dictatorship" insofar as private agricultural land management is concerned.

FOOTNOTES TO CHAPTER 16

1. Limits of time and knowledge do not permit exploration of the private guild units which have become so enmeshed in the administration of some of the national and state public lands as to constitute vital parts of the administrative, policy-making, and operating systems. However, the full division of powers and the real system of federalism that have developed around this resource will remain partly obscured until the roles of the livestock advisory boards of the grazing districts, the National Forests, and the state land departments, of the Timber Protective Associations, and of the grazing associations (in the Great Plains states) are delineated.

2. William B. Greeley, *Forests and Men*, Garden City, Doubleday, 1951, pp. 19–20.

3. Stewart H. Holbrook, *Burning an Empire*, New York, Macmillan, 1952, pp. 132 ff.

4. Luther H. Gulick, *American Forest Policy,* New York, Duell, Sloan & Pearce, 1951, p. 145.

5. The Weeks Act restricted the fire protection program to the watersheds of navigable streams but the Clark-McNary Act took a broader view of national constitutional power by extending the grant system to all forested and cut-over land. See the 1950 report of the Chief of the U.S. Forest Service, p. 3.

6. 1951 Report of the Chief of the Forest Service, U.S. Dept. of Agriculture, p. 56.

7. 1952 Report of the Chief of the Forest Service, pp. 37–38.

8. Testimony of Assistant Chief Forester Harper before the subcommittee on Agricultural Appropriation Bill of the House Committee on Appropriations, Jan. 1952. Hearings, 82nd Cong. 2nd Sess. Part I, p. 653.

9. These were California, Idaho, Maine, Massachusetts, New Hampshire, New York, Oregon, and Pennsylvania. 1950 Report of the Chief of the Forest Service, p. 12.

10. Pest control programs and operating relationships are described by Dr. W. L. Popham, assistant chief of the Bureau of Entomology and Plant Quarantine in (1) a talk given at a meeting of Western Forestry and Conservation Associations in Portland, Dec. 8, 1949 and (2) his testimony at the hearings of the House Subcommittee on Appropriations for the Department of Agriculture, 82nd Cong., 2nd Sess. p. 1050. See also a mimeographed pamphlet entitled "Spruce Budworm Situation in Oregon and Washington—1949 Season" by A. Lindsten, Oregon State Board of Forestry, and W. J. Buckhorn, J. F. Wear, J. M. Whiteside, and K. H. Wright of the Bureau of Entomology and Plant Quarantine, dated Portland, Oregon, Sept. 1, 1949.

11. The Conservation Foundation, in its 1952 publication, "Forests for the Future," p. 15, estimates that on the state and locally owned commercial forest lands totaling about twenty-seven and a half million acres cutting practices are good or better on forty-seven percent, are fair on ten percent, and poor or worse on forty-three percent. This is a much better situation than exists on private lands but much inferior to that of the National Forests. No overall estimates of other management practices of state and community forests or of their use for grazing purposes are available.

12. See the Biennial Report for 1950–52 of the State Forester, pp. 28–30, for a brief summary of the Oregon state forest rehabilitation programs.

13. The estimate of state-owned timber is reported in the 30th Biennial Report of the Commissioner of Public Lands, p. 28.

14. The lands granted for the state capitol buildings, now about 111,000 acres, are under the management of a third state agency, the State Capitol Committee.

15. See the "First Report of the Committee on State Government Organization," Jan. 1952, to Gov. Arthur B. Langlie, pp. 22–24; see also the scathing criticism by Alfred McBee, Special Assistant Attorney General, in a special report on "Department of Public Lands of the State of Washington," dated July 1, 1952.

16. Gulick, *op. cit.,* p. 147.

17. See the so-called Anderson Bill. Senate No. 1920, 81st Cong., 1st Session.

18. The decision of the U.S. Supreme Court late in 1949 sustaining the Washington law places such state regulation upon a firm constitutional basis. Dexter v. State of Washington, 338 U.S. 863. See *State Government,* Vol. 23, p. 2, Jan. 1950.

19. A much more drastic statute was enacted in Idaho in the mid-thirties but it has never been enforced. In its summary of state laws regulating cutting practices

the Conservation Foundation gives sixteen states as having some kind of regulation. But these include those with tax legislation only.

20. It is interesting to note that in Washington, where enforcement is well under way, the U.S. Forest Service is used by the state to enforce the regulations against private operators within the National Forest zones.

21. This is the conclusion reported by Conrad McBride from data collected in 1952 through a questionnaire circulated by the Council of State Governments.

22. When the comprehensive report on the condition of the Western Range was made (Sen. Doc. No. 199, 74th Cong., 2nd Sess.) the states owned in excess of 58 million acres and the counties had foreclosed on an additional seven million acres of range land. Since these lands had been administered with the object of sale or lease, concern over conservation of the basic resource had been absent. "It is estimated that the grazing capacity has been depleted approximately one half from virgin conditions and that about 28 million acres are severely eroded and an equal amount is materially eroded." (p. 477) No general summary of the present situation is available. Consequently the factual conclusions contained herein are based on limited first hand observations in states of the Pacific Northwest and in Utah, on the judgement of federal range and forest officers who have worked on range management in a number of western states, and on a few studies of limited aspects of the range situation.

23. 36th Annual Report, 1940–42, State Land Board and Rural Credit Department, pp. 4–5.

24. Note should also be taken of the interest shown by Idaho in 1940 in obtaining a full scale study of its state owned lands, looking toward their improved management, by a technical advisory committee on land management of the Idaho State Planning Board. This project was carried through by a group of state and federal officials (chiefly the latter) representing functions having to do with land use. It was partly financed, and its summary and recommendations were published, by the late Northwest Regional Council in 1941 under the title: "Management of State Owned Lands in Idaho." The full report exists in manuscript form in the files of the Idaho State Land Department.

25. This is a common legal impediment to proper state school land management. Even where school people take a long range view of the returns from this great estate, as in Washington, the legal prohibition concerning the use of revenues for land management requires special legislative appropriations for such elementary tasks as inventory and classification. Where these have not been forthcoming, as in Washington, conservation management cannot be attained.

26. 31st Biennial Report, Idaho State Land Department, 1950–52, p. 19.

27. In view of the proposals being revived during the current Hooverian renaissance, Commissioner Nash's full length statement makes very interesting and cogent reading. His general position seems to have been approved by the then Governor, H. C. Baldridge. See 20th Biennial Report of the State Land Department of Idaho, 1928–30, pp. 16–32.

28. C. H. Craig and C. W. Loomer, "Collective Tenure on Grazing Land in Montana," p. 10; Bulletin 406, Feb. 1943, Montana State College Agricultural Experiment Station, Bozeman, Montana.

29. *Op. cit.*, p. 17. No summary of grazing association history since 1943 has been available. The writer does not know whether or not the early favorable record of improved range management and harmonious private-state-federal relations has continued.

30. See for example Miller vs. Schoene, 276 U.S. 272 (1928), in which the U.S. Supreme Court speaking through Mr. Justice Stone upheld the validity of a Virginia statute which ordered the destruction of trees afflicted with cedar rust when they were close enough to contaminate apple orchards.

31. Erling D. Solberg, *Rural Zoning in the United States,* Bureau of Agricultural Economics, U.S. Dept. of Agriculture, Agricultural Information Bulletin No. 59, Jan. 1952, Washington, D.C. The information in this publication is the principal source of facts used in the discussion of this topic.

32. Solberg, *op. cit.,* pp. 34 ff.

33. *Ibid.,* p. 53.

34. The raw statistics about "rural zoning" seem very impressive. But most of the 175 enabling statutes are designed chiefly to prevent building development of an urban character from encroaching upon the countryside along the highways or to bring some order into the suburban accretion beyond the city limits. Most of them have little or nothing to do with the management of agricultural or forest lands. Thirty-one laws in seventeen states exempt all agricultural activities from zoning, and in many of the other states in which agricultural zones are permitted the ordinances are directed toward the regulation of such activities as hog ranches, livestock feed and sales yards, etc., which might be offensive to suburban or town dwellers. See *Ibid.,* pp. 30–31, 43–44, 46.

35. The state creation of conservation agencies in the Theodore Roosevelt era never entered the province of private resource regulation.

36. These data rest in part on 1953 estimates furnished the Portland, Oregon, regional office of the Soil Conservation Service. In part they are taken from page 8 of the recent study by W. Robert Parks, *Soil Conservation Districts in Action,* Ames, Iowa, Iowa State College Press, 1952. In summarizing the work of the Soil Conservation Service and its relations with the soil conservation districts in the quest for securing conservation practices on private land, I have relied principally on this study of Professor Parks.

37. Robert Salter, the new chief of the SCS, has testified recently affirming the importance of the PMA payments in furnishing farmers the financial means for the change-over to conservation farming. See House Committee on Appropriations, Hearings before the subcommittee on the Agricultural Appropriations Bill for 1953, 82nd Cong., 2nd Sess. Part I, p. 508.

38. There is some evidence that the department, as the district plan got under way, considered the use of this new unit as a device through which all of its action programs might be channeled. This was expressed by Secretary Wallace in a memorandum to Chief H. H. Bennett dated Dec. 10, 1937, cited and partly quoted by Parks, *op. cit.,* pp. 190–191.

39. The actual application of this area justification has been honored in the breach. More than half the districts consist of a county or group of counties. See Charles M. Hardin, *The Politics of Agriculture,* Glencoe, The Free Press, 1952, p. 71.

40. In Missouri centralized control includes (1) the withholding of state aid where districts do not comply with the state commission's policies, (2) the approval of all district rules, regulations, and operating forms and documents, (3) the approval of farmer-district agreements and contracts, and (4) the approval of all contracts and legal instruments. In Missouri state primacy over the district was cemented into our federal system by a special amendment to the appropriation act for the Department of Agriculture, beginning in fiscal year 1945 at the behest of Chairman Cannon. It stipulated that any agreement between a soil conservation dis-

trict and the U.S. Department of Agriculture must have the prior approval of the Missouri "central state agency."

41. *Op. cit.,* pp. 212–213. For another account of the political activities of the district supervisors and their association, see Hardin, *op. cit.,* chap. 5.

42. In 29 states the joint employment of the Extension soil conservationist has developed, in the judgment of Professor Parks, into a "major contribution to developing unity of effort. . . ." *Op. cit.,* p. 207.

43. It is true that the PMA, and the AAA before it, never succeeded in making this structural adjustment, though the latter took the first steps in that direction by regionalizing within the Washington organization. The Eisenhower administration in 1954 was attempting to reverse this process, and was dismantling the regional offices of the SCS. State field headquarters were to be the centers for field supervision.

44. SCS Field Memorandum No. 475, April 29, 1937, entitled "Emphasizing Complete Farm Planning."

45. Parks, *op. cit.,* pp. 197–8.

46. The facts concerning land use regulations in Colorado have been reported in considerable detail by Stanley W. Voelker in a study sponsored by the Great Plains Council, published in March 1952 as Technical Bulletin 45 of the Colorado Agricultural Experiment Station, Colorado Agricultural and Mechanical College, Fort Collins, Colorado. Professor Parks, however, lists eight districts in Colorado as having such regulatory ordinances. *Op. cit.,* p. 152.

47. *Ibid.,* p. 149.

48. See chap. 6 in his *The Politics of Agriculture.*

17

The Management of Water Resources under the American Federal System

By Charles McKinley

I

Division of Legal Powers over Water

To understand the "going" interlevel relationships affecting water resources between national, state, and local governments, one must keep in mind the distribution of the principal legal powers over water. Because navigation is an aspect of commerce, the national government through its primacy in matters of interstate and foreign commerce has jurisdiction over the navigation of domestic waters. This national jurisdiction reached beyond the coastal and tidal streams more than a century ago, first into nontidal navigable waters and finally encompassing "both the upper non-navigable reaches of a navigable waterway and . . . its non-navigable tributaries, if the navigable capacity of the non-navigable waterway is affected or if interstate commerce is otherwise affected."[1] Indeed the doctrines developed by the Supreme Court in the *New River* case (1940) and in *Atkinson v. Oklahoma* (1941) have found even broader constitutional justifications for national water control through the commerce clause. These judgments assert the doctrine that flood control and watershed development as well as navigation are parts of interstate commerce. To quote from the latter case:

> But there is no constitutional reason why Congress or the courts should be blind to the engineering prospects of protecting the nation's arteries of commerce through control of the watersheds. There is no constitutional reason why Congress cannot, under the commerce power, treat the watersheds as a key to flood control on navigable streams and their tributaries. Nor is there a constitutional necessity for viewing each reservoir project in isolation from a comprehensive plan covering the entire basin of a particular river.[2]

These recent cases also appear to give a firm support to the federal development of hydro-electric power "as a paying partner" in the control of commerce even when the chief or sole purpose of the dam is either flood control or the generation of electricity.

But the national jurisdiction over navigable streams does not impair the state's proprietary control over the beds of navigable streams or its right to determine who may legally use the waters. However, the state's control over water appropriation is "subject to the paramount power of the United States to control it for the purpose of navigation."[3] Moreover, the state may not destroy the right of the United States as the owner of lands bordering on a stream to its continued flow when required for the beneficial uses of government property.[4] The national government obtained these riparian rights on vast areas of land acquired by war and purchase. When it has divested itself of such lands, as through the Homestead acts, Congress has passed these national water rights along to the new owners as it saw fit. Its control over its landed properties as to riparian rights did not cease when states were carved out of the federal territories unless it so willed. The Supreme Court has held that Congress did so decide by various statutes culminating in the Desert Land Act of 1877, with the result that "all non-navigable waters then part of the public domain became *publici juris,* subject to the plenary control of the designated states, including those since created out of the territories named, with the right in each to determine for itself to what extent the rule of appropriation or the common rule in respect of riparian right should obtain."[5]

Thus it has happened that states through their acceptance of the old common law doctrines of riparian ownership rights or the western miner-improvised doctrine of prior appropriation, or some combination of both, determine who may appropriate the water for beneficial use.

The national government has further cemented state control of water rights by requiring in the Reclamation Act of 1902 that the programs therein contemplated should not be permitted to "affect or in any way interfere with the laws of any state or territory relating to the control, appropriation, use, or distribution of water used in irrigation, or any vested right acquired thereunder and the Secretary of the Interior, in carrying out the provisions of this act shall proceed in conformity with such laws, and nothing herein shall in any way affect any right of any state or of the federal government or of any landowner, appropriator, or user of water in, to or from any interstate stream or the waters thereof. . . ."[6] Administrative practice of the Bureau of Reclamation has been to file notices of appropriation under the state laws, whether for water on a navigable or on a nonnavigable stream, and to pay for water rights acquired under state law.[7] The army on the contrary is not required by Congress to file for water rights.

The states' jurisdiction over water applies not only to surface streams and lakes but also to underground water supplies. These, if in the form of streams, may be used under the same legal doctrines that apply to surface waters; if in the form of what the courts have called "percolating" waters, the right to use may either attach absolutely to the land ownership, or to prior appropriation, or it may take the form of limited ownership right, subject to reasonable use or the correlative rights of other owners.[8] The growing scarcity of unappropriated surface waters in the arid West has recently brought a notable increase in the use of ground waters for irrigation and other purposes—a use greatly stimulated by low cost electricity for pumping, improved pumping mechanisms, and high prices for agricultural products.

Wherever water is scarce, therefore, the legal jurisdiction of the state over its use has compelled the establishment of state administrative and judicial machinery (1) to adjudicate water rights and (2) to administer the distribution of water to the rightful users. In the second task as well as in other ways the state and its local agencies have been brought into intimate and constant contact with the agencies of the national government which administer the planning, development, and control of its water resources.

In the contrasting situations where the problem is to prevent surplus water from flooding occupied areas, state and local governments will also play an indispensable legal role whenever the necessary remedy calls for flood-plain zoning. Although this remedy is used reluctantly, it is in many of our most important and most menaced areas the only economic means for preventing disaster during severe floods.[9]

II

The Evolution of Water Resource Programs and of Interlevel Relationships

In the first quarter of the nineteenth century both national and state governments were actively interested in the development of inland waterways along with complementing forms of land transport. But the central government's entrepreneurship in internal transportation works, except for the launching of the "national pike" to link the Atlantic seaboard with the Ohio and ultimately the Mississippi valley, was expressed pretty largely in "planning" documents.[10] Not until the Civil War period did it begin the improvement of inland waterways. Even then it gave virtually no aid to protect farms and communities from floods. In the meantime the states launched ambitious schemes for internal transportation improvements in which canals played the dominant role. The states asked and received national assistance through numerous specific land grants for project sites and for sale, through the authorization to charge tolls, and through the Treasury purchase of stock in the canal companies chartered by the states.[11] This era of canal and road construction left many states with large debts, some of which were never paid.[12]

When concern for inland water transportation revived, it was the national government through the Corps of Engineers that took over almost complete responsibility for it. True, local and occasionally state port agencies on the bays and lower river locations began dredging for harbor and channel improvements and performed other services intended to increase the shipping business of their communities. Early in the twentieth century, however, the Corps of Engineers assumed the major responsibility for such navigation works, a share that has today become almost a monopoly.

These revived navigation and related functions were for years performed on a project by project basis. It was not until President Hoover's administration that the Corps, on congressional instructions, began surveys of all navigable streams on a basinwide, multiple-purpose basis. Even then, the first "308" studies took little cognizance of fisheries, pollution control, recreation byproducts, or watershed management. While they included studies of hydroelectric potentials, irrigation, and hydrological data as well as navigation and flood control (the latter having been made a full-fledged army responsibility by Congress in 1917) their emphasis still reflected the Corps' dominant interest in navigation.

Local attempts to prevent floods in the Mississippi delta country date back to 1717 when the New Orleans settlers built the first levees along the Mississippi.[13] The long story of local self-help beginning first with the abutting riparian land owners, then the parishes, and later levee districts aided by state engineering advice, had been one of continual if disjointed effort, a costly ever-expanding levee system, buoyant hope, and catastrophic disappointment.[14] Southern politicians (J. C. Calhoun among them) began by 1850 to make organized demand that the national government take over the construction of the Mississippi River levee system, which had already cost the local folk an estimated forty million dollars. The Civil War, the post-war economic demoralization, and the onset of increasingly devastating floods ruined the levee system and threatened the depopulation of the lower valley.

The national government finally came to the rescue in 1874 by setting up the Mississippi River Commission, a unit in the Corps of Engineers. This agency worked through local levee boards. While these were state appointed, they were in fact local units of government, supported by the taxing and bonding powers of their respective local districts. The Commission gave advice on levee location, set the construction and maintenance standards, and contributed approximately half the funds, until, in 1917, Congress adopted a new contribution ratio of two federal dollars to one local dollar (plus locally furnished rights of way and maintenance costs). The Mississippi River Commission also took command of defense and rescue when floods descended.

Nevertheless the people in the delta country pressed for assumption of full national responsibility on the Mississippi. So effective were they in organizing regional, vocational, and economic interest groups in favor of the principle of national responsibility that when the catastrophic 1927 flood wrecked the lower river protective system and dramatized human suffering by an unprecedented loss of life and property, the American Bankers Association and the U. S. Chamber of Commerce joined in the "full responsibility" hue and cry. The latter's national referendum answered by 1,053 of its local chambers voted by more than ten to one that the national government not only should take over the whole cost of building and maintaining the levees of the lower river, but also should assume full responsibility for installing and maintaining all other flood control works on this river.[15] The Reid Act of 1928 was a partial but generous response to this nationalizing sentiment.

Perhaps it was also a landmark in the dawning recognition that flood control on our major rivers must be sought in system-wide (though not as yet watershed-wide) control programs. For the Mississippi's seriously endangered and damaged area, from Cairo to the Gulf, was only a minor fraction of the vast drainage area producing the flood waters.

It is difficult to generalize about present interlevel relationships in river and harbor and flood control activities within the forty-eight states. The legal-administrative arrangements are very diverse and the actual processes of informal administrative interlevel behavior have received very scant study. Nevertheless it appears that only in a minority of states, chiefly in New England, the Great Lakes region, and a few other areas, are the contacts of the Corps of Engineers in its river and harbor and flood control work principally with or through state administrative agencies.[16]

A few states have developed more or less comprehensive water plans of their own. These include California, which in 1931 originated the famous Central Valley Project as a state enterprise, then abandoned it to the national government, and has recently reentered the water development field by authorizing state construction of the Feather River and Sacramento-San Joaquin Delta Diversion projects.[17] In New England, state surveys of water resources looking toward the development of hydro-electric power on the Connecticut River system seem to have been a favorite interest of the four affected states between 1870 and 1927. This culminated in a good deal of sentiment during the latter part of that period, and also in the early thirties, for state public power development. Activity in that direction, however, did not get beyond the planning and data collection stages. The state of Massachusetts, prior to the assumption of federal responsibility, built a number of flood works on the Connecticut, augmenting the protective effort of cities and private groups.[18] On the Missouri River most of the ten states have a "principal water development board or commission" which "is responsible for formulating statewide programs for the conservation, development, and use of the state's water resources."[19] But information is not available to indicate how fully they have performed this assignment. Undoubtedly state activity there in both land and water planning was stimulated by the national government's adoption and prosecution of the 1944 Pick-Sloan plan for the Missouri basin. However, "only a few states have entered into the construction of projects. . . ."[20] Montana's water conservation board is the only state agency that has seized upon the potential opportunities for small water projects—projects of great importance to the stability of this Northern Plains region—and has developed a "sustained program for the construction of irrigation projects and other water facilities."[21]

Before the enactment of the Water Pollution Control Act of 1948 the interest of Congress in water pollution was confined to its effect upon navigation. It forbade the dumping of refuse that would obstruct navigation and the wasting of oil in navigable waters. Enforcement of these restrictions brought the Corps of Engineers into many direct negotiations with local governments.

The new 1948 pollution program gave the U. S. Public Health Service a task which had been a matter for exclusive state concern until that time (with a few exceptions such as the work of the Tennessee Valley Authority). We are witnessing today the beginning of a new pattern of cooperation between the national, state, and local governments and private industry. Delicate questions of jurisdiction have been avoided in the regulatory phases of this new national antipollution effort on interstate streams. Thus the 1948 act requires the head of the department that includes the Public Health Service, after finding a public nuisance which endangers the health of residents in another state, to obtain the consent of the appropriate water-pollution control agency in the nuisance-creating state before he may ask the Attorney General to sue for nuisance abatement.[22] It is too early to know how this relationship will work out, or what other problems of interlevel cooperation will develop out of this new national excursion into water sanitation. The grant-in-aid features of the program are as yet of very modest proportions. Nevertheless there is good reason to expect that the pattern of interlevel cooperative relationships will be as successful as has been true of the other national health grants-in-aid.

Many of the states have facilitated land drainage through permissive provision for local action. This is of some interest to the Bureau of Reclamation's irrigation projects where drainage problems have arisen. The Corps of Engineers is acutely interested in state and local drainage law and administration because the Flood Control Act of 1944 authorized it to expand its local flood control work to include primary drainage canals and nonnavigable tributary channels so as to permit drainage of bottom-lands adjacent to major flood control works. The flood control and navigation functions of the Corps of Engineers have stressed direct national-local relationships. Most of the states leave negotiations and contractual relationships with the Corps either to counties and cities or to special districts. This practice has no doubt expedited the inauguration of construction projects by the Corps. But it has likewise failed to assure that after construction the local agencies will live up to the obligations they assume when projects are built. If the Columbia River states may be taken as illustrations, only one state, Washington, has become a partner to flood control project agreements or has any obligation to supervise local performance (and that is limited to the selected projects in which it invests). Too often annual inspection reports by the army district engineer are ignored, while revetments or dykes, once built, are allowed to erode or are undermined through misuse or failure to maintain them. The state engineers or conservation departments have no authority to intervene nor is it likely that they would readily do so even if endowed with such powers. The State of Washington does have a flood control fund it uses chiefly to help local agencies repair or maintain existing structures, usually on a forty to sixty per cent sharing of cost. Nevertheless the state officer charged with allocation of these moneys depends on the county, city, or local flood control district engineer to supervise the investment of these state funds. He has no engineering staff to perform such duties.

A few years ago Oregon created a special state commission with (*inter alia*) construction, investment, and contractual functions to further the Willamette watershed program.[23] But it has never undertaken these tasks. Instead it has been content to act as a lobby for obtaining more national funds for Willamette river projects and as a booster for advertising their beneficial effects.[24]

Formerly in the regulation of navigation the army dealt almost exclusively with local and private groups affected. It was the municipalities and counties that chiefly built the bridges across navigable streams whose design, location, toll charges, draw span operation, and the like must be approved by the Corps of Engineers. But as the state highway agencies took over more and more bridge building functions and as the army moved up stream for the building of reservoir structures, often involving highway relocation, the state and the Corps have developed many direct administrative relations.

The Flood Control Act of 1944 and the Rivers and Harbors Act of 1945 require consultation with the states during the survey and planning phases of river programs by both the Corps of Engineers and the Bureau of Reclamation.[25] Both agencies must now, during the conduct of their respective river investigations, furnish the states with information developed and give them opportunity for consultation and cooperation in the investigations. After the reports are finished, the governors have ninety days for review and comment. In 1946 Congress made a special requirement that each of these national water development agencies consult also with the state agency in charge of wildlife resources (as well as with the U.S. Fish and Wildlife Service) with a view to forestalling any damage to wildlife resources in their project developments.[26] Doubtless these consultative, informational, and reporting requirements are being meticulously fulfilled. Nevertheless, in the Pacific Northwest at least, there is little evidence that the states have made consequential contributions to these water plans.

The chief agency through which Bureau of Reclamation programs are translated into farming is the irrigation district, first developed by Utah. Each of the seventeen western states now explicitly permits its districts to contract with the Bureau for the repayment of irrigation works built under federal reclamation statutes. The district becomes the nation's agent for enforcing repayment by the individual water user of his share of construction charges and of operation and maintenance costs.

The Bureau operates the reservoirs, canals, laterals, syphons, and pumps until most of the cost assessed the irrigators has been repaid. Even after canals and laterals are transferred to the district, all major reservoirs are retained under Bureau management. Consequently relations between the district and the Bureau are intimate and continuous. State governments generally do not exercise administrative supervision over the districts once they are organized and in business. Thereafter the state enters the picture only to distribute water in accordance with adjudicated rights. For this purpose a system of water masters or water commissioners has grown up. In some states, however, even these officers are only loosely linked to state administrative control.[27]

There are many other manifestations of the administrative intimacy of the national reclamation agency and the local irrigation district. The physical irrigation plant of the district is operated and mantained by the Bureau not only during the ten year "development period" now provided by law but also in most cases for l any years thereafter. Even the districts that do manage their structures look to the Bureau for technical assistance.

While some districts grumble about the delayed transfer of physical operations to the district, there is no district demand that the states should take the Bureau's place.[28] The future prospect resembles the past situation—namely, a prolonged period of direct national control and tutelage of the districts.

An irrigation enterprise requires a complementing system of drainage structures to prevent water-logging of the land and other evils. Consequently the Bureau of Reclamation must frequently deal with local drainage agencies. Unless the irrigation district is also endowed with drainage functions, as in some states, the Bureau encounters many of the same difficulties of local ephemeralism and neglect of drainage structures that have so often dogged the path of the Corps of Engineers.

It has become an increasing practice of the Bureau to utilize the technical skills of the state colleges and universities in the analysis of problems encountered in the planning and operation of its projects. The pattern of special contractual arrangements with the engineering schools, the farm economists, the agronomic specialists, and others set by the Tennessee Valley Authority has recently made great headway in the relations between the Bureau and the state institutions of higher learning in the West. Often when both the state water agency and the Bureau are interested in obtaining special basic data on the topography or hydrology of a particular local watershed they share the cost of map work or of gauge installation. This is in addition to the state's regular cooperative contract, long firmly established, with the U.S. Geological Survey for the collection of water data or for topographic mapping. A state agency may also develop the recreational opportunities created by a Bureau reservoir. Thus, in the Grand Coulee balancing reservoir area where a spectacular recreational byproduct is available, the Bureau and the governor of Washington have recently signed an agreement under which the state will develop and manage this new recreational asset of arid northeast Washington.

These are a few illustrations of the ways in which the meshing of national-local and national-state functions takes place as an inescapable part of the process of managing water resources. There are many others—so devoid of political drama as to be unknown to most citizens—which I cannot discuss here.

But I must briefly notice one byproduct of the functions of the Bureau of Reclamation, the Corps of Engineers, and the TVA which is a matter of special public interest, importance, and controversy. This is the production of hydro-electric energy and its conduct to market load centers via nationally owned transmission lines. Congress has given the Department of the Interior the job of disposing of surplus hydro-electric energy produced not only by certain Bureau-built structures but also by the generating facilities in army-built dams. Despite the revival of the "bus bar" and "falling water" sale policies favored by the private utilities and Herbert Hoover, it is not likely that the Eisenhower Administration will sell or dismantle established regional transmission systems. Nor is the long run force of social pressure and historic tendency on the side of such policies.

The national hydro-electric function has also helped mutiply the rural electric cooperatives, public utility districts, and municipal electric distribution departments. National transmission agencies, such as the TVA, the Bonneville Power Administration, and the Southwest Power Administration, have dealt with these public and quasi-public local entities as directly and intimately as has the Bureau of Reclamation with irrigation districts. They have helped organize cooperatives and local distribution districts and aided in the acquisition or construction of distribution systems. They have advised on engineering, utilization, and other operating problems. They have administered the preference clauses of national statutes in allocating scarce energy to public agencies as against competing private utilities. They have (sometimes) regulated resale distribution rates to prevent the ultimate consumers from carrying the legitimate burdens of tax payers. And they have applied regional rate policies which greatly widen the areal distribution of cheap hydro-electric energy.

In the pursuit of these authorized purposes the use of legal discretion has placed federal administrators squarely in the middle of the economic and ideological conflict over public and cooperative versus private ownership of electric utilities. Hence in the present apotheosis of "private enterprise," administrative discretion has shifted to narrow views of congressional intent. Congressional intent via appropriation acts and committee reports has also become astringent with respect to the preference clause, regional equalization of low-cost energy benefits, and the administrative paternalism recently characterizing national-local public agency relations in the marketing of surplus hydro-electricity. It remains to be seen what effects these changes in national policy will have upon the nexus of national-local relations that grew up after 1933.

Already a partial reversal is noted in the policy under which the national government, in the sale of energy generated in its river structures, has removed control of resale rates of private utility distributors from the jurisdiction of the regulatory authority of the state. The congressional transfer of such resale rate control to the TVA in the area covered by its transmission system, though at first challenged by the State of Alabama, was later explicitly accepted by that state and by Tennessee. But in the Tennessee Valley this acceptance became innocuous as the major private utility systems were bought out by the TVA and by the public and cooperative distributors. In the Pacific Northwest a similar potential clash with state regulatory agencies was avoided until recently by the refusal of the private companies to accept long-term contracts, with resale control included, offered by the Bonneville Power Administration. The recent Eisenhower-McKay twenty-year contracts with the private utility distributors of the Columbia Valley include provisions for federal control of resale rates which are transparent shams.[29] Thus the Bonneville Power Administration program avoids conflict with state regulatory agencies.

This conflict over the hydro-electric policy lies at the base of much of the present agitation for a greater state share in interstate river system planning and the concomitant proposals for river basin planning by interstate compact agencies. Since the canal days, the states with a few exceptions have avoided investing in major river structures. They have been content to let local agencies furnish the fiscal collaboration required for flood control and for navigation. They have let the farmers in the irrigation districts shoulder that part of the cost of reclamation projects not met by the nation and the consumers of electricity.[30] With a few exceptions the states have been content since their transfer of federal grant lands to private promotional companies under the ill-fated Carey Act of 1894 to rely for the larger water development programs either on the national government or on the private initiative of riparian owners in the East and of the prior appropriators in the West.

The present opportunity to push the states into a dominantly negating role in determining water and land management plans and operations exists largely because of the failure of Congress and the executive to put the national administration in order. Congress and the President have shied away from the recommendations of the Hoover Commission report on this matter. They have ignored the "second best" suggestions made by the President's Water Resources Policy Commission and especially its proposals for a more equitable sharing of costs and a more integral process for water development planning under which the states would obtain the kind of participation their present responsibilities warrant. Congress has refused to change its committee system so as to facilitate the adoption of integrated land and water resource policies. The difficulty here is not solely one of a *federal* system: it is equally a reflection of a constitution which so divides responsibility for national policy formulation as to invite irresolution and conflict.

In the most recent moves toward institutionalizing the integrated planning of land and water development by major river basins the states have been given a position of great influence.[31] I refer to the Missouri and Columbia

Basin Interagency Committees. In the case of the committee for the Missouri the basic water plan had already been adopted by Congress after the governors of the region approved the improvised reconciliation of the conflicting Pick and Sloan plans. By the time the committee was constituted the fundamental pattern on the main stream had been fixed.

On the Columbia, however, the situation was not crystallized when its committee was set up in the spring of 1946. Since then the governors have had ample opportunity to contribute their ideas about the proper elements of a comprehensive, multiple purpose program for the Columbia River system. They have been receiving since 1944 the full information which the departments of the Army and Interior have developed on the basis of the work done by the Corps and the Bureau of Reclamation, the Bonneville Power Administration, the U. S. Geological Survey, and other federal agencies in the assembly of information for development projects and system-wide reports. The revised "308" report of the army was launched shortly after the Flood Control Act of 1944 made it mandatory to give the states for their comment full information in process as well as final reports. About the same time Interior began the preparation of its comprehensive Columbia River Basin report. In the autumn of 1948 the army report was ready for review by the states and for discussion by the Columbia River Interagency Committee. The latter had also been kept fully informed of the discussions between Interior and the army to reconcile their somewhat divergent views. When these were harmonized the committee considered the resultant comprehensive river development plan. On March 18, 1949 by formal resolution it indicated its "general concurrence" in the bidepartmental agreement, the gist of which it quoted.[32] This resolution of concurrence was approved unanimously, including all the governors present. Within the next few weeks each of the basin-state governors (in the cases of Wyoming and Utah the state engineers) sent a letter to General Pick, Chief of Engineers, giving his official comments upon the army's "308" review report. Not a single governor objected to the inclusion of Hell's Canyon Dam as one of the chief flood control and power projects in the "main control" plan.[33]

The subsequent repudiation of this committee agreement in 1951 coincided with the announced intention of the Idaho Power Company to build a group of power projects on the Snake River which would irreconcilably conflict with the federal Hell's Canyon project.[34] This *volte face* came in the summer of 1951 as the interagency committee prepared to publish a synopsis of a comprehensive river program for public informational purposes. The new governor of Idaho (Jordan) then announced his unalterable opposition to the Hell's Canyon dam; he was aided and abetted by Governor Langlie of Washington who now objected both to Hell's Canyon and to the proposed navigation-power dams on the lower Snake.[35] When the proposal was made by Governors Jordan and Langlie that the committee throw out Hell's Canyon and Ice Harbor (lower Snake project) it was acquiesced in by all the governors and all the federal field members, except one department alternate, without discussion of its consequences on the rest of the "308" program for preventing floods on the lower Columbia, for meeting the tremendous growth in power demand, or for attaining slack water navigation. It took the subsequent pressure of the Secretary of the Interior and of the President to rally the federal members against the summary excision of the Hell's Canyon project from the comprehensive plan.

This episode illustrates the ability of the state governors negatively to dominate the decisions of federal-state field committees. There is little doubt that most of the federal agency representatives believed that the Hell's Canyon and Ice Harbor projects were essential to the comprehensive program unless and until other projects could be found at comparable economic cost to perform the flood control, power, and navigation services inherent in these two. But each federal agency wanted the political support of the governors for its own programs and would therefore not stand up against them. The departments of Agriculture and Commerce and the Federal Security Agency all were interested in many activities having little or nothing to do with big river projects. The army had by agreement relinquished to the Bureau of Reclamation its claim to constructing Hell's Canyon; its willingness to let Ice Harbor go temporarily was tied to the expectation that other and larger projects such as Libby and the Dalles dams would keep its construction forces busy until a more propitious time for renewed effort on the lower Snake. Even the Department of the Interior, since it was concerned with much more in the State of Idaho than the proposed Hell's Canyon project, was amenable to drastic compromise with Idaho's private utility-minded governor. This has been shown by its subsequent proposal to assure the Idaho Power Company a twenty year monopoly in the transmission of energy from the Hell's Canyon site. The governors unanimously took the position that any project heretofore included in the agreed-upon comprehensive system-wide plan to which any member of the committee objected should be thrown out until there should be complete agreement. This position was accepted by a majority of the federal agency representatives. Thus was the "liberum veto" incorporated into the unwritten constitution of this federal-state regional water planning body!

This recent experience of the Columbia Basin Interagency Committee also bears upon the probable success of suggested federal-state agencies to be created by interstate compact for the planning and operation of water development on the Missouri and the Columbia. There is no doubt that the recent review of experience with interstate compacts in the United States has corrected the former underestimates of this device as a means of dealing with many important interstate matters.[36] It is assuredly better voluntarily to agree on the division of scarce waters between two or more states than to invite the expensive, long drawn out litigation before the Supreme Court which is the alternative. But the increase in the number of interstate compacts for the settlement of state property rights in water does not prove their superiority

over other governmental arrangements for the planning and management of
land and water resource development on interstate river systems.

The recently ratified compact for the upper Colorado basin is the most
hopeful example cited. But this is largely a refinement and extension of the
water allocation functions of the earlier water compacts. Each state member
retains its own control over the waters that are assigned to it.[37]

The compact proposed in August 1950 by the Interstate Commission on
the Delaware (Incodel) for a multiple purpose program to supply water for
the New York-New Jersey-Delaware-eastern Pennsylvania region and to regulate stream flow has been rejected by Pennsylvania.[38] Yet if there is any
important interstate river system for which the interstate compact might seem
a good developmental vehicle it is the Delaware. The major water needs of
the tributary region are municipal and industrial. There are no important flood
dangers, no appreciable hydro-electric development possibilities incompatible
with urban water supply priorities. There is no important federal ownership
of watershed lands. The small area encompassed includes the greatest urban
concentration in the United States, possessed of ample resources to finance,
without national aid, the whole comprehensive river-structure program. Yet
efforts which began in the mid-twenties to weld through the interstate compact
the interests of the four affected states into a common program have thus far
failed. Nor have these efforts included watershed land treatment along with a
river structure program. The newest compact plan for river planning is that
invented by the Council of State Governments for the Missouri basin. Its
essential features will be outlined and evaluated in the final section.

III

EVALUATIONS AND CONCLUSIONS

A sure-footed evaluation of the impact of our federal system upon the
management of land and water will be very difficult until detailed case studies
are available, touching a sufficient sample of states and localities to show more
completely the interlevel governmental process in this area of administration.
Studies of state management of state owned lands are very few, as are studies
of recent state and local adventures in the regulation of privately owned agricultural and forest land. While much has been written about irrigation, flood
control, stream pollution, and government production of hydro-electricity, the
processes of interlevel administration of these and other associated water resource functions have rarely been explored. And the interweaving of private or
group interest demands with public policy decisions on both the administrative
and legislative fronts is even more sketchily documented. Natural resource
functions were not included in the only full-dress, objective investigation of
federal-state-local relationships in a single state that has been made—namely
the University of Minnesota study under William Anderson and Edward
Weidner.

The value judgments and conclusions already implied in this chapter and those presently to be hazarded must largely rest therefore upon fragmentary samples, personal observations, and second-hand experience picked up through many conversations with local, state, and federal officials.

Inadequate as is the written record it is clear enough that some gross private abuses of resources were early recognized by the states and even by their predecessors, the colonies. Regulations to control methods of fishing and hunting appeared before we became a nation. New York's leadership in conservation of land and water resources in the second half of the nineteenth century was far in advance of her sister states and the nation.[39]

Though Major John Wesley Powell was the first public official to grasp fully the problems involved in the use of the grasslands of the Great Plains, it was in Montana some years before the coming of the New Deal that agricultural practices in harmony with the facts of Great Plains nature were first tried out on a community-wide, cooperative basis. Here the local people inaugurated a number of the best land practices, later to be incorporated in the nationwide programs of the "action agencies" of the federal government.[40] It was Montana, also, which set up its own water conservation board to develop, with state funds and gifts and loans from the national government, many small irrigation projects of special value in stabilizing its grassland agriculture. Its work became a model for later national programs, though few states emulated it. These examples of state and local initiative show that in resource conservation there is some basis for Justice Holmes' oft quoted remark about the experimental values to be found in the "insulated chambers" of the states. But it seems equally clear that state experiments were few and that the insulation was often so thick that the good examples failed to be generally copied until they were incorporated into national policy and spread through the forty-eight states by education and financial inducements. The rate and completeness of "cultural diffusion" of the best practices in the management of land and water have been immeasurably increased by national leadership. In that process, moreover, many national improvements upon the limited state and local models have been made.

In the southeastern states where for a hundred and fifty years the philosophy of states' rights has been endemic, state concern for resource conservation, expressed in law and appropriate administrative facilities, has lagged years behind parallel national action. Significant innovations for the better treatment of soils, forests, wildlife, and waters have for the most part come from national government suggestions and have been aided by money, technical assistance, facilities, and example.[41]

In the realm of water resources the need for large amounts of capital for development and control has been a special factor working for state and local dependence upon national action.[42] Despite the present din about the danger of national bankruptcy if federal funds continue to be so used, this situation is not likely to be basically altered. It is true that much has been done by the central government that could and should have been paid for in larger measure by local and private beneficiaries. This applies precisely to those aspects of water management (flood control, navigation, and the non-power aspects of irrigation) about which the new states' righters of north and south, east and west are strangely silent.

A sober estimate of the role of the states in the management of land and water resources recognizes that their greatest prospective opportunity lies in their exercise of police, taxing, and educational powers to improve private and local resource use. It is the way water is used, polluted, or wasted, the manner in which private owners of timber land, range pastures, and arable farm land use the resource of which they are social trustees, that will primarily tell the story of the efficacy of the states in the management of these resources. By properly shaping their tax systems, by expanding rural land zoning and use regulations, and by their laws governing tenant-owner relations they can provide new incentives to private owners which may hasten the day when these resources are managed with greatest social efficiency.

The states' place in the federal system will be also measured by their policies for improving the habitat for game and fish, for regulating hunting and fishing to balance yield with harvest, for preserving to the public the great outdoor recreational opportunities afforded by many water development projects, and for meeting these social needs in the design and handling of their publicly owned land resources. These state functions are essential to the highest resource use in the United States. Without their exercise in a manner consistent with national needs and national policy, conservation goals will not be reached. There is no doubt also that the constant interchange of information and ideas on these subjects between national, state, and local agencies is essential. Neither can it be questioned that at many points the complementary programs of national, state, local, and private agencies must be made to dovetail if maximum utility is to be attained.

Yet with rare exceptions the individual states or local combinations of states ought not to supersede the national government as builders of the expensive river, watershed, and related projects on interstate river basins or as the managers of the vast "wild land" interstate watersheds that collect the precipitation which keeps our western streams alive. In that vast semi-arid region where water is the key to human occupancy, the mountain and high-elevation lands, mostly in national ownership, act as the collecting basins for the precipitation which produces eighty per cent of the stream flow for all our western rivers. These lands must remain in national ownership and control to assure attention to interstate regional interests through conservation management. And state lands which often lie in small tracts scattered through this national estate must be managed in harmony with these standards, behind which most of them now lamentably lag. Far from adopting a policy of transferring national forest and range lands to the states, as some propose, the states ought either to assume their responsibility by placing their own wild lands on a sustained yield basis or turn them back to the national government for such management. Even the federal government, however, will not solve the range land problem until it breaks the undue influence of the national livestock associations and their subsidiary state organizations upon the grazing fee system (to which appropriations are tied) and upon the management policies of the national grazing districts.

The evidence that maximum utilization of the nation's water calls for river system, multiple-use development is too convincing to permit a reversion either to project-by-project planning or to plans on a state-by-state basis. Major drainage areas must be encompassed within unified plans, and river systems must be planned, scheduled, built, and managed as unities to obtain the best economic and social return. Moreover, the adoption and continued expansion of national policies by which some of the multiple uses are not required to reimburse their costs to the national treasury (flood control, fisheries protection, recreation, pollution control, and part of irrigation) make either the states or private enterprise unsuitable instruments to shoulder the primary responsibility for these tasks. Nor should we forget that the national legal jurisdiction over water power site development makes any general alienation of these to the states, localities, or private parties a dubious "give away" of the national heritage wherever hydro-electric development has significant regional development values. As the Water Resources Policy Commission has shown, only national development can assure in this situation maximum development and consumer use. Here river development policies must go hand-in-hand with transmission and rate policies which transcend local, state, or narrow private interests.

The complementary function of watershed management as it relates to the handling of timber, grass, and soil must remain a joint national-state enterprise so long as (1) title to so large a portion of the nonarable, rough, timbered, or range land remains in national ownership and (2) the states alone may legally determine the regulation of privately owned agricultural and other types of land.

That the states should also play a regularized consultative role in the planning of river basins is now generally conceded and is partly established by national law and administrative practice. This can be improved and a more genuine partnership established provided the states equip themselves to play a constructive role. The states should also follow Montana's example by helping local communities to plan, finance, and manage small irrigation or drainage projects looking toward the stabilization of agricultural communities and the fullest long run use of every acre of good agricultural land.

Direct national-local collaboration in such programs as irrigation, navigation, flood control, and drainage is essential. The states are in a legal position to increase the returns from that collaboration if they will wisely exercise their potential functions. If the states had not so generally and hastily jettisoned their resource planning agencies the moment national funds were withdrawn when the National Resources Planning Board was killed, they might have developed information, plans, and state-local advisory relationships of great benefit to many districts and towns concerned with local water projects. In this way they might have guided more constructively the habitual local pressure-congressional intervention-acquiescing set of relationships that so often determines which local water projects shall be built by the Corps of Engineers and the Bureau of Reclamation. And they might also have provided greater assurance of local responsibility for the effective maintenance and use of these projects once the national treasure has been invested in them.

Looking toward a future of markedly increased population pressure, the time may come when the present constitutional division of powers between the states and the nation over land and water may require either the transfer of legal authority over the use of these resources from the states to the nation or the intervention and application of more stringent control devices for bridging the federal gap in the interest of urgent national need. Burdened as we have been with farm surpluses it is difficult to conjure up a time when the highest productivity of all our land will be required. Yet we have been told that by 1975 our population requirements will call for the equivalent of one hundred million new acres of land.[43] At that or some more distant time we may have either to restore the original Soil Conservation Service policies for bringing private land owners to complete farm plans for all their acres or find some other kind of sanction for attaining the goals implicit in those policies. We may also need drastically to revise the present legal systems by which the states allocate water rights. These have had no necessary correlation with the best use of water.

The fact should now be faced that our prospective population-income requirements and our totally new position in global affairs necessitate that the national government in the future take increasing responsibility for seeing that our physical resource base of land, water, and minerals is so developed and used as best to meet our social requirements. The current recrudescence of states' rightism in its application to such resource policy responsibilities is a sad anachronism. The common problems of development and management cannot be bounded by state lines. There must be a framework of national policy, just as there must be continued national financial investment and grants-in-aid, to meet the necessary goals of national policy. A federal system at best throws many legal obstacles in the way of this necessity. But in the United States the experiences of the last half century on *many* fronts show a large measure of success in welding the behavior of all levels of government, as well as much private "sovereignty," into consistently constructive programs of land and water management without undue administrative or social friction. Clearly, the outlook at present does not call for relinquishment of either nation-owned resources *or* national policy responsibility to the states.

But what of the Council of State Governments' recent suggestion for a regional pseudo-polity, a *via media* between state and national sovereignty over the Missouri and perhaps other river basins?[44] Under this plan a new genus of interstate compact commission, with the nation as a member, would become the sole official basin-wide land and water planning agency. It alone would formulate the basin policies for congressional authorization; it would propose the projects for construction; it would adopt the reservoir operating policies to govern the management of these river structures. The nation would still underwrite or finance, build, and operate the major river and watershed improvements through existing national administrative organizations. No affirmative decisions could be taken without the agreement of the compact commission's national representatives and those of a majority of the states. Stated from the reverse view, either the national government or a majority of the states could prevent any affirmative decision or action.

For a comparison of national and state influence on this proposed commission, as related to the share of capital investments required of each for basin-wide development, the estimates of the Missouri River Basin Interagency Committee for a long-range program are illuminating. The 1952 report of that committee allocated to the national government approximately eleven and a quarter billion dollars, to the states about seven million (or six one-hundredths of one per cent), and to the local flood control and watershed conservancy districts slightly less than four hundred million.[45] (Since each local district can customarily veto any local flood or watershed project in whose costs it shares, it can stop any such project not to its liking.)

Implicit in the relinquishment by the nation to the proposed commission of jurisdiction over resource programs heretofore recognized as within national competence is the notion of a kind of alien status for the national government in whose decisions Senators, Representatives, and citizens from the ten Missouri states are evidently presumed to have no appreciable influence. As a matter of fact, river basin planning by national agencies and by Congress is already hypersensitive to local desires and pressures so that programs are often unduly deflected from integrating and economic objectives. Under the existing situation, moreover, there is some recognition of the differences in importance and political power of social interests within the basin, for congressional representation in the House bears a rough relation to the number of people in each state. The proposed Missouri compact would reduce that equitable influence because it embraces the "equal sovereignty" principle regardless of the fact that there are and will remain great variations in population of the several states whose welfare is affected by the recommended river basin programs.

The composition of an interstate compact agency is bound to push the process of policy formulation away from regional goals and toward state and local particularism. Unlike the political processes within the states where the governor and some other statewide elected officers, from the manner of their selection, feel political obligations which pull them toward statewide integrating adjustment of interests, no state member of an interstate compact commission will feel a region-wide loyalty buttressed by a politically organized regional constituency. If compromise is reached it will tend to maximize the particularistic interests at the expense both of regional balance and of the national interest. The national government, still footing most of the bill for capital investment, will become the fiscal victim of particularistic pertinacity. Even though the unanimity rule customary in the compact device is modified under the proposed Missouri Basin scheme, a heavy premium still attaches to the obstructionist attitude.

In the process of bargaining the psychology stimulated by the compact system will greatly heighten the impetus to press to the utmost the case of special or local interests. Since the bargainers are acting as ambassadors for their respective states, they can use the cloak of state patriotism (perhaps unconsciously) with greater freedom from criticism than in comparable intrastate conflicts. What in the latter situation would readily be recognized by the voters and organs of opinion as clashes of narrow selfish or parochial interests becomes suffused with emotions of sovereign honor which sanction a protective tenderness by a state's official spokesman toward Lilliputian or sinister purposes.

Moreover, should the compact be found deficient in any of its provisions, the rule of state unanimity would again exercise its customary obstructive influence in the process of amendment. It would be seized upon as a bargaining weapon with which to exact the highest possible price.

That such difficulties are not fanciful is well illustrated by the history of state attempts in New England to deal with water resources through compacts, which Professor William Leuchtenburg has exhaustively studied. His recent book traces the efforts during the past quarter century to manage the Connecticut River. The failure to solve acute flood and pollution problems or to provide for the joint use of flood reservoirs for power, recreation, or pollution abatement he ascribes to two main causes: (1) the conflicting responsibilities of the national water resource agencies and the hostility of the Corps of Engineers toward multiple-purpose development and (2) the "inadequacy of state action and the limitations of the compact device."[46]

Leuchtenburg's general evaluation of this experience challenges the compact device in the following conclusion:

> The concern to have the states rather than the federal government control water resources development, the impetus to the movement for interstate compacts came from forces—private utilities opposed to public power sites, industries opposed to effective pollution abatement programs, farm groups opposed to the flooding of arable land—which believed that the states, or a combination of states, would be less successful than the federal government in halting the opposition to these private interests. The interstate compact was not a device chosen by state governments which on their own initiative were developing the resources of the Connecticut Valley, but was hit upon as a means to prevent such development by the federal government. Insofar as state governments actively sought interstate cooperation, it was because powerful economic interests within the state cut across state lines. . . .

The main problem in developing a river valley is the resolution of conflicts between different water users. Shall farm land be flooded to permit the generation of power? Shall a reservoir be used for power or recreation? Shall a river be used as a sewer for industrial wastes or for fishing and swimming? These issues are difficult to resolve at best; the inadequacy of the interstate compact is that while ostensibly it seeks to resolve such issues, it actually tends to exacerbate them, either by postponing a decision, or by working out a temporary makeshift at the expense of sound resource development.[47]

The American federal system, in which state boundaries are practically unalterable and both state and national powers highly developed, does not lend itself to the creation of a genuine intermediate regional polity. The interstate compact contrivances thus far suggested for meeting the need for regional public policy formulation and administration of land and water resources appear to be cumbersome, jerry-built structures lacking in region-wide political responsibility, parasitic on national finance, and negative or unduly dilatory in decision-making. In the absence of a *bona fide* regional polity, our best hope for formulating and implementing resource policies consistently with both regional and national needs is through the perfection of the collaborative institutions of nation-state-locality already functioning or incipiently developed, and the improvement of the structures and performance of the national and state executive and legislative systems.

FOOTNOTES TO CHAPTER 17

1. "Water Resources Law," Vol. 3 of the *Report of the President's Water Resources Policy Commission,* Washington, U.S. Government Printing Office, 1950, pp. 15–16.

2. 313 U.S. 525.

3. Arizona v. California, 298 U. S. 558 (1936).

4. U.S. v. Rio Grande Irrigation Co., 174 U.S. 690, 703 (1899). Cited in "Water Resources Law," *op. cit.,* p. 32.

5. California Oregon Power Co. v. Beaver Portland Cement Co., 295 U.S. 142, 163 (1935).

6. Sec. 8, 32 Stat. 396, 43 USC. 383.

7. "Water Resources Law," *op. cit.,* pp. 46–47.

8. *Ibid.,* pp. 159–160.

9. For example the Missouri Basin Survey Commission reports (*Missouri: Land and Water,* Washington, U.S. Government Printing Office, 1952, pp. 130–131) that Kansas City cannot be adequately protected from the damage wrought by recurring floods like that of 1951 by means of reservoirs and levees alone. There are simply not enough reservoir sites on the contributing watersheds, and to raise levees, bridges, etc. to the required height would be prohibitively costly.

10. Gallatin's report of 1806 made at Jefferson's instance was the first national transportation plan and was notable for its comprehensive character. A second national plan of canals, water-way improvements, and turnpikes was produced by the Board of Engineers of the Army, created in 1824. It was abolished in Jack-

son's regime. See Clifford J. Hynning, *State Conservation of Resources,* Washington, National Resources Committee, 1939, pp. 48–50.

11. "Water Resources Law," *op. cit.,* pp. 75–76.

12. The panic of 1837 caught eighteen states with a total public debt of sixty million dollars for canals "little of which was ultimately recoverable." Hynning, *op. cit.,* p. 47.

13. See Arthur D. Frank, *The Development of the Federal Program of Flood Control on the Mississippi River,* New York, Columbia University Press, 1930, pp. 27 ff.

14. The detailed story for the Yazoo-Mississippi delta country after 1819 has been recently told by Robert W. Harrison in his *Levee Districts and Levee Building in Mississippi,* Mississippi Agricultural Experiment Station, Oct. 1951.

15. Frank, *op. cit.,* chap. 9, gives a full account of this nationalizing effort.

16. In addition to California, this list includes Connecticut, Maine, Massachusetts, Rhode Island, New Jersey, New Hampshire, Vermont, Ohio, Indiana, Michigan, Washington, Iowa, New York, and Pennsylvania. The other states rely chiefly on local initiative and financial responsibility. This seems most uniformly the case in flood control. Because a number of the states have no fixed legislative policy, but deal with each problem that arises by special legislative act, it is impossible on the basis of the scant information available accurately to tell what their practices have been. For information on these matters reliance has been placed chiefly on a summary of state legal policies prepared a short time ago by the U.S. Corps of Engineers for internal use, the incidental information secreted in the seven monographs on resource management in Kentucky, Tennessee, Mississippi, Alabama, South Carolina, Florida, and North Carolina, prepared by the staffs of the state universities in those states in cooperation with the TVA, and on information collected personally in the Pacific Northwest.

17. Vincent Ostrom, "State Administration of Natural Resources in the West," *American Political Science Review,* Vol. 47 (June 1953), pp. 483–84.

18. William E. Leuchtenburg, *Flood Control Politics: The Connecticut River Valley, 1927–1950,* Cambridge, Harvard University Press, 1953, chap. 2.

19. *Missouri: Land and Water,* Report of the Missouri Basin Survey Commission, 1953, p. 83.

20. *Ibid.,* p. 187.

21. The Water Conservation Board's small projects now serve a total of 385,000 acres. This record has been made possible by loans and grants from the national government (which has defrayed slightly more than two thirds of capital costs) and by technical assistance from the federal agencies. *Ibid.,* pp. 187–189.

22. "Water Resources Law," *op. cit.,* p. 341.

23. Chap. 110, Oregon Laws of 1939, Sections 1 and 4, pp. 253 ff.

24. See Ostrom, *op. cit.,* p. 484, for a quotation to this effect from one of the Commission's bulletins.

25. 58 Stat. 887 and 888, and 59 Stat. 10.

26. Par. 2, 60 Stat. 1080, 17 USC, 662.

27. In Wyoming the state's water distribution agents, called water commissioners, are the political appointees of the county boards. The legislature has refused to listen to the repeated complaint of the state engineer that he cannot control their actions unless they are responsible to him. In Idaho associations of districts or com-

panies annually elect a water master, whom the state engineer then deputizes as his representative if he can make bond.

28. However, Secretary McKay is reported to have told the western governors at their regional conference at Albuquerque in 1953 that he favored the transfer of federal irrigation projects to the states when reimbursement is complete. Portland *Oregonian*, Nov. 3, 1953, p. 6.

29. In the contracts recently signed with four major private utilities the resale rate control provisions (which are identical) give the Administrator of the BPA the right, in case he is supplying the firm power requirements of the company, to negotiate with the company for rate changes if he determines that its rates are not reasonable or are discriminatory. If no agreement is reached he may cancel the contract *"on four years' notice."* But the company, on receipt of cancellation notice, may then "have the action of the Administrator reviewed by the U.S. District Court" . . . to "determine if such rates and charges are in fact unreasonable and discriminatory." Even if the federal court would accept jurisdiction, which is doubtful, these stipulations afford virtual freedom from resale rate control.

30. There are a few conservancy or improvement districts, notably those provided for in New Mexico and in Colorado, under which the urban beneficiaries and the owners of non-irrigated land are taxed to help in a repayment obligation. Nebraska, South Dakota, and North Dakota laws also permit the creation of conservancy districts. See "Water Resources Law," *op. cit.*, pp. 172–174.

31. The states were not, however, given official recognition when Congress ordered the Tennessee Valley Authority to prepare and present to it a system-wide plan for the development and control of the Tennessee. Nor did that agency in practice consult the states about the policy issues relating to the flood control and power programs. Almost the only aspect of its navigation program about which state advice and cooperation were sought was in TVA's intervention in the grain rate case, brought in 1951 by three barge lines, against 131 railroads whose rate policies handicapped the development of the river traffic on the Tennessee. In this matter TVA made the analysis of the facts and issues and then sought and obtained intervention of five states plus some eighteen private intervenors. In its earlier freight rate studies and rate proposals, aimed at discriminatory railway rates which impeded the growth of river traffic and regional economic development, the states evinced little official interest. These facts and conclusions are contained in a very able study of the "Relations between the TVA and the States" by Elliott P. Roberts, who has kindly permitted me to see his manuscript.

32. See the letter of March 28, 1949 from the Chairman of the CBIAC to Chairman H. H. McCoy of the Federal Inter-Agency River Basin Committee.

33. It is true that Governor Robins of Idaho expressed the opinion that "Scriver Creek and Garden Valley units of the Mountain Home project" proposed by the Bureau of Reclamation "should precede construction of the proposed Hell's Canyon project because the irrigation and power features of the Mountain Home project are integrated in a manner required for the orderly development of reclamation in Idaho." He and the other up-stream governors also staked out a number of extravagant claims for the use of power revenues not only for ultimate federal reclamation subsidization but for state prosecuted projects also. Governor Langlie of Washington, in giving his general approval to the main control plan, made no criticism of Hell's Canyon or any of the lower Snake River dams. His interest appeared to center on entering a claim for turning over the federal projects, when amortized, to the states so that they might share in the "unencumbered profits from the sales of electric energy produced within the Columbia Basin area. . . ." As spokesman for a

down-stream, urban state, he entered a mild objection to the idea of using hydro-electricity too completely as a milch cow for irrigation. Governor Douglas McKay's brief letter took no exception to any part of the plan and closed: "I wish to commend the Corps of Engineers on an excellent report, and to *heartily endorse the project.*" (Italics mine) House Document No. 531, 81st Congress 2nd Sess. Vol. I, pp. xv–xxvii.

34. The Federal Power Commission representative insists that there was no repudiation because the "general concurrence" was not a commitment to any particular project. Such a construction renders the "concurrence" meaningless unless subsequent modifications of projects would harmonize with the basic multipurposes for the whole program.

35. The lower Snake dams are opposed by the Columbia River fishing industry, a force to which the governors of both Washington and Oregon are sensitive.

36. Frederick L. Zimmermann and Mitchell Wendell, *The Interstate Compact since 1925,* Chicago, Council of State Governments, 1951.

37. Jean S. Breitenstein, in *State Government,* Vol. 22, pp. 214 ff. It should be noted that this agreement undoubtedly owes its perfection to the crisis confronting the upper Colorado river basin growing out of the report of the Bureau of Reclamation in 1946 which showed that there was an insufficient supply of water to build all the projects that had been inventoried. The Secretary of the Interior and the Director of the Bureau of the Budget issued instructions that no new "major projects dependent upon the Colorado would be approved for federal construction until the basin states had made an apportionment among themselves."

38. The Pennsylvania criticisms of the proposed compact illuminate some of the difficulties of this mode of river planning. See *Report of Pennsylvania Water Resources Committee,* Feb. 1953, and *Delaware River Basin Report,* Pennsylvania Water Resources Committee Engineer's Study Committee, Jan. 1953.

39. See Hynning, *op. cit.,* p. 29.

40. Joseph Kinsey Howard, *Montana High, Wide and Handsome,* New Häven, Yale University Press, 1953, chap. 26.

41. See the following monographs for incidental information confirming this judgment: Paul W. Wager and Donald B. Hayman, *Resource Management in North Carolina,* Chapel Hill, University of North Carolina, 1947; Jos. M. Ray and Lillian Worley, *Alabama's Heritage,* University, University of Alabama, 1947; Vera Briscoe, James W. Martin, and J. E. Reeves, *Safeguarding Kentucky's Natural Resources,* Lexington, University of Kentucky, 1948; Robt. B. Highsaw, *Mississippi's Wealth,* University, University of Mississippi, 1947; Christian T. Larsen, *South Carolina's Natural Resources,* Columbia, University of South Carolina Press, 1947; Lee S. Greene, Virginia Brown, Evan W. Iverson, *Rescued Earth,* Knoxville, University of Tennessee Press, 1948; Hubert Marshall and Robt. J. Young, *Public Administration of Florida's Natural Resources,* Public Administration Clearing Service, Gainesville, University of Florida, 1953.

42. In the heated discussion of the utility of river valley "authorities" few have noticed that South Carolina and Texas have created these ill-named agencies for some minor watersheds (the Santee Cooper in the former and the Brazos and Colorado in the latter). But in both cases the initial capital for these state water developments came from federal sources. See Larsen, *op. cit.,* pp. 165 ff., and C. P. Patterson, S. B. McAllister, and G. S. Hester: *State and Local Government in Texas,* New York, Macmillan, 1940, pp. 397–405.

43. *Report of the President's Water Resources Policy Commission,* Vol. 1, p. 158.

44. Revised Draft, Missouri River Basin Compact, Prepared for the Missouri River States Committee by the Council of State Governments, Jan. 1953.

45. Summarized from the tables in the Oct., 1953 Report of the Missouri Basin Interagency Committee, entitled: *Program for Land and Water Development of the Missouri River Basin.*

46. William E. Leuchtenburg, *op. cit.,* pp. 250 ff. After much federal pressure an interstate pollution control compact for New England was adopted in 1946 but Leuchtenburg notes that headway made by the compact commission and the states has been exceedingly slow. Exhibit "E," Minutes of the eighth meeting, New England-New York Inter-Agency Committee, May 8, 1952.

47. Leuchtenburg, *op. cit.,* pp. 250–253.

18

Patterns of Trade Regulation in a Federal System

By Milton Handler

I

Probably no field better exemplifies the pragmatic nature of the adjustments necessary in a federal system than the regulation of industry by the states and the nation. To paraphrase Holmes, the life of federal systems has not been logic; it has been experience. No single unifying principle comprehends the distribution of power among the state and national governments. There is no consistent, uniform, or logical pattern. The division of responsibility varies with the business regulated; in some fields it is the national government, in others it is the states which have assumed the primary role.

While both the nation and the states derive their authority from the Constitution, the boundaries delineating their respective spheres of action are elastic and ever-changing. The Constitution confers upon the Congress the power to regulate commerce among the several states and with foreign nations. There is reserved to the states the control of intrastate economic activities. The tenuous distinction between intrastate and interstate commerce, however, does not disclose the true line of demarcation between state and federal action. Intrastate activities which affect commerce among the states may be federally regulated. In the absence of conflicting federal legislation, the states may control local phases of interstate commerce in those respects in which national uniformity is not required, provided the free flow of commerce from state to state is not substantially impeded or unduly burdened and there is no discrimination against such commerce. Even where the same activity is the subject of federal control, concurrent state regulation is normally permissible if there is no plain conflict between the two enactments. Federal law in such circumstances is, of course, supreme and Congress can oust the states or relinquish to them some of its own authority over interstate commerce. Congress thus can deeply penetrate the reserved precincts of state authority; it can surrender vast power to the states by express delegation or through inaction; the dual power can be concatenated into a pervasive plan of regulation by concurrent and cooperative action; the two systems of regulation may coexist without coordination or integration; there may be a partial exercise of power by either federal or state governments or by both. The combinations and permutations are manifold. The important point is that current constitutional interpretation permits of viable accommodations of the dual authority of state and nation over industry.

Such accommodations were not always possible. There have been periods in our constitutional history when interstate commerce was narrowly conceived in terms of the physical movement of goods across state lines; when a sharp dichotomy was drawn between manufacture and sale; when state regulation of interstate activities was rarely tolerated; when the conflicting claims of state and nation were not wisely reconciled by an appraisal and adjustment of competing state and national interests. Happily, as Mr. Justice Rutledge has pointed out, "the history of the commerce clause has been one of very considerable judicial oscillation and the present judicial outlook tends toward the removal rather than the creation of constitutional barriers to effective federal or state action."[1] The fluctuations in constitutional theory, however, are mirrored in the assumption of duties by the states and the nation, and the differing contours of various regulations can be accounted for by the differences in their vintage. The element of time is thus a further dimension of the constitutional division of authority.

II

The erection of constitutional fences around intrastate and interstate commerce can manifestly be a serious impediment to effective regulation. The old dispensation tended to create a no man's land beyond the practical reach of either the states or the nation. The exclusion of manufacture or production from federal control destroyed the efficacy of national regulation. The theoretical possession of power by the states in the aggregate was of no avail to a single state acting alone. Cooperation by all the states was practically unattainable. Any state by offering asylum to those seeking to avoid regulation could frustrate the efforts of its sister states. Similarly, the exclusion of the states from the regulation of interstate commerce resulted in a practical immunity from all control, since Congress could not feasibly provide legislative solutions for the manifold local problems arising in a country of our magnitude. The new dispensation with its greater judicial tolerance of both state and federal action merely creates a favorable legal climate within which both governments can function; it does not of course guarantee effective exercise of power by either state or nation, alone or in combination. The states can only act within their territorial borders. Successful regulation will frequently require wholehearted cooperation from other states or the federal government. Despite the breadth of the federal regulatory power under the modern conception of what is interstate commerce or affects it, there still remain important areas of economic activity which can only be regulated by the states. Inaction by either government will therefore preclude complete coverage. But successful regulation presupposes more than a full exertion of power by both governments; cooperation must extend to the realm of administration as well as legislation. Laws which are not vigorously enforced and wisely administered are only precatory in their effects.

There being no central, logical principle which determines whether the obligation to regulate devolves upon the states or the nation, or how those obligations shall be discharged, we must turn to the pages of history for the explanation of the diverse patterns of control and administration.

III

The issuance of patents and copyrights is an exclusive function of the federal government. The right to grant such monopolies is specifically vested in the Congress by the Constitution, and Congress has never shared their judicial protection with the states. The federal courts have sole jurisdiction over patent and copyright controversies. Trademarks, on the other hand, are concurrently protected by the states and the nation. A suit for the infringement of a federally registered trademark may be brought either in the state or federal courts. The substantive law of trademarks is essentially the product of judicial decision rather than legislation and both state and federal courts have shared in its development. The advantages of federal registration are available only to marks used in interstate commerce. State registry laws are primarily designed for marks which are used locally; they generally permit the concurrent registration of marks already on the federal register. Since rights in a trademark are based upon use and not registration, since most branded merchandise is advertised and marketed nationally, and finally since the courts afford protection to unregistered marks, state legislation is of minor significance and is largely unnecessary.

For one hundred and fifty years Congress had never undertaken to regulate the important business of insurance despite the national character of its operations. This task thus fell to the states. As early as 1851 the states commenced the regulation of insurance with the acquiescence of the federal government. The constitutionality of state regulation was repeatedly challenged as an infringement of the commerce clause. In 1869 the Supreme Court refused to invalidate a Virginia statute requiring foreign insurance companies to obtain a license as a prerequisite to doing business in that state.[2] Holding that insurance was not commerce, the Court sustained the state licensing law. Under the shelter of that ruling, consistently followed by the courts for seventy-five years, the states established elaborate machinery for the administrative supervision and control of the insurance business. In 1944 the constitutional foundation of these comprehensive state codes was undermined by the decision of the

Supreme Court in *United States* v. *South-Eastern Underwriters Asso.*,[3] holding insurance subject to the federal antitrust laws. To fill the vacuum thus created, Congress immediately passed the McCarran Act[4] in which it declared that the continued regulation and taxation of this business by the states was in the public interest, that insurance should continue to be subject to such laws, and that the application of the antitrust laws should be suspended for a period of approximately three years, after which they should apply only to the extent that the insurance business is not regulated by state law.

Here then is a national business almost exclusively controlled by the states. That the federal government could, if it desired, occupy this field and that its own regulations would be supreme, is indisputable. The federal antitrust laws remain applicable to boycotts, coercion, and intimidation. The states initially were more alert to the need of remedial legislation than the nation. Spurred by a favorable construction of the Constitution and by federal inaction, they expanded their controls beyond the theoretically permissible limits of state action. Congress now has validated their trespass by relinquishing to them a substantial part of its own constitutional authority. At any time the power so granted may be withdrawn or conditioned upon the imposition of standards or regulations formulated by Congress.

It is plain that not logic but purely practical considerations account for this alignment of functions. The states having occupied the field for so many years without federal intrusion, it would be quite infeasible, without serious dislocation, for the central government to supersede the states entirely. However, the McCarran Act could be more explicit in the standards which the states are to observe, and might provide for some form of federal supervision in the administration by the states of federally prescribed standards. There should be a continuing interest in the national government in the regulation by the states of an industry of national proportions. A more effective scheme of cooperation could be devised with the primary responsibility still devolving upon the states.

What has been done with insurance could be repeated in the case of other industries if Congress so willed. But it does not follow that this pattern of regulation could be successfully utilized in other fields in which the conditions are not parallel. During the many years of federal noninterference, the states developed vast experience and valuable traditions in regulating this complex and highly specialized business. The industrialized and populous states have been able to impose their standards upon the out-of-state companies which were anxious to tap their rich markets. The sphere of influence of such states is thus not narrowly confined to their own territorial limits. Under these circumstances, state regulation has enjoyed a higher degree of success than is normally possible.

At almost the opposite end of the spectrum is the regulation of railroad transportation. Here too the states responded to the need before the federal government. By 1885 railroad commissions had been created by twenty-five states and twenty-eight states had enacted some form of regulatory legislation.

The action of any state was necessarily confined to the operations of carriers within its own boundaries. There was no coordination or cooperation among the states. State enactments were constitutionally inoperative to the interstate aspects of railroad transportation. In 1887 Congress entered the field with the enactment of the Interstate Commerce Act. In order to make effective its regulation of interstate transportation, it became necessary for Congress to control local transportation affecting commerce among the states. While there has thus been a constant attrition of state regulation, and the role of the federal government has been dominant, the regulation of transportation is still a concurrent function of both governments.

IV

Antitrust provides a still different story. The states again acted first. It was inevitable that the transformation in the nineteenth century of an agricultural into an industrial economy would have its initial impact upon the states. It was also inevitable that the regulation of trade before the nation became a single market should have been the primary concern of the states. With the industrial and marketing revolution that followed the Civil War, the states lost their significance as economic entities. Local regulations attuned to the needs of petty trade could not cope with the sprawling affairs of big business which spilled over state lines. The hostility of any one state to monopoly could be circumvented by removal to the more favorable environment of another state. After being attacked in Ohio, Standard Oil created a holding company in New Jersey. Unlike the insurance field, the competition among the states lay in depressing and not elevating standards. Federal action became imperative. The Sherman Law was accordingly enacted in 1890. Five years later the Supreme Court, by its decision in the *Knight* case,[5] holding the statute inapplicable to the monopolization of manufacture, returned the monopoly problem to the states which had already demonstrated their inability to cope with it. Fortunately, this solecism in constitutional interpretation was subsequently corrected. Without such correction, monopoly would go unregulated and the freedoms which the Sherman Law was intended to safeguard would be unattainable. Today, under the modern concept of commerce, the Sherman Act extends to any economic activity, however local, whose effect is to stifle or restrain commerce among the states. The statute in recent years has been invoked against combinations in such diverse lines as real estate brokerage, sugar beet production, practice of medicine, taxicab transportation, insurance, gasoline filling stations, gathering and dissemination of news, investment banking, and real estate mortgage loans and building construction.

There has been, however, no express ouster of the states from the control of local monopolies. Broad as is the scope of the federal law, there are still activities which are beyond its reach, but their economic significance dwindles as the frontiers of federal authority are pushed forward. Conflict in the administration of state and federal law and the delicate constitutional adjustments which are necessary where there is a concurrent exercise of power have largely been avoided by state inaction. The state antimonopoly laws are essentially dead letters, enforced rarely and at best sporadically.

In theory, there is full coverage by both state and federal law. Administration is concurrent, not cooperative. The division of power follows the erratic line separating purely intrastate from activities in or affecting interstate commerce. In practice, the coverage is far from complete. A quarter of a century ago, it was commonly believed that the aims of antitrust were unattainable because the statute was unenforceable. The complaint today is that enforcement is too vigorous and that the restraints of antitrust upon business are too severe. There has been singular success in attacking restrictive arrangements among trade groups or confederations. Less progress, however, has been made in curbing the omnipresent tendency toward industrial concentration. Perhaps the recent amendments to section 7 of the Clayton Act may reverse the trend.

Neither the successes nor failures of antitrust, however, are attributable to the constitutional distribution of power. Some sectors of the economy enjoy a practical immunity through failure of enforcement which in turn stems from inadequacies of manpower and appropriations. It is by no means clear that the country favors a stringent policy curbing concentration or that it would support a program of drastic disintegration. Turning to the state level, an almost total absence of enforcement has encouraged restrictive arrangements in purely local trades. This, however, is no longer a serious problem in view of the constant expansion of federal authority and the almost exclusive reliance of the country on federal antitrust enforcement. Here it is the states which through inaction have in effect ceded part of their power to the central government. Few important business activities are immune from federal antitrust attack. Hence, to attain reasonably full coverage, it is enough to strengthen the arm of the federal enforcing officials rather than to resuscitate the waning powers of the states which they never exercised anyway. But in the regulation of unfair competition, the jurisdiction of the Federal Trade Commission is so much more limited that there is ample room as well as a direct need for concurrent and cooperative state action.

In one branch of antitrust the primacy of state law has been acknowledged by the federal government. The Sherman Act condemns vertical price-fixing. Most states have not only legalized resale price maintenance agreements but require nonsignatories to observe the prices stipulated in contracts made with others. As state fair trade legislation by itself could not apply to interstate transactions, it was doomed to futility until Congress, first in the Miller-Tydings Act,[6] and again recently in the McGuire Act,[7] gave controlling effect to state law. For years the advocates of resale price maintenance sought statutory change in the federal law without success. The state legislatures were more responsive to their entreaties and it did not take long for the nation to be blanketed by these separate state enactments. The stage was thus set for renewed pressure upon the Congress, not to alter the federal law as such but to permit state law to govern interstate transactions. The principal contribution of the states, thus, has been in relaxing the requirements of antitrust, not merely within the boundaries of their own authority but in the national sphere as well. Ironically, this has occurred during the period of heightened federal antitrust enforcement. Perhaps some day the pattern of state-federal cooperation, which is now constitutionally secure, will be employed to further the aims of the antitrust laws upon which our national policy of trade regulation so dominantly rests.

V

The incorporation of companies has been left almost entirely to the states notwithstanding the clear constitutional competence of Congress to require federal incorporation of concerns doing a nationwide business. It is not the constitutional distribution of power but rather inertia and sufferance that accounts for this allocation of function. Deference to the states has encouraged a regressive competition in the standards imposed by them to govern corporate charters and powers. This is an inexorable corollary of inaction by the central government under a federal system in respect of questions of national import and dimension. No disability, of course, prevents the states from concerting their actions in the enactment of uniform legislation; but where strong pressures are exerted against such a synthesis, only some species of federal intervention will produce uniformity. This intervention need not eliminate state administration; it can be confined to the formulation of national policy to be executed by state agencies.

For many years utility regulation was left exclusively with the states. Much of the operations of utilities are local but they frequently have a substantial impact upon interstate commerce. With the advent of the utility holding company and a growing tendency of utilities to transmit electric power across state lines, federal intervention became necessary. In the thirties the federal government commenced regulating the purely interstate aspects of this business and subjected the holding company to its control. Thus today we have a detailed system of state regulation supplemented by federal legislation. Here again the primacy of state action is not entirely dictated by constitutional considerations. This is a field that the states first occupied and that they doubtless would be loath to yield. The federal government has been deterred from assuming a larger responsibility because of the monumental nature of the task. The present pattern of state-federal control is workable if the states maintain an effective system of utility regulation; otherwise further federal action may become necessary.

There are many other instances of concurrent regulation—sometimes, as in the case of food and drugs, the state legislation supplementing the federal enactment, and sometimes the reverse, as in the regulation of motor carriers and the telephone industry. Here the object is a workable synthesis of federal and state activity rather than the assertion of federal supremacy.

One of the most interesting patterns of combined state and federal regulation is found in the regulation of the petroleum industry. Competition in the marketing of petroleum is secured by enforcement of the antitrust laws by the federal government. During the N.R.A. the industry was federally regulated. Production today is controlled by state proration laws. Cooperation among the oil producing states is assured by an interstate compact approved by Congress. Under this compact production quotas are assigned to each state by a joint state body which it created. These quotas are based in large measure on the estimates of demand made by the United States Bureau of Mines. Within each state production is prorated among oil well operators by an appropriate state agency, ostensibly to avoid "waste" and in the interest of "conserving" an irreplaceable natural resource. Shipments across state lines of oil extracted in violation of state law are made a federal crime. State and federal power are thus pooled to effectuate a system of regulation which is predominantly of state initiation and responsibility and which appears well designed to serve the interests of those regulated. Though ostensibly designed to prevent waste and to conserve an important resource, these regulations in effect control production, and by keeping production in reasonable balance with demand, protect the price level in a manner not disadvantageous to the industry.[8]

Many other illustrations of state and federal regulations could be cited but their effect would only be cumulative. Both state and nation have responded to different needs and pressures. The force of events and not any abstract principle accounts for these diverse patterns of state-federal relationships. Undoubtedly, greater logical symmetry could be achieved if a master plan for the distribution of functions had been or were to be consciously and deliberately formulated in light of the capacity and interests of state and federal governments. And such a master plan might well conduce to more effective regulation and more efficient administration. The very nature of federalism introduces, of necessity, irrelevant considerations in the execution of any plan of regulation.

Whether optimum efficiency in the social control of business is better attainable under a unitary central government than in a federal system is an unreal issue so far as the United States is concerned. It is our conclusion from this brief study that there are enough tools in our legal arsenal to enable the states and the federal government, either alone or by a synthesis of their efforts, to regulate industry effectively in the public interest. The Constitution as presently interpreted interposes no obstacle. A rich variety of procedures exists for the pooling of state and federal power. Suitable devices for joint or cooperative administration of concurrent and supplementary legislation can readily be contrived. Given the will to do the job, there can be little doubt that the inherent difficulties in a federal system present no insuperable obstacle to the effective control of our economic affairs.

The deficiences in our methods of regulation do not stem today from any

constitutional disability. The time is past when the inadequacies of social control could be laid at the door of the Constitution or its authoritative interpreters. Ample latitude is afforded to both state and federal authority. Indeed
current constitutional theory moves in the direction of overcoming the inadequacies of regulation resulting from defective legislation or government inaction. Thus in the field of antitrust, the vacuum created by state inaction has
been substantially filled by an expanding conception of the commerce clause.
Hence the onus for insufficient controls falls primarily upon the legislative
branch of government in state and nation, and secondly upon the agencies of
enforcement and administration. If we fall short in the regulation of utilities,
the fault lies not in the federal structure of our government but rather in inadequate legislation or supine administration. Such shortcomings as there may be
in state regulation of insurance or the combined state and federal control of
petroleum are likewise attributable to legislative action and are just as likely
to exist in a centralized as in a federal state. Hence the builders of new federations can be encouraged by our experience in knowing that effective regulation
is not incompatible with a federal system, although theoretically more difficult
of attainment than in a unitary state. The nub of the problem is not the structure of the regulating governments but rather an understanding of the need
for regulation, the will to meet the need, and the imagination and courage without which all administration becomes pedestrian and ineffectual.

FOOTNOTES TO CHAPTER 18

1. Prudential Ins. Co. v. Benjamin, 328 U.S. 408, 420 (1946).
2. Paul v. Virginia, 8 Wall. 168 (U.S. 1869).
3. 322 U.S. 533 (1944).
4. Act of March 9, 1945, c. 20, 59 Stat. 33.
5. United States v. E. C. Knight Co., 156 U.S. 1 (1895).
6. Act of August 17, 1937, c. 690, 50 Stat. 693.
7. Act of July 14, 1952, c. 745, 66 Stat. 632.
8. In the discussion of the preliminary draft of this chapter, Vincent M. Barnett,
Jr., raised even stronger doubts than are reflected in the text about the significance
for public regulation generally of the cooperative pattern as applied to oil production. It was an instance, he said, "where the interest being regulated wants and
welcomes such regulation. This attitude facilitates the concert of action which Mr.
Handler talks about . . . the industry is well-entrenched in both the state governments and in the national administrative agencies." Altogether, said Mr. Barnett,
the situation was "a good interstate example of the way in which a strong group
interested in being regulated for its own advantage can bring about the concert of
action which has been described here." The foregoing caveat was echoed by James
W. Fesler, who remarked: "One is safer in placing authority for regulation—in
areas such as insurance, petroleum, and some of these other matters—in the
national government than in the states." He added: "The question of the relation
of private and selfish interest groups to the distribution of government power is
one we need to examine." (Editor)

SECTION TWO

OVERALL ASPECTS OF FUNCTIONAL
RELATIONSHIPS

19

Decision-Making in a Federal System

By Edward W. Weidner

Federalism has been thought of as the golden mean between excessive centralization and excessive decentralization. It has also been thought of as an inherently imperfect and defective form of government that stymies a positive solution to the pressing governmental problems of the twentieth century.[1] At base, both of these viewpoints picture national-state relations as a give-and-take situation in which there is disagreement and possibly conflict. A common assumption is that in this give-and-take situation the interests of state and national governments are competing or opposed. The one school of thought sees such competition resulting in a highly acceptable compromise, while the other sees it as destroying any possibility of a systematic attack on national domestic problems.

It is a thesis of the present discussion that in the federal system in the United States there are relatively few direct clashes or compromises between state and national governments on large issues of national domestic policy. Furthermore, in the administrative sphere positive cooperation is the pattern rather than aloofness or conflict. The disagreements and conflicts that do arise and that may be encouraged by federalism's structural features are not basically clashes between state and national governments. Instead, they are clashes between much smaller groups of people and the opposing groups are located within a single governmental level as often as not.

While this thesis is essentially different from that developed fifteen years ago by Jane Perry Clark in her monograph entitled *The Rise of A New Federalism,* it is complementary, not contradictory, to it.[2] Jane Clark pointed out that a cooperative federalism existed in which nation and state combined their resources the better to carry out their responsibilities. The presence of cooperative federalism is certainly in evidence today, but certain patterns of disagreement and conflict are with us as well. Indeed they always have been. If an understanding is to be gained of how federalism affects political behavior, it is essential that elements of disagreement be analyzed and understood as well as patterns of cooperation, and that such elements be analyzed in terms of the forces that produce them and their consequences.

A second assumption is implicit in the older view of national-state relations as a give-and-take situation of disagreement and conflict between levels of government as such. A theory of leadership is implied. Political and administrative leaders of national and state governments are thought of as rather forceful and direct. Supposedly they develop and support fairly clear-cut public policies for which they become known. Furthermore, the assumption is that they use all the means at their command to gain acceptance for the public policies they support, including coercive techniques. Given the assumed competing interests of national and state governments, a compromise becomes necessary but only as a last resort. In any event, it is believed that leadership is not based upon the idea of "getting along" with officials of the other level of government at almost any price, nor is a community of interests assumed. A further thesis of the present discussion denies the validity of this view of leadership.

The entire process of agreement and disagreement, of cooperation and conflict, is here viewed as a decision-making process. Put another way, the basic datum in political science is the political act or the individual in an action situation. Each act has its own general environment or ecology varying all the way from factors rather remote from the action situation to the immediate conditioning factors or foci of attention and the actual stimulus that presents a problem to an individual. The problem that an individual faces is essentially a decision-making problem. Something happens that creates tension, frustration, insecurity, or expectations of indulgence. A greater or lesser period of hesitation sets in and then a choice or decision is made. The decision is made in a value context, that is, the very reason for tension or frustration as the result of a stimulus is the need of or striving for values. Men are essentially goal-oriented although there are wide differences in the extent to which they are conscious of their long-range goals or have a systematically thought-out value framework. There are also wide differences in the degree to which they are able to implement their values or desires, and of course the intensity with which particular values are held varies greatly.

The decision or choice results in one of two kinds of behavior or both. An individual's attitude may change; this is essentially a subjective matter with the individual involving a tendency to participate in a certain way. Secondly, the patterns of participation (that is, human interaction) may be altered; these are overt or external to the individual. Presumably the change in attitude or participation is designed to remove the tension of the individual, and a new state of gratification or equilibrium sets in, a state that the individual hopes will be more compatible with the ends he is seeking.

Unfortunately for purposes of analysis, political acts seldom occur in a separate, neat sequence. The more usual situation is that many of them are occurring simultaneously, often involving a series of individuals in a multitude of decisions. Rather than causes and effects there are a series of interrelations. Before responses can be made to certain stimuli, other stimuli present still further problems. Patterns of attitudes and participation must be adapted quickly and often imperfectly to only a select few of the many stimuli. In national-state relations this pressure of events and pressure of other individuals and groups is an ever-present phenomenon. Decision-making in a federal system thus takes place in the context of many varied groups, formal and informal, large and small.

If attention is concentrated upon areas of agreement and cooperation on the one hand, and areas of disagreement and conflict on the other, a study of decision-making in a federal system is very suggestive of major factors that affect or are related to political behavior. To study decision-making in a federal system is to study the kind of choices that are made under different circumstances, the factors that may have shaped the choices, and the resulting or related patterns of attitudes and participation. These choices, factors, and patterns vary with the probability of cooperation or conflict; a theory of behavior must take account of such variances. Viewed from the standpoint of public policy, change may take place under conditions of either cooperation or conflict but the secondary effects of these conditions may be quite different. Conflict is normally avoided as much as possible and cooperation sought, but only within a limited frame of reference. Cooperation may come at too high a price. By selecting for analysis a group of decisions concerning which agreement and cooperation are to be found and another group concerning which disagreement and conflict are present, we are limiting our investigation, but in a manner that contributes to its usefulness in building empirical theory while at the same time the enquiry has important policy implications.

I

There are countless causes for disagreement and conflict in a federal system. Personalities play a part. So do bothersome procedures, differences in the age and general background of administrators, poor communication, frequency of contact, and so on. However, all these factors are secondary in importance. They are relatively easy to deal with: procedures may be changed, frequency of contact increased, personnel shifted. This is not to say that such variables are never troublesome, for they are very troublesome on occasion. Rather, they are secondary in the sense that they are not of crucial importance to the participants in federal-state relations. The main concern of these participants, and, for that matter, most men, is to have their values implemented to as great an extent as possible. Hence it is not surprising that the fundamental reason for disagreement and conflict in a federal system is that there is a lack of consensus as to what values should be implemented. This is true in both the legislative and administrative spheres.

While differences on public policy or values are to be expected in a country containing as many heterogeneous elements as are to be found in the United States, it does not necessarily follow that officials in the several states will take

one policy position and those of the national government another. Indeed, on
an *a priori* basis it would seem surprising if this were the case, given the diversity of conditions in the several states and the fact that the union is made up
of all states. "States' rights" is only one of numerous values held by state
officials, and it is relatively unimportant to many of them. The prime thing
that the states have in common is their existence; it is possible that if an issue
were presented that threatened the very existence of the states their political
officials might be brought together. In actual fact, a major issue of this kind
has not been presented. Consequently, usually national government officials
can find many of their state counterparts who support national policy objectives and many others who oppose. And among the states, differences in values
are the rule.

The framers of the Constitution clearly expected value or policy disagreements among the states as well as between the central government and one or
more states. In his famous essay on faction, Madison wrote:

> Hence, it clearly appears, that the same advantages which a republic has over
> a democracy, in controlling the effects of faction, is enjoyed by a large over
> a small republic,—is enjoyed by the Union over the States composing it. Does
> the advantage consist in the substitution of representatives whose enlightened
> views and virtuous sentiments render them superior to local prejudices and
> to schemes of injustice? It will not be denied that the representation of the
> Union will be most likely to possess these requisite endowments. Does it con-
> sist in the greater security afforded by a greater variety of parties, against the
> event of any one party being able to outnumber and oppress the rest? In an
> equal degree does the increased variety of parties comprised within the Union,
> increase this security. Does it, in fine, consist in the greater obstacles opposed
> to the concert and accomplishment of the secret wishes of an unjust and in-
> terested majority? Here, again, the extent of the Union gives it the most
> palpable advantage.
>
> The influence of factious leaders may kindle a flame within their particular
> States, but will be unable to spread a general conflagration through the other
> States. A religious sect may degenerate into a political faction in a part of the
> Confederacy; but the variety of sects dispersed over the entire face of it must
> secure the national councils against any danger from that source. A rage for
> paper money, for an abolition of debts, for an equal division of property, or
> for any other improper or wicked project, will be less apt to pervade the
> whole body of the Union than a particular member of it; in the same propor-
> tion as such a malady is more likely to taint a particular county or district,
> than an entire State.[3]

Thus Madison emphasized that one of the main characteristics of the federal
system would be the wide variation in the public policies that would be followed in the several states. To guard against the possible excesses of certain
states the central government was given a core of power over matters deemed
to be of nationwide concern. The states were expected to disagree among
themselves over how the central government exercised its powers, and they
were also expected to pursue different policies in matters that were reserved
to them for decision.

Federalism implies that there is a variety of political values in a nation for which allowance needs to be made. It is more than a neutral centralizing or decentralizing device. Historically it has been a unifying device that took cognizance of the fact, among others, that agreement was lacking as to political goals and values, and hence single public policies for a society would be developed only in those matters over which the central government was given jurisdiction. State participation in public policy would automatically mean lack of uniformity and recognition of alternative and even competing political values. Viewed in this context, "states' rights" and the division of powers and responsibility for public services between the national and state governments become matters affecting substantive policy. They are matters upon which citizens will disagree in the proportion that their values or goals vary. The appointment of a President's commission to make recommendations on national-state relations may be an excellent political device but by the very nature of the subject with which it deals it cannot be a nonpartisan body whose recommendations will be supported by all or nearly all men of good will.

Given the diverse policy objectives of the several states, it becomes unrealistic and impossible to expect of them any unified approach to important public problems. The United States learned at an early date, under the Articles of Confederation, how true this was. As a result of the experience with the Articles, the framers of the Constitution sought to vest the new central government with effective power over those matters that, in their opinion, required a single, unified policy or that required a minimum standard of performance. Foreign affairs and defense from external attacks were thought to be areas in which a single policy was necessary, while interstate commerce and the preservation of peace in the face of possible internal disturbances were thought to be areas in which minimum standards or assurances were needed.

The experience of 170 years ago is confirmed by contemporary events. The states have been unable to follow a single course even in such comparatively noncontroversial areas as are covered by the so-called uniform state laws. If minimum standards are desired for the nation as a whole in a particular policy area such as health or welfare, it is the central government that must act to assure these ends. To leave the matter exclusively to the states means that there will be a variation in standards from very low to quite high. To set up a system of joint national-state participation means that standards and practices will vary much more than in a system of central action alone. It also means that some disagreement and conflict are inevitable because officials in various states will not all see eye-to-eye with those of the national government in terms of the objectives of the program.

This is not to blame the states in any way for their actions. Rather it is to recognize that public policy is in large part the result of the values that men hold and that these values vary from individual to individual and group to group. It would be unexpected and surprising if the several states followed identical or even similar courses of action on important public issues. The normal expectancy is that they will differ in greater or lesser degree among themselves in regard to policies they enact and in regard to the policies of the national government.

II

As we have already seen, two broad categories of values are immediately noticeable in a federal system. There are those values that attach to units of government or agencies or individuals within the units, and there are those values that attach to programs or types of substantive policies. The latter may be called principled, programmatic, or organization goals; the former may be called expediency or conservation goals.[4] Programmatic goals are normally those concerned with adequate standards of public service—minimum standards in health and welfare, better public education, a more extensive system of interstate highways, more service to farmers, and so on. Expediency goals refer to the preservation and extension of influence of individuals, agencies, or units of government—for example, the defense of state government against "encroachment" from Washington, the desire of an individual for more power for its own sake, or the protection of an agency from supervision by those deemed unfriendly to it.

It is in the nature of a federal system that there are many occasions when the one set of values conflicts with the other. The states are not creatures of the national government and thus need not accept many of the programmatic or expediency goals that are put forth by those in control nationally. The constitutionally guaranteed semi-independence of the states lends encouragement to the development of strong expediency values relative to them, their leaders, and agencies. At the same time, the trend toward an increase in national-state relations helps strengthen the hold of programmatic values on many state and national administrators. The inevitable result is disagreement and conflict of three kinds: between competing expediency values, between competing programmatic values, and between expediency and programmatic values. The interplay of these goals is such that it is not unusual to find a programmatic value being defended in terms of expediency objectives and vice versa. Thus many who hesitate directly to attack programmatic values such as the so-called welfare state do so indirectly by defending states' rights since they feel that if welfare services were turned over to the states entirely they would be much less extensive and effective. On the other hand a welfare agency may battle for independence from supervision by the governor in order that it may better pursue certain types of welfare policies in cooperation with welfare personnel at the national level.

The net effect of a federal system is not by any means in the direction of increasing value conflict. Rather, while the system results in increasing the likelihood of certain disagreements over goals, it results in decreasing the likelihood of other and often more basic value conflicts. The federal system of the

United States has withstood the shocks of wars and depressions and the changing centuries and meanwhile it has provided an organization that has helped weld a strongly unified nation where formerly there were independent states and unorganized territory. This has been an effective demonstration of the ability of a federal system to contribute toward modifying values and reducing value conflict. The expediency values attached to the several states are not nearly as intensely held as those attached to independent nation-states.

Disagreement or conflict in national-state relations is limited. It is not a matter that normally determines election results or on which there is a clear public opinion. General issues of national-state relations have concerned only a small minority of individuals and groups in recent decades, usually a group of public officials at each level and a few interest groups outside the framework of government. When an important new substantive policy for the national government is under consideration, national-state relations may take on a broader significance, as was the case in welfare and labor policy during the thirties. As a whole, however, interest groups and public opinion have not found states' rights an attractive theme unless by the defense of states' rights they could defend some programmatic value. Nonetheless, for those public officials daily engaged in national-state relations the issues arising therefrom may be crucial.

The values that individuals hold are so diverse that there is no definable "state" point of view in intergovernmental relations as a whole. Even if the forty-eight governors were considered to be spokesmen for their entire states, there does not emerge a single state approach to intergovernmental relations. Occasionally all the governors will agree on a minor point or two but they have never agreed that a specific general reallocation of activities should take place between national and state governments. This is understandable since some of them are Democrats, some Republicans; some are liberals, others conservatives; some have national political ambitions, others do not; some come from poor states, others from well-to-do areas. These are only a few of the variables that affect the approach governors take on national-state relations. Much of the publicity arising from recent political events, Governors' Conferences, and the Council of State Governments tends to give the impression that all governors demand that certain functions and tax resources of the national government be turned over to the states. The impression is erroneous. It is true that the governors probably defend states' rights as vigorously as any other group of public officials; they tend to stress expediency values relative to state government. In part this is a function of their role as chief executive and chief party leader. Nevertheless, such a set of values may be subordinate to many other considerations, and consequently consensus is not easily forthcoming.

If the governors as a group cannot produce a state point of view on intergovernmental relations, there is little likelihood that it will be found elsewhere. State legislators or elected state administrators show no more tendency to agree than the governors. Political parties remain rather vague on the subject and public opinion gives no evidence of a state viewpoint. Therefore, the most that can be said is that state political officials who hold elective and/or general executive posts tend to defend state government as such more vigorously than others, but that this expediency value is often secondary to a number of other values these individuals hold.

If an analysis is made of the national government, similar conclusions are reached. Although there is only one unit of government here compared to the forty-eight states, a single approach to national-state relations is never found. Of course, to the extent that the President speaks for the entire government and has a clearly defined policy on relations with the several states, a "national" policy may be referred to. But such a policy is not binding on Congress, and in actual recent practice Congress, the various departments and agencies, and the President have not followed a unified policy on intergovernmental relations. No comprehensive policy has been put forth by the President or the Congress; for the most part a piecemeal approach has prevailed. The reason is not hard to find. A unified policy requires agreement or compromise on basic programmatic and expediency values and such a general agreement is difficult if not impossible to secure even when the President has a large majority in Congress. The major political parties are too diverse in composition, the interest groups too strong relative to special programs, and the determinants of values too varied.

Nevertheless in one way the national situation differs somewhat from that in the states. Since defending the national government per se is usually thought of as centralization and is condemned, the political officials of the nation, at least outwardly, are less oriented toward expediency values than their state counterparts. Within this framework, however, the President is usually more committed to defending the national government than other top officials of his party or of the nation.

To summarize, the states disagree among themselves as to the major public policies they pursue and as to the desirability of particular national policies. They also differ even on smaller issues of national-state relations which may appear to be purely procedural in nature. The explanation is that public policies and even national-state procedures reflect particular values and on these there is lack of agreement. But it is not accurate to speak of the attitudes or policies of the several "states" or "national government." Public policies, and consequent disagreement and conflict, are not the product of entire units of government. Particular individuals, more or less associated in groups and to be found both within a unit of government and without, are the central force behind the molding of public policy.

Therefore, we turn to an analysis of some of the groups that are playing crucial role in national-state relations and the kinds of values their member hold. In making this analysis, the concept of an interest group developed by David B. Truman will be especially helpful: an interest group is any group formally organized or not, "that, on the basis of one or more shared attitudes makes certain claims upon other groups in the society for the establishmen maintenance, or enhancement of forms of behavior that are implied by the shared attitudes."[5] Our concern will be to examine interest groups whose members share values or goals resulting in claims on others relative to national-state relations.

III[6]

While it is not possible to speak of a state or a national attitude on intergovernmental relations, there are many interest groups that have rather distinct approaches to the subject. It has already been suggested that as a group state elective and/or general executive officials tend to have more intense expediency values relative to state government as a whole than other groups of officials or employees. As part of its regular program the Council of State Governments tries to further these values; on many occasions its leaders have taken the initiative to get the state governors or other top officials to favor particular provisions in legislation before Congress that emphasize the prerogatives of the states or to encourage the President to appoint certain types of individuals —namely those generally considered pro-states' rights—to commissions or other posts. The Council has probably been more states' rights in its attitude than the recent governors of Minnesota. It would seem a reasonable hypothesis that it has been more states' rights than most state elective officials throughout the nation. Put more accurately, state officials find a large variety of values pressing upon them as they carry out their responsibilities, of which states' rights is usually a minor one. The Council, on the other hand, performs a limited number of functions. In addition to its technical assistance activities, its main emphasis has been placed on states' rights.

The most striking interest groups in national-state relations are those of a professional nature. Formally, these interests are evidenced by the many professional associations that have as members national, state, and often local government employees and occasionally members of the profession who are not employed in government. Professionalism has been introduced into almost all the principal services that state and national governments perform. Education was probably the first, soon after the middle of the nineteenth century. There followed such fields as agricultural extension, public health, highway administration and engineering, and social work, and more recently airport management, employment security, and others. The process of professionalizing has even gone so far that the professional fields have tended to split. Thus, in addition to a general education profession, there are separate groups interested primarily in vocational education, higher education, secondary education, and so on.

As each professional group has its own peculiar way of organizing it is difficult to generalize about the structure and membership of professional associations. For purposes of analysis, considerable clarity may be gained by thinking of a professional interest group as any group, whether formally organized or not, that shares a professional attitude on the basis of which claims are made on others "for the establishment, maintenance, or enhancement of forms of behavior that are implied by the shared attitudes."[7] In observing national-state relations it is immediately noticeable that there is a marked parallel in the behavior of the members of each of the several professions relative to the type of values held, the occurrence of administrative cooperation and conflict, and the decisions made—all this despite the different functions of government involved and the wide differences in formal organization of professional associations.

One of the basic motivations of a professional interest group is the furtherance of programmatic values. If the profession is social work, for example, it will be concerned with high professional standards and conduct in social welfare and the raising of minimum standards of welfare aid. The secondary effect of such goals is of course to promote the well-being of the social work profession—an expediency consideration that is also an agreed-upon goal—but the genuine programmatic interest is clear. From the moment of entrance into schools of social work to the first in-service training and on to regular employment, social workers are placed in an environment where certain programmatic values are accepted without much question. It is partly a matter of conformity but also a matter of mutual interests. Some of the vocational guidance tests are based upon this idea of mutual interests.

Any group, professional or otherwise, that seeks to implement certain values finds a number of allies in the form of those groups that share some concern for the same goals. Social workers have had ready support on many matters from their clientele, the recipients of welfare services. Liberal and labor groups generally have demanded higher minimum welfare standards and certain segments of the two major parties have indicated their sympathy for action in such a direction. A number of state legislators and congressmen have been favorably disposed, and often the warmest support in legislative bodies will come from those on legislative committees dealing with welfare matters. The position of any one governor or President is less predictable and his policies can be changed more quickly. Also, of all public officials, the chief executives must keep the "general interest" in mind most often.

It is easy to secure the cooperation of those who share the same values. National, state, and local professional officials in social welfare find they see eye-to-eye on most important matters, and consequently their decisions to cooperate reflect basic agreement on welfare programmatic values and agreement on expediency goals relative to their profession. Other values pale in importance to these as far as national-state relations in welfare are concerned. Professional employees do not feel strongly about defending the unit of government for which they work. The states' rights argument is not persuasive although there may be some expediency values associated with the welfare agency itself. Cooperation not only extends across national, state, and local levels in the administrative work but also includes clientele activities, party and legislative groups, and others who for the moment at least feel that certain welfare programmatic values are especially worthy of their support. The help that the professional welfare group receives from such outside sources is considerable and greatly strengthens its hand.

From the standpoint of social workers, conflicts over social welfare policies are of three types. There is the ever-present tendency for a large profession to subdivide, particularly under pressure from special clientele interests. Thus child welfare and welfare for the aged tend to be separated (or be kept separate) from a general welfare program. Secondly, at the professional or agency level, welfare values must compete with values associated with the other main substantive services of government such as education, health, and highways. Here the social worker comes in occasional conflict with professionals in other fields. The third and main area of conflict is the political. The citizen and the politician must pick and choose among many expediency and programmatic values of which welfare is only one. To convince citizen and politician that welfare values should have a high priority is the task the social worker assigns to himself.

All three areas of conflict affect national-state relations. In a general way all three have the same effect, namely, to lessen direct national-state conflict and to promote conflict among or within the main substantive services of each level of government. From the standpoint of both political leaders and professional employees, the disagreements within and among the professions are probably less serious than those between the professional and citizen and politician. It is particularly in conflicts of a political type that the very nature of federalism presents a special problem. Under a unitary system, the social worker would be involved in a simple direct clash between professional welfare workers and political leaders, be the latter located in the legislative body, the office of the general executive, or in departmental offices. With federalism the clash occurs at both the state and the national levels, and federalism's structural features make available to the combatants additional goals, tactics, and strategy.

In Minnesota the governor and his staff, the budget officer, and the director of the state welfare agency have traditionally been political officials who have not shared the typical programmatic values of professional social workers. The main division in attitude therefore tends to come between the welfare director and his professional employees rather than between the director and the budget office or governor's staff. In general the political officials feel that professional employees engaged in administering national grant-in-aid programs tend to play off supposedly rigid national standards against state political control they do not like. Since a prime objective of professional employees is to further the governmental service with which they are connected and not necessarily policy control at the state level, they tend to read somewhat more into national minimum standards than is actually there. The professionals are also active in appearing before the state legislature from time to time in an attempt to have legislation modified to anticipate changes in national standards. Often they are optimistic in their forecasts of probable national action. Viewing national standards with a different set of values than the professionals, political officials tend to underestimate the demands of the national agency or overestimate the deleterious effects such restrictions may have on the discretion left for state policy-makers. A similar set of circumstances exists at the national level as to the weight national officials give to state demands—the professionals underestimating them, the political leaders overestimating them. The situation portrayed in welfare is equally true of national-state relations in most other functions.

Considerable empirical data exist to support these conclusions. In a mail questionnaire sent to a cross-section of officials in Minnesota's state government, counties, municipalities, and urban school districts, the following question was asked: "What is your evaluation of the cooperativeness of public officials in the national government with you? (check): no contacts ———, very poor ———, poor ———, fair ———, good ———, very good ———." At the local government level, comparisons were made between the responses of administrative officials and legislative officials and in every one of the three types of local units in the sample, the administrators were markedly more of the opinion that the national officials were cooperative. A comparison of the responses of 302 municipal administrators (engineers, police chiefs, fire chiefs, assessors, and health officers) with those of 280 city councilmen by means of the chi square test indicated that the difference in attitude was very significant beyond the one per cent level; that is, this difference could have occurred by chance less than once in one hundred times. Comparing the responses of 239 county administrators (engineers, superintendents of schools, sheriffs, county agents, assessors, and welfare executives) with those of 199 county governing body members by the same test also yielded a very significant difference beyond the one per cent level. Furthermore no significant difference appeared between the attitude of state administrators and that of county, school district, or municipal administrators. However, county and state administrators felt that the officials of the national government were more cooperative than their school district and municipal counterparts. They are also the officials who have the most contact with the national government. While the questionnaire was not sent to state legislators, a number of interviews indicate that there is every reason for assuming that these officials would have reacted in much the same way as the local legislators did. Seventy-nine per cent of the 275 national administrators queried by questionnaire thought that state cooperation with them could be rated as good or very good. Only about two-and-a-half per cent thought it poor or very poor.

It is difficult to develop a measure of professionalism so that questionnaire and interview data can be classified on the presence or absence of this characteristic. The closest approximation used in the Minnesota study was the breakdown by type of official, together with general education, professional education, age, and various experience breakdowns. All these groups showed a positive orientation to the cooperativeness question; for example, the more education and the more frequent the contacts the more cooperative the national officials were rated.

Since the data from the Minnesota study are being reported at length elsewhere, our present purposes will be served by summarizing the quantitative data in regard to professionalism drawn from about 650 questionnaires and an equal number of interviews of public officials, national, state, and local. The main findings are these:

1. Administrators rate national-state relations as being more cooperative than do legislators, and within the administrative group those who would commonly be thought of as professional rather than amateur or political lean more heavily in the same direction.

2. Administrative officials think that administrators of other governmental levels cooperate best and legislative officials think legislators do.

3. Professional officials at all levels of government tend to favor more centralization and expansion of their own function than of other activities. Here the programmatic values of professional administrators are revealed. At least state and local professional officials seem to value their activity more than their unit of government.

4. Local administrators are much more critical of the extent of control of their departments by the local legislative body and the executive office than are members of the local legislative body or the executive office; the latter groups would like to see their control somewhat increased. This is hardly surprising. Moreover, local administrators see much less danger in the existing extent of state administrative supervision over their departments than the local political officials do, and there is even some tendency on the part of the former group to favor an increase in it. Here again is a tendency that cannot be explained in terms of expediency values; expediency values would dictate that local administrators should oppose control of their departments both from within and without their units of government. While by far the majority of administrators are satisfied with the existing levels of control both from within and without, four to five times as many want to increase state administrative supervision as want to decrease it. Also, more favor an increase in state administrative supervision than in local control, and more favor a decrease in local control than favor a decrease in state administrative supervision. Chi square analysis indicates very significant differences beyond the one per cent level.

At this point an apparent contradiction arises between national-state and state-local relations. About two-thirds of the state administrators answering questionnaires agreed that the extent of national administrative supervision was about right, but the remainder split about four to one in favor of decreasing it. A number of factors account for this contrast between national-state and state-local relations. In the first place, quite a few state administrators included in the sample have very few relations with the national government, and it was noticeable that the ratio was cut to about two-and-a-half to one in the case of administrators in such departments as education and welfare where contacts are quite frequent. Secondly, state administrators feel less need for national administrative supervision since within their numbers various technical competencies are likely to be found and since there are enough of them in each department to set up a strong defense for professional standards against executive or legislative interference. At the city level a similar tendency is noted in large cities in contrast to the situation in small cities where more administrative supervision is desired by the semi-isolated professionals. Yet neither of these factors explains the entire difference.

States' rights, outwardly at least, are valued more intensively and extensively than local self-government, and here seems to lie some of the explanation. They are valued more partly because of the superior legal position that states hold in their relations with the national government, compared to that held by local governments in their dealings with the states. A subordinate role for local government is accepted much more readily than a similar role for the states. The states, according to the law and theory of federalism, are permanent partners in governance with a set of powers that cannot be taken away except by constitutional amendment. They are the proving grounds where the loyal opposition gains experience and experiments. To subordinate them to the national government is counter to the tenets of federalism and thus runs counter to customary values, and in the eyes of some officials an increase in national administrative supervision appears to lead in this direction.

In fact, however, the difference in national-state and state-local relations is more apparent than real. The difference shows up almost entirely on general questions or issues such as asking a respondent whether he favors an increase in administrative supervision. As actual case studies of intergovernmental relations are examined, the difference all but disappears. In other words, the difference occurs in reacting to general symbols and not to actual events. For example, the enactment of general regulations and their acceptance by officials of lower levels of government is much the same in national-state and state-local relations. So are the processes of audit and review and the possible consequences of finding officials violating regulations. Intergovernmental relations are at base human relations and require some mutual adjustment if they are to be cooperative in nature in the long run. This adjustment takes place in much the same manner in national-state and state-local relations despite the legal differences of federal and unitary systems. In this adjustment, professionalism plays an important role because the participants from both state and national governments share many of the same goals.

5. Administrative and legislative officials alike are of the opinion that the main clash of values occurs within a unit of government rather than between units. This is true even in regard to the issues arising from intergovernmental programs. The professional is especially prone to this point of view.

The conclusions outlined so far, based on both quantitative and case study material, have been largely descriptive. They have indicated that the values and identifications of different types of public officials vary widely, and consequently the decisions they make vary. The two most significant values for purposes of this analysis were found to be the expediency values attached to a unit or level of government and held especially by some political officials, and the programmatic values, attached to the performance of certain governmental services and held especially by professional officials. This is not to deny that there are some who defend states' rights or local self-government through a genuine concern for decentralism and not on the basis of expediency. Nor is it to deny that some professionals develop strong expediency values in connection with their own agencies—the Corps of Engineers is a case in point. Indeed the activity of the Corps of Engineers is a good example of intergovernmental action that promotes intragovernmental discord—in this case, within the national government. However, situations where the programmatic values of professional administrators are overridden by their expediency values are not frequent except as professionals develop expediency values in connection with their entire profession rather than a single agency.

Furthermore, problems arising from intergovernmental programs have been described mainly as problems within units of government rather than between levels. Professional administrators are especially prone to perceive the situation in this manner. Yet there are those who perceive the situation in opposite terms—as a national-state conflict—and they may act upon their perceptions. Some political officials, especially a few governors, respond in this manner.

Explanatory conclusions can be drawn as well. As has already been emphasized, professionalism creates a powerful set of programmatic values the existence of which explains much of the behavior of professional and non-professional public officials in intergovernmental relations. But there is a larger point. To use the suggestive terminology of John M. Gaus,[8] we are in an era of vastly increased physical and social technology, an era in which the catastrophes of war and depression can strike quickly. As a result, new programmatic values have been emphasized by those who want to take advantage of services that are now available because of the advances in physical and social technology and by those who demand governmental activities designed to lessen or avoid the ravages of wars and depressions. The technicians themselves have become attached to and encourage the creation of programmatic values. In such a situation, the cry of states' rights sounds a hollow note. The stronger the programmatic values, the less states' rights and federalism can become important independent values even for state public officials. States' rights come to be judged by the programmatic values that are implemented by the states and not by a set of independent expediency values.

IV

In a clash of values involving national-state relations some individuals try to affect and succeed in affecting the policies of others. Such political acts are acts of leadership, and leadership plays a central role in decision-making in a federal system. By definition leaders try to influence others; the idea of manipulation is present. But manipulation is not sufficient; some success or influence must result.[9] We have already noted in discussing programmatic and expediency values some of the patterns of leadership in the federal system of the United States and some consequences flowing therefrom. We now turn to an analysis of the methods of leadership and the motives underlying their use.

Leaders, or those who perform acts of leadership frequently, have available to them two general methods, namely, authoritative means and nonauthoritative means. Authority is the formal and effective power "to make decisions which guide the actions of another." This means that the individual affected "sets himself a general rule which permits the communicated decision of another to guide his own choices (i.e., to serve as a premise of those choices) without deliberation on his own part on the expediency of those premises."[10] In contrast, nonauthoritative means do not involve an abdication of choice. "Persuasion and suggestion result in a change in the evidential environment of choice which may, but need not, lead to conviction."[11]

In a unitary system, the political and administrative leaders of the central government are vested with a rather complete set of authoritative means to use in their relations with subordinate units of government. Often there is the power to remove local officials and even appoint others in their place if they do not perform in an acceptable manner; there are powers to issue orders and make general rules that govern the very minute details of local action. Furthermore, the officials at the higher level can substitute, if they wish, direct central legislation and administration. Federalism sets severe limitations on the authority of central government officials in dealing with the lower governmental units. Constitutionally they are forbidden to alter in any way the power of officials in lower units to act. This means they cannot expand or contract such power, and they therefore cannot substitute central administration for local administration on matters that are within the authority of the lower units to perform. Today most national-state relations are based on grants-in-aid or the voluntary exchange of technical information and assistance. Most state-local relations, legally at least, are based upon the state's constitutional unitary authority over local government; there is no formal dependence on local officials accepting state policy decisions voluntarily.

However, when a comparison was made of national-state and state-local relations as observed in the State of Minnesota, no important differences were found in the frequency of use of authoritative and of nonauthoritative means by the two supervisory levels. Both national and state administrators stressed nonauthoritative means. Advice, consultation, technical assistance, information—these were the devices that had an appeal alike to the state and national administrator in charge of state-local or national-state relations, be the program in the field of welfare, education, health, highways, or in some other field. The more authoritative devices went unused, or were used only with the advice and consent of the officials to whom they were to apply, or were used as an unwelcome last resort in one or two rare cases.[12] Occasionally, strong statements and hot words were used by the supervised in describing the supervisors, particularly if one was a professional and the other a nonprofessional official. Almost never was the reciprocal found true.

There are a number of explanations of this phenomenon. "Pulling rank" or flaunting authority are not devices that win many friends, and most individuals with experience in human relations became accustomed to dealing with others in a more friendly, permissive manner. So it is in intergovernmental relations. The more experience an official has, the greater the likelihood that he has cooperative relationships with those of other levels of government. Political and administrative realism lead to other factors of explanation. The success of a program depends in most instances on the lack of use of authoritative devices in carrying it out. Politically, the superior unit of government is open to attack. If a national administrative official were to offend unduly the administrators from a state, there might be immediate repercussions in the congressional delegation of the state as well as official protest from the governor to the President. State officials have powerful political levers over national action just as local officials have a real check over state administrative supervision through the legislature and governor. These checks are enough of a threat to make frequent use of authoritative means of supervision unlikely. Yet administrators as a group are less concerned with the possibilities of such an attack from the flanks than they are with direct conflict or cooperation with their counterparts on the other governmental level. Here administrative realism enters. No program involving national relations with the forty-eight states is going to be successful if the national officials have to be checking up constantly on the states to see if they are complying with every detail of national standards. Nor is it going to be successful if the national administrators have to make all the important decisions through the use of authoritative methods. A national-state program must be based on the assumption that the great majority of states are going to cooperate to the best of their ability without close supervision, and that therefore the prime role of the national government is to assist the states and to help them carry out the program more effectively. To follow any other course is to increase the cost of administration and decrease its effectiveness. State administrators would rebel against a system that was apparently based on a lack of trust in them, although they do not object to occasional audits to see if their agencies are in accord with national policy. Similar considerations affect state-local relations.

The use of nonauthoritative devices by political and administrative leaders in national-state relations is supplemented by a further practice, namely, the cooperative development of program policy.[13] State and national administrators almost never develop rules and regulations or program changes by themselves without consultation with and participation by local and state officials, respectively. The practice is quite standardized. For example, a problem-area arises either in the minds of state or national officials involving a national-state program. Within a short time, the problem finds its way to the agenda of a meeting of state administrators from the several states, a meeting at which national officials will probably be present but withhold much comment. If it is a problem of large proportions, it may be referred to a special committee of state administrators and a report brought in at a subsequent meeting. It will be discussed and debated informally around the country and in regional or state meetings of administrators. Appropriate clientele or other interest groups are likely to be consulted. Finally, the state administrators will recommend a course of action to national officials, usually with prior knowledge that their suggestion will be acted upon without substantial change.

This practice of developing policy from below is based upon much the same line of reasoning as the preference for nonauthoritative devices. In a national-state program, more cooperation will be forthcoming from the several states if their officials have taken an active part in the framing of the regulations and the making of decisions that outline the main course of national policy. State administrative officials must accept part of the responsibility for national policy, and this makes the task of the national official easier when it comes to enforcing minimum standards. It may also place the state administrator in a peculiar position if top state political leaders object to a policy he had a part in developing. In order to defend himself, the state administrator may blame the national government for a policy he helped write.

In thus decentralizing decision-making on public policy, national administrators are acting in accord with rather vague and undefined notions of democracy and therefore receive support from traditional cultural values. At the same time, they are not risking much in terms of lack of control over the direction of public policy because professionalism is prevalent in the states and leads to agreement on many values between national and state officials. To be sure, many of these national-state relations occur essentially between national professional and state political officials, since the heads of state agencies tend to be political rather than professional in orientation. But to a considerable extent the political heads of agencies must rely upon their professional subordinates for advice and help, and consequently the influence of professionalism is not without its effect.

V

The conclusions reached and the hypotheses for future research put forth in these pages are of a very limited nature. They refer to conditions within the United States and many of the data have been confined to national-state and state-local relations as observed in Minnesota. In the United States with a particular tradition of freedom and democracy patterns of political behavior may be present that are not duplicated elsewhere. Our federal system and political party structure present many unique features. In like manner the State of Minnesota has many political patterns that are not found in some states. In recent times it has never been a boss-ridden state but rather one of loosely organized political parties and independent voting. It has been neither a very well-to-do state nor a poor state. And over all, its state administration has been of a fairly high quality from the standpoint of professional standards.

Under the conditions that prevail in the United States and in Minnesota, public officials who would be leaders in national-state relations must base their acts on the idea of getting along with officials of the other level of government by using voluntary, nonauthoritative methods. In particular, two theorems are suggested. The more the administrative leaders of the national government use nonauthoritative methods in their dealings with the states and, secondly, the more decision-making related to national-state programs is participated in by state officials, (1) the more cooperative will be the continuing relations, (2) the less chance there will be of the program being seriously curtailed or altered in a direction contrary to the values of the national administrators, and (3) the greater will be the probability that the values of the national administrators will be implemented in the long run. The converse of these propositions is likewise true.

Power as a value and expediency values in general have less hold on those engaged in national-state relations than various programmatic values. The picture of a power-mad individual seeking to strengthen his personal influence over his associates by every means at his command because he values power so highly is a false picture, or at least not a typical one, in national-state relations. This is especially true of administrative leadership in an era of professionalism but the tendency is observable among political officials as well. Program values are the usual goals for which power is sought with expediency values supplemental or subordinate thereto. Perhaps in an era of contracting governmental services expediency and power values would be prized more highly. Since such conditions did not prevail at the time the observations reported here were made the present data do not deny or confirm this possibility.

In conclusion, some comments are ventured on current suggestions for "improving" national-state relations. One of the most popular suggestions is that national-state relations be coordinated by the national government so that a single policy would prevail in all fields. If this idea were followed, national-state relations in highways would follow the same general policy and procedure as national-state relations in welfare, and so on. A second proposal is that the success or failure of intergovernmental relations be judged by the degree of harmony and cooperation that prevails between each set of national and state officials. Thirdly, particularly since the Eisenhower Administration took office, there has been much talk of the desirability of decentralization and a movement "back" to the states.

A common difficulty besets all these suggestions. Coordination, harmony or cooperation, and decentralization or states' rights are not necessarily good or bad in and of themselves. They are usually neutral concepts and are good or bad only in relation to other and more fundamental objectives an individual or group is seeking. To the extent that they are valued in and of themselves, they almost always hold a secondary place in the value framework. A program may be highly successful yet not present a picture of harmony and cooperation between state and nation. This often happens in the early years of a program when program goals remain unanswered or not agreed upon. Complete harmony is simply not possible if there is conflict over program goals. On the other hand, harmony may come at a high price. The professional administrators of national and state governments may have very harmonious relations but this good feeling may be a means of masking their fundamental disagreement with the general political officials of both levels and of suppressing policy issues that the latter would prefer to have brought to light.

As for coordination, all national-state relations cannot be coordinated until policy goals are agreed upon. The important problem is not coordination but coordination *for what*. The President and Congress have found it impossible to give a single answer. The policy and procedures in connection with national-state relations are not coordinated because no one in authority can agree on a single set of goals or objectives. Similarly decentralization. Decentralization for what and with what policy results? Decentralization cannot be considered apart from programmatic values that are affected thereby, particularly with an increase in the nationwide economic and social problems confronting government. Decentralization or states' rights, if applied to a number of activities, would mean virtual elimination of effective governmental action. Decentralization is thus often advocated by those who oppose governmental activity in a particular area and believe that decentralizing it would make action ineffective; it is also frequently supported by those from rich states as opposed to those from poor areas, by those not in political power nationally, and by those voicing a general political philosophy rather than by those confronted with very detailed and practical problems.

The patterns of national-state relations can be changed or "improved." But since these patterns reflect the values of individuals engaged in these relations, any change in the patterns is likely to heighten value conflict, at least temporarily.

FOOTNOTES TO CHAPTER 19

1. William Anderson, *Federalism and Intergovernmental Relations, A Budget of Suggestions for Research*, Chicago, Public Administration Service, 1946, pp. 32–3.

2. New York, Columbia University Press, 1938.

3. *The Federalist*, No. 10 (Modern Library ed., 1937, pp. 61–2).

4. The terms "principled" and "expediency" have been suggested by Harold D. Lasswell and Abraham Kaplan, *Power and Society*, New Haven, Yale University

Press, 1950, p. 42; the terms "organization" and "conservation" have been put forth by Herbert A. Simon, *Administrative Behavior*, New York, Macmillan, 1947, pp. 112–3 and 117.

5. *The Governmental Process*, New York, Knopf, 1951, p. 33; see also chapter 2 generally.

6. The material that follows in this and the next section is based heavily upon the data collected by Research in Intergovernmental Relations in the United States as observed in the State of Minnesota, a group research project at the University of Minnesota from 1946 to 1951. For more complete documentation of some of the points made here, see the series of ten research monographs published by the University of Minnesota Press as the result of the study, particularly the forthcoming analytical volume which will be number nine in the series. William Anderson and the present author were directors of the project.

The functional fields covered are indicated by citing the six volumes in the series which deal with particular activities: No. 1, *Intergovernmental Relations and the Courts*, by Forrest Talbott; No. 2, *Intergovernmental Relations in Highways*, by R. A. Gomez; No. 3, *Intergovernmental Relations in Education*, by Robert L. Morlan; No. 4, *Intergovernmental Relations in Public Health*, by Laurence Wyatt; No. 5, *Intergovernmental Relations in Social Welfare*, by Ruth Raup; No. 6, *Intergovernmental Relations in Employment Security*, by Francis E. Rourke.

7. Truman, *op. cit.*, p. 33.

8. *Reflections on Public Administration*, University, University of Alabama Press, 1947, p. 9.

9. Influence is here defined as effect on policies of others (Lasswell's and Kaplan's "exercise of influence"). Leadership is a subset of influences involving purposive manipulation. Compare Lasswell and Kaplan, *op. cit.*, pp. 71, 74–75, 152.

10. Simon, *op. cit.*, p. 125. Compare David Easton, *The Political System, An Inquiry into the State of Political Science*, New York, Knopf, 1953, p. 132: "A policy is authoritative when the people to whom it is intended to apply or are affected by it consider that they must or ought to obey it."

11. Simon, *op. cit.*, p. 127.

12. For an analysis of the devices of administrative supervision and their persuasiveness in actual practice, see Edward W. Weidner, "State Supervision of Local Government in Minnesota," *Public Administration Review*, Vol. 4 (1944), pp. 226–233.

13. In the discussion of the fiscal aspects of federalism, not specifically in connection with the material in this chapter, John E. Burton presented a somewhat different picture of national leadership in grant-in-aid programs, as a phase of his plea for procedures that would "establish the minimum service in various fields that we want a state to perform, and on the basis of general compliance which can be audited on a much broader basis than the detailed audit that now goes on by federal administrators." In developing his point of view about a more broadly-based system of grants with compliance on a broader basis, he contrasted it with "compliance set in detail and in the back room, as it were, as now—a field agent of a federal bureau works with some deputy or department head in the state government and receives compliance. Many times what he achieves is no part of the law, no part of the regulation. But because the state is on the receiving end, a sort of attrition goes on and finally they agree to certain conditions." (Editor)

20

Fiscal Aspects of Federalism

By Roy Blough

Federalism is a system of allocating governmental powers among central and local governing jurisdictions. The powers to be allocated are of two general kinds: police powers and financial powers. It is with the latter group—the powers of performing and financing governmental services—that this chapter is concerned. The police powers have only a minor fiscal interest, for the cost of *governing* is only a small fraction of the total cost of *government*.

In examining any system for allocating financial powers, three questions immediately come to the fore: Who is to benefit? Who is to pay? Who is to decide who is to benefit and who is to pay? These questions may be asked with respect to various meanings of "who." "Who" may mean "what income classes" or it may mean "what occupation groups." In a discussion of federalism "who" means "what governmental unit, central or local"; the concept is one of geographical jurisdiction.

The problem of geography in relation to decision-making is not limited to a federal system of government as such. It is met with in all forms of governmental relationships throughout the range from a weak military alliance at one extreme to a highly centralized unitary government at the other. For example, a grant-in-aid of funds to a city by a state government, or a grant-in-aid to economically underdeveloped countries by the United States or an international organization, gives rise to philosophical and technical problems that are similar to each other and to those presented by a federal grant-in-aid to the states, although only the last involves a federal system of government. The fiscal approach thus encourages the observer to consider the problems of federalism as covering a much wider range of governmental structures than the political system of intergovernmental relationships that is defined as the federal system.

This chapter does not seek to examine the fiscal aspects of geography and decision-making for the whole range of governmental relationships or even for different varieties of federalism.[1] It relates specifically to present-day federalism in the United States. This example of federalism, while presenting a formidable task to those who would understand it, is too distinctive to serve as the basis for more than the most cautious generalizations regarding federalism in other countries. The emergence of a federal state in Europe, for example, would undoubtedly give federalism a much different type of test than it has had in the United States and the financial problems, while basically similar, would almost certainly be more complicated and difficult.

Fiscal problems in the United States are affected by the fact that it represents a particular variety of federalism, one which has developed predominantly by a process of growth and budding-off rather than through the uniting of originally diverse elements. Much of its strength derives from the fact that the lines of authority drawn by the Constitution between state and federal action have proved not to be permanently rigid but to have a degree of flexibility; they have shifted as the clear pattern of public interests was seen by the Congress and the Supreme Court to require such a shift. The fiscal restrictions placed by the Constitution are relatively minor but even they have evolved with the growth of population, advances in technology, and changes in our national pattern of values.

Finance has at the minimum the two aspects of expenditures and revenues. A third, that of borrowing and repaying debt, is common although not inevitable. The revenue side clearly falls in a special category since, with possible minor exceptions, the only purpose of raising revenue is to make possible the performance of the functions of government in a stable economy. The expenditures side requires attention to such technical matters as budgeting, purchasing, accounting, and disbursing. At bottom, however, it is concerned with the functions of government themselves inasmuch as these are reflected in the services and goods which government expenditures purchase. Information regarding amounts of expenditures, the purposes for which made, units of government by which made, and so on, must be available before it is possible to speak intelligently regarding the amounts and forms of taxes that should be imposed and the governmental units by which they should be imposed.

A study of fiscal aspects may help answer two questions of concern to a larger study of federalism. The first and central question it should answer is this: Accepting federalism as the desired system of governmental organization and operation, what fiscal arrangements can be developed which will most effectively promote its successful functioning? In the consideration of this first question a second one will be found intruding itself from time to time: What limitations do the realities of fiscal action place on choices regarding federalism? That is, what decisions that otherwise seem attractive are found to be impracticable or otherwise undesirable because of difficulties in using the fiscal machinery?

The stubborn fact that government and the services of government are possible only if they can be paid for makes finance one of the central factors determining the success or failure of a federal system of government as well as any other governmental system. In United States history the failure of the

Articles of Confederation to insure adequate financial support for the central government is recognized as a major cause of the breakdown of the confederation. Today a more pertinent question is whether under our federal system of government state and local financing methods can stand the strain which public demand for governmental services places upon them. The financial impotence of the central government is only a dim memory recorded in the history books. Yet there are movements even now under way that have for their avowed purpose the undermining of the financial powers of the national government. The fiscal aspects of federalism are, it would seem, more than merely an interesting issue. It was significant how much stress the congressional act setting up a commission on intergovernmental relations in 1953 placed upon fiscal problems.

I

AREAS OF BENEFIT, TAXATION, AND DECISION-MAKING

Simple Model

What answer to the fiscal questions—who should benefit, who should pay, and who should decide—is most consistent with the central philosophy of federalism? The appropriate answer would seem to be that the geographical area benefitted by a service is the area that should pay for it and also the area that should decide whether and at what standard of adequacy the service should be rendered. This may be illustrated by a simple and therefore unrealistic model. In this model it is assumed that there are some needs for public service that are generally recognized to have nationwide signficance, not so much in the sense that persons everywhere in the nation have the same problems and aspirations—this would not be enough—but rather in the sense that the interests of persons throughout the nation are substantially affected by whether the services are performed in part of the nation. Decision-making on problems relating to such nationwide interests would in this model be made by the federal government. Moreover, since the benefits of governmental activity undertaken to promote these interests would be shared throughout the nation, the taxes to support such activity would be levied by the federal government and collected throughout the nation. Certain other interests, according to this simple model, would be of statewide or narrower concern. (Throughout this chapter state-local fiscal relations are disregarded.)[2] Since only persons within the state would be substantially affected by services undertaken to promote these interests, the unit of decision would be the state, which would finance the service by taxes tapping sources of revenue within the state. In this simple model, finally, it is assumed that all interests to be promoted by governmental action are deemed to be of these two kinds, nationwide or statewide, and the further assumption is made that no difficulties would be met in levying and collecting the taxes required to finance the required expenditures.

Similarity of Early U. S. to Simple Model

Although this simple model of federalism obviously is unrealistic, the actual practice during a considerable portion of our national life did not differ widely from it. To be sure, it may be doubted whether all activities left to the states were of only statewide interest and all activities undertaken by the central government were of truly nationwide interest. But the division was fairly well defined; there were few cases of joint action by the federal government and the states, or by two or more states. The low level of public expenditures could be met by relatively simple tax systems. The federal government, outside of periods of war and emergency, kept to a pattern of taxation which included only import duties and excise taxes. States and their subdivisions relied almost entirely on the taxation of property. While the situation perhaps was never quite as simple as this description would indicate, it was not far from the truth up to shortly after the turn of the present century.

Evolution of Last Half-century

To a considerable extent since about 1900, and especially since 1920, the actual situation has increasingly departed from the simple model of federal-state relations described above. The reasons are well known, if sometimes overlooked, and need only to be recalled briefly to mind. With the improvement of transportation resulting from the spread of railroads, the automobile and the hard-surface road, and the airplane, the nation physically is more closely linked than were most states a century ago, and it continues to become a smaller unit year by year. The growth of cities has reflected and stimulated the growth of commerce and industry. Markets for many products are nation-wide. In the expanding economy per capita incomes and levels of living have risen and have created insistent demands for rising standards of public activities and for new services, many of which have been made necessary by industrial employment and urbanization. The uniting of the nation for the successful fighting of two world wars united the nation also for peacetime economic and political tasks and added to the understanding of the mutual interdependence of the different regions of the nation. Finally, the United States shared and largely contributed to a growing worldwide concern for justice and equity and an increased awareness that a person can be his brother's keeper through public as well as private action. These forces in combination have resulted in tremendously increased government expenditures and have enlarged the geographical areas of interest in and benefit from the services of government.

Present-day Complexities: Benefits

A few illustrations will suffice to show how the nation as a whole is interested in the quality of locally applied services. In the case of public highways, the introduction of the automobile and the hard-surface road have made it a matter of concern for New Yorkers going to Florida, for example, that roads in the intervening states be adequate and linked into a readily useable through route. The use of motor trucks for interstate shipments likewise has made the road system a matter of general concern both for supplying markets and tapping sources of supply. Airports are a relatively new development and in their case clearly the interests served may be nationwide and even worldwide.

The growing mobility of the population widens the area of interest in several important government services. Health conditions are of increasingly widespread concern because of the ease with which communicable disease can sweep across the country. Moreover, persons who do not receive proper health care may become a public burden later in other states to which they may move. The training of soldiers for the army, likewise, has made health conditions within states and localities a matter of national concern.

With respect to social security and relief of poverty, it was observed during the depression that persons migrated from the states which had low standards of care and became a burden on states which had higher standards. Moreover, social unrest is a communicable disease which if it were to receive a substantial start in one region might spread widely. Finally, the competition of states for industrial plants may lead them to underbid each other in standards of social insurance benefits and in rates of tax imposed to support them, with the result of lowering standards below acceptable levels in all states. With respect to education, a high degree of population mobility means that the standards of education that children receive are not the concern solely of their home state, for poorly educated persons moving to other states may prove to be a liability there.

War and depression also have shown the mutuality of interest among states in the level of production and economic activity. Thus the importance of maximum production for war has demonstrated the national interest in a well-trained, well-educated labor force. Moreover, recessions cannot be quarantined within state boundaries. They may spread across the nation and even across the world. Unemployment often results from factors more nearly nation-wide than local in character, and indeed may be a consequence of national policy. The maintenance of purchasing power and other programs designed to protect the economy thus are matters of national and not purely state interest. These examples should make clear that to an increasing extent the standards of many government services within any state are matters of major concern far beyond the borders of the state and often are of truly national importance.

If the conclusion is sound that the area of interest determines the area of decision-making, it is clear that many forms of governmental services for which the federal government formerly felt little or no interest or responsibility have now become appropriate subjects for central decision-making. With respect to such matters the federal government has open to it several courses of action. It may decide to take no action at all in the hope that the interest of the states will be in accord with national interest and sufficiently strong that they will without central intervention act to promote the national interest. The tendency not to act is in practice strengthened by reluctance to expand the field of national action.

With respect to many matters of relatively minor importance in which the nation has an interest, this policy of nonintervention is the one actually followed by the federal government. For major matters, however, nonintervention may not be acceptable, for states often have proved to be unable, and sometimes unwilling, to provide a standard of governmental service sufficiently high to achieve what the nation may consider to be a minimum standard of performance in the field. It must be recognized that there are matters in which the states have not had a satisfactory record of action in the absence of federal prodding.

Where intervention was found desirable the federal government might follow one of several courses of action. It might take over and carry on the entire activity in a field in which it has substantial interest, thus in effect relieving the states of responsibility in that field. Or the federal government might arrive at a division of a field of activity, leaving to the states decision and action with respect to a clearly defined portion of the field. The federal government on its side would exercise complete control and action with respect to those aspects which are necessary to assure performance of that minimum of services which the national interest required. Division of a field of services is often virtually impossible since usually one closely related set of services is being provided. When one administration is adequate to perform a function, adding another may be disruptive and surely will add expense. Accordingly, the position taken by the federal government might be not actually to enter the field, but to insist that the level of performance by the states be adequate to protect the national interest, leaving the states freedom to provide whatever additional service they may desire. This insistence by the federal government on a minimum standard carries with it, of course, responsibility to assist the states in financing the service. This in turn raises such problems as how to assure that the minimum standard is performed efficiently so as not to waste federal funds, how to avoid interfering with state decisions outside the legitimate area of federal interest, and how to allocate the cost equitably. As will be seen later, the methods and devices available for solving these problems leave much to be desired.

In those cases where the benefits are wider than the state but continue to be largely regional and not national, the application of the principle would call for regional areas of decision and financing. The lack of such regional machinery makes federalism work less perfectly than might otherwise be the case. Compacts among the states have proved to be a cumbersome type of machinery which has been applied in relatively few cases, such as the allocation of water resources or the joint operation of port and other facilities. There is no present prospect for the establishment of a regional level of government. In passing it may be noted that regional development at national expense was adopted at a relatively early date as a federal function and was actively carried on at a time when federal funds for relief purposes, for example, were deemed to be both undesirable and unconstitutional.

Present-day Complexities: Taxes

The same forces that have enlarged the area of benefit have altered and greatly complicated the sources of tax revenue. More than one jurisdiction may have valid claims to impose the tax on a person, business, piece of property, transfer, or income, while the burden of a tax may fall outside the area of the unit which imposes it. As tax sources have come increasingly to be based on an ever more complicated national economy it has become less and less possible to say with assurance upon whom the burden of any particular tax really falls. The difficulties are greatest with respect to local taxes but are present also with respect to state taxes. A few examples may help to clarify the point.

In the case of the property tax the problem may be illustrated by a railroad or a public utility which extends physically into a number of different taxing jurisdictions. For example, a hydro-electric plant which depends for its power on water accumulated in several states and for the profitable sale of its electricity on access to a large regional market should not be the tax monopoly of the local district or even the state in which it is physically located.

In the case of taxes on personal income, a taxpayer may reside in one state, work in another state, and spend his money in two or more states. Clearly, more than one jurisdiction has some kind of claim to tax his income.

In the case of taxes on the passage of property at death, the person may have died in one state, may have been domiciled in another state at the time of his death, may have owned real estate in a third state, may have rented a safe deposit box to store his securities in a fourth state, while the property may be transferred to an heir who resides in still a fifth state. The property may consist of securities representing wealth and income throughout the nation and may have been accumulated during residence in a number of states. It is arguable that each of the states involved has some claim to tax the passage of the estate from the decedent to the heir.

In the case of corporation taxes, the corporation may be incorporated in one state, may be licensed to do business in a number of other states, may have factories located in several states, may buy its raw materials from other parts of the country or abroad, and may sell its products throughout the nation or even throughout the world. Meanwhile, its stockholders may live far removed from its offices. Out of the joint efforts of all persons connected with the corporation a profit is derived. Many jurisdictions would seem to have some claim to taxes on this profit.

A simple answer to these jurisdictional questions is that every state should have the right to tax what it can. To this answer it may be objected that the result might well be confiscatory double taxation by two or more jurisdictions or, at the least, gross inequity among taxpayers, since in some cases several jurisdictions would be involved, while in others, only one would tax. Moreover, many states with an equitable claim may not be able to assert a tax in view of physical and constitutional restrictions. Finally, under complicated jurisdictional situations, a tax imposed by one state may very well rest as a burden on taxpayers in other states thus violating the principle that benefits to an area should be financed by persons in that area. In today's complex economy the bases on which our simple model rests no longer exist.

II

COMPLAINTS REGARDING FEDERAL-STATE FISCAL RELATIONS

One approach to the fiscal problems of federalism in the United States is to examine the complaints that are made about the fiscal situation and particularly about federal-state fiscal relations. As usual with respect to policy matters, the views that are expressed are often conflicting.

A frequent pair of complaints more or less common to all times and places is that taxes are too high and that there is too much government. In a sense, these are two sides of the same complaint since one is the cause of the other. Some complainants, however, are chiefly concerned about the load of taxes they pay while others are chiefly concerned at the impact on their businesses or their other activities of the operations of government. The objection to "excessive" taxation or government is often the motivation that underlies the complaints about federal-state fiscal relations that are discussed in the following paragraphs.

Over the past two decades there have been persistent attacks on the "excessive" spread of federal activities.[3] It is charged that the federal government is assuming functions reserved to the states, is taking the government away from the people, is exercising a stranglehold on state operations by forcing states to carry on certain activities in a specified manner, and otherwise is upsetting the allocation of powers that the Founding Fathers wisely provided. In particular, the grant-in-aid programs of the federal government have come under attack as encouraging wasteful and extravagant expenditures, encroaching on state prerogatives, and achieving no real purpose since, it is urged, the only result is to give the taxpayer's money an unnecessary round trip to Washington.

On the other hand, there have been persistent efforts to enlarge the scope of federal activities and to increase federal grants to states. These efforts have generally been made by groups interested in promoting and raising the levels of certain governmental services, such as health, education, housing, and poor relief. They have also come in some cases from financially weak states that feel the need of greater aid in financing services in which the federal government has shown an interest.

A major source of complaint has been the situation commonly referred to as "conflicting taxation" or "double taxation" or "overlapping taxation." As previously mentioned, both the federal government and the state governments have reached out into the previously untaxed area between them so that now it would be difficult to devise a major source of revenue not being used at one or both levels. Moreover, most of these revenue sources are used by both the federal government and the states. Many studies have been made of overlapping taxation and it has been vigorously criticised; nevertheless the trend to an increasing amount of overlapping taxation has continued.[4]

An argument that some critics of overlapping taxation have put forward is that the total volume of taxation has become too high; eliminating overlapping taxes, it is urged by these critics, would reduce the total revenue that could be collected, thus forcing down expenditures. The general argument against high taxes has been noted above. Advocates of federalism who want effective government are not likely to be persuaded by this argument that double taxation is therefore harmful.

Another argument is that for two jurisdictions to levy the same kind of tax is double taxation and inherently wrong. The argument has appeal—double taxation sounds wrong and in the "good old days" was not imposed—but the logic of the argument is weak. Most if not all taxes fall in the final analysis upon income although they differ in the way in which the burden is distributed.

Another objection voiced against overlapping federal and state taxes is that taxpayers as the result of such overlapping are required to prepare and file an excessive number of tax returns, which imposes on them an inordinately high cost of "tax compliance." The criticism is a valid one since there are few or no examples of the use of the same tax returns by both federal and state governments. Its importance is easily overstated, however, since the basic data for one return are available for preparing other returns involving the same kind of tax. The extra expenses involved in filing the extra returns do not loom as a major consideration in determining tax policy. It should be noted that overlapping taxation does not result in an increase in the total number of different kinds of taxes levied, since the taxes which one level of government did not impose would be even more necessary than at present as a source of revenue for the other level.

The high cost to taxpayers of tax compliance resulting from overlapping taxation is accompanied by a high cost to government of double administration, since two levels of government are administering the same kind of tax falling on the same taxpayers. This criticism also is a valid one but, again, is not of major importance; moreover, it could be obviated, as will later appear.

A further argument against overlapping taxes is that when two or more jurisdictions use the same tax the total load of that tax becomes excessive. The validity of this argument depends on the rates imposed by the two governments. If each jurisdiction sets its tax rate with no regard to other taxes being imposed on the same tax base, the total load of that tax may indeed become excessive. While examples certainly could be pointed out where this seems to have occurred, the state and federal governments usually are fully aware of and sensitive to the situation faced by the taxpayers. It may be noted that a very few states imposing very high tax rates might substantially reduce the rates which the federal government would be prepared to impose on the same tax base.

The argument against overlapping taxation which seems to be the most persuasive to the present writer is that the imposition of federal taxes of kinds which the states can successfully use results in placing unnecessary limits on state financial powers. The implications of this argument will be discussed at a later point.

Finally, state and federal officials alike prove to be critical of the tax exemptions enjoyed by the other level of government. The states point to the exemption of the federal government from property taxation and stress the resulting loss of potential revenue and the "threat" to the financial independence of the states that results. Particularly mentioned in this connection are the national domain of forests and grazing lands on the one hand, and the recently acquired government property holdings for public power operations and for military training centers on the other hand. Exemption from sales tax of purchases by government and of sales on government reservations are among other exemptions brought under attack. It should be observed that a good deal has been done by the federal government to meet this criticism either by permitting state taxation or by paying equivalent amounts to the states in lieu of taxation.

On the other side, the President and other federal administrative officials and members of Congress, as well as persons outside the government, have from time to time attacked the exemption from the federal income tax of the interest on state and municipal securities. Many lawyers now hold the view that although taxation of such interest was held unconstitutional in earlier years, a non-discriminating income tax applying to it would now be upheld. The exemption is, however, imbedded in the statutes and all efforts to remove or weaken it have failed. The objection to the exemption has been based on various grounds, notably that the exemption gives great financial benefit to taxpayers in higher income brackets which is not passed on to states in lower interest rates and that investors who should and otherwise would invest in equity securities of private enterprise are induced instead to invest in tax exempt securities.

III

FINANCIAL POWERS OF THE STATE

The most crucial practical problem of federal-state fiscal relations concerns the ability of the states to finance governmental services, to which reference was made above. If the states have ample ability to support the programs in which they feel an interest, the federal government will find it necessary to intervene only when the states oppose or neglect the national interest. But if state financial abilities are so limited that the scope and quality of state activity are substantially restricted, despite the good intentions of the state, the need for federal intervention and assistance is greatly increased since the national interests are likely to be adversely affected.

The limits placed by the United States Constitution on state taxing power are relatively minor. The prohibition of taxes burdening interstate and foreign commerce may deprive states of substantial revenue but the imposition of such taxation would almost surely destroy the national character of the economy and thereby destroy also the foundations of the high levels of production and consumption that we enjoy. Other federal constitutional restrictions protecting taxpayers against discrimination should have little if any effect in reducing state ability to raise revenue.

The states themselves have placed various constitutional restrictions on state and local taxing powers. These restrictions must be disregarded in the present discussion since they can be removed by the states themselves and do not involve federal-state relations.

State taxing power is undoubtedly reduced by the large number and high rates of federal taxes. In the absence of federal taxes on personal incomes, corporate incomes, alcoholic liquors, tobacco, gasoline, admissions, etc., the states could raise their rates without causing undue economic harm. Nevertheless, the amounts by which state taxing powers are reduced by federal taxes can easily be overemphasized. The experience has been that the states did not make any more use of these taxes when federal rates were low or nonexistent and have in general raised rather than lowered their tax rates as new federal taxes have been imposed or risen in rate.

It is important to recognize, moreover, that if the federal government were to withdraw from tax fields it now occupies, the states would in the case of most taxes be able to increase their tax rates by only a fraction of the rates now imposed by the federal government. There are two major reasons for this conclusion. The first is that the imposition of a high rate by a state may well result in the migration of the tax base to other states, especially where there is considerable possible mobility in the tax base. The threat of such migration has proved to be a very powerful political weapon in state legislatures. State tax rates on transfers at death or by gift, individual incomes, corporate profits, gross receipts, and manufacturing are particularly likely to be held low and correspondingly nonproductive by this consideration.

A second problem for the states is the difficulty of administering effectively some kinds of taxes, particularly at rates so high as to stimulate strong efforts at avoidance or evasion. Perhaps the most notable examples are the high excise taxes on liquor and tobacco. The federal government has found that the only way these taxes can be imposed is on the manufacturers. Despite tremendous efforts on its part, the illicit manufacture and sale of liquor is probably very large. Only a few states could raise much revenue from the manufacture of distilled spirits or tobacco, because production is concentrated and in each of these states competition of manufacturers in other states would operate to hold the tax rate down. While these taxes present particularly great difficulties, in part because of the very high federal rates, most other excises as well as the corporation taxes and the personal income tax present problems of adequate administration and enforcement.

A second significant aspect of the problem of the financial abilities of states is the great variation among them in their capacity to raise revenue. Despite the existence of free movement of persons and goods within the United States, per capita income has continued to vary tremendously among the states. Accordingly, rates of taxation necessary to perform a service at a given standard may be comfortably low in high-income states but forbiddingly high in low-income states. With respect to services that confer only local or statewide benefits, the nation at large need have little concern about the capacity of states to finance such services. But where, as in an increasingly large variety of services, the benefits are to some extent dispersed over a large region or the nation as a whole, the inability of states to finance such services is a matter of deep concern to the region or the nation. Programs of great national importance may not in fact be carried out at levels deemed necessary to meet the national minimum. The implications of this point for federal help in financing selected services in the poorer states are reinforced by an argument along a quite different line. While differences among the income levels of states undoubtedly in the main reflect differences in productivity, it is arguable, and persons from low-income states make strong use of the argument, that incomes in a national economy are derived from a much wider area than the taxing jurisdiction which is in a position to collect taxes on such incomes. Accordingly, it is contended, the poorer states are equitably entitled to some of the tax revenues from businesses that are concentrated in a few industrial and commercial centers.

A third significant aspect of the financing powers of states concerns the effects of depression in multiplying the financial problems of states and localities. Indeed, on the basis of the experience of the thirties it may be concluded that depressions constitute a substantial threat to federalism. During a period of depression demands in the states for governmental services mount at the same time that tax revenues fall, the capacity to bear taxes is at a minimum, and increases in tax rates would discourage economic activity and reduce private purchasing power. The credit of states and localities—often strained to its legal limits in good times—may be seriously impaired by the unwillingness of investors and financial institutions to extend credit when revenues are low and the outlook is dark. Finally, the states, unlike the federal government, are not able to use monetary powers to make up deficiencies in taxing and borrowing powers. For all these reasons, some states and local governments during a depression period may not be able to meet even their basic requirements for services, with the result that the federal government must come to the rescue in support of functions that in better times were effectively handled at state and local levels. A breakdown of this kind occurred during the thirties; it might again if serious depression were to develop.

IV

MEASURES PROPOSED TO MEET THE PROBLEM OF STATE FINANCIAL WEAKNESS

The measures proposed to solve fiscal problems of federalism have a considerable range of objectives. Since the major problem is that of state financial weakness, the following discussion concentrates on measures designed at least in part to deal with this problem.

Centralization of Functions

The federal government might take over, determine, administer, and finance certain important functions. Where this involved services to people such a shift would usually entail loss of efficiency in operation, loss of interest on the part of the local public, as well as the enlargement of the federal bureaucracy, the shift of political controversy to the federal level, and a weakening on pressures against extravagant levels of expenditure. For these reasons this kind of "solution" to the problem of lack of state financial power has not been acceptable either to students of the subject or to politicians.

Federal-State and Interstate Cooperation

A rather modest approach to strengthening state financial powers would be for the central government to cooperate with the states and for the states to cooperate with each other in allocating the bases of complicated taxes and in administering the taxes. The difficulties of states in administering complicated taxes can be greatly eased; much has already been done by making federal tax returns available to state tax administrators and by joint audit procedures with which the federal government has been experimenting. Similarly, states have sometimes cooperated in the auditing of national businesses although for some reason this cooperative procedure has not thrived. While it is not possible to allocate tax bases in an entirely equitable manner for reasons previously described, considerable success has been achieved in securing agreement among states regarding allocation formulas to be applied to various kinds of taxes. Such allocations permit the states to impose taxes on a reasonable share of the tax base without the danger either of exempting the taxpayer or of confiscating his property through overlapping state taxes.

There are several other methods which may be considered examples of federal-state and interstate cooperation. One possible method would be for state governments simply to add a percentage to the federal rate of tax with the central government collecting the tax and remitting the proceeds to the state. The state governments have shown little interest in having the federal government collect taxes for them in this manner. A somewhat similar proposal is for the federal government to impose a tax in excess of its own needs, assigning definite shares of the tax to those states to which the tax base could be allocated. This method, like the one previously mentioned, would presumably reduce the costs of administration to states and the cost of compliance to taxpayers. State governments prefer to keep tax collection in their own hands, fearing that some future Congress might repeal the state share and preferring to maintain their own bureaucracies rather than strengthen the central bureaucracy.

Another method by which the federal government could assist the states is through allowing a credit against the national tax for tax payments to the state. Thus, in the case of the federal estate tax, a credit is allowed against the federal tax for death taxes paid to the state governments up to a large fraction of the federal tax. This credit operates to give the states part of the revenue and to prevent them from competing with each other for wealthy taxpayers by promising low estate tax rates. The state governments have complained that their share is too small. They have opposed extending the crediting device to other taxes on the ground that this would bring them to an increasing degree under the power of the federal government. This is true in the sense that the crediting device in effect forces the states to impose the tax up to the limits of the credit since if they fail to do so they lose revenue without any saving to the taxpayer.

Proposals to Separate Tax Sources

A persistent proposal for reforming federal-state fiscal relations is to eliminate overlapping taxation by assigning certain taxes to the state governments and other taxes to the federal government, each level to have the monopoly of taxes assigned to it and thus to avoid imposing the taxes assigned to the other governmental level.[5] Some variants of this proposal would achieve the separation of sources through constitutional amendment while others would rely on agreement between the federal government and the states. A normal part of the proposal is that there be no grants-in-aid or subsidies paid by the federal government to the states.

Partial separation of sources is practised by many states in their relations with local governments. There is no state that has complete separation of sources, including the absence of state aids. The most ambitious plan for separation of sources appears to have been the one adopted by constitutional amendment in California several decades ago. Although it was widely hailed at the time of its adoption, it has long since been abandoned.

The reasons urged for the separation of federal and state tax sources are largely those based on the objections previously mentioned to overlapping federal and state taxes. Expense and trouble to the taxpayers, greater total cost of tax administration, inadequacy of state and local revenues, dependence of states on the federal government, an excessive level of taxes—these were the principal objections to overlapping taxes and they form the basis for urging the separation of tax sources. Other motives underlying the proposal are the desire to reduce and hold down the size of federal expenditures, opposition to federal grants-in-aid, and the desire of state political leaders to strengthen their positions. The argument that is pertinent to the state power to finance, which is the point of emphasis in this discussion, is that state taxing power could through separation of source be increased so that states could more readily meet from their own tax sources the demands placed upon them for governmental services without the necessity for relying on the federal government. The validity of this argument depends on whether in the assignment of taxes the states received better sources of state revenue than they gave up, and how effectively they could tax these resources. A brief examination of the major tax sources will indicate how difficult it would be to increase substantially the state taxing power without much more seriously impairing the large taxing powers that the federal government obviously must have, if for no other reason than to assure survival in time of war. It must be borne in mind that separation of sources would not reduce total expenditures, at least not significantly. Revenue lost from one tax would have to be made up from other taxes.

The personal income tax is the largest single source of revenue of the federal government. To assign this tax to the states would require the federal government to find some fifteen to twenty billion dollars more revenue from other sources. The states, however, would be unable to derive more than a substantial fraction of this amount of revenue from additional use of the income tax, for reasons discussed above.

In separation-of-sources proposals the taxes on corporation profits are usually assigned to the central government. These taxes would be perhaps the most difficult for the states to handle successfully since the corporations do business in a great many states. The devices which corporations could use in shifting their income from one location to another would make it extremely difficult for the states to impose corporation taxes at rates at all comparable with those of the present federal tax.

The estate tax is frequently urged for assignment to state governments. The argument is frequently made that since the state governments control the transfer of property at death they should enjoy a monopoly of taxing such transfers. Since virtually all laws relating to property, contracts, incomes, and so on, are state laws, the special argument for death taxation, on examination, loses much of its force. If the purpose of advocating the withdrawal of the federal government from the taxation of estates really is to benefit the states financially, its advocates have failed to think the problem through. If the federal government were to withdraw from death taxation the states would get far less revenue than the federal government would lose. The major reason for adopting the tax crediting device in the early twenties was to protect state revenues from death taxation from the underbidding of other states which were making a strong appeal to wealthy taxpayers to move to those states in order to avoid death taxation. There can be little doubt, in fact, that many advocates of turning the estate tax over to state governments hope that thereby the tax would be virtually destroyed through interstate competition. The states may well derive more from the estate tax today under the crediting system than they would if the federal government retired from the field; modifications of the crediting system could readily be devised which would greatly enlarge state revenue. The claim of the states to the entire estate tax is also weakened by a fact previously mentioned, namely, that the property subject to this tax is often accumulated in many states.

Among the excise taxes, the most productive is the tax on alcoholic liquor. If the federal government withdrew from the taxation of liquor, the state governments could not possibly recapture the same amount of revenue because of the enforcement problem, as previously explained. Likewise, with respect to the taxation of tobacco, the assignment of this revenue source to the states would undoubtedly result in a much lower total collection of taxes. The same is true of most other taxes, although to a lesser degree.

There thus seem to be very strong reasons for not assigning any of the major sources of federal revenue to the state governments. If the total needs for revenue were not so great, the loss of revenue arising from assigning tax sources to the states might not be particularly serious, but under existing circumstances the federal government would certainly be very loth to give up major sources of revenue, particularly when the states could not use them effectively. There are undoubtedly a few taxes that could usefully be assigned to state governments. The federal government entered the gasoline tax at a late stage. While its tax is collected at less cost than are the state taxes, the states have developed efficient collection systems for gasoline taxation and in any event are not likely to leave the field. Likewise, there is no reason why the federal government might not leave the admissions taxes to the states or localities. The same may be said for some other miscellaneous forms of excise tax, although the amounts of revenue involved would not be of major proportions.

Whatever its merits, separation of sources would be extremely difficult to achieve. The federal government can of course withdraw from any form of taxation unilaterally. Such withdrawal would not give the states any protection against the federal government reentering the field whenever Congress decided it was desirable to do so. Moreover, a real separation of sources would require that the states also withdraw from certain taxes which the federal government is now imposing, for example, the tax on corporation profits. Many states would be very reluctant to give up this profitable source of revenue. They might be forced to do so by a constitutional amendment, but such an amendment could be passed only by a vote of three-fourths of the states themselves. The states might be induced to withdraw from certain forms of taxation by special grants from the federal government, but this would bring the states under federal control in a manner which the advocates of separation of sources usually deplore. Moreover, the amount of compensation granted to states in exchange for withdrawal from certain forms of taxation would require reexamination from time to time. There could be no permanent assurance either that the federal government would continue to pay the compensation or that states would continue not to use the tax.

The advantages to the states of a separation of tax sources would by no means be uniform. Some states are very poor with respect to the sources of taxation which might be turned over to them. For example, the rural states would find the admissions tax of relatively little value to them as a revenue producer. The revenues from the estate tax would also be highly concentrated in a few states. For perhaps most of the states, separation of sources has relatively little to offer for what they might be asked to relinquish in exchange for it.

Even if separation of sources were achieved, there is no assurance that any problems would remain solved for any considerable period of years. The proponents of allocation of revenue sources assume that it would be possible to determine the revenue needs of state and local governments not only for today but also for decades to come. To be adequate, the separation of sources plan would have to be drawn along such lines that all jurisdictions would be able to finance their expenditures by imposing reasonable, nonconfiscatory rates that would not have harmful effects. There is no possible way of assuring that any present-day solution would be adequate for the future.

On balance, even if the practical hurdles could be surmounted it must be concluded that the separation of tax sources between the federal and state governments would not be a satisfactory solution to the problem of financing a federal system of government in the United States. It may well be desirable for the central government to withdraw from the use of some taxes which it now imposes. It is not possible, however, to count on any such withdrawal to meet the modern problem of enlarging state financial powers in the face of growing demands for the services of government. Nor would it be generally advantageous to states to accept federal withdrawal of grants-in-aid as the price for federal withdrawal from the use of relatively minor tax sources. Some states might benefit from the exchange but those which are relatively poor would find that they were worse off than before as the result of the bargain.

Grants-in-Aid

In this discussion of ways of increasing state financial power there remains consideration of federal grants-in-aid, that is, of federal payments to the states for the support of functions which the states are carrying on and in which the federal government has an interest.[6] Grants-in-aid in some form have been used by the federal government from its beginning, with annual money grants dating from 1887. The great increase in the use of grants has come since 1930, when they amounted to about one hundred million dollars.[7] In the fiscal year 1952 the federal government paid grants-in-aid to state and local governments that totalled 2,212 million dollars, which was equal to 7.2 per cent of total state and local expenditures of 30.9 billion.[8]

The use of grants-in-aid by the federal government has grown up largely on a program by program basis. A recent list includes eighty-one appropriation titles, which gives a general idea of the numerous programs for which aid is granted.[9] Most of these programs are relatively small. The two largest groups of programs are for public assistance, which accounted for over half the total, and highways, which accounted for about one-fifth.

Numerous formulas are employed for grant distribution. For the most part the states must match the federal grant with state funds according to some fixed proportion. In some grants states with relatively low financial ability pay a smaller proportion of the federal grant, thus helping to "equalize" the burdens on states for financing the program.

The grant-in-aid is generally recognized to be a significant device from the viewpoint of federalism. It is praised by some as a method of promoting federalism and condemned by others as a threat to federalism. On the side of its advocates are the arguments that it permits joint sharing by state and federal governments of the cost of projects having both statewide and nationwide interest, that it permits the administration of the program to be carried on by the governmental unit best qualified to do so with administrative standards kept high through federal review, that it makes it possible for national interests to be promoted and national minimum standards of service to be maintained—that, in short, it is an instrument for cooperative action.

The position that the grant-in-aid threatens federalism derives from the fear that the states will be brought under the complete domination of the federal government, thus destroying the local freedom of action that is essential to a federal, as distinct from a unitary state. Examples are presented by the advocates of this position to show that extravagant levels of expenditures are induced because the people of the states want to be sure to get their full share of the national tax dollar and feel that someone else is paying most of the bill, that states are in effect forced into the programs for which grants are paid at the expense of other programs that may be of equal or greater importance, and that state administration is strait-jacketed by federal requirements.

In view of these conflicting considerations the desirable course would seem to be not to abandon grants-in-aid but to seek to minimize the dangers and maximize the advantages and, when this is not feasible, to adopt a grant policy that gives the maximum net advantage. In this connection, it may be noted that such need as may be found by the federal government for the use of grants to promote national interests is likely to be greatest in the early stages of a new program before some of the states have become fully aware of its value to them. As time goes by it should be possible to reduce matching grants toward, if not to, a situation in which the lower the per capita income of the state the higher the grant as a percentage of total expenditures for the program, with the states with the highest per capita incomes receiving only a nominal grant or no grant at all. At the same time it should be possible to combine related programs in a general field such as welfare into a single program for purposes of paying grants-in-aid, thus reducing the pressure on the state to devote an undue part of its resources to a specific narrow program.

A question of considerable importance is whether the federal government should help remedy the financial weaknesses of state governments by levying federal taxes and allocating the revenues among the states not merely for particular programs but for the general financing of state and local governments. If the states wanted this and the federal government could determine with some precision the source by states of the revenues it collected, the arrangement would be one in which the states used the federal government as an agent. The states have shown no interest in such a scheme. Arrangements that have been proposed have taken the quite different form of the "block grant," which is financed out of the general revenues of the central treasury and distributed among states on an equalizing basis in accordance with "need." To be acceptable in a federal system, such a distribution would have to be made without conditions except such as might be found necessary to assure honest expenditure on public purposes. The payment of an equalizing block grant might be defended on the ground that people in low-income states contribute more to the incomes of people in high-income states than *vice versa,* a point that has been argued but, so far as the writer is aware, not proved. The payment of such a grant might be defended with less difficulty on the ground that the maintenance within each state of an adequate level of general governmental services is of national interest. Care must be taken in considering the national interest not to confuse it with "common interests." To illustrate, all families might have the desire in common to own expensive automobiles, but this would not make the fulfillment of these desires a matter of governmental interest; likewise the fact that people throughout the nation may desire the same high standard of state and local governmental services does not make this desire a matter of national interest. It is when persons outside the state are adversely affected because the service is not rendered that an element of national interest appears.

It is quite possible that in time of depression the decline of state and local financial powers might become so acute that a breakdown in state and local governmental services accompanied by undesirable nationwide repercussions could be prevented only by the federal government coming to the financial rescue. Under such circumstances general grants of funds by the federal government might be necessary for the protection of federalism itself, since a breakdown of state or local functions during a depression with a resulting reliance on the federal government to carry out these functions might mean that the functions would never again return to state and local hands. It may be that a special kind of grant-in-aid needs to be provided for depression periods or perhaps a system of loans could be devised whereby the federal government would make funds available to state and local governments during depression which the states would repay when prosperity returned. Such a system would need to be developed in advance and there is no sign at the present time that any plan of this kind is under consideration.

The need during periods of normal business to pay block grants for financing state and local functions in which the nation had no special interest would be a sign of something rather seriously wrong with the tax system or the economic system. It would seem preferable to try whatever other alternatives were available before resorting to such grants in times when the economy is operating at normal levels.

An extreme application of the block grant approach would be the centralization in the federal government of the financing of all levels of government. Persons who are relatively uninformed concerning government are sometimes attracted to this idea, and on occasion it has had more knowledgeable support. The attractiveness of the idea presumably lies, on the one hand, in the avoidance of overlapping taxation and its disadvantages and, on the other hand, in letting the federal government take all the worries and political unpopularity of imposing taxes. There are, however, several fatal defects. Clearly it would not be equitable to finance the widely varying costs of local and state governments from national taxation with respect to those expenditures from which the benefits are largely or altogether only local or statewide in character. The independence of the states and the cities would be destroyed by the rigid federal controls on local and state expenditures that would be found necessary to avoid the tremendous wastes that would arise if the federal government were to finance all expenditures which a state or local government might decide to make. The chaos of political controversy that would arise in allocating funds and determining proper expenditures can be readily imagined. Moreover, it should not be expected that such an arrangement would result in a smaller number of taxes being imposed, since the pressures for revenue would not be reduced.

Proposals to Limit Federal Financial Powers

In a somewhat different category are proposals to set constitutional limits on federal income, profit, and death and gift tax rates. One of the arguments made for setting such limits is to permit greater use of the taxes by the state and local governments. A study of the proposals for tax rate limitation makes it clear, however, that the central purpose has not been to protect state finances but rather to reduce federal activities and shift the distribution of the tax burden to excise, sales, and other nonprogressive taxes. To the extent that either of these purposes was achieved, the financial position of state governments would be harmed, not benefited. The reduction of federal activities would throw a greater burden on the states, while the greater federal use of the other taxes just mentioned would reduce the possibility of their use by the states. The inability of states to make extensive further use of income, profit, and death transfer taxes was examined above in commenting on the fallacy of assuming that any type of form of tax could be imposed at equally high rates and would provide equal yields at all levels of government including especially the state level.

V

CONCLUSION

In conclusion let us return to the two questions asked earlier in the chapter. The first of these questions was how fiscal measures could be used to promote federalism. A number of methods have been discussed which would help strengthen the taxing powers of the states. Not all of these are accepted cheerfully by strong defenders of states' rights. But the time is far past, if ever it existed, when it was possible to view federalism solely in terms of states' rights. We live in a complex national economy in which enormous demands for expenditures for both peace and war are placed on government. There seems to be no overall solution to the fiscal problems of federalism. Instead it is necessary to use various methods in conjunction with each other to promote the goal of having as strong a state financial structure as is possible alongside the federal government.

With respect to the question concerning what restrictions fiscal possibilities place on federalism, it is clear that the diffusion of benefits and tax burdens and the limitations of state financing power prevent us from making a rigid distinction between federal functions and taxes on the one hand, and state and local functions and taxes on the other. At least so far as the functions of government that require money are concerned, federalism must exist in a kind of mixed world in which there will be some state functions financed by states, some federal functions financed by the federal government, and a great many functions financed by both federal and state governments with the decision-making power divided between them.

If these conclusions are correct, the problems of federal-state relations that have accumulated over the past two generations will not be quickly solved. Such solution as may be expected will be wrought out through piecemeal development of institutions now in use. Some possible developments of this character have been suggested in the preceding pages.

There has been a persistent belief in some quarters that the piecemeal approach does not give sufficiently quick or comprehensive results and that we should look to large overall solutions developed through study commissions. If the succession of studies in the past is any indication, the problem is not one to be solved through broad drastic solutions. Indeed, we must be prepared to live with a permanently unsatisfactory situation despite such improvements as may be achieved. Federalism is not a perfect system of government; it is simply the least imperfect among the possible governmental alternatives available to us for achieving the objectives of organized society.

FOOTNOTES TO CHAPTER 20

1. For a selective bibliography on federal-state tax relations, see Library of Congress, Legislative Reference Service, "Selected Bibliography on Federal-State-Local Tax Relations," in Committee on Ways and Means Report on *Coordination of Federal, State, and Local Taxes,* House Report No. 2519, 82nd Cong., 2d Sess. (1953) pp. 113–116. For a bibliographical summary of past efforts to resolve intergovernmental fiscal problems in the United States, see L. L. Ecker-Racz, "Federal-State Tax Relations: Résumé of Action and Study," presented at Tax Institute Symposium on Proper Jurisdictional Limitations of Federal, State, and Local Taxation at Princeton, New Jersey, December 3–4, 1953. Among general works of major interest are: U.S. Treasury Department, Committee on Intergovernmental Fiscal Relations, *Federal, State, and Local Government Fiscal Relations,* Senate, Senate Document No. 69, 78th Cong., 1st Sess., (1943); James A. Maxwell, *The Fiscal Impact of Federalism in the United States,* Cambridge, Harvard University Press, 1946; and *Federal-State-Local Tax Coordination,* U.S. Treasury Department, Tax Advisory Staff of the Secretary, Washington, 1952, which is also published in House Report No. 2519, above.

2. In disregarding state-local fiscal relations except incidentally in this chapter, it is assumed that anything which the state undertakes is of statewide concern and that the local interests are adequately represented by the state government. The state-local problem has many of the same characteristics of the federal-state problem.

3. See for example Harley L. Lutz, *Bring Government Back Home,* New York, National Association of Manufacturers, 1950.

4. For a recent, detailed study of overlapping taxes, see U.S. Treasury Department, Analysis Staff, Tax Division, (Washington) January 1, 1954. 144 pages, mimeographed; also Treasury Department, *Federal-State-Local Tax Coordination.*

5. See in addition to previously cited publications, *The Coordination of Federal, State and Local Taxation,* Report of the Joint Committee.

6. See *Federal Grants in Aid,* Chicago, Council of State Governments, 1949.

7. *Annual Report of the Secretary of the Treasury, 1953,* p. 573.

8. U.S. Bureau of the Census, *Summary of Governmental Finances in 1952,* p. 9.

9. *Annual Report of the Secretary of the Treasury, 1953,* pp. 570–573.

PART FOUR
Supranational Union in Western Europe

21

Introduction

By Arthur W. Macmahon

Supranational union in Western Europe belongs essentially in the stream of national federalism. It seeks to create an entity and already involves strands of the fabric in an area strongly marked by elements of common culture and of economic interdependence. Approaching the question on the level of novel methods of national aggregation, we may disregard the vaster and different issues of overall international organization. The term supranational has implications, however. Anything that emerges in Western Europe will be touched by the pride, power, and hesitations of nations in an age of nationalism, although in the post-colonial period the main zest has passed to other continents. Whatever is done in Western Europe, therefore, even if it advances far toward cohesion, will have lessons of international significance.

The connection is the closer because of the extent to which international affairs fall into regional vortices. One can trace this tendency in many forms: in the impulse that led the United Nations Economic and Social Council in 1947 to create such a body as the Economic Commission for Europe; in the way in which specialized agencies of global scope establish regional centers, like the Office for Europe of the World Health Organization. Developments of this sort make the point more persuasively although less dramatically than the regional defensive pacts for they rise to meet the needs of institutions that are world-wide in their main basis and emphasis.

Within the European regional frame are crisscrossing lines of organization that complicate the problems dealt with in the following chapters. The rifts lie partly in the different territorial groupings that exist or may be conceived. There is the Europe of the nearly thirty countries that belong to the United Nations Economic Commission for Europe, theoretically bridging the barrier of the iron curtain. There is the Europe of the fifteen countries that are members of the Council of Europe and the Europe of the slightly larger numbers that belong to the Organization for European Economic Cooperation and the European Payments Union which it originally sponsored. There is the Europe of the six countries—France, the Federal Republic of Germany, Italy, Belgium, the Netherlands, and Luxembourg—that have established the Coal and Steel Community, drafted the treaty for a Defense Community, and devised and discussed plans for a Political Community. This is the Europe of the Six where some degree of federal union became an early possibility. One calls it Little Europe in contrast to the combinations that have been mentioned. Outside of it stand, notably, the United Kingdom with its Commonwealth links and the Scandinavian countries, vaguely joined in a Nordic Union and bound by various relatively informal understandings. Over Western Europe laps the structure of the North Atlantic Treaty Organization, institutionalizing in a partly political way the area that not improperly may be called the Atlantic industrial basin. Somewhat in rivalry with the tendencies that it involves is the European idea that sees in Africa, still so largely linked politically to countries in Europe, a reciprocal partner in economic development and in the formation of a complex of power which, if it could also enlist the Commonwealth, might present another great balancing force in the world. Within Europe itself, it is probably premature to ask where Western Europe ends as one looks eastward and down the Danube. The issue may well be temporized by elastic clauses in any arrangements that are presently made. The postponement of the main question seems justified by the assumption that a galvanizing hope within many minds in the eastern countries, going beyond mere relief from existing regimes, is the thought of membership in a united Europe.

In addition to the problems raised by these alternatives of territorial combination is the question of the practicability of organizing functionally by sectors, already illustrated in the European Coal and Steel Community. In other functional fields the same tendency exists expressly or at least in the implications of many existing relationships or proposals although they are mainly of a less formal and authoritatively supranational character. Can separately organized sectors achieve their objectives in isolation? Can the Coal and Steel Community succeed in the face of the fact that it covers only fifteen per cent of the industrial production of the six countries and yet is dependent on factors that ramify through their economies and involve many governmental powers and agencies? These queries raise many problems in the relationship of the vertical or specialized mode of organization to a more horizontal and comprehensive type of supranational structure. They present the political issue of responsible popular control as well as technological issues in the coordination of public policies.

Territorial difficulties are also involved. Initially any functional union with supranational regulative powers is likely to be confined to an area in which the sense of identity is strong enough to make it realistic at least to talk about more inclusive forms of political association. Under these conditions the limited organization of the function is attended by profound problems of liaison with adjacent countries. To the extent that specialized agencies can be projected more easily than political unions, the solution of the problem of liaison by the admission of new countries to full membership in the functional union creates a new frontier of problems in the relationship of functional to general political organization.

I

I need not speak of the long history of projects for European union; phases of that story are recalled in the chapters by Robert Bowie and Carl Friedrich. It is appropriate by way of introduction here to give the immediate background of the movements for functional and more comprehensive political union among the six countries of Western Europe. The potentialities of close association were found within this area. As part of the background we must first note the forces at work in the rise of the Council of Europe and its effort to serve as a matrix of policies and projects and a focal point in larger patterns of relationship.

In 1946 at Zurich Winston Churchill called for the creation of some sort of united states of Europe, paying tribute to its earlier prophets. He argued that such an integration would not be inconsistent with the United Nations. It would provide the indispensable basis for the partnership of France and Germany, crucial in the peace of Europe. The first step, he said, was to build a European parliament. The Union of European Federalists, founded by Henry Brugmans later in the same year, associated forty elements in sixteen countries. At its conference in mid-1947 it declared that, although the continent should not reconcile itself permanently to division into two hostile camps, union could be envisaged only for part of Europe. In the following year the elements espousing union had so multiplied and the risks of splintering had become so pronounced that an international committee was formed to bring them together. This impulse was projected in the so-called Congress of Europe at The Hague in May 1948. Its main resolution, protean in possible meanings, declared that "The time has come for the nations of Europe to transfer some portion of their sovereign rights, and henceforth to exercise them jointly so as to coordinate and develop their resources." The Hague Congress touched off a series of official statements including reminders from the Labour Government that while the United Kingdom was linked to Europe it was also the center of the Commonwealth. Following the meeting at The Hague, a more comprehensive organization was formed under the name European Movement, with Churchill, Blum, Spaak, and de Gasperi as its original presidents and with branches in different countries. Its executive committee sketched the possible bases of union in a communication to the various governments. Suggestions on constitutional, economic, and cultural aspects were developed at conferences during the following year.

Among the organizations thus loosely brought in concert, perhaps the most notable in point of crucial leverage subsequently was the group that evolved into the Socialist Movement for the United States of Europe, led by André Philip who also headed the propaganda work of the European Movement. The influence of this organization, especially pointed and telling among French socialists, was important because, apart from doubts connected with the arming of Western Europe and the Defense Community, it had to combat the fear that at the national level the economic powers essential to socialist objectives might be crippled in the name of supranational laissez faire ideals and commitments to a common market while at the same time political obstacles would prevent the conferral of effective positive powers on a supranational government. It was doubtless partly for this reason, and not merely because of historic British foreign policies and Commonwealth connections, that the ascendant Labour Party failed to bring its immense postwar prestige on the Continent effectively to bear in favor of the European Movement.

The establishment of the Council of Europe in 1949 was partly an outcome of the pressures and proposals that have been mentioned. Much of the immediate impetus was provided by the auspices that had convened the Congress at The Hague. Contributory factors of an official character were at hand in the association of five countries under the treaty concluded at Brussels in 1948. Early in the following year the ministers in this organization sponsored the call for a conference of ten countries. From this meeting and subsequent negotiations came the statute of the Council of Europe. It held its first sessions in the late summer of 1949. Even before it met Greece and Turkey had applied for membership; in the next year Iceland was admitted to full and the Saar to associate membership. The Federal Republic of Germany, admitted on an associate basis in 1950, was received in full membership in 1951.

This relatively loose but inclusive organization of Europe came into being before the realistic prospects of federal union had narrowed to six continental countries. It came at a time when relationships through the larger area were being cultivated by the Organization for European Economic Cooperation— evoked originally to collaborate in the Marshall Plan, first announced in 1947 —and by the North Atlantic Treaty Organization under the pact of 1949. The existence of these agencies helped the trend but qualified from the outset any expectation that the Council of Europe would become the single main center of counsel and clearance.

The statute of the new organization stated that "the aim of the Council of Europe is to achieve a greater unity between its Members for the purpose of safeguarding and realising the ideals and principles which are their common heritage and facilitating their economic and social progress." It specified that "matters relating to national defense do not fall within the scope of the Council of Europe." This stipulation did not prevent the discussion of political matters of moment in the Council's Consultative Assembly which early won from the Committee of Ministers the right to control its own agenda. In 1953, for example, the Consultative Assembly recommended positions to be taken at the forthcoming four-power conference at Berlin and in 1954 the work of the Council was helpful in laying the basis for an agreement between Germany and France on permanent autonomy for the Saar. The reporter at the Assembly's meeting in May who summarized the proposed solution and its acceptance as a platform of discussion by the governments concerned remarked that "the Europeanization of the Saar would not constitute an injustice provided it became truly supranational. That is why the German representatives on the committee on general affairs insisted on the Saar question being linked to that of the establishment of a European Political Community."

The ferment of the Council of Europe lies primarily in the Consultative Assembly and secondarily in the secretariat. The representatives in the Assembly are chosen by the several national parliaments, almost invariably from among their own members although this is not a formal requirement. They reflect the different party groups except communists. In the Assembly the members vote as individuals. It has been noteworthy how far the voting, when not purely personal, follows party rather than national lines. The significance of this fact must be discounted, of course, by the extent to which the process of election to an advisory body such as the Consultative Assembly, broad in range of discussion but without final power, tends to recruit and to retain interested individuals sympathetic to European integration.

The recommendations of the Consultative Assembly if approved by a two-thirds vote, with a majority of the 132 members in attendance, go to the Committee of Ministers. This body brings the foreign ministers together twice a year, and oftener through deputies, with a tendency for the latter to be on permanent assignment to the work. The ministers must act unanimously in approving the recommendations as proposals to the member governments. In the first five years of its existence, the Consultative Assembly adopted 155 recommendations, 62 resolutions (apart from those on matters of internal organization), and seven opinions. Of the total number of recommendations, less than one-third had been fully implemented by the ministers. In calculating the score in a record that in large measure was one of frustration, it should be noted that many of the recommendations were on the same subjects, to which the Assembly kept returning. At the same time the very inconclusiveness of its procedures tempted it to disperse its attention. During the five-year period the Council had been instrumental in drafting six conventions which had been ratified by many of the governments but this action was hardly the full sign of its influence.

On the question of the relations of the two organs—the Consultative Assembly and the Committee of Ministers—Chancellor Adenauer, as president of the latter body at the time, portrayed the situation at the meeting of the Assembly in May 1954. "It is up to the Assembly," he said, "to offer suggestions, to submit proposals, and to make recommendations. In so doing, it will be able not only to express itself in connection with all fundamental matters of European politics, as the meeting in September 1953 excellently showed, but should bring its discussions to bear on all questions of topical interest affecting European life. Only thus does it represent a European forum." At the same meeting the ministers submitted a program of work. They accompanied it with a combined admonition and apology. "As far as the Assembly is concerned," said the statement, "it should continue to make suggestions to our Committee for action by member governments. There will be discouragements. Notwithstanding the possibility of concluding partial agreements, the operation of the unanimity rule in the Committee and the diverse customs and traditions of member countries often raise obstacles against implementation in full of the Assembly's proposals." The statement congratulated the Assembly "on the particularly important work it has done in connection with the Saar question" and expressed the hope "that a solution based on that work will soon be reached." This formula, as already noted, was more likely to be acceptable if supranational auspices were available.

Meanwhile the Organization for European Economic Cooperation remained separate, conducting its affairs through a large expert staff and ramifying in the important educational work of the European Productivity Agency and in seventeen or more vertical bodies for particular branches of economic activity. The possibility of some formal interlocking with the Council of Europe was early broached in that body. In 1952 the Consultative Assembly recommended that negotiations should be started with a view to a merger of the organizations. The Committee of Ministers reported in 1954, however, that, desirable as simplicity might be for the man on the street, "there are certain difficulties in the way of a merger which, in the Committee's view, over-ride this consideration." One difficulty lay in the somewhat different memberships. The ministers believed that satisfactory methods of liaison had been arranged. Looking to the future, they said: "The Council of Europe will retain its political initiative and its right to make general declarations on questions of European economic organization. But at the same time the Committee of Ministers will be able, if it considers desirable, to refer to OEEC or to other competent organizations, for specialized study and report, economic proposals put forward by the Consultative Assembly."

The play of interagency comment was illustrated by the OEEC's criticism in 1954 of the Consultative Assembly's so-called Strasbourg Plan "on the coordination between the economies of the member states of the Council of Europe and those of the overseas countries having constitutional links with them." The resolution of the Consultative Assembly in presenting the plan had taken note of the argument "that Europe imports from the dollar area a large part of its raw materials and has been able to pay for them since the end of the war only because of the generous assistance afforded by the United States." It pointed out that the United States, though presently importing only ten per cent of the raw materials it consumed, was expected to import twenty-five per cent within as many years. The resolution declared that it was "essential for Europe to stimulate the development of the production of raw materials outside the dollar area and, in particular, in the area under consideration." Accordingly the plan recommended, first, the establishment of a European bank for the development of overseas territories, which would work in cooperation with the International Bank for Reconstruction and Development; second, long-term contracts and international agreements on basic products, covering both quantities and prices, to give the producer greater security and to encourage the expansion of output; third, the introduction of a preferential system. The last-mentioned feature especially was criticized in the appraisal submitted to the Council of Europe in May 1954 at the request of the ministers. "The upshot of this system," it said, "might well be the formation of a solid bloc isolated from the dollar area and a recrudescence of protectionism." Nor did the report approve the idea of a European bank for the development of overseas territories. It would not conjure up new European savings and it might complicate the work of the International Bank. On the floor of the Consultative Assembly, the spokesman for the OEEC warned against a policy that might intensify discrimination against the United States and Canada. "These wider considerations," he said, "reinforce the judgment of the OEEC that the right objective in economic policy was, is, and will be for Europe to move forward, in cooperation with the United States and Canada, towards a freer system of trade and payments for the free world as a whole." The improvement of Europe's economic position, he added, lessened the force of the original arguments for the Strasbourg Plan. Meanwhile, however, its main ideas had been endorsed afresh by the Second Westminster Conference, as it styled itself, convened in January 1954 under the auspices of the European Movement. Its resolutions recalled the initiating role played by the original Westminster Conference in 1949 and the declaration of that body that "the aim of a European economic system linked with the associated overseas countries is not to build up high tariffs against the rest of the world." Thus again was signalized the problem of regional and global factors.

The Council of Europe, obviously, was an active but far from exclusive center of European thinking and intergovernmental discussion. What about its relation to the movement for supranational organization? Almost at the outset the Consultative Assembly unanimously declared that "the aim and goal of the Council of Europe is the erection of a European political authority with limited functions but real powers." This formula had so many meanings, however, that when a committee was directed to explore its implications, it could not agree. Some may have imagined that the Council itself could be made the basis of a firm but still inclusive organization with federal characteristics. Britain's peculiar position, however, would have made such expectations fantastic even if no other obstacles existed. It may be remarked in passing that in the formative stage of the Council, Britain's influence had been thrown against the idea of an Assembly, chosen individually by parliaments, in which different parties would be represented. Yet Britain became a chief proponent of the Council. It valued it as a flexible association of wide membership precisely for the reasons that made it view with concern the separate development of an entity or entities within part of Western Europe. When the movement for closer union, quickened by the proposal of the common market for coal and steel, began to run functionally within a smaller area, Britain supported the view that the Council should at least be a coordinating influence in all European supranational developments.

That hope, indeed, was voiced in 1950 by the Consultative Assembly and the Committee of Ministers. In the following year, compromising with the trend, the ministers decided that partial agreements could be concluded within the framework of the Council. Meanwhile the device of functional union was being discussed not only for coal and steel but also for a common army, and diverse schemes, often misleadingly called pools, were bruited in a number of economic and administrative fields. The Consultative Assembly was sometimes a seedbed for such proposals. In the face of this functional stress, while still asserting its ideal to be the means of concert, the Council was forced to seek the modest fulfillment of that ideal by such methods as the formula suggested early in 1952 by the British foreign minister and associated with his name as the Eden Plan. This formula called for as much overlapping of membership as possible between the Consultative Assembly and such new special assemblies as might arise, for joint meetings, and for permanent delegations from the non-member countries with opportunities to participate in debate and in the committee work of supranational bodies.

II

The launching of the European Coal and Steel Community in the summer of 1952 afforded the prime test of the functional or sector mode of union. In mid-1954, less than half way through the transitional period allowed by the treaty for the full achievement of the common market, two questions were apparent. The first turned on limitations inherent in the functional approach. Among other issues it involved the relationships of a specialized supranational body to the overall economic policies and controls of the member governments. The second question, being a matter of attitudes, was less inherent but hardly less crucial. Could a supranational authority associated with a particular industrial sector avoid being so impressed by industrial points of view that it might lack the will to force changes in business practices inconsistent with the full objectives of the plan? This difficulty might impede programs essentially laissez faire in spirit, intended to get rid of barriers, not to mention the troubles that might beset programs entailing a more positive use of governmental powers.

Behind these questions were broad choices of emphasis in the strategy of development. Should the outlook combine caution with vigor in shunning any effort to broaden the political context until the functional agency was thoroughly established? And should the initial expansion proceed primarily through the organization of related industrial sectors? Or did the viability of a functional plan require that it be put as quickly as possible in a framework of broader supranational political powers and responsibility?

The functional plan's territorial scope raised different issues. What working relations could it develop with areas outside the member states? What should be its policy about the admission of additional countries? Still another type of problem arises in the external relationships of a regional union. How can the ideal of an internal common market achieved by a supranational authority within the composite area of a number of countries be adjusted to international ideals and commitments such as those of the General Agreement on Tariffs and Trade?

In the discussion of the draft of Tom C. Clark's chapter on the inauguration of the Coal and Steel Community, Herbert Wechsler called attention to an angle of the problem of emphasis and timing in the relationship of a specialized functional agency to a more broadly political type of organization. Mention of it here, along with a canvass of outstanding developments, may contribute to the reader's perspective in approaching the chapters that follow. Mr. Wechsler confessed that he had come to the discussion disposed to favor a conservatively ad hoc functional procedure. "Then, listening to Mr. Clark," he said, "there arose in me an apprehension that moved in the opposite direction from his own views and views I held myself. I would like to put this question to Mr. Clark: Is there a danger that if the Schuman Plan proceeds according to its own genius there is a prospect that the industrialists of Europe, far from getting a stake in the progressive unification of Europe, and particularly in political unification, may, on the contrary, create the result of retarding the ultimate political unification of Europe because of the necessity of meeting their own needs and be less receptive to real political control than if any such structure should be set up in the context of true political union?" Mr. Clark's rejoinder deprecated "a political emphasis at this stage of its development." After the device had proved itself in the especially favorable as well as important fields of coal and steel, it might well be expanded into related industrial sectors. "Practically," Mr. Clark insisted, "unless this plan can be made to work and successfully applied to the coal and steel industry, it cannot be applied to anything." He added that he did not "look for any supremacy of the industrial order under present social conditions."

Note may be taken here of viewpoints expressed in May 1954 by the Consultative Assembly of the Council of Europe after sitting in joint session with the partly overlapping membership of the Common Assembly of the Coal and Steel Community and after hearing a statement by Jean Monnet, president of the Community's High Authority. The Consultative Assembly unanimously approved the comments and resolution submitted by its economic committee, dealing with the Community's second general report on its activities in the year that ended in April 1954. The resolution began by accepting the Community's statement that trade in coal and steel across national boundaries within the area of the Community had increased and "that the general trend of world prices in coal and steel has to a greater extent than before the establishment of the common market been reflected in price developments within the Community." These phenomena were viewed as objective signs of market flexibility. The resolution observed further "that the efforts of the High Authority to eliminate discriminatory practices, particularly in respect to transport, have been successful." The resolution went on to declare by way of exhortation rather than direct criticism, although not without a touch of challenge, that the High Authority was urged "to define, as soon as possible, its lines of policy with regard to cartels and monopolistic organizations within the Community."

The treatment of the cartel problem by the Coal and Steel Community provides a clue to the strategies embodied in the treaty that created the Community and applied in the policies of the High Authority, at least during the inaugural period. The prohibitions of the treaty regarding cartels were not absolute. They looked to results rather than form. Thus the second general report pointed to the obligation imposed by the treaty of "progressively establishing conditions which will in themselves ensure the most rational distribution of production at the highest possible levels of productivity." In discharging this obligation, declared the report, "It is necessary gradually to carry out structural alterations, in order to put an end to the *autocratic rule of cartels, and to control the use which concentrations are making of their power.*" (Italics in the original)

In the application, the High Authority has been empirical, tentative, and intentionally progressive in handling the problem of business organization. An illustration was its treatment of the preexisting sales organization in the Ruhr in relation to a scheme of maximum prices. The general report in 1954 stated that the Community was continuing to set maximum coal prices for the Ruhr field in Germany and for the Nord and the Pas-de-Calais field in France. In the Ruhr certain conditions, including the large number of varieties of coal, were held to warrant the continuance of the sales organization which the industry had created. The report observed that "The present selling system in the Ruhr precludes any form of effective competition between the enterprises or agencies of that coal field, the organization of which, in view of the nature and volume of its production, has a predominant influence on the common market as a whole." As to the French field, it pointed out that "the present methods of distributing coal through trade between the countries of the Community, together with the tariff regulations still applicable to international transport, are a limiting factor on effective competition in the French market, where the influence of the Nord and Pas-de-Calais is predominant." Therefore, after considering possible alternatives and "taking account of the development of the common market and of the special problems of the moment," the High Authority decided to continue a system of maximum prices but to confine it to the two crucial fields.

The policy of advance by tactical concession, leeway, and persuasive pressure was further illustrated in the enforcement of regulations for the publication of iron and steel prices and their observance in the making of sales. When the requirement for publication first went into effect, some of the published prices were higher than had prevailed before. A declining demand, however, invited many sales at lower than the published levels in violation of the rules. These were modified, however, to permit sales to be made at a margin of deviation from the published rates and to permit these rates to be changed on shorter notice. At the same time the High Authority announced that it was watching the situation closely, that it had instituted spot checking, and that it would not hesitate to apply the sanctions of the treaty against enterprises that did not comply with their obligations as defined in the new regulations.

Notwithstanding the High Authority's firmer attitude toward cartels on the one hand and on the other its piecemeal but persistent whittling away of discriminations inherent in the policies of separate governments, the philosophy of the common market in the European context is not likely to be one of drastic laissez faire. There are at stake too many social considerations such as the maintenance of existing levels of employment in marginal mining areas hitherto dependent upon subsidies. Instead of the outright dropping of all such supports in the name of the common market, the evolution of the policy is likely to continue to take the course of a shift from national measures to devices of an equalizing and supporting nature conducted jointly with the Community. In the meantime the High Authority pursues an eclectic policy.

The transitional provisions set forth in the treaty allowed the High Authority to agree to the temporary retention of assistance, subsidies, or special charges already introduced by the governments before the common market was proclaimed. In this spirit the High Authority proceeded cautiously. In the case of Germany, as Mr. Clark notes, the government yielded to the Community's demand that it should not enforce a sales tax on imports imposed, it was said, to offset a French tax rebate to exporters. Furthermore, after the common market had been in force for a year, the High Authority secured Germany's agreement to drop certain special charges it sought to impose on the German collieries in behalf of various classes of consumers such as railways, inland water transport, deep sea fishing, and domestic householders. In abandoning the scheme under pressure, certain substitute arrangements were permitted in behalf of the lowest-income consumers in view of existing provisions of a collective agreement between the collieries and trade unions.

In the case of preexisting subsidies, such as aid to the marginal mining area in Belgium, the High Authority permitted temporary retention, accompanied by financial aid from the Community pending the development of rationalization programs. The circumstances suggest that in the long run as well as immediately the rationalization of the industry will take account of the human as well as political considerations involved in the displacement of labor that is relatively immobile, especially in societies that with much reason cherish other values than mobility. On the general question of outlook and policy, note may be taken of the statement of the president of the High Authority, Jean Monnet, before the joint meeting of the assemblies of the Coal and Steel Community and the Council of Europe in May 1954. "Since the Six countries had common interests," he said in the words of the official paraphrase, "they had naturally afforded each other mutual assistance: thus the German and Dutch coal-mining industries were helping to finance improvements to the Belgian collieries. Similarly, as a result of the conditions under which Italy was allowed to purchase iron scrap, the Italian steel industry was receiving a large measure of assistance."

Jean Monnet also pointed out that "it was thanks to the levy that the High Authority had been able to raise a loan in the United States; this loan was only a beginning, and the fact that it had been granted provided a glimpse of how high Europe's credit would be when all European countries were united." The object of the loan in part was to improve workers' housing. In the general rationalization of the industries covered by the plan it was not possible to predict how far and in what ways the Community might be active in the fields of financing. It did not have power to control improvements financed from corporate surpluses but it had power of approval over new security issues and might use its financial resources to reduce capital costs of rationalization programs by guaranteeing private loans.

In the absence of higher coordinating machinery of a political nature, the Community established ad hoc relations with adjacent national states and with certain international bodies. Various non-member countries accredited standing delegations to the High Authority. An official representative of the United Kingdom participated in debate and in the work of technical committees. At the end of the second year, however, negotiations were still pending on a scheme of closer working relations that might well be crucial in setting a pattern for the non-member governments. A British delegate at the Consultative Assembly in May 1954 remarked that, if the members of the body from countries other than the six that belonged to the Coal and Steel Community had spoken their minds during the discussion of the Community's report, they would have said: "We are really waiting to see what kind of association Great Britain intends to make with the Community before we decide what we should do."

On the question of the Community's external relations, a resolution of the Consultative Assembly urged that the Community make "efforts to harmonize the tariff policy of the member states at the lowest possible level" and it voiced the hope that "the High Authority will take measures to prevent the development of transport rates designed to prevent the free import of coal and steel into the Community." In the course of the debate, a member of the High Authority declared that it "had taken no restrictive measures concerning either coal or steel, and that if any shortage should arise it would always follow the instructions of the O. E. E. C." As for the General Agreement on Tariffs and Trade, the Community had maintained relations with the thirty-four signatory countries, which at a meeting had granted a waiver from the most favored nation clause to permit the six member countries of the Coal and Steel Community to fulfill their obligations within it as an entity.

As to the main question of the practicability of the principle of functional organization within a regional area, a few things may be said about attitudes in the Coal and Steel Organization toward a more general form of union. Jean Monnet, as architect of the Community and its first administrator, imaginative but practical, had concepts that probably made him unconcerned about handicapping a new going project of limited scope by proposals for political union with economic implications that would alarm many interests. The progress of the Coal and Steel Community during the first two years was at least enough to prevent an acute sense of exigency about its limitations. Nevertheless, below the record of its initial accomplishments were teachings of experience as well as logic that pointed to a growing recognition within the organization of the limitations inherent in its nature. The interdependence of the elements appeared ever more clearly. Looking beyond the period of introductory tactical accommodation, the Community faced the need for a more comprehensive supranational influence upon intertwined economic conditions and policies in the member countries.

III

The inauguration of the Coal and Steel Community, traced in the chapters by Mr. Diebold and Mr. Clark, combined with the signing in May 1952 of the treaty for a Defense Community to precipitate the drafting of an instrument for a limited political union among the six countries that were parties to the functional arrangements. In the concluding chapters, Robert Bowie comments on the context, development, and main features of this plan and Carl Friedrich considers its significance in the light of the constitutional theory of federalism as a process. It is enough here to provide elements of framework for their analysis, including an indication of the course of events and the nature of the organizational issues in the period after a draft treaty for a European Political Community was laid before the governments of the six countries in March 1953.

The treaty for the Defense Community expressly contemplated the drafting of a limited political union. The motive in part was to provide responsible oversight. Article 38 stipulated that when the treaty came into force the assembly for which it provided should act as a constituent body in devising a more inclusive form of union. The article directed that in its constituent capacity it should "study (a) the creation of an Assembly of the European Defense Community elected on a democratic basis; (b) the powers which might be granted to such an Assembly; and (c) the modifications which should be made in the provisions of the present Treaty relating to the other institutions of the Community particularly with a view to safeguarding an appropriate representation of the States." The article directed further that in performing the task certain principles should be respected. "The definitive organization which will take the place of the present transitional organization," it said, "should be conceived so as to be capable of constituting one of the elements of an ultimate federal or confederal structure, based upon the principle of separation of powers and including particularly a bicameral representative system." An additional guide was the statement that "the Assembly shall also study problems to which the co-existence of different organizations for European co-operation, now in being or to be created, gives rise, in order to ensure that these organizations are co-ordinated within the framework of the federal or confederal structure."

As things turned out, the drafting of an instrument of political union did not wait on the consummation of the Defense Community. After the treaty was signed in May 1952, the international committee of the European Movement suggested a procedure by which article 38 could be carried out ahead of schedule. Since the Assembly of the Coal and Steel Community was similar to the body immediately proposed for the Defense Community, the committee urged that the governments of the six countries agree to instruct the Coal and Steel Assembly to undertake the role of a constituent body. Along the same line, the Consultative Assembly of the Council of Europe, at its meeting in May 1952, suggested two alternative procedures, of which the more rapid should be adopted: "either the Assembly for which provision is made in the Treaty setting up the Coal and Steel Community, as soon as this Assembly has been established, or the Assembly of the Council of Europe, sitting with restricted membership in accordance with the distribution of seats provided for in the Assembly for the European Defense Community."

It was natural that in the Council of Europe the possible territorial scope of any proposed union should be conceived broadly. The resolution said that the duty of the constituent body was to draft the statute "of a supranational Political Community which would remain open to all Member States of the Council of Europe, and which would offer opportunities of association to such of the states as are not full Members of this Political Community." But a shift was in progress that had its reflex in the outlook of the Council of Europe. The change was summarized in a later report of the general affairs committee of the Consultative Assembly when commenting on the draft treaty for a political community. "Originally," it said (recalling a resolution it had adopted in 1951), "the Consultative Assembly saw the European Community as a strictly limited body, designed to secure only democratic control of the European army, and thus to increase the chances of the ratification of the European Defense Community. This followed logically from the policy of piecemeal engineering, of federation by sectors, which had been the recourse of those who wanted European unity, after they had understood that Great Britain was unable to follow them in that course. But with the Luxembourg Resolution of 10th September, the situation changed. This Resolution marked the point at which those who were prepared to form a Federation initially limited to the six Powers decided to go ahead." From this point a political community limited in area was conceived more broadly than as a device to secure the democratic control of a common army.

The resolution of the six foreign ministers adopted at Luxembourg on September 10, 1952 was not merely a turning point; it was also destined to be a point of reference and a rallying point in the future. In this resolution the ministers of France, the Federal Republic of Germany, Italy, Belgium, the Netherlands, and Luxembourg decided that the drafting of the design of a political community should be entrusted to the Assembly of the Coal and Steel Community, already in operation. In performing this constituent role the Assembly should draw enough additional members from the national delegations of the six countries in the Consultative Assembly of the Council of Europe to bring the membership up to the number specified for the Assembly of the Defense Community if that plan was in effect. The Luxembourg Resolution also stated that "the final aim of the six governments has been and still is the establishment of as comprehensive a European Political Community as possible." And by way of guiding principles the resolution quoted the language of article 38 in the pending Defense Community treaty.

The drafting of a treaty that would be the constitution of a political association was accordingly undertaken by the Assembly of the Coal and Steel Community, expanded for this role under the self-given name Ad Hoc Assembly. The German Social Democratic members declined to serve. Observers were present from the countries in the Council of Europe other than the six directly involved. The framing of an instrument of 117 articles and two protocols was accomplished between September 1952 and March 10, 1953. In the course of this intensive work materials comprising fifteen volumes were developed. Helpful preparatory work had been done by an unofficial committee of legal experts set up early in 1952. Its recommendations on a number of constitutional issues were embodied in resolutions and commentaries published in the autumn under the auspices of the European Movement. As background information for this committee, Robert Bowie and Carl Friedrich at Harvard University, with foundation support, directed a series of comparative analyses of existing federal systems.

The Ad Hoc Assembly itself worked mainly through a Constitutional Committee of twenty-six members, acting in turn through a smaller working party deployed in four subcommittees. A tentative draft was discussed in the Ad Hoc Assembly in January, was subsequently revised, and was considered and altered further in plenary Ad Hoc Assembly sessions in March. In the meantime various features of the tentative draft were debated in the Consultative Assembly of the Council of Europe, with stress upon the importance of liaison. Later the Consultative Assembly approved the mainly favorable report of its general affairs committee which analyzed the text adopted by the Ad Hoc Assembly on March 10, 1952 and presented to the governments of the six countries.

The Ad Hoc Assembly was not dissolved. Before it adjourned subject to call, it passed a resolution which directed its Constitutional Committee, with the aid of the headquarters staff of the working party, "(i) to keep in close touch with Governmental action on the draft Treaty embodying the Statute of the European Community; (ii) to take the necessary steps to enable the Governments, where necessary, to benefit by the experience gained in working out the draft Treaty; and (iii) to report to the Assembly at the appropriate time."

The subsequent course of events was forecast in the overtones of the words of the French foreign minister on behalf of his colleagues in receiving the draft from the Ad Hoc Assembly. He remarked that in such an undertaking a division of labor was appropriate between "men with bold and independent minds and governments whose honor and impediment it is to carry the responsibility." He complimented those who had worked on the draft. "You need have no doubt that we shall at all times call upon their experience and their devotion which we so highly esteem. Our responsibilities, which are convergent, must go hand in hand but must not be merged." At a meeting of the ministers in May to discuss questions of procedure in considering further the problem of a political community, it was decided not to take the Ad Hoc Assembly draft as the basis although it would be used among other documents. In practice, during the following months the notations of the viewpoints expressed by the foreign offices of the several countries were largely assembled in terms of the divisions and categories of the draft. In this sense the draft served as a framework; its provisions were unintentionally accepted as starting points for much of the discussion.

Nevertheless the relative disregard of the draft evoked a letter of protest signed jointly by the president of the Ad Hoc Assembly and the chairman of its Constitutional Committee on June 24, 1953 and addressed to the ministers. The letter pointed out that "neither the Ad Hoc Assembly nor the Constitutional Committee wishes to claim that the draft in its present form has a definitive character. It is the evident and indisputable task of the participating Governments to examine the text, to subject it to a critical analysis, and to amend it, so far as appears necessary." At the same time the letter insisted that the draft was "not merely, as has sometimes been stated, the outcome of work by a study group. Rather it is the outcome of work accomplished by a European Parliament convened at the instance of the six Foreign Ministers." To treat it as no more than an important preliminary work would slight its background and history and "the political responsibility" of those who had assisted in preparing it. The letter declared: "Now that the draft has been adopted in the Ad Hoc Assembly by an overwhelming majority and without a single dissentient, and supported in the Consultative Assembly by an equally impressive majority, there is surely ample justification for making it the basis of the deliberations of the Council of Ministers." In addition, it urged that the working party of the Constitutional Committee "should be invited to participate in these deliberations in a manner in which the details would form the subject of agreement." This last demand, however, was qualified by the recognition (as stated in a later exchange of letters) that the members of the working party were "bound by the mandate received from the Ad Hoc Assembly not to submit themselves to instructions from governments" and that "their contribution should consist of giving explanations on reasons which led the Ad Hoc Assembly to take certain decisions, especially on the most controversial matters."

The efforts to bring the ministers together for discussions of the political community were complicated by political motives and mishaps. The early meeting on questions of procedure was to have been followed by one at Rome on matters of content, after which substitutes for the ministers and experts could take over the task. A change of government in Italy, however, led to the cancellation of the ministers' meeting. They did meet in Baden-Baden in August 1953 at a session timed with an eye to the September elections in the Federal Republic of Germany where the Government staked its success upon the record of its espousal of European integration. "The milestones along this road," Dr. Adenauer had said in a debate on foreign policy in July, "are the entry of the Federal Republic into the Council of Europe, the conclusion of the Treaty setting up the Coal and Steel Community, the Treaty establishing the European Defense Community, and not least the work accomplished toward the evolution of a European Political Community, as the crown over both the other great unions." Adenauer's electoral victory helped to galvanize the movement afresh. Nevertheless it should be noted that the ministers at Baden-Baden, while endorsing the idea of a directly elected parliamentary body, had defined the objective of the plan as a whole to be the creation of "a community of sovereign states exercising supranational functions as defined in the treaties in force or by future treaties."

The substitutes for the foreign ministers with their staffs finally met at Rome for three weeks in the early autumn. Their report of a hundred-odd pages to the ministers was not a draft of a constitution. It consisted of summaries of the views of the different delegations on a number of issues, largely grouped (as has been said) in terms of the arrangement of the Ad Hoc Assembly's draft without purporting to take it as a base and with many matters held over for later discussion. The ministers were to consider the report in October but, time proving too short, the three-day meeting at The Hague did not take place until late November. Even then decisive action was impeded by the fact that involvements at home required the French minister to be absent much of the time. It was agreed to set up a special commission for the European political community, with its seat in Paris and composed of substitutes for the ministers aided by staffs from the foreign offices. This body began its work in December and in March 1954 presented a report of more than two hundred pages. Again, however, the report was a statement of the views of the officials of the several countries on various issues. It was to have been considered at a conference of ministers in mid-March. The gathering was indefinitely postponed, however, partly because of pending Belgian elections, partly to wait on the maturing of an incipient settlement of the Saar question, and especially because of the problem of French action on the pending treaty for the establishment of the European Defense Community.

Through all these steps an inhibiting factor was the conservatism of the permanent staffs of the foreign offices. So pronounced was this attitude, especially in the country that was most crucial, that observers might well ask whether the drafting of even a very modest version of federal union could succeed unless the formulative process could somehow by-pass the several officialdoms. But although this observation is supported by logic and experience, one must not belittle the degree of popular national conservatism and the hesitations of parties and politicians.

On May 4, 1954 an important declaration was made by the interim committee of ministers on the treaty for the European Defense Community. It promised that as soon as the treaty was ratified steps would be taken to substitute for the Assembly under the treaty "an Assembly elected by direct universal suffrage," to which the governing bodies of the Defense Community and the Coal and Steel Community would be responsible. The immediate occasion of the statement, no doubt, was the wish to reassure the French socialists on the eve of a perhaps crucial party decision in favor of the ratification of the Defense Community treaty. A prerequisite of socialist support was the promise of democratic control of the common army; the other prerequisites—British association in the plan and American guarantees—presumably were met by the convention for military participation entered into by the United Kingdom in mid-April, 1954 and a nearly simultaneous statement by the President of the United States.

The action of the ministers to which reference has just been made indicated the possibility that the preparations for a political community of the six might proceed by working from the assembly of the Defense Community as a core. Under these conditions it would be likely to confine itself to minimum objectives. Nevertheless the supporters of European union have come to attach much importance to the dynamic potentialities of growth that inhere in a popularly based supranational legislative body.

IV

It would be premature as well as inappropriate here to enter into a structural analysis of a constitutional draft which, in the face of the tortured issues that confront even a limited union among nations, was at best accorded the status of a tentative working paper. Carl Friedrich touches critically upon some of its features, including the provisions for amendment and the attempt to devise a form of executive which would satisfy the need for unity and stability while remaining responsible through the legislative body. We need not examine in detail the positions taken by the several countries after March 10, 1953 in discussions among the ministers' substitutes and their staffs. Even on matters where opinions were expressed, the views were informal, tentative, partly tactical, and wholly inconclusive. It is enough to mention a few items that illustrate the nature of the issues of organization and competence.

A significant instance was the trend of thinking about the upper house of the legislature. The Ad Hoc Assembly's draft proposed that its members should be elected by the several national parliaments. Like the members of the Peoples' Chamber, they would vote as individuals and in person and they were not to accept any mandate as to the way in which they cast their votes. Representation was apportioned on the same basis and scale as in the directly elected lower house, that is, by the assignment of fixed numbers of seats in very rough relation to the respective populations of the countries. The legislative powers of the two chambers were to be substantially the same but the senate was to have the initiative in choosing the executive. The draftsmen believed that the upper chamber would incidentally provide a valuable link to the Council of Europe through the representatives who would be chosen by the national parliaments. The spokesmen for the Constitutional Committee extolled the fact that, in seeking to devise institutions for a novel organization, they had rejected the formula of equal representation of member states in any organ of the supranational government, save as it would be present, as a matter of regrettable but seeming necessity, in a council of national ministers that mostly would have to act unanimously on important matters. Such were the outlines of the design for the senate as approved on March 10, 1953.

In the subsequent exchanges of official views about the nature of the upper chamber, it was tempting to invoke the analogy of the German Bundesrat. In truth, the degree of dependence of the new supranational government upon the administrative organs of the member states made the analogy a persuasive example since it would allow official representatives of the several governments to participate continuously in the policy-framing process from the standpoint of the implementation of the measures under discussion. But in its historical evolution the German prototype points to a chamber with at most a suspensory veto in legislation. Such a limitation might partly redeem the proposal for a supranational chamber of states that gained the tentative support of at least two of the subministerial delegations. The German representatives may well have introduced the idea of a chamber of states in order to meet French reluctance about the supranational scheme as a whole. In the chamber of states the countries were to have an equal vote cast by delegates appointed by their governments and subject to binding instructions. At the same time the proposal seemed to contemplate that the council of national ministers would be retained with the high prerogatives conceded in the Ad Hoc Assembly's draft and with the added power of initiative in choosing the executive. Therefore the upper house, if recast in the imagined manner, seemed an almost superfluous and complicating reinforcement of the potent national elements represented in the council of ministers, while it also sacrificed the chances for liaison with the

Council of Europe through senators who might simultaneously be their country's representatives in the Consultative Assembly.

As for the principle of control embodied in the council of national ministers, there seemed little hope for its elimination from any early plan for supranational union. At best, one could expect (with some support from the early experience of the Coal and Steel Community) that a council of ministers would be helpful rather than obstructive in promoting adjustments of as well as with the policies and operations of member states. Looking into the future, optimists speculated on the possibility that the council of ministers might survive in a role like the conference of state prime ministers in the federal system of Australia.

In accepting an organic provision for a body of national ministers with wide veto powers, which indeed has seemed unavoidable in any scheme of union likely to be acceptable at the present time, there is of course the risk pointed to by Herbert Wechsler in the discussion. American experience, he said, indicated "that whereas power distribution clauses in constitutions are subject to variations of interpretations through the years, the political structure provisions of the constitution tend to have a rigidity through the years and for the obvious reason that political power is unwilling to surrender advantages." It is perhaps reassuring to recall that the United States managed to move peaceably from the Articles of Confederation to the Constitution.

That the lower house in the proposed political community would be an elective body was taken for granted. The acceptance of the principle of universal and direct suffrage, however, left secondary issues of method on which the delegations continued to disagree. Should it be elected directly at the outset or, as the spokesmen of one foreign office argued, should it be chosen in the first instance by the national parliaments in order, among other reasons, to allow it to work out a sufficiently safeguarded electoral law? In any case, what types and degrees of specifications should govern the choice of electoral methods by the several countries? Should there be the requirement, urged by at least two delegations, that for purposes of national liaison a proportion of those elected to the lower chamber must be members of their own country's parliament at the time of election?

Throughout, while the ideal of a common market was affirmed in general terms, there continued to be disagreement about the nature and extent of the powers that it would be desirable and practicable to confer at the outset in addition to those that would be acquired through the affiliation of the functional agencies. The Netherlands, for example, and to a hardly less extent its associates in the Benelux customs union, insisted that from the outset there should be additional positive powers of an economic nature. They tended to favor a program with definite commitments and a schedule under which the burden of proof would rest on countries seeking delays in the movement toward a universal common market within the regional union. Such a broad and positive emphasis, even for ends largely negative in character, was not likely to be satisfied if, in the event of the approval of the Defense Community treaty, a fresh start in building a political community began from the Defense assembly as the animating center. For in those circumstances the supranational competence was likely to be limited to the fields and powers of the functional authorities. From the other extreme, criticism was heard that the Netherlands program, though sweeping in one sense, was unduly colored by the ideals of a customs union, lacking in positive purposes and powers.

Even in the minimum role of coordinating the specialized agencies many structural alternatives remained subject to debate. What, for example, should be the relationships of their executive organs to an overall supranational executive? These problems, like many other phases of the plan, were complicated by the time and setting of the effort to frame a political community. The undertaking that began in 1952 was at once aided and embarassed by a double circumstance. The purpose was to draft the constitution of a durable union of considerable potential range. Yet much of the impetus came from considerations involved in two functional unions: one already in existence and preoccupied in the hardy adventure of consolidating its supranational controls within its important but limited field; the other pending as a treaty, far-reaching in its implications and caught in the uncertainties of internal politics and international crises. As things stood, common defense and the proposal for a European Defense Community became the critical factor. The failure of the treaty would be likely to complete the ironic process of turning impetus into impediment. Only the future could show whether the substitute arrangements for joint defense would contain elements that might become points of attachment and growth, as in the development of a popular assembly. The field of defense, after all, was as difficult as it was compelling. Meanwhile and in the long run view of union, the common needs and compatibilities alike lay deeper.

THE ECONOMIC BACKGROUND AND FUNCTIONAL DEVELOPMENTS

22

The Relevance of Federalism to Western European Economic Integration

By William Diebold, Jr.

"Federal" is a word that occurs with disconcerting frequency in the discussion of Western Europe's economic problems. The frequency is disconcerting because it implies that so many different things are somehow "federal." Perhaps they are, but in that case the concept is not very useful as a point of investigation. Sharper delineation is needed, even for the somewhat loose-jointed commentary this chapter offers on the relation between federalism and the measures of Western European economic cooperation that are already in effect or are being seriously contemplated.

I

THE APPROACH

Federalism concerns the unity of an area and also the separateness of its constituent parts. In terms of the wielding of economic power, federalism is largely a matter of the functions assigned to a central authority that will apply to the whole area, and the functions assigned to the governments of the smaller constituent parts, applicable by each only to its own area. In Western Europe any movement toward federalism must emphasize the creation of an economic area larger than that of the existing countries and the yielding of national powers to supranational bodies. The first of these elements taken alone is not necessarily federal; for instance, a larger economic area can be created by the removal of national barriers to trade and payments without any transfer of powers to another body. Total yielding of national powers to a supranational agency would also not create federalism. The existence of two levels of government, each wielding certain powers over economic affairs, and the corollary existence of two kinds of economic area, a common one and the constituent separate ones, are the marks of federalism as the word is used in this chapter. Moreover, to be federal, for present purposes, the government of the common

area must be truly supranational, not the creature of the participating govern
ments.

Too rigorous application of these criteria would make for an arid analysi
and would lead to infinite complications. For instance, an intergovernmenta
body that works by majority rule has in it a trace of what might be calle⸀
federalism that is clearly absent from a body in which each government has ⸀
veto. To take another example: "economic areas" do not necessarily coincid⸀
with national boundaries; to the extent that a government does not prohibᵢ
international economic transactions, their existence creates some kind of "eco
nomic area." Though there would be some use in a careful classification ⸀
measures of economic cooperation according to the degree of semi-, quasi-, an⸀
even crypto-federalism to be found in them, this chapter presents no elegan⸀
taxonomies. Its approach is more general, allowing comment on some ilᐧ
defined phenomena without losing sight of the essential characteristic of fed
eral measures as distinguished from other forms of integration:[1] the exisᵗ
ence of two levels on which governmental economic decisions can be made, th
national and the supranational.

II

FEDERALISM AND ECONOMIC COOPERATION

The center of most Western European economic cooperation has been th⸀
Organization for European Economic Cooperation, the body composed of th⸀
governments receiving Marshall Plan aid. Never endowed with supranationᵃ
powers, the OEEC has been an agency through which governments havᵉ
reached agreement on many issues and worked out solutions to common probᐧ
lems. By means of its secretariat and a variety of special committees the OEE⸀
has stimulated some of these agreements, laid the bases of others, and to som⸀
extent supervised their execution.

During the first few years of its existence, the OEEC was responsible fᵒ
bringing about agreement among recipient governments on the allocation ⸀
American aid. This was not wholly an autonomous function, since the allocᵃ
tion had also to be approved in Washington and since the whole process waᵉ
influenced by the views of ECA. The allocation was arrived at by negotiatiᵒ
among the members of the OEEC, not by fiat of the organization's staff. Judᶢ
ing by the testimony of participants, a part of this process took on a rathe
special character. The aim of the negotiations was the reduction of nationᵃ
requests for aid so that the total would fit the amount provided by the Unite
States. To justify their claims to aid, spokesmen for each country had to appeᵃ
before a committee made up of delegates of the other members of OEEC. Thᵉ
committee was skilled at questioning estimates of the expected performance ⸀
each national economy during the coming year and at criticizing the prograᵐ
and policies adopted by the governments asking aid. It became awkward anᵈ
embarrassing for delegates to defend policies on investment, taxation, coᵣ

umption, and foreign trade that appeared to the consensus to be inadequate
or misdirected. Fifteen days out of sixteen the defenders were sitting on the
other side of the table, criticizing someone else's request for the limited supply
of aid, so too outrageous a resort to a double standard was discouraged. At the
committee's elbow was the OEEC secretariat, providing analyses and opinions
apt to weigh in the scales on the side of common standards and reasonable
judgment.

One has only to look at the record of some countries to see that this process
of review and trial by peers was not decisive in bringing about wise recovery
programs. Nevertheless delegates of many countries to the OEEC agree that
his process, and the anticipation of it, had a real influence. Never supranational in form, and certainly not federal, this arrangement was still somewhat
different from conventional intergovernmental negotiations. When the emphasis
of American aid to Europe shifted toward military assistance and nonmilitary
aid was dubbed "defense support," the OEEC lost its role as allocator and with
it the kind of direct influence on annual national economic programs that it had
previously exercised.[2]

Could we look behind the scenes, other intergovernmental bodies might be
found to have developed practices that to a considerable extent circumvented
he unanimity rule. For instance, minorities may accept a majority decision to
avoid stopping the works. Or permanent delegates may come to personal
understandings so that each recommends the same policy to his government.
Such situations, and the OEEC review process, have an element of what might
be called proto-federalism. It may be unimportant, it may come to nothing, but
if a European federation were ever formed, these practices might look like
origins.

Apart from the Schuman Plan, the principal measures of Western European
cooperation have concerned international trade and payments. The European
Payments Union, created in 1950 as the successor of several less ambitious
arrangements, has made possible the multilateral clearing of current accounts
among the OEEC countries and between them and the sterling area. Apart
from the limitations inherent in any agreement that covers the financial ties of
only a part of the world economy, EPU's chief difficulties come from circumstances that make certain countries extreme debtors or creditors of the rest of
the group. On the debtors' side, these circumstances are often the product of
domestic financial conditions, and especially inflation. As first conceived by
ECA officials, the Managing Board of the EPU was to have had powers that
would have enabled it to exert pressure on member countries' domestic financial policies. This proved unacceptable to the European countries and when
the agreement was signed it gave the Managing Board much weaker powers.
The Board has seven members of different nationalities who act by majority
rule but in some cases their action requires the approval of the Council of
the OEEC, where the rule of unanimity prevails.

Starting with the German balance of payments crisis in the first year of

EPU's life, the Managing Board has been able to exercise some influence over the domestic policies of extreme debtor countries. As a condition of getting extra credits beyond the quotas stipulated in the EPU agreement, these countries have had to agree to certain domestic measures. Extreme creditor countries, too, have sometimes agreed to take certain steps as part of an arrangement for their continued membership in the EPU and the receipt in gold of half their surpluses with the union. To cut down the number of crises, the Managing Board of EPU consults with countries that appear to be heading toward the limits of their quotas to work out means of avoiding that result.

These are not federal functions. The Managing Board is not a supranational agency, but it has a certain independence of action which appears to have been effective on occasions. To a certain degree the EPU creates a common economic area (the current payments among members) subject in part to a common regime different from that applying to the rest of each component part (a member's whole balance of payments on current account).

The counterpart of the EPU is the OEEC's program for the liberalization of trade. Started shortly before EPU came into effect, this program had no central body comparable to the Managing Board until 1952 when a Steering Board for Trade was created with largely advisory powers. At no time has there been any serious effort to put a supranational body in charge of the trade liberalization program. The Steering Board, the OEEC, and foreign governments have put pressure on each country to remove quotas on enough trade to meet the levels of liberalization agreed on from time to time but no sanctions have been taken against those who failed to do so. Although the methods of measurement used in the liberalization program are misleading, substantial progress has been made in the removal of quotas. The plan suffered a setback in late 1951 when France and England reimposed many quotas for fear of the effect of rearmament on their economies but it is a sign of the effectiveness of the method that other countries held the line at that time and subsequently advanced to new heights of liberalization. Britain has worked its way back to nearly the general level of liberalization but France is still badly behind.

For all its limitations, the liberalization program is one of the main accomplishments of European economic cooperation. It and the EPU are the principal steps that have been taken under OEEC aegis toward the integration of Western Europe. They are not federal arrangements. They do not necessarily move toward federalism. The removal of barriers to trade and payments is in this respect ambivalent; it can form part of a federal form of integration or of one that adheres to traditional methods of cooperation among sovereign states. Possibly this is one reason there has been progress under these heads; by signing up no one committed himself beyond the immediate arrangements, yet adherents of either approach could regard the immediate measures as contributing to the line of development they favored.

Another way of getting at the relevance of federalism to Western European economic integration is to look at some of the obstacles to greater integration and the efforts that have been made to overcome them. The importance of various obstacles has changed as recovery progressed, but their basic elements have been fairly constant. Protected interests have objected to greater foreign competition. Governments have feared that domestic economic programs would be upset, that new difficulties would confront them, that political opposition would be increased, that production judged essential to defense would be deranged, or that any one of a hundred things would happen that they would rather not have happen. Removal of barriers to trade and payments deprives governments of some of the most effective and most easily used methods of coping with balance of payments difficulties.[3] There is also fear that domestic programs of full employment or economic stability will be harder to carry out if foreign transactions are freed from controls. Countries with high costs, due perhaps to inflation, may prefer limiting trade to the politically more difficult measures needed to adapt their economies to freer competition or to check inflation.

In short, even with strictly private interests set aside, there is a kind of public interest—however misconceived we may think it—opposing further removal of barriers to trade and payments. It hinges first of all on fear of the dislocation likely to result from the changed flow of trade and financial movements that would follow the removal of barriers, and secondly on the uncertainty that in the new situation the government will be able to do as much to meet its responsibilities as it would if it continued in the old way. The latter is certainly often a shortsighted view since many governments are already not in a good position to meet their responsibilities should there be crises, and closer connections with foreign economies might prevent some crises or make it easier to deal with some aspects of them. But the attitude exists and it is enhanced when there are important differences in the dominant lines of policy being followed by different countries. Governments relying heavily on direct controls and fairly detailed manipulation of the economy have feared that extensive liberalization would expose their countries to disturbances and unemployment flowing from countries with "uncontrolled" economies where markets had freer play. Governments of these latter countries, at the same time, took the view that the general use of controls perpetuated problems instead of solving them and so distorted the price system that liberalization of trade and payments could not perform its proper function. To overcome some of these obstacles and to evade others, several attempts have been made to integrate single sectors of the Western European economy instead of removing barriers across the board. These efforts had a double purpose: to make headway by concentrating effort on a single sector, and to undertake the adjustment of the productive structure of each country concomitant with the removal of trade barriers, thus minimizing the fear of dislocation.

In the summer of 1950, Dirk Stikker, the Dutch Foreign Minister, suggested a general plan for integration by sectors. When a certain industry had been chosen for integration, experts would work out means of dealing with the problems arising in each country from the complete removal of barriers to trade among the participants in the products of that industry. A European Integration Fund would help countries adapt their industries to the new common market. For some firms this might be a matter of modernization and rationalization; others would have to shift into new lines of production or go out of business altogether; the fund was to help in the retraining and, if necessary, the relocating of workers. Stikker's proposal said little about how the Fund was to be constituted. Its use was to be governed by the OEEC Council but not subject to the unanimity rule.

There has been no final, formal action on the Stikker Plan. Though the circumstances of its demise are obscure, some of the contributing factors are clear. Limiting integration to a single industry, though it has some clear practical advantages, also has some real disadvantages; these arise mostly from the concentration of adjustments in a limited area which may reduce a country's flexibility and its chances to offset contraction of one kind of production by immediate expansion of another. There were doubts about how the integration fund would be used. Officials of some governments objected to the amount of planning and governmental control they thought would be required to integrate industries under the Stikker Plan. In short, although the Stikker Plan recognized some major obstacles to the removal of trade barriers, the means it presented for overcoming them were not attractive enough to produce results.

There have been some other attempts at the sector approach. The OEEC tried through industry committees to coordinate national investment programs but failed to produce any substantial results. Discussions of agricultural integration—"the green pool"—have gone on since 1950 but have not led to any serious suggestions for effective action. Agriculture is one of the sectors of the Western European economy least apt for integration. Every government pursues a number of objectives that require special measures of farm policy. The political responsibility for the results of these programs is clearly recognized and of great importance for staying in office. Except where there is an export interest, the main feature of the agricultural policies is protection of the farmer's position and income by trade barriers, price manipulations, and various forms of subsidy. It would be most surprising, therefore, to find much support for major measures of liberalization. More likely to succeed is the tendency that has been clear from the beginning: to make the green pool some kind of producers' organization, possibly modified by arrangements for the exchange of surpluses and the easing of certain kinds of international transactions. This kind of economic integration would be unlikely to lead to a better allocation of Western Europe's productive resources. Nor would it be likely to bring about much change in national farm policies since governmental protection and assistance would be the economic underpinning of the pool and the political support for the bargaining position of each national group of producers.

In these circumstances the only way to get effective agricultural integration would be to create international or supranational responsibility for farm programs. This would hardly be possible without creating a high degree of political responsibility as well. The Dutch, who produced one of the first official proposals for a green pool, seem to dislike currents in the negotiations that lead toward domination by producers; they have given up the sector approach in favor of a general common market under a political authority. The French, who at one time favored a supranational organization to run the green pool, appear to have shifted to support an intergovernmental organization.

This sketch of the sector approach carries us a step farther in our search for the relevance of federalism to economic integration. The sector approach aims to overcome some of the obstacles to the removal of trade barriers by arranging for some sort of common action to adapt protected economies to a common market. These measures of adaptation would simultaneously remove obstacles to liberalization and cushion the impact of liberalization in each country. To some extent, therefore, adoption of the sector approach would transfer responsibility for some economic matters from national governments to the group of governments of the countries forming the common market. This responsibility might be exercised by an international or by a supranational agency. The need for effective, flexible action would make for a supranational arrangement. But unless political responsibility for the repercussions of the adjustment measures and of the creation of the common market could also be transferred, the arrangements would work only so long as governments felt able to withstand adverse domestic pressures by pleading *non possumus*. Failure to work out satisfactory methods of adaptation by intergovernmental action or to get countries to accept the transfer of responsibility to a supranational body is the key to the failure of the sector approach.

No comment on Western European economic integration is complete without a reference to Benelux. That effort, being somewhat different in character from those we have already examined, can also contribute its mite to the theme of this chapter.

Almost at the outset, the wartime agreement to form a customs union of Belgium, The Netherlands, and Luxembourg was expanded to make the objective an economic union. Had this been fully achieved, the result would have been hard to classify according to its federal attributes. Constitutionally there might have been no federalism at all while economically the existence of a common area for many activities coupled with the retention by national governments of basic political responsibility and many economic powers would have suggested some features of federalism. But matters never reached that point. The Benelux countries had the same major difficulties in removing barriers to trade between them that other countries faced which were not committed to such far-reaching projects. They made more progress than the other countries but serious barriers remained, especially to the export of Dutch farm products to Belgium and (because of payment difficulties) to the sale of Belgian manufactured goods to Holland. The customs union agreement had been premised on the idea that the two countries would start more or less even at the end of the war, both with a good chance to reshape their economies. In fact, circumstances varied markedly when the first steps toward union were taken. Perhaps inevitably the view emerged that economic union could be realized only after conditions in the two countries had been "equalized" in critical areas, and their major policies coordinated. Just as inevitably, since there were two governments responsible to different electorates and facing different problems, equalization of conditions came only slowly, almost haphazardly. It was a poor idea to start with; equalization as a prior condition of union would mean that the union would bring no changes and so would lose much of its reason for being (the rest would be the assurance it gave for the future). Put another way, the insistence on equalization meant that union was expected to force greater changes than the countries were prepared to accept.

The steps toward union taken by Belgium and Holland were always the results of negotiation between the two governments and there have been few attempts to move outside this framework. An arrangement made in October 1950 provided that if the two governments could not agree on a maximum price for farm products moving from one country to another, the price was to be set by arbitration. In December of the same year, before the agreement went into effect, the Belgian government had to back out because of the opposition of its farmers. Arbitration was again introduced in July 1953 as part of an agreement establishing conditions under which new trade barriers could be erected when an industry in one of the countries was hurt by imports from the other. Some support has been shown for the creation of a joint Benelux body with the power to act in certain economic matters. Nothing has come of this idea, however, and much of the present activity is concentrated on discussions among industrialists to see if they can work out arrangements that would make possible (i.e. virtually innocuous) the removal of trade barriers.

Benelux differs from the other cases we have surveyed. Only three countries are involved and they agreed almost ten years ago to form an economic union. Yet the pattern of limited progress is very much the same: unwillingness to accept the dislocations of removing all trade barriers; inability to coordinate national policies to the point where the dislocations would be minimized; unwillingness to transfer responsibility for measures of integration to some body outside the national government. This pattern is the epitome of the history of federalism in postwar Western European economic cooperation—except for the Schuman Plan.

III

THE SCHUMAN PLAN: PARTIAL FEDERALISM

The Schuman Plan differs fundamentally from all the other measures of Western European economic cooperation in being federal. The treaty creating the European Coal and Steel Community establishes the High Authority as a supranational body with certain powers over the coal and steel industries of the six participating countries; other powers remain in the hands of the national governments and some are to be exercised by the Council of Ministers in which each of the six governments has a single seat, but not always a veto. Certain disputes about actions taken under the treaty can be settled by the Court, another supranational body. A Common Assembly chosen by the parliaments of the member countries reviews the work of the High Authority and may depose it. A Consultative Committee composed of spokesmen for interest groups completes the array of institutions.

The Schuman Plan has affinities with the sector approach, coordination of investment, removal of trade barriers, and other efforts at cooperation, but it is not so much a prolongation of these approaches as a quite separate case. The cliché that the Schuman Plan is a political measure, not an economic one, ignores the central point that, in large part, the plan depends on economic means to achieve political results. The truth, much more complicated than the cliche, is as briefly stated: political and economic elements are inextricably mingled in the Schuman Plan. Political propulsion got acceptance of supranational features that were rejected in other schemes for economic cooperation. There was nothing inevitable about the Schuman Plan; indeed it was unpredictable. Its future, too, is unpredictable, depending not only on how the coal and steel pool works, but also on exogenous political factors.

Our concern here is with some issues related to federalism that the Schuman Plan raises concretely. To start with, how supranational is the High Authority? Has it the strength and powers to function effectively? To what sort of political control is it subject?

In form the High Authority is wholly supranational. Its members are chosen as individuals, given a mandate by the treaty, and forbidden to receive instructions from governments. In practice, the High Authority inevitably starts with some national taint in its make up. The members are nationals of the participating countries; each was, in effect, chosen by his own government but had to be acceptable to the other governments.[4] Later, cooption is to play an important part in the choice of members but that is some time off. Although Europeans outside the High Authority still often speak as if the members represented the countries of which they are nationals, spokesmen of the High Authority maintain that it is working effectively as a group of individuals carrying out a supranational mandate and reaching a consensus on major issues before acting. This does not mean, of course, that the men on the High Authority have somehow wholly detached themselves from their pasts as civil servants, steel producers, union officials, etc. in their native countries. Nor is such a superhuman feat necessary to make the High Authority an effective supranational agency; federalism calls for a mingling and balancing of the interests of constituent parts as a means of determining a common interest, not a complete abstraction from them.

The real strength of the High Authority will be revealed only in time. The treaty gives it a wide range of powers reinforced by national commitments to take major steps toward integration. The High Authority has a broad mandate on many basic issues and a series of rather explicit mandates on specific issues. There are legal tangles and areas of uncertainty but in general the structure is clear. Whether the arsenal of means of enforcement provided in the treaty will suffice to enable the High Authority to impose its will if governments resist is a matter not susceptible of very enlightening discussion in the abstract. Any treaty can be undone by its makers.

Similarly the effectiveness of the High Authority's sanctions against an offending firm or private group will depend on circumstances. But there are some broad considerations worth noting. However effective the enforcement measures may prove to be, the need to use them extensively would show that the Schuman Plan was not working effectively, since economic processes do not take place properly if they can be kept going only by a series of punishments. The High Authority's problem is to create conditions in which there are inducements and pressures moving private interests toward integration. So far as possible the pressures should come from circumstances that the High Authority has helped create rather than from direct disciplinary action.

The iron, coal, and steel industry of Western Europe is massive, complicated, and crisscrossed by intricate and subtle relationships. It is meshed with the whole economy and political shape of the area and has dynamics of its own. It will not be easily governed. A statement by the High Authority to the Council of Ministers in October 1953 gives some indication of the kind of difficulty that arises from trying to fit new arrangements onto this complex.

> One must not be surprised at the loyalty buyers show to their traditional suppliers and it must be underlined that learning and comparing the new price schedules, like learning new rules of competition, runs into real difficulties.
> Furthermore, the national organizations of producers tend to protect their national markets.
> Finally, in the present state of business, competitive adjustment of prices to the schedules of other firms is used for the most part to hold old markets rather than to conquer new ones.[5]

These difficulties among others are cited by the High Authority as reasons why "we are not yet in the presence of a true common market" but have only a "limited interpenetration of markets." Part of the trouble stems from an effort by steel producers to keep up prices in the face of a fall in demand. This may change but the High Authority's problem of making economic conditions respond to its decisions will persist. It is no secret that price fixing by national producers' groups in the steel industry plays its part in the situation described by the High Authority and will not easily be changed by fiat.

The cartel question in its many forms will present the High Authority with a continuing series of difficult decisions. Among the private groups in the steel industry there is some tradition of integration that does not exist among the national governments, and indeed of federalism as well. The federalism of cartels entails a constant conflict of the parts among themselves, each striving for an advantageous position and calling on its government for help, while at the same time cooperating with foreign producers. But this kind of federalism is more apt to obstruct than to help the creation of a common market to which the High Authority has dedicated itself. The High Authority has to emphasize the unification of the market and the breaking down of some of the factors that in the past made for the kind of federalism found in some cartels.[6]

One of the most discussed questions about the Schuman Plan's federal structure concerns the political responsibility of the High Authority. The Common Assembly possesses only the authority to discuss annually the High Authority's work and to vote it out of office. Constitutionally it has none of the more flexible controls that would come through voting the budget for instance. But in practice the Assembly, through its committees, seems to be in closer contact with the High Authority's work than the treaty's provisions indicate. How much this may influence the action of the High Authority is unclear. Another form of political control over the High Authority is through the Council of Ministers. Though the Council has no general supervisory power over the High Authority, it is the agency by which the governments of member countries let the supranational body know their views. Moreover the functions of the Council and the Authority are intermeshed in complex and variegated ways.[7] The Council's role, and therefore the power of the governments, is particularly important in times of shortage or surplus, when the most drastic powers of control over production, trade, and prices come into play.

There are other complicating factors. The Assembly has no legislative power; challenges to the High Authority's interpretation of the treaty are to be settled by the Court, another supranational body; the Council of Ministers can often act by simple majority but on major issues can rarely overrule France and Germany if they vote together. No clear lines of political responsibility emerge. On the other hand, one cannot realistically picture the High Authority as a powerful supranational body freed of political responsibility. Conceivably it might become that in time. For the immediate future, the difficulty and inherent slowness of its primary tasks, coupled with the political limitations outlined, make it likely that the High Authority will have to show much caution and, to some extent, act as if it were at least loosely responsible to the majority view among the governments of the member states. This does not solve the problem of agreed political control of the Coal and Steel Community. Should the European Political Community be created, it would clarify matters, without perhaps wholly resolving them, especially if the Coal and Steel Community had developed marked habits and relationships within it that proved to be not altogether malleable by a new agency within which a different balance of powers was taking shape.

Closely related to political control of the supranational body is the kind of policy that it is to follow. Federalism by itself requires no particular cast of policy. It does however ensure that policy will be uniform, so far as federalized matters are concerned. This is one of the reasons there are not more federal institutions in Western Europe and that Britain is not in the Schuman Plan. It is not that governments decried uniform policies but that they did not value uniformity above the right to adopt whatever policies they deemed best, since they would be held responsible by their electorates for the result. The executive of the British Labour Party only put this view in extreme form when it said: "No Socialist Party with the prospect of forming a government could accept a system by which important fields of national policy were surrendered to a supranational European representative authority, since such an authority would have a permanent anti-Socialist majority and would arouse the hostility of European workers."[8] Governments favoring free market policies would be bound to reach the same conclusion if they felt a supranational body would be dominated by the views of socialists or believers in the extensive use of direct controls. Establishment of clear lines of political control over a supranational executive like the High Authority would not remove this difficulty for a country that feared it might be in a minority at a crucial time. Basic difficulties, for federalism and for economic integration, will arise if countries participating in a federal arrangement that covers only part of their economies pursue, outside the federalized area, policies that diverge basically from those adopted by the supranational agency.

The main lines of policy that will be followed by the Coal and Steel Community cannot now be determined. The treaty stipulates many principles and some conditions that give a general orientation, mostly toward an economy aimed at more competition and less governmental intervention than has existed in the past. However, to enable the organs of the Community to deal with a variety of cases and to function effectively in all phases of the business cycle, as it must if it is to be flexible, the treaty gives the High Authority a good bit of discretion to do or permit things that would create quite a different kind of economy. Fears that the Community would be too *dirigiste* or too *laisser faire* have been important sources of opposition to the Schuman Plan. The High Authority has started by professing its allegiance, in word and action, to the dominant philosophy of the treaty, but the hard cases are yet to come. A certain similarity in the general orientation of economic policy among the countries in the Community has helped but this uniformity may be less general than it sometimes seems and in any case is not immutable.

Another set of problems rises from the fact that the Coal and Steel Community is a partial federal economic union. It is partial in two senses. First, it does not cover all of the economic relations among the member countries that affect the coal and steel industries. Second, each member country has part of its economy in the pool and part outside.

The problems that would arise if a country in the Community decided to devalue its currency demonstrate the first of these difficulties. Devaluation is a matter wholly outside the jurisdiction of the High Authority yet it would have a strong impact on the relative position of the pooled industries in different countries. Costs would go down, initially at least, in the devaluing country and its coal and steel would become cheaper in the other countries of the Community. They would not be free to levy special taxes or tariffs or to ban imports. The devaluing country's imports from the rest of the Community, becoming more costly, would be apt to shrink. The price change might not reflect long run changes in real costs but would upset competitive conditions and thereby the structure of production that was taking shape in response to the single market. Calculations the High Authority had made for the guidance of investments would be askew; what had seemed justified investments might now be losing propositions requiring either protection or subsidy, in violation of the treaty, or failing to justify investments just made.

The treaty provides an escape clause for cases like this; integration, however, cannot be created by escape clauses. The High Authority might also be able to find emergency powers enabling it to deal with the most disturbing immediate manifestations of the dislocation, but only at the expense of setbacks in progress toward the kind of single market envisaged in the treaty. The real question is not whether the Community could meet such a crisis but whether it could effectively pursue its main aims while unable to control such major factors having a direct bearing on its activities.

Problems also rise from the second sense in which the Schuman Plan is only a partial union. The coal and steel industries that are in the common market are still part of the economies of the countries where they are located. Each is enmeshed not only with the rest of the pool but also with the unpooled elements in its national economy. Customers, suppliers, bankers, and labor with which the coal and steel industries deal are cut off in varying degrees from the economies of other countries in the Community. Governmental economic policies that are not governed by the treaty have direct and serious effects on the pooled industries. The High Authority stressed the basic significance of this situation in the statement to the Council of Ministers already cited:

> . . . . the development of our Community calls for a general policy of expansion and of normal competition for the industries in the common market.
>
> But this common policy is not possible unless internal contradictions in the policy of each country are eliminated first.
>
> Each of your governments has entrusted to the Community an essential part of the activity of its country and a fundamental element in the development of its economy. Look at the facts and ask yourselves if you assure the enterprises in the common market normal conditions of development and normal conditions of competition.
>
> . . . .
>
> Do you take adequate care to avoid affecting in a contradictory manner the prices of products which influence the costs of coal and steel, and the prices of products which assure them of markets?
>
> Does your general monetary policy permit each of your industries, for the

good of our Community, to take full advantage of its real costs and its technical achievements?

Turning from the conditions necessary for the functioning of the common market to the conditions necessary for the development of our industries, would it not be a dereliction to neglect the high level of investment necessary to a satisfactory expansion of the production of coal and steel?[9]

The statement mentions key issues and needs little elaboration. Governments have given up the right to fix coal and steel prices (except in the sense that for nationalized enterprises a government agency has the same rights in the pool as a private entrepreneur), but what they do to fix or influence other prices may have an important effect on the coal and steel industry. Money and credit policy will affect the costs and the market of the coal and steel industries as well as their access to domestic capital. The direction of government investment programs or of the incentives offered to private investors would also shape the prospects of the pooled industries, in sales and supplies as well as in capital. Changes in social security or measures that generally lower or raise wages throughout the economy will not leave the coal and steel industries unaffected. Nationalization would raise new problems.

Some of the complications arising from different methods of levying taxes have already given concern to the High Authority. The equalization of wages, once much discussed as an aim of the Coal and Steel Community, dropped out of the negotiation of the treaty when it was realized that wages in the coal and steel industries of each country had much more to do with the general level of wages in that country than with the wages in the same industry in other countries. The pooling of the coal and steel industries also affects the unpooled part of the economy, for instance by price changes resulting from access to a larger market. The governments of the Community have lost some of their ability to manipulate their national economies by giving up some of their power over coal and steel.

All these examples add up to much the same thing: the diversity in unity inherent in a federal system poses economic issues that concern not only the long run effects of the coal and steel pool but also its short run effectiveness. The drive that made the treaty possible was a drive, largely political, toward unification of markets and of control over basic resources. The discrepancies arising from partial pooling coupled with continuation of separate national economies were pushed into the background by the emphasis on the main drive.[10] They may, however, prove to be the crucial element in the future of the Schuman Plan.

These discrepancies have been regarded by some as flaws likely to prove fatal to the Community. Divergent national actions in the unpooled sectors will, in this view, undo or nullify the effects of pooling. Others have welcomed the discrepancies as the modes by which the Coal and Steel Community's dynamism will spread to the rest of the European economy. According to this view, the pressure to make the pool work effectively will force countries at least to coordinate their policies in other fields and perhaps to adopt new federal arrangements. Both these contradictory views are plausible. There is no cogent *a priori* criterion for choosing between them. The validation of either will depend on what happens in the pooled economy, what kind of difficulties arise from the discrepancies, and how the countries affected balance the advantages and disadvantages of adding to or subtracting from their supranational arrangements. There is a third possible alternative. The idea that the Schuman Plan must spread or contract rests in part on simple logic, but in human affairs it is very misleading to assume that a process must move to its logical conclusion. An illogical coexistence of partial federalism and partial separation of national economies seems a fairly likely eventuality, at least for quite a while to come.

IV

PENDING ISSUES

Europeans are discussing with some seriousness a number of possible steps toward further economic integration that have some federal elements. They fall into three main classes. Some would pursue the method of the Schuman Plan, creating new supranational agencies for other portions of the Western European economy. Concerning this method, nothing needs to be added to what has already been said about the coal and steel pool and integration by sector. The second line of approach aims at creating a political federation within which economic integration may progress. Monetary integration and the breaking down of financial barriers between European countries, which are the main features of the third approach, may or may not include federal measures. Both these latter approaches require brief comment.

The proposals for a European Defense Community and a European Political Community provided the recent content of the movement toward greater federalism in Western Europe. Adoption of the EDC treaty contemplated a federal structure of defense roughly comparable to the Coal and Steel Community. The economic powers assigned to the defense commissariat under the treaty concerned the procurement of military supplies and the allocation of part of the defense appropriations of the participating countries. How far their economic implications would reach is problematical. If they led to defense economies or to heavier defense expenditures they would obviously have an influence on the Western European economy but not necessarily on its integration. Effective provision for common defense would undermine the argument that certain industries in each country need protection for national defense. This would weaken one of the obstacles to the removal of trade barriers within the Defense Community but would not enhance the chances of integration between the Community and outside countries.

Within the Defense Community, the concentration of orders for military supplies in certain plants or areas might be the strongest factor making for integration. To the extent that strictly military items were involved, the broad economic significance would not be great. In the case of industries that produce both military and civilian goods, like the manufacture of vehicles, machine tools, aircraft, some kinds of machinery, chemicals, textiles, and electrical equipment, the economic significance of concentration of orders under the Defense Community would be much greater. How much integration would take place in these industries is a matter for speculation. Economy would indicate concentration of production and division of labor, but strategic considerations, political pressures, and the desire to avoid dislocation and disturbance would tend to check too great a departure from the established pattern of industrial production.

Adoption of the treaty for a European Political Community would change basically the conditions discussed in this chapter. Willing creation of a federal polity would imply that the peoples of Western Europe had accepted a concept of their own unity that would be almost certain to lead in time to a substantial degree of economic integration. Even somewhat hesitant adoption of the EPC treaty would probably set in motion forces that would pull together the economies of the member countries, provided the treaty was not greatly abridged and allegiance to it did not deteriorate. More immediately, creation of EPC would affect some of the problems discussed in this chapter by providing organized supranational political responsibility for the Coal and Steel Community and the EDC. Presumably the political climate would make for greater economic integration as a result. But the formal change alone would not assure this. A federal parliament and cabinet, bound to conciliate the national governments in the Political Community, might move less rapidly toward integration of the coal and steel industries than the High Authority with its less clear political responsibility.

The major economic provision of the EPC treaty is the stipulation (with some escape clauses) that over six years the Community "shall establish progressively a common market . . . , based on the free movement of goods, capital and persons." A European Readaptation Fund is to be used to help bring about necessary adjustment. Dutch insistence appears to be responsible for these provisions. The Dutch view has been that economic integration was a necessary foundation for federal political union and military strength. Put another way this is to say that much of the content of government is economic. If the countries of the EPC seriously undertake to create a common market, they will face problems that have already arisen in the Schuman Plan, Benelux, and the work of the OEEC. Some they will be better able to cope with since they will be forming a common market for all products instead of selected ones. Other questions, though, will remain highly apposite and serious. They point to a basic issue already noted: the extent of the powers that a federal government would need to bring about effective economic integration. For instance, will the EPC countries accept the removal of trade barriers without first equalizing conditions in their countries? And if they try to do that will six countries make more headway than the three of Benelux? Can they maintain a common market if each pursues a separate monetary and financial policy? The treaty takes note of this last question and calls on the Community to "foster the co-ordination of the policy of the Member States in monetary, credit and financial matters." It has already been noted that one country at least asks for a stronger mandate.

This leads to the third approach to economic integration that is being seriously discussed in Western Europe: emphasis on monetary integration as the basic, if not universal, solvent. The rubric covers a wide variety of proposals that have in common three principal, interrelated aims: to permit free movement of funds throughout Europe; to preserve this freedom without resort by governments to trade barriers to protect their balances of payments; to maintain the dominance of the price system and free markets in the Western European economy, confining government regulation largely to measures of monetary and fiscal policy. There is wide agreement on the desirability of these aims, subject to important differences in view about priorities when these ends conflict with other social, economic, or political aims, as well as about the extent to which these goals can really be attained. Not all of the three aims would have to be fully achieved for a significant degree of monetary integration. Indeed, one of the main virtues claimed for the approach is that it is dynamic and flexible. Once a fair degree of convertibility at proper exchange rates is attained, costs and prices are affected in ways that bring about improved allocation of resources. Nevertheless the process could be seriously undermined or the results distorted by numerous and very restrictive trade barriers or by failure of governments to rely primarily on monetary and fiscal measures, instead of on direct controls and price manipulations, to meet their problems. In a sense, monetary integration aims at creating a facsimile of the gold standard, with modifications to allow for varying degrees of deliberate intervention in the process. The question is whether semi-automatic operations and effective pressures for correction can be successfully combined with retention of the amount of governmental power to manage national economies that is politically necessary.

The possibilities of solving these problems and the merits and implications of the various methods cannot be examined here. So far as federalism is concerned, monetary integration is basically ambivalent (like the removal of trade barriers). That is to say, monetary integration might be achieved by national states without a supranational body or it might be a major feature of a federal system. As we have seen in the discussion of the Schuman Plan, it would be difficult for a federal economic system to work effectively without a good bit of monetary integration. This does not mean that the integration would necessarily have to be brought about by supranational action; indeed it might be very hard to do it that way. But if one were drafting a constitution and wanted to assign to the federal government all the powers it needed to prevent a member state from upsetting economic integration, one would have to give it very extensive powers over monetary policy. Many of the proponents of the monetary approach regard as a major virtue the fact that it would make unnecessary the creation of additional supranational authorities along the lines of the Schuman Plan because they fear that any of these agencies (and presumably a federal government as well if it were endowed with adequate powers) may lead to suprastate *dirigisme* or socialism. In this sense, monetary integration might be a substitute for federalism.

Some specific proposals for monetary integration, however, have distinctly federal elements. The most extreme is the proposal for a common currency to be managed by a European central bank or currency commission. By accepting such an arrangement, a government would give up major powers over its national economy. Milder proposals would create some kind of international body not directly responsible to governments—perhaps a Federal Reserve Board or a committee of central bank heads—that would be given more limited powers to influence national monetary policies. Robert Triffin has argued that without creating federal agencies virtually the same economic effects as would result from a common currency can be attained by convertibility at fixed exchange rates, so long as the rates are proper ones.[11] The big difference, of course, is that it is easier to break out of an agreement for maintaining convertibility at fixed rates than to withdraw from a common currency area where issue and credit policies are controlled by a supranational agency. Another approach recommends flexible exchange rates as the best means of maintaining monetary integration while differential inflation or deflation occurs in member countries. This suggestion presumes that countries will be unwilling to give a supranational body more direct control over their internal monetary affairs. But then it is sometimes suggested that a federal body would have to have some degree of control over the exchange rates, partly as a disciplinary measure and partly to check disintegration.

Two basic considerations are likely to influence the willingness of governments to accept measures of monetary integration that put powers in supranational hands. First, those who will be held politically responsible for a satisfactory level of employment cannot afford to give up the power to use monetary and fiscal measures to cope with the business cycle. Second, monetary integration does not automatically dissipate the difficulties of areas that previously had trouble with their balances of payments. The difficulties are transmuted but poor areas are still poor, rich areas are still rich, some are more productive than others, flexibility varies, and the desire to consume more than you produce continues to create a problem. Regional balance of payments difficulties within a single country are somewhat mitigated by the movement of labor and capital, a variety of special factors, and an acceptance of the idea that one part of the country can be taxed for the benefit of another. Both these basic considerations emphasize the correlation of political responsibility with economic powers which has emerged in this chapter as a fundamental structural problem of economic federalism.

V

THE AREA OF FEDERALISM

External relations—completely ignored so far in my treatment—have played an important part in shaping Western Europe's measures of economic integration. Britain's position is well known. While the supposed conflict between the United Kingdom's obligations to the Commonwealth and the sterling area and the requirements of closer Western European economic cooperation has sometimes been exaggerated, the pull of overseas interests has been a real factor in keeping Britain aloof from efforts to make European integration the primary goal. Britain's great concern with world trade and especially with its dollar problem has concentrated attention on a broader area than Western Europe. Unwillingness to give up control of industries basic to national life—a view shared by Conservatives and Labourites—was mainly responsible for Britain's refusal to enter the Schuman Plan, but fear of the loss of autonomy in dealing with the rest of the world on these matters also played its part.

In France during the heyday of *"faire l'Europe"* there was much skepticism about British concern for overseas ties and sometimes a certain scorn for an insular lack of mental suppleness in not finding ways to combine the two sets of responsibilities. Now there is a new emphasis on France's overseas interests and the limits these put on the kind of arrangements it can agree to in Europe. Not only the attitude but the very language echoes the British position: "The truth is that France is not solely a European power but a world power. She cannot merge with countries strictly limited to the continent. She can only associate herself with them, coordinate her policy with theirs in certain areas which are of common interest and, for the rest, maintain her personality and her independence."[12] This view may not in the end dominate French policy but it reflects real issues.

Other countries have also been concerned with their extra-European relations, though in somewhat different ways. The large creditors in EPU, for a long while Belgium and now especially Western Germany, have wanted to receive a larger share of their surpluses in gold, partly in order to be able to set off their surpluses in Europe against deficits elsewhere. In the view of some of its advocates, monetary integration would eventually make the EPU unnecessary. As an initial step, any great "hardening" of the terms of payments for debtors would make their EPU relations more nearly comparable to their transactions with the rest of the world. Indeed, the whole emphasis on monetary integration raises questions about the external relations of the area. Western Europe might achieve monetary integration while the area as a whole continued to have a "dollar shortage"—shorthand for a complex of factors, of which the most relevant at this point are continued discrimination against imports from the dollar area and control over payments into that area. In this case the question rises: Who is going to control the area's gold and dollar reserves, deciding how they shall be allocated among countries, for what imports they shall be used, and the minimum level below which they may not be depleted? Unless there are uniform policies or some form of central control of the reserves, the competition for dollars in intra-European trade might well set in motion disintegrative tendencies. If, on the other hand, Western Europe achieved monetary integration and dollar convertibility for the whole area, then some of the economic rationale for Western European integration would disappear, for it is based on the assumption that Western Europe is not economically viable cut up into national units. Moreover, if European currencies, including the pound, are generally convertible into dollars, then European monetary integration would be different from the monetary integration of the whole free world only to the extent that the European countries achieved a greater harmonization of national policies or set up supranational financial institutions.

The Schuman Plan raises a whole series of questions about relations with countries outside the union but at present gives little guidance for their solution. The special problem of relations with the United Kingdom is now under negotiation with no clear indication of where it is heading. French African iron ore is not part of the pool but its use is subject to some rules laid down in the treaty. A special arrangement assuring Italy of certain quantities of this ore played a part in Italian adherence to the plan. Germany is more interested in Swedish iron ore than in the *minette* of Lorraine and questions were raised in the Bundestag whether Germany's commitments in the treaty would still leave it free in times of shortage to send Sweden whatever coal was required to assure ore supplies for the Ruhr. The Swiss have agreed to invest in the German steel industry in return for an assurance of minimum supplies over a period of years. Germany, France, and other countries in the Community are greatly concerned with exports of steel products and machinery to overseas markets. Will they gain more by continuing to compete or by combined operations? An export price agreement is already giving the High Authority difficulties. Is there to be a common foreign trade policy for the Community? In times of shortage or surplus will the regulations imposed by the Community seriously impair each member's freedom of action in dealing with the rest of the world? The treaty's provisions on external relations are much less definite and clear than on most internal matters. The High Authority's powers over foreign relations seem to be weaker than in domestic affairs. This is plainly an area where practice will be more important than prescription in shaping policy. Leaving aside the question of construing treaty provisions, the central issues are whether the Community will come to deal with the outside world as a unit and whether separate national dealings with the outside world will check the growth of a wholly unified Community coal and steel economy.

The areas covered by major measures of European economic integration are not identical. The EPU covers the payments of the OEEC countries with the sterling area; the trade liberalization program does not. Tariff reduction is not dealt with on a European basis at all but in multilateral negotiations under the General Agreement on Tariffs and Trade in which a large number of countries participate. The Schuman Plan and the EDC and EPC proposals apply only to six countries. The differences are reminders that the geographical unity of Western Europe does not carry over into economics. There are plausible reasons for thinking of some matters—notably transportation—as area problems, but in matters of trade and payments the factors that make one grouping more logical than another have no special geographical base. The reasons for choosing the area are political and pragmatic—the belief that a degree of cooperation can be achieved within a certain group that is not possible among a larger number of countries. Because integration implies some degree of exclusion there is always the risk that measures of integration, or of preferential economic cooperation, will substitute one misallocation of resources for another by drawing countries to focus on a single economic area rather than on the potentialities of their global relations. The risk may often be worth running when the potential gains from measures of integration are clear and especially when steps can be taken to moderate the effects of integrating on a limited basis. For federal arrangements this is a double problem: How the federal agency shall conduct itself toward the rest of the world and how much freedom of action each member state shall have.

VI

CONCLUSION

Federalism is relevant to Western European economic integration because it offers a form of organization for international economic relations that appears well suited to some of Western Europe's principal needs. The essence of federalism is the combination of unity and diversity reflected in the two levels of government. Since the countries of Western Europe recognize that some of their economic problems might well be dealt with in common but are not prepared to submerge their national existences in a European state, some degree of federalism seems a likely method of proceeding; it has the added advantage, at least in form, of permitting change as time passes, with additional powers being assigned to the central agency if that seems desirable.

By its nature, federalism can solve only certain kinds of economic problems. Insofar as Western Europe's economic problems can be solved by removing barriers to trade and payments among the countries of the region and otherwise creating larger economic areas, federalism can help, provided, of course, that governments will give up the necessary powers to a supranational agency. Subject to the same conditions, federalism can help when the problem involves some harmonization of policies in a number of countries. To the extent that the solution of Western Europe's economic problems depends on the pursuit of certain kinds of policy rather than others—whether this be socialism vs. competitive capitalism, direct controls vs. market economy, hard vs. soft money, etc.—federalism by itself has nothing to do with the matter. In some situations creation of a federal agency may so alter the balance of forces that it makes possible a different kind of policy than that previously existing under national regimes; but there can be no guarantee that in the long pull the direction established by this shift will be decisive. Treaties creating federal institutions can also give an initial direction to policy, but if the treaties are to be flexible enough to survive the economic vicissitudes that may occur over a long period of time, they will have to permit areas of discretion on key matters that may drastically alter the original direction. For this sort of issue, federalism provides only a form and does not by itself indicate what the content of policy will be.

The central practical problem in devising a federation is the allocation of powers between the two levels. So far as economic integration is concerned, this becomes a matter of deciding how much integration is wanted and then what powers the federal government must have to take the initial steps needed to create that amount of integration and to protect the essential measures against nullification or subversion by national action in other fields. The interaction of economic processes makes it almost impossible to draw a logical line short of giving the central government quite extensive powers. This may be a harder problem on paper than in fact. Whether certain powers are needed depends on whether the action of national governments creates certain difficulties. For instance, if all members of a federation pursued the same general type of monetary policy and kept their finances in order, a federal government would not need to take action in this field; but if national governments acted so as to cause serious difficulties, the federal agency would need very extensive powers to be able to correct the condition. In practice many problems may work out in ways not indicated by a paper division of powers, perhaps because the component parts accept guidance from the center that could not be legally enforced, or because unforeseeable processes in economic or political life (resulting maybe from creation of the federation) make for the satisfactory solution of certain problems without recourse to a testing of power between the two levels. Furthermore, a federation may function satisfactorily in spite of considerable diversity of conditions in its parts. It should be borne in mind, though, that divergences that are acceptable or even almost unnoticed in established federations may seem serious obstacles to a new federation where national attitudes and pressures are still strong.

Although federalism seems well adapted to dealing with some of Western Europe's problems and has recommended itself to a number of individuals and groups, it has played no important part in the steps toward economic integration of the area except in the Schuman Plan. Apart from the coal and steel pool, integration has been largely a matter of the removal of barriers to trade and payments. Although new kinds of measures had to be invented for Europe's special situation, the basic process is a traditional part of cooperation among nations and required no measures as drastic as the creation of federal institutions. Many of the obstacles to the further removal of barriers are of a sort that might be dealt with more effectively by federal measures than under existing arrangements. But some of the same factors that made these obstacles serious made governments unwilling to give up the power to deal with them nationally. Removal of the obstacles would affect national payments positions, full employment policies, and trade with the dollar world, and would cause changes in national economic structures. National governments are politically responsible for such matters and the minimum condition of yielding control over them would be the transfer of political responsibility to a supranational body. This is more than any politically dominant group has been willing to do. Even if the principle were accepted, nations might still refuse to enter such a federation for a variety of reasons. Among them might be the expectation that the country would be overruled by the majority on basic direction of policy, or that membership in a federation would hinder development of the most advantageous relations with the rest of the world.

The Coal and Steel Community, on the other hand, is a major federal measure of economic integration. It was created because basic political motives combined with economic considerations to make it appear advantageous. In France it was accepted as a better way of dealing with Germany than past methods, which were failing fast. Instead of futilely trying to check German growth, the Schuman Plan aimed at tying Germany closely to Western Europe and at removing some major elements of power from purely German control. Schuman's view that this was the best way to cope with France's perennial German problem was not fully accepted by important segments of French opinion; a shift in the basic political decisions would alter the prospects of the coal and steel pool and probably check its growth. In Germany, the Schuman Plan was accepted partly for its economic advantages, partly as a measure of integration, and partly as a means of putting Germany on an equal footing with other Western European countries. Thus at the basis of the Schuman Plan is a series of truly federal equations, concerning the relations of the parts to one another and of each to the federal agency.

The growth of German power upsets these equations in French eyes but seems their logical solution to Germans. It is not surprising to find that the French, lacking confidence in the untried federal institutions, should feel that a balance of power within the Coal and Steel Community is necessary. The dilemma, which faced the French in the EDC as well, is that the growth of German strength seems likely to go on in or out of a federal arrangement. In exercising its supranational mandate the High Authority must make decisions that will affect the balance of national power within the pool; for example in connection with investments in French and German industry. This kind of issue raises questions about the division of real power in a federation in relation to the formal distribution of powers.

If the Schuman Plan can survive this tug of war with reasonable satisfaction to all parties, it will have proved the viability of federal arrangements for some kinds of economic and political integration in Western Europe. Quite apart from the French-German struggle, the coal and steel pool poses another set of questions about federalism as a method of economic integration. Although the High Authority has extensive powers, the powers remaining to the member governments, particularly in the field of finance, can frustrate the purposes of its actions. Within each Schuman Plan country there are a series of points at which the pooled and the unpooled elements in the national economy come together in ways that create problems that may be solved by measures moving in one or the other direction. Whether in both these areas the Schuman Plan will turn out to be an active center from which integration spreads, or whether its own integration will be hampered and hedged round by the limitations set by unpooled elements, may prove to be the central issues on which the future of Western European economic integration will turn.

FOOTNOTES TO CHAPTER 22

1. "Integration" is another word that invites abuse. To avoid diversion from the main theme, let me say only that when I say "integration" I refer to a process of increasing connections between economic activities now divided by national frontiers. The process moves toward, but need not reach, the end that can also be called "integration": replacing separate national economies by a single economy for Western Europe; the essence of a "single economy" would be that decisions on economic matters, whether made by public authorities, private concentrations of power, or the processes of the market, would ordinarily apply to the whole area.

2. The need for governments to report on the extent to which they had met OEEC production targets, the quotas they had removed from imports, and other matters probably influenced national policies to some extent, as did some OEEC reports, but the process was less direct than in the review of annual programs and there have been fewer indications of the influence.

3. EPU removes the need for discrimination among participants on balance of payments grounds by making the currencies of all member countries equally "hard" (or "soft") for all other members, but it does not eliminate the need for a country to be concerned with a continuing deficit in its payments to the group as a whole since once it exceeds its quota with the union it has to pay all further debts wholly in gold. This and most of the other matters dealt with in this section are discussed more fully in my *Trade and Payments in Western Europe*, New York, Harper & Brothers for the Council on Foreign Relations, 1952.

4. The two Frenchmen and two Germans on the Authority were both chosen in the same way as other members. A second Belgian was nominated by international trade union organizations.

5. Communaute Européenne du Charbon et de l'Acier. Haute Autorité. *Déclarations de la Haute Autorité devant le Conseil des Ministres*, Luxembourg, 12 Octobre 1953 (mimeographed), p. 4.

6. A line of investigation that might be relevant to European federalism would be a study of the organization of the coal and steel industries to determine the extent of regional and local concentrations of production and the nature of the exchanges among them. One might find a kind of industrial analogue of federal

structure that might not be completely superseded by the creation of a common market.

7. See the list of over one hundred powers of the High Authority classified according to the requirements for advice, agreement, etc. by other parts of the Community, in *La Communauté Européenne du Charbon et de l'Acier,* par un Groupe d'Étude de l'Institut des Relations Internationales de Bruxelles; Cahiers de la Fondation Nationale des Sciences Politiques 41, Paris, Colin, 1953, pp. 36–53.

8. *European Unity;* a statement by the National Executive Committee of the British Labour Party, May 1950, p. 8.

9. *Op. cit.,* p. 7.

10. There is, however, a clear recognition of this kind of federal problem in the treaty's provision that while the High Authority's decisions "shall be binding in all their details," it may make recommendations that are binding as to objectives but "leave to those to whom they are directed the choice of appropriate means for attaining these objectives."

11. Robert Triffin, "Système et Politique Monétaires de l'Europe Fédérée," *Economia Internazionale,* Vol. 6, No. 1–2 (1953), pp. 207–14.

12. XXX, "Union Francaise et Institutions Européennes;" *Politique Etrangère* (September–October 1953), p. 275. This article is one of the first results of a study of the relation of the French Union to European integration undertaken by the Centre d'Études de Politique Étrangère at the request of the French government. An article by René Servoise in the same issue of the periodical implies a view more favorable to the gradual linking of the French Union with an integrated Europe.

23

Problems of Economic Integration

By Ingvar Svennilson

The division of the world into a large number of independent national units is, of course, above all a political phenomenon. An integration, partly or completely, of such units is, therefore, also mainly a political problem, and it is probably safe to say that independent countries have never seriously approached economic integration unless under strong political pressure.

It is also doubtful if a full clarification of the advantages and disadvantages of economic integration or a careful planning of the various steps by which such an integration may be approached will promote progress in this direction. The theory that a reconciliation of interests can more easily be achieved if all the economic consequences of alternative actions have been forecast is probably not a very realistic one. Great changes in the relations between countries may perhaps occur more easily if undertaken as a leap in the dark. Subsequent difficulties may perhaps be solved more easily if they are tackled as they appear. And the habit of collaboration and of making compromises may grow stronger through practice. This all supports the view that a discussion of the economic implications of integration is not of primary importance.

And yet experience of the last few years seems to show that from a political point of view it is necessary to face the main economic conditions for and the consequences of integration. Since the war there has been so much loose talk, so much uninformed enthusiasm, so many false starts, that there is a great risk of the whole idea of integration becoming discredited. There now seems to be a need to assess past experiences and to make clear what are the main objectives of integration and by what methods they can be attained.

Such a discussion introduces the problem of how far economic cooperation between independent nations can be brought about without a certain minimum of political integration. One of the main lessons of the past years seems to be that we cannot advance very far towards a freer and more stable international economy without to some degree giving up the political autonomy of individual countries and developing new international institutions where joint solutions can be negotiated or even joint decisions be taken.

The result of an economic discussion will, thus, be that the ball is passed back to the politicians. If they refuse to play, they must face the risk of the international markets remaining unstable and restricted. Let us hope that in the end they will realize that this is a consequence of an economic nationalism that the Western World can no longer afford.

International integration may be taken to mean the extreme opposite to national isolation. But the word may also be used to indicate a *movement* towards less restricted international economic relations. It is in this more relative, and, if you wish, dynamic sense that I am going to use the word here. In the extremely nationalistic world in which we live, this seems to be the most realistic way of treating the subject. We would be happy if such a movement could get under way, even if it could only slowly build up a more completely integrated world.

The problems I am going to discuss are related to the tactics and strategy of such a movement. Every movement towards integration should, at least if it is to be successful, be organized as a combined movement in several directions at the same time. Experience of international economic policy in the first few years after the last war seems to show that if you advance too far in one direction, while progress in other directions is neglected, the whole process of integration easily comes to a standstill. There is even a risk of breakdown, retreat, and failure.

In this way arises the problem of coordinating the policies aiming at economic integration. It is a few of these problems that I am going to discuss.

I

The Importance of Large and Stable Markets

The starting-point for any discussion of the economic motives for integration must be modern industry's need for a large market where it can sell its products. This need was seen clearly even by Adam Smith some two hundred years ago. The advantages of a large market have never been demonstrated more clearly than in the famous exposition of the division of labor between pin-makers with which he introduced his treatise on the "Wealth of Nations." His conclusions about the relation between mechanization and the size of the market are just as valid today.

It is implicit in the idea of a large market that it should also be stable. The entrepreneur must, when he plans his investment and production, be able to count on the market remaining large; otherwise he will not be induced to exploit its advantages to the full. The importance of stability has grown with the progress of modern industry towards a higher level of mechanization and capital intensity. Mechanization, or high capital intensity in general, usually means an increase in the optimum scale of output of manufacturing industry. But it also means less flexibility in the choice of product, once the initial investment in product and process research, plant, machinery, and sales promotion has been made. If a part of the market should later be cut off, large capital losses are inevitable, and the existence of such risks may prevent industry from attaining the full advantages of large-scale production.

One main problem of economic integration is, therefore, how to find this large and stable market. Can it be found in a better integrated international market or only by a more complete integration of national economic systems to form larger "home-markets"?

II

HOME-MARKET AND INTERNATIONAL MARKETS

One of the main distinctions of home-markets, as opposed to international markets, today, is their greater freedom with regard to the movement of goods and their relative stability. It is true that restraints of trade may exist also in the home-market. But they are rather the exceptions that confirm the general rule that freedom of the market prevails. More and more countries are following the example of the United States in trying to control or eliminate various types of restrictive practices in their home markets. In the international markets, on the other hand, cartels are so far given free play; in this respect you can, for once, speak of the freedom of international trade.

In the last decade another factor has developed which has created a sharp difference between home markets and international markets. Within most national areas the new economic policy of stabilization and full employment has improved the conditions for industrial activity in a revolutionary way. It is difficult to find a country today which does not, at least publicly, adhere to these new principles. We are just beginning to harvest the fruits of this new policy. At the high level of capital costs typical of modern industry, enormous gains in terms of industrial efficiency follow from a high and stable level of employment. A comparison of the United States industry before and after the war shows, for example, how much efficiency can be increased when industry is allowed to run at full speed. Something similar is now happening in Europe. Under such economic conditions the risks run by new investments are reduced, and this will encourage the use of still more capital-intensive methods of production.

As is well known, there has been no corresponding development in the international market. While in the national field we rely more and more on a coordinated economic policy, international economy is still very much a prey to uncontrolled market forces. The energy that is invested in the balancing of the various national economies is getting quite out of proportion to the amount of cooperation in the international field.

It is true that domestic stabilization should improve the chances for a stable and free international trade. But in the first place there are still considerable risks that some countries will not maintain their employment and consequently their demand for internationally traded goods on a high level. And secondly, internal stability is often bought at the price of supplies from other countries. Because of forceful multiplier effects within international trade, even small initial changes may give rise to wide fluctuations. The international market is, therefore, still subject to fluctuations in demand which may easily give rise to a serious crisis for international trade.

Besides these cyclical fluctuations in market conditions there is in international trade, as it is organized today, another kind of instability which is especially harmful to the economic management of industry. The sudden introduction of import restrictions in order to safeguard the national balance of payments has come to be a very grave risk for exporting industries. Markets where large sums have been invested in a sales organization may suddenly be cut off, leaving the exporting industry with a large surplus capacity.

In spite of all efforts it must also be admitted that the development towards a demolition of the various restrictions on international trade has made only slow progress. Tariff reductions have only gone half-way or even less and the outlook for further progress is very uncertain. The balance of payments problems have not been solved and this blocks the way towards a general convertibility. Under these conditions important international institutions, such as the International Fund, have been unable to fulfill their functions.

Not to be misunderstood, let me declare from the start that I regard a solution of these worldwide problems as the most important task of international economic policy. We all know that their solution very much depends on the ability of the United States to assume the leadership corresponding to its prominent position in the world economy. This wide field of international relations is, however, not my subject here.

As a starting-point for the following discussion it should only be stated that the need for economic integration within groups of countries will depend on the progress that is made in creating a stable and free worldwide setting for international trade. If progress in this direction could be expected to be rapid, the need for closer integration within groups of countries would completely disappear. The world would then be not only the home but also the home-market of everybody. But if the efforts to achieve worldwide economic co-operation fail, or even if progress in this direction is slow, or is checked half way, there is a case for integration within groups of countries which want to widen their "home-markets."

Certainly a conflict may arise between group formations and the creation of a stable worldwide economic system. Groups of nations may become just as exclusive as individual nations. We may even conceive that the world economy may be split up into a number of more or less closed blocks. If such a risk exists the present nationalistic organization may seem to be preferable. But a group formation may also be conceived to fulfill the opposite function, one of strengthening the economy of various parts of the world in such a way as to make them strong enough to make a contribution to the creation of a free world economy instead of forming stumbling blocks on the road towards international cooperation. It is the possibilities of group-formation in such an international spirit that I am going to discuss here.

III

THE LOCATION OF WORLD INDUSTRY AND INTERNATIONAL TRADE

Over the last fifty years the role of home-markets, as compared with the international market, has been steadily increasing in importance. This is a consequence of the spread of industrialism to new areas of the world which would have appeared even without any trade restrictions. This tendency will very likely continue, as world industrialization is only in its infancy.

Fifty years ago some European countries were still the main suppliers of industrial products to less developed parts of the world. In subsequent decades this special position of a few industrialized countries in Europe has tended to disappear. In the first place other countries have been able to adopt old, well known industrial processes, and the commodity composition of world trade has as a result tended to change. The exports of more advanced industrial countries have shifted towards products which are more difficult to produce or which are completely new. It is mainly in the more advanced countries that new processes and products have been developed; as these processes or products have become "old," they have increasingly been taken up in a wider group of countries. In this way, each separate product passes through a kind of cycle. In an early stage production is restricted to a few countries and the share of exports in total output is large. Later, as new countries start production, exports fall in relation to the output for the home-market. The length of this cycle has probably been shortened, as a large number of countries have become more qualified as imitators of the techniques developed in pioneering countries. New products and processes take the place of old ones in world trade, but the general effect for all types of commodities has been a reduction of the share of the output of industrial products that flows into international trade.

These tendencies are reflected in the distribution of world trade on broad commodity groups. Textiles and miscellaneous manufactures have declined. Chemicals and steel products have held a stable share in world trade while engineering products, such as machinery and transport equipment, have been increasing in relative importance. There have, however, also been rapid changes within each main group, from well known staple goods towards new products and more difficult specialties. This tendency can, for example, be seen within the textile group.

Chemicals probably provide the best example of these dynamics of world trade. It has been estimated that before the first World War one-third of all output of chemicals went into international trade. At the end of the interwar period this share had declined to about one-sixth, and since the second World War it has been less than one-tenth. At the same time old products have yielded to new products. The history of dyestuffs, a field in which before the first World War Germany almost had a monopoly, affords a good example. Exports were large, but declined as after the war other countries built up their own dyestuff industries.

Special natural advantages or a far-reaching specialization have, of course, in many cases served to maintain international trade in some "old" products. But advantages in technical skill have tended to be evened out, and an industrial country that wants to maintain large exports has gradually become more dependent on its ability to develop new processes and new products which may temporarily give a competitive advantage. A large and stable home-market provides a favorable background for such pioneering activities.

IV

Advantages of a Large Home-market

Small countries may have special advantages in the possibilities of a close internal, political, social, and cultural integration. But in a world where the international market is restricted, unstable, and quickly changes towards new products, their possibilities of exploiting the most modern techniques are becoming more and more precarious.

Technical processes in the last fifty years have tended to increase the optimum scale of output for each single product. Ford's innovation in standardized mass-production was made forty years ago and has spread to other industries. The continuous strip mill from the middle twenties provides another example of how the output of one single unit may far exceed the consumption in a small country. Modern chemical industry, with its heavy investment in research and plant and its multitude of by-products, shows the same advantages of scale. Modern industry is thus in many fields outgrowing the market of small countries.

The rapid succession of new products in the international market gives the large country a great advantage. When a product is becoming "old" and its production is spreading to other countries, it is an advantage to be able to fall back on a large, often protected, home-market; for a firm in a small country it is more uncertain whether the initial investments can be completely covered before international competition cuts out profits. For a firm in a large country the home-market may provide a basis for dumping; hence its position is stronger when it comes to bargaining within an international cartel.

These differences in the position of countries with large and small home-markets have resulted and will probably continue to result in a specialization in different types of industries. Countries with a large home-market specialize in industries where economies of scale are of special importance, and especially those where a rapid product innovation takes place. There are always a number of other industries where the product will remain more tailor-made, such as heavy electrical equipment and shipbuilding.

The latter type of production is, however, on the whole relatively labor-intensive. It is thus best suited for countries with a relatively low wage-level. Small countries such as Sweden, where wages are high, easily find themselves in a dilemma. On the one hand, their cost structure favors a highly mechanized and therefore large-scale production; on the other hand, such a production will outsize their home-market, and they will find it difficult to compete with larger countries in the international market.

V

SMALL AND LARGE COUNTRIES IN WORLD TRADE

In this world, where production for the home-market is declining in importance and the economies of size are growing, it is not surprising to find that in relation to world trade the large industrial countries—such as the United States, the United Kingdom, Germany, and France—hold a very different position from that of smaller countries. One of the most striking features of world trade is the almost complete isolation of these large countries from each other. Their exports of industrial products are mainly directed towards smaller industrial countries or less developed parts of the world. The trade in motor-cars provides a good example of this tendency. In Paris you almost only see French cars, in London British cars, in Bonn German cars, and in New York American cars. The Soviet Union completes, in an excellent way, this picture of a world economy where a few countries, which together dominate world industrial output, only provide markets for each other's products to a very small extent. It is to the economic relations between these large countries that the word *disintegration* can most properly be applied.

The smaller industrial countries, on the other hand, are not only highly dependent on the supply of industrial goods from the larger countries but also maintain a comparatively intensive trade among themselves.

A few figures from inter-European trade may serve to illustrate this tendency: five smaller countries, Italy, Belgium, the Netherlands, Sweden, and Switzerland, represent together a market which—measured by their incomes—is less than one third of the joint market of the United Kingdom, France, and Germany. *Ceteris paribus,* one would therefore expect the trade between the three big countries to be more than twice as large as their exports to the group of smaller countries. The relative order of magnitude of these two currents of international trade is, however, just the opposite. If we call the exports of the big countries to each other A and to the five small countries B—B is twice as big as A for textiles, 2½ times as big for chemicals, 3 times as big for machinery, and 6 times as big for motor-cars and other transport equipment.

From this situation we can draw the following conclusions: A liberalization of world trade in order to create a larger open market first of all means that the larger countries must open their frontiers to imports from each other and from smaller countries. If this dominating part of the world market remains closed, there is a strong case for the smaller countries to join the market of a large country or for groups of smaller countries to integrate into larger units.

VI

PRIORITIES IN ECONOMIC INTEGRATION

There is one lesson that has been brought home in the years since the last war, and that is that no progress towards a free stable market can be made without a more permanent solution of the problems of international payments.

It is only since the last war that we have begun to see more clearly that trade restrictions are largely explained by balance of payment difficulties. In the twenties and the thirties it was usual to speak of the nationalistic and pro-tectionist attitude as a kind of disease which had affected a large number of countries. This view did not, however, always go to the root of the prob-lem. The impact of some important factors on the international payment situa-tion of various countries was not taken fully into account. First of all, there was a large number of less developed countries which had started to develop their industry and which needed large imports of capital for this purpose. But such capital was not always available and as a substitute they had to introduce import restrictions. These countries were mainly the agricultural and raw-material countries which had suffered a heavy setback in their terms of trade against industrial countries. Most countries in Eastern Europe, for example, were in this position. Secondly, the dollar was becoming a scarce currency, even though this did not become so evident as after the second World War. We have now learnt how the existence of one important scarce currency may lead to import restrictions not only in respect of imports from the scarce-currency country, but—if currencies are convertible—also between other coun-tries in order to acquire more of the scarce currency. Thirdly, the great world depression in the thirties led to a heavy decline in demand in the international market and forced many countries to restrict their imports. These factors, no doubt, provide the main explanation for the protectionist tendencies that pre-vailed before the war.

The same factors are still active in the international markets: the need for development of less developed countries, the restrictions in international capi-tal movements, the special market risks for countries dependent on a few export products, the insufficient supply of dollars, and the risk of at least a recession if not a depression in world trade. Further, currency reserves are in most countries smaller than before the war. In my view, it is therefore quite clear that any considerable progress towards a free and stable international market cannot be made if countries do not start to cooperate more closely in the field of international payments.

In the eight years that have passed since the war, a number of experiments have been made aiming at European integration. Some of them have failed completely, others have been a moderate success, while others have been more successful. In the first group must be counted the European customs union and some of the proposals for regional customs unions, for example, between the three Scandinavian countries. It is my conviction that in this last case, which I know best, one of the main reasons for failure was that the proposal was not combined with a joint solution of the payment problems of the three Scandinavian countries. So long as one country within such a group has greater difficulties than the others in balancing international payments, there is little chance of opening the frontiers within the group by other means, such as tariff reductions. The same would be true within a wider group, such as the fifteen countries of Western Europe; but the Scandinavian case may be used to demonstrate the nature of the problems.

Of the three Scandinavian countries Norway is, on the whole, less developed than the others and wants to build up its own industry. Large investments are needed for reconstruction and for a fuller exploitation of waterfalls and other natural resources. It can, therefore, be expected that Norway will need to import capital in order to balance its payments with the same ease as Sweden and Denmark do. Within an integrated Scandinavian economy this difference could be evened out by free capital movements. In order to arrive at a free Scandinavian market some corresponding arrangements would have to be made in the payment relations between the three countries. This could be done by establishing a system for joint settlement of international payments which would have to be combined with arrangements for short- and long-term credits between the three countries. Tariffs in Scandinavia are on the whole very low and even without a complete customs union trade could flow relatively freely; a reduction of tariffs could, with advantage, be effected according to a long-term plan.

The problem of freeing trade within such a group is complicated by the scarcity of dollars. Some countries in the Scandinavian group earn more dollars directly and could probably more easily make their currencies convertible into dollars. As was the case before the war, a solution of this problem on a national basis might break up the free trade within the joint market. The competition for scarce currencies might start over again and might be fought with the help of trade restrictions. All such difficulties would disappear if the approach to the problem of convertibility could be made jointly. But such a solution would evidently presuppose a coordination of dollar imports during a transitional period, a sharing of dollar assets in a way similar to that within the sterling area.

What I have said about the Scandinavian case is intended to demonstrate some conclusions that must be drawn if we regard international payments as the central problem of economic integration. For my part, I think that similar principles must be applied to the wider European area if lasting progress is to be made towards a free and a stable market.

VII

INTEGRATION AND INTERNATIONAL SOLIDARITY

The conclusions at which I have arrived here will probably shock many who have been playing around with more innocent ideas about economic integration through such devices as custom unions. It is quite clear that a joint settlement of international payments in combination with long-term capital movements will require a great amount of political solidarity between the countries concerned. In my view, the realization of the fundamental importance of the payments problems lays bare the *sine qua non* without which all work on economic integration is rather futile: If countries are not prepared to coordinate their whole economic policy, all integration will stop half-way. I think it is better that this basic condition for economic integration should be seen clearly right from the beginning. Useless work and failure of schemes may be very harmful to international understanding. A realization of the full implications of integration puts the sincerity of the partners to test as regards their own willingness to pay what it costs; charity should begin at home.

We have hardly realized the degree of solidarity that has been developed in the last few decades within the modern welfare state. Through fiscal, monetary, and social policy, through the national policy of foreign trade and payments, various groups within a national system have become tied to each other by strong economic links. The economic situation of one group within a country will be influenced by the management of other parts of the economy over which it has very little control. If agriculture is managed ineffectively, industry has to pay. If exports of one type of commodity decline in quantity or in price, the whole nation will suffer. And this situation is accepted in the name of national solidarity.

But the solidarity of the modern welfare state is not extended outside the frontiers of the home country. The American taxpayers' aid to Europe since the last war is a remarkable exception to this rule. But economic integration means, as I see it, nothing less than that people in different countries are prepared to pay for each other's mistakes or bad luck, just as they must be prepared to share with others the results of their own hard work or undeserved success. A joint settlement of international payments would mean as close a tie as this between the participating countries. To revert to the Scandinavian case, Swedes and Norwegians would have to pay for a less favorable trend in Danish farm exports and the other two partners would have to pay for an expansion of Norwegian investment.

This leads to the conclusion that a free and stable market between a group of countries can only be established if the participating countries are prepared to develop a system of joint consultation, or even joint decision in common political institutions, on various aspects of economic policy. What types of institutions will have to be developed will evidently depend on the disparity or similarity of countries within the group. Within a European framework the political integration will probably have to go very far in order to arrive at a stable arrangement. Within the more homogenous Scandinavian group, one could probably get a long way on the basis of consultations, unwritten gentlemen's agreements, or negotiations. The essential role of foreign payments would probably make it necessary to establish a joint central bank for currency transactions which could represent the common area in wider international payments schemes. The equalization of social and fiscal policy would, on the other hand, probably not have to go further than between the various parts of the United States.

VIII

NATIONALISTIC IMPERFECTIONS OF AN INTEGRATED MARKET

One of the most important experiments in economic integration that has been made in recent years is the European Coal and Steel Community. It is remarkable because it has faced the fact that the creation of a joint free and stable market must be accompanied by the creation of joint political institutions. On the other hand, it has by-passed the payments problem. But this has only been possible because coal and steel represent such a small sector of the total international trade of the participating countries. The conflict between the free movement of goods and the general balance of payments of the respective countries will, therefore, probably not become serious. But this certainly does not mean that integration by sectors of industry can be extended indefinitely without raising the payments problem. Sooner or later these problems will come to the fore and raise the usual problems of coordination of economic policy.

This case of group integration is, however, of special interest from another point of view. As this is the first serious experiment in a more complete integration, it gives us a first opportunity to study some of the many obstacles that arise on the road towards a more perfectly integrated market. If I mention a few of these difficulties it is not because this experiment should be looked upon as a failure. They only demonstrate very clearly that old national systems cannot be dissolved over night, that it is not enough to remove the more apparent restrictions to trade, and that the development of a more completely integrated market can only be brought about by a process that probably will take a considerable time.

In the first Schuman plan, the supranational character of the High Authority of the Community was very clearly defined. During the subsequent negotiations on the Charter of the new organization this structure was weakened, while the influence of the national governments was strengthened. I also think it is fair to say that later experience has demonstrated how unrealistic it would be to expect the divergent national interests not to appear in the work of such an organization. It can only be expected to develop slowly from a center for bargaining between national interests to a truly supranational structure. It can be added that a development in this direction will require very qualified leadership in the new international institutions.

The case of the Coal and Steel Community also shows that the creation of an integrated market is dependent on the good will not only of national governments but also of private industry in the participating countries. If private industry remains passive or obstructs the work of creating an integrated market, progress in this direction will of necessity be slowed down. It is especially difficult to create the competitive spirit which is the main condition for a more perfect integration without the active support of private industry. In the European steel industry, cartels have always been strong and old attitudes towards restrictions can only be expected to disappear slowly, especially if they are identified with national interests. But a removal of the barriers to trade evidently becomes quite useless if they are replaced by restrictive practices of private industry. The case of the European steel market thus exemplifies in a very striking way the dependence of integration on attitudes in industry and the importance of reconditioning attitudes through the education of industrial leaders.

IX

Main Conclusions

My discussion of the problems of economic integration can be summarized in the following points:

There is no contradiction between the work of creating a free world market and the endeavors to bring groups of countries closer together.

The five largest industrial countries in the world have almost completely isolated their industrial systems from each other. In this respect, the division of the world into a number of isolated economic blocs is almost a reality. Work on a unified world market is useless if these large countries are not prepared to open their frontiers to imports of manufactured products.

If the five large countries do not change their attitude, small countries will be forced into group integration in order to be able to take advantage of modern industrial techniques and raise their standards of living to a high level.

A free and stable international market cannot be created unless the problems of international payments are solved, whether on a world basis or on a group basis.

The most effective way to introduce an open and stable market within a group of countries is by joint settlement of international payments and the free movement of capital within the group.

This cannot be done, however, without extending the solidarity of the modern welfare state to other countries which participate in a group formation. This solidarity must find expression in joint institutions for consultation or even joint decisions about economic policy.

Even if other trade restrictions are removed, nationalistic market imperfections will probably for a long time remain important obstacles to a free flow of goods across the frontiers. These obstacles can only be overcome by education of industry to a new and less nationalistic attitude and by skilled and patient administration of international institutions.

24

Inaugurating the Coal and Steel Community

By Tom Charlton Clark

On August 10, 1953, without fanfare and under the same pressure that characterized its activities throughout the year, the Schuman Plan celebrated its first anniversary. Western Europe's only real movement toward economic and political integration through the pooling of its coal, iron, and steel industries was well under way.

It was, indeed, a tremendous year, marked by unforeseen problems, national tensions, economic adjustments, and the host of hard tasks confronting any new organization. By all fair standards it had been a success. It is the purpose of this chapter to examine some of the important steps taken, appraise solutions, and estimate future trends not only for the Plan itself but the possibility of its extension to other industrial sectors.

By no means can it be said that the High Authority, which is the name given the Plan's administrative organization, was not forewarned about its problems and difficulties. Opponents and critics had been loud, long, and detailed as to why the Plan would not work and the specific, unsurmountable obstacles on which its collapse was inevitable. Among these were: lack of currency convertibility which would restrict sales to national boundaries, thus defeating establishment of the common market; uniform prices stabilized at a high level under cartel practices so deeply rooted they could not be eradicated; development and expansion stifled by a bureaucratic regimentation of impractical economists and political dreamers; nationalization or socialization of the industries would shortly follow their inevitable bankruptcy in the hands of incompetent officials of the new supranational organization; an overwhelming political emphasis would aggravate national tensions and the industries would flounder in a morass of confusion, thus ruining all hope for a united Europe.

These dire predictions were voiced not only in Europe but also by some Americans who attempted appraisals against the background of their industrial experience at home and who were not equipped by training or knowledge to reckon with the resourcefulness of the Schuman Plan leaders and Europe's real sense of desperation should this Plan fail. During the treaty's ratification by the parliaments, they were voiced by every conservative right-wing block which found itself strangely and for once in complete agreement with their left-wing Communist colleagues. At this juncture it is, indeed, too early to assert that all of the fears expressed were fictitious and without merit. They still stand as possibilities; but as eventualities they become more remote as time goes on for, based upon the foundations laid, attitudes adopted, and procedures employed, the ultimate success of the Schuman Plan seems fairly well assured. At least not one of the bogies raised has become a reality. This accomplishment has been brought about not only by the guiding genius of Jean Monnet but also by the tolerance and cooperative efforts of the entire staff assembled from the six member countries.

I

The first meeting of the Plan's Council of Ministers took place in Paris on July 24, 1952, being notable not only for the range and importance of the questions resolved but also for length—an unbroken session of seventeen hours.

The selection of the site proved the most controversial issue, each nation clamoring to play host with its own pet location. At one point during a 2:00 A.M. recess on the 25th, newspaper reporters picked up the information that Turin had been selected—as indeed it had been at that time—and the Paris morning papers carried that announcement. However, the matter was reconsidered and Luxembourg selected as the temporary site through a strategic move of the wily old Bech, then Foreign Minister of Luxembourg. Following hours of fruitless wrangling, it was finally decided that no one of the six claimed sites would be chosen and that anyone claiming a site for his own country barred himself from the consideration. Bech thereupon promptly withdrew the claim of his country and this move permitted Luxembourg to be named, which it was unanimously and, it now seems, quite logically.

The ministers also picked the members of the High Authority, some of the members of the Court, fixed Strasbourg as the meeting place for the Assembly, and set August 10 as the effective date for the formal operation of the treaty. As the treaty's provisions spelled out in considerable detail the chronological series of events which were to follow the effective date at certain specified intervals, this date has more than an anniversary significance. For example, the first meeting of the Assembly was to be held thirty days thereafter with a second in four months; the common market on iron ore, coal, and scrap was to open in six months, and on steel two months later. Thus the timetable was set and with the exception of the common market for steel, which was delayed about twenty days—from April 10 to May 1—it was religiously kept. As the early months passed, there were many arguments and some good reasons for postponement of these dates but it was also recognized, with a realism unusual for Europe, that the same arguments would be just as valid at a later date for a further postponement. Thus the schedule was adhered to.

The first few months were turbulent. There was no staff, no housing, no buildings in which to go to work, no telephones, no stationery—nothing except the will of nine members of the High Authority to make a go of it. At the outset, these men became embroiled in a dispute with the Council of Europe at Strasbourg which added little to the stature of either organization but did establish that the High Authority was a vitally new supranational body with certain sovereign powers which it intended to guard jealously and exercise effectively.

Under the stimulus of Paul-Henri Spaak, former Belgian Prime Minister, who had been elected its president, the Assembly, as its first move, set up an Ad Hoc Committee to prepare a constitution for a political union of Western European states—a work completed in draft form in March 1953 and submitted for the consideration of the foreign ministers of the six countries.

As these political skirmishes were quite removed from the economic and industrial realities of coal and steel and as they seemed to overshadow in importance and attention the hard spade work necessary for the opening of the common markets, there were many early doubts about getting the working parts of the treaty under way. However, the idea of national sovereignty dies hard and in one sense the Schuman Plan symbolizes that death. At the same time it symbolizes the birth of a new sovereignty concept—that of a united Europe. With two exceptions, the members of the High Authority were either politicians or economists. Only Monnet and Daum, the French representatives, had had practical industrial or commercial experience. It was, therefore, too much to expect that the High Authority members would immediately concentrate on the unfamiliar problems of strange industries which seemed, in any event, to be producing at capacity and which were in no case sick or needing particular attention. In addition, as the European approach to the problem of unification has been traditionally political, it was only natural that the High Authority should at the outset try that approach. Nevertheless, much real organization work was accomplished during those early months and a competent staff, familiar with the practical problems of the industries, was selected. The membership of the Court was completed and the various committees and commissions called for by the treaty were established. This selection of staff was accomplished without regard for national allegiance, political influence, or industry affiliation. The influence of no one of the six countries outweighs that of any other in any of the staff functions.

The staff of the High Authority has been organized without division between coal and steel, each department or division—in the High Authority's terminology—handling products in both sectors. The work is channeled through eleven such services: Economic, Production, Investment, Marketing, Transportation, Labor, Statistical, Juridical, Financial, Investigative, and OEEC liaison. The directors of these services take their orders from and are responsible to Jean Monnet, the president.

To maintain contact with the realities of the industrial order, advisory committees—or "commissions" as the High Authority calls them—have been set up, composed of experts from industry, labor, and government. There are commissions on Investment and Productivity, Development of Markets, Supplies and Requirements, Workers' Housing, Transportation, and also a commission to deal with the levy on coal and steel production from which the Community receives the income for its operations. The members of these commissions are mostly hardheaded realists lending their services on a part-time basis, and their views impart a down-to-earth check on the soaring tendencies of the political enthusiasts.

Against the charge of a huge bureaucracy, the High Authority can point to a total permanent staff of about five hundred of whom more than half are in auxiliary work, such as interpreters and translators, publications, and documents reproducing work. The other half are in the technical divisions, services, Court of Justice, or occupied with the reports and statistical work for the commissions. The large translating and interpreting staff is made necessary by the language problem—there being four official languages: French, German, Italian, and Dutch. All papers and documents must be precisely and accurately translated. Meetings of the High Authority are usually conducted in French and German but a considerable amount of English finds its way into the discussion. It has been reported that at an initial meeting of the Council of Ministers for the settlement of the language matter, the discussion was actually carried on in English, which, among that group, had supplanted French as the most widely used foreign language.

The expenses of the Community are covered by a levy on the coal and steel production within the Community. The treaty specifies that it may not exceed one per cent of the average value of the products. Under a formula, the levy is applied to different classes of products so that the effect of a cumulative tax is minimized. Collections commenced on shipments made after January 1, 1953, and the rate of levy—.3 per cent at the beginning—was gradually increased to .9 per cent effective July 1. At this rate and assuming a production and prices in the fiscal year 1953–54 the same as in the previous year, the levy should yield an income estimated at the equivalent of forty-seven million dollars.

The total budget for the four institutions of the Community—i.e., High Authority, Common Assembly, Council of Ministers, and Court of Justice— for the same period amounts to about ten million dollars, leaving a surplus, with accumulations from the first 6 months' collections, of about forty million dollars. It is this sum, which can go on accumulating at this rate in future years unless the levy is lowered, that worries certain parts of the industry and, at the same time, encourages the High Authority. What is this fund to be used for?

II

Problem of Investment and Finance

No other problem facing the High Authority is more important than finding investment capital for its industries and for workers' housing. European credits are generally available only at prohibitive rates of interest—from 9 to 12 per cent—and only on a short term basis—from three to six months. The few capital markets in Europe that have survived the two wars in this century, such as the Swiss, can only furnish a small part of these credits which the High Authority had estimated to be in the nature of five hundred million dollars per year for the next several years. Indeed, this is the minimum if more and cheaper coal is to be dug—thus removing Europe's dependence on U.S. imports—and if steel mills dating from around the turn of the century are to be modernized and turned into low cost efficient units. Fortunately, no dollars are required as practically all of the machinery and equipment can be furnished from European sources, thanks to the American foreign aid program and Europe's industrial recovery.

It was with this problem in mind that the levy was set at practically the maximum limit. The treaty is quite specific as to the purposes for which the funds realized by the levy may and may not be used. They may not be used to make loans to the industries but they may be used to guarantee loans obtained by individual concerns. It was, therefore, the stated purpose of the High Authority to build up a fund to be used for guaranteeing loans and establishing confidence in the credit of the Community. As the High Authority explained in its report on January 10, 1953:

> Investors in the countries of the Community hesitate to invest in operations offering no protection against the uncertainties in the national economies. Within the framework of the financial structure of the Community, new methods will be established in an attempt to overcome this hesitation by making investments productive and by accompanying them with irrevocable guarantees.
>
> These were the reasons why the High Authority fixed the rate of the levy so that it will amount to 0.9 per cent by July 1, 1953. It is essential that the Community prove its financial capacity. Until such time as the levy is in effective operation, doubts may persist in the mind of future lenders.

Offsetting the charge that the High Authority planned to move toward the socialization or "internationalization" of the industries, the report further stated:

> This assistance from the High Authority is only supplementary and, in accordance with the Treaty, will in no case take the form of an acquisition of ownership or participation rights by the High Authority. The High Authority will not become a kind of holding company for the coal or steel enterprises of the Community.

Obviously, the High Authority is looking to the U. S. capital market and the IRBD. Its ability to obtain money from such sources would seem to hinge on factors over which it has no control and which, in fact, remain within the powers of the member governments. The size of a guarantee fund is of little interest to a United States investor if he is required to accept interest and principal in unstable or depreciated currencies not convertible into the dollars he invested;

the guarantee fund itself is in those currencies. The IRBD has explained it can only make loans to its members, and as the Community is not a member the Bank is precluded from making a direct loan to it. However, the Bank could make loans to the governments, earmarked for the coal and steel industries in those countries; and such loans could be guaranteed by the High Authority in favor of the Bank as well as the governments, thus, perhaps, permitting the High Authority to obtain money on more favorable terms than otherwise available. This procedure might involve another section of the treaty (Article 54) under which the High Authority could issue an opinion that such financing might involve "subsidies, assistance, protection or discrimination contrary to the present Treaty," thus permitting the High Authority to block a project. Only when a concern uses its "own funds" is its program of expansion or rehabilitation freed from High Authority control.

The thinly disguised purpose of Mr. Monnet's trip to the United States in May 1953 became apparent with the publication of President Eisenhower's exchange of letters with the heads of the committees on foreign affairs in the Senate and House. Widely interpreted at the time as offering U. S. money to the High Authority, on closer inspection they came down to a hope. The President's letter said:

> It appears to me that a portion of the financing of this development program by the United States Government or one of its agencies, out of moneys available for such purposes and under conditions insuring proper use and ultimate repayment, would foster European integration in a tangible and useful way.

To this, the House Committee report stated:

> Subject to proper qualification, it is the hope of the Committee that the Community may be able to obtain a portion of such loans from United States sources.

It seemed likely that the amount of money obtained from official government sources on a loan basis would be more in the nature of a token, prestige item than a substantial share of the large sums required. The European coal and steel industries have made good profits since the war and are themselves in sound financial condition. If the governments would take the necessary measures to remove some of the currency restrictions, there is no valid reason why those industries cannot secure the necessary loans on their own account. This is not in depreciation of the High Authority's guarantee, which is, indeed, a significant item.

III

OPENING THE COMMON MARKETS

In broad terms, the common market means the substitution of one area comprising the territories of the six member states for the six separate territories which existed before. The fixing of this common market had a number of negative as well as positive aspects; certain old practices had to be abandoned and certain new ones established. Among the practices abandoned were:

1. All customs duties and quantitative restrictions on the free movement of CSC products.
2. Elimination of discriminatory transportation rates.
3. Elimination of dual pricing under which different prices applied to domestic and export sales.
4. Removal of all government control of prices, production, distribution, and export.
5. Elimination of all combines, agreements, and understandings in restraint of trade, in principle and in substantial degree.
6. Elimination of government subsidies and special grants to the industries involved, likewise in principle and degree.

On the positive side the new practices included:

1. Tariff regulations embracing the Community's external boundaries.
2. Prices and terms of sale applicable throughout the entire community and regulations for their filing and publication.
3. Measures for the licensing of currency to buyers, thus establishing convertibility so far as sales, purchases, and transport of the Community's products are concerned.
4. Rules against nondiscrimination because of nationality or class of buyer.
5. Opening the market to free competition.
6. Equalization of transportation rates and charges.

The accomplishment of these tasks within a period of about four months, and they were all accomplished, was a feat of no mean proportion. Superimposed on the staff work involved were almost daily negotiations with nonmember countries, press conferences and interviews, meetings with industry, consumer, and labor groups, over all of which hung the disruptive threat of the tax problem referred to below. Without the cooperative efforts of all three groups and a common will to make the Plan succeed, the work could never have been accomplished.

The common market on iron ore was the easiest, France being the only substantial exporter of that product to other countries of the Community. Europe's high grade ores come from Scandinavian countries and French North African possessions, which are excluded from the treaty, and Europe relies on imports to achieve a high rate of production. Consequently there is little competition within the Community on the sale or production of iron ore. Two things, however, the iron ore common market should do: intensify French production which, under restrictive governmental controls, still lags behind her 1929 output, and permit a freer exchange of Ruhr coal for that ore. Freight cars bringing duty-free German coal to Lorraine now can take back duty-free Lorraine ore—all at non-discriminatory freight rates.

Coal presented a more difficult problem. Although the resources of the Community are adequate to take care of its requirements, the coal stays underground. For a variety of reasons production lags in all Western European countries, including England, and 1952 production was still below that of 1929. Under normal conditions this deficit could be made up by eastern countries, but since that trade is blocked or restricted it has been made up by the United States. The High Authority thus found itself with adequate resources but a deficit supply. It proceeded to act as if there were no European shortage, a sustainable position so long as the United States put up the difference. The alternative open to the High Authority was to declare a shortage and invoke Article 59 under which it would have had to fix prices and allocate availabilities among different classes of consumers and for export. This would have involved a rationing and priority system the High Authority was in no position to evolve or enforce, particularly within the time allowed. Consequently, it merely set maximum prices for the different producing basins and put in operation the per-equation or subsidy scheme under which high cost mines, particularly Belgium, are to be closed down or modernized over the next five or six years.

It is too early to say that the substantial betterment of Europe's coal position during the Plan's inaugural period was due to the opening of the common market. Nevertheless, production had increased, U. S. imports had dropped, prices were stable, and consumers were satisfied—facts to which the High Authority could proudly point and also assume some credit.

Iron and steel scrap will forever be a worldwide problem and Europe does not escape its implications. As the Community exports about 25 per cent of its steel production and as the scrap charge can run from 25 to 90 per cent of the steel produced, depending on the prices of scrap and finished steel, Europe has to import scrap, such requirement for 1953 being estimated at about a million tons. Peculiar to the scrap market is the fact that no one produces it. It is assembled, collected, gathered, and prepared, but it is not produced. Consequently, the sole incentive in the scrap business is the lure of profit. The trade is worldwide and large fortunes are won and lost in very short periods of time, depending on demand to which the price very sensitively reacts.

Each Schuman Plan country prior to the common market had internal controls on the price of scrap, which ranged from about $18. per ton in Holland to about $50. per ton in Italy. These were the maximum prices the scrap merchants were permitted to charge for sales within the country. In addition, all exports were subject to license. On top of this came the world market price for scrap which at the time of the opening of the scrap common market amounted to $60. to $65. per ton, a high price sustained by the practices of one country bidding against another in a tight world market.

Representatives of the steel industry worked out the formula for scrap in the actual construction of which only two real problems emerged. The first— a free or a controlled market—was settled by the High Authority by fixing a maximum price of $36. per ton including a merchants' allowance of $1.50. This action pacified French fears of Italian raids on their supply once export licenses were removed. The second problem related to the organization of a central scrap buying agency which would negotiate the price consumers would pay for scrap imported from outside the Community, thus eliminating the merchants' practice of playing one country off against another.

After the High Authority had reviewed several nonacceptable suggestions, a plan was finally evolved similar in operation to the system which had prevailed in Germany. Under this plan there are three groups: consumers, merchants, and a combined group of both. A High Authority representative sits in the meetings of these groups and their decisions are subject to High Authority review and sanction. The consumer group, which is the most important, negotiates the price with the merchants. It does not negotiate any contracts, 'terms, quantities, or deliveries—merely the price. It then makes this price known to the consumers who are free to buy from any merchant they choose and free to pay any price they want. If they pay less, it is to their advantage. If they pay more, it is for their account and a special equalizing subsidy only applies up to the maximum price. The subsidy fund is created by a voluntary contribution from scrap consumers at a fixed rate per ton set by the central price negotiating group and is based on the quantity of imported and internally purchased scrap consumed by the producer in a past period. This fund is then used by the group to equalize for an importer the difference between the maximum price of $36. per ton and the price of the imported scrap. Only consumers who make contributions to the fund are entitled to participate in the subsidy. The rate of contribution is currently set at $2. per ton and will vary, dependent on the price negotiated.

This ingenious scheme has much to recommend it. Cartel buying and monopoly control of supply are avoided. The burden of equalizing the cost between domestic and imported scrap is rationally spread over all scrap consumers who remain free to purchase from any source and have the option of contributing or not as they choose. The whole operation is subject to High Authority scrutiny and (at least as seen at the end of 1953) the plan is in successful operation.

The common market for steel posed the most complicated problems. Steel is produced in a variety of forms and shapes for which there was no standard nomenclature in the six countries. There were wide variations in the domestic prices, and the methods of computing prices, as well as the terms and conditions of sale, were completely dissimilar. In Belgium a zone price applied throughout the country while Germany used a single basing point, except for certain areas where zone prices applied. France had a combination of pricing and Italian products were sold f.o.b. mill. A greater hodge-podge could scarcely be imagined.

The overall problem had many points of similarity with that confronting the U. S. Steel Industry in working out its Code of Fair Competition under the

N.I.R.A. In effect, the Schuman treaty sets out a multiple basing point system with sales at delivered prices calculated from the basing point nearest in terms of transportation charges to the place of delivery. Each company files its prices and terms and conditions of sale with the High Authority and disseminates them widely in printed form to the trade. The High Authority also issues its own publication of them, thus assuring wide publicity, an innovation for Europe where prices not set by government fiat have customarily been fixed by cartels or combines. Under the treaty, governments may no longer interfere with prices; and cartels, combines, and all agreements in restraint of trade are prohibited.

The High Authority met the problems of opening the steel common market primarily by putting them up to the steel industry. Committees of industrialists were formed, each to handle a specific subject, and representatives of the High Authority staff, familiar with industry conditions, sat in their meetings. These committees covered such subjects as nomenclature, extras (supplemental charges for special forms, treatment, analyses, packaging, et cetera), transport rates, basing points, sales through merchants and agents, et cetera. Although not all of their work was finished by May 1, 1953, the official opening date, enough was completed to permit the filing by each company of its own prices for its own basing points, together with extras and terms of sale. The High Authority declined to fix any prices, either maximum or minimum, and also refused to set any limitation on the amount of freight a producer could absorb, thus leaving the market completely open.

As might be expected, the first prices and extras came out with a certain uniformity. For basing points within each country, they were in fact the same but, as among the various states, there were slight but significant differences. The German prices came down about 5 per cent; those in France and the Benelux countries went up from 2 to 3.5 per cent, with no change in Italy. Actually the net overall effect amounted to a reduction as dual prices were eliminated and the German reduction, which applies to about 40 per cent of the Community's finished products, more than offset the other increases. A comparison of the lowest first filed prices for a few principal products reveals the following:

	Basing Point Base Prices Exclusive of Taxes (Dollars per Metric Ton Thomas Steel)		
	Bars	Sections	Wire Rods
Germany	90.25	87.95	92.85
France	90.30	88.85	91.55
Belgium	91.50	91.50	91.70
Luxembourg	90.50	90.50	87.00
Netherlands	91.75	87.00	85.90
Saar	92.60	91.15	93.35
Italy	121.60	121.60	116.80

Comparisons with U.S. prices are difficult because the U.S. has no distinction between prices for Thomas and open hearth quality steels. Generally speaking, the European prices for Thomas steel are comparable with the U. S. prices for open hearth, but European prices for open hearth are from $10. to $15. per ton higher than their steel of Thomas quality.

After many confusing details have been clarified, it will be found that the Schuman Plan pricing method does not radically differ from the method used by the U. S. industry from August 1933 to May 1935 under the Steel Code. Sales are at delivered prices calculated from basing points; basing point base prices will be filed and published; reductions in delivered prices will be allowed in case actual shipment from mill to destination is made by water, rail-water, or truck; and deductions and discounts will be standardized for different classes of jobbers, agents, and dealers. Even in the matter of cut prices and price reductions the two systems appear comparable.

The U. S. Steel Code, like the codes generally, was designed to eliminate unfair competition by prohibiting sales at lower than filed and published prices. Changes in price were only permitted by public filing after a ten-day waiting period, which, of course, under a "price leadership" principle, gave every other producer the opportunity of filing the same higher or lower price within due time. No producer could cut or reduce a price without extending the same cut to all purchasers. Under the Schuman Plan, the same filing requirement prevails but the time limit is five days. Two other provisions, however, could make prices under the Schuman Plan more solid, and the price structure more rigid, than any combine or cartel agreement of the past.

The first relates to the High Authority's power to fix a maximum limit on the amount of freight a producer can absorb in making a sale on a basing point other than his own at a destination far removed from his mill. Thus a French producer in the Lorraine area, selling on a Milan base to a destination in Northern Italy, with a small amount of freight in the delivered price, might have to absorb from $12. to $14. freight (the difference between freight included in price and actual freight paid on the shipment) to effect delivery. If the High Authority were to fix the maximum limit at $8. per ton, it would eliminate the French producer from the market. Abuse of this power would permit the High Authority to control a great many market areas to the advantage of certain producers and the exclusion of others. However, as mentioned, the High Authority has not for the present invoked this power.

The second restraint on price mobility relates to a provision which requires producers to stick rigidly to their filed prices for all "comparable" transactions. In other words, assuming the same product and approximately the same quantity, the price must be the same to all purchasers, under penalty of a fine by the High Authority or a suit for damages by a disgruntled purchaser. The only way for a producer to cut his price is to file a new one, but then all purchasers are immediately entitled to the reduction.

What constitutes a "comparable" transaction remains to be defined and a looked for price flexibility could be introduced by a sensible interpretation. For example, the High Authority could say that sales of the same product to noncompeting purchasers does not constitute comparable transactions, thus permitting a different price on sheets to automobile companies and railroad car builders. On tinplate, one price could be made to a can manufacturer and another to a maker of bottle caps and closures. Unless some such interpretation is adopted, the prices will remain rigid despite the absence of cartels and combines. The requirement for filing and publication of all prices, including cut prices, can be liberalized by the High Authority under its absolute authority in this regard, which specifies that it shall be made "to the extent and in the form prescribed by the High Authority."

The transport charges are the darkest and most difficult area. In certain sections of Western Europe, water transportation with interlocking canals and rivers is as highly developed as truck highway movements in the United States. Many of the mills in Belgium and Holland can accommodate both barges for inland shipment and ocean freighters for export and import. Boats and barges move on the Rhine as thickly as trucks on American highways. Trucking itself is not so highly developed, except in Germany where double bottoms are common and even triple bottoms not rare. Not one of the European countries has anything corresponding to the Interstate Commerce Commission or similar commissions existing in our individual states. As a result, there has been no such thing as filed and published rates. This is to be corrected by the treaty which provides:

> The rate scales, prices, and tariff provisions of all sorts applied to the transport of coal and steel within each member State and among the member States shall be published or brought to the knowledge of the High Authority.

There are three steps in the adaptation of transport charges: (1) removal of discriminatory rates because of country of origin or destination, (2) elimination of preferred rates and rebates to certain shippers and consumers, and (3) harmonization of rates on the various products between countries. Only the first two requirements have been accomplished and it is anticipated the third will take at least the full transition period—i.e., five years. The stolid government bureaucracies which operate the railroads will want some time to bring about an equalization of rates.

In this transport area the High Authority's progress seemed tardier than in any other. Prices and extras have been filed and published for the opening of the common market but transport charges—rail, water, and truck— the third ingredient of the delivered price, have lagged behind. Also, regulations on delivered price reductions for shipment by means other than all-rail and by customer-owned or supplied conveyance have been slow in emerging. As a result, the market was thrown in confusion for some weeks after the common market opened. Purchasers continued to rely on established sources of supply. In the absence of official rate publications by the High Authority, they were bewildered to read announcements that French buyers in Bordeaux could purchase more cheaply from German producers in the Ruhr with a water shipment than they could from French mills in Lorraine, particularly when no such quotations were forthcoming. There are perhaps more than five hundred separate water and truck tariffs which have to be published, and as they come out the buyer is required to thread his way cautiously through the maze. As a result, he continues to buy from traditional sources in his own country and only the most progressive—the Belgians and Germans—have ventured into other markets as producers or looked for other suppliers as consumers.

Indeed, it is reasonable to assume, so far as steel products are concerned, that perhaps two or three years must elapse before both producers and consumers become aware of the different market potentialities now open to them. To stimulate this awareness the High Authority must take more constructive steps in explaining how a multiple basing point system operates and the possible market advantages open to processors of steel products. Not enough attention has been concentrated on how purchasers can benefit from lower prices in the new market with better delivery, quality, and service. It is doubtful whether many producers are prepared for the challenge of meeting this new market with sales staffs and a knowledge of who uses particular products, such as tinplate and special sections, and in what quantities. In the absence of such activity by individual companies, the High Authority itself might well undertake a few constructive market research studies and restrain its facile statements about serving a market of 155 million people. If those householders bought steel rails, ship plates, and piling, the allusion would have more merit. Actually, the direct purchasers of products from the coal and steel industry are relatively few compared to the United States—perhaps not one-third the number—and it is this market which has to be stimulated before comparisons can be drawn. What then will this steel industry do in this transition period? The answer is not hard to find. It will look to exports as it has in the past.

IV

THE TAX PROBLEM

The significance of the tax problem is basic for a comprehension of the most difficult situation confronting the CSC. It raises questions of sovereignty, retained and surrendered powers, subsidies and, indeed, overall survival because it cuts across the internal revenue and taxing systems of the member nations. The treaty abolishes all custom duties and quantitative restrictions on the movement of products from one state to another, and prohibits any discrimination because of nationality or geographical location. These barriers have been effectively removed but what has not been removed or, as yet, overcome is the idea that a shipment from one of these countries to another is an export shipment. Restraining the demise of this idea are the tax laws of the member states. The theory of these laws is that they represent the progressive accumulation of all such taxes on the materials purchased and used to produce the particular goods to which the tax is applied and that this progressive accumulation is always for the account of the consumer. A steel producer, to make his steel bar, has purchased iron ore, coal, coke, refractories, lubricants, *et cetera,* and the taxes paid by him on all such transactions are a determinable amount. On his domestic sales he passes this tax on to the next purchaser but on export sales his "foreign" purchaser naturally refuses to pay it. The state, therefore, remits the accumulated aggregate to the seller. With a view to encouraging export trade, the revenue laws of those states are built around a system of rebates of the sales taxes or, as they are called, "turnover taxes" applied to sales made within the state.

In France the turnover tax on sales of steel products amounts to about 14 per cent of the invoice value, while in Germany a tax of like import comes to 4 per cent. If the products are sold to a purchaser in another country these taxes are rebated to the seller. It is as if Pennsylvania had a sales tax of $14. a ton applicable to all sales within that state and Illinois one of $4. All purchasers in Pennsylvania, whether they bought from a producer within or outside of Pennsylvania, had that tax tacked on to the price they paid and likewise with all purchasers in Illinois. So far as the consumers are concerned there is no discrimination. Within a given state they all pay the same price. From the point of view of the producers, however, entirely different problems are raised.

In Europe the terms direct and indirect taxes have meanings different than in the United States. Direct taxes, i.e., those exactly levied against an individual or company are always debatable, arguable, and contestable, based, as they are, on a system of bookkeeping which involves receipts, costs, depreciation, and other maneuverable items. Indirect taxes, on the other hand, are levied on specific transactions supported by tangible documents evidencing sales, of which there are many copies. The possibility of evasion and the area for discussion and adjustment on indirect taxes are, therefore, much more restricted than is the case with direct taxes.

In this sense the respective tax systems of these two countries perhaps may be said to reflect certain characteristics of the two peoples. For revenue, the French Government relies primarily on the nondebatable and profusely documented indirect taxes, while the Germans rely on the accurate documentation of overall operations according to bank statements, costs, sales, profits, *et cetera.* Under these circumstances French indirect taxes are high and German low, and there would be no difficulty except for the newly established free movement of the goods from one state to the other. When this occurs, the French producer nets 14 per cent more on his sales in Germany than he does in France; and the German producer, for the same transaction, only 4 per cent more (assuming, of course, that all other factors, including freight, are equal). The problem is not what the consumer pays but rather what the producer realizes, and this tax inequality, say the Germans, produces a discrimination CSC was designed to eliminate. Producers as well as consumers were to be put on the same basis, leaving efficiency of operations, service, and quality as the primary competitive factors, unencumbered by unequal and discriminatory revenue tax systems. Furthermore, they argue that within the Community there is no such thing as "exports"—the terms "exports" and "common market" being mutually exclusive. In addition, they say the tax rebate is nothing more than a subsidy specifically forbidden by the treaty, which they are ready to abandon.

The following will serve to illustrate:

German Sale in France:

Delivered Price	100
German tax rebate	4
Mill Gross	104
Freight absorbed	10
German Mill Net	94

French Sale in Germany:

Delivered Price	100
French tax rebate	16
Mill Gross	116
Freight absorbed	10
French Mill Net	106

Thus the Germans argue that on every sale the French make in Germany they net considerably more than the Germans net on such sales in France,—a situation which may encourage cross-hauling but hardly promotes competition or a reduction of prices, the principal goals of the Schuman Plan.

This problem raised its ugly head shortly after the opening on February 10, 1953 of the first common markets. It assumed such proportions that it threatened to wreck the further establishment of the Community. The German press was vociferous in its demand that the inequality be removed, claiming that the elimination of tariffs had been defeated by the imposition or rebate of these taxes which produced the same net effect. The German Parliament promptly rushed through a bill permitting the Ministry to impose a sales tax of 12 per cent on CSC products imported into Germany, which, if absorbed by the French seller, would bring his mill net to the same figure realized by the German producer. While the situation had arisen over the question of coal, that product, because of its relatively low price, served only to force attention on the coming problem with steel which, being a more finished and costly commodity, bore a higher rate. On coal, iron ore, and scrap the High Authority had issued a decision that producers and sellers were not permitted to include in, or charge as a part of their prices, any taxes on which they were entitled to rebate, exemption, or waiver, a decision which did not meet the contentions of the disputants. The question now became whether the High Authority could make its decision stick. Would it have to bow to the action of one of its member states in a field in which the states unquestionably retained their sovereign power? To settle the issue, the High Authority moved with alacrity, resourcefulness, and courage.

It immediately appointed an independent committee under the chairmanship of Prof. Tinbergen, of Holland, to investigate and report on the subject. Meanwhile it postponed the opening of the steel common market from April 10 to May 1 and conducted its own negotiations to find a solution. The Tinbergen Report, although scholarly, complete, and thorough, did little to clarify what everyone knew was a complicated matter. Generally, it favored the decision already taken by the High Authority but it did point out that substantive tax problems requiring specific adjustment would have to be met and eventually settled if the free movement of goods within the common market was to be successful. After accepting the report, the High Authority issued a directive to the governments asking for remedial recommendations and suggestions by the end of this year, in the meantime continuing in effect its decision that all such taxes could not be charged to purchasers. Now the matter was up to Germany.

A sigh of relief went up from the High Authority when the German Ministry announced it would not invoke the power granted by the Parliament to impose the retaliatory compensation tax without fully exploring the matter with the High Authority and that for the time being, pending further clarification by the end of 1953, it would abide by the High Authority's decision. Thus passed a most significant crisis for the High Authority; a sovereign state had recognized the super-sovereignty of the new supranational organization and had agreed to abide by the latter's decision—a real milestone in European unification not measurable in terms of victory and defeat but rather definite progress toward a common goal. The steel common market was duly opened on May 1, with Mr. Monnet tapping a Luxembourg blast furnace at 12:01 A.M. on that day to pour the first truly European pig iron. But the tax problem remained to be settled and became the assignment of a special commission.

V

CARTELS AND COMBINATIONS

Even the word *cartel* is anathema in the Community's jargon; the High Authority's department which deals with combines, agreements, operations in restraint of trade and, finally, cartels, was first called the *Investigative Service*. But denying existence of cartels does not quite get away from them or Europe's traditional practice of operating under them. Nevertheless, despite appearances and some published reports to the contrary, it can truthfully be said that there are no cartels operating in the coal or iron and steel industries in the Community at the present time.

To support this statement it might be well briefly to examine what the European understands by a cartel and its necessary elements. Among its main characteristics are (a) a definition of the specific products covered, (b) production quotas assigned individual members, based on production capacity, past sales, or some other criteria, (c) a markets division, with some sacrosanct and others open, and (d) most important, a system of penalties for infractions of quotas, prices, or other parts of the cartel agreement. These are basic indicia for the operation of a cartel and unless they are all present in one form or another, particularly the system of penalties, the Europeans maintain, with good cause, that a cartel does not exist. By these standards no cartel is in operation in the Community's products or among its industries.

Perhaps the matter most prominently referred to is the so-called export cartel on steel products from which it is commonly deduced that the High Authority not only sanctions cartels but is itself operating a huge one. Nothing could be further from the truth or further from the motives and purposes of the High Authority. In the first place, the CSC treaty, except in certain exceptional cases, has nothing to do with exports from the Community or with export sales. Its powers over prices and combines are limited to operations within the new common market. It is true that in the Spring of 1953 a group of French and Benelux producers, alarmed at some remarkably low French export quotations, met to discuss the matter. Later the Germans were brought in. Out of this meeting came an understanding that there would be a minimum export price on three products for an indefinite period. No sanctions were attached, no quotas set up, no markets divided, and anyone could withdraw at any time. Actually, within about forty-five days the minimum had been shaded and the effectiveness of the understanding is very doubtful. Without any obligations to do so, some members of the arrangement transmitted its substance to the High Authority for information or such action as it might have competence to take. When questioned at the Assembly meeting in June, the High Authority replied it was aware of the matter and had it under advisement. It said it hoped to be in a position to give a final answer by September 30. This incident has been widely interpreted to mean the High Authority has sanctioned and supported cartels, a completely unsupportable position on the basis of the facts.

The anti-cartel road of the High Authority, its task of removing discriminations and opening up the market to the play of free competition, are among the most difficult problems confronting it. On the one hand are the innocent, classical economists who believe that grades of coal and various iron and steel products should be priced and sold like shoes, textiles, and refrigerators, with a wide range and variety of prices dependent on quality, style, and fashion. There are others who immediately smell collusion and agreement if the price of steel billet comes out the same from two or three producers even though all of the machinery and equipment in the three mills are identical, the same amount paid for ore, limestone, and coke, and the wage rates are covered by the same agreement. Without one dominant concern in an industry, the principle of "price leadership" is difficult to establish or maintain and some such principle will necessarily have to be established in the Community. Coupled with these problems is the fact that the managements of these companies have had much experience with cartels, have been raised in their tradition under governments which always have sanctioned them and still do so, and also that their vendors as well as most of their customers are members of one. The question is, therefore, the extent to which the High Authority can insulate the coal and steel industries from the cartel operations and influences which surround it and at the same time keep these industries free from cartels.

To accomplish this job the treaty gives the High Authority all the power it needs. The provisions against combines, agreements, and acts in restraint of trade have been drafted on the experience of the Sherman, Clayton, Federal Trade Commission, and Robinson-Patman Acts. They are carefully drawn, complete and adequate, with severe penalties for a breach of the statute. In addition, any injured customer has the right to damages in the Community's Court for infraction of the rules. The operation of these provisions is up to the High Authority and the Court's prosecutor. So far they have acquitted themselves very well and give every promise of stamping out every evidence of a cartel operation which appears. With a competent staff alerted to the problem, a vigilant enforcement may be expected.

VI

SCHUMANIZATION OF OTHER INDUSTRIES

It seems axiomatic that the Schuman Plan—the idea of "pooling" Europe's coal and steel industries—cannot operate for any other industries until it successfully operates for those industries. From this basis it follows that, before the idea can be used on any other federating front, whether financial or political, it must first prove its adaptability to the industrial area. Such is the logic of Europe. This is the dilemma confronting Europe's new leaders.

Under the impetus of enthusiasm and smooth speed with which the High Authority has operated, the fact that all significant parts of the treaty do not come into effect until several years hence has been overlooked. The transition period started on February 10, 1953 with the opening of the first common markets. The treaty contemplates a five-year period thereafter in which subsidies are to be gradually reduced, tariffs eliminated, and favorable conditions of competition created. All of this was not to be accomplished automatically at one swoop but gradually over a period of time. Precisely for this reason accomplishments to date must be evaluated against this reference—and the accomplishments are of no mean proportion.

However, the High Authority had hardly started its work before the "pool" idea spread to other fronts and meetings were being held on agricultural products—the "green pool." There were also some preliminary talks in the petroleum and chemical fields but no progress was made. A Dutch parliamentarian courageously but quite impractically has suggested the elimination of all customs and quota restrictions on all products. The Geneva United Nations Economic Commission sensibly suggested an undertaking on passenger cars, busses, and trucks, with a preliminary standardization of models and designs, but no one has picked up the idea. Indeed, the principle could well be extended across the basic industrial front and it is high time that the idea of national self-sufficiency be abandoned. Nations incapable of fighting alone cannot economically exist alone. In Western Europe, France is the only country that can feed herself and none of the nations except Germany can produce enough industrial goods to take care of home requirements and at the same time buy food with the income from exports. The importance of the colonial possessions of Belgium and Holland is too frequently overlooked. It is also time that U.S. foreign aid stop assisting the development of an industrial self-sufficiency for each Western European nation if at the same time one of its aims is to bring about a united Europe. With plenty of wire drawing and pipe capacity in Europe there is no reason why U.S. funds should be used to fix up obsolete wire drawing concerns in Italy or install a new pipe mill in Austria merely because those countries, on a purely national basis, have inadequate facilities to care for home requirements. Judged by the length of time it took to get the Schuman treaty into operation—one year for negotiation, another for ratification, and a third to start it—all other pooling ideas should get under way without delay.

The Schuman Plan is a nucleus, a toe hold on the industrial unification of Europe. It is definitely a move in the right direction but to be fully successful four basic conditions have to be met. This cannot be done overnight. But if it is done within or by the end of the five-year transition period, a full realization of the original aims and objectives on an industrial as well as a political front may well come about.

The first requirement is that the "pool" idea be extended to other basic industries, particularly those from which the industrial sector in the Coal and Steel Community principally buys and those to which it principally sells. This would include the refractory, ceramic, petroleum, electrical equipment, and heavy machinery industries on the one side and all principal steel fabricating and steel consuming industries on the other. The steel industry cannot for long live in isolation from its vendors and customers in an economic area of government subsidies, cartels, custom duties, and discriminatory freight rates, etc., applicable to them but not to the steel industry. A free and competitive common market for steel products can have little effect on the European automobile industry if the inter-country commerce in cars, busses, and trucks is blocked or hampered by high tariffs (those in France now amount to 50 per cent of the value) and quantitative restrictions. The same applies to shipbuilding and heavy industrial equipment.

The second necessity is the free convertibility of the currencies of the six countries or that illusory dream—a common currency. Although the governments are now making foreign currencies available to purchasers the banking complications are onerous, with the principal difficulty lying in the French franc. The currencies of the other five countries are at or near par while in those five countries the French franc is discounted from 15 per cent to 20 per cent. Naturally, a Belgian purchaser resents having to buy French francs at par to pay for French steel products when he can buy all the French francs he wants for other purposes at a very substantial discount. To establish currency convertibility is not a simple matter; but to have a free exchange of goods in a common market you must have free currencies with which to pay for them— the seller must have confidence that he can use the currency he receives to purchase for equivalent value the goods and raw materials he needs.

The third requirement is investment capital and this could be the key to unlock the entire Pandora box. Large amounts are required to increase production and modernize facilities. The capacity of steel mill finishing equipment, particularly for flat rolled products, is several million tons out of balance with crude steel availabilities. This means more open hearths, more Thomas converters, which in turn means more blast furnaces, coke ovens, and finally more coal and iron ore. Along with this credit problem for heavy equipment is that for workers' housing which alone could use several hundred million dollars over the next years. If the High Authority, through its unique position of having an assured income considerably in excess of its administrative expenses and its authority to guarantee loans from the fund thus created, can succeed in finding the necessary capital for the coal and steel industries— which it must do in the first instance—it might also be able to attract the equally necessary capital for other industries which must be included to make the pool idea successful. If the High Authority can raise money on good terms with reasonable rates of interest, this could, indeed, be the key.

The fourth condition is the effective suppression of cartels and the establishment of a competitive market free of discriminations and governmental restrictions. As stated above, the High Authority has all powers required to blot out the traditional combine arrangements and to move effectively against price controls, but its success in this area could be nullified by uncooperative governments if the tax problem is not amicably settled. As this cuts across the internal revenue systems in the various countries and as the High Authority has no powers in this field, the problem is up to the governments where it currently rests. Indeed, this problem looms larger for the steel consuming and fabricating industries than for the steel industries as the taxes are progressive and the amounts higher on more finished products. Naturally, no immediate and automatic solution can be found to this problem but the door must be opened and a way discovered.

THE PROJECT OF A POLITICAL COMMUNITY

25

The Process of Federating Europe[1]

By Robert R. Bowie

I

INTRODUCTION—THE FEDERAL PROCESS

The most striking instance in the world today of a movement for bringing together a number of sovereign states in a federal relationship is that now developing in Western Europe. No prediction can at present be made regarding the future course of this movement. There does evidently exist a situation which brings to bear powerful compulsions to unity upon the states of Western Europe. But the course of history is strewn with the failures of projected federal unions. The obstacles are always great and the pitfalls numerous. Attempts to unify Europe are nothing new, but this latest endeavor does present certain aspects that are in some sense unique and will repay careful examination.

It is important, first, to note the general nature of federal movements. Historically, federalism has been a process for creating wider political communities to promote specific interests common to several existing states. For the successful formation of a federal union, the component states must recognize that certain of their interests and problems are common and that they cannot be dealt with effectively by the separate states or by cooperation of sovereign entities. Diagnosis of such a situation has often been slow and painful, and the federal remedy is not likely to be applied until the ills have become acute and less radical remedies have failed.

In historical retrospect it becomes apparent that states have generally moved toward federation under the compulsion of defense and economic needs. In the United States, for instance, defense needs were clearly the primary reason for the formation of the Articles of Confederation. Economic rivalry and antagonism among the states constituted an additional impulse in the drafting of the federal Constitution. Likewise in the case of Switzerland, Germany, Canada, and Australia, federal unions developed from the inability of the individual states to provide adequate defense against actual or possible external threats to their existence, and the fact that needs for markets and vital supplies outran the capacity of any one state to satisfy them effectively. In all these, and similar cases, military and economic problems had become common to all, could no longer be handled by each state in isolation, and obviously required the interposition of some authority common to all the states concerned.

Even after the need is fully acknowledged there remain stubborn difficulties in the way of realizing federation. Existing state bureaucracies prove resistant to new arrangements affecting their prerogatives and reluctant to admit their inadequacy to deal with the pressing problems. Those persons and vested groups that profit by narrow markets and protectionism oppose economic changes, although these are in the general interest. Prevailing loyalties and patriotisms tend to foment resistance to the establishment of any new authority above the existing governments. Against such inertia and opposition, the needed support for federation has generally come into being only when the impelling necessity and threat of disaster have become apparent to influential and important segments of the population.

The general pattern of compulsive need and latent or overt resistance is apparent in Europe today. Both need and resistance are of such intensity, the requirements for speedy action and the massive and deep-rooted forces of the opposition are so great, that the movement is charged with dramatic conflict. The proponents of federation have resorted to novel and ingenious devices in order to make progress. They have first resorted to partial measures with an immediately practical bearing, the desirability of which was almost beyond dispute. Proceeding from these incomplete measures, they have gone ahead, relying on the dynamic conception of federalism as an evolving process in which each step entails some necessary further development. In this way they are banking on the progressive continuance of the process for ultimate success.

The purpose of this chapter will be, by reference to the general European problem and to specific measures toward union which have been undertaken, to show how initial steps lead into subsequent ones and are supplemented by them, and to indicate some of the tasks and problems that remain.

II

The Situation in Europe

A. Before 1945

The ideal of a united Europe is, of course, much older than the specific postwar needs which have given it its present impetus. But in the past it has moved only small groups of intellectuals and had little impact upon the actual course of European development.

It is a commonplace that Europe was united before it became divided. Europe was Christendom, for a long time bound together in theory, and even to some degree in fact, by the ties of Church and Empire. It was the abode of a common Classic-Christian civilization. The forces of the modern age shattered this unity, at least in its political and economic aspects. Europe became, in the modern era, a cluster of national states—kingdoms, empires, eventually republics—corresponding to national cultures which were diverse and deeply rooted in their respective native soils. These embodied deeply felt emotions of national greatness. Europe's states were highly competitive, and European history for centuries has been largely the record of their conflicts. With its unparalleled expansion, Europe's conflicts became worldwide and distant continents were often involved. Despite the tempering influence of alliances and a slowly evolving body of international law, the situation by 1914 was one of almost unrelieved international anarchy, resulting in the two great wars of our century.

Europe's remarkable growth in wealth and power had enabled it to survive the recurrent internecine wars of the earlier modern period, but it suffered almost mortal wounds from the wars of 1914 and 1939. It experienced revolutionary decline in its power position, economic well-being, and general morale. Communist imperialism thrust a wedge deep into the heart of the continent. West of Russia there remained by 1945 not a single major power center on the continent. A relatively impotent Europe lay helpless between the two emergent super-powers, the U.S. and the USSR, its fate largely in the hands of non-European peoples. As important as its economic and political decline was the spiritual malaise that affected much of its population.

Throughout the period when Europe's unity was being shattered the aspiration to regain it has been voiced, often with overtones of nostalgia for the era of Europe's Christian and Romanic past, but increasingly sounding a modern note. Thus Sully in 1638: "To render France happy forever is his [Henry IV] desire and she cannot perfectly enjoy this felicity, unless all Europe likewise partakes of it." And William Penn, proposing a Parliament of the Rulers of Europe, in 1693: "It would prevent the spilling of much blood. The reputation of Christianity would in some degree be recovered in the sight of infidels. It would save money. It would avoid the ravages of war. It would encourage travel. It would provide the security of Christendom against the inroads of the Turk."

Subsequent generations also had their advocates of unity: Voltaire, Rousseau, the Abbé de St. Pierre, Kant, Jeremy Bentham, Lamartine, Victor Hugo, Cobden. On the practical side, the very imperfect "Concert of Europe" was only a feeble step toward the realization of unity, and its breakdown on the eve of 1914 made a European civil war inevitable. After World War I, the Pan Europa movement led by Count Coudenhove-Kalergi, which proposed a confederation of all the sovereign states of Europe excluding Britain and Russia, attracted considerable support among peoples and officials, including the French Prime Minister, Herriot, and the Foreign Minister of the Weimar Republic, Stresemann. In 1930, another French Foreign Minister, Briand, officially put forward a plan for confederation without the loss of national sovereignty. He said: "To unite in order to live and prosper; that is the imperious necessity which henceforth confronts the nations of Europe." These proposals, of course, produced no concrete results; instead nationalism became stronger and more virulent. But such blueprints did prepare a climate of opinion destined, after World War II, for wider and popular acceptance.

B. After 1945—The Impulse to Unity

The plight of post-1945 Europe was such that the unity concept moved into the foreground of popular thinking, with both an emotional and a practical appeal. Europeans generally were bitterly disillusioned with nationalism and its fruits; they felt that if Europe was to survive it was essential to find some way to bury past hatreds and to live and work together in peace. The post-war situation of Europe may, perhaps, best be seen as the inevitable termination of one phase of its history, a phase in which it had run its course as world metropolis and which must give way to a very different one if Europe was to endure. The realities of World War II and its aftermath renewed interest in the idea of unity—this time as something relevant to the concrete needs of Europe.

There was first the unprecedented destruction wrought by the war. Looking about them, Europeans were profoundly shocked by the ravaged face of their continent and deeply disillusioned with the political doctrines which could have had such consequences. There was a dawning realization that the historic compartmentalization of the continent into national states, each a law to itself, had reached a point of no return and, in fact, threatened the ultimate destruction of all. There was a growing recognition that in a crowded subcontinent of three hundred million people the perpetuation of old animosities and antagonisms among a score or so of sovereignties could only lead to further internecine wars and a chain reaction of endless catastrophe. It was seen as especially important that France and Germany should somehow reconcile and merge their vital interests. The truth was driven home that only through a new ordering of its corporate life could the distraught European community be saved from eventual suicide.

There existed other compelling reasons for European action. The technological changes of our time that enormously multiplied man's power over natural forces, the extension of greater centralized authority over larger areas, the declining competence of the nation state to deal with large-scale economic and military problems, the loss of much of Europe's colonial domain, and the rapid development of new productive areas overseas which challenged Europe's one-time monopoly of important markets—all these factors posed new and pressing problems for European statesmanship.

The war-depleted economies of Europe presented a special problem. The tasks of reconstruction which faced European nations, victors and vanquished alike, were too huge and too general to be undertaken by any nation alone.

The need for European economic integration, however, went deeper than the war. For in the shrunken world which modern technology had created the separate states of Europe had become too small. Tariffs, quotas, restraints upon movement of persons, transport barriers, currency restrictions, and private cartels all operated to divide Europe into a series of airtight markets, each too small for efficient output and distribution. Any one state was powerless to correct the situation. Each state was forced to consider only its separate interests and to impose additional barriers to commerce with other states. It became clear that only a European authority could rise above separate national interests and seek the common interest in a wider market and freer trade.[2]

The most obvious and dramatic challenge to Europe's survival was that of the rapidly rising post-war Soviet power. This was already far ahead of its 1939 levels, in both economic and military respects. The statistical picture of Western Europe vis-à-vis the Soviet orbit shows that the former still has the potentiality of matching this new power, but only if united and progressing. For the latest economic reports indicate clearly that the USSR is increasing its industrial output at a much more rapid rate than is Western Europe and may eventually be in a position to match and surpass Europe's present living standards while bearing the load of even heavier military expenditures.

In the face of the Soviet threat it was clear that no one nation in Europe could possibly afford to maintain the necessary level of armed forces for its own security, nor conduct its own defense alone. War had become an increasingly complicated and expensive process, and no one state had the resources in terms of money, material, or men to face the Soviet danger. No one state would be able, in terms of strategy alone, to maintain an effective defense against a Soviet attack. Furthermore, a coalition was no answer. An aggregation of national forces would not produce as efficient a fighting force as a single balanced force made up of components from several European states. If each state attempted to maintain its own separate military forces, they were certain to be based on a balance among the various military elements within that state. The aggregate of these separate forces would not necessarily constitute a genuinely balanced total force for the entire area to be defended. Inexorable military logic demanded that there be more than associated national forces—that there be, in fact, a fully integrated European force responding to common institutions and directed by a common will.

Thus circumstances in Western Europe in the years following the war corresponded closely to those which often in the past have led nations to undertake the initial steps toward federation. The impulse to unity arose as a response to a challenge that went to the very foundations of social existence.

The post-1945 period has witnessed something new in the history of the European unity movement—the convergence of thought and action on the concrete and desperate realities of the day. Not philosophers only, but also men of experience in grappling with the stubborn post-war problems saw the need for unity—men such as Schuman, Pleven, and Monnet in France, Adenauer in Germany, Spaak in Belgium, and De Gasperi in Italy. This need was eloquently voiced by Winston Churchill in a speech in Zurich in 1946:

> This noble continent is the home of all the great parent races of the Western World. It is the fountain of Christian faith and Christian ethics. It is the cradle of Western civilization. Yet it is from Europe that have sprung that series of frightful nationalistic quarrels, which we have seen, twice in our own lifetime, wreck the peace and mar the prospects of all mankind.
>
> And what is the plight to which Europe has been reduced? Some of the smaller states have indeed made a good recovery, but over wide areas a vast quivering mass of tormented, hungry, care-worn and bewildered human beings gape at the ruins of their cities and homes and scan the dark horizons for the approach of some new peril, tyranny or terror. Among the victors there is a babel of jarring voices; among the vanquished the sullen silence of despair. But for the generosity of the United States, which have now realized that the ruin or enslavement of Europe would involve their own fate as well, the Dark Ages would have returned in all their cruelty and squalor. They may still return.
>
> Yet all the while there is a remedy which, if it were generally and spontaneously adopted, would, as if by a miracle, transform the whole scene, and would in a few years make all Europe as free and as happy as is Switzerland today.
>
> What is this sovereign remedy? It is to recreate the European family, or as much of it as we can, and provide it with a structure under which it can dwell in peace and safety and freedom. We must build a kind of United States in Europe. In this way only will hundreds of millions of toilers be able to regain the simple joys and hopes which make life worth living.

III

FIRST STEPS TOWARD UNION

The Churchillian call in Zurich evoked a significant response. Organized movements on a larger scale than ever before were soon afoot and in 1947 and 1948 came together to form the European Movement, itself a sort of confederation of private organizations. Nor was action by governments lacking.

In 1947, in response to the Harvard address by Secretary of State George C. Marshall, sixteen European countries and Iceland created the Committee for European Economic Cooperation to work together in planning a common effort, with United States aid, toward economic recovery. When the Marshall Plan became effective in 1948, this Committee became the Organization for European Economic Cooperation (OEEC) through which the member governments have worked together in administering U. S. economic aid and for other joint economic ends, with authority residing in a council composed of government representatives.

In March 1948, the United Kingdom, France, and the Benelux nations entered into a Treaty of Economic, Social, and Cultural Collaboration and Collective Self-Defense, generally called the Brussels Pact. This treaty imposed an obligation to render assistance to any member suffering armed attack and established a Consultative Council "so organized as to be able to exercise its functions continuously."

This phase in the evolution of unity in Europe culminated in the formation of the Council of Europe in 1949, initially with ten and later fifteen members. The Council consists of a Consultative Assembly made up of parliamentarians from the member states and of a Committee of Ministers representing governments. The Assembly has authority to conduct debates and make recommendations. The Committee of Ministers has the sole authority to take action and then only under a rule of unanimity.

The OEEC, the Brussels Pact organization, and the Council of Europe are all essentially forums for discussion and for promotion of cooperation among the sovereign states of Europe. None of them could take any action affecting a member state without that state's consent. Thus, in these bodies, the work could proceed only as rapidly as the most hesitant was prepared to move. The less hesitant soon came to feel that progress was not rapid enough.

The needs of the times would not wait, and efforts at cooperation alone were palpably not meeting them. Yet two factors conditioned the desire for more rapid progress toward federation. One was that a number of countries, notably Britain and the Scandinavian states, while prepared to join bodies such as the Council of Europe, were simply not ready at this time to delegate to any supranational institution power to affect their affairs without their consent in each instance. Any such institutions must therefore have a membership more limited than the Council of Europe or the OEEC. Second, it was clear that there could be no speedy establishment of full-blown federal institutions resting on a base of popular suffrage. It was doubtful that the people of any European country were yet ready for such a step. Futhermore, the working out and the actual setting up of such institutions was certain to take time. In the United States, the Articles of Confederation persisted for a decade before dire necessity drove the leaders of the American states to prepare a constitution for a genuine federal union.

To deal with the situation, European statesmen, especially Foreign Minister Schuman of France and Chancellor Adenauer of the Federal Republic, developed a new approach. It proceeded from the basic premise that Europe must create federal institutions with real authority if it is to achieve economic well-being, political stability, and military security. It recognized that creation of a federal state is a process, not an event, and that even after its formation its powers develop and evolve over a long period of time. Yet the problems —economic, political, and military—were urgently pressing for solution. Under these conditions it was decided to proceed piecemeal toward federation. Instead of trying at once to create a full federal structure endowed with all necessary powers, the plan was to set up institutions patterned on the federal model, but with authority limited to a specific function. Agencies to tackle the immediate problems could provide the foundation for an eventual complete federal structure.

This method meant proceeding to build now a "Little Europe," restricted to those countries which were ready for an immediate, though limited, transfer of sovereign powers. "Big Europe" would have to come later. But its advent might be hastened by the example of supranational institutions operating successfully on a restricted scale. Similarly, their successful operation would lead to a gradual broadening of their powers and of their democratic base.

IV

Toward Economic Unity

In dealing with Europe's post-war economic difficulties, international bodies such as the Organization for European Economic Cooperation (OEEC), the European Payments Union (EPU), and the Council of Europe had performed useful functions. But while they provided a basis for voluntary cooperation, they acted only by the unanimity rule and could proceed only as rapidly as the most reluctant member. It was becoming clear that if Europe was ever to solve its basic economic problems, there must be achieved a more organic unity through European agencies capable of acting effectively in the common interest.

The obstacles to such genuine economic unity were and are formidable and deeply rooted. The very maturity of the European economies was a source of special difficulties. The long history of tariffs and other measures to protect national markets had created an enormous range of vested interests deeply concerned with their continuance. Opposition was certain to arise from varied quarters—from entrepreneurs whose business would face new competition, from workers who would fear the loss of their jobs or painful readjustments of their mode of life, from officials whose careers were closely associated with the regulation of traditional economic practices, and from advocates of a socialized or planned economy on a national scale.

Furthermore, the fact that governments today are much more deeply involved in the economic life of their peoples than they were in the recent past greatly complicates the task of creating a federal arrangement. When the Swiss and American federal republics were formed, the state interfered to a relatively slight extent in the actual operations of the economy.[3] At that time, transfer of control over trade or commerce from state to federal government was not seriously disrupting and did not entail the much broader range of controls which are common today. But at present, and particularly in Europe, a state accepts responsibility for the health of the economy; it manages the budget, taxation, currency and credit, regulation of internal and foreign trade, and to a considerable extent of domestic industry, as interrelated means for discharging this function. To transfer this entire responsibility to a new federal state would burden it with tasks with which it could not cope, at least in its initial stages.

Under these conditions, M. Schuman, in May 1950, suggested a unique initial approach to the problem.[4] He proposed the creation of a European Coal and Steel Community (CSC) providing for the delegation to European institutions of authority to regulate the coal and steel industries of the member states. He stated that the plan had three major purposes: (1) to promote French-German trust and *rapprochement* by putting their primary industrial materials —coal and steel—under common European institutions; (2) to make a start toward freer intra-European trade by opening up a single market for these two basic industries; (3) to establish the nucleus of federal institutions. Six countries—France, West Germany, Italy, and the Benelux nations—have joined in establishing this Community. The preceding chapters have treated the economic and other details of the plan; a few summary comments here will suffice.

In one sense, the selection of the coal and steel industries of these countries was a natural first step toward federation. The Community embraced the principal industrial complex of Western Europe, including much of the heavy industry of the Ruhr and Rhineland, the Saar, Alsace-Lorraine, northeastern France, Belgium, and Luxembourg. Yet to separate out these particular industries for European control was no easy task. In many ways they were woven into the fabric of their separate national economies. Inevitably there were many loose ends, and the project could scarcely be expected to endure without further steps toward more comprehensive economic integration. But it was the essence of the plan that, half measure though it was, it would be a beginning. Its very incompleteness would create the necessity for new measures for joining other segments of the economies of the Six under supranational control, and eventually for a genuine parliament to insure popular confidence and support and to assume new responsibilities. Thus the plan would start in motion a process of growth toward wider functions and authority. The essential thing was to make a beginning toward unity before the opportunity was lost.

The plan became effective by treaty in August 1952 when the High Authority took up its functions. The first six months were devoted to setting up the institutions of the Community, organizing the staff, and preparing for opening of the common market.

The CSC was patterned on the structure of a federal state. A High Authority of nine members was to act as executive and administer the common market. Although its members are named by the states, this body is designed to act independently on its own judgment and has both the authority and responsibility to deal directly with the coal and steel enterprises rather than with the member governments. There is also a Common Assembly, representing the parliaments of the member states, with a limited control over the High Authority which it can depose by a vote of no confidence. A Council of Ministers, representing the governments of the member states, also exercises certain restricted powers, somewhat as a second chamber. A Court of the Community is established to ensure adherence by the organs of the Community to the terms of the treaty and to enforce decisions of the High Authority in conformity with the treaty.

The function of the CSC is to create a common market, though restricted to coal and steel. In its final form, the common market will permit commerce in coal, steel, iron ore, and scrap to flow among the six states without regard to national boundaries. Within this market these products will not be subject to tariffs and similar barriers. They will be priced without discrimination. Railroad and other freight rates will be computed on the same basis for shipments to all parts of this market. Buyers will be able to obtain the necessary currencies for purchases anywhere in the market. In periods of scarcity, the available supplies will be shared among all six countries according to allocations set by the High Authority. Cartels and monopolies in these products will be outlawed. Skilled coal and steel workers will be free to move across the national boundaries of the six countries.

This common market constitutes a radical change from the past. Full establishment will require many adjustments in these industries and in national laws and practices. The treaty provides for a five-year period of transition to enable these changes to be made without undue disruption. Tariffs and quantity limits and many forms of discrimination have already been removed. In some cases existing subsidies are allowed to continue temporarily, but will be withdrawn progressively. Taxes on coal and steel yielding currently about fifty million dollars have been imposed, and the High Authority is working out an investment program to improve productive efficiency and output. Thus the CSC has taken a long stride toward a single competitive market and, under present plans, will achieve it fully in a few years.

An important purpose has been served by the Community in accumulating experience and creating a climate of opinion favorable to federal institutions. It has taught by example the benefits even of limited economic unity. It has begun to create a group of European officials whose loyalty is wider than national loyalty, whose horizons are wider than national horizons. It has provided a symbol and center around which new loyalties could group themselves. It is significant in this connection to note that within the Common Assembly party groupings crossing national lines have already been formed. The Coal and Steel Community is the living sign of a future Europe which would beckon others toward European solutions for other problems.

Naturally much hinges on its success. In little more than three years the initial idea has borne fruit to an amazing extent. The CSC has now been in operation since the middle of 1952 as a federation of limited scope. Its institutions are functioning effectively. The decisions of the Community have so far been loyally accepted by the member states.

V

Toward European Defense

The CSC, as indicated above, was designed as the first step toward a more comprehensive union of the six nations. The original intent had not been to hurry on into other types of union until experience with the CSC had provided some basis and justification for further ventures. But the next step came more quickly than had been anticipated. While the CSC treaty was being negotiated, the Communists struck in Korea (June 1950). This attack, and the fear that Europe might be the next victim of aggression, drew attention to the pitiful weakness of Europe's defenses. It became increasingly evident that effective defensive strength in Europe would require a greater degree of integration of existing military forces and the addition of West German military strength to the joint effort.

Federation for defense represented an even more radical step than the CSC. Yet it seemed imperative, in view of the drastically changed conditions of modern warfare, that there should be a common, balanced force for the defense of Western Europe. So costly had become the weapons and techniques of modern fighting that no West European state alone could afford an adequate defense establishment. The experience of the wartime coalition had demonstrated the possibilities of the coordinated, multinational force. It seemed apparent that a common army on which the total resources available for defense were expended to create a reasonably balanced force, would be superior to a group of national armies, none of which could afford all the kinds and amounts of force essential to effective defense under modern conditions.

A further consideration of great weight strongly influenced official thinking in this matter. An effective West European defense force could scarcely exist without the Germans, yet Europeans generally felt that the creation of a German national army would constitute a potential danger to all Europe, and that any authorized German armed force must be within the framework of international arrangements and controls. This could clearly be most effectively accomplished through a federal arrangement.

Even more than in the case of economic union, federation for defense raised grave difficulties. Defense matters touch the sensitive core of national pride and the merging of armies is not at all comparable to the merger of mines and mills. Moreover, today's armies are massive establishments based on compulsory service and consuming ten per cent or more of the gross national income and one third of the total budget. The transfer of military authority from states to a federal body is certain to have a heavy impact on the economy and on other aspects of national life. To discharge its responsibilities, the federal union would need to kindle and maintain genuine loyalty on the part of the citizens of the individual states who serve in its military forces or make financial sacrifice for their support. It would also seem to call for some overriding political authority within the federal group to harmonize military and foreign policies.

Confronted with these dilemmas, French leaders drew upon the example of the CSC for a solution. In late 1950, M. Pleven proposed the creation of a European army, integrating French, German, Italian, and Benelux units under joint six-power institutions. After extended deliberation and negotiation, a treaty for a European Defense Community (EDC) was signed in May 1952. By May 1954 it had been ratified by the Federal Republic of Germany, Belgium, the Netherlands, and Luxembourg. Before the end of the summer, however, the French Assembly had refused to ratify the treaty. Nevertheless it may be useful to summarize the significant features of the plan as contemplated in the treaty.

The institutional plan of the EDC was to be similar to that of the CSC, with avoidance of overlapping to the greatest extent possible. The EDC would be headed by a Commissariat as the executive agency, with responsibility independent of the separate member governments. The CSC has now demonstrated that such a body can make decisions contrary to the wishes of one or more of these governments. The EDC Assembly would be the same as that of the CSC, with three additional representatives each for France, Germany, and Italy. The Council of Ministers would exercise powers analogous to those of the corresponding CSC organ. It would be the instrument through which the member governments would retain some very considerable powers. The EDC would have the same Court as the CSC, with the same general purpose.

The functions to be discharged by the Commissariat of the Defense Community without unanimous approval of the group of ministers were to be substantial. The Community would prepare a common budget for the common forces. The receipts part of this budget would be subject to unanimous approval in the Council of Ministers, but the Community would have real power to determine how money—once allocated by the states for defense purposes—would be spent. It would be in charge of all procurement and weapons research and standardization. It would also have some power directly to control military production in the several states and to require some economic measures to be taken in the event that its production program was not fulfilled. It would be empowered to negotiate for foreign end-item aid and also financial aid to be spent outside the monetary zones of the member states. It would supervise and might gradually come wholly to control the training of the forces and other measures for putting them in readiness. It would establish and administer military schools for the forces, which would be integrated. Units required for any effective large-scale operations would be multinational. Finally, the states would have divested themselves of the responsibility for defense which they would have entrusted to the Community and also of the means readily to discharge it themselves.

The powers which the member states were to retain, or which required the unanimous approval of the Council of Ministers, would include the capacity to use the forces of the Community, the authority to finance its activities, and to determine the size of the forces to be mounted by it.

The EDC was to be closely tied to other European states through NATO. There would be a defense guarantee binding the two organizations. In addition, the Community's forces, like the forces of other European countries, would be under the command of the NATO Supreme Commander in Europe. Provision would exist for joint sittings of the Councils of the Community and of NATO, and NATO procedures would be employed to reach an initial determination of the financial contribution each member state would make to the Community so as to render such contributions commensurate with the NATO effort.

Even closer ties were to exist with Britain. There was to be a defense guarantee between that country and the Community. Special arrangements would be made for joint training of Community and British forces in the field and for the closest general cooperation among them. Special efforts to standardize equipment and weapons would be made. Finally, a British representative would frequently sit with the Council of the Community and Britain would have permanent representation near the Commissariat.

The EDC, like the CSC, illustrates the sort of "chain reaction" involved in any successful move toward federation. If established it would have necessitated expanded powers before long to be effective. In view of the vital nature of its activity, it would eventually require the support of institutions of a political character constructed on a broader democratic basis.

VI

TOWARD POLITICAL UNION

The two organizational plans just described (CSC and EDC) were drafted in response to very real problems of such character as to elude the competence of single states and require joint action. Both represent a partial transfer to supranational organs of powers normally exercised by sovereign states. Thus both of them would tend eventually to create a situation in which the need for democratic political organs expressing the combined popular will of the six nations will be strongly felt. Realization of this need gave rise to a special provision of the EDC treaty (Article 38) under which the Assembly of the Defense Community was assigned the constituent role of preparing and submitting to the governments a stronger framework for a federal or confederal structure, to be based on a bicameral legislature and on the separation of powers between it and the executive. Originally, it had been intended to undertake this task only after the EDC treaty had been ratified. During the summer of 1952, however, the foreign ministers of the six countries decided to request the Assembly of the CSC, augmented as provided in the EDC treaty, to draft a statute for a European Political Community (EPC). This work has proceeded, and by March 1953 a draft statute was ready and was presented to the six governments.

This draft statute would, in essence, create a parliamentary form of federal union as an umbrella under which the CSC and EDC would function. Its most striking feature is the legislature, the lower house (Peoples' Chamber) to be elected by universal popular suffrage, and the Senate to be composed of delegates selected by the parliaments of the member states. Representation in the

Senate would be weighted somewhat in favor of the larger states. The executive would be a Council headed by a President chosen by the Senate, who then would name the other members, subject to the approval of the Peoples' Chamber. Either the Senate or the Chamber could remove the President and other members of the Council which, however, would have the right to dissolve the Chamber following a vote of censure lacking the required majority.

The Council of National Ministers, as provided in both the CSC and EDC, would continue with certain additional powers. It would thus retain a central position and, in this respect, the draft statute falls short of its purpose to create stronger federal institutions.

The Court established by the CSC and EDC would be retained as the Court for the EPC and would act both as a constitutional and as an administrative tribunal.

The EPC statute—even in the form submitted in March 1953—is an imperfect effort to achieve true federalism for the six-nation community. Although a logical and practical next step, it has become the subject of heated debate which focuses some of the basic issues of the federalizing process. There is the uncertain scope of the Community's financial powers; its authority to create a common market "progressively" among the member states; the question of the unanimity rule in the Council of Ministers and the relation of that body, representing the separate governments, to the more truly federal organs of the Community; the need of harmonizing the foreign policies of the member states and creating a common political will. There is also the difficult problem of the relation of the EPC, once it is realized, to other European states and to Britain in particular. Observers from the Council of Europe sat with the committee in working out the statute, which provides for close liaison and consultation between the organs of the Community and the Council of Europe.

Since the statute was submitted there have been occasional meetings of the foreign ministers of the six nations to consider it, but in the late spring of 1954 there had been no agreement on the final form of the statute. France has proved somewhat more reluctant to proceed to the creation of a genuinely federal union than the other nations. Progress was largely held up awaiting full ratification of the EDC treaty. There were evidences at this stage, however, of the continued vitality of the idea of a European Community, and also the need of a fostering spirit on the part of the United States and Britain to prevent the movement from foundering on nationalist forces and obstructions.

VII

INHERENT DIFFICULTIES

It has earlier been pointed out that certain difficulties and obstructions are inherent in the federalizing process in general. It may be well at this point to note briefly a number of major problems which have a close bearing upon the federal movement in Europe and which present difficulties to be surmounted if a successful federal union is ever achieved.

The natural stress within the last few years upon a close federal integration of six of the central nations of the continent should not obscure the broader problem. Europe outside the USSR contains some twenty-five state entities enjoying *de jure* or *de facto* sovereignty, seven of which are in the Soviet orbit. What is under way is not so much the federating of Europe as the creation of a new federal state within Europe. In view of the probably prolonged division of Europe by the iron curtain, and the wide range of national cultures and interests even within free Europe, it would be premature to assume that a federated Europe is in prospect. In fact, the successful federation of the Six in a "Little Europe" might even be a divisive factor and prejudice ultimate attainment of a wider union. On the other hand it might become the central core from which such a union could evolve. If this were ever to extend to the present satellite countries, the growing divergence between their systems and those of the West European countries would create obstacles to federation.

The territorial scope and federative character of the union are aspects of the problem that particularly concern Britain and the Scandinavian countries. Even though Churchill fathered the post-war concept of European union, Britain has been most reluctant to be drawn into any federal arrangement which would involve a partial surrender of sovereignty to federal institutions. The same is true of the Scandinavian countries. Yet all are interested in the achievement of a closer association of European countries; Britain, in particular, could scarcely be dissociated from any European development.[5] The so-called "Eden Plan" of March 1952 would have remodelled the Council of Europe so that its organs could serve as the ministerial and parliamentary institutions of the new six-nation communities. This scheme, however, would seem to have been overtaken by the evolution of the EPC to date. But it illustrates the discrepancy between the concepts of "Big" and "Little" Europe.

At the heart of any European federation, whether little or big, there must be a France and Germany which have put aside their historic differences and agreed upon whole-hearted cooperation. Without a healing of this most persisting European schism there can be no meaningful European union. Yet France hesitates to be absorbed into a union which, with some show of justification, she fears may eventually be dominated by a more powerful Germany. She, like Britain, has large overseas interests and responsibilities not readily reconcilable with such a union. The Federal Republic of Germany is less hesitant to federate, but might, in some post-Adenauer phase, introduce an element of instability and aggressiveness into the policy of the union because of its ambitions to reunify Germany and recover the lost eastern territories. The problem of associating a reunited Germany with a European federal union would inevitably raise grave difficulties in the relation of the Western powers to the USSR, as amply demonstrated by the diplomatic controversy over Germany of the last few years, most lately exemplified in the Berlin four-power talks of January-February 1954. In fact, any type of European federation or associative action seems certain to encounter the unqualified hostility of the Kremlin.

An important aspect of European integration is the economic one, yet there are special difficulties here. Europe, even in its decline from world metropolitan status, is far from being a self-sustaining area and its trade is, and must remain, closely interlinked with areas outside upon which it is still dependent for primary raw materials and for markets. European economic integration can help but can never entirely solve Europe's broader economic problem. The relationships between a European "economic community" and extra-European economic areas vital to its existence must continue to be a matter of continued concern.

VIII

CONCLUSIONS

The European experience to date represents an effort to achieve federation by a unique process adapted to the peculiar needs and situations existing in post-war Europe.

The distinctive feature of this process has been in developing federal institutions, stage by stage, through successive agencies, wielding limited powers in specific fields. This method has made possible an immediate start in applying the federalist solution to pressing current problems. It relies on a cumulative process of growth and gradual fulfillment. It assumes that existing residues of traditional and nationalist thinking may best be changed through actual experience and example.

This method provides an inner compulsion toward growth. Once certain functions are delegated, once partial communities are established, their initial success can create pressures to widen their functions and cure their deficiencies. The commitment embodied in the steps already taken leads to the next logical step. The rapid start with the Political Community treaty shows how effectively this compulsion can operate.

But the method also involves serious risks. The same deficiencies which provide motives to go further can, if not cured, undermine the communities already created. A process of this sort cannot stand still; it must go forward or seriously recede. That is the risk inherent in it.

What, then, are the prospects? No one can say for certain. In terms of need, certainly, European unity has an aspect of ultimate inevitability. No other method has been proposed to enable Europe to achieve security, economic health, and social stability, or to attain the permanent and essential reconciliation of France and Germany.

Decision cannot wait upon ideal conditions which are not likely to materialize. Drift and indecision would only mean increasing insecurity, rising economic pressures, social tensions, political radicalism, and "crisis governments."

French rejection of the EDC treaty was a setback to the movement toward integration. But it would be premature to conclude that the movement has come to a halt. Indeed the program worked out to replace EDC, while less supranational in character, may provide opportunity for further progress toward integration. The plan for majority action by the Council under the revised Brussels Treaty, and the efforts to develop within that framework a common armament pool like that under EDC, show the vitality of the integration idea. In the economic and political fields there also persist roots which could grow. Even so, vigorous and sustained efforts will be needed to restore the full momentum of the integration movement and to secure action in these various directions.

It is not too much to say that the future of Europe hangs on the early success of these efforts. The situation will not stand still. The present historic opportunity can be lost by indecision or delay. Realities demand that the states upon which these compulsions operate should overcome their fears and hesitations and go forward, without faltering, in hammering out tighter bonds of union. The solid achievement of federation, even on a partial basis for only a part of Europe, will be the surest indication that the future is not without hope.

FOOTNOTES TO CHAPTER 25

1. The views expressed in this chapter are those of the author; they do not necessarily represent the views of the Department with which he is connected.

2. It is significant that the United States Congress, in its endeavors to assist economic recovery in Europe, quickly recognized the importance of unity. The original ERP Act of 1948 referred to the need for "economic cooperation" in Europe. The Act of 1949 declared the "unification of Europe" to be a goal of American policy, and the MSA Acts of 1950 and 1952 were even more specific in urging "economic unification and political federation."

3. It is true that during the 17th and 18th centuries, governments in Europe under the influence of the mercantilist or cameralist doctrines were wont to impose comprehensive and vexatious regulations upon trade and industry. But the nineteenth century witnessed a widely increased practice of economic liberalism with its stress on free enterprise. This trend has been, to a large degree, reversed during the last forty years with the tendency toward state intervention in the economic field.

4. The plan was actually conceived by M. Jean Monnet, author of the so-called "Monnet Plan" for the modernization of the French economy, and now President of the High Authority of the CSC.

5. In the words of British Under-Secretary for Foreign Affairs Nutting: "The only condition which we seek to impose upon . . . (federal) development is that it should be within the orbit of a body of which Britain is a member and through which Britain may be associated with it."

26

Federal Constitutional Theory and Emergent Proposals

By Carl J. Friedrich

The rise of modern constitutional government has been accompanied by the establishment of any number of federal schemes. The parallel is so impressive that federalism clearly is one of the most important aspects of modern constitutionalism. Federalism, when spoken of in general discussions, is used rather vaguely to mean any kind of linking of autonomous units. The word may therefore refer to a league or confederation of "independent, sovereign" states as well as to a federal system. Genuine federal systems are found in Australia, Austria, Canada, the German Federal Republic, Switzerland, and the United States. Beyond these, the matter becomes controversial. In the satellite countries of Eastern and Central Europe, the problem turns upon whether their "constitutions" are genuine constitutionalism (see below); in other cases, such as the Commonwealth, other problems are involved.[1]

I

When the foreign ministers of the six nations composing the Coal and Steel Community decided to establish a corresponding European Defense Community and to include in this project a program for a Political Community as well, they provided in article 38 of the Defense Community treaty that this Political Community should be, *inter alia,* of "an ultimate federal or a confederal structure." The perplexities of the discussion over federalism are reflected in this indecisive phrasing. Torrents of ink have been spilt over this alternative. It all goes back to a discussion in *The Federalist* and the later discussions in Switzerland, Germany, and elsewhere which were cast in terms of sovereignty. It is the dichotomy of *Staatenbund* and *Bundesstaat* which the constitutional jurists fought over throughout the nineteenth century, with consequent confusions in terminology, since a federation is evidently a *Bund* and yet those advocating the federal principle plead for a genuine federation. Yet

John C. Calhoun and other Southern advocates of the confederal principle as the sound interpretation of the American constitution had made it clear that they thought of the union as a federation of states (or a confederation of them) rather than a state built on the federal principle.[2]

The same argument arose in the discussions between the occupying powers over the future political organization of defeated Germany. The French made themselves the advocates of a policy imposing upon Germany the confederal principle, that is to say the establishment of separate states, Baden, Wuerttemberg, Bavaria, and so forth, which might then be permitted to federate into some sort of confederal union. Great Britain favored the reestablishment of a federal state of the close-knit pattern of the Weimar Republic. The United States and the majority of the Germans favored something in between. Thus the Basic Law of the German Federal Republic of 1949 became more federal than Weimar, less federal than some had insisted it should be.[3] To these remarks, recalling some recent arguments over the issue of federalism and involving high policy of the major powers, there might be added a brief reminder that the United States of America were presumably originally neither clearly federal nor clearly confederal, or the dissensions which culminated in the War between the States (as the Southern version has it to this day) could not have taken the form they did. The United States became, however, clearly federal after 1866, and are more unitary today than at that time.[4]

These and other comparable uncertainties elsewhere suggest that there is something basically misleading about the confrontation of the federal and the confederal as a sort of a dichotomy which would enable us to divide the world of political entities involving federal aspects into those which are states and those which are not. The error springs, evidently, from the particular use made of the term *state* in this connection. It is perhaps symptomatic that the issue has been recurrently sharpest among those who attached especial importance to the conception of the state as a primary term calculated to serve a useful purpose in describing political phenomena. Should it not have been seen as a warning that we speak of a political entity as more or less federal, that is to say that we recognize that quantitative gradations can be discerned by the student of federal systems?[5]

But apart from the difficulties resulting from the preoccupation with the state as the focal point of political interest, there is to be noted the related difficulty of seeing federalism as a static structure and then trying to deal with divergent patterns in terms of these static structures. Thus particular arrangements for the distribution of competencies between the authorities at the center and those in the component units have been selected by some for special emphasis, and there has been much insistence upon particular minimum powers for the central authorities and the like. *The Federalist,* contrasting as it did the new Constitution with the preceding confederation, helped to entrench this particular approach. But the history of the United States, as well as other federal constitutions, demonstrates clearly that these patterns do not stay put, that Canada assigning residual power to the central authorities sees these authorities severely restricted in developing new powers by the interpretation put upon the British North American Act by the Privy Council, while the United States under the opposite arrangement has witnessed a steady expansion of the competencies of the central power. However, it is presumably true that a certain minimum of powers is essential. These may, however, be different powers for different federal systems.

II

The Federalist repeatedly refers to previous federal experience, especially to the Netherlands and twice to Switzerland. It had been these two countries which in early modern times inspired the elaboration of a genuine theory of federalism by Johannes Althusius. In his celebrated *Politics* (1603), he built his unique theory of constitutionalism upon an all-embracing concept of federal union on successive levels of community. The village was for him a federation of families, the town a federation of families and guilds, the province a federation of towns, the kingdom a federation of provinces, and the empire a federation of kingdoms. Swiss, German, and Dutch political realities were the basis of this striking system of politics in terms of federated communities. And as Gierke has shown, this theoretical system bore a close resemblance to medieval political structures. There are traces of a comparable approach in Dante and Thomas Aquinas, though the references in these writers to a composite political structure ought to be read in reference to the feudal and ecclesiastical hierarchies of the time. Althusius' conception of the federally organized community was, by contrast, constructed in terms of the concept of sovereignty as Bodin had expounded it. Or rather in terms of a conception of sovereignty derived from the Bodinian notions.[6]

For Bodin's own concept of sovereignty tended toward an interpretation of federal unions as either confederations of states or as states. Bodin had insisted that Switzerland was nothing but a confederation and that the several component units were fully sovereign states—an analysis which flies in the face of the established matters of fact but which eventually predominated. Similarly, Bodin had described the Holy Roman Empire as an aristocratic *respublica* or commonwealth in which the princes and estates recognized by the Golden Bull jointly exercised sovereignty. In thus interpreting the medieval constitution of the Empire, he had evidenced the inherent contradiction between the classic doctrine of sovereignty and federalism which has already been noted.[7]

Not only Althusius but Grotius as well developed a federal theory in conjunction with a concept of sovereignty. This is even more significant, in a way, because Grotius maintained the idea of state sovereignty, as contrasted with the Althusian doctrine of popular sovereignty. The reason is, according to Gierke, that Grotius like Althusius adopted the social contract as the basis of all corporate entities and hence conceived the political commonwealth (*staatliche Gemeinwesen*) as an immortal and perpetual association of less comprehensive communities. But no clear conception of federalism results, such as animates the work of Althusius. Only he perceived clearly that federalism presupposes a dual sphere of genuine autonomy, and he could do this because by vindicating the collective sovereignty of the people he had in fact destroyed the classical Bodinian doctrine by a process of inversion.[8]

The theory of federalism went thereafter into an eclipse, along with that of popular sovereignty. Neither Locke nor Montesquieu expounds one; the latter's famous doctrine of the *pouvoirs intermédiaires* is actually very much akin to Bodin's doctrine of the dependent jurisdiction of all corporations and associations. His view is in line with all those jurists who expounded the Roman concept of the corporation.[9]

Federalism had a rebirth in the political philosophies of Rousseau and Kant. This fact is significantly related, of course, to their emphasis on constitutionalism and democracy. It has lately become fashionable to belittle this emphasis, even to interpret Rousseau's thought as the seed-bed of totalitarianism. There is an element of truth in this perspective, but it must be seen in relation to the actual kinship between democracy and totalitarianism, for the latter is the corruption of the former. The genuine penchant of Rousseau is evident in his well-known recognition that democracy is possible only in small communities and that a democratic order must therefore be a federal union of such democratic communities—not perhaps a very original idea for a writer with Swiss antecedents, but an unusual view in his time. This idea is carried further by Kant, who after abandoning the radically democratic basis of Rousseau's federalism stressed the federal solution as the only possible one for a group of republics or constitutional states. Kant clearly recognized the formidable implications of a world state and its potentialities of universal tyranny. But Kant, like Rousseau, failed to carry his idea of federal union back to the lower levels of government. The states composing the federal world order are unitary systems in which the corporate entities are instituted by the state and possess no genuine autonomy.[10]

It was Proudhon who revived the Althusian notion of an all-engulfing federalism (though there is no evidence that he ever read him). Even his formulations sound at times like translations from Althusius, including the emphasis on contract. He speaks of a *contrat fédéral* and claims that its essence lies in the fact that under such a system the contracting parties (*contractants*), the heads of families, the communes, the cantons, the provinces, and the states do "not only oblige themselves bilaterally and mutually (*synallagmatiquement et communativement*) toward each other, but they also in forming such a pact reserve for themselves (*individuellement*) more rights, more freedom, more authority, and more property than they give up." We find here in Proudhon the same doctrine as in Althusius: federalism is characterized by the permanent give and take between the inclusive community and the component communities, and this organic interrelation, cooperation, and exchange is a universal principle of political organization. However, Proudhon leans toward a rather loose and imprecise construction which leaves the component communities the final authority. This presumably is due to his anarchist starting point. Thus he asserts that, according to his principles, the contract of federation has "as its object to guarantee to the component states their sovereignty." He consequently insists that the powers (*attributions*) of the federal authorities can never exceed in number and in reality those of the provincial authorities. Apart from the difficulty involved in making this kind of comparison, there is no foundation in fact for the assertion.[11] True federalism, the federalizing process under constitutionalism, solves this problem of the two competing autonomies by the constitutional device of vesting in the amending power (derived as it is from the constituent power) the prerogative of determining from time to time whether and how the powers should be altered. It is for this reason that such importance attaches to the problem of constitutional amendments under a federal system—and also that we find ourselves obliged below to comment critically upon the draft treaty for a European Community. Every federal community, to be truly federal, will organize its amending process in such a way that it calls for the effective cooperation of the inclusive and the component communities in amending the basic law. This is actually the situation in the existing federal systems, notably Australia, Switzerland, the German Federal Republic, and the United States.[12] In Canada, the absence of such a provision has led to considerable controversy and the provinces claim the right to be consulted.

III

The spread of federalism which Proudhon predicted has taken place on all levels of those societies which have progressed in a constitutional and democratic direction. The attempts of jurists to narrow the focus of federalism and to restrict it to thinking in terms of the "federal state" have not succeeded. New federal systems, like India and Europe, are in the making. Older federal communities, like the United States and Germany, are evolving novel solutions to the difficult problems of associated territories, resulting from war and conquest, such as Puerto Rico and Berlin. France has entered upon the road of federalism in connection with the problems of her overseas possessions. So has Britain overseas.

What does all this suggest? It suggests that federalism should not be considered as a static pattern, as a fixed and precise term of division of powers between central and component authorities. Instead, federalism should be seen as the *process of federalizing a political community,* as the process by which a number of separate political organizations, be they states or any other kind of associations, enter into arrangements for making joint decisions on joint problems, or reversely the process through which a hitherto unitary political organization becomes decentralized to the point where separate and distinct political communities arise and become politically organized and capable of making separate decisions on distinct problems. But this broad characterization of the process of federalizing a political community is not sharp enough at the periphery, because as stated it would appear to cover an alliance at one end of the scale and a decentralized unitary state at the other. What is the peculiar federal aspect which distinguishes federalizing from these other processes of governing and deciding? It is essentially the fact that unity is combined with diversity in such fashion that there coexist spheres of autonomy for the inclusive community and the exclusive communities.

In a sense, no such sharp line of demarcation could or should really be drawn from our point of view; for the federalizing process may indeed commence in the forming of a league, such as the Council of Europe or the North German Confederation—not to speak of the confederation which preceded the United States of America. The same applies to decentralization, as in the Austro-Hungarian Empire or the Kingdom of Prussia, or even more significantly in the British Empire, leading to the British Commonwealth of Nations which is presumably a league today, though this turns on how one interprets the role of common Crown. In this connection, the "balance of power" in its broadest sense is of decisive importance. That a league does not eliminate the problem of "balance of power" was amply shown by the experience of the League of Nations.[13] Indeed it may be argued that the presence of an effective "balance" is essential in the formation of federal systems, so as to overcome the internal strains that may arise from rivalries among the states involved in the community which is to be federalized.

Autonomy is here taken in its original meaning as signifying the power and authority, the legitimate right, to govern oneself, but not excluding the participation in a group of similar entities which form in turn an autonomous community. In other words, the autonomy of a community is not considered as impaired by participation in a wider community *if* the sphere of authority of the wider community is instituted, maintained, and altered only with the effective participation of the component community, as likewise the autonomy of the inclusive community is considered unimpaired if its sphere cannot be altered without its effective participation. It is evident that this intertwining of participating communities can only be accomplished within the context of a constitution, and furthermore that it necessarily and significantly divides governmental power and authority over the citizens of such federal (or federated) communities. It is likewise evident that such composite communities will only arise when a comparable pattern of composite needs and interests (objectives) prevails; for this is the meaning of community.

The emphasis on "community" as contrasted with "state" is, of course, decisive. It is in keeping with the federal trend in Europe, where community is spoken of as the uniting base in coal and steel, defense and general politics. It is the Coal and Steel *Community,* the Defense *Community,* and finally the European *Community.*[14] Community is taken here not in terms of the dichotomy so popular in sociology between community and society (or association), but rather in the broader and yet better focused sense of the Aristotelian *koinonia,* where the most inclusive community is that of the *polis* as the archetype of political community.

Only if this coexistence and interaction of a set of political communities as autonomous entities is present do we have genuine federalism. Apparently, such a congeries of autonomous communities is incompatible with the prevailing concepts of sovereignty. It has often been observed that nothing like an Austinian sovereign can be discovered in the United States. The remark holds even more true of Switzerland. Autonomy is incompatible with "sovereignty," as classically defined: indivisible and penultimate (the German doctrine of *Kompetenz-Kompetenz* is merely a version of this, of course). The term autonomy is, we may recall, Kantian; Kant uses it to describe the individual's freedom *under* law. But it is evident that there is also a usage in which sovereignty means simply autonomy, as when the American states are spoken of as sovereign, and in this sense sovereignty is, of course, not only not incompatible but identical with the view here expounded. It may well happen that this will be the "semantic" solution in Europe. Certainly the present trend in various constitutional provisions, such as art. 24,2 of the Basic Law of the German Federal Republic which provides for the transfer of the sovereign rights *(jura majestatis, Hoheitsrechte),* is to envisage a division of sovereignty, although the provisions of the basic law apply only to a "system of collective security" which has rightly been described as a league under international law. The emphasis placed upon the *supranational* character of the authority of the High Authority for Coal and Steel, as well as the corresponding institutions of the European Community and the Defense Community, clearly show that an autonomous sphere is being envisaged both for the inclusive European and for the component national communities; in other words true federalism is implied.[15]

IV

The coexistence of these autonomous political communities, including the inclusive community which comprises them all, cannot, as we just said, be organized except in terms of an explicit constitution of the type now familiar in the West. Such a constitution is a system of effective, regularized restraints upon the exercise of governmental power.[16] This implies, of course, that the government is organized in a particular fashion; but to say that a constitution is the pattern of organization is to miss the crucial point regarding modern constitutionalism. For if constitutionalism is the process by which a constitution is made, including its advocacy and its defense, there can be little doubt that the rise of modern constitutionalism is intimately linked with the problem of how to secure effective and regularized restraints upon governmental action. This is not to deny that there are numerous other conceptions of a constitution which may serve a useful purpose in other contexts, notably the one which speaks of the constitution of an unconstitutional government, as is the case with Aristotle's definition; he thinks of tyranny as having a constitution. In defining constitutionalism as a system of effective, regularized restraints upon governmental action, we have approached a constitution in terms of the function it is supposed to serve in the political community. This means that a constitution is seen as process.

Function and process are closely related and are a modern version of the teleological-genetic approach to social phenomena. Like the latter, the functional-procedural approach is value-oriented without being value-preoccupied. The central value toward which the constitution is oriented is freedom but this value is not the only one; security, for example, is another important value, differentiating constitutionalism from all forms of anarchism. This is the meaning of Proudhon's claim that federalism solves the problem of freedom and authority. Federalism, as a species of constitutionalism, is oriented toward the specific value of the freedom and security of federally recognized communities. Historically these have been territorially defined communities but this aspect is not necessarily implied in the concept. The now forgotten yet highly imaginative idea of the Austrian socialists Otto Bauer, Herrnritt, and Karl Renner for a solution of the nationality problems of the Austrian empire by organizing it in terms of corporative national bodies without defined boundaries but with defined cultural loyalties—a solution which Esthonia tried to utilize in solving its problems in the twenties of this century—is indicative of the broader possibilities of federalism, as was indeed recognized by Althusius, and underlies the practice of many federated associations.[17]

A federal constitution then is a subdivision of the general kind of process involved in modern constitutionalism. The function it is supposed to serve is to restrain the powers wielded by an inclusive community, as well as those of the communities included in it. It is, in a sense, based upon the principle of the division or separation of powers applied on a spatial basis. This aspect of the matter, however, may be hidden by the fact that the need for cooperation is uppermost in the minds of those who establish a federal system out of constituent and previously "sovereign" and "independent" units. They tend to overlook what is obvious in the reverse process of federalizing a preexistent united community, namely that there is felt a strong need for restraining the inclusive community and its powers *in all but a few select spheres of joint interest and joint need*. If we now ask ourselves what is the function of the process of federalizing a community, it is clear that this function consists in combining the inclusive community and the included communities for joint and separate action according to a prearranged plan: its constitution. It thus seeks to combine a maximum of freedom with the necessary authority. But it is not a fixed and unalterable plan.

Since the spheres of joint interest and joint need are likely to undergo a steady evolution in the direction of either greater or lesser joint interest and need, such a constitution is in this respect (as in many others) subject both to formal amendment and to judicial and other official interpretation which may at times be almost imperceptible, except to those immediately concerned. Since these changes are related to the very basis of the federalizing process itself, it is important *not to confuse the process itself* with particular divisions of power and authority which may be characteristic of it under particular circumstances of time and place. A great many of the arguments over whether a particular structure is federal or confederal result from precisely this sort of confusion. Thus Mr. Spaak, in presenting the draft treaty to the foreign ministers on March 10, 1953, observed almost apologetically that this proposed constitution was partly federal and partly confederal.[18] Although politically a highly relevant observation, it is meaningless in terms of the analysis here given. The real issue is whether the European Community's authority is supranational or intergovernmental. The proposed draft treaty clearly envisages federalizing the six nations to which it applies by recognizing that they constitute an inclusive community which it undertakes to organize for the purpose of making autonomous decisions, that is to say, of wielding autonomous powers through its own authorities whose legitimation is derived from the community as a whole, not its component units. At the same time it likewise recognizes that these component units continue to constitute separate political communities with very substantial autonomy in all matters not specifically delegated to the government of the inclusive community. The same is true, of course, in the Coal and Steel and the Defense Community treaties. It is perhaps the most serious obstacle to the final conclusion of a treaty establishing the European (Political) Community that numerous individuals, groups, and certain nations, reared as they have been in the conventional notions of sovereignty, cannot grasp this sort of federalizing process and continue to interpret it as either an association of states or as a decentralized state (in the manner of Bodin).[19]

While the relation of federalism to constitutionalism is thus to be seen as based upon the idea of mutual restraint of the inclusive community and its component units, its relation to democracy is another source of controversy. For those who would, in the manner of absolutism, identify democracy with the absolute and unrestrained will of the majority of a given community are confronted with an unresolvable dilemma by federalism. This probably explains in part the general penchant of radical democrats all over Europe, such as are found in the Labour Party of Great Britain and various Socialist elements of continental Europe, to oppose the federalizing of Europe. For there is no doubt that the "sovereign will" of the British or German electorate might be thwarted if it has to adjust to what other people want or reject. More specifically, socialism may become more difficult of achievement if it has to be achieved on a European plane. The difficulties of federalism in this respect are analogous to those in the field of constitutionalism. They are resolvable in a comparable way. All that is required is to recognize that a given group of individuals A1, A2, A3 . . . and another group B1, B2, B3, . . . "belong" not only to community A and community B but also to community AB which includes them both, it being understood that communities are defined in terms of *common* needs, interests, etc. If that is recognized, the "will" of these individuals cannot then shape communal action through effective participation adequately, unless community AB as well as community A and community B are properly organized. Democracy, far from clashing with federalism, requires it where a composite community, comprising subcommunities, exists.

From a pragmatic standpoint, an effectively centralized government, a decentralized government, a federal government (state), a federation, a confederation or league of governments (states), an alliance, an alignment, a "system" of independent governments (states) such as the European family of nations, and, finally, completely unrelated governments (states) such as Rome and China in the days of Caesar—all these could be represented as differences of degree in the relation of governments to the territory affected by them; the two extremes are complete unity and complete separateness, both marginal cases. Federalism as a process needs to be seen as a number of transitional phases in the middle section of this series; it constitutes a form of political organization suited to communities in which the territorially diversified pattern of objectives, interests, needs, and traditions can be effectively implemented and served by joint community efforts in the pursuit of common objectives, interests, needs, and the cultivation of common traditions. It is therefore this patterning of objectives, interests, and needs which occasions the federalizing of existing community structure either in the direction of greater diversity or of greater unity.

V

If we now inquire what are these common objectives, interests, and needs, we find that they were different for different federations, but there appears to have been always at work the common objective of security, more especially of resisting some outside pressure or threat of a military nature, a potential conquest, as it were, to which all of the potential member communities were alike exposed. Likewise, in cases where the federalizing process involved a loosening of preexisting unity, the continuing need of common defense, at least in part, explains the residue of community which the government at the federal center represents. This common rule of past federalism appears to hold again in the case of the federalizing process which has been going on in Europe in recent years. It might be argued, however, that there is involved here also a kind of "negative" factor springing from past and present rivalries between the communities entering into the federal community. Such rivalries may be associated with a sense of insecurity on the part of the weaker members or they may spring from a continuing desire for predominance or the two may be intermingled. The psychology of France at the present moment seems to be of this complex variety; it is difficult to say how far expressed fears of German predominance may hide actual apprehensions over the prospect of losing her own existent predominance. In any case, federalizing appears as a possible way of overcoming a sense of insecurity prevalent among the partners of a proposed federal union. In cases such as these there may be some advantage in having a strong outsider as the "balancer" of the power balance within the federal system, as suggested above. Such a system is unlikely to evolve into a genuine federal union; the case of Austria-Hungary in relation to the German *Bund* may be cited as a case in point.[20] It is to be expected that there are and may remain security problems (insecurity feelings) between communities which formerly were rivals on the international scene. Some of the weaker members may well be fearful of being absorbed, so that the federalizing process may appear as a species of peaceful penetration and expansion on the part of the stronger member or members. It is instructive, however, that the extended controversies which centered on this issue in the long debates over the large versus small state issue in the Philadelphia Convention proved to have been of relatively small consequence, this particular matter of size not having proved to be a primary problem in the development of American federalism. Likewise, in the case of Germany, Prussia in spite of her early predominance has actually disappeared, having already been brought close to dismemberment in the course of the Weimar Republic's efforts at *Reichsreform*.[21] It would seem that the security of the three small states—Belgium, Netherlands, and Luxembourg —in the Community of the Six is reasonably insured by the close balance of the other three—France, Germany, and Italy—and that these are so closely equilibrated, even though France and Germany are stronger than Italy, that significant predominance, though a convenient argument in the political battle over the community's federal constitution, is not likely to be a primary problem. The primary issue, in other words, is not internal but external security and defense.

Alongside this recurrent common objective of common resistance and common defense, nationalism has in modern times been a powerful factor in providing common objectives, reinforced by common traditions, for a group of independent political communities to federalize.[22] This factor was recurrently and characteristically reinforced by the economic advantages of a larger market for mass-production industries. The latter objective with its symptomatic development of a multitude of common interests may, as a matter of fact, be considered the more important factor in the case of the United States, Australia, and Canada, though nationalism was certainly not absent in these instances.[23]

Special difficulties have arisen in the case of the federalizing process in Europe on the score of nationalism, of course, since it operates here as a divisive force. However, the fact that nationalism is found here on the side of local autonomy does not diminish its importance in the federalizing process in an inverse sense; for the defense and economic needs of Europe call so insistently for European unity that without the national sentiment and traditions not a federal but a unitary government would presumably arise from the communal interests and needs of Europe as a whole. Certainly nationalism has operated to prevent the uniting of Europe on any other basis.[24]

When the particularistic local objectives are sufficiently strong and compact to hold together the territorial subdivisions of the more inclusive community, sustaining them or molding them into autonomous communities, while at the same time the common objectives are sufficiently strong and compact to hold the inclusive community together too, then the federalizing process will set in and manifest itself in a structure which may be called federational. There is a typical form which such composite communities adopt as best suited to the organizing, dividing, and restraining of powers. These structural particularities are not unrelated to the fact that, historically speaking, federal systems evolved from leagues or associations of governments (states). It was so in the United States, in Switzerland, and in the Netherlands. In view of this, it is not surprising to find that typically the organizational features of a league are found prevalent in the governmental structure of federal communities.[25] In a sense it could be said, therefore, that the institutional pattern of a league survives in a federal system. It shapes the structure in the direction of "organized diversity." Hence, the understanding of federalism calls for a brief institutional analysis of such leagues.

VI

A comparative study of many such composite communities reveals that there usually are found (1) a charter or constitution defining the "unity in diversity," and more especially setting up the organization of the federal authorities, namely (2) an assembly of representatives of the constituent communities, making rules (legislating) to implement the charter, (3) an executive establishment of some sort to carry out the decisions of the assembly, and (4) an arbitral or judicial body interpreting the charter.

In the early phases of the unifying process which leads to federalism (when there exists a league or a confederation that is being established), all these assemblies have one characteristic in common, the equal representation of the member communities, although there are occasional slight exceptions.[26] The rationale for this equality is that if the smaller communities had not been given equality they would either have refused to join or would have broken away. It will be recognized that these are precisely the issues which have been confronting the Europeans in trying to find an equitable solution to the problem of representation in terms of some species of equalizing proportionality, since the component communities vary so much in size. An interesting compromise has been worked out between this complete equality of the communities and the equality of the citizens of the inclusive community. Usually in the more advanced stages of the federalizing process two representative bodies are combined, one to represent the component communities as equals, the other the citizens of the inclusive community as equal. This is the situation in Australia, in Switzerland, and in the United States, to mention only a few. But in the draft treaty as proposed in March 1953 for a European Community (as in the Coal and Steel Community), neither the equality of the communities nor that of the European citizens is fully recognized; instead a compromise on both positions has led to the establishment of two houses, both based upon the principle of proportionality modified in the direction of equality (or equality modified in the direction of proportionality, if one prefers). As a result, the need for equality has reasserted itself in the retention of a Council of National Ministers. (See below.)

As far as the common executive is concerned,[27] communities in the process of federalizing typically develop an executive establishment for the inclusive community which tends to become the spearhead of the process itself. Characteristically, this executive is not intergovernmental but separate and apart from the governments of the component communities. The trend is promoted not only by the vested interests growing up around such an executive (whether in the form of positions, prestige, or material advantages) but also by the greater insight into the objectives, interests, and needs of the inclusive community. The advantages of a developed and responsible bureaucracy which are recurrent in the growth of modern organization, and more especially of government, thus accrue to and tend to advance the inclusive federalized community.[28] Naturally, the characteristics of this executive will be influenced by the nature of the task assigned to it on the basis of the objectives, interests, and needs of the federal community. It thus may be military, or economic, or more broadly political, or even ecclesiastical. Typically, a federal executive may be selected with the active participation of representatives of the component communities which may also be charged with participating in the execution of federal decisions under federal supervision of varying degrees of efficiency. Thus, in the proposed European Community treaty, as in the Coal and Steel Community, the federal executive is chosen by the joint action of a legislative body of a composite nature as just described, and the execution may either be carried out by administrative services of the European Community or by the administrative services of the several component states.[29] Furthermore, none of the component communities can be represented by more than two members in the federal executive. These provisions parallel constitutional practices in Canada and Switzerland.[30] But the treaty does not provide for minimum representation as is the case in Canada and Switzerland. (By contrast, the executive of the Council of Europe is essentially intergovernmental, i.e., a secretariat of a league, thus indicative of an early phase of unification preceding federalism where the functions of the executive are not so much executive as diplomatic and liaison functions between governments which have remained completely "sovereign.")

All federal systems finally possess a judicial or arbitral body to settle disputes concerning the meaning and interpretation of the charter which the other federal authorities and custom are not able to compose.[31] Typically, the participation of the component communities in the selection (and dismissal) of such a body and/or its members is vigorous in proportion to the extent of local autonomy. Such participation may be restricted to participation in the legislation under which the judicial body operates, as in the United States, or it may leave to authorities of the local communities a substantial share of the appointing power. But however created, the judicial body is characteristically a court of last resort, and as a consequence tends to forward the federalizing process, where it is centralizing, and retard it, where it is decentralizing in its general direction. But in either case its impact is limited in scope. Under the draft treaty for the European Community as submitted in 1953, the High Court is chosen with the participation of the Senate representing the component communities, upon nomination of the several states on an equal basis. This court is, of course, not restricted to an arbitral function since the Community has legislative functions; the scope of its jurisdiction is therefore broadly that of the inclusive community's field of activity.[32] Primarily, its jurisdiction is concerned with "conflicts between the states, or between one or more states and the Community." But it also has significant powers over individuals who are citizens of the member states. This direct jurisdiction is of very great importance in establishing the "Community." (The position of the Court in the Coal and Steel Community is similar.)

VII

These few brief references to some of the provisions of the European Community treaty as approved by the Ad Hoc Consultative Assembly in 1953 are not intended to serve any more technical purpose than to indicate by concrete illustration how the federalizing process which we have identified as the realistically important core of federalism presumably will work out, if the Community becomes effectively organized. It may not be amiss, however, to indicate briefly some of the issues which have been causing special difficulties. One very typical and central issue is that of the admission of new communities (states) to the Community, as well as the "right of secession." The latter is by many felt to be the touchstone of whether we have a federal or a confederal community. Unquestionably it is an important issue and the decision of the drafters to omit reference to it is an important victory for the more radical proponents of the federalizing of Europe. Indeed, the issue has been raised by some of the opponents of ratification of the draft treaty. But in the light of the foregoing analysis it is clear that the issue is not decisive. At the beginning of the federalizing process the ability to secede (regardless of the formal right) will obviously exist; it will decline as the process goes forward and will tend to disappear as the inclusive community is extended to ever widening spheres of the common life.

Another issue is that of the conditions of adherence. Evidently, there is much to be said for making the European Community of the Six grow to be coincidental with the European Council's sphere of the fifteen, and more especially to include Great Britain in the European Community. Yet, as a matter of fact these other communities, and more especially Great Britain, do not, for a variety of reasons, at present desire to enter into the Community; that is to say, they are not ready for the federalizing process which it involves. In recognition of these contradictory "wills," the proposed treaty does two things, both quite in keeping with a realistic conception of the federalizing process. On one hand, it makes it very easy for any European state to join the Community; all it needs is the "will" to do so and the readiness to maintain the basic rights and fundamental freedoms agreed upon by the Council of Europe.[33] On the other hand, the European Community is prepared to recognize associated members who, because of mutually acknowledged close ties of interest and need, are ready to enter into close treaty relations with the Community. Such associated members would actually acquire the right to participate in the decisions of the Community, both on the legislative and the executive level, in a variety of ways, notably in the Council of Ministers and the Senate. This rather novel status obviously is intended to facilitate the early involvement of as many of the component communities of Europe as possible in the federalizing process.[34]

The Council of Ministers has been mentioned earlier in this chapter only as an adjunct of the European executive. Actually, a good deal of the most pointed controversy has raged over this particular body. Composed as it would be of ministers of the component communities to whose separate parliaments it would be responsible, its extended jurisdiction scattered through the proposed constitution and usually based upon unanimous agreement, this council has seemed to many (including the writer) to be a most unfortunate institution.[35] By its defenders, however, it is seen as a most important link to the several communities and their governments. The Germans see it as the starting point for a development paralleling their own in which such a council has played a vital role from the day of the Empire to the present.[36] The smaller countries see it as a valuable instrument of protection against being ruled by the larger ones. Finally, the French look upon it as a guardian against domination by the Germans. Actually, all that the establishment (or rather maintenance) of such a council signifies is a brake on the federalizing process. It will slow a variety of decisions and open the door to extensive administrative logrolling. But it may be considered doubtful whether some of these effects can be adequately assessed at the present time in terms of whether they imperil or insure the success of the proposed federal community. For experience shows that the federalizing process can be imperiled both by too great speed and by too great delays. What should in any case be clear from our general analysis is that to assess the establishment of such a council in terms of the formal dichotomy of a federal versus a confederal structure is to engage in dogmatism.

This may be illustrated by two concrete further instances of provisions that are part and parcel of the federalizing process as here envisaged. One is the problem of citizenship and the mobility within the federal territory connected with it. There were those who argued that only establishment of a European citizenship would meet the requirements of a "true" federal union, while others insisted that such citizenship was completely out of the question. The proposed Community treaty sets forth a rather ingenious compromise which, it must be admitted, is still being hotly debated after having secured acceptance only with considerable difficulty. This compromise provides that any European who has completed his military service in the European forces or who is born after the treaty comes into effect will have complete freedom of movement and enjoy the right to establish domicile in any member state under the same conditions as its nationals. The question of citizenship as such is left open.[37] This is considerably less than the dual citizenship characteristic for such close-knit federal communities as the United States, or even the degree of economic equality found in Switzerland. But if accepted it would constitute a substantial step forward in the direction of federalizing Europe. It may, however, be questioned whether a less radical proposal, which would include all the citizens of the component communities, would not be preferable at this time. If European citizenship is beyond the reach of practical politics, then the elimination of passports, the right to reside and to acquire citizenship in another of the member communities upon preferential terms, and the like might prove more valuable in the long run, while at the same time appearing more acceptable at present. For to grant complete equality even to members of the armed forces may cause serious tensions in the communities affected.

The other concrete and highly controversial aspect of the proposed community we might speak of in this connection is that of overseas territories and colonial possessions. It is well-known that these possessions caused considerable trouble in connection with both the Coal and Steel treaty and the European Defense Community treaty. Indeed, with reference to the latter they have proved one of the two most serious stumbling blocks.[38] The question as to how to fit them into the European Community is indeed formidable. In the past, federalism has not been troubled by this issue. In Australia, Canada, Germany, Switzerland, and the United States, such possessions were either nonexistent or of such limited importance as to cause no serious problem.[39] But for France and Belgium the issue is a vital one. The obvious alternative is to say: either these possessions are brought into the European Community or they are left outside (as is the case of the two treaties just mentioned). Unfortunately neither of these alternatives recommends itself as a solution. For either would confront the colonial power with unprecedented problems for which she is unprepared. These problems are part and parcel of the universal problem of the evolution of such colonial and dependent territories throughout the world. For they aspire to equality, if not to independence, and either including them in or excluding them from the European Community would precipitate this issue. The draft of the proposed treaty submitted in 1953 seeks to compromise it. It leaves to the several states the right to exclude, by unilateral declaration, any territory from the treaty's application. It also gives to a member the right to "adapt" legislation and other decisions to the non-European territories under its jurisdiction which it has not excluded from the union.[40] It also permits such a member state to make applicable by special act such European statutes as it wishes to its excluded territories, but only by agreement with the Community. It is evident that these somewhat complicated provisions are intended to provide a considerable variety of possible transitions for these dependent and associated territories. It may be added that the provisions for association with the Community (see above) also envisage the possibility that non-European states might become thus associated, if they have constitutional bonds with the associated or member state. It is evident that this provision would, for example, make it possible for a state in the French Union, or a member of the British Commonwealth such as Canada, to become an associated member of the European Community.[41] These several provisions make the European Community treaty a better instrument for the effective federalizing of the national communities involved than is the Defense Community treaty. Both those provisions for overseas territories and those for limited equality of economic status are clearly inspired by the notion that federalizing Europe is an extended process and that for these perplexing issues of how to transform a group of completely autonomous communities into a federal community a series of transitional steps must be made available so as to facilitate the process.

If federalism implies the process of federalizing a group of communities and thus building a federal community, then obviously the relative flexibility of any formal constitutional arrangements is of crucial importance. As the history of past federal experience amply demonstrates, there must exist adequate opportunities for changing the constitution. At the same time, such amendments of the constitutional charter ought (a) not to be too easy, lest public confidence in the federal system be undermined, and (b) to provide for the full participation of the component communities as well as the inclusive one in the process of amendment. For it should always be borne in mind that a federal system arises from, that is to say, is constituted by a federal community, a composite community in other words. In such a composite community, the "constituent power" is also composite and the amending power needs to be molded here, as always, upon the structure of the constituent power.[42] The proposed constitution of the European Community fully recognizes the complexity of its own composition. In fact, it subdivides the constitutional amendments into three different categories: basic amendments, institutional amendments, and ordinary amendments.[43] The basic amendments are those concerned with the changes in the competency (power or jurisdiction) of the Community and with fundamental rights and liberties of the individual. The institutional amendments are those which are concerned with a modification of the relations between the institutions of the Community, that is to say the separation of powers, be this a modification of the division of their respective competencies (powers or jurisdiction) or be it a change which would seem to affect the guarantees which the member states find either in the composition or the functioning of these institutions. The remainder is left undefined and would not seem to concern anything of real consequence for the federalizing process as such. These ordinary amendments are accomplished by regular legislative process and need not detain us here. As concerns the others, the apparent compromise is based upon the following division: basic amendments are made very difficult, indeed, by requiring the unanimous consent of the Council of Ministers for a proposal to be made by the Executive Council of the Community which then has to be submitted to all the national parliaments as well as the parliament of the Community, so that any one of the component communities is put in the position of being able to block an extension of the competencies (jurisdiction, power) of the Community.

If one recalls the history of constitutional amendments in the United States, where only three-fourths of the components' assent is required, this seems a most questionable provision, calculated to impede if not to thwart the federalizing process. Indeed, these provisions could be made an argument for maintaining that federalism would not be achieved for the European Community under this treaty, were it not for the fact that the Court is given the power to decide which procedure is applicable for a particular amendment as well as the power to interpret the constitution generally. Unfortunately, institutional amendments also call for the unanimous consent of the Council of National Ministers, although not that of the national parliaments. Considering that every one of the component states has a parliamentary system of government, this does not appear to be much of a relaxation, for it can be assumed that usually and according to the rules of the game the government and the parliamentary majority which supports it move in harmony with each other.

The rigid arrangements for these amending processes would not be as serious as they in fact are if the grants of power to the European Community were broadly phrased and fundamentally adequate for a federal community. Such is unfortunately not the case. Coal and steel and defense apart, the provisions of the treaty are severely restrictive. They only make a beginning in the matters of a common foreign policy and common market, virtually rule out a common currency and credit system, and are wholly unsatisfactory in the field of federal finance where the treaty makes the Community depend upon contributions by the component states to implement a wholly unsatisfactory provision for taxes. For all taxes require the unanimous consent of the Council of National Ministers as do these contributions. No account was taken, apparently, of the unfortunate experience of the German Empire with such a system of contributions which proved a stumbling block to sound finance.[44] It is obvious that the European Community is completely hamstrung, financially, by these requirements. This is the more serious since the Community is presumably going to be in charge of defense which at present calls for about a third of the resources of all the component states. To set the stage for an annual wrangle between the component units under the handicaps of a unanimity requirement would seem to invite disaster, as well as to jeopardize the federalizing process as such.

It is the cumbersome, not to say unworkable, amendment process that forces one to take a most critical view of the proposed constitution as that of a viable federalism. It is, of course, possible that the vigor of European sentiment in the component communities will overcome these obstacles, but it is more likely that discouragement followed by disgust will be the result, as it has been in the sequel of the ill-constructed Council of Europe in which constructive change is likewise made virtually impossible by the requirement of unanimous action by the Committee of Ministers.[45]

VIII

Federalism can be, and often has been, a highly dynamic process by which emergent composite communities have succeeded in organizing themselves by effectively institutionalizing "unity in diversity." That such a community, emergent and composite, exists in Europe today is fairly evident. That it has as yet found an appropriate constitutional crystallization is more than doubtful. While the Coal and Steel Community and the proposed Defense Community, implemented by the Political Community as suggested in the draft treaty of March 10, 1953 which we have analyzed, represent steps in the direction of launching this composite community upon the road of an effective federalizing process, serious doubts must be entertained as to whether Europe has yet reached this stage in its evolution. Certainly the Council of Europe, the Organization for European Economic Cooperation, the European Payments Union, and the North Atlantic Pact all remained on the level of treaty arrangements under international law. Whether they launched Europe upon a genuine federalizing process remains uncertain.

This process, thoroughly dynamic in character, implies, as we have tried to show, the effective organizing of an inclusive community possessing its own *autonomous* sphere. Nor may this sphere be so narrow as to be at the mercy of the component communities in fact. Thus, such a community must, for example, be authorized to levy its own taxes so that the revenue required for its operations be not dependent upon the cooperation of every one of the component communities. In the case of Europe, such a community and its organs would be supranational, since the component member communities are national communities. No merely intergovernmental arrangements will suffice. To be sure, in the case of the Coal and Steel Community (as well as that of the Defense and Political Community proposed), there are elements of such supranational structure; nevertheless, in the light of the shortcomings of the proposed treaties, serious doubt must be entertained as to whether these supranational elements in the treaties suffice to launch the six nations upon a genuine federalizing process. Certainly, a comparison between the proposed European set-up and the existing federal systems suggests very grave deficiencies.

John Milton once wrote, in a rather different context and to different purpose, in contrasting the commonwealth he dreamed about with the United Netherlands as they existed then, that it would be "many commonwealths under one united and intrusted sovereignty," rather than "many sovereignties united in one commonwealth." This was the ancient alternative which thinks in terms of "sovereignty" which must be one and indivisible. A conception of federalism in dynamic terms seeks to avoid this alternative, fits the notion of federalism as process into the notion of constitutionalism as process, and understands the relation between the inclusive community and the component communities as a system of regularized restraint upon the exercise of governmental power so as to make power and responsibility correlative with the structure of a composite and dynamic community, its interests, and needs.

FOOTNOTES TO CHAPTER 26

The following notes are limited to specific references. For a general bibliography, see *Studies in Federalism,* edited by R. R. Bowie and C. J. Friedrich, Boston, Little, Brown, 1954, and published in French under the title *Etudes sur le fédéralisme,* Editions du Comité d'Etudes pour la Constitution Européenne, 7 vols., Bruxelles, Movement Européen, 1952–53. (These studies will be cited as SF hereafter.)

1. See for all this the author's *Constitutional Government and Democracy,* Revised edition, Boston, Ginn, 1950, chaps. 7–13, where the theory of constitutionalism underlying this paper is developed. For the Commonwealth, cf. the illuminating recent discussion in *The American Political Science Review,* Vol. 47 (1953), pp. 997–1040, with contributions by H. Duncan Hall, K. C. Wheare, and Alexander Brady; they write, however, in terms of a looser concept of federalism devoid of the requirement of a "written" constitution.

2. The classic discussion in *The Federalist* occurs in Nos. 9, 10, 39, 40, and 41, but the terminology is somewhat antiquated; for Hamilton speaks there of the United States as a confederacy, and of its constitution as confederate-republican—a term derived from Montesquieu. It must be remembered also that Hamilton was seeking to persuade people who were reluctant to enter into the union. For the discussion of federalism in Germany in terms of sovereignty, see Rupert Emerson, *State and Sovereignty in Modern Germany,* New Haven, Yale University Press, 1928, especially chapter 3, entitled "Federalism." For Calhoun, see John C. Calhoun, *A Disquisition on Government* (1851). His argument was taken over by Max von Seydel, "Der Bundesstaatsbegriff," in *Zeitschrift fuer die gesammte Staatswissenschaft,* Vol. 28 (1872), pp. 185–256, who insisted that sovereignty was indivisible, and that therefore the component states remained sovereign; the argument was turned around by P. Laband and G. Jellinek who insisted upon the sovereignty of the Reich. See for all this Emerson, *op. cit.,* pp. 96 ff.

3. See for the problem, Hermann von Mangoldt, *Das Bonner Grundgesetz,* Berlin, Vahlen, 1950–53, Part II, pp. 125–131, 182–203, 216–222, 262–292 (on the Federal Council), 368–443 (legislation), and *passim.* Cf. also the author's

"The Constitution of the German Federal Republic" and "The Evolution of Post-war Government," in Edward H. Litchfield and Associates, *Governing Postwar Germany*, Ithaca, Cornell University Press, 1953.

4. Besides the leading texts on constitutional law, see the literature cited in C. J. Friedrich, *Constitutional Government and Democracy*, Rev. ed., 1950, chap. 11. (Cited hereafter as CGD.)

5. See Emerson, *op. cit.*, chaps. 1 and 2, and the literature cited there.

6. See my introduction to *Johannes Althusius'* (*Althaus*) *Politica Methodice Digesta*, reprinted from the third edition of 1614, Cambridge, Harvard University Press, 1932, *passim*, and the chapter on the history of the idea of federalism in Otto von Gierke's *Johannes Althusius und die Entwicklung der naturrechtlichen Staatstheorien*, (1880), chap. 5 (translated by Bernard Freyd as *The Development of Political Theory*, New York, W. W. Norton, 1939). Gierke's treatment is influenced by his preoccupation with the German *Bundesstaat* discussion; this in turn is linked with the problem of state sovereignty. See Emerson, *op. cit.*, ch. 4. S. Brie's well-known *Der Bundesstaat*, Leipzig, 1874, gives a brief history of federalism, limited by the same preoccupation with the "state." The doctrine of the *res publica composita* which was developed by Althusius' followers,—Gierke notes especially Hoenonius, Besold, and Hugo (whom Brie had hailed as the founder of the *Bundesstaat* theory), *op. cit.*, pp. 245–247,—is credited with embodying the idea of the "federal state" as contrasted with Althusius' general theory of federalism. From our standpoint this was not progress but a retrogression, due to the introduction of the "state" concept.

7. For Bodin, see Pierre Mesnard, *L'Essor de la philosophie politique du XVIe siècle*, Paris, Boivin, 1936, pp. 473–546, and a recent and as yet unpublished dissertation by Kenneth D. McRae, "The Political Thought of Jean Bodin" (1953) in the Harvard archives which supersedes earlier writings. The discussion of Switzerland is found in Jean Bodin, *Six Livres de la Republique* (1576).

8. For discussions in Grotius, see *De Jure Belli ac Pacis* (1625) where they are scattered throughout; see especially Book II, chs. 5–6,4; 8; 15, 5 & 12; 20. The discussion in Gierke is found on p. 215 of the work cited.

9. Montesquieu's views are found in Book IX, chaps. 1–3. He links federalism primarily to the need for defense. Montesquieu expresses the view that it is suited for republics, rather than monarchies, and notes its value in restraining tyrannical usurpations.

10. For this see C. J. Friedrich, *Inevitable Peace*, Cambridge, Harvard University Press, 1948, especially chapter 6 which deals with Saint Pierre, Rousseau, and Kant. To the literature cited there must now be added J. L. Talmon, *The Rise of Totalitarian Democracy*, Boston, Beacon Press, 1952, a brilliant study devoted to the "totalitarian" ingredient in Rousseau and his followers. Talmon's emphasis of this side of Rousseau characteristically keeps him from considering the federalist aspects of Rousseau.

11. For the quotation see *Du principe fédératif et de la nécessité de reconstituer le parti de la Révolution* (1863), republished with an introduction and notes by Jean Charles-Brun, Collection des chefs-d'oeuvres méconnus, 1921, pp. 104–105. Proudhon's viewpoint, like that of Althusius, is based upon the universalisation of the principle of contract, and as he points out the particular kind of contract which the *Code Civil* calls *synallagmatique*, or bilateral, *communative*, or mutual (as contrasted with unilateral, onerous, or gratuitous contracts). That is to say, Proudhon based his federalist thinking upon civil law conceptions of contract which are at variance with common law views. As Roscoe Pound has said: "As the civil

law has been at its best in the law of contracts and has treated torts on a contract theory, the common law has been at its best in the law of torts and has treated contracts on a tort theory." (*Encyclopedia of the Social Sciences*, 4, p. 329.) The same holds for Althusius, of course. On Proudhon's importance see also the interesting article by Michel Moushkély, "La théorie du fédéralisme," in *La technique et les principes du droit public*, Etudes en l'honneur de Georges Scelle, Paris, Librairie générale de droit et de jurisprudence, Vol. I, 1950, where this point is not stressed, however.

12. SF XVI.

13. See C. J. Friedrich, *Foreign Policy in the Making*, New York, W. W. Norton, 1938, especially chap. 5, for a theory of balance.

14. The term was the subject of a magisterial inquiry by Robert M. MacIver, *Community*, 3rd ed., London, Macmillan, 1924, but in juxtaposition to the state which the same author discusses in *The Modern State*, Oxford, Clarendon Press, 1926.

15. An English translation of the text of the *Treaty Constituting the European Coal and Steel Community* (ECSC) and of the *Treaty Constituting the European Defense Community*, (EDC) are available in a U.S. Senate Document, dated June 2, 1952 and issued for the Committee on Foreign Relations. For the point here made see the preambles. For the Basic law, see Mangoldt, *op. cit.*, p. 164.

16. CGD, chap. 7.

17. See R. Herrmann von Herrnritt, *Nationalitaet und Recht*, Vienna, Manz, 1899; Karl Renner, *Das Selbstbestimmungsrecht der Nationen*, Leipzig, Deuticke, 1918; and Otto Bauer, *Die Nationalitaetenfrage und die Sozialdemokratie*, 2nd ed., Vienna, Wiener Volksbuchhandlung, 1924. See also Henry Meyer Magid, *English Political Pluralism*, New York, Columbia University Press, 1941, *passim*. Harold D. Lasswell and Abraham Kaplan, *Power and Society*, New Haven, Yale University Press, 1950, p. 225, have characteristically no way of appreciating the role of the federalizing process, since their approach is in terms of power primarily.

18. See *Draft Treaty for a European Community* (hereafter cited as DTEC), p. 150. The same, of course, may be said of the ECSC and the EDC. See *Documentation* on the European questions in general, published by the Council of Europe, November 1952.

19. The point here made finds expression in the "Resolution on Institutions" of The Second Hague Congress of the European Movement, October 1953, when it insists upon the "supranational" authority of the executive and legislative powers the draft treaty proposes. In the same sense the High Authority of the Coal and Steel Community has been highly insistent upon the supranational character of its authority.

20. The development of this point owes much to discussion with J. Liska, at present writing a dissertation on equilibrium theory. He put the matter rather pointedly this way: "The enemy is to be 'disarmed' or 'neutralized' either by military destruction, a politico-military encirclement, or by a federal embrace, . . . there can be a very tenuous dividing line between federal integration and war . . ."

21. See for this Arnold Brecht's *Federalism and Regionalism in Germany*, New York, Oxford University Press, 1945, and the literature cited there.

22. It is therefore only natural that the leading advocate of European unification since the twenties, Count Coudenhove-Kalergi, should have recently urged the development of a European nation of which he delineates the beginnings in his book *Die Europäische Nation*, Stuttgart, Deutsche Verlagsanstalt, 1953. The term

European Nation has cropped up in various speeches and is countered by the entrenched nationalists, like de Gaulle, by such remarks as de Gaulle's recent quip about Jean Monnet when in speaking of him he remarked that the European army was advocated only by "men without a country" (*N. Y. Times*, November 13, 1953).

23. The economic aspects of European unification are especially stressed by two organizations, the European League for Economic Cooperation and the European Committee for Economic and Social Progress, the former including representatives from all the fifteen nations composing the Council of Europe, the latter only representatives from the six nations composing the Coal and Steel Community. Some of the work of these organizations as well as other significant aspects of economic unification are documented in *Europaarchiv,* now in its ninth volume, a most valuable source. Among official publications, those of the OEEC (Organization for European Economic Cooperation) are most important, as are those of the High Authority for Coal and Steel.

24. See C. J. Friedrich "European Unity and European Tradition," in *Confluence,* Vol. 2 (1953), and the publications of the European Institute for Cultural Cooperation in Geneva, especially *Bulletin du Centre Européen de la Culture,* Mars 1952.

25. See CGD, pp. 191 ff.

26. This and the following institutional analogies which are really developmental patterns are discussed in CGD, chap. 11, where some literature is given. For the legislative power under existing federalisms, see SF I.

27. See SF II.

28. Cf. besides CGD, chaps. 2–6, Robert K. Merton's *Reader in Bureaucracy,* Glencoe, The Free Press, 1952, and the literature cited in those books.

29. See DTEC, arts. 7, 105, 106, 56–66, 69 & 74, 88–9, and elsewhere. For the ECSC, see arts. 6, 14, 16, 86, 88; cf. EDC 112–116.

30. SF II.

31. SF III, *passim.*

32. See DTEC, art. 38 ff., especially art. 41. This set of provisions is in sharp contrast to the situation of the Council of Europe; the treaty establishing it contains no comparable provisions. It thus is even weaker than many leagues, or confederations, have been in the past. The proposed judicial body for protecting the fundamental rights of the citizens in the several participating communities, while accepted by an increasing number of participating states, has not come into full operation. See *Europe Today and Tomorrow,* International Bulletin of the European Movement, for current progress in this field. It is, however, in keeping with the situation in the ECSC. See arts. 31, 33, 36–44, 92.

33. See DTEC, art. 116.

34. See DTEC, arts. 90–93. There is an apparent analogy here to the statute of Puerto Rico under the American constitution, as recently worked out; Puerto Rico describes herself as an associated state. But in point of fact Puerto Rico is subject to federal legislation, as well as the U.S. Constitution, and its status cannot be compared at all. See *The Annals,* Vol. 285 (January 1953), "Puerto Rico: A Study in Democratic Development."

35. See, *inter alia,* the following articles: 24,2; 44; 60,2; 69,2; 70,2; 70,3; 78; 80; 84,2; 84,3; 87; 91,1; 93; 99; 104; 111,2; 112,2; 116,2; 116,3; 117,5. Note also the corresponding provisions in the two protocols attached to the treaty. A

similar council with comparable powers is recognized in the ECSC (arts. 26–30 and in the EDC (arts. 39–50).

36. CGD, chap. 11, pp. 201–4, and the literature cited there. Interesting comments on the debate over the retention of this system are found in von Mangoldt *op. cit.,* pp. 262–273. There continues to be vigorous disagreement among Germans over the wisdom of continuing this institution.

37. In terms of Aristotle's conception of citizenship, as developed in his *Politics,* the fact of voting and thus participating in the affairs of the European community as equals is the decisive one, and all the citizens of the six member countries become Europe's citizens by this determining fact. See *Politics,* Bk. III, ch. 2.

38. See ECSC, art. 79 (limiting treaty to European territories) and EDC, arts. 10–1, 13, 120–2. The problem is also briefly discussed in SF XIV.

39. See SF XIV, *passim.*

40. See DTEC, art. 101. The analogy to Puerto Rico is more significant in this instance because here too it is recognized that federal legislation may be "locally inapplicable." Formally, the determination of this inapplicability is left to the U.S. Congress, but in point of fact it is determined by the Puerto Rican authorities themselves, advising the Congress through their authorized representative in Congress. It is a question, though, whether this right should not now be formalized, as has been urged in the Trusteeship Council of the United Nations. See for all this, Rupert Emerson, "Puerto Rico and American Policy Toward Dependent Areas," *The Annals,* January 1953, pp. 9–15 and C. J. Friedrich, "Autonomy for Puerto Rico," *Dalhousie Review,* Vol. 33 (1953), p. 12.

41. See DTEC, art. 90.

42. See CGD, chap. 8, where the doctrine of the constituent power in its relation to the amending power is elaborated.

43. See DTEC, arts. 110–114. By contrast, the treaty establishing the Council of Europe can only be amended by regular treaty procedure, involving the unanimous consent (through ratification) of all member states. The ECSC and the EDC are similarly organized as to amendments. See art. 96 and art. 125 respectively. However, there is a limited right of minor amendments given to the Council (of National Ministers) by both the ECSC and art. 95 and the EDC treaty art. 125. On the whole the provisions for amendment in both treaties are so rigid and so definitely tied to ratification by unanimous vote of all the member communities that a serious doubt remains as to whether these treaties do in fact create "communities" of an inclusive sort.

44. See SF VII, and the literature cited there.

45. The unsatisfactory arrangements for amendments were the subject of a suggestion for improvement in the Resolution on Institutions, adopted by the Second Hague Congress, dated October 10, 1953, which after declaring itself in favor of the draft treaty, nonetheless felt it desirable to state that it "considered it indispensable that these institutions could be revised by procedures sufficiently flexible to permit their adaptation and functioning." (Translated from the French by the author.) See Deuxième Congrès de La Haye, Resolution sur les Institutions #4, Dec 12, (Def.)

Participants in the Bicentennial Conference on Federalism

(*Bicentennial Conference No. 2*)

Arden House—January 11–14, 1954

WILLIAM ANDERSON, Professor of Political Science, University of Minnesota. President, American Political Science Association, 1942. Member of the committee on federal-state relations of the Commission on the Organization of the Executive Branch of the Government (Hoover Commission), 1947–48. Member of Commission on Intergovernmental Relations, 1953–54. Author, in addition to standard texts on municipal and national government, of *The Units of Government of the United States,* 1934; *Federalism and Intergovernmental Relations,* 1946. Co-Director (with Edward W. Weidner) of the six-year project for the study of intergovernmental relations as illustrated in Minnesota.

FRANK BANE, Executive Director, Council of State Governments, since 1938. Director of Public Welfare, Knoxville, 1923–26. State Commissioner of Public Welfare, Virginia, 1926–32. Director, American Public Welfare Association, 1932–35. Executive Director, Federal Social Security Board, 1935–38. Director, division of state and local cooperation, Advisory Commission of Council of National Defense, 1940–41.

VINCENT M. BARNETT, JR., Professor of Political Science, Williams College. Recently Economic Counsellor, U. S. Embassy, Rome, Italy. Executive Assistant to the Program Vice Chairman, War Production Board, 1943–45.

JOHN E. BEBOUT, Assistant Secretary, National Municipal League. Executive Secretary, New Jersey Commission on Constitutional Revision, 1942. Executive Vice President, New Jersey Constitution Foundation, 1942–45. Director, Citizens League of Cleveland and Cleveland Bureau of Governmental Research, 1945–46. Author: *Documents and Readings in New Jersey Government,* 1931; *The Making of the New Jersey Constitution,* 1945.

ADOLF A. BERLE, JR., Member of the New York Bar and Professor in the Columbia Law School. Assistant Secretary of State, 1938–44. Ambassador to Brazil, 1945–46. Author, among other works, of *Natural Selection of Political Forces,* 1950.

FREDERICK L. BIRD, Director of Municipal Research, Dun and Bradstreet, Inc. Chairman, Temporary Commission on the Fiscal Affairs of State Government (N.Y.). Author: *The Recall of Public Officers,* 1930; *Taxation and Public Policy,* 1936; *The Port of New York Authority,* 1948, and other works.

ROY BLOUGH, Principal Director, Department of Economic Affairs,

United Nations. Director of tax research, U. S. Treasury Department, 1938–46. Member, President's Council of Economic Advisers, 1950–52. Professor of Economics, University of Chicago, 1946–52. Author of: *Facing the Tax Problem* (with others), 1937; *The Federal Taxing Process*, 1952.

AHMED SHAH BOKHARI, Ambassador of Pakistan, as head of its permanent mission to the United Nations since 1950. Professor of English Literature at the National College, Lahore, for many years. Director General of the All-India Radio during war years. Leader, Pakistani delegation, Indian Office Partition Negotiations, London, 1947. Commonwealth Relations Conference, Toronto, 1949.

ROBERT R. BOWIE, On leave as Professor of Law in the Harvard Law School, serving as Director of the Policy Planning Staff, U.S. Department of State. Assistant Attorney General of Maryland, 1941–42. Special Assistant to the Military Governor for Germany. Member of the committee on regulatory commissions of the Hoover Commission, 1948. General Counsel and Special Adviser to the U.S. High Commissioner for Germany, 1950–51. Co-director (with Carl J. Friedrich) of the Harvard project for research on federalism in conjunction with the European Movement.

ALEXANDER BRADY, Professor of Political Science, University of Toronto. Author of: *Democracy in the Dominions*, 1947, and other studies.

JOHN BARTLET BREBNER, Professor of History, Columbia University. Engaged in survey of Canadian-American Relations under Carnegie Endowment for International Peace, 1932–43. President Canadian Historical Association, 1939–40. Author: *New England's Outpost—Acadia before the Conquest of Canada*, 1927; *The Explorers of North America*, 1933; *The Neutral Yankees of Nova Scotia*, 1937; *North Atlantic Triangle—The Interplay of Canada, the U.S. and Great Britain*, 1945.

ARNOLD BRECHT, Professor of Political Science, graduate faculty, New School for Social Research. Held high executive positions in Germany as a non-partisan official, 1910–33. Author, among other studies, of *Prelude to Silence: The End of the German Republic*, 1944; *Federalism and Regionalism in Germany*, 1945.

JOHN EDWARD BURTON, Vice-President of Cornell University and Chairman, New York Power Authority since 1950. Budget Director of New York State, 1943–50. Member, Governor's Committee on State-Local Fiscal Relations, 1945; committee on federal-state relationships of the Commission on the Organization of the Executive Branch (Hoover Commission), 1947–48. President, National Association of State Budget Officers, 1946. Member of Commission on Intergovernmental Relations, 1953–54.

SIR CECIL THOMAS CARR, Counsel to the Speaker of the House of Commons since 1943. K.C.B. 1947. Barrister at Law, Inner Temple, 1902; Bencher, 1948. Editor: *Revised Statutes* and *Statutory Rules and Orders*, 1923–43. Chairman, Committee on Electoral Reform, 1944–47. Author: *Delegated Legislation*, 1921; *Concerning English Administrative Law*, 1941; and other studies.

GORDON R. CLAPP, Chairman, Tennessee Valley Authority, and formerly its general manager. Chairman, United Nations Commission for Economic Survey of the Middle East, 1949. Member of the President's Advisory Commission on Education, 1949.

CHARLES EDWARD CLARK, Judge, United States Circuit Court of Appeals, 2nd Circuit, since 1939. Professor of Law, Yale Law School, 1919–

29; Sterling Professor and Dean, 1929–39. Vice Chairman of commission on reorganization of Connecticut state departments, 1935–37. Chairman of President's advisory commission on the relation of federal laws to Puerto Rico. Draftsman of Uniform Principal and Income Act for Commissioners on Uniform State Laws, 1931. Author of *Cases on Pleading and Procedure* and other works.

TOM CHARLTON CLARK, recently head of the coal and steel section in the Office of the U.S. Special Representative in Europe, Paris. Now in the private practice of law. LL.B., Western Reserve, 1928; Instructor of Politics at Princeton, 1929–31. Doctorate from University of Vienna, 1932. Engaged thereafter in the practice of law, including connection with Cravath, de Gersdorff, Swaine and Wood, 1932–34, and the Bethlehem Steel Corporation, 1935–43.

HENRY STEELE COMMAGER, Professor of History, Columbia University. Pitt Professor of American History, Cambridge University, 1947–48. Harmsworth Professor of American History, Oxford University, 1952–53. Author: *The Growth of the American Republic* (with S. E. Morison), 1931; *The Heritage of America* (with A. Nevins), 1939; *Majority Rule and Minority Rights*, 1943; *The American Mind*, 1950, and other works.

ROBERT E. CUSHMAN, Goldwin Smith Professor of Government, Cornell University. President, American Political Science Association, 1943. Director, Cornell Research in Civil Liberties since 1943. Author of *The Independent Regulatory Commissions*, 1941, and other works.

LAWRENCE E. de NEUFVILLE, Assistant to the President, Free Europe Committee, Inc., New York City. Formerly with Office of Military Government and U.S. High Commission, Germany; Mutual Security Agency (European Headquarters), 1951–53.

KARL W. DEUTSCH, Professor of History and Political Science, Massachusetts Institute of Technology. Visiting Professor at the Center for Research on World Political Institutions, Princeton University, 1953–54. Author of: *Nationalism and Social Communication*, 1953; *Political Community at the International Level: Problems of Definition and Measurement* (a study prepared for the Center for Research on World Political Institutions), 1953.

WILLIAM DIEBOLD, JR., Director of Economic Studies, Council on Foreign Relations. Office of Strategic Services, 1943–45. Department of State, Division of Commercial Policy, 1945–46. Author: *New Directions in our Trade Policy*, 1941; *Trade and Payments in Western Europe*, 1952.

NOEL T. DOWLING, Harlan Fiske Stone Professor of Constitutional Law, Columbia University. Special Assistant Legislative Counsel, U.S. Senate, 1921 and 1927–28. Special Assistant to the General Counsel, Agricultural Adjustment Administration, 1933. Consultant, Tennessee Valley Authority, 1935. Consultant to the State Department, 1950–52. Author of *Cases on Constitutional Law* and other works.

LAZLO ECKER-RACZ, U.S. Treasury Department. Chief of municipal finance section, FERA, 1933–36. Fiscal Consultant, Michigan Tax Study Commission, 1938–39. Economist and Adviser, U.S. Mission to Hungary, 1945–46. Director, Tax Advisory Staff of U.S. Treasury Department, 1950–53.

CHARLES FAIRMAN, Nagel Professor of Constitutional Law, Washington University, St. Louis. Colonel and Chief, International Law Division, Office of Theater Judge Advocate, ETO. Author of *The Law of Martial Rule*,

1930; *Justice Miller and the Supreme Court, 1862–90*, 1939, and other works.

JAMES W. FESLER, Professor and Chairman of the Department of Political Science, Yale University. Author of *Executive Management and the Federal Field Service*, 1937; *The Independence of State Regulatory Agencies*, 1942; *Area and Administration*, 1948.

JOHN FISCHER, Editor-in-Chief, Harper's Magazine. Chief representative of the Board of Economic Warfare and Foreign Economic Administration in India, 1943–44. Author: *Why they Behave Like Russians*, 1947; *Master Plan U.S.A.*, 1951.

PAUL A. FREUND, Charles Stebbins Fairchild Professor of Law, Harvard University. Legal Staff, Treasury and RFC, 1933–35. Special Assistant to the Attorney General, Office of the Solicitor General, 1935–39, 1942–46. Author: *On Understanding the Supreme Court*, 1949; co-editor, *Constitutional Law, Cases and Other Problems*, 1952.

CARL J. FRIEDRICH, Professor of Government, Harvard University. Director, School for Overseas Administration, 1943–46. Governmental affairs adviser in the Office of Military Government, Germany, 1946–49. Author, among other works, of *Responsible Bureaucracy*, 1932; *Constitutional Government and Democracy*, 1941; *Inevitable Peace*, 1947; director and editor (with Robert R. Bowie) of *Studies in Federalism* prepared in conjunction with the European Movement; published in French, 1953, English version published in 1954.

JOHN M. GAUS, Professor of Government, Harvard University. Executive Secretary, Wisconsin Executive Council, 1931–33. Member, Wisconsin State Planning Board, 1943–47. Member, Madison Area Planning Council, 1945–47. Member of the committee on agricultural activities, Commission on Organization of the Executive Branch (Hoover Commission), 1948. President, American Political Science Association, 1945. Author of *Public Administration and the U.S. Department of Agriculture* (with L. Wolcott), 1940; *Reflections on Public Administration*, 1947.

MILTON HANDLER, Professor of Law, Columbia University. General Counsel, National Labor Board, 1933–34. Assistant General Counsel, Lend-Lease Administration, 1942–43. Associate public member, National War Labor Board, 1944. Author of: *A Study of the Construction and Enforcement of the Federal Antitrust Laws* (TNEC monograph No. 38); *The Antitrust Laws—A Symposium*, 1932; *Cases and Materials on Trade Regulation*, etc.

CHARLES M. HARDIN, Associate Professor of Political Science, University of Chicago. Consultant, Production and Marketing Administration, U.S. Department of Agriculture, 1945, 1949; T.V.A., 1948; Farm Foundation, since 1949. Author of *The Politics of Agriculture*, 1952.

HENRY MELVIN HART, JR., Professor of Law, Harvard University. Associate General Counsel for O.P.A., 1942–45. General Counsel, Office of Stabilization Administrator, 1945–46. Member of Attorney General's Committee on Administrative Procedure, 1939–41. Author (with Herbert Wechsler) of *The Federal Courts and the Federal System*, 1953.

RICHARD HARTSHORNE, Judge, United States District Court, New Jersey District. Professor of Constitutional Law, New Jersey Law School. President of the Interstate Commission on Crime, 1935–43. Chairman of

New Jersey Commission on Interstate Cooperation. Member of the Board of Managers of the Council of State Governments. Member of the joint conference committee in charge of federal-state conference on law enforcement problems of national defense. Delegate to the 8th international conference on the unification of penal law. Author: *The Handbook on Interstate Crime Control,* 1938.

PAUL R. HAYS, Professor of Law, Columbia University. Arbitrator, New York State Board of Mediation since 1937; member, 1940–44. Arbitrator and Special Representative, National Defense Mediation Board, 1941–42. Member, Board of Legal Examiners, U.S. Civil Service Commission, 1941–44. Visiting Professor of Law, Free University of Berlin, summer of 1952. Author: *The Judicial Function in Federal Administrative Agencies* (with N. T. Dowling and J. P. Chamberlain), 1942; *Cases and Materials on Civil Procedure,* 1947; *Cases on Labor Law* (with Milton Handler), 1950; revised 1951.

ARTHUR N. HOLCOMBE, Professor of Government, Harvard University. Chairman, Appeals Board, War Production Board, 1942–45. President, American Political Science Association, 1936. Author: *State Government in the United States,* 1916, 1926, 1931; *The New Party Politics,* 1933; *The Middle Classes in American Politics,* 1940; *Dependent Areas in the Post-War World,* 1941; *Human Rights in the Modern World,* 1948; *Our More Perfect Union,* 1950, and other works.

ALLAN HOVEY, JR., Executive Director, American Committee on United Europe, New York City. Formerly with Office of Secretary General, United Nations. Study Director, Council on Foreign Relations, 1952.

JAMES WILLARD HURST, Professor of Law, University of Wisconsin Law School. Board of Directors, Social Science Research Council, 1948–52. Author of: *The Growth of American Law: The Law Makers,* 1950.

PHILIP C. JESSUP, Hamilton Fish Professor of International Law, Columbia University. Assistant Solicitor, U.S. Department of State, 1924–25. Assistant Secretary General, UNRRA and Bretton Woods Conferences, 1943–44. Later Ambassador-at-large for the United States. Author: *U.S. and World Court,* 1929; *International Security,* 1935; *A Modern Law of Nations,* 1948, and other works.

ARTHUR S. LALL, Consul-General for India, New York City, with the rank of minister. Alternate delegate for India to the 7th and 8th sessions UN General Assembly. Alternate delegate to the 15th session of the Economic and Social Council, 1953. Chairman of the UN Committee on Contributions for 1953. A writer of poetry, short stories, and book reviews.

FREDERICK PADDOCK LEE, Member of the Bar of the District of Columbia. Assistant Legislative Counsel, U.S. House of Representatives, 1919–23. Legislative Counsel, U.S. Senate, 1923–30. Professor of Law, Georgetown University, 1929–35. President, Montgomery County (Md.) Civic Federation, 1931–33. Chairman, Montgomery County Charter Board, 1942–44.

RALPH E. McGILL, Editor, *The Atlanta Constitution.* Chairman, Selective Service Board, 1940–44. Member of advisory committee, War Labor Board, for Georgia. Special advisor and consultant to Department of State.

CHARLES McKINLEY, Professor of Political Science, Reed College, Portland, Oregon. Consultant, National Resources Committee, 1935–39. Staff member, President's Committee on Administrative Management, 1936. Member of the Portland City Planning Commission since 1934 and President 1935–40. Executive secretary to administrative council, U.S. Department of Agriculture, 1940–42. Consultant, North Pacific Planning Project, U.S. State Department, 1943–44. Member, Regional Advisory Council, Bonneville Power Administration since 1943. Consultant, Department of Interior Pacific Northwest Coordination Committee since 1947. President, American Political Science Association, 1954. Author: *Uncle Sam in the Pacific Northwest: Federal Management of Resources in the Columbia River Valley,* 1952.

ARTHUR W. MACMAHON, Eaton Professor of Public Administration, Columbia University. President, American Political Science Association, 1947. Staff member, section on cooperation with states, Council of National Defense, 1917–19. Editor, New York City Charter Commission, 1921–23. Staff member, President's Committee on Administrative Management, 1936–37. Consultant on administration, U.S. Department of State, 1943–45. Member, Loyalty Review Board, 1947–50. Author: *The Administration of Federal Work Relief* (with others), 1941; "Taking Stock of Federalism in the United States" in *Problems of Modern Government,* 1941; *Administration in Foreign Affairs,* 1953.

JAMES A. MAXWELL, Professor and Chairman of the Department of Economics and Sociology, Clark University, Worcester, Massachusetts. Economic Adviser to Royal Commission on Financial Arrangements, 1935. With State Department, 1944–46. Author of: *Federal Subsidies to the Provincial Governments in Canada,* 1937; *The Fiscal Impact of Federalism in the United States,* 1946.

SPENCER MILLER, JR., Assistant Secretary of Labor for international affairs. Director of Workers Educational Bureau of America, 1921–42. New Jersey State Highway Commissioner, 1942–45. One-time President of the village of South Orange, N.J. Author: *American Labor and the Nation,* and other works.

FRANZ L. NEUMANN, Professor of Government, Columbia University. Member of the faculty, Deutsche Hochschule für Politik, 1928–33. Special assistant, Office of Strategic Services, 1943–45. Chief, German research section, U.S. Department of State, 1945–47, and consultant thereafter. Author, among other works, of *Behemoth: The Structure and Practice of National Socialism,* 1942; editor, Montesquieu's *The Spirit of the Laws,* 1949.

JAMES K. POLLOCK, Professor and Chairman of the Department of Political Science, University of Michigan. Chairman, Michigan civil service study commission, 1935–37. Election official, Saar Plebiscite, 1935. Special adviser to General Clay, U.S. Military Government for Germany, 1945–46, 1947, 1948. Special Adviser to the U.S. High Commissioner in Germany, 1950. Member of Commission on Organization of the Executive Branch (Hoover Commission). President of the American Political Science Association, 1950. Author: *Money and Politics Abroad,* 1932; *The Government of Greater Germany,* 1938; *What Shall be Done with Germany,* 1944; and other works. Editor: *Change and Crisis in European Government,* 1947.

THOMAS REED POWELL, Story Professor Emeritus of Law, Harvard University. Previously Ruggles Professor of Constitutional Law, Columbia University. President, American Political Science Association, 1937. Author: *Separation of Powers,* 1913; *Indirect Encroachment on Federal Authority by the Taxing Powers of the States,* 1919; *The Supreme Court and State Police Power,* 1932, and others.

IVAN CLEVELAND RAND, Justice, Supreme Court of Canada. Attorney General of New Brunswick, 1924–5. Member of the New Brunswick Legislature, 1925. Canada's representative on the United Nations Special Committee on Palestine, 1947. K.C. 1924.

HUBERT RIPKA, New School for Social Research. Member of the Czechoslovak Cabinet, 1940–48. Formerly Professor of History in Charles University. Author of: *Munich Before and After; Russia and the West; The Small and Great Nation; Czechoslovakia and the New Europe. A Federation of Central Europe,* (mimeographed, 1953).

INGVAR SVENNILSON, Professor of Political Economy, University of Stockholm, Sweden. Consultant and director of special studies under the Economic Commission for Europe and other special bodies of the United Nations System, including chairmanship of the Ad Hoc Committee on Restrictive Business Practices.

FRANK TANNENBAUM, Professor of Latin American History, Columbia University. Member of staff of Commission on Law Observance and Law Enforcement, preparing report on penal institutions. Staff of Institute of Economics, making studies in Mexico and Puerto Rico, 1928–30. Author: *The Labor Movement,* 1921; *Wall Shadows,* 1922; *Darker Phases of the South,* 1924; *The Mexican Agrarian Revolution,* 1928; *Osborne of Sing Sing,* 1933; *Peace by Revolution,* 1933; *Whither Latin America?,* 1934; *Slave and Citizen,* 1947; *A Philosophy of Labor,* 1951.

KYAW THET, Lecturer in History, Rangoon University. Burmese Fulbright scholar, Yale University.

DAVID B. TRUMAN, Professor of Government, Columbia University. Assistant head, division of program surveys, U.S. Department of Agriculture, 1943–44. Deputy Chief of morale division, U.S. Strategic Bombing Survey, Pacific, 1945–46. Consultant, Carnegie Corporation, 1946. Author: *Educational Functions of Municipal Research Bureaus,* 1936; *Administrative Decentralization,* 1940; *The Process of Government,* 1951.

RICHARD W. VAN WAGENEN, Associate Professor of Politics, Princeton University, and director of center for research on world political institutions. Staff of the American Legislators Association and Council of State Governments, 1935–37. Pennsylvania Economy League, 1937–38. New Hampshire Foundation, 1935. Assistant Deputy U.S. Secretary, Allied Control Council for Germany, 1945–47.

AARON WARNER, Associate Professor of Economics, Columbia University; in charge of economics work in the School of General Studies. Regional Director, NLRB, 1937–41. Director of Field Operations, Enforcement Division, OPA, 1941–43.

HERBERT WECHSLER, Professor of Law, Columbia University. Assistant Attorney General of the United States in charge of War Division, U.S. Department of Justice, 1944–46. Technical adviser to U.S. members, International Military Tribunal, 1945–46. Author: *Criminal Law and its Administration* (with J. Michael) 1940; *The Federal Courts and the Federal System* (with H. M. Hart, Jr.), 1953; Reporter, *American Law Institute Model Penal Code.*

EDWARD W. WEIDNER, Professor and Chairman of the Department of Political Science, Michigan State College. Director of the Bureau of Government Research. Co-Director (with William Anderson) of the six year project for the study of intergovernmental relations as illustrated in Minnesota.

KENNETH CLINTON WHEARE, Gladstone Professor of Government and Public Administration, Oxford University. Member of Oxford City Council since 1940. Member of Hebdomadal Council since 1947. Constitutional adviser to National Convention of New Foundland, 1946–47, and to conferences on Central African Federation, 1951–52. Author: *The Statute of Westminster*, 1931, 1933; *The Statute of Westminster and Dominion Status*, 1938; *Federal Government*, 1946, 1951, 1953.

FREDERICK L. ZIMMERMANN, Assistant Professor of Government, Hunter College. Research Director, New York State Joint Legislative Committee on Interstate Cooperation, 1936–51. Consultant, U.S. Department of State, 1943, 1947–49. Special Adviser, Atlantic States Marine Fisheries Commission, 1945–51. Consultant, Council of State Governments and Interstate Commission on the Delaware.

ARNOLD J. ZURCHER, Executive Director, Alfred P. Sloan Foundation. Professor of Political Science, New York University, and head of its Institute of Public Affairs and Regional Studies. Author: *Experiment with Democracy in Central Europe*, 1933; *The Governments of Continental Europe*, (with J. T. Shotwell and others); 1940; *Post-war European Federation* (with R. N. Coudenhove-Kalergi and others), 1943; Editor, *America's Place in the World Economy*, 1945. Member of Board of Directors, American Committee on United Europe.

The following were prevented by illness or other compelling reasons from attending the Conference:

PAUL H. APPLEBY, Dean, Maxwell Graduate School of Citizenship and Public Affairs, Syracuse University.

HODDING CARTER, Editor and Publisher, The Delta Democrat-Times, Greenville, Mississippi.

CARL B. CHATTERS, Executive Director, American Municipal Association.

EDWARD S. CORWIN, McCormick Professor of Jurisprudence Emeritus, Princeton University.

NORMAN COUSINS, Editor, Saturday Review of Literature.

RAFAEL DE COLINA, Ambassador, Head of the Mexican Permanent Mission to the United Nations.

CALVIN B. HOOVER, Professor and Chairman, Department of Economics, Duke University.

SAM HOUSTON JONES, Lawyer, St. Charles, Louisiana. Former Governor. Member of Commission on Intergovernmental Relations.

FRANK C. MOORE, Director, Government Affairs Foundation, Inc. Former Lieutenant Governor of New York State.

WHITNEY H. SHEPARDSON, President, Free Europe Committee, Inc.

H. ALEXANDER SMITH, United States Senator from New Jersey.

CHARLES E. WYZANSKI, JR., Judge, U.S. District Court for Massachusetts.

Index

Administrative patterns,
 at various levels, 21, 22
 direct type of federal administration, 20,
  21, 270, 427
 existing fiscal relations factor, 20
 fiscal relations, 22
 state inferiority, 53
Advantages and disadvantages, 5, 10, 15
Agricultural policy and administration,
  See also Land resources management.
 cooperation, emphasis on, 283–289
 cooperative systems,
  extension work, 287–289
  grants-in-aid, 283, 284, 287
  market regulation through, 289
  public domain management, 285, 286
 Department of Agriculture policy, 286
 economic emphasis,
  acreage control, 291, 302
  conservation, 292–294
  limitation of production, 290, 291
  "parity," 290
  soil conservation, 292–294
  sub-marginal land policy, 292
  watershed control, 292–294
 extension,
  Agricultural Extension Service, 287
  area condition recognition, 288
  county agent system, 287, 288
  individual activity emphasis, 288
  local determination policy, 288
 functions, distributions of, 281–284
 government reorganization effect, 297,
  298
 land use coordination,
  areal level jurisdiction, 295
  continuous planning for, 295
  farm organization programs, 296, 297,
   302, 303
  Office of Land Use, 295
  World War II effect, 296–298
 legislation,
  factors affecting, 282, 283

Agricultural policy—(Continued)
 legislation—(Continued)
  land dispersal and conservation, 283,
   285, 287, 318
  land grant institutions, 283
 national resources,
  land dispersal, conservation, 283, 285
  public domain, 283, 285
 operating units,
  farm as basic unit, 298
  federal functions of, 299
  local consumer services, 298
  national-state relations, 298
  regions, as watersheds, 298
 policy coordination efforts,
  areal levels, jurisdiction, 295
  Office of Land Use Coordination, 295
  unified planning service, 296
  World War II effect, 296–298
 policy at the local level, 288
 post-World War I policy, 289–294
 pre-World War I policy, 284–289
 public domain,
  agencies concerned, 285–287, 315
  inter- and intradepartmental agencies,
   286, 287
 rural zoning, 316
 summary,
  collective action effectiveness, 299
  community concern, as, 299–301
  individual action emphasis, 299
  land grant institutions' part, 300, 301
  national-regional action, 301
  needed policy improvement, 300
  policy unification need, 299
 World War II effect, 296–298
Alternatives to federalism,
 federal pattern, 9, 10, 54, 410, 433, 453
 separate individual countries, 9, 54
 unitary constitution, 9, 54
Ambivalence of federalism, 3
Amending federal instruments,
 ease or difficulty question, 4, 526
 participation in process, 514, 526

Date Due